Classics in progress

Essays on ancient Greece and Rome

Classics in progress

Essays on ancient Greece and Rome

edited by
T. P. Wiseman

Published for THE BRITISH ACADEMY
by OXFORD UNIVERSITY PRESS

Oxford University Press, Great Clarendon Street, Oxford OX2 6DP

Oxford New York

Auckland Cape Town Dar es Salaam Hong Kong Karachi
Kuala Lumpur Madrid Melbourne Mexico City Nairobi
New Delhi Shanghai Taipei Toronto

With offices in
Argentina Austria Brazil Chile Czech Republic France Greece
Guatemala Hungary Italy Japan Poland Portugal Singapore
South Korea Switzerland Thailand Turkey Ukraine Vietnam

Published in the United States
by Oxford University Press Inc., New York

© The British Academy 2002

Database right The British Academy (maker)

First published 2002
Paperback edition 2006

British Library Cataloguing in Publication Data
Data available

Library of Congress Cataloging in Publication Data
Data available

Typeset by Alden Bookset
Printed in Great Britain
on acid-free paper by
Antony Rowe Ltd.,
Chippenham, Wiltshire

ISBN 0-19-726323-2   978-0-19-726323-5

Contents

List of figures

Notes on contributors

Jonathan Barnes is Professor of Ancient Philosophy at the University of Geneva. At the moment he is mainly concerned with the history of logic. His next book will be *Porphyry: Introduction*.

Mary Beard is Reader in Classics at the University of Cambridge and Fellow of Newnham College. She is the author of *The Invention of Jane Harrison* (2000).

Alan K. Bowman is Student of Christ Church and University Lecturer in Ancient History, University of Oxford. His main research interests are in Roman imperial history and papyrology. His publications include *Egypt after the Pharaohs* (2nd ed. 1996).

Averil Cameron is Warden of Keble College, Oxford, and a historian of late antiquity and Byzantium. She is co-editor of the three final volumes of the *Cambridge Ancient History*, covering the period from the third century AD to *c*.600.

Paul Cartledge is Professor of Greek History, Chairman of the Faculty of Classics and a Fellow of Clare College in the University of Cambridge. His most recent books are *The Greeks: Crucible of Civilization* (2000) and *Spartan Reflections* (2001); he is currently working on a social and economic history of Classical Greece and a history of Greek political thought and theory.

Michael Crawford is Professor of Ancient History in the History Department at University College London; he is quite certain that Classics is not a discipline. His publications include *Roman Statutes* (two volumes, 1996).

John K. Davies is Rathbone Professor of Ancient History and Classical Archaeology at the University of Liverpool. He has worked extensively on Greek history, especially on economic, cultic and administrative aspects.

Pat Easterling is Regius Professor of Greek Emeritus in the University of Cambridge. Her main research interests are in Greek literature, particularly drama, and its transmission; her most recent book is *The Cambridge Companion to Greek Tragedy* (1997).

Jasper Griffin is Professor of Classical Literature at Oxford University and a Fellow of Balliol College. His main research interests are in Homer, Attic tragedy and Augustan poetry; his most recent book is a commentary on book 9 of the *Iliad* (1995).

Philip Hardie is Reader in Latin Literature in the University of Cambridge, and a Fellow of New Hall. His book *Ovid's Poetics of Illusion* was published in 2002.

Malcolm Heath is Professor of Greek in the University of Leeds. His research interests include Greek tragedy and comedy, ancient literary scholarship, criticism and theory, and rhetoric in late antiquity. His book *Interpreting Classical Texts* will be published in 2002.

Mary Margaret McCabe is Professor of Ancient Philosophy at King's College London. She is especially interested in Plato, and her most recent book is *Plato and his Predecessors: the Dramatisation of Reason* (2000).

Peter Parsons is Regius Professor of Greek at Oxford University. His main research interests are papyrology and the Greek poetry of the Hellenistic period.

Malcolm Schofield is Professor of Ancient Philosophy, University of Cambridge. He is co-editor of *The Cambridge History of Greek and Roman Political Thought* (2000).

R. R. R. Smith is Lincoln Professor of Classical Archaeology and Art at Oxford University. His main research interests are in Greek and Roman art, the sculptured monuments of Aphrodisias in Caria, and the archaeology of Asia Minor. His publications include *Hellenistic Royal Portraits* (1988), *Hellenistic Sculpture* (1991), and *Aphrodisias 1: the Monument of C. Julius Zoilus* (1993).

Oliver Taplin is a Professor of Classics at Oxford University, and Tutorial Fellow of Magdalen College. He is particularly concerned with the ancient and modern receptions of Greek epic and drama. He was editor of *Literature in the Greek and Roman Worlds* (2000).

T. P. Wiseman is Emeritus Professor of Classics in the University of Exeter. His main research interests are in Roman history, historiography and myth, and his most recent book is *Roman Drama and Roman History* (1998).

Preface

You might think that 'classics', as the name of a discipline, is like 'physics', 'ethics', 'politics', even 'gymnastics'. But no: those pursuits define themselves as straightforward Greek words, derived from *phusis* (nature), *ethos* (custom), *polis* (city), *gumnos* (naked). The etymology of 'classics' is Latin, and metaphorical. *Classicus* meant 'top-rank' — originally 'wealthy enough to equip yourself to serve in the armoured phalanx of the citizen army' — and its opposite was *proletarius*. Applied to literature, it referred to 'first-class' authors, as opposed to the mere rank and file.[1]

The English version is essentially an eighteenth-century concept, Greek and Latin 'classics' providing, in Lord Dacre's elegant formulation, 'a set of selected texts from a golden age which present a model of life and letters for posterity: a balanced rational life, traditional letters'.[2] It is hardly an adequate phrase to describe the modern study of Greco-Roman civilisation itself, one and a half millennia of literature, politics, philosophy, law, religion and art, but for want of a better alternative the name has stuck.

What this book offers is a selection of the sort of work done by classicists nowadays, with a deliberately eclectic emphasis on its range of subject matter and its multifarious engagement with contemporary intellectual life. The idea is not to provide anything like an exhaustive survey, but to offer examples of the interest and variety of the subject.

The point is perhaps best made by contrast. In 1954, Basil Blackwell published a volume entitled *Fifty Years of Classical Scholarship*, consisting of seventeen essays by distinguished classicists. The chapter headings were: Homer, Early Greek Lyric Poetry, Greek Tragedy, Greek Comedy, The Greek Philosophers, The Greek Historians, Greek Orators and Rhetoric, Hellenistic Poetry, Roman Drama, Late Republican Poetry, The Augustan Poets, Roman Oratory, The Roman Historians, and Silver Latin Poetry.

---

[1] Aulus Gellius, *Noctes Atticae* 19.8.15, quoting Cornelius Fronto (tutor to Marcus Aurelius). See below, p. 24.

[2] H. Trevor-Roper, *Sunday Times* 11 December 1977, 39; *OED* s.v. 'classic' §B.1.a.

The editor, Maurice Platnauer, contributed the following preface:

> In April of this year the Classical Association held its Jubilee meeting; and the close of the half-century seems a fitting occasion for the publication of a book which sums up the advance made along the main lines of classical scholarship during that period. This advance has not been so rapid, and certainly not so spectacular, as has been that of, say, physics; yet advance there has been, and that not only thanks to the discovery of new material but also because of what scholars hope is a sounder re-interpretation of the material they already have. As Anatole France once wrote, 'Chaque génération imagine à nouveau les chefs-d'oeuvre antiques et leur communique de la sorte une immortalité mouvante.' It is just this *immortalité mouvante* that the contributors to the present volume now illustrate for the contemporary reader.

Nothing more. No further explanation was necessary. The 'main lines of classical scholarship' were self-evidently literary, 'les chefs d'oeuvre antiques' from Homer to Tacitus and Juvenal. Beyond the reign of Hadrian, which is where the Oxford Greats syllabus ended, it was someone else's business.

Platnauer was 67 when he wrote that. He had grown up in late-Victorian and Edwardian England, when a classical education was taken for granted as the intellectual training of a gentleman. Homer and Sophocles, Horace and Cicero, were studied as character-forming paradigms, and the world of antiquity was a mirror of one's own:

> A nineteenth-century Englishman could ignore the differences produced in time and interpret his society in Roman terms. He could look for Cicero's virtues in his legislators and see the faults of Spartacus in Feargus O'Connor. He could regard India as a province, the North-West Frontier as Hadrian's Wall, and hope that the subjugation of the Zulus would be followed by the civilising effort that justified the defeat of Boadicea.[3]

It takes a long time for such assumptions to become obsolete, and all but two of Platnauer's contributors were born before 1914.

In 1954, however, in an egalitarian Britain whose empire was already a thing of the past, traditional 'Classics' were not easy to defend. A whole generation of idealistic young men and women, who would become the head teachers and educational administrators of a post-war society, took it for granted that the subject had lost its relevance to modern life. If *they* had wanted to use a French quotation, it would have been 'nous avons changé tout cela.'

---

[3] R. R. Bolgar, 'Classical Elements in the Social, Political and Educational Thought of Thomas and Matthew Arnold', in R. R. Bolgar (ed.), *Classical Influences on Western Thought AD 1650–1870* (Cambridge 1979) 327–38, quotation from 337–8.

In 1960 the universities of Oxford and Cambridge ceased to require Latin as an entrance qualification. From now on the subject would have to compete for timetable space on its own intrinsic merits, and the spread of comprehensive schools in the sixties made its survival precarious. The classicists, who knew what their subject's intrinsic merits were, fought back hard, and the organisation of JACT (Joint Association of Classical Teachers) and the Cambridge School Classics Project were brilliant examples of curricular re-thinking.[4] But it was a struggle against the tide, and in popular prejudice the subject remained, however unjustly, a byword for the obscure and obsolete. As late as 1986, David Cannadine was urging his fellow historians to face the dreadful prospect 'that history may become the Classics of the twenty-first century: self-absorbed and self-enclosed, and thus doomed to self-destruction'.[5]

Such changes happen in pendulum swings. Today, Latin is popular again, the primary-school course *Minimus* welcomed by parents who value the subject as something they were deprived of which they want their children to have. Now that only a few old men remember the 'classical education' of the Edwardian age, the appalling ignorance of language among the young people of contemporary Britain has evoked a belated awareness of the value of Latin teaching.[6] And a subject that makes its students think their way into value systems different from their own is properly valued for reasons precisely opposite to the Victorian paradigm of empire.[7] Not that the ancient world is unique in offering that educational benefit; what makes it special is the inescapable fact that its texts and its experiences form the origin of western culture and western thought.

Research into those texts and those experiences has proceeded with vigour, notwithstanding the decades of hostility and resistance. What has gone is the ingenuous assumption that 'the classics' form a self-contained and self-sufficient discipline. Nowadays, the word can be taken as shorthand for 'the languages, history, literature, art and thought of the Greco-Roman

---

[4] Martin Forrest, *Modernising the Classics: a Study in Curriculum Development* (Exeter 1996).

[5] David Cannadine, 'The State of British History', *Times Literary Supplement* 4358 (10 October 1986) 1139–40, quotation from 1140.

[6] For a Romance linguist's view, see Rebecca Posner in Richard Jenkyns (ed.), *The Legacy of Rome: a New Appraisal* (Oxford 1992) 396: 'The Latin model of grammar, for all its defects, is infinitely better than none; it fulfils the descriptive requirements of simplicity and elegance, and, to an unprecedented extent, of adequacy. It even makes a shot of being explanatory. Most of all, it is readily teachable. Let us hope that this legacy will not be thoughtlessly cast aside.'

[7] *Classics from 5 to 16* (Curriculum Matters 12, HMSO, 1988); see especially para. 41 on 'attitudes and values'.

world', part of the common intellectual enterprise of scholarship, and it is in that sense that it appears in the title of this book.

We begin with the here and now, the unselfconscious use of Greek and Latin writers by contemporary British and Irish poets (Chapter 1), and then look at the way the concept of 'classic authors' changes over time, both by constant redefinition (Chapter 2) and by the discovery of new texts (Chapter 3). But the subject is not only textual, and Chapter 4 explores the visual aspect, a territory shared with archaeology and art history. Two chapters follow which exemplify the complexities of the surviving evidence, whether literary (5) or epigraphic (6). In Chapters 7 and 8, the traditional limits of 'classical antiquity' are disputed in both time and space. Part of the intention in the first half of the book is to realign the reader's expectations. This is not a static and predictable subject.

The central chapter takes a systematic look at one particular sub-discipline, Greek history, and the historical theme is continued with three chapters — 10 and 11 on democratic Athens, 12 on republican Rome — reflecting issues of politics and ideology that engage the modern world no less urgently than the ancient. The 'classic authors' are represented by close readings, in different styles, of a poem of Horace (Chapter 13), a passage of Virgil (Chapter 14), and two Socratic arguments in Plato (Chapter 15). The philosophical tradition continues into the world of Christian doctrine (Chapter 16), and the book's concluding study presents the rhetorical education of the fourth century AD, not as the end but as only midway in the literary culture of Hellas, between Homer and the Byzantine emperor Manuel Palaeologus. The overall structure is deliberately loose: you will always find that the next chapter is different.

Finally, I should like to thank the contributors (a wonderfully supportive team) — those who delivered early, for their patience, and those who delivered late, for their perseverance in overcoming the time-consuming obstacles which the management of higher education in Britain now puts in the way of scholarship.

T. P. W.
August 2001

1
Contemporary poetry and Classics

Oliver Taplin

i

In 1973 an enterprising garland-maker collected together some 850 translations from *The Greek Anthology*.[1] Most of the versions by the fifty or so
contributors were specially commissioned, and they included some excellent
epigrams, some by poets already quite well known, including Fleur Adcock,
Tony Harrison, Peter Levi, Edwin Morgan and Peter Porter.[2] While only a few
of them were actually professional scholars, more than a few had received a
classical education, and had evidently translated with some knowledge of the
original Greek.

I have picked on this volume as marking a transition, from an age when a
project like this had been primarily the preserve of scholars, and when classical
poetry was predominantly the preserve of the few, to our age, when it has been
opened up to a wide range of creative artists, though with rare exceptions not
working from the original language. It is this efflorescence in the last quarter of
the twentieth century — an era when Classics has probably had less presence
in education than at any time since the Renaissance — that is the centre of my
attention in this attempt to snap the moving target of contemporary culture.[3]

---

[1] *The Greek Anthology and Other Ancient Greek Epigrams*, edited with an introduction by Peter Jay
(London 1973).

[2] Two of these were developed into separate publications: Peter Whigham, *The Poems of Meleager*
(Berkeley 1975), and Tony Harrison, *Palladas: Poems* (London 1975).

[3] I am restricting myself to poetry from the British Isles and Ireland, a more limited subject than my
title might seem to promise. I am also concentrating mainly on poets born between about 1925 and
1950. The reasons for these approximate limits will emerge. There are certainly interesting things,
and interestingly different things, to be said about twentieth-century American poets and Classics.
And the relationship between post-colonial poetry from the former British Empire (I realise that
some would include Ireland under that description) and the classical world is a fascinating subject,

The new liberation of inspiration that I hope to reveal is epitomised by a comparable enterprise of anthologising some twenty years later than Jay's. In 1994 Michael Hofmann and James Lasdun persuaded forty poets to pool contributions based on extracts from a text which was proving especially congenial to the 1990s. The fruit of their success, *After Ovid: New Metamorphoses*,[4] collects a significant proportion of the best-known — and the best — poets of the time, including Fleur Adcock (the only one also in *The Greek Anthology*), Fred D'Aguiar, Amy Clampitt, Carol Ann Duffy, Seamus Heaney and Les Murray. Few of these forty had, so far as I can establish, the opportunity even to loathe, let alone enjoy, a traditional classical education beyond, at most, basic Latin. There is nothing in the Editors' introduction about the significance or insignificance of a knowledge of Latin for their selection of poets. Furthermore, this limitation — that few of them worked seriously from the Latin text — in no way hindered the volume from becoming a major success, and being well received by reviewers.

Set this, then, beside *The Greek Anthology*: a major canonical text (by any definition of the word) beside a relatively obscure one; poets working from other translations rather than from the original; significant literary impact as compared with a praiseworthy but little-noticed 'footnote'. Of course there is nothing inherently superior about a translation which is made directly from the original language. Translations made through other translations have a distinguished pedigree going back to the Renaissance;[5] and the practice was endorsed by the father-figure of modern translation, Ezra Pound. But it is telling that no one any longer regards it as even a consideration worth noticing, let alone as an invalidation. Up to the 1960s enough people learned Greek at school — and Latin as a matter of course — for it to be the general rule that translations should be made from the original: now it is the exception.[6]

---

which deserves separate treatment. Derek Walcott has deservedly come in for special attention. There have recently been two good and relevant collections of essays: Gregson Davis (ed.), *The Poetics of Derek Walcott: Intertextual Perspectives* (*South Atlantic Quarterly* 96.2, Spring 1997), and T. Hofmeister (ed.), *From Homer to Omeros: Derek Walcott's Omeros and Odyssey* (*Classical World* 93.1, September–October 1999).

[4] For a characteristically stream-of-consciousness rumination, pretty disparaging of Hughes (though warm about Duffy), see John Henderson in P. Hardie, A. Barchiesi and S. Hinds (eds.), *Ovidian Transformations* (*Proceedings of the Cambridge Philological Society* Suppl. 23, Cambridge 1999) 301–23.

[5] For some examples see A. Poole and J. Maule, *The Oxford Book of Classical Verse in Translation* (Oxford 1995) xliv.

[6] The bare statistics of those taking A-Level Latin are enough to make the point. According to the records of the DfES (to whom I am very grateful for the information), there were 7,901 candidates in 1965, 5,120 in 1970, 2,575 in 1980, and 1,237 in 2000.

ii

After Ovid marked the first emergence of a major figure on to the scene of twentieth-century translation of classical poetry into English: the then Poet Laureate, Ted Hughes. He went on to add twenty more stories to the four he had already contributed, and turned them into what was to become literally a best seller, *Tales from Ovid* (1997). There is no prefatory note; and Hughes did not, so far as I know, record his method of translation, or declare to what extent he engaged directly with the Latin. He had at least O-Level Latin, which he needed in order to gain admission to Cambridge to read English in 1948, and some French; but ignorance of their original languages never inhibited him from translating poets who wrote in Russian, Czech, Hungarian, Serbo-Croat, German, Spanish or Portuguese.

In his last years Hughes also turned to Greek literature: *The Oresteia* from Aeschylus and *Alcestis* from Euripides were published almost simultaneously, some months after his death in October 1998.[7] In the case of the *Oresteia* I can detect no evidence that Hughes worked from the Greek; but I have found two revealing indicators that he based himself on one particular translation.

First and foremost, all but the last two lines of Clytemnestra's enigmatic but lethal speech at *Agamemnon* 958–74 is transposed from the end of the scene, when Agamemnon is treading on the purple cloths, to earlier in the dialogue, between lines 930 and 931 of the transmitted text. This transposition is a generally ignored conjecture of A.Y. Campbell, which is not to be found in any standard edition of the play, but which was championed by Philip Vellacott in his Penguin translation of 1956 (much reprinted), where a special Appendix (pp. 195–7) was devoted to it. Another indicator, though less telling, is that Ted Hughes has Aegisthus say 'I was the third brother,' while nearly all modern texts and versions of line 1605 follow the transmitted text, which says that he was the thirteenth (literally 'ten plus third brother'). Vellacott, however, adopts an emendation to say 'I was the third child of Thyestes.' Whether or not Hughes used any other versions, I think it is clear that he relied heavily on the old Penguin, a translation which few who have scholarly interests would recommend over those of (for instance) Lattimore,

---

[7] It seems that Hughes translated the *Oresteia* in 1995, interrupting work on his *Alcestis* to do so. In private conversation in 1998 he said it was 'the best thing I have ever done. I read it and wonder how I ever did it': I owe this 'table talk' to K. Sagar, *The Laughter of Foxes: a Study of Ted Hughes* (Liverpool 2000) xxxi. The *Oresteia* was put on, directed by Katie Mitchell, at The National Theatre in London in winter 1999–2000; *Alcestis* was first performed by Northern Broadsides, directed by Barrie Rutter, in Halifax in September 2000.

Lloyd-Jones, Fagles, or for *Agamemnon* Louis MacNeice, on whom see further below.

This all stands in stark contrast with the previous version put on at the National Theatre, eighteen years earlier, the one by Tony Harrison. It is no organisational accident that the Hughes in 1999–2000 was performed in the traverse space of the Cottesloe Theatre, while that by Harrison (directed by Peter Hall) was staged in the much larger and more open Greek-form Olivier Theatre. The programme even reproduced a page of Gilbert Murray's Oxford Classical Text covered in Harrison's annotations (and I personally discussed the Greek of several key passages with him during the rehearsal period).

While he has also translated directly from Czech and French, Harrison has translated most, and most proudly, from the language which so dazzlingly opened his eyes and mind while still at school, as will be explored more fully below. It seems to me that as an achievement in poetic translation Harrison's *Oresteia* has not always received the recognition it deserves.[8] At the time of its production it was described as 'surely the best acting translation of Aeschylus ever written'.[9] But many readers, it seems, stumble over the translation's idiosyncrasies and never reach an appreciation of, for example, the tense vigour of the rhyming stichomythias, or the tight metrics and labile diction of the choral lyrics. This seems to be the case even with Michael Silk, who compares the Ted Hughes version with Pope's *Iliad* and claims that it is 'at its best, the most powerful and compelling English version of a Greek tragedy in existence'. It is, he goes on, 'English with none of the quaint and numbing (if sometimes brilliant) Anglo-saxonism of Tony Harrison'.[10]

Hughes's diction and metric are, by comparison, homogeneous throughout, whatever the dynamic of the original. One need only compare any passage of choral lyric in the two versions to see this. I have selected *Agamemnon* lines 773–81, but similar points would emerge from any number of juxtapositions. First, the close 'crib' by Hugh Lloyd-Jones:[11]

---

[8] Nor, come to that, has the music for the production by Harrison Birtwistle, which has never been published. It can still be heard, however, on the video of the television film made for Channel 4. (It is a sad irony that this is only available from Films for the Humanities and Sciences, Princeton, NJ, and not from Channel 4 itself.)

[9] Oswyn Murray, *Times Literary Supplement* 11 December 1981, reprinted with revisions in Neil Astley (ed.), *Tony Harrison* (*Bloodaxe Critical Anthologies* 1, Newcastle upon Tyne 1991) 262–74, quote at 267. There is a substantial discussion of the whole production, including the translation, by R. B. Parker in M. Cropp, E. Fantham and S. Scully (eds.), *Greek Tragedy and its Legacy: Essays Presented to D. J. Conacher* (Calgary 1986) 337–57, esp. 348–51.

[10] *Times Literary Supplement* 17 December 1999, 16–17.

[11] Published by Prentice-Hall (Englewood Cliffs, NJ 1970), reissued by Duckworth (London 1982).

Justice shines
beneath smoky rafters
and honors the righteous life;
but the gold-bespangled halls where there are hands unclean
she quits with eyes averted
and goes to what is holy, having no respect for
the power of wealth made counterfeit with praise.
And she guides all things to their appointed end.

Next, Hughes:

Justice lives in poverty.
She survives. She measures
What is necessary.
She honours what ought to be honoured.
She seeks out clean hearts, clean hands.
She knows what wealth and power
Grind to dust between them. She knows
Goodness and the laws of heaven.

Thirdly, Harrison:

Justice shines through hovel smoke
She loves the man who's straight
Justice eats off plates of oak
Scorns dainties off gold plate

Hands bespattered with shed blood
Raise gilded rafters to the skies
Justice searching for the good
Leaves with averted eyes

Justice doesn't kneel to fame
Kiss affluence's feet
Isn't dazzled by a name
Gold-coined but counterfeit

Justice isn't put out of her stride
Justice can't be turned aside

The contrasts are extreme: the staccato phrases and heavy stopping of Hughes against the unpunctuated Harrison, the vague moralising against the cascade of metaphors and images. Other considerations may be lurking here. This is the last stanza immediately before Agamemnon's triumphant return from Troy. The iconoclastic, anti-monarchist Harrison makes the most of this 'antifanfare' for the king: the royalist, male-sympathising Hughes plays down anything that might reflect badly on the sovereign, even papering over the 'gold-bespangled halls'.

There can be little room for dispute that Hughes comes worst out of this particular comparison. This is not to deny that there are powerful passages scattered through his *Oresteia*, especially perhaps where he seasons the original with his own taste for the visceral. Clytemnestra descanting on the purple dye of the cloth she has laid out for her husband, for example:

> . . . the ocean
> From which pour the streams of purple dye
> To flush our fabrics with all the colours of blood —
> Bring scarlet of the lungs,
> The liver's deep indigo,
> The artery's hot crimson,
> Inexhaustible, like life itself
> Teeming from the sources in the great deeps.

But all the polychrome physiology is pure Hughes. It would seem that in his last years he turned to translation because it unclogged the well of his Muse, and gave him the material on which to embroider some of his leading pre-occupations. These included the co-existence of blood-lust with spirituality, the 'tragic' turns within his own life-story, and 'human passion *in extremis* — passion where it combusts, or levitates, or mutates into an experience of the supernatural'.[12]

But for this present train of thought the two most notable things are that Hughes turned to central classical texts, and that he felt no call to apologise in any way for his lack of contact with the works in their original languages. To put it another way, he did not associate his translations of Latin and Greek with Classics as an academic subject, neither the study of the ancient languages, nor of the Greek or Roman worlds in any sort of historical or anthropological sense.

iii

One contemporary English poet is perhaps more celebrated than any other for making a virtue out of not knowing the original Greek: Christopher Logue in his 'Accounts of Homer's *Iliad*', as he himself calls them.[13] He has told how he started out by consulting five reputable versions, from Chapman to Rieu; and how he formed the opinion that the more Greek the translator knew, the worse the result.[14]

---

[12] *Tales from Ovid* (London 1997) ix.
[13] *Patrocleia* (1962) and *Pax* (1967), combined with *GBH* to form *War Music* (1981); *Kings* (1991); *Husbands* (1994).
[14] Introduction to *War Music*.

But what is far more subversive than the abandonment of stock epithets or modernisation of similes — and what has proved, I suspect, most attractive to his admirers — is his stripping away of all overlays of 'civilisation', of 'humanism', in order to get down to a bedrock of brute rivalry and violence, of masculine greed, lust and objectification of women. This has recently been called 'the desanitisation of Homer', and heralded as 'a revolutionary intervention...both aesthetically and ideologically'.[15] This claim, however, that the alleged humanity of Homer is merely a veneer, is by no means unheard of in professional scholarship. In some ways it was already present in F. A. Wolf's *Prolegomena* (1795), and it is explicit in Moses Finley's *The World of Odysseus*:[16] 'The *Iliad* is saturated in blood, a fact which cannot be hidden or argued away, twist the evidence as one may in a vain attempt to fit archaic Greek values to a more gentle code of ethics.' I would be surprised if Finley's book was unknown to Logue when he first began work in 1959.

Although Christopher Logue's versions have won praise from scholars as various as Jasper Griffin and George Steiner, he does not seem to have any interest in locating himself in relation to the wider reception of Homer or to Homeric scholarship. While he is concerned to assert his sense of poetry against the lack of poetry in more 'accurate' translations, he does not say whether his programme of desanitisation is in any way motivated by a wish to rescue Homer from the piety or sentimentality of the professional pedants. Again, as with Hughes, Classics with a capital C is no part of the picture, at least not explicitly so.

While Logue's debonair attitude to scholarship may owe something to Pound, it is interestingly different from that of the generation of poets before him as well as the one after him (Logue was born in 1926). All such periodisation is, of course, liable to artificiality, but it does seem fair enough to mark off four poets who were born between 1904 and 1909 as a shifting 'group': Wystan Auden, Cecil Day Lewis, Louis MacNeice and Stephen Spender.

All four went to major English Public Schools and Oxford. Day Lewis and MacNeice actually read Mods and Greats; and all were at schools where, as a matter of course, they will have received or had imposed on them a

---

[15] Lorna Hardwick, *Translating Words, Translating Cultures* (London 2000) 55–61, quote at 60–1. This thoughtful collection of essays was published after I had drafted this chapter, but I have tried to adapt to its main convergences.

[16] New York 1954; rev. ed. London 1977 (quote at 118). For Finley on self-assertion see 113–20; on women, 126–8. For even stronger meat see E. Vermeule, *Aspects of Death in Early Greek Art and Poetry* (Berkeley 1979) 83–116 ('The Happy Hero').

traditional grounding in classical languages and literature.[17] This background was something they could take for granted among their friends, and among a good proportion of their primary public. Generally speaking, classical material and allusions in their poetry are widespread but not made much of. It may be worth noting, though, that in the two chief poems where Auden directly engages with classical literature it is to take fundamental issue with Homer and Virgil respectively.[18]

MacNeice stands out, however. His poetic life-blood is infused with a classical awareness, especially of Homer and Horace. 'He is perhaps the only poet today whose work is directly in the classical tradition,' Auden said of him in 1939.[19] This was soon after the publication of *Autumn Journal*, a kind of reformulation of Wordsworth's *The Prelude* for the 1930s. In the course of the poem, and especially in sections IX and XIII, MacNeice explores with depth and wit his whole knotted relationship with the Greek and Roman world and with his classical education. Although he had earned his living as a lecturer in Classics (in Birmingham and then London) for the previous eight years — 'an impresario of the Ancient Greeks', in his own phrase — he explores much that he dislikes or distrusts in his own education and profession. It is almost as if it means too much for his own foundations for him to allow himself to be sentimental or apologetic.[20]

It so happens that in 1936, early in his poetic span, MacNeice translated Aeschylus' *Agamemnon*. He undertook this, at Auden's suggestion, for performance by Rupert Doone's experimental Group Theatre, and it was published just before its not very successful production.[21] This translation

---

[17] Christopher Stray's *Classics Transformed: Schools, Universities and Society in England, 1830–1960* (Oxford 1998) is a valuable contribution (if over-fond of deflationary frivolities). In chapter 10 he traces the security of Latin in schools between the wars.

[18] 'The Shield of Achilles' in *The Shield of Achilles* (1955), and 'Secondary Epic' in *Homage to Clio* (1960).

[19] I owe this to Peter McDonald's interesting essay '"With Eyes Turned Down on the Past": MacNeice's Classicism', in K. Devine and A. J. Peacock, *Louis MacNeice and his Influence* (*Ulster Editions and Monographs* 6, 1998) 34–52, quote at 35.

[20] McDonald (n. 19) has good observations, drawing out three threads in MacNeice's classicism: tight technique, religious preoccupations, and the darker side of the imagination. There are also good observations on MacNeice in M. Beard and J. Henderson, *Classics: a Very Short Introduction* (Oxford 1995) 119–21.

[21] The music was by an unknown young composer, Ben Britten. There is information about the event in J. Stallworthy, *Louis MacNeice* (London 1995) 193–6, and M. Sidnell in Cropp, Fantham and Scully (n. 9 above) 323–35; the latter overlaps with M. Sidnell, *Dances of Death: the Group Theatre in the Thirties* (London 1984) 209–16. For an extract of MacNeice's unpublished and uncompleted translation of Euripides' *Hippolytus*, see G. Nelson, *Oxford Poetry* 11 (2000) 50–68.

was very much done from the original Greek, line for line indeed; and it was submitted to be scrutinised by his mentor, E. R. Dodds. MacNeice, like Hughes and Harrison, has had superlatives applied to his version— 'the most successful version of any Greek tragedy that anyone in this country has yet produced'[22] — and it makes for an interesting comparison with them. Here are the lines discussed above:

> But Honest Dealing is clear
> Shining in smoky homes,
> Honours the god-fearing life.
> Mansions gilded by filth of hands she leaves,
> Turns her eyes elsewhere, visits the innocent house,
> Not respecting the power
> Of wealth mis-stamped with approval,
> But guides all to the goal.

This is smooth-shaven and finely judged (and again immeasurably better than the Hughes). In some undated notes MacNeice maintains that the English rhythms for translating Greek metres should be 'severe, intricate and irregular', and insists (probably reacting against Gilbert Murray) 'you must not use any sustained & regular English metre'.[23] It seems to me, none the less, that compared with the sustained metre of Harrison his stanza lacks a certain vividness and musicality; and it lacks oral performability (for example 'wealth mis-stamped with approval'). It seems that MacNeice's training was so strong that, faced with an actual classical text, exactitude proved stronger than poetry.

None of the major English poets born between, say, 1915 and 1935 seems to have shown a strong awareness of any relationship to 'the classical tradition'. As we have seen, Ted Hughes used it as a source of material, but in a way that was unaffected by its pedagogic associations. Apart from him, the leading figures are probably Philip Larkin and Geoffrey Hill.[24] Hill has learnedly turned to northern Europe and to Christianity rather than to pagan antiquity for raw matter; but Larkin (who got a 'D' in his School Certificate Latin) was positively anti-classical. He once put his attitude bluntly: 'To

---

[22] Hugh Lloyd-Jones, reported in E. R. Dodds, *Missing Persons: an Autobiography* (Oxford 1977) 116.

[23] I owe this to McDonald (n. 19) 39.

[24] I am aware that there are significant poets from this period who do not really fit my rough generalisations, though there are factors that help explain their untypicality: for example Thom Gunn (moved to USA in his twenties), Edwin Morgan (dedicated Glaswegian), Fleur Adcock (New Zealander), Peter Porter (Australian). This suggests that the story of the ways in which Classics fed into the cultural life in England may be significantly different from elsewhere (see further below on Ireland).

me, the whole of the ancient world, the whole of classical and biblical mythology mean very little, and I think that using them today not only fills poems full of dead spots but dodges the poet's duty to be original.'[25]

This anti-classical or non-classical 'generation' (in so far as my periodisation is valid) may be the product of little more than individual coincidence. But these poets were educated in what was to prove the final era in which Classics held an automatic and often obligatory elite status in schools in England. This death-grip produced a revulsion in many of those subjected to it. It may also be relevant that this 'generation' was formed at the time when F. R. Leavis was at his most influential in his attempt to clear the pedestal of all idols, including the classical, so that he could place the Great Tradition there in sole majesty.

iv

Whether or not I am justified in discerning this period of indifference or downright hostility to classical inspirations, I am more confident that many poets born between 1935 and 1955 have been more positively disposed. Douglas Dunn, for example, David Constantine and Carol Ann Duffy all include substantial classical material, though in an eclectic, occasional way, and according it neither apology nor any special awe. So, not least, does Seamus Heaney, as I shall trace later.

One thing that most of this 'generation' of poets have in common is that they did not go to famous Public Schools. On the other hand most did take Latin, at least as far as O-Level: the difference is that the subject was not imposed with such heavy constraint or expectation as it had been on previous generations. The period between the education reforms of 1944 and the 1960s was a kind of golden age for selective grammar schools and for independent 'Direct Grant' schools, during which both catered for the bright and motivated children who had been selected by the reviled '11 Plus' examination. In rivalry with the more privileged Public Schools, and often in superiority to them, Latin and Ancient History, and to some extent Greek, were taken seriously. Even though still generally taught by unenlightened traditional methods,[26] they seem to have introduced future poets to a resource which enriched rather than alienated them.

---

[25] This is the version of his 'self-introduction' (in D. J. Enright's *Poets of the Nineteen-Fifties*, 1955) which is cited in Larkin's *Required Writing: Miscellaneous Pieces 1955–1982* (London 1983) 69.
[26] Stray (n. 17) 293–6.

Set in this context, Tony Harrison is not quite so isolated a figure as he is sometimes made out to be. A scholarship boy picked out from a working-class background to go to a Direct Grant School,[27] he was taught Classics in a far from progressive way (as also, indeed, at Leeds University), but he was still inspired by it. 'At that time of my life when I most hungered for articulation and models of eloquence, at the maximum point of my need and hunger, I was brought face to face with Greek tragedy.'[28] Ancient Greece, and to a lesser extent Rome, became for him a poetic essential, in a way that has only one clear companion in twentieth-century Britain, Louis MacNeice. As with him, such an obsession is bound to be ambivalent, producing a love mixed with revulsion.[29] Harrison has remained an avid researcher, but unlike MacNeice he has kept away from the official academic world, at least since his early labours towards a post-graduate degree on the reception of Virgil. He has also turned away the usual round of formal lectures and visiting professorships, the chief exception being his year as President of the Classical Association in 1987–1988, which coincided entertainingly with the furore over the television film of *v.*

Harrison's attitude towards Classics, of simultaneous intimacy and distancing, is in fact characteristic of his relation to many of his obsessions. It is in keeping with this that he has found inspiration among the fringes and fragments of the classical worlds no less than, indeed more than, from the glorious canon. True, he has drawn matter from Homer, especially in *The Gaze of the Gorgon* (television film/poem 1992), from Marcus Aurelius in *The Kaisers of Carnuntum* (play, 1995), and above all from Athenian tragedy.[30] But he has also turned to minor poets who give sidelong glances on the mainstream, especially in *Palladas: Poems* (1975) and *U.S. Martial* (1981). *The Trackers of Oxyrhynchus* is made round a satyr-play by Sophocles, of which only one line existed before substantial fragments on papyrus were excavated in 1907. It remained the preserve of specialist scholars until Harrison opened up its possibilities, a revelation

---

[27] Some background is painted in Ken Worpole, 'Scholarship Boy: the Poetry of Tony Harrison', in Astley (n. 9) 61–74, reprinted from *New Left Review* 153 (1985).

[28] For the importance of learning Latin and Greek at school, see his 1988 Presidential Address to the Classical Association, 'Facing Up to the Muses', in Astley (n. 9) 429–54, quote at 437.

[29] There are good observations in Sean O'Brien, *The Deregulated Muse* (Newcastle upon Tyne 1998) 51–3; also Rick Rylance in Sandie Byrne (ed.), *Tony Harrison: Loiner* (Oxford 1997) 137–60, esp. 152–4.

[30] Notably *The Oresteia* (1981), *Medea: a Sex-War Opera* (opera libretto, 1985), *Trojan Women* (in *The Common Chorus*, 1992), *Prometheus* (feature film/poem, 1998). On *Prometheus* see Hardwick (n. 15) 127–39.

paralleled by the moment within the play when wooden crates of dry papyri fly open to release the satyr chorus.[31]

Drawing on even more obscure source material, *The Labourers of Herakles* (1995, published 1996) incorporates 24 fragments of the tragedies of Phrynichus in ancient Greek (several consisting of only a single word), virtually the entire surviving oeuvre. Phrynichus, who was an elder contemporary of Aeschylus, connects vividly with two of Harrison's recurrent concerns. First, he notoriously composed a tragedy about a recent atrocity, the sacking of Miletus by the Persians, a dramatisation that affected the Athenians so strongly that they punished Phrynichus for it. Secondly, he is said to have been the first tragedian to introduce a female character and/or a female chorus: women as witnesses and mourners are a recurrent motif in Harrison's theatre works.[32]

V

Harrison has made it a special mission to prove the poetic worth of his local Yorkshire speech. But he is far from alone among poets in not coming from London or the Home Counties, and in speaking with a regional accent. The recent contributions by contemporary poets from Ireland might well, indeed, be claimed to outweigh all of those from Great Britain put together.

Any kind of analysis of recent Irish poetry is bound to enter a minefield, especially because discussion has inevitably been pulled towards political or ethnic divisions. I shall rush in, none the less. Some poets have aligned themselves with Republicanism, for example John Montague and Seamus Deane: others acknowledge their Unionist associations, for example Michael Longley and Derek Mahon. But there are many complications and crosscurrents, the products of geographical mobility, mixed loyalties and political temperament.[33] Thus, to give only a few random examples, Tom Paulin grew up in a Unionist world, but has his own brand of Republican sympathies; Paul Durcan is fully Irish, but is fiercely hostile to Irish nationalism; Ciaran

---

[31] *Trackers* was performed at Delphi in 1988 and published in 1990, then revised for performance in London and elsewhere in 1990, and republished in both versions in 1991. There are essays on *Trackers* in Astley (n. 9) by me (458–64) and Marianne McDonald (470–85); discussion of it is recurrent in Sandie Byrne, *H, v & O: the Poetry of Tony Harrison* (Manchester 1998) esp. 71–2, 129, 223–4.

[32] I have written about this in 'The Chorus of Mams', in Byrne (n. 29), 171–84, esp. 179–82.

[33] For me personally it was a revelation when I heard E. R. Dodds give a talk in about 1975, based on a draft chapter of *Missing Persons* (n. 22): he began by explaining that his father was 'Scots–Irish' and his mother 'English–Irish' ('almost extinct'), while his own sympathies were 'Irish–Irish'.

Carson locates his Gaelic culture in the North. Scarcely one of the dozen or more significant Irish poets of the generation born between 1935 and 1955 has an ethnic, political or religious identity which is wholly univocal. One thing that almost all these poets do have in common, however, is the same kind of relationship to classical raw material as I have already characterised in British poets of the same era: a kind of eclectic and easy-going allusion and incorporation.[34]

Partisans might attempt to construct a schism in this area. Poets with British affiliations might be aligned with traditional classical education and its imperialist associations; MacNiece supplies the model. Trinity College, Dublin has always been the pre-eminent centre of classical studies in Ireland — the Anglican foundation, which was debarred to those obedient to the Catholic hierarchy until 1970. On the other side, the 'Irish-Irish' might point to their exclusion from the colonial educational system, an exclusion marked most vividly by the hedge-schools that developed in the eighteenth and early nineteenth centuries.[35] However much or little truth there is in the romantic anecdotes surrounding these — ragged boys spouting Latin and so forth — they have planted the idea that the ordinary rural folk of Ireland have had, and may still have, a special access to and love of ancient Greek and Latin.

This is part of the background to the very first production put on by the Field Day Theatre Company in 1980: Brian Friel's *Translations*. This powerful dramatisation of British linguistic and cartographic imperialism is peppered with hedge-school Greek and Latin.[36] Field Day went on to mount two plays of more direct Greek inspiration, both by poets: Tom Paulin's *The Riot Act* (1984), a version of Sophocles' *Antigone*,[37] and Seamus Heaney's *The Cure at Troy*, which follows Sophocles' *Philoctetes* quite closely in the

---

[34] I would single out as a particularly powerful instance Eavan Boland's *The Journey* (1987), built on Sappho, fragment 1 and Virgil *Aeneid* 6. Although she has lived her adult life in Dublin, Boland has increasingly turned away from public politics. (A poet from the North who has analogously turned to more personal and feminist preoccupations is Medbh McGuckian.)

[35] See W. B. Stanford, *Ireland and the Classical Tradition* (Dublin 1976) 25–31 for the hedge-schools, 45–69 for Trinity College, Dublin.

[36] The play's ideology and, by association, Heaney and Paulin were the subject of a challenging, if skewed, attack by Edna Longley in *The Crane Bag* 9 (1985), reprinted in *Poetry in the Wars* (Newcastle upon Tyne 1986) and extracted in S. Deane (ed.), *The Field Day Anthology of Irish Writing* 3 (Derry 1991) 648–59.

[37] Paulin has also written a play based on *Prometheus* called *Seize the Fire* (1989), commissioned by the Open University.

dialogue sections, interspersing these with largely original lyrics. Several other Irish poets have turned to making plays out of Greek tragedy, including Brendan Kennelly (*Antigone* 1985, *Medea* 1991, *Trojan Women* 1993) and Derek Mahon (*Bacchae* 1991).[38]

None of these versions has been made primarily for academic reasons, and none of them uses the classical source as a bid for some kind of cultural respectability. It seems, rather, that a generation of poets, whose education included some Classics but was not dominated by the subject, has found a rich source of inspiration for composing contemporary drama for a divided island which has been going through a period of terrible conflict and suffering. Something of this is expressed in the choral prologue that Heaney adds to Sophocles at the start of *The Cure at Troy*:

> . . . my part is the chorus, and the chorus
> Is more or less a borderline between
> The you and the me and the it of it.
>
> Between
> The gods' and human beings' sense of things.
> And that's the borderline that poetry
> Operates on too, always in between
> What you would like to happen and what will —
> Whether you like it or not.

Classical material is, then, scattered through the works of nearly all this generation of poets, whether from the North or the South. John Kerrigan has tracked down Ovidian echoes in Coffey, Deane, Durcan, Heaney, Hewitt, Longley, Montague, Muldoon, Paulin, and above all Mahon — and that was before *After Ovid*, to which half of these were contributors.[39] There is one of these poets, however, whose classical material is most ubiquitous and potent: Michael Longley. He has drawn persistently on the texts he discovered while reading for his degree in Classics at Trinity College, Dublin.[40] This material

---

[38] Also an Aristophanic *Birds* by Paul Muldoon (1999). There is a balanced discussion of these Irish Greek plays in Hardwick (n. 15) 79–95. For a Nationalist account see M. McDonald, *New Hibernia Review* 1 (1997) 57–70; on the other side, D. O'Rawe in *Theatre: Ancient and Modern* (Open University 2000) 109–24, makes some good points but descends into distasteful carping.

[39] J. Kerrigan, 'Ulster Ovids', in N. Corcoran (ed.), *The Chosen Ground: Essays on the Contemporary Poetry of Northern Ireland* (Bridgend 1992) 237–69, an article which includes an extraordinarily wide range of poets.

[40] Recalled, with special affection for W. B. Stanford, in 'River & Fountain' (1992) in *The Ghost Orchid*.

has proved both flexible and resilient, changing with Longley's changing preoccupations.

In his early poems from the 1960s and 70s he showed a particular affinity with Latin love elegy, especially Propertius and Tibullus, though also with the *Odyssey*, especially for the figure of Odysseus as lover of women. His appeal to the elegists has continued; and in *The Ghost Orchid* (1995) Ovid's *Metamorphoses* becomes prominent, partly in response to the invitation to contribute to *After Ovid*. A change has come over his response to Homer, however, and it is given a new potency, first in *Gorse Fires* (1991), continued in *The Ghost Orchid*, and again in *The Weather in Japan* (2000).

What Longley does is to take an extract from the *Odyssey*, or less often the *Iliad*, and turn it, largely in direct translation, into a complete poem of any length up to about thirty lines. While the sense of place and the reunion of lost loved ones are the Odyssean themes in some of these poems, he is drawn also to Homeric passages which bring out the pathos inherent in a world of violence — the reality, the humanity and the waste of killing.[41] As translations these poems seem to me to be as close to the expression and tone of the original Greek as any other translation of Homer into English in the last quarter of the twentieth century (even perhaps from the whole century). While retaining a trace of the scope and scale of the epic, they have the tightness and concentration of lyric, which is Longley's genre. And the present, and more particularly the present of Northern Ireland, is quietly and movingly insinuated through the use of dialect words and of words which are loaded with association from 'the Troubles'.[42]

The following brief example, 'The Helmet' (from *The Ghost Orchid*), draws on the Hector and Andromache scene in *Iliad* 6, directly translating lines 466–474 (omitting 470), and then turns Hector's prayer in 476–81 into the single last line of reported speech. With this touch the double life of the paramilitary as family man and as ruthless killer also comes suddenly into painful focus.

---

[41] Now I know his work better, I regret not including Longley in the rapid survey of recent Homeric reception in my 1999 Presidential Address to the Classical Association, 'Greek with Consequence'.

[42] *Cf.* S. Matthews, *Irish Poetry: Politics, History, Negotiation* (London and New York 1997) 1–3; also Hardwick (n. 15) 54–5.

When shiny Hector reached out for his son, the wean
Squirmed and buried his head between his nurse's breasts
And howled, terrorised by his father, by the flashing bronze
And the nightmarish nodding of the horse-hair crest.

His daddy laughed, his mammy laughed, and his daddy
Took off the helmet and laid it on the ground to gleam,
Then kissed the babbie and dandled him in his arms and
Prayed that his son might grow up bloodier than him.

vi

Lastly to turn to another poet born in 1939, who shared a reciprocally formative relationship with Longley in their early poetic days: Seamus Heaney.
He was another scholarship boy at a selective school, where he gained an A
grade in A-Level Latin (as well as in four other subjects) before reading
English at Queen's University, Belfast. There are classical allusions right from
Heaney's earliest poetry, but — in keeping with what has emerged elsewhere
in this study — there has been a quantitative and qualitative shift in his latest
work. It is once again as though classical poetry has been liberated as a source
of inspiration and interaction.

Before the 1990s Heaney's classical connections were relatively sparse
and relatively recherché. Thus, most notably, Hercules' less than well-known
encounter with the earth-dependant Antaeus is thematic in *North* (1975).[43]
Other motifs that recur are Orpheus; the *omphalos*, navel-stone of the earth;
Helicon, mountain of poetic inspiration; Hermes, both as god of trade and as
the *psychopompos*, who accompanies souls to the underworld; and the underworld experiences of Aeneas and of Virgil (with Dante).

There is, however, a palpable 'change of gear' at around 1990, the time
of *The Cure at Troy* (p. 14 above).[44] *Seeing Things* (1991) actually begins
with a close and sensitive translation of lines 98–148 of *Aeneid* 6, where
Aeneas plucks the golden bough: this is clearly connected with Heaney's
poems in response to the death of his father (in 1986). He has turned again to

---

[43] On this see John Lucas, in E. Andrews (ed.), *Seamus Heaney: a Collection of Critical Essays*
(London 1992) 130–1; and Seamus Deane, in C. Malloy and P. Carey (eds.), *Seamus Heaney: the
Shaping Spirit* (Delaware 1996) 29–30. There is a brief but helpful survey of Heaney and the Classics
by Bernard O'Donoghue in *Omnibus* 36 (1998) 21–23.

[44] On *The Cure at Troy* in the larger context of Heaney's poetry, see Alan Peacock in Andrews (n. 43)
233–55, and Phyllis Carey in Malloy and Carey (n. 43) 137–56 (relating it to the plays of Havel).

central, iconic Virgil even more unashamedly and intimately ('my hedge-schoolmaster Virgil') in 'Bann Valley Eclogue', published in the *Times Literary Supplement* on 8 October 1999. To celebrate the imminent birth of a child on the dairy farm of his natal valley, the 'Poet' conducts a dialogue with 'Virgil', working in the chief motifs and even the Latin words of the 'messianic' fourth *Eclogue*.

Another treasury opened in *Seeing Things* is the *Odyssey*. Heaney's friendship at Harvard with Robert Fitzgerald, whose death is memorialised with Odyssean echoes in a poem in *The Haw Lantern* (1987),[45] played a part in turning him towards the Greek epic. It is even his 'Bedtime Reading' in the sixth of the seven sonnets in the sequence 'Glanmore Revisited'.[46] The marital bed of Odysseus and Penelope had been introduced in the previous sonnet, and the nurse Eurycleia's recognition of Odysseus' scar in the third. In *The Spirit Level* (1996), Heaney's next — and at the time of writing most recent — collection, Odysseus among the ghosts in Hades is invoked in the powerful poem 'Damson': 'Like Odysseus in Hades... / But not like him...' [47]

The work of Heaney that relates to classical literature most of all to date is the sequence of five poems, in varying metres, that stand at the very centre of the 1996 volume. Entitled 'Mycenae Lookout', they have Aeschylus *Agamemnon* line 36 as their epigraph — 'The ox is on my tongue.' They reach towards some of Heaney's fiercest and deepest responses to the Troubles in Northern Ireland; but this is achieved through the mediation of the dynastic saga in the *Oresteia* and its civic repercussions. I shall attempt to trace their sequence.[48]

In the first poem, 'The Watchman's War', the 'I' is identified with the watchman of the prologue of *Agamemnon* by echoes such as the ox on the tongue, the 'sheepdog', and watching for the beacon.

> Up on my elbows, gazing, biding time
> In my outpost on the roof...

---

[45] On this see H. Hart, *Seamus Heaney: Poet of Contrary Progressions* (Syracuse, NY 1992) 188–9.

[46] I looked briefly at some of these poems in 'Greek with Consequence' (n. 41).

[47] Another classical 'hero' who figures in *The Spirit Level* is Socrates, whose death scene is both made near and distanced in the second section of 'The Poet's Chair'. The figure of Socrates already informs 'A Daylight Art' in *The Haw Lantern*.

[48] I have not attempted to search for bibliography on these poems: indeed the only relevant secondary literature I have read is Helen Vendler, *Seamus Heaney* (London 1998) 168–74. Heaney visited Mycenae on his first-ever visit to Greece in summer 1995, a journey curtailed by the announcement of his Nobel Prize. This itinerary may be relevant to the sense of locality in the third poem, and is surely recalled in the details of the Athenian Acropolis in the last.

But this watchman is an implicated witness, overhearing the ardour of Clytemnestra's love-making, and recognising its affinity to the blood-lust of the Trojan War. The opening of the second poem, 'Cassandra', spells out the connection:

> No such thing
> as innocent
> bystanding.

In this jerky, harsh, four-letter-worded poem, the Watchman is repelled by Agamemnon's macho lust, yet also aroused by Cassandra's vulnerability. Although so different in tone from the Aeschylean tragedy, there are at least two clear echoes: 'And then her Greek / words came'; and Cassandra's departure to her own slaughter inside with a virtual quotation of *Agamemnon* 1329:

> saying, 'A wipe
> of the sponge,
> that's it.'

In the third poem, 'His Dawn Vision', the Watchman is moved by the early-morning landscape of Mycenae to a saddened sense of guilty disengagement. This then gives him a vision of a future empire — Rome — and of yet more internecine murder, as one man strikes another down 'amorously, it seemed'. Next, in 'The Nights', he acknowledges with bitter humour his complicities with Clytemnestra and Aegisthus: he is even the confidant of their sex-lives. He associates himself with Atlas, who has to carry the floor on which the gods noisily fornicate. And in the end this means that he betrays Agamemnon:

> I moved beyond bad faith:
> for his bullion bars, his bonus
> was a rope-net and a blood-bath.
> And the peace had come upon us.

Lastly, in 'His Reverie of Water' Aeschylus is almost left behind. The thought moves from baths to the secret wells of citadels to siege and sack. Then in the final three stanzas, memories of the sinking of a bore-hole come welling up, and the sequence ends with a cleansing image of 'gushing taps'.[49] So within the scope of this sequence Heaney encompasses, among other themes, tragedy and comedy, violence and gentleness, the rise and fall of empires, the apprehension and hope of cease-fire. The inspiration of the

---

[49] Vendler (n. 48) 174, refers to a well-sinking in Heaney's childhood, which is recalled in his *Preoccupations: Selected Prose 1968–1978* (London 1980) 17, 20.

greatest of all Greek tragedies, along with other classical resonances, is woven in and out without apology or distortion.

In the meandering course of this chapter I have taken into account hardly any poets born after 1950, and none after 1960. For one thing, I do not have the confidence to predict which of them will still be widely read in the mid-twenty-first century. Yet if a successor ever comes to write a similar survey in a hundred years' time, then those poets who are now young will by then be as distant in time as Wilde, Yeats, Housman and Edward Thomas are from us. That sobering thought brings home how much what is meant by 'Classics' has changed in the past century. And how the cultures of ancient Greece and Rome have continued in ever-shifting ways to filter up through the strata of dead generations, and to flow as fresh wellsprings for poets.

I am grateful to Lorna Hardwick, Fiona Macintosh and Bernard O'Donoghue for helpful comments.

2
A taste for the classics

Pat Easterling

i

Anyone with a professional, or at least a serious, interest in what we are used to calling 'classical literature' is liable nowadays to encounter problems of definition. At the extreme, they can be formulated along such lines as: What implications does a value-term like 'classical' carry in contemporary English? What does 'Classics' as a discipline suggest, if not the traditionalist attitudes and assumptions of an élite past culture, offering a badge of membership in a no longer sought-after club? And if one tries substituting 'ancient' for 'classical' (as in 'ancient history') that too raises questions. Why privilege Greece and Rome over Egypt or Persia or China? Why speak confidently of 'the ancient world', as if it were coterminous with the Roman empire? Finally, literature itself has become a problematic category for contemporary criticism — and the Greeks and Romans, in any case, didn't have a word for it.[1]

All this is worlds away from the notion of the 'best authors', used more or less unselfconsciously by educators well into the twentieth century as a way of defining the classical canon.[2] 'Best' implied a shared set of values —

---

[1] Teresa Morgan, *Literate Education in the Hellenistic and Roman Worlds* (Cambridge 1998) 90–1. Some of the issues currently debated in relation to 'Classics' are discussed in Yun Lee Too and Niall Livingstone (eds.), *Pedagogy and Power* (Cambridge 1998).

[2] This concept was enshrined in the regulations for the Classical Tripos at Cambridge from 1849, when the reformed ordinances were approved, and stayed there until the late 1950s. The notion of 'best periods' was naturally linked with it, as in R. W. Browne's *History of Greek Classical Literature* (London 1853) 1: 'The Classical literature of a nation includes, strictly speaking, only the works of its best authors. Its Aera is that during which the national intellect is in its greatest vigour and health; when the language, which is the exponent of that intellect, exhibits the most perfect refinement and purity, when Poetry, Philosophy and History are in their most flourishing condition.' For an eloquent defence of the Victorian syllabus see R. Burn, 'Course of Reading for the Classical Tripos', in *The Student's Guide to the University of Cambridge* (Cambridge 1862).

moral, social, aesthetic — for rating both Classics as a discipline and the classics of ancient literature. Postmodernist poetics on the one hand and institutional politics on the other have finally dismantled this reassuring framework. But the effect of the upheavals has not been merely to disrupt old certainties. What has been emerging, along with new and more capacious definitions of 'the ancient world', has been a closer understanding of the complex processes of reception. The recognition that the canon is (and always has been) open to reinvention, and that even the most 'central' texts themselves are infinitely mutable, as one generation's readings inform another's, has had the effect of releasing new energies. The role of the interpreter is now seen as more exploratory, less hierophantic and certainly less secure,[3] while its potential for achieving richer and more nuanced results has been growing.

This chapter explores aspects of the debate about canonicity, first by reviewing some basic 'canonical' vocabulary, then by taking a test case (the use of quotations) by which to illustrate the tensions inherent in the notion of literary authority, first in the ancient world and then in the Renaissance, and to make some suggestions about 'staying power'.

ii

It is worth starting with terminology, because there is an oddity at the very beginning of the story, namely that 'canon' ($\kappa\alpha\nu\dot{\omega}\nu$), a perfectly good ancient Greek word meaning 'measuring rod', 'rule', 'standard' and 'model',[4] was not used by Greeks or Romans (who took the word over) in the modern sense of a set of the most highly valued authors or works of a particular cultural tradition, or as in current slogans like 'the Western canon'. The source of this usage is no doubt the early[5] Christian application of the terms 'canon' and 'canonical' to those books of the New Testament which were accepted by the church as the standard or rule of faith. The Christian practice in its turn had a highly significant model, the Hebrew canon of the Old Testament. But the

---

[3] See e.g. Charles Segal, 'Cracks in the marble of the classic form: the problem of the classical today', *Annals of Scholarship* 10.1 (1993) 7–30, esp. 18–21; Charles Martindale, *Redeeming the Text: Latin Poetry and the Hermeneutics of Reception* (Cambridge 1993).

[4] The sculptor Polyclitus used it as the title for his manual on proportions; in literary contexts it was used of a writer who could serve as the 'standard' of a genre or of writing in a particular dialect, e.g. Herodotus in Ionic, Thucydides in Attic (Dion. Hal. *Pomp.* 3).

[5] From the fourth century AD onwards. For the NT canon see R. M. Grant, 'The New Testament canon', in P. R. Ackroyd and C. F. Evans (eds.), *The Cambridge History of the Bible* vol. 1 (Cambridge 1970) 284–308.

modern non-biblical use of 'canon' goes back only to the eighteenth century.[6]

When the Dutch scholar David Ruhnken published an essay in 1768 in which he applied the term to lists of approved (pagan) Greek and Latin authors,[7] he was not intending to imply that there was a 'god-given' selection of ancient works, destined from the start to survive. Nor did he believe it was easy to establish orders of merit: as he remarked, *Verum quid perfectissimum sit, judicare, quam anceps est et difficile.*[8] What interested him was the question of ancient lists and their origins: he had read Quintilian's passing reference (*Inst. Or.* 10.1.54) to the scholars of Alexandria — specifically Aristophanes of Byzantium and Aristarchus — as responsible for listing past Greek authors according to genre, but he saw that neither the history nor the function of the lists was self-evident. Indeed, long before the Alexandrian scholars got to work on the rescue and cataloguing of what survived of the work of earlier Greek authors, there were popularly familiar lists of one kind or another that may have helped the whole process of classification to get started. It was not after all such a big step from the Three Graces and the Nine Muses to the Seven Sages and the Nine Lyric Poets. And once lists were in being, for whatever purpose, they had a notorious tendency to mutate: Diogenes Laertius, for example, quotes a source which knew 17 candidates for inclusion in the list of the Seven Sages.[9]

What is hard to tell at this distance is whether the Alexandrians made systematic selective lists according to criteria of value and importance, which then influenced the choice of works most commonly read and studied, or whether their lists developed out of their library catalogues, which recorded what was *available* from the past. This itself, of course, would have been the product of some kind of filtering process, 'the test of time'. And if a grouping like the Nine Lyric Poets was already in being,[10] it would certainly have an effect on which lyric poets' works were still obtainable several hundred years after they were composed. In the case of drama there is a strong presumption

---

[6] See Rudolf Pfeiffer, *History of Classical Scholarship* I (Oxford 1968) 206–8 for more details.

[7] *Historia critica oratorum graecorum*, published along with Rutilius Lupus, *De figuris sententiarum et elocutionis* (Leiden 1768).

[8] Ruhnken (n. 7) cviii: 'but how difficult and uncertain it is to judge what is most perfect!'

[9] Diogenes Laertius 1.41, citing Hermippus. Lists and numerically defined groups are a fascinating subject for the cultural historian. They go back early in Greek traditions and no doubt served multiple purposes, as ways of organising experience (the Three Fates, the Nine Muses), passing on moral and religious teaching (the Three Precepts, as at Aesch. *Supp.* 708; *cf.* the Twelve Tables, the Ten Commandments and the Seven Deadly Sins), and claiming authority by implicit appeal to the power of certain numbers.

[10] So Gregory Nagy, *Pindar's Homer* (Baltimore 1990). Nagy argues strongly for the importance of panhellenic relevance as a qualification for survival.

that the performance repertoire had a great deal of influence on which play-wrights and which plays were best known centuries after their first produc-tions.[11] Mention of performance is a useful reminder that the formation of public taste was more strongly influenced, at different periods, by rhapsodes, actors in tragedy and comedy, choirs and solo singers of various kinds, mime and pantomime artists, orators, rhetors and contestants in poetry competitions than by scholars; the importance of the latter was in the development of the technology by which texts were edited and transmitted.

At all events there is no hint of the discipline of biblical canonicity — not surprising in the absence of a doctrine of revelation. A passage in Josephus brings out very sharply the difference between the Greeks' cavalier treatment of their literary and historical sources and the Jews' reverence for their works of scripture 'which defile the hands':[12]

> We have given practical proof of our reverence for our own Scriptures. For, although such long ages have now passed, no one has ventured either to add, or to remove, or to alter a syllable; and it is an instinct with every Jew, from the day of his birth, to regard them as the decrees of God, to abide by them, and, if need be, cheerfully to die for them. Time and again before now the sight has been witnessed of prisoners enduring tortures and death in every form in the theatres, rather than utter a single word against the laws and the allied documents.
>
> What Greek would endure as much for the same cause? Even to save the entire collection of his nation's writings from destruction he would not face the smallest personal injury. For to the Greeks they are mere stories improvised according to the fancy of their authors . . . [13]

If 'canon' terminology is problematic in the ancient (secular) context, alter-native vocabulary is hard to find, and this perhaps suggests that we should beware of trying too hard. The examples of technical language commonly cited by modern scholars all seem to have had limited currency in antiquity: the Latin *classicus* ('top-rank', 'superior') which gave English 'classical' and 'classic' could be used of a writer,[14] but it does not have to imply that there was a

---

[11] *Cf.* P. E. Easterling, *The Cambridge Companion to Greek Tragedy* (Cambridge 1997) ch. 9.

[12] This translates a phrase in the Mishnah, which according to Grant (n. 5) 114, 'in effect indicates canonical status. Of the various interpretations of it which have been offered the most probable is that the books so described were, so to say, impregnated with a contagious quality of holiness which had to be washed away so that it might not be conveyed to mundane objects.'

[13] *Contra Apionem* 42–5, trans. H. St. J. Thackeray (Loeb, slightly adapted).

[14] Aulus Gellius 19.8.15: . . . *uel oratorum aliquis uel poetarum, id est classicus adsiduusque aliquis scriptor, non proletarius*: 'or some orator or poet, I mean a top-rated and first-class writer, not one of the common herd'. The phrasing suggests that *classicus* is being used rather self-consciously as a metaphor (from property-rating). It seems that *classicus* had to wait till the Renaissance to gather standard literary significance.

precisely defined *classis* or category in which he would be ranked. Quintilian uses *ordo* and *numerus* when discussing the groupings made by the Alexandrians, and his use of the verb *recipere* suggests admission to a select category (10.1.59), but he also insists on the multiplicity of options open to readers (10.1.57–8). Expressions like 'admitting' and 'including' (ἐγκρίνειν) may have been used by Greeks for approved authors, but the only texts that give us proof of a really technical application of such a term are very late ones: the *Suda* entry on the orator Dinarchus, identifying him as one of the 'included' (οἱ ἐγκριθέντες), and a remark in Photius about Aeschines having been 'included' by the Atticist lexicographer Phrynichus (*Bibl.* 20b25). At best this might suggest that a wide range of authors was 'included' in their various generic groups as most appropriate for study; at its narrowest it could refer quite specifically to the selection of Attic orators intended for students to imitate (and orators are a special case, as we shall see).

Another term found in specialised contexts is οἱ πραττόμενοι, the 'dealt with', 'handled' [authors],[15] that is, supplied with commentaries, presumably because they were regularly used and studied and readers needed help in understanding them, particularly as the time-gap widened between composition and reception. Most categorical, though not particularly specific, is the use of τὰ βιβλία (βυβλία), 'the books', to refer to the works (covering a period from Homer to Demosthenes) that formed the basis of Hellenic culture (*paideia*) at a time — from the late first century AD onwards — when 'Greekness' was being significantly reinvented, and admiration for Attic authors in particular became a dominant factor.[16]

The common thread in all this vocabulary is education: the regular objective of this 'including' and 'handling', and of the identification of appropriate works as examples, was to provide students at different levels with models to imitate. Even at the most elementary level of school exercises, the commonest type of text for copying and (no doubt) for learning by heart was the maxim (*gnōmē, sententia*) which always had a normative, if not always a particularly ethical, function.[17] Over and over again the notion of usefulness

---

[15] *Scholia in Dionysii Thracis artem grammaticam* ed. A. Hilgard (= *Grammatici Graeci* 1.3) Leipzig 1901, 20.1 and 21.17–19; schol. on Nicander, *Theriaca* 11.

[16] Dionysius *Rhet.* 8 (= Usener-Radermacher 295–323). See Morgan (n. 1) 74–9; Tim Whitmarsh, 'Reading power in Roman Greece: the paideia of Dio Chrysostom', in Too and Livingstone (n. 1) 192–213; Simon Goldhill (ed.), *Being Greek under Rome* (Cambridge 2001), esp. the introduction and chs. 3 and 6.

[17] Modern parents might find a good deal to object to in a collection like the Menandrean monostichs (single-verse quotations from Menander, Euripides and others, edited under the title *Menandri Sententiae* by Siegfried Jäkel, Leipzig 1964), particularly in the sections on women and money.

is invoked, and there is no difficulty in guessing the implied answers to the question 'useful for what?' The aim is to achieve effectiveness in speaking and writing (the 'communication skills' of modern educators),[18] which constituted the most reliable indicator of *paideia*, the qualities possessed by a cultivated person (*pepaideumenos*). At all levels, effective use of language was thought to rely on correctness, and for students with the financial resources to go beyond acquiring basic literacy there was the special challenge of imitating the most admired Greek writers in the Attic dialect, and an ever more systematic tradition of rhetorical training to foster it. Although the general approach is a highly instrumental one, moral and social values clearly come into the equation when the 'best' models are being identified.

Quintilian, at any rate, is in no doubt about his agenda: he wants his Roman students of oratory to read authors who are good to imitate, and the criteria are moral as well as stylistic. The word-power for which the trainee orator must strive is to be more than that of the spin doctor: the students 'must become familiar with the best, and their minds must be formed and their style developed through much reading rather than the reading of many authors'.[19] So, however little weight we might want to give to the idea that ancient education and culture were subject to strictly 'canonical' discipline, there is no escaping the conclusion that the emphasis on imitation of correct models had a strongly convergent intent.[20] But how did imitation work in practice?

iii

When we start to look into the choice of models, there are several factors that complicate the situation in interesting ways. Many of the most admired models were poets, while the end-product of the imitator was typically

---

Some samples: 'Women in general are extravagant by nature' (153), 'A woman's advice is not usually profitable' (163), 'Much harm comes from women' (666), 'Don't trust your life to a woman' (142). Even though there are counterbalancing maxims like 'A good woman keeps her household safe' (140), the general message is pretty misogynistic. On the importance of the gnomic texts see Morgan (n. 1) ch. 4.

[18] *Cf.* Sheldon Rothblatt, *The Modern University and its Discontents* (Cambridge 1997) 362, for the importance to sophisticated societies of the arts of communication, negotiation and mediation.

[19] 10.1.59: *optimis adsuescendum est et multa magis quam multorum lectione formanda mens et ducendus color.*

[20] This is quite compatible with the model of 'core and periphery' as a way of understanding ancient education, persuasively argued for by Morgan (n. 1) in preference to a 'curricular' model which would presuppose a more institutionalised system of syllabus and examination.

meant to be in prose; the indispensable Homer was not an Attic author; tensions and contradictions of all kinds can be traced between the convergent and normative character of the ancient educational process and the stylistic inventiveness of some of its products, Plutarch, for example, or Heliodorus, or Clement of Alexandria. The use of quotation, so important an element in the ancient theory and practice of imitation, makes a useful test case.

Quoting the classics can easily be construed as derivative and mechanical, particularly as the use of well-known sayings and quotations (*gnōmai*) was a prescribed element in the preliminary exercises (*progymnasmata*) of the rhetorical schools, and later antiquity produced many collections of such material — *anthologia* and *florilegia* — from which elegant 'blooms' could be selected without any necessary familiarity with the original texts or contexts. But the essential question is whether these quotations were adaptable to a truly diverse range of purposes. We need only consider a collection like Stobaeus' *Anthology*, made up of many earlier collections of quotations, to see how versatile they could be. It is interesting that scholars are not sure whether its author, John of Stobi in Macedonia, probably to be dated to the fifth century AD, was a pagan or a Christian; the quotations are from pagan authors, but for centuries the collection was used with approval by Christian writers.

If we are to do justice to ancient practice, the term 'quotation' needs to be quite broadly interpreted, to include not only citations from known works or authors and utterances attributed to famous sages of the past, but also a wider category of sayings and proverbs, usually anonymous or attached to a variety of different authors, expressed in varying formulations and in verse as well as prose. The habit of using such sayings, whether attributed to an author or not, had been common in Greek texts from the earliest times and was no doubt an important pre-literate mode of communicating cultural values. The surviving ancient collections are fairly catholic in their range, and there are plenty of examples of what started as a quotation with a specific literary origin ending up as an anonymous saying.[21] One factor that makes the dividing line between 'saying' and 'quotation' hard to draw is that

---

[21] See Renzo Tosi, *Dizionario delle sentenze latine e greche: 10.000 citazioni dall'antichità al rinascimento* (Milan 1991) ix–xix. For the tradition of 'sayings' and its importance in Greek culture from the earliest times see Joseph Russo, 'Prose genres for the performance of traditional wisdom in ancient Greece: proverb, maxim, apothegm', in Lowell Edmunds and Robert W. Wallace (eds.), *Poet, Public and Performance in Ancient Greece* (Baltimore and London 1997) 49–64, with an interesting discussion of categories and terminology.

by far the largest category are on general topics relating to life and death, wealth, moral and social conduct, and so on, and are not typically as idiosyncratic as are many of the best known Shakespearean quotations in modern English-speaking cultures. Lines like 'Is this a dagger which I see before me?' or 'Beware the Ides of March' would have had less staying power in the ancient world than more versatile ones like 'All the world's a stage' or 'Brevity is the soul of wit.'

An interesting question at once arises in relation to canonicity, if no paramount need was felt either to name the author of a quotation ('as Homer says') or to reproduce the words exactly; there is plenty of evidence, from variants in manuscript traditions, from doublets in the anthologies and from attributions of the same saying to several different sources, that the appropriation of past wisdom did not crucially depend on name-dropping. What seems to have mattered most was the adaptability of the words used; but of course it would be hard to deny that citation without naming, or more oblique allusive reference, might often be making an implicit appeal to shared familiarity with approved authors. Even so, the most important factor of all is the extraordinary pervasiveness of the practice of quoting: this itself may have been more durable than any particular significance attached to the content or associations of what was cited.

Starting from the bottom up, we can note the strong and long-lasting pedagogic preoccupation with quotations, as in the Menandrean monostich collection, or the collections of verses attributed to Theognis, Phocylides and others,[22] which is partly to be explained in utilitarian terms. Short passages — a line or two of verse, or a pithily expressed prose saying — were easily memorised and good to use as copybook materials, practical vehicles, therefore, for the inculcation of rules of behaviour and linguistic correctness. But the very memorability of their form, combined with the arresting, paradoxical or enigmatic content of some at least of these quotations, must

---

[22] For the Menandrean collection (iambic trimeters) see n. 17 above; for Theognis (elegiacs) and the shadowy Phocylides (hexameters) see M. L. West's edition (Berlin and New York 1978), and his note 'Phocylides', *JHS* 98 (1978) 164–7; the hexameter collection attributed by scholars to 'Pseudo-Phocylides' (an Alexandrian Jew of probably the first century AD) appears in the Teubner edition of Theognis, edited by Douglas Young (Leipzig 1971). Hesiod's *Works and Days* was a popular source of quotations in educational texts; see e.g. Isocrates, *To Nicocles*. In the later Byzantine period the Distichs of Cato, translated from the Latin by Maximus Planudes, were also widely used. The original Latin text (from late antiquity) was popular with Renaissance teachers in the West; *cf.* Robert Black, 'Humanism', in C. Allmand (ed.), *The New Cambridge Medieval History*, vol. 7 (Cambridge 1998) 259.

have given the more interesting ones (for example, 'Those whom the gods love die young')[23] an imaginative appeal that was hard to confine within a narrow didactic programme.

Moving on from first encounters with the Classics to something more ambitious and theoretical — a text, indeed, that had an extremely powerful influence on all subsequent thinking about effective communication — we find Aristotle discussing the use of what he calls *gnōmai* in the second book of the *Rhetoric*. Chapter 21 is devoted to a detailed analysis of the function of these 'maxims' (in fact the three examples he chooses are all easily recognisable as quotations from heroic poetry, the first two from famous passages in the *Iliad*, the third probably from the Epic Cycle), and shows how powerfully they can be made to work:[24]

> One should even make use of common and frequently quoted maxims, if they are useful (*chrēsimoi*); for because they are common, they seem to be true, since all acknowledge them as such. For instance, someone who is exhorting his soldiers to face danger before they have offered sacrifices may say: 'The best of omens is to defend one's country,'[25] and if they are inferior in numbers, 'The chances of war are the same for both,'[26] and if advising them to destroy the children of the enemy even though they are innocent, 'Foolish is he, who having slain the father, suffers the children to live.'[27]

These examples, all identified as 'useful' (by far the most important criterion of value for quotations), show how easily they can be adapted to the relevant circumstances, and this very adaptability to different moral standpoints may in fact be one of the secrets of their success, however problematic in principle such frank pragmatism might seem.

Aristotle goes on to discuss the effectiveness of challenging a famous old saying: this is the rhetorical device, much used by the poets,[28] which

---

[23] Menander *Mon.* 583 (= *Dis Ex. fr.* 4), Stobaeus 4.52.27, *cf.* Plautus, *Bacchides* 816–17.

[24] *Rh.* 2.1395a10–19, trans. J. H. Freese (Loeb, slightly adapted).

[25] *Iliad* 12.243: Hector's famous reply to Polydamas before the attack on the Achaean wall.

[26] *Iliad* 18.309: again Hector speaking to Polydamas, when Achilles has returned to the fighting.

[27] *Cypria fr.* 33 Bernabé; Tosi (n. 21) no. 1590. Quoted by Aristotle in *Rh.* 1.1376a7 as an example of a traditional saying that can be used to give weight to an argument. In two fragments surviving from Polybius 23.10 the quotation is given to Philip of Macedon in contexts described in highly dramatic language: in 10.10, when he orders the killing of the sons of his executed rivals, and in 10.15, when he finds himself haunted by the need to have one of his own sons killed. Here the saying has taken on a 'tragic' and prophetic significance.

[28] Often to powerful effect, as by Aeschylus (*Ag.* 750–62), Simonides (*PMG* 542 11–26), Sophocles (*Trach.* 1–5). In each of these cases the critique of the 'old saying' has an important structural role to play in the whole text.

simultaneously appropriates the authority of past wisdom and marks out the speaker's point as different, original, surprising. The technique can be used, he says, to make one's *ēthos* appear better, if (for example) one contradicts a saying like 'Love as if you were bound to hate' and replaces it with 'Hate as if you were bound to love' (21.13).[29]

Passages like these bring out the fundamental challenges that faced the speaker and writer who attempted to persuade: how did you manage to convince your audience or your readers that you were 'genuine' and to be trusted, when your training had prepared you to turn the most basic moral sentiments either way with the aid of an apposite quotation? Evidently the authority of the past was felt to be worth harnessing, but how did one succeed in rising above patent artificiality at one extreme or mere cliché at the other? This was where the quality of the models came in, and the need to form one's taste, moral as well as aesthetic. For anyone aspiring to write convincingly and creatively it cannot have been enough to rely on more or less random selection from handy collections of *gnōmai*: one had to go through the strenuous exercise of engaging closely with models admired for their stylistic power. So Quintilian advises in the case of Archilochus: 'Of the three writers of iambic verse "admitted" by Aristarchus, Archilochus will be the one most relevant for the development of *hexis* [a trained habit to be cultivated by the good speaker]. He has a supreme gift of expression, his maxims [*sententiae*] are strong and at the same time terse and vibrant, and he is full of blood and sinew . . . '(10.1.59).[30] The importance of *using* the fruits of one's reading and not merely flaunting them is implicit in all the most influential texts on rhetoric, forcing the would-be speaker or writer to wrestle with the problem of finding a voice of his own at the same time as acknowledging the riches of 'the books'.

Some of these issues are explored from a rather different standpoint by Plutarch in a remarkable essay entitled 'How the young man should study poetry' (*Mor.* 14d–37b), which makes the case for using quotations for educationally valuable purposes and at the same time demonstrates how

---

[29] *Cf.* Sophocles, *Ajax* 679–82, with Jebb's fascinating note in the Appendix to his commentary (Cambridge 1896) 231–2. The saying was attributed to Bias of Priene by Aristotle (*Rh.* 2.1389b23–5) and by some to Chilon; Tosi (n. 22) 1311.

[30] *itaque ex tribus receptis Aristarchi iudicio scriptoribus iamborum ad ἕξιν maxime pertinebit unus Archilochus. summa in hoc uis elocutionis, cum ualidae tum breues uibrantesque sententiae, plurimum sanguinis atque neruorum . . .*

this should be done. What Plutarch stresses most of all is the reading process, which he sees as essential preparation both for the conduct of life and for the study of philosophy. He is not concerned with rhetorical studies, but he shares Quintilian's interest in *discrimination*: reading the poets will help young people to develop their critical judgement (*krisis* 20d).

Plutarch's own method shows the importance of discrimination at every stage. The first principle to be kept ready at hand by the student is the proverbial saying 'The poets tell many lies' (πολλὰ ψεύδονται ἀοιδοί; cf. Aristotle, *Metaph.* 1.2). Poets will create fictions both intentionally and because they know no better, and the student will have to learn to isolate truth from fiction and note when the poet himself gives clues to correct reading. So in the *Odyssey*, if the reader finds himself getting distressed by the pathetic account of Agamemnon and Achilles in the underworld he will be able to quote a couple of lines from book 11 (223–4): 'Go back to the light as fast as you can, and keep all these things in mind, so that later you can tell them to your wife,' on which Plutarch comments (16e) that Homer put this in 'gracefully', as a fanciful and therefore fitting tale to tell to a woman. But he then cites examples of the downright deluded things Homer and other poets say about the gods and the underworld — and in answer to these you need to have lines from Empedocles or Xenophanes ready to quote, which deny that any human being has the power to know the truth about the gods (17e–f).

The next stage is to learn how art and fiction work, so that one can take pleasure in good imitation and recognise that a poet may quite properly put wicked sentiments in the mouths of bad people (18d–f). The fact that the poets come up with contradictory sayings gives an opportunity for comparison and discussion, and might indeed lead one to challenge them on their own terms (21a):

> When Pindar has very harshly and provocatively said 'You must do everything in your power to destroy your enemy' [*Isthmian* 4.48], [we may reply] 'But you yourself say "The bitterest end awaits sweet things gained unjustly"' [*Isthmian* 7.47]. And when Sophocles [says] 'Sweet is profit, even if it comes unjustly' [*fr.* 833R], [the reply is] 'Well we've heard *you* say "False words bring no fruitful harvest"' [*fr.* 834R].

This 'dialogic' engagement with the classic authors is one of Plutarch's main preoccupations: he explicitly rejects allegorical readings, which are liable to explain objectionable things away (19e–f), and favours instead a robustly critical willingness to answer back (26b):

> One ought not timorously, or as though under the spell of religious dread in a holy place, to shiver with awe at everything, and fall prostrate, but should rather with confidence acquire the habit of exclaiming 'wrong' and 'improper' no less than 'right' and 'proper'.[31]

At the extreme Plutarch recommends altering key words in famous quotations to suit one's own sense of what is acceptable (33c–34b). Although his main concern is with the moral implications of what a person reads, he understands that the discriminating reader has to attend to the nuances of language and usage, and there is plenty in this essay to show how using quotations could fulfil a crucial double function, developing the power to transform as well as the power to connect.

The power to transform is displayed with great verve in the works of the early Christian apologist Clement of Alexandria, born in the mid-second century a generation after Plutarch's death. Like Plutarch, Clement had been brought up on 'the books', probably at Athens in a pagan household, and was equally at home with the use of quotations, though his agenda was radically different. For him the point of using the quotations (often, no doubt, derived from ready-made and sometimes tendentious anthologies) was to demonstrate the follies of pagan religious belief, while allowing that the sages and poets of the past had given indirect or veiled utterance to true wisdom (*Stromateis* (*Patchwork*) 4.24) and showing in detail what they had 'stolen' from the Holy Scriptures, the new and also definitive source of authority (*Str.* 5.107–40). He is at his liveliest when engaging in satirically 'dialogic' critique of the poets in his *Exhortation to the Greeks* (*Protrepticus* 2.27–8):

> Now listen to the loves of your gods and the extraordinary stories of their uncontrollable passions; and hear about their wounds, their binding in chains, their fits of laughter, their fights and their periods of slavery . . . Call Poseidon and the whole chorus of women he raped: Amphitrite, Amymone, Alope, Melanippe . . . and thousands of others. Call Apollo, too [names of his victims follow]. Above all, let Zeus himself come, the one you call 'father of men and gods' [*Iliad* 1.544 etc.]. So utterly was he abandoned to lust that he desired all women, and satisfied his desires for them all . . . And I'm surprised, Homer, by your verses: 'So spoke the son of Cronos and nodded assent with his eyebrows / the king's ambrosial locks streamed / from his deathless head; and he made great Olympus shake' [*Il.* 1.528–30]. He's very dignified, Homer, the Zeus you portray, and you give him a nod that wins reverence. But look, [Clement uses the patronising address *anthrōpe* for Homer: 'old man' or 'mate', perhaps?], if you once show him the girdle, Zeus is exposed, and his locks are shamed . . .

---

[31] Trans. Frank Cole Babbitt (Loeb).

The reference to 'the girdle' — any woman's girdle, perhaps — neatly reminds the reader of *Iliad* 14, where Hera entices Zeus with the aid of Aphrodite's *kestos* (described at 214–21), and adds to the deconstructive tease. Here there is a definite gain if the reader can share the allusion, but sometimes, when Clement is drawing on a 'pre-packaged' set of quotations, he turns their very detachability to advantage, as a source of both (appropriated) authority and freedom in his handling of the pagan past.

iv

Another way of approaching the use of quotations and the transmission of a canon is to look back from the vantage point of the Renaissance[32] and observe how quotations worked at a period when the rediscovery of the classical past was peculiarly urgent and inspiring — and at the same time potentially inhibiting.

An obvious starting point is Erasmus' collection of 'adages' first published as *Adagiorum Collectanea* in 1500, expanded as *Adagiorum Chiliades* in 1508, and reprinted with new material in successive editions throughout his lifetime (the last appeared in 1536).[33] Erasmus is well aware of the difficulty of categorising 'adages', and although a large number of his examples are what we would call proverbs he includes many well known quotations. A guiding principle for him, as for all the educators we have been considering, is the importance of brevity and memorability; in the Introduction to the *Adagia* he explores their functions and effects with considerable finesse, showing how the capacity to condense important (and often contradictory) ideas is crucial to the lasting power of the best of them. A sample will illustrate his method and also the originality of this approach: he used the ancient material and his elucidation of it to 're-create a mental climate', as Margaret Mann Phillips neatly puts it, and at the same time when he traces the parallels between pagan and Christian thought he does so from a markedly modern standpoint.[34]

---

[32] For the context see Anthony Grafton and Lisa Jardine, *From Humanism to the Humanities: Education and the Liberal Arts in Fifteenth and Sixteenth-Century Europe* (London 1986); Jill Kraye (ed.) *The Cambridge Companion to Renaissance Humanism* (Cambridge 1996).

[33] See Margaret Mann Phillips, *The 'Adages' of Erasmus: a Study with Translations* (Cambridge 1964) ix–xiii.

[34] Phillips (n. 33) 14, also 25–34.

Here is a passage where Erasmus quotes Plutarch quoting Hesiod (Introduction vi):[35]

> He [Plutarch] suggests that these sayings, brief as they are, give a hint in their concealed way of those very things which were propounded in so many volumes by the princes of philosophy. For instance, that proverb in Hesiod 'The half is more than the whole' [*Works and Days* 40] is exactly what Plato in the *Gorgias* and in his books *On the State* tries to expound by so many arguments: it is preferable to receive an injury than inflict one. What doctrine was ever produced by the philosophers more salutary as a principle of life or closer to the Christian religion? But here is a principle clearly of the greatest importance enclosed in a minute proverb, 'The half is more than the whole.' For to take away the whole is to defraud the man to whom nothing is left; on the other hand, to accept the half only is to be in a sense defrauded oneself. But it is preferable to be defrauded than to defraud.

In the same section of his Introduction Erasmus characterises the 'intrinsic usefulness' for modern readers of the old sayings as follows: 'A knowledge of proverbs contributes to a number of things, but to four especially: philosophy, persuasiveness, grace and charm in speaking, and the understanding of the best authors.' The important point for our purposes is his emphasis on the multiple functions the material serves, and this notion of 'usefulness' must remain a constant in the canonicity debate, irrespective of how precisely it is defined.

There is also the problem of the 'anxiety of influence'. Alain de Botton[36] has recently used Montaigne as a sort of test case — as an author whose work is full of classical quotations, and who also discusses the need for independence with great subtlety, irony and originality. As de Botton points out, in the sixteenth century it became 'an act of intellectual good taste and the ultimate stamp of authority to back up any assertion with a quote indicating that an ancient philosopher, Plato or Lucretius, agreed with you; had said something similar in Greek or Latin . . . centuries before.' Montaigne's quotations in the *Essays* bear this out: he cites Plato 128 times, Lucretius 149, and Seneca 180, and plenty of other authorities — Cicero, Plutarch, Horace — crop up often, too. But he is preoccupied with the need to speak 'utterly alone'. There are a couple of passages in *On the education of children*, showing Montaigne at his most playfully creative, which bear closely on this issue:

> There are some men who are so foolish as to go a good mile out of their way in pursuit of a witty remark, or who, 'instead of suiting their words to their subject drag in

---

[35] Trans. Margaret Mann Phillips in *Collected Works of Erasmus* (Toronto 1982) vol. 5, 14–15. Erasmus' quotation of Plutarch (*Mor.* 36a–b) is from memory.
[36] 'What are the humanities for?', *European Review* 7.1 (1999) 19–25, quotation at 23.

extraneous matters, to which their words will fit'. [Quintilian 8.3.76: Montaigne's text quotes the Latin but without naming his sources.] And as another author says, 'There are some who are tempted by the charm of an attractive phrase to write about something they had not intended' [Seneca, *Letters* 59.5]. I prefer to twist a good saying in order to weave it into my argument, rather than twist my argument to receive it. Far from that, it is the business of words to serve and follow, and if French will not do it, Gascon may. I would have the subject be paramount, and so fill the hearer's mind that he has no memory of the words. The speech that I love is a simple and natural speech, the same on paper as on a man's lips: a pithy, sinewy, short and concise speech, sharp and forcible rather than mincing and delicate: *Haec demum sapiet dictio, quae feriet* ['Striking speech is good speech' *Epitaph* of Lucan], rather rough than tedious, void of all affectation, free, irregular and bold; not pedantic, not friar-like, not lawyer-like, but soldierly rather, as Suetonius says Julius Caesar's was, though I do not see very well why he calls it so.

And again:

> The tutor should make his pupil sift everything, and take nothing into his head on single authority or trust . . . For if he embraces the opinions of Xenophon and Plato by his own reasoning, they will no longer be theirs but his. Who follows another follows nothing. He finds nothing, and indeed is seeking nothing. 'We are not under a king: each man should look after himself' [Seneca, *Letters* 33.4]. . . .
> It is no more a matter of Plato's opinion than of mine, when he and I understand and see things alike. The bees steal from this flower or that, but afterwards they turn their pilferings into honey, which is their own; it is thyme and marjoram no longer. So the pupil will transform and fuse the passages that he borrows from others, to make of them something entirely his own; that is to say, his own judgement. His education, his labour, and his study have no other aim but to form this.[37]

Montaigne's image of the bees evokes a famous passage on inspiration in Plato's *Ion* (534b1–6), which draws on the language of the lyric poets to make the comparison between bees and poets seem richly apposite.[38] Despite the signal in Montaigne's previous sentence that the reader should indeed be thinking of Plato, the reference to 'thyme' in his bee image surely triggers an association with Horace's industrious bee gathering nectar from the thyme (*Odes* 4.2.27–32: *ego apis Matinae/more modoque/grata carpentis thyma per laborem/plurimum circa nemus uuidique/Tiburis ripas operosa paruus/carmina fingo*). This too is a celebrated image, from a poem which begins with Horace's refusal to compare his own homely poetry with the soaring flight and majestic flood of Pindar's: Horace is 'small' like the bee, his scope is modest, and his eloquence depends on laborious effort.

---

[37] The translation is by J. M. Cohen (Harmondsworth 1958) 79–80 and 56.

[38] *Ion* 535a7–b7, with the notes of Penelope Murray, *Plato on Poetry* (Cambridge 1996) 116–18.

Even so, his choice of simile echoes one of Pindar's own: in *Pythian* 10.53–4 the 'choice bloom of victory odes darts like a bee from theme to theme'.

Did Montaigne's reading, one wonders, include Plutarch's use of the bees as figures of the discriminating reader's ability to draw out profitable meanings from dangerous-seeming passages (*Mor.* 32e–f) or of the student's selective reception of showy lectures (*Mor.* 41f)? Or perhaps he knew how St Basil had adapted the image to suit the idea that pagan literature can be profitable to Christian students, if they treat it selectively, as the bees visit flowers, and 'take only what is suited to their work and leave the rest behind' ('To the young, on how to benefit from Greek literature' (4.36–46), a favourite text of Renaissance humanists).

Whatever may have been Montaigne's immediate sources, this is an extremely loaded image to use in a passage discussing a writer's relation to his past, and although what we have here are allusions rather than exact quotations, they fulfil very similar functions in making connections with that past, condensing it, indeed, into the present, while effecting radical transformations. The interesting thing is the adaptability of the bee figure to so many different ends: the flitting movements can be associated with sophisticated artistic selectivity as in Pindar, with low-level laborious effort as (ironically) in Horace, with moral or religious discrimination as in Plutarch or Basil; and in Montaigne the stress is on the transformation of old texts into new ones. The one constant is the desirability of the bees' honey, and closely related to this is the implied commitment to certain admired authors, Horace most of all, and the implied approval of ancient criteria of taste while staking a claim for originality and independence. As Rodney Stenning Edgecombe puts it, in an illuminating reading of Gray's use of 'received wisdom' in the 'Elegy Written in a Country Churchyard', 'Such interleavings of source upon source arrive as so much glory trailed by words as they enter a poem.'[39]

The point of Edgecombe's examples is to show that there are better models than 'the anxiety of influence' for the various ways in which a writer may relate to his literary past; my main concern here is with the question of *value*, which is perhaps implicit in his 'glory trailed by words'. I have already used terms like 'taste' and 'quality' (p. 30 above), and what I want to suggest is that Quintilian was right to stress the importance of 'blood and sinew'.[40] It is hard to see how notions of 'usefulness' and multifunctionality, so important for the long-term survival, in whatever form, of literary texts,

---

[39] 'A typology of allusive practices', *Colby Quarterly* 34.1 (1998) 25–38, quotation at 26–7.

[40] See n. 30 above. For a robust discussion of value and other criteria in the canon debate see Charles Martindale (n. 3) ch. 1.

can be completely value-free or divorced from the particular way the words are made to work.

George Eliot has a neatly literal evocation of 'taste' in chapter 5 of *Adam Bede*, in her description of the worldly but highly sympathetic Mr Irwine:

> Clearly, the Rector was not what is called in these days an 'earnest' man . . . His mental palate, indeed, was rather pagan, and found a savouriness in a quotation from Sophocles or Theocritus that was quite absent from any text in Isaiah or Amos. But if you feed your setter on raw flesh, how can you wonder at its retaining a relish for uncooked partridge in after life? and Mr Irwine's recollections of young enthusiasm and ambition were all associated with poetry and ethics that lay aloof from the Bible.

Eliot's ironic play (in chapter 16) with quotations from *Prometheus Bound* and Horace's *Odes* to articulate the relationship between Mr Irwine and his errant pupil Arthur illustrates the quite unexpected uses to which 'canonical' material can be put.[41]

Even in the contemporary world, when the conventional educational hierarchies have broken down, and the very notion of 'best authors' — in any language — is fiercely challenged, the scope for transformation, more often of a subterranean and allusive kind than through anything as obvious as straight quotation, remains limitless. It seems appropriate to end with a quotation, this time from a contemporary playwright, whose works show him to be keenly interested in the processes of reception and in using quotation himself. In Stoppard's *Arcadia* (1993) the tutor, Septimus Hodge, encouraging his pupil Thomasina not to mourn the losses of ancient tragedies, remarks:

> We shed as we pick up, like travellers who must carry everything in their arms, and what we let fall will be picked up by those behind. The procession is very long and life is very short. We die on the march. But there is nothing outside the march so nothing can be lost to it. The missing plays of Sophocles will turn up piece by piece, or be written again in another language.

(Act I, Scene 3)

---

[41] Details in P. E. Easterling, 'George Eliot and Greek tragedy', *Arion* 1.2 (1991) 60–74.

3
New texts and old theories

Peter Parsons

i

The Renaissance reader of Quintilian's textbook of oratory (known in manuscript to Petrarch and first printed in 1470) gained access, among other things, to a canon of classical Greek literature, the books that the aspiring gentleman-orator must absolutely read.[1] First comes epic verse: Homer, then Hesiod, the two great originals; among poets of the Hellenistic age, Apollonius, Aratus, Theocritus, Nicander. All these were available to our reader; they had survived the Middle Ages in manuscript, and by 1500 all were in print. But others ranked with them — Antimachus for elegy, Panyasis and Pisander for epic, Euphorion for his riddling mythologies — were not available then or later: their work had perished, quotations apart, in the dark millennium since the fall of Rome. And so for the rest of Quintilian's digest. Callimachus, 'the leader of elegy', exemplar of allusive sophistication; Archilochus the muscular satirist, father of invective; Stesichorus' lyric epic, Alcaeus' songs of war and wine, the pathos and wit of Simonides, the Old Comedies of Eupolis and Cratinus, the New Comedy of Menander, the histories of Theopompus and Ephorus, the speeches of Hyperides and the philosophy of Theophrastus — all these were gone.

Indeed, whole genres had vanished. In the second century AD, Athenaeus had read (or made one of his characters claim to have read) eight hundred plays of the Middle Comedy;[2] the gastronomic titbits he excerpted from them survived, the plays themselves perished. And even authors who did survive most often survived in mutilated form. The ancient biographers

---

[1] Quintilian, *Institutio oratoria* 10.1.46–131.
[2] Athenaeus 8.336d. On the interpretation, H.-G. Nesselrath, *Die attische Mittlere Komödie* (Berlin 1990) 69–71.

recorded at least 70 tragedies by Aeschylus, more than 120 for Sophocles; only seven of each surfaced at the Renaissance.

So too with Latin.[3] Lucretius and Virgil lived on, but not their archetype Ennius; Horace's satires, but not those of Lucilius; Seneca's tragedies, but not those of Pacuvius; Catullus (in a single manuscript), but not his fellow neoterics; Propertius and Ovid, but not the famous elegist and political suicide Cornelius Gallus. Here too the survivors were often mutilated: Ovid's only tragedy had gone into the dark; of the great historians, most of Sallust, three quarters of Livy and substantial portions of Tacitus. Thus what was to become, from the Renaissance on, the 'canon' of Greek and Latin literature had its roots in a void.

This was in its way not unexpected. When Horace proclaimed his work 'more long-lasting than bronze',[4] there was a deliberate paradox, in a world in which the physical book, a papyrus roll, was notoriously at risk from worm, mould and fire. It was a world without mass production; and although there was demand enough, and copyists enough, to produce Homer in commercial quantity, rarer works might have a more tenuous hold on immortality. When the Palatine library in Rome was burned down, the emperor Domitian sent copyists as far as the great library of Alexandria to make replacements.[5]

Every library contained its rarities: Apollodorus of Athens was so charmed by an otherwise unknown poem which he 'came upon' in a library that he copied out substantial excerpts from this crabby epic of Coan mythology.[6] The discovery of a unique book was a matter of practical reality in the ancient world; the notion has continued in *The Book of Mormon* and postmodern fiction. Even with the undisputed masters, some works became, or remained, more popular than others. That, and other factors, had their consequences at the end of the High Empire: book production dwindled, and what remained remained by lucky chance or deliberate selection, most probably by schoolmasters for a syllabus of set books. Schools, libraries and monasteries sheltered the survivors as the old order collapsed; but many perished on the long march, the victims of war or fashion or pious neglect. Thus two poems of Callimachus, exemplars of the exquisite to his Roman admirers, could still be read until 1205, when the thugs of the Fourth Crusade destroyed the library which contained them.[7]

---

[3] H. Bardon, *La littérature latine inconnue* (Paris 1952, 1956).

[4] *Odes* 3.30.1.

[5] Suetonius, *Domitian* 20.

[6] A. Bernabé (ed.), *Poetae epici Graeci* vol. 1 (Leipzig 1987) 131–5.

[7] N. G. Wilson, *Scholars of Byzantium* (London 1983) 205.

Renaissance scholars collected and printed what they could find. For them and their successors, the hope of finding more remained, as western and eastern libraries were visited and catalogued. Yet returns soon diminished; and the new science of archaeology, which reinvented whole areas of the classical past by its finds of statues and vases and inscriptions on stone, could apparently do little to help, for (with the exception of Herculaneum, where a whole philosophical library had been entombed, black and brittle, by the eruption of Vesuvius in AD 79) the main sites of Greece and Italy were too wet to preserve papyrus and parchment. The stream had dried up, and it remained dry until, in the late nineteenth century, a new spring was discovered in the desert.

In Egypt, Greek immigrants and their Greek-speaking descendants had ruled the country (first as a Hellenistic kingdom, then as a province of the Roman and Byzantine empires) for a millennium, from Alexander the Great to the Arab conquest. In Egypt, no rain falls south of Memphis, and perishable materials remain fully preserved under the sand. It gradually became apparent that the cities of the Egyptian Greeks preserved in quantity original books and documents in a way not possible in their motherland. First, there were chance finds sold to collectors: in the 1890s, the British Museum acquired three substantial lost works of Greek literature — Aristotle's *Athenian Constitution*, the cantatas of Bacchylides, and the louche comic sketches of the 'old dirt-peddler' Herondas. And then, systematic excavation. At one site alone, Oxyrhynchus, 'City of the Sharp-nosed Fish', once a county town of perhaps 20,000 people, the excavators found discarded papyri piled in rubbish-tips twenty feet deep; ten years' digging rescued some 100,000 fragments, and a first sample published in 1898 included parts of an unknown Gospel and a poem of Sappho.[8]

These finds have opened new doors. The documents, perhaps 90 per cent of the total, display a Greek colonial society in unprecedented detail; the extent of this archival material, and its randomness (for most of it comes from a congeries of casual discards), allows a privileged sampling of life, law, trade, government and mentality.[9] The literary texts — fragmentary books in roll form or codex, written in carbon ink still black on papyrus and parchment — represent a dip into the libraries, private or public, of the Greek diaspora

---

[8] 'Sayings of Jesus', now known to be part of the lost Gospel of Thomas: latest text in D. Lührmann, *Fragmente apokryph gewordener Evangelien* (Marburg 2000) 119–25. Sappho *fr.* 5 Voigt.
[9] See Chapter 8 below.

before the great libricide of the Middle Ages. Over the last hundred years, one literary papyrus has been published, on average, every ten days; the agglomeration provides, for Greek literature at least, a small new renaissance.

Fig. 3.1. Oxyrhynchus Papyrus 2652. Menander, the father of situation comedy, was almost entirely lost until finds of papyri restored substantial portions of his work. A sketch (perhaps part of an illustrated edition) of the goddess Ignorance, from his play *The Girl Who Has Her Hair Cut Off.*

This material has brought back from the dead long-lost authors like Sappho, Menander (Fig. 3.1) and Callimachus. For Greek drama, Egypt has provided *Trackers*, a 'satyr play' by Sophocles,[10] and Euripides' *Hypsipyle*, a romantic tragedy of recognition and rescue; for Greek history, Aristotle's *Constitution of Athens* and the anonymous author (perhaps Cratippus) who continued Thucydides; for the last Greek literary invention, the novel, new excursions into melodrama and comedy — Calligone's adventures among the Amazons, Iolaus disguised as a eunuch priest (a classic plot which looks back to Terence and forward to *The Country Wife*). Our generation is the first since the fall of Rome to see Archilochus encounter his Lolita in a field of flowers,[11]

> covering her with my soft cloak, holding her neck in my arms,
> as she stopped in fear, like a fawn in flight.

It is the first to meet Menander's love-lorn soldier complaining to the wet cold Athenian night:[12]

> Have you ever seen a more miserable man?
> Seen a more unlucky lover?
> Now I stand at my own front door,
> in the alley, and I mooch up and down,
> both ways, right up to now which is midnight,
> when I could be sleeping and holding my beloved.
> She's indoors, in my house, and I have the chance
> and I want it like the craziest lover —
> but I don't do it...

We can at last follow Heracles crossing Ocean in the golden cup of the Sun, in Stesichorus' lyric epic (Fig. 3.2),[13] and killing head by head the triple monster Geryones:

> ... an arrow with death on its head,
> smeared with blood and gall,
> the agonies of the Hydra,
> flashing-necked, destroyer of men. Silently,
> stealthily he drove it into his forehead.
> Through the flesh and bones it sliced, by god's will.
> Right through held the arrow
> to the very top of his head.
> It soiled with bright blood
> his corslet and gory limbs. So Geryones leant his neck

---

[10] Tony Harrison has staged the play and the drama of its finding: see above, pp. 11–12.

[11] Archilochus *fr.* 196a West[2].

[12] Menander, *Misoumenos* A4–12 (Sandbach p. 351; Arnott 2 p. 356).

[13] Stesichorus, *Geryoneis* S 15 col. ii Page-Davies.

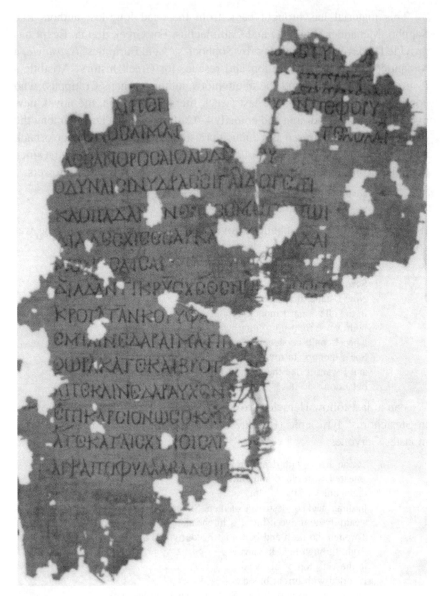

Fig. 3.2. Oxyrhynchus Papyrus 2617 *frr.* 4 and 5. Heracles attacks the three-headed Geryones, in Stesichorus' poem (translated on pp. 43, 45).

> to one side, as when a poppy
> which, degrading its delicate form,
> all at once dropping its petals...

We can now admire the mythical temples of Delphi as Pindar imagined them:[14] the first temple made of laurel branches; the second built by bees from wax and feathers, until a great wind carried it to the people beyond the North; for the third,

> ...by the all-skilful
> hands of Hephaestus and Athena,
> what was the shape that showed itself?
> Bronze the walls and bronze the pillars that stood beneath,
> and on its pediment six golden
> Sirens sang.
> But the sons of Cronus
> opened the earth with a thunderbolt
> and hid the holiest of all works,
> amazed at their sweet voice,
> for strangers who came wasted away
> far from children
> and wives, on that honey-minded song
> suspending their soul...

Latin fares less well (in Egypt the language belongs to the military and the administration, until around AD 300 the homogenising policies of the Roman government made it into a school subject); but someone left Sallust's *Histories* on the tip, and a ditch full of rubbish at the frontier fort of Qasr Ibrim has yielded some graceless epigrams by the poet-politician Cornelius Gallus. Gallus had been a figure of legend, the inventor of love-elegy and of that long-lived fantasy, *la belle dame sans merci*; but only a single line survived to match the great name. 'Virgil wrote a poem for him: how much immortality does a man need?' — so Tom Stoppard's A. E. Housman.[15] But scholars did feel the need for more, and now they have, in a fragment of eight lines, enough to reveal a cruder sharper poet, more in debt to his rough-hewn Roman predecessors than to the smooth-versed Greeks, than their speculations had ever pictured.

Not just authors. Whole new genres emerged: the lyric epics which Stesichorus constructed on the fringes of Greek Italy, the lyric diatribes which Cercidas used to preach his Cynic philosophy, the nationalist pamphlets in which noble Alexandrians face martyrdom by their coarse

---

[14] Pindar, *Paean* 8 *fr.* 52i.62–79 Maehler.
[15] Tom Stoppard, *The Invention of Love* (London 1997) 98.

Roman oppressors, the comic narratives whose low-life characters anticipate the picaresque novel in a mixture of prose and verse. New authors remind us that in Greek literature chance and choice have preserved Bach but not Handel, Mozart without Salieri. Now we can read Bacchylides alongside Pindar, Cratinus alongside Aristophanes; the papyri give us not just the masters but poetasters and speechifiers, exercises and handbooks; we come closer to the Library of Linus, as the comic poet Alexis depicted it, where the young Heracles bypassed Orpheus, Hesiod, tragedy, Choerilus' epics, even Homer himself, even the coarse comedy of Epicharmus — and chose a cookbook.[16]

The material is not just new; it comes to us without that haze of reception and interpretation which darkens the reading of older texts. Thus new texts are particularly apt to realign old ones: old Pindar finds himself interpreted and recreated in the new Callimachus,[17] old Homer sanctified and modernised in the new Simonides;[18] we now read Euripidean tragedy with knowledge of its new stepchild, Menandrean comedy,[19] and new Menandrean comedy with knowledge of its galumphing future in the farces of Plautus.[20] One new author shakes the kaleidoscope. Now that we possess some Stesichorus, we can recognise again a guiding thread of Greek literature: the successive revolutions which revivify the old material of myth in new literary forms — Homer, Stesichorus, tragedy, Hellenistic poetry.

Hunters of allusion have tended to over-confidence, assuming a closed world in which the ancients had read only what we have read. But of course any new text may reveal a new intertextuality. Theocritus, in the third century BC, looks back to the Thessalian princes whose patronage had sustained Simonides three hundred years before. Their patronage earned them immortality, for the poet 'made them great names among later men.' This phrase comes from Simonides himself. But in Simonides it describes how Homer made immortal the heroes of the Trojan War. By using it, Theocritus identifies himself with Simonides and so with Homer, his patrons with the Thessalians and so with the Trojan heroes. That is clear; but we did not know it until 1992, when a new papyrus (Fig. 3.3) revealed the lines of Simonides.[21]

---

[16] Alexis *fr.* 140 KA.

[17] T. Fuhrer, *Die Auseinandersetzung mit den Chorlyrikern in den Epinikien des Kallimachos* (Basel 1992).

[18] D. Boedeker and D. Sider (eds.), *The New Simonides* (New York 2001) 71–2, 94–5, 106–119, 182–4.

[19] N. Zagagi, *The Comedy of Menander* (London 1994) 54–7.

[20] E. W. Handley, *Menander and Plautus: a Study in Comparison* (London 1968).

[21] Theoc. 16.45–6; Simonides *fr. eleg.* 11.17–18 West².

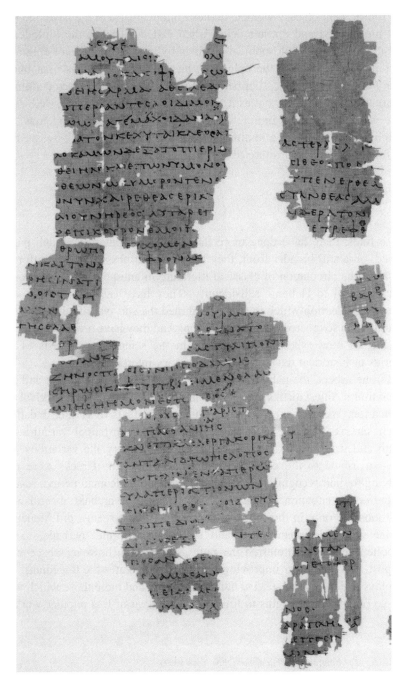

Fig. 3.3. Oxyrhynchus Papyrus 3965: the long-lost elegy by Simonides on the battle of Plataea, at which the Greeks finally defeated the invading Persians.

Horace, bent on easy women, quotes Philodemus: 'Let me have one who isn't high-priced and doesn't delay when called.' That is the Philodemus who diversified his philosophical writings by composing elegant epigrams; the philosophy, but not the epigrams, has been found in his own buried library at Herculaneum.[22] 'Let her be fair and stand tall,' Horace continues: apparently his own taste, but as it now appears a literary taste as well, since these words too turn up in a new papyrus of epigrams by Philodemus.[23] A compliment or an irony, a reminiscence or an allusion: in any case, we now see more clearly the furniture of the poet's mind.

ii

These finds, then, have done more than restore a scatter of golden pages. Indeed, on a still broader front, they have made it possible to study for the first time the circulation of classical literature in antiquity, in its relation to education and to Hellenic self-identity. They have cast new light on the process of selection which in part determined the survival of authors in late antiquity and so created the modern canon. And they have provided, and will provide, as new experimental data do in the sciences, new tests of old theories of historical development and literary interpretation.

In one aspect, the papyri are an epiphenomenon of Hellenistic and Roman culture. Any statistics must be qualified by the accidents of survival and publication. We can, even so, find patterns. The texts of Homer and Plato which survive from the third century BC show substantial variations of length and wording; by the end of the second century the variations subside — a tribute to the coherent scholarship which the Greeks were now applying to their recognised classics. Throughout the Roman period, readers far prefer the situation comedy of Menander to the archaic absurdism of Aristophanes; only in the fourth century and after, it seems, did Menander decline and Aristophanes rise and survive — a tribute, perhaps, to the schoolteachers, who preferred the pure Attic Greek, however obscene, to the post-Attic, however improving. Euripides dominates the tragedians, and the plays which were to survive outnumber more and more those which were not; so popular taste begins to limit the circulation of less popular works.

---

[22] D. Sider, *The Epigrams of Philodemos* (New York 1997).
[23] Horace, *Serm.* 1.2.119–24; *The Oxyrhynchus Papyri* LIV (London 1987) 3724 *fr.* 1 iii 15 (= Sider (n. 22) 210).

Oxyrhynchus, to take a unitary site, produces more than a thousand texts of Homer, a hundred pieces of magic, but only thirty-odd pieces of the novel, and (so far) only one cookery book. The top twenty authors include none who wrote later than 200 BC: no doubt conservative taste, and the school curriculum, favoured these, the real classics on which the cultural identity and hegemony of the later Greek diaspora partly depended. A minority did read contemporaries or near-contemporaries: Plutarch, for example, whose only mention of Oxyrhynchus depicts it as a stereotype of ferocious barbarism, was being read by those same barbarians within a generation.[24] The novel makes a respectable showing, but certainly not enough to sustain the theory, based on eighteenth-century England, that it was a bourgeois best seller. In Egypt overall, the statistics illustrate the cultural changes of the early Christian period — the inroads of Latin, the triumph of the modern book (codex) over the book-roll, the decline in circulation of classical literature. The early medieval world finds its best exemplar in two codexes (from the same library?) of the early fourth century: one contains Thucydides book 4 alongside *Susanna* and *Daniel*; the other Cicero's *Orations against Catiline*, and elegant but anonymous verses on the self-sacrifice of Alcestis, alongside a Hymn to the Virgin in Latin and the canon of the Mass in Greek.[25]

A different use of new knowledge is experimental: it tests the categories by which we organise it. All intellectual advance, clearly, consists in making patterns; and though as human beings we know that experience is tangled and complex, we seek as scholars for simple schemata. Patterns appeal if they conform to intuitively agreeable principles: that simple precedes complex; that processes are linear and entropic; that the pattern should accommodate all the data, and only those data. It is such principles that new knowledge tends to subvert. For that reason, novelties are not always welcome. It is still the custom of text-editors to treat the early evidence of the papyri as a footnote to the late evidence of the medieval manuscripts. Scholars at first doubted the authenticity of the *Athenian Constitution*[26] and the authorship of the Lille Stesichorus;[27] some hastened to declare

---

[24] Plutarch *De Iside et Osiride* 380b–c.

[25] A. Carlini, *Museum Helveticum* 32 (1975) 33–40 (Thucydides, Bodmer papyrus XXVII); 38 (1981) 81–120 (*Susanna* and *Daniel*, Bodmer papyri XLV–XLVI). R. Roca-Puig, *Psalmus responsorius; Ciceró, Catilinàries; Alcestis, Hexàmetres Llatins* (Barcelona 1965, 1977, 1982).

[26] K. von Fritz and E. Kapp, *Aristotle's Constitution of Athens* (New York 1950) 3–4. Apart from those who wished to attribute the work to an author later than Aristotle and his school, a few thought it a modern forgery.

[27] P. J. Parsons, *Zeitschrift für Papyrologie und Epigraphik* 26 (1977) 12.

the Cologne Archilochus,[28] and the Gallus of Qasr Ibrim, to be ancient forgeries (the Gallus even a modern forgery),[29] because they differ in style or theme from what is expected — as if such expectations rested on anything more than a handful of quotations.

Partly as cause and partly in coincidence, the rise of papyrology has accompanied the decline of certainty. The year 1891, which saw the publication of the Aristotle and the Herondas, may serve as a landmark. The golden age of *Altertumswissenschaft* stood at its height; only one year before, Wissowa had begun the revision of Pauly's encyclopedia, which was, like the new scholarship, to combine every aspect of the ancient world in a single science. A hundred years on we may view the scholarship of that age, romantic, positive, confident, with surprise as well as envy. Two world wars, the fragmentation of high culture, Einstein and Heisenberg, Freud and Wittgenstein, have all contributed to weaken those moral and scientific certainties. An accumulation of minor discrepancies undermined the foundations of Newtonian physics. The papyri have served in the same way, to test the *fable convenue*. In consequence, they have not only shown the extent of scholarly ignorance; they have also shown up the fragility of scholarly methods.

By 'methods' I mean no more than the simple procedures which often seem so commonsensical, and indeed necessary, if we are to find a pattern in an epoch or an oeuvre or even a single work. Let me recall some examples from the traditional activities of classical scholars: constructing a text, a commentary, a biography, a literary history.

First, the text. Greek and Latin texts as we read them now stand at the end of a long tradition of corruption and restoration: corruption during the long process of copying and re-copying by hand, restoration by the science and intuition of scholars since the Renaissance. Romantics cherish the idea of reading the very words their poet wrote; close readers need some assurance that what they read closely is authentic. Classical scholars traditionally have shared the sentiments of an eighteenth-century colleague from another culture of classics and scholarship, whom his friend Yuan Mei addressed thus:[30]

---

[28] Summary in B. Kramer and D. Hagedorn, *Kölner Papyri* II (Opladen 1978) 14–20.

[29] G. Giangrande, *Quaderni Urbinati di cultura classica* 5 (1980) 141–53; F. Brunhölzl, *Codices Manuscripti* 10 (1984) 33–40 (his theory of a modern forgery has been generally rejected: see R. G. M. Nisbet, *Collected Papers on Latin Literature* (Oxford 1995) 432).

[30] Arthur Waley, *Yuan Mei* (London 1956) 163. (I had remembered the verses, but not the source; I am most grateful to Professor D. L. McMullen of Cambridge University for identifying them.) On the last line, Waley comments: 'The Zen-master Ch'ing-liao (died *c.* AD 1152) was watching some meal being cooked in a bucket, when the bottom of the bucket fell out. The monks cried out, "What a sad waste!" But Ch'ing-liao said, "On the contrary, the shock was well worth the loss of a bucket of meal."'

> You tell me that collating texts is the great passion of your life —
> To sort them out with as fine precision as a sieve sifts rice;
> That to get a single right meaning is better than a ship-load of pearls,
> To resolve a single doubt is like the bottom falling off the bucket.

The papyri sometimes do restore the original. Pindar reflects that humankind is prone to stumble; 'it is always better to watch everything that lies before your foot.' The sense is certain, but in the text as it survived the Middle Ages a word has dropped out — a word of two syllables, meaning 'watch'. A papyrus now supplies the word, an obvious word (βλέπειν) but as it happens not one of those ('see', 'notice', 'look at', 'gaze') that scholars had conjectured.[31] At the beginning of Euripides' *Phoenissae*, Jocasta addresses the Sun which has shone on the tragedies of Thebes:

> Sun, you who cut your path through the stars,
> and take your stand in a chariot welded with gold,
> Sun, who whirl your fire on swift horses...

Grand rhetoric, which might suit the tragic heroine, though she continues in a much more matter-of-fact tone; but not Euripides' rhetoric. Three early papyri omit the first two lines, which makes it very likely that they were added by an author or an actor who thought more of verbal gestures than of characterisation.[32]

More often the papyri show that our texts were corrupted early, and how hard Greek scholars of their own classics needed to work at them. They show the complexity of traditions, where one manuscript that has variant readings noted in its margins may father a diversity of different copies which may themselves be contaminated and cross-fertilised: a far cry from the simple logical stemmatics of Lachmann, which suppose that any manuscript carries a clear series of genes which can prove its relationship to any of its ancestors or descendants. Above all they show a family tree dominated by missing links.

In earlier days, if some Byzantine reader recommended a reading which no earlier manuscript attested, we would have assumed that it was his own guess. Now we find that some of these readings turn up in papyri of the Roman period; they were there in the tradition, but not visible.[33] About

---

[31] Pindar, *Isthm.* 8.13 in E. Lobel, *The Oxyrhynchus Papyri* XXVI (London 1961) 2439 *fr.* 1. The conjectures are listed by E. Thummer, *Pindar: die Isthmischen Gedichte* vol. 2 (Heidelberg 1969) 131.

[32] M. W. Haslam, *Greek Roman and Byzantine Studies* 16 (1975) 149–74.

[33] See, for examples in Theocritus, A. K. Bowman et al., *The Oxyrhynchus Papyri* L (London 1983) 101.

200 BC, a copyist charged with reproducing Menander's *Sikyonios* added at the end some verses in his own person: 'Do not laugh at my handwriting... Anyone who laughs, I'll break his leg... How gladly I have rested my three fingers.' These are the three fingers that hold the pen; and we intuit that the line is a stock colophon. Indeed, the line does turn up again — in two Byzantine manuscripts more than a thousand years later.[34] Such is the nature of our evidence: most of the streams run underground.

Second, the text's interpretation in context. I quote three examples.

In better days it was widely held that the *Suppliants* of Aeschylus was his earliest, indeed very much his earliest, play. There were good reasons: static action, huge choral sections, limited use of the second actor, much as might have been imagined for the earliest stages of tragedy. So it was until 1952, when Edgar Lobel published part of a *didaskalia*, a record of dramatic performances at Athens. The papyrus is broken, and on the more likely reconstruction the actual date at which Aeschylus won with the *Suppliants* is lost; but it was a year in which 'Sophocles' won second prize. Now the famous Sophocles first competed in 468 BC: the best ancient tradition is agreed on that.[35] So, if Sophocles was already active, the *Suppliants* can't be earlier than about 470 — later than the *Persians*, contemporary with or later than the *Seven Against Thebes*. Not therefore 'very early': Aeschylus was now in his fifties.[36]

Now it's easy to be wise after the event; and the event may be so unwelcome that we seek to evade it (for example, by referring this papyrus to a re-performance of the play after Aeschylus' death). But after the event we can ask why we have gone astray in a judgement which concerns much more than a detail, since it has implications for the whole question of the origins and development of Greek tragedy. Certainly the judgement rested on inadequate evidence. The play was the third part of a trilogy: who knows what the economy of the whole looked like? Fewer than ten per cent of Aeschylus' plays survive at all: how far can we judge his overall development? But there is a more important point. The judgement rested on a doubtful premise, that of simple linear development. Artists do change, but not necessarily in linear mode. Aeschylus may have responded to the mood of the moment, or the nature of the subject, or the provocations of a competitor.

---

[34] G. M. Parássoglou, *Scrittura e civiltà* 3 (1979) 16–18.

[35] Marmor Parium, *FGrH* 239 A56; Plutarch, *Cimon* 8.7. For the confused tradition in the chronographers see Sophocles T 32–5 Radt.

[36] E. Lobel et al., *The Oxyrhynchus Papyri* XX (London 1952) 2256 *fr.* 3 (= Aesch. T 70 Radt).

No song of Sappho is more famous than φαίνεταί μοι κῆνος ἴσος θέοισιν, 'He seems to me the equal of the gods.'[37] Catullus translated it;[38] Longinus *On the Sublime* quoted it,[39] as a poem distinguished by the selection and compression of detail — see how objectively she catalogues the symptoms of love: the eyes dim, the ears humming, cold sweat, shivering all over. The text survives only in the quotation, and towards the end it dissolves in a broken context, as Sappho sums up those symptoms: 'I seem to be little short of dying.' One thing is certain, from the metre, that this last intelligible sentence lacks its last word. Various scholars tried to restore it from the corrupt letters following. Some thought of an epithet: perhaps a dialect form of the poetic adjective 'distraught'. Others thought of a name, a vocative addressed to the subject of the poem. One name had a special success: Agallis (a known name, but not a known name of a friend of Sappho). It became so popular that the standard text printed it, and even the great Wilamowitz insisted that the problem was now solved.[40]

In 1965 our colleagues in Florence published four square inches of papyrus, which quotes precisely the end of this stanza.[41] There was the missing word — not 'distraught', not a name, certainly not 'Agallis', but the rather prosy pronoun 'myself': φαίνομ' ἔμ' αὔται 'I seem to myself.' Well, it's good to know; chance has allowed us to 'resolve a single doubt'. More important is the unargued aesthetic premise on which Agallis rode to fame. The scholars of the nineteenth century will have felt that the name of the beloved must appear somewhere; what more natural than to cap the catalogue of symptoms by naming, at last, the unnamed? That is a true Romantic climax. But, as we now see, that is not necessarily the Greek way.

Consider finally the third *Georgic*. Virgil begins by asserting the novelty of his theme. All the old mythological subjects are vulgar; Virgil will triumph by bringing back the Muses to Mantua, and there found a temple and games in honour of Augustus:[42]

---

[37] Sappho *fr.* 31 Voigt.

[38] Catullus 51.

[39] [Longinus] *Subl.* 10.

[40] E. Diehl, *Anthologia lyrica Graeca* vol. 1 (Leipzig 1925) 330, from W. R. Paton, *Classical Review* 14 (1900) 223. U. von Wilamowitz-Moellendorff, *Sappho und Simonides* (Berlin 1913) 56.

[41] [V. Bartoletti], *Dai papiri della Società Italiana* (Omaggio all'XI Congresso internazionale di papirologia, Florence 1965) 16 (= Sappho *fr.* 213B Voigt).

[42] Virgil, *Georg.* 3.17–20.

> illi uictor ego et Tyrio conspectus in ostro
> centum quadriiugos agitabo ad flumina currus.
> cuncta mihi Alpheum linquens lucosque Molorchi
> cursibus et crudo decernet Graecia caestu...

> In his honour, I, the victor, conspicuous in Tyrian purple, will put in motion a
> hundred four-horse chariots by the river. For me all Greece will leave Alpheus and
> the groves of Molorchus and compete in races and with the raw boxing-glove.

Singular images: to the literal mind, a mix of pictorial incoherence and mythological opacity.

Now, for the first time in the history of scholarship, we know the words that lay behind the words. In 1977, a literate mummy in Lille disgorged fragments of a long and characteristically perverse poem by Callimachus. He celebrates, in alien metre and dialect, a victory in the chariot race at the Nemean Games, by his sovereign and countrywoman, Queen Berenice of Egypt; and he celebrates it by narrating at length how Heracles founded the games on his mission to kill the lion of Nemea.[43] On this mission Heracles was entertained (and Callimachus exercises all his skill in rustic chic) by an old peasant named Molorchus.

Thus the ancient reader of Virgil had three clues. *Omnia iam uulgata* (line 4): Callimachus was the literary archetype for the rejection of the commonplace.[44] Molorchus: this poem of Callimachus was the classic source for the hospitable peasant and his history. The third book: Callimachus' poem begins the third book of his *Aitia*, as Virgil's lines begin that of the *Georgics*. The allusion is palpable, but notably oblique: the scene shifted to Italy, the chariot-race transformed from sport to metaphor. One notion, one name, one number: enough to alert the knowledgeable, and so to hint what kind of poem Virgil thinks he is writing. Modern scholars, until now, had lacked the clues. Some, in desperation, even resorted to biography to explain the topographical touches—Virgil must have been writing in Greece, or after a recent visit to that country.[45] We know better: the gesture is textual, not touristic. Such fabrics of allusion play a central role in Greek as in Latin literature. Whether we glimpse them depends largely on chance. This time we see clearly, not just the intertext but the devious and asymmetrical use made of it, something we should never have dared to hypothesise if we had facts less clear than these.

---

[43] H. Lloyd-Jones and P. Parsons, *Supplementum Hellenisticum* (Berlin 1983) *frr.* 254–69.

[44] Callimachus, *Epigr.* 28 Pf.

[45] J. Conington and H. Nettleship, *The Works of Virgil with a Commentary* vol. 1 (5th ed. revised by F. Haverfield, London 1898) xxiv.

Third, biography. The biographical approach to literary interpretation has had a long run. In this respect, as in many, the nineteenth century continued to explain Greek literature in the categories that the Greeks themselves had established (a good historicist principle vulnerable to an obvious anthropological objection, that a nation is perfectly capable of misinterpreting its own literature). Hence the search for personal references and biographical patterns. That began quite early. In Euripides' *Palamedes* the chorus lamented 'You have killed, you Greeks, the nightingale of the Muses.' Some Roman readers understood this to refer to the death of Socrates, though a scholarly spoilsport pointed out that Euripides died before Socrates.[46] Classical scholars have trodden ancient paths with modern industry. Not, of course, naively. *Quellenforschung* cast doubt on much inherited information. And yet there has been a strong sense of 'No smoke without fire.' If we today react against biography, that is partly the spirit of the age. But it is also that the recovery of the fragments of ancient scholarship gives us a much clearer picture of its character than the marginalised snippets of the medieval tradition.

The Derveni papyrus, our oldest surviving papyrus and the only one found in Greece itself (it had been thrown on a funeral pyre, and baked enough to resist the wet climate), shows how things might be in the fourth century BC.[47] It takes an Orphic poem, which relates the early history of the universe in terms of generations of gods, and interprets it allegorically, each god as a physical element and the whole as a treatise in cosmogonical physics, all done with a single-minded perverseness which recalls the mad commentator in Nabokov's *Pale Fire*. The third century BC produced a grand crop of serious scholarship; it produced also Satyrus' *Life of Euripides*, of which substantial parts have been recovered on papyrus.[48] It is rich in sensations. 'The man above money, in the *Danae*, must be Socrates': this assumes that all a playwright's work must be autobiographical. 'The women so hated Euripides that they attacked him at the festival of the Thesmophoria': this is the plot of an Aristophanic satire, taken as a statement of fact. 'Euripides was torn to pieces by the dogs of Archelaus, as the worthy and most ancient of the Macedonians relate': here a cliché masquerades as an authority. The papyrus has shown us, close to source, the artless journalistic

---

[46] Eur. *fr.* 588 N; Diog. Laert. 2.44.

[47] A. Laks and G. W. Most, *Studies on the Derveni Papyrus* (Oxford 1997).

[48] A. S. Hunt, *The Oxyrhynchus Papyri* IX (London 1912) 1176; G. Arrighetti, *Satiro: Vita di Euripide* (Pisa 1964).

irresponsibility with which ancient critics could satisfy their appetite for tattle about their dead celebrities.

Fourth and last, literary history. Such history looks for periods and movements. 'Archaic', 'classical', 'Hellenistic': handbooks still operate with those terms. But for Hellenistic, at least, the line is now much harder to draw. Rudolf Pfeiffer saw the third century BC as a new epoch, though as an epoch of revival, not, like his predecessors, as a donnish decline; the reassessment of the literature of the past was an essential part of this, the writing of commentaries an essential feature of that. The model, that is, was the Renaissance: a Greek 'revival of learning', with Callimachus as its Petrarch.[49]

Much of this may be true; but the papyri have shown that the Hellenistic, like the Renaissance, crossed boundaries. The Derveni papyrus explains an obscure text (or rather, obscures the text by explaining); Aristarchus would have despised its allegories, but still it represents a commentary of sorts.[50] The local epic *Meropis*, which Apollodorus came upon in a library, is normally assigned to the archaic world of the sixth century BC; yet its verse plays tricks with Homeric diction in a way that we have been used to associate with the third century.[51] A new fragment of the Hesiodic *Catalogue of Women* refers to the fatal love of Ceyx and Alcyone, how they were turned into birds and have remained faithful to each other ever since[52] — a Hellenistic motif, we call it when it recurs in Ovid.

A papyrus of Simonides (Fig. 3.3) offers an elegy on the battle of Plataea:[53] a proem invokes Achilles, and notes how Homer made immortal the heroes of the Trojan War; then a transition, with a formula that we know from the *Homeric Hymns*; then the narrative, the Spartans marching out with the Dioskouroi and Menelaos at their head. This is no doubt typical of the 480s (the Persian War is the Trojan War of the time), but the construction of the poem is far from typical. Essentially, it represents the rhapsodic form: hymn, transition, heroic narrative. But here the old heroes move into the hymn, the new heroes occupy the narrative; the whole structure is transposed into elegiacs, and compassed in (at a guess) two hundred lines. Miniaturisation, crossing of genres — wouldn't we be tempted to call that Hellenistic?

---

[49] R. Pfeiffer, *History of Classical Scholarship* I (Oxford 1968) 170.

[50] Laks and Most (n. 47) 26–30.

[51] Above, p. 40.

[52] R. Merkelbach and M. L. West (eds.), *Hesiodi...fragmenta selecta* (3rd ed., Oxford 1990) *fr.* 10(a) 87–97.

[53] Simonides *fr. eleg.* 11 West².

Once again, the textbook scheme of modes and periods turns out to be much too simple for the reality.

The twentieth century has added to our stock of Greek and Latin literature, slowly and piecemeal. The flow continues. In the last year of the century we acquired our first consecutive text of the philosopher-shaman Empedocles[54] — at last a steady view of a poet who, in the fifth century BC, at the interface of religion and science, set out his own guide to the principles of physics which create this world (four elements mixed by Love and Strife) and the rituals of purification that we need to enter the next world. We knew that Lucretius had read him; now we see how closely. Lucretius refers to mankind as a 'twin race' (2.1082, *geminam prolem*); 'twin' must mean 'male and female', but most editors thought the expression bizarre and emended it away; now we know that the poet meant what his manuscripts say, for 'twin race' (δίδυμον φῦμα) duly turns up in Empedocles. In 2001 we acquired a new collection of 'epigrams', those pithy poems which represent the most vital art form of the Hellenistic revival: nearly a hundred poems, all but two unknown, by Posidippus and perhaps by contemporaries, on carved gems, ominous birds, lifelike statues, deaths and dedications, horse-races and shipwrecks and miraculous cures and people's funny ways — all life passes by in snapshot.[55]

Such finds remind us how much is lost, and how here and there the lost may be found: new pleasures, new contexts, new interpretations, new blood for the Classics.

Some of the material in this chapter first appeared in *Proceedings of the XXI International Congress of Papyrologists* (Copenhagen 1994) 118–23. I am grateful to the publisher for permission to present the material in reworked form here.

[54] A. Martin and O. Primavesi, *L'Empedocle de Strasbourg* (Berlin 1999).
[55] G. Bastianini and C. Gallazzi, *Posidippo di Pella: Epigrammi* (Milan 2001).

4
The use of images:
visual history and ancient history

R. R. R. Smith

It might seem obvious that art and images can add something to our understanding of ancient culture, but quite what they add and how it is to be assessed and mediated are less obvious. This chapter explores some of the great gains made by recent work in this area and some of the remaining deficiencies. Gains have resulted from application of historically based questions, while deficiencies arise from the still largely untheorised nature of this subject's research and discourse.

Introduction

The Greek and Roman world poured an astonishing amount of its surplus into expensive monuments and elaborate public images, and their study is naturally an important part of classical archaeology. Unlike many other archaeologies, this subject studies a world extremely well documented by abundant and diverse literary and textual evidence, and it is thus part of the wider classics project. There is great potential especially in its growing closeness to ancient history. Some of the best recent classical art history and archaeology has tried to work with questions conceived from historical points of view, and some of the best recent ancient history now integrates written and visual evidence.[1] There remains much to do on both sides. Some of the history, the current state, and the broader use of ancient visual studies are the subject of this chapter.

---

[1] See, for example, the different ways images are used in the following recent works: S. R. F. Price, *Rituals and Power: the Roman Imperial Cult in Asia Minor* (Cambridge 1984); P. Zanker, *The Power of Images in the Age of Augustus* (Ann Arbor 1988); R. Osborne, *Greece in the Making, 1200–479 BC* (London 1996).

Classical archaeology began as art history with Winckelmann in the mid-eighteenth century, and was defined as a modern academic discipline in the late nineteenth century by its big excavations and the monuments they revealed, which could be connected directly to things mentioned by classical authors such as Pausanias and Pliny. Greek and Roman art and architecture have remained ever since as leading strands in the discipline. In the mid-twentieth century, the subject's connections to a wider archaeology were strengthened and emphasised, especially in textless periods and zones such as early Greece and the countryside. This was part of the project of the self-styled 'new archaeology' in its classical form — to make classical archaeology look more like other archaeologies. In the countryside, indeed it does. In the city, sanctuary and cemetery, where images and monuments stood everywhere, it emphatically does not.[2]

The connection with classical literature has been one aspect of ancient images that has been studied intensively from the beginning. Ancient art and literature share after all a wide range of subject matter — for example, the exploits and characters of gods and heroes. The relationship was once seen simply as that of art illustrating texts, and the art was treated as a directly parallel, if lower, form of cultural undertaking to that of the literature.[3] Today the nature of the relationship between visual and literary representation is seen as a more complicated matter, a precise connection to a particular literary text being merely one interpretative possibility instead of an agreed starting point. Many would prefer to see now a shared stock of gods, heroes, stories, events, and ideas whose representation was formulated independently in many different ways according to the different needs of varied media, contexts, and audiences. The simple and direct connection of the subject to literary classics has thus receded in the best recent scholarship in this area.[4]

---

[2] For good recent critical discussions of the discipline from a wide variety of perspectives: A. M. Snodgrass, *An Archaeology of Greece: the Present State and Future Scope of a Discipline* (Berkeley 1987); F. Coarelli, 'L'archéologie classique dans la culture européenne d'aujourd'hui', *Revue Archéologique* 2 (1994) 294–310; P. Zanker, 'Nouvelles orientations de la recherche en iconographie: commanditaires et spectateurs', *Revue Archéologique* 2 (1994) 281–93; I. Morris, 'Archaeologies of Greece', in Morris (ed.), *Classical Greece: Ancient Histories and Modern Archaeologies* (Cambridge 1994) 9–47; T. Hölscher, 'Klassische Archäologie am Ende des 20. Jahrhunderts: Tendenzen, Defizite, Illusionen', in E.-R. Schwinge (ed.), *Die Wissenschaften vom Altertum am Ende des 2. Jahrtausends n. Chr.* (Stuttgart and Leipzig 1995) 197–208; M. Shanks, *Classical Archaeology of Greece* (London 1996); A. H. Borbein, T. Hölscher and P. Zanker, *Klassische Archäologie* (Berlin 2000).

[3] On which see recently, for example, A. M. Snodgrass, *Homer and the Artists: Text and Picture in Early Greek Art* (Cambridge 1998).

[4] For example: L. Giuliani, *Tragik, Trauer, und Trost: Bildervasen für eine apulische Totenfeier* (Berlin 1995); Snodgrass (n. 3); F. de Angelis and S. Muth (eds.), *Im Spiegel des Mythos: Bilderwelt und Lebenswelt. Lo specchio del mito: Immaginario e realtà* (Wiesbaden 1999).

Fig. 4.1.   The middle-aged men who ran fifth-century Athens as they wanted to be seen. An anonymous, 'democratically' composed group of 'elders' in procession on the Parthenon frieze, north side, slab 10 (marble, H: 1.05 m). 430s BC. Acropolis Museum, Athens.

What I want to describe here are some aspects of an important new strand in the subject, developed in the last generation, that looks at the monuments and images as parts of an enlarged culture history of the Greek and Roman world — a history that recognises that image-bearing structures and objects such as the Parthenon, the Prima Porta Augustus, and Palmyrene grave reliefs (Figs. 4.1–4.3)[5] do not merely supply parallel evidence of what we read about in Thucydides, Virgil and Palmyrene inscriptions, but were powerful expressive components of their own time,

[5] Parthenon frieze, north 10: F. Brommer, *Der Parthenonfries* (Mainz 1977) 33. Prima Porta Augustus: D. Boschung, *Die Bildnisse des Augustus: das römische Herrscherbild* 1.2 (Berlin 1993) 179, no. 171, with earlier literature. Palmyrene relief: *Sotheby's Sale Catalogue: Antiquities and Islamic Works of Art* (New York, Sale 7489, 14 June 2000) 122, no. 124.

Fig. 4.2.   The emperor Augustus in armour, his right arm raised to calm a fictive mass audience. The cuirass features the return in 20 BC of the standards lost to the Parthians in 53 BC, set in a mythical-allegorical frame. The youthful portrait is of Augustus' main type, created in 27 BC. Marble statue (H: 2.09 m), from Livia's villa at Prima Porta. After 20 BC. Vatican, Braccio Nuovo.

with distinct agendas, and actively shape our understanding of whole areas of ancient culture in ways that we need to work hard to understand, define and control.

Fig. 4.3. A veiled Palmyrene woman with a face of exaggerated Hellenic beauty, wearing elaborate heavy jewellery of local style. Limestone relief bust (H: 69.5 cm). *c*. AD 200–250. From the art market in New York. Private Collection, USA.

The following is thus a highly selective account of how ancient images have been studied in the classical context and how recent work in this area is of use and interest to a broad history of Greek and Roman political, social, and religious cultures. It highlights both strengths and weaknesses in the discipline as seen from this one single point of view: what use is visual history for ancient history?

Art, images and figured objects

To designate as 'art' the bewildering variety of image-bearing objects that inhabited the ancient world is perhaps to get off on the wrong foot, to lead one into an arguably false way of looking at the material. The thousands of statues, for example, that stood in Greek and Roman cities and sanctuaries were active markers in a loud public discourse, and represented a huge financial investment in expressive symbols—in large, useless, finely fashioned lumps of stone and metal. 'Ancient art' is a convenient collective misnomer for all these figured artefacts, but we should be aware that this is a very different, bigger and shaggier, beast from art in our own time, and we should resist sidelining it to art history alone as if it were somehow separate from or above other parts of the historical process.

In the past, there has been occasional discomfort that art and images make up so large a part of the archaeology of the ancient world. On the one hand classical art history tended to bleach out the archaeological support of the subject in order to get at its creative artistic core, while on the other hand some archaeology seemed content to leave the visual and stylistic aspects of ancient monuments to another discipline. This used to be a traditional habit, for example, of Roman archaeology as practised in Britain: real archaeology deals with things like camps, roads and belt buckles, not flighty representations. Today such practice looks curious, because in the meantime its obvious allies in other strands of non-classical anthropological archaeology have embraced the study of art and visual culture with great vigour.[6]

Part of this unhelpful, ahistorical division between visual representation and material remains in classical archaeology was driven by period-specific attitudes: art history is Greek, archaeology is Roman. And assumptions and practices on both sides used to reinforce these absurd positions. Greek art historians seemed to be preoccupied with artists and their creative

---

[6] In 1994 a special issue of a prominent journal posed the following question to a range of archaeologists: 'Is there a Place for Aesthetics in Archaeology?', *Cambridge Archaeological Journal* 4.2 (1994). Although most answers were affirmative, both the bald formulation of the question and the perceived need to ask it at all were parts of an earlier archaeological mind-set. See now, for example, T. Dowson, *The Archaeology of Art* (London 2001).

innovations, while archaeologists of the early Roman empire, for example, seemed to find more in pottery assemblages than in the friezes of the Ara Pacis.

Undoubtedly different skills and kinds of research are needed for reading images, but they were first of all part of the wider material and visual environment of antiquity. None were images for their own sake. They were all parts of objects or structures with other functions that are prior and primary — pots, pins, mirrors, altars, tombs. Even statues were at first large stone and metal totems that happened to be in figured form, and they marked in their scale and expense the importance attached to the religious, political and social concerns they represented. These were real, active players with a dynamic three-cornered relationship between buyer, figured object and audience. Even those that look most like 'art' to us — that is, paintings and pictures — usually turn out to be parts of something else, such as Roman house-walls or Egyptian mummies.

If we take the monuments and images out of Greek and Roman archaeology and concentrate on such things (obviously important in themselves) as settlement, trade objects, diet and domestic space, the subject can be made to resemble any other archaeology, but in doing so we would not only have taken out a very large part of the artefactual record of Greek and Roman antiquity, but also filtered out what was a central defining feature of the culture under investigation. Very large quantities of expensive, ostensibly useless figured monuments, reliefs, pictured walls and floors, and statues were an unmistakable peculiarity of Greek and Roman culture.

The period of continuous, unbroken deployment of large marble statues, for example, gives not a bad definition of a recognisable period of antiquity — say 600 BC to AD 600. Large marble statues start and stop in the ancient world abruptly around these dates. Two relatively recent discoveries can illustrate this phenomenon. A colossal naked male statue in the 'kouros' format was set up in the early sixth century BC in the sanctuary of Hera on Samos by one Isches son of Rhesis, and belongs within the first generation of large marble figures set up in the Greek world (Fig. 4.4).[7] At the other end of antiquity, an over-lifesize marble statue of a provincial governor called Flavius Palmatus was set up in Aphrodisias in Caria in the late fifth or early

[7] H. Kyrieleis, *Der grosse Kuros von Samos* (*Samos* 10, Bonn 1996). During the preparation of this chapter, the discovery on Thera of an important new female grave(?) statue was reported in *The Guardian* 29 November 2000, p. 18 (with illustration). It is of marble, of large scale (H: 2.30 m), and of early date (mid-seventh century BC), making it probably our earliest large marble statue so far discovered in the Greek world.

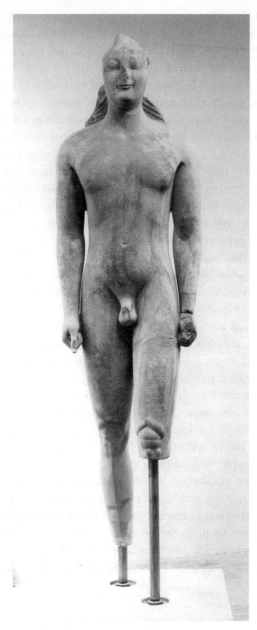

Fig. 4.4. From the first generation of large public marble statues in the Greek world. A colossal naked youth or *kouros* (H: 4.75 m), dedicated by Isches son of Rhesis. From the sanctuary of Hera on Samos. Early sixth century BC. Samos Museum, Vathi.

sixth century AD (Fig. 4.5).[8] Isches' naked kouros stands in a highly period-specific style and pose, while Palmatus wears a typical late antique senatorial toga suit with full accessories. So different as styled images, they are remarkably similar as functional artefacts — large, finely crafted public marble statues.

Among other cultures, ancient or modern, only ancient Egypt has deployed large stone images in any comparable profusion, and there are crucial and obvious differences. Greek and Roman absolute quantities were surely very much higher, and Egyptian stone statues were mostly conceived as high reliefs attached to a back pillar that affirmed their essential character as figured objects. Egyptian statues were also more often set up inside temples and sanctuaries unvisited by a wide public. Freestanding figures in the round, lifesize and larger, in marble and bronze, made in their many tens of thousands, displayed in permanently accessible public places, and conceived as real figures occupying a space continuous with that of the viewer were an unmistakable defining component of Greek and Roman culture.

My general point so far is simply that it is not a good idea to try to separate out ancient images from the wider visual and material history of antiquity.

Two traditions in 1975

To articulate the discussion, some basic, crude taxonomy of the last half-century of studying ancient images is needed. I am not concerned with the great pioneering publications of the big digs — the site volumes of, for example, Olympia, Pergamon, Delphi and Delos — that are the pride of the subject. Those excavations and the accompanying volumes defined classical archaeology in the late nineteenth century and continue majestically to the present.[9] They are works of meticulous, detailed, cautious, empirical classification. Although their premises are derived essentially from the more general works that I do want to talk about, their conclusions are generally closely hemmed in by obtuse archaeological data and circumstance.

---

[8] K. T. Erim, in J. Inan and E. Alföldi Rosenbaum, *Römische und frühbyzantinische Porträtplastik aus der Türkei: Neue Funde* (Mainz 1979) no. 208.

[9] *Olympia* I–V (Berlin 1890–1897) and *Olympische Forschungen* I– (Berlin 1944–); *Altertümer von Pergamon* I– (Berlin 1885–); *Fouilles de Delphes* I– (Paris 1902–); *Exploration Archéologique de Délos* I– (Paris 1909–). There soon followed others, for example: *Corinth* I– (Cambridge, Mass. 1929–); *Athenian Agora* I– (Princeton 1953–).

Fig. 4.5. From the last century of ancient marble statue production. The governor of Caria, Flavius Palmatus, wearing a Constantinopolitan fashion hairstyle and an elaborate late Roman senatorial toga. He stands in the stiff, board-like pose demanded by contemporary court ceremony. Marble statue (H: 1.96 m), from Aphrodisias. Late fifth or early sixth century AD. Aphrodisias Museum.

Two works published in the same year, 1975, may be picked arbitrarily to represent for us two major strands in the study of classical images. Martin Robertson's great *History of Greek Art*[10] was the culmination and the best of the tradition we may call the pure art-historical or Plinian tradition — 'Plinian' after Pliny the Elder's *Natural History*, which preserves the first art history organised primarily by artists. Paul Zanker's inaugural lecture at Göttingen on the portrait reliefs of Roman freedmen[11] may be taken as standing near the beginning of a different approach that we may call simply the historically based tradition — that of interpreting ancient images firstly in relation to the interests and mentalities of their buyers and audiences. It is here of course that the main gains for ancient history come, but I want first to look at the other tradition a little more. Just as the historically based tradition has roots in some excellent work of the 1940s to 1960s,[12] so the 'Plinian' tradition continues today, ignoring or sometimes deprecating the new tradition as sociology.

Artists and development

The Plinian or art-historical tradition ascribes the main motive force in ancient images to the creative interest of the artist. The maker/creator is prior. This tradition has impeccable authority. The world's first art histories were written in the Hellenistic period and traced a linear development of constant innovation along a trail blazed by a canon of great artists towards ever better representations — either towards realism, in one art-historical theory, or to a higher ideal beauty in another version. These art histories established the influential idea of ancient art as an autonomous cultural phenomenon. They are preserved in Pliny (*Nat. Hist.* books 34–36), from where they reached Vasari, Winckelmann, and twentieth-century classical art histories, of which Robertson's is by far the best, most recent full-scale example.

This kind of art history is disappointing for ancient historians not only because it does not address or answer many of the questions that they as

[10] M. Robertson, *A History of Greek Art* (Cambridge 1975) 2 vols.

[11] P. Zanker, 'Grabreliefs römischer Freigelassener', *Jahrbuch des deutschen archäologischen Instituts* 90 (1975) 267–315.

[12] P. H. von Blanckenhagen, 'Elemente der römischen Kunst am Beispiel des Flavischen Stils', in H. Berve (ed.), *Das neue Bild der Antike* (Leipzig 1942) 310–41; R. Bianchi-Bandinelli, *Storicità dell'arte classica* (2nd ed., Florence 1950); id., *Rome, the Center of Power: Roman Art to AD 200* (London 1970); id., *Introduzione all' archeologia* (Rome, Bari 1976) esp. ch. 7: 'Problemi di metodo: la storia dell'arte come interpretazione storica della forma'.

historians are interested in, but also because it explicitly repudiates any close connection between the course of history and the course of art, sometimes asserting pugnaciously that art has its own independent dynamic. Classic art, on this view, is something not open to lowly socio-historical explanations. Robertson's book is superbly accurate with the facts as far as they can be known, and it is impossible, in honesty, to go further in this direction, but his account, complete with frequent Renaissance parallels, carries all the advantages and disadvantages of treating ancient art as somehow cognate to European art, 1300–1900.

The two ideas already implicit in Pliny, of individual artistic innovations and linear formal development, are usually made to work together — artistic individuality within an overarching common development. But they can also be seen as contradictory: if the artists were so innovative and individual, why is the development (supposedly) so even? One powerful variant of the pure art-historical tradition, which sees itself as radically opposed but is in fact merely a subset of it, privileges the unstated Hegelian and Darwinian elements of autonomous development or evolution over the creative abilities of the individual, who is banished altogether; and art is then held to progress under its own higher, unseen formal imperatives of inevitable, even predictable, phases of development. This was the approach, for example, of Rhys Carpenter in the 1950s and of the Bryn Mawr school he founded. For this school of thought, the artist was dead long ago: Greek sculpture was, in Carpenter's most famous dictum, 'an anonymous product of an impersonal craft'.[13] This approach is merely a subset or variant of the originating art-historical tradition because it is wholly at one with it in seeing art as prior. From the historian's point of view, it is all much the same whether the motive and shaping force of an image was its artist or an impersonally creative 'art'.

There is no Pliny or ancient art history for the Hellenistic and Roman periods. This was and is a theory for the classical period, 500–300 BC. This has entailed several things. Firstly, the ancient sanction for the artist-driven view of the fifth and fourth centuries BC has given what was really a tendentious account of ancient image-formation the rank of immutable truth for that period. Secondly, without artists properly recorded for the succeeding periods, the art-historical tradition has fallen back on the forces of autonomous chronological development to explain everything from 300 BC to

---

[13] R. Carpenter, *Greek Sculpture: a Critical Review* (Chicago 1960). The full quotation (p. v) is as follows: 'The present volume contains singularly little comment on the lives, reputations, and accomplishments of the old Greek masters and, instead, pays what may seem undue attention to sculpture as an anonymous product of an impersonal craft.'

AD 600 (only occasionally positing great masters, whom the evidence rarely allows us to see). Thirdly, this theory, so manifestly unsuited to explaining the complexities of Hellenistic and Roman visual culture, has left a wide opening for the more historically based theory, and much of the ground-breaking work in the last generation (as we will see) has been on the figured world of these later periods.

The maker's share

The Plinian tradition (artists plus development), so confident in its ancient sanction, has never stopped to justify theoretically its answers to some simple and obvious questions. How large was the artist's share in the for-mation of an ancient image? This tradition simply assumes that it was close to 100 per cent. The artist made the thing physically and technically, and was responsible for its texture, finish, and, according to some calculated ratio of craft-skill and price, its quality. But who or what shaped its basic forms, style and externals of dress, attributes and iconography? How much was shaped by earlier images, how much by changing externals of life and by shared experience, how much by the maker? The Plinian tradition invites us to see ancient artists, like modern artists, as responsible for the totality of their works and as creators standing outside, commenting on or ignoring con-temporary society and history as they chose. This is an obvious distortion.

Today the artist is prior. Artists need no commission. Their names appear first on gallery labels, the subject and occasion of the image second, if at all. They must constantly strive for difference and originality, and they inhabit a narrow zone of public culture. Little or none of this was true for ancient artists. Ancient artists could be rich and important people, but they stood very much within their society, serving its needs and expressing concerns which they shared. They sought not rupture and originality but modulation within and enlargement of an agreed visual tradition and repertoire. In so far as an image was 'original' — that is, not meant to look like others — one might say the originality of the ancient artist was of a socially negotiated kind. And we cannot expect to have preserved the works of any subversive visual com-mentators, if they ever existed. Ancient images are perhaps better seen as the crystallised product of infinite and continuous oscillations between buyers, workshops and public. They are therefore speaking about society's concerns — or that section of society that would see the image — and not those of the artist *qua* artist. The historically based tradition takes this as a given: history and the buyer are basic. That is, the whole range of external circumstances, ideas and mentalities surrounding the commission — occasion, purpose, display, subject — needs to be considered first.

This may sound like Marxist determinism, but the ancient artist still had a large role — usually to make real, convincing, palpable and technically fine (within an available budget) the representation of more or less collective social, religious, political ideas. And the full effect of an ancient image is hardly described, or its meaning fully interpreted, by listing correctly all such extrinsic parameters that frame it. That is, ancient images are very far from being merely the sum of a set of historical circumstances that are easily verbalised. The images still retained an irreducible intrinsic aesthetic core — their often breathtaking, physical, in-your-face impact. This realist shock value, heightened by sharp technique, was the artist's, and it was what the best of them were prized for. The effect and meaning of this intrinsic visual core can be described, defined and historically controlled and understood only by reference to other images. That intellectual process is what we may call visual history.

Autonomous formal development has been an even more powerful organising idea than creative artists, but again some obvious theoretical questions are never really addressed. For example, how should development be correlated with different levels of production and price? How does style development correlate with craft development? That is, how does the evolution of 'style' correlate with perceptible changes in craft technique and methods of manufacture? And more obviously, how much time — five, ten, fifty years — should be allowed to how much development? Documented examples show, when available, that while craft-artefact evolution can follow a broad observable Darwinian progression (pottery shapes, for example), changes in figure representation and style rarely follow a single gradualist line that is *a priori* self-evident.

Some new premises

Alongside Plinian art history, there has emerged a broader history of ancient visual culture. This scholarly approach has switched the emphasis of explanation from artists to buyers, from creators to consumers, from style to expressive concerns, from development to historically charged changes, from higher Hegelian form to details of local context — that is, from art to history. In order perhaps to persuade other parts of the discipline, the new approach has seemed concerned not to spell out the oppositional character of its basic premises, evidently feeling that its methods can somehow be reconciled with and added to the earlier tradition. Some aspects are of course compatible — for example, detailed observation and carefully differentiated description and classification — but in truth the two approaches have quite different and opposed theories and assumptions about what most decisively informed the style, shape and essential character of ancient images. The explicit resolution in theory and practice of the methods and assumptions of the two approaches is some way in the future. At the moment most scholars working in this area combine them in an unselfconscious, untheorised way according to intellectual taste, the questions chosen and the evidence available.

It may be useful then simply to provide a bald preliminary list of some of the basic theoretical ideas and assumptions embedded in the historically based approach. In antiquity artists and development were secondary, consumers and context were primary. Under 'consumers' are understood both the range of buyers and patrons and the range of audiences, targeted, intended or merely possible. Under the large parameter of 'context' are understood all aspects of possible audience as well as of site, occasion, purpose and function extrinsic to the artefact as image. The visible stylistic evolution and variety of ancient images were not simply the result of personal artistic creativity but more decisively of important historical change and difference. Changing styles represented the changing self-perception of ancient societies — the more homogeneous and collectivist the society (fifth-century Athens, for example), the narrower the range of styles; the more complex the society, the greater number of concurrent styles (the Roman empire, for example). The meaning of ancient images was relative not absolute, relative to their historical and physical circumstances, to their audience, to their place in a tradition, an evolving visual language or system of representation. The same visual form can mean quite different things in different times and places, so that detailed reconstruction of context — purpose, setting, audience — is essential before reasonable interpretation can begin. Level of production and social level are very important, and since much of surviving ancient art is middle-level, not elite, some idea of whose interests and agenda are being expressed is needed before images can be properly assessed.

Beyond the effects of these broad historical circumstances, there was in the very best work also no doubt something due to the individual contributions and personal styles of great artists. But we have very few works surviving from such levels, and not enough evidence or sure cases that would allow us to test how large or marked a phenomenon such personal individuality was. The individual hands of most of the Athenian vase painters detected confidently by J. D. Beazley, but by few others, while of real potential interest from the point of view of the practice and organisation of a major ancient craft, do not seem strong evidence for the depth or width of this phenomenon — rather the reverse.[14]

We will look at some specific examples of these ideas in practice later, but their basic aim is to make the useful but often ahistorical taxonomies of modern archaeology speak usefully in historical terms.

Archaeology and epistemology

This may all sound straightforward and what ancient historians should want from visually inclined archaeologists, and indeed there is now plenty of excellent work in this line (further below). But some more needs to be said on the deficit side concerning the epistemology of the subject. There are some weaknesses in its practice that are perhaps of interest both to historians and to archaeologists.

The epistemology of classical archaeology has often been (for reasons of modern academic history) a lax affair, and the new historical approach in its desire not to be confrontational has been insufficiently radical in tightening it up; in fact, for its own intellectual convenience, it has often simply gone along with the old paradigms and habits. I do not mean the pluralist, sometimes *ad hoc* interpretations that have proliferated in the last generation, especially in anglophone scholarship, under an assumed general umbrella of 'post-modernism'. Though on occasion ill-supported and unhistorical, such work has provided a useful alternative voice in the discipline and rests on intellectual foundations quite different from those under discussion here.[15] I mean simply the old ways in which names, dates, provenances and facts of the subject have been and continue to be diagnosed, verified and known — ways that remain common in varying degrees to all current approaches. There is more here than merely problems of evidence and the general difficulties and uncertainties that beset any area of ancient historical studies. There is at best a dangerous level of optimism about our facts, at worst some serious bluffing — that is, unverifiable assertion and intellectual obscurantism.

---

[14] For some varied criticism of the exaggerated role vase-painters as individuals have played in the subject: M. Beard, 'Adopting an Approach II', in T. Rasmussen and N. Spivey, *Looking at Greek Vases* (Cambridge 1991) 12–35, at 15–19; Shanks (n. 2), 30–41; B. Sparkes, *The Red and the Black: Studies in Greek Pottery* (London 1996) ch. 4.

[15] The best combine a historical framework with (more or less post-) modernising aims, for example: N. Spivey, *Understanding Greek Sculpture: Ancient Meanings, Modern Readings* (London 1996); A. F. Stewart, *Art, Desire, and the Body in Ancient Greece* (Cambridge 1997); J. Elsner, *Art and the Roman Viewer: the Transformation of Art from the Pagan World to Christianity* (Cambridge 1995).

Classical archaeology has an impressive and complex set of classifications of different categories of object arranged in a place-time grid, according to their original manufacture and their date in an evolutionary sequence. The problem is that because much of this works demonstrably well, it has been assumed that it should be made to work for all categories, in all places and at all times. The sad but interesting historical truth is that it does not, and that there is no easy way for those not directly in control of the primary evidence to know which archaeological facts can really be relied on and which cannot.

The standards of evidence and verifiability often deployed would, I think, surprise scholars in other fields. 'A statue by Onatas of Aegina(?)' should in normal academic language mean that the statue in question has a more than 50 per cent chance of having been made by Onatas. That is, there is some good evidence that it was probably made by Onatas, but also some room for doubt. In classical archaeology such a formulation often conceals a different range of meaning: that although there is no hard evidence for the connection, the work has often been associated with Onatas, or that the attribution is a pure hypothesis (preliminary guess) of the writer's. This is a perhaps trivial (and fictional) example, but the practice is pervasive.

Some undocumented artefacts in classical archaeology can be closely dated (for example, imperial portraits) or closely provenanced (for example, Corinthian pottery). But when things cannot safely be so classified, it needs to be explicitly recognised and honest parameters, however wide, need to be set and justified. How can we assess the statement that a marble statue 'is dated *c*.250 BC'? Does this mean that it really is dated by some external evidence, or that an archaeologist has assigned it that date? And if the latter (as usually), on what basis? And does the '*circa*' mean around 250 BC as opposed to around 300 or 200 BC, or does it mean 260–40 BC, or 275–25 BC? That is, what are the real, verifiable external parameters? 'Bronze statuette, Lakonian': does this mean the statuette was found in Lakonia? Or that it can be seen on technical or iconographical grounds and with some degree of certainty to have been made there? Often it means neither. Such a caption will usually mean either that 'Lakonian' is a preliminary hypothesis for the statuette's place of manufacture, or more commonly that it belongs with a group of other bronzes that seem to belong together and have commonly been labelled 'Lakonian' but where they were actually made is not yet known.

Spurious precision helps nobody. Such preliminary ideas and hypotheses presented as researched data are unusable for further historical inquiry. Nothing but sand-castles and compound hypotheses can be built on them.

The data-sets of classical archaeology look like an appealing body of historical evidence, but they are constructed with an arcane epistemology that conceals some very fluid and shifting boundaries.

This is not said in a spirit of intellectual moralising, rather because such pseudo-precision about all artefacts conceals some important aspects of rupture and continuity in the material record that are enormously interesting from a historical perspective. While such statements do no harm as pre-liminary hypotheses for further work of the same kind to refute or adjust — what date, what place of manufacture? — they are seriously misleading about the overall shape and character of ancient material and visual pro-duction and its differential rates of change. According to the unstated principles of Hegelian/Darwinian classical archaeology outlined above, everything can be dated, more or less precisely, in the same way according to its place in a constant development. But this is manifestly untrue. This theory conceals and falsifies the broad and very interesting zones of static cultural production that archaeology can attest so well, and which much of the figured monuments of antiquity inhabited (for example, Hellenistic grave reliefs or later Roman mosaics: see nn. 20 and 22). Traditional archaeology dislikes these zones and tries to break them up into periods, phases, groups and sub-groups.

One might say that a few epistemological sleights of hand are nothing to worry about, the broad picture is approximately correct, and anyway archaeologists are often proved right. But there is much more genuine uncertainty and flexibility in many areas than is currently allowed for. And while archaeologists are sometimes proved right, the list of serious errors is surely longer — that is, cases where dates, names, identities and provenances have been confidently diagnosed on conventional criteria which later evidence has proved decisively wrong.

Some examples. The fifth-century portrait type identified as the Spartan general Pausanias turned out in fact to be of the poet Pindar.[16] The portrait of a late republican Roman aristocrat turned out to be of the Hellenistic comic poet Poseidippos.[17] Many Greek 'originals' turn out to have been made in the Roman period (very embarrassing for traditional art history, with its

---

[16] G. M. A. Richter, *Portraits of the Greeks* (abridged and revised edition, R. R. R. Smith, Oxford 1984) 177–80, figs. 139–40; J. Bergemann, 'Pindar: das Bildnis eines konservativen Dichters', *Mitteilungen des deutschen archäologischen Instituts: Athenische Abteilung* 106 (1991) 157–89.

[17] K. Fittschen, 'Zur Rekonstruktion griechischen Dichterstatuen. 2. Teil: Die Statuen des Poseidippos und des Ps.-Menander', *Mitteilungen des deutschen archäologischen Instituts: Athenische Abteilung* 107 (1992) 229–71.

claim to be able to detect the authentic work).[18] Many Hellenistic-looking marble statues in fact belong in the Roman period—for example, many himation-wearing males and many of the massively constructed and tightly draped female figures from the cities of Greece and Asia Minor.[19] So too several kinds of Hellenistic-style marble grave stelai may begin *c*.200 BC but they also continue well into the Roman imperial period.[20] Many painted mummy portraits from Roman Egypt that were long dated by their abstracted and simplified style to the fourth century have been shown recently on other criteria to belong rather in the second century.[21] Much fine classical-looking silverware and figured mosaic in fact belongs in the fourth to sixth centuries AD.[22] The story, so resolutely resisted by the traditional method, is one of lots of different continuities, spilling over dates thought to be epochal for all products—510, 323, 31 BC, AD 285, 410.

All this is to say, the dates of some kinds of figured objects can be known with some precision, while the dates of others, for good and historically interesting reasons, can be known only very broadly. In the latter cases,

---

[18] A good example is the Acropolis Alexander, long thought to be a fourth-century original, but easily shown by detailed comparison with two other versions of the same type, in Berlin and Schloss Erbach, also to be a later copy: K. Fittschen, *Katalog der antiken Skulpturen in Schloss Erbach* (Berlin 1977) 21–5, no. 7, pl. 8 (Erbach), Beilage 2 (Athens) and 3 (Berlin); R. R. R. Smith, *Hellenistic Royal Portraits* (Oxford 1988) 60, cat. 2, pl. 2, 1–8 (all three versions).

[19] The material is most easily accessible in: A. Linfert, *Kunstzentren hellenistischer Zeit: Studien an weiblichen Gewandfiguren* (Wiesbaden 1979); R. Kabus-Preisshofen, *Die hellenistische Plastik der Insel Kos* (Berlin 1989). For such statues in a historical setting, *cf.* P. Zanker, 'Brüche im Bürgerbild: zu bürgerlichen Selbstdarstellung in der hellenistischen Städten', in M. Wörrle and P. Zanker (eds.), *Stadtbild und Bürgerbild im Hellenismus* (Munich 1995) 251–63.

[20] E. Pfuhl and H. Möbius, *Die ostgriechischen Grabreliefs* (Mainz 1977–9) 2 vols.; *cf.* D. W. von Moock, *Die figürlichen Grabstelen Attikas in der Kaiserzeit: Studien zur Verbreitung, Chronologie, Typologie, und Ikonographie* (Mainz 1998).

[21] B. Borg, *Mumienporträts: Chronologie und kultureller Kontext* (Mainz 1996). Also recently on mummy portraits: E. Doxiadis, *The Mysterious Fayum Portraits: Faces from Ancient Egypt* (London 1995); S. Walker and M. L. Bierbrier, *Ancient Faces: Mummy Portraits from Roman Egypt* (London 1997).

[22] F. Baratte, *La vaisselle d'argent dans Gaule de l'antiquité tardive (IIIe–Ve siècles)* (Paris 1993). The most important finds are the Kaiseraugst and Sevso hoards: E. Alföldi-Rosenbaum, H. A. Cahn and A. Kaufmann-Heinimann, *Der spätrömische Silberschatz von Kaiseraugst* (Derendigen 1984); M. Mango and A. Bennet, *The Sevso Treasure: Art Historical Description and Inscriptions* (*Journal of Roman Archaeology* Suppl. 12.1, Ann Arbor 1994). Mosaics: D. Levi, *Antioch Mosaic Pavements* (Princeton 1947) 2 vols.; J. Balty, *Mosaiques antiques de Syrie* (Brussels 1977); K. M. D. Dunbabin, *The Mosaics of Roman North Africa: Studies in Iconography and Patronage* (Oxford 1978); ead., *Mosaics of the Greek and Roman World* (Cambridge 1999). For an astonishing series of pavements, many recently discovered, made for pagan, Jewish, Christian and Muslim patrons, but showing an extraordinary continuity of craft tradition, second to eighth centuries, from the Roman to the Ummayad period, see M. Piccirillo, *The Mosaics of Jordan* (Amman 1993).

the knowable limits can be wider than one, two or three centuries. Some epochal dates are important for some categories of image, not for others. The visual and material record shows clearly that where the modern world places high value on change, innovation and individuality, the ancient world often preferred similarity, continuity and collective ideas.

My point here is simply that the well-classified data-sets of classical archaeology are rich, inviting and ready-made, but they are shaped and controlled by strong unstated theories about how ancient images came to be the way they are, and that those theories may not be obviously the best ones.

Historical perspectives: the classical ideal and horrors of war

We may turn now to the more obviously historical use of ancient art and the difficulties that it poses. Ancient images have often proved simply too powerful and volatile as evidence for easy historical use. Ancient art is generally a highly successful and seductive medium, but its range of expression and meaning is not so easy to tie down without quite a lot of disciplined effort. I bypass the old use of images in books of ancient political history and biography that most of the time simply got names and places wilfully wrong — 'portrait of Hannibal', for example, might be illustrated by the image of an Antonine charioteer (there are no extant portraits of Hannibal from antiquity).[23] This tradition is still alive on book covers and in TV documentaries about Roman emperors illustrated by a general scattering of evocative, contextless, often misidentified images. This was an old-style laziness that signified simply a lack of real interest in ancient visual culture. For serious historians today, however, that is all in the past. But even when basic facts are got right, it can still be too easy to engage in a direct and unproblematic way with such apparently straightforward images. They speak so clearly and loudly, but it remains easy to get them at least half-wrong.

Some simple examples. The heads and naked bodies of statues of the mid-fifth century BC look obviously 'ideal', an improvement on reality, a representation of something more noble than ordinary life. And that is how ancient art history interpreted them, and what they meant in the Roman period to the people who admired and bought fine marble replicas of them.

---

[23] One example from many: G. Audisio, *Hannibal* (Paris 1961) 176, fig. p. 177. That this commonly illustrated bust from near Capua (now in the Naples museum) is in fact a private portrait of the mid-second century AD is not something difficult to discover.

A noble ideal, *supra verum*, is indeed their correct meaning in their later, Roman context. But statues of the mid-fifth century BC had in their own time and cultural context a very different agenda and a different contemporary reception and meaning. The explicit aim, premise, and theory of such representations was *alētheia* — 'truth' or observed reality.[24] We may think that the statues do not look very real, but that is mainly because we know the much more real-looking statues that came after them. In its day this was a brash new hard-hitting realism. The gap between its stated aim and its obvious artificiality is where we locate style, and more historically, contemporary social ideology. The strong effect of this peculiar brand of period-specific and culture-specific realism is what stunning new finds such as the Motya Charioteer and the Riace Bronzes have given us (Fig. 4.6).[25]

In spite of often-repeated warnings, it remains difficult for modern viewers not to look into ancient images and pictures as uncomplicated windows on to the ancient world, unproblematic reflections of what it was like. This was of course the aim of antiquity's realist visual grammar — to conceal highly structured, coded, often tendentious representations beneath an aura of truthful inevitability. Things were just like that. With imperial Roman monuments we are naturally on our guard for loaded statements ('propaganda'), but we are still easily caught off balance. In a small and well-known vignette on Trajan's Column (scene 45), many have seen wild Dacian womenfolk torturing with fiery torches some naked, bound, heroically muscled Roman soldiers: a clear *exemplum* of the barbarity the imperial armies have come to crush (Fig. 4.7).[26] Such a reading follows our expectations, our natural empathy with a brilliantly conceived monument and the suffering it depicts. But it is in fact clear in this scene that it is not Romans who are being tortured. Two of the three bound naked figures (clearest in the topmost figure) have a Dacian-style beard, and the prisoners are therefore really Dacians being tortured by local provincial women, who are now on the side of Rome. The women are probably to be considered as proximate victims of some Dacian atrocity. The scene is thus a visual celebration of revenge properly taken, and so rather out of step with our expectations of the role of a work of fine art.

[24] J. J. Pollitt, *The Ancient View of Greek Art: Criticism, History, and Terminology* (New Haven, London 1974) 125–38, s.v. *alētheia-veritas*; *cf.* R. R. R. Smith, 'Art Theory and Criticism in Antiquity', in M. Kemp (ed.), *Oxford History of Western Art* (Oxford 1999) 58–61.

[25] Motya charioteer: N. Bonacasa (ed.), *La statua marmorea di Mozia* (Rome 1980); V. Tusa, in H. Kyrieleis (ed.), *Archaische und klassische griechische Plastik* (Mainz 1986) vol. 2, 1–11. Riace bronzes: L. Vlad Borelli (ed.), *Due bronzi di Riace* (*Bolletino d'Arte*, Suppl. 1984).

[26] S. Settis (ed.), *La colonna traiana* (Turin 1988) 172, pl. 68.

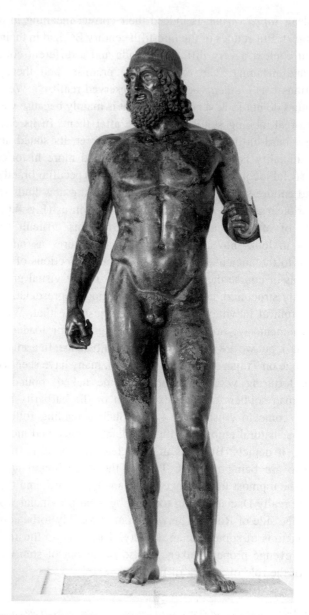

Fig. 4.6. Classical ideal or fifth-century Hellenic norm? The impact of a body like this results from astonishing top-of-the-line technical quality and a realism specific to Greek culture of the fifth century BC. Bronze statue (H: 1.98 m) of an unidentified hero, from Riace Marina, S. Italy ('Riace A'). Mid-fifth century BC. Museo Archeologico, Reggio di Calabria.

Fig. 4.7. Barbarian atrocity or rightful revenge? Five local women torture three naked and bound male prisoners with torches — captive Romans or captive Dacians? Column of Trajan, spiral marble frieze, scene 45 (H: *c.* 75 cm). AD 106–113. Rome. Photo after plaster cast.

On the Column of Marcus Aurelius a grisly execution scene (scene 61), often illustrated, seems here a surely straightforward representation of the horrors of war, so painful for the philosophical emperor, so sadly portrayed on his column (Fig. 4.8).[27] But again this is a modern and sentimental point of view. The pained spiritual style of the sculptured heads is a technical illusion, and the horror of war was simply beyond the range of meaning to be located in a Roman triumphal monument. This is rather a representation of just punishment duly carried out by the dutiful imperator, visited on barbarian leaders who (we may surmise) have broken their word. The explanatory collateral ancient text here is not Marcus' pained private meditations but Caesar's briskly reported accounts of executions and mutilations of Gauls and Germans in illegal revolt.[28] The modern visual parallel is not 'All Quiet on the Western Front', but something more like 'Robocop' or 'Death-Wish'. The best positive visual parallels in the ancient world are to be found in Assyria and Egypt.

A free, ahistorical, or historically unmediated viewer-response to such images can of course carry conviction. The execution scene from Marcus' Column could still usefully be deployed today to represent the horrors of war. This is testimony to the power and volatility of ancient images, and to how much we still share their visual language. (The same is shown by the quickness and instinctiveness with which the modern viewer is moved to criticise or laugh when ancient images — such as low-level northern provincial grave reliefs — fall outside our expectations of a convincing legible image.) But as historians of course we force ourselves to look differently. And this is my general point here: ancient images have to be located in their correct place in an evolving visual language (such as that of fifth-century male body norms) and within an attested range of meaning and associations (such as that of the good and just war).

Ideas, finds, documentation

To turn now to solid gains. What in recent scholarship on ancient images is useful and interesting for ancient historians? Three things stand out: useful new interpretative ideas, new finds and excellent documentation. Well-published new finds that make a difference, filling real gaps in our knowledge, continue to revitalise the subject in all periods — from the colossal archaic kouros set up by

[27] E. Petersen, A. von Domaszewski and G. Calderini *Die Marcussäule* (Munich 1896) 73–4, pl. 70.
[28] Caesar, *Bellum Gallicum* 3.16 (Veneti, 56 BC), 4.14–15 (Germans, 55 BC), 8.44 (Uxellodunum, combatants' hands cut off, 51 BC).

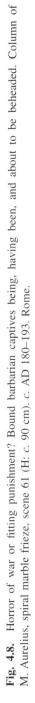

Fig. 4.8. Horror of war or fitting punishment? Bound barbarian captives being, having been, and about to be beheaded. Column of M. Aurelius, spiral marble frieze, scene 61 (H: *c.* 90 cm). *c.* AD 180–193. Rome.

Isches in the Heraion on Samos (Fig. 4.4) through the tomb paintings of late classical and Hellenistic Macedonia to the late Roman mosaics of Nea Paphos.[29] Such extraordinary and high-quality new data are obviously important. There has also been a quantum leap in the quality and quantity of publications of categories of material not properly assembled before, now set out in thoughtful, detailed, well-illustrated monographs and catalogues.[30] These provide the subject with well-edited bodies of primary evidence represented in high-quality photographs, plans and reconstructions. The subject lives from good consistent visual documentation. Complete documentation of all examples, good and bad, of a particular image type is necessary before a good historical interpretation can be attempted. In terms of major recent projects that undertake such total documentation, one thinks for example of the *LIMC* collection of mythological iconography, of the *Kerameus* series on pot painters, of the revitalised corpora of Roman sarcophagi (*Die antiken Sarkophag-Reliefs*) and of imperial portraits (*Das römische Herrscherbild*), of the remarkable new *Häuser in Pompeji* series documenting Pompeian wall-paintings in their full archaeological setting.[31] At the same time, a rich profusion of excellent new museum and exhibition catalogues has set various areas of the discipline on a new footing.[32]

Most important in this context, however, are the new controlling ideas by which this abundance of material is organised and understood — that is, the usually unstated theory of what has been called here the historically based tradition. A lot of its key ideas have emerged at the same time in different places and in areas of ancient visual studies. It is thus a broad-seated change of

[29] Isches: see n. 7. Macedonian tomb painting: M. Andronicos, *Vergina: the Royal Tombs* (Athens 1984); id., *Vergina II: the 'Tomb of Persephone'* (Athens 1994); S. Miller, *the Tomb of Lyson and Kallikles* (Mainz 1993); R. Ginouvès (ed.), *La Macedoine* (Paris 1993). Nea Paphos mosaics: W. A. Daszewski, *Dionysos der Erlöser: Griechische Mythen im Spätantiken Cypren* (Mainz 1995).

[30] At random, for example, two catalogues: S. Steingräber (ed.), *Etruscan Painting: Catalogue Raisonné of Etruscan Wall Paintings* (New York 1986); K. Fittschen and P. Zanker, *Katalog der römischen Porträts in den Capitolinischen Museen* (Mainz 1983–5) 2 vols., which has set a new standard for the documentation of ancient sculpture.

[31] *Lexicon Iconographicum Mythologiae Classicae* 1–8 (Zurich 1981–97); *Forschungen zur antiken Keramik. II. Reihe: Kerameus* 1– (Mainz 1975–); *Die antiken Sarkophargreliefs* (1890–); *Das römische Herrscherbild* (Berlin 1939–); *Häuser in Pompeji* 1– (Tübingen 1984–).

[32] Our understanding, for example, of pre-Imperial Italy and Rome, has been transformed by the material and visual evidence presented in the following exhibitions and catalogues: *Roma Medio-repubblicana: Aspetti culturali di Roma e del Lazio nei secoli IV e III a.C.* (Exhibition catalogue, Rome 1973); *Enea nel Lazio: Archeologia e mito* (Exhibition catalogue, Rome 1980); M. Cristofani (ed.), *La grande Roma dei Tarquini* (Exhibition catalogue, Rome 1990); G. Pugliese Carratelli (ed.), *The Western Greeks: Classical Civilization in the Western Mediterranean* (Exhibition Catalogue, London 1996); and now M. Torelli (ed.), *The Etruscans* (Exhibition Catalogue, Venice 2000).

intellectual orientation in the discipline that has been combined in varying degrees with older methods that are partly inconsistent with it. Generally, this approach to visual history has produced the most tangible results in the long 'non-Plinian' periods of antiquity — the Hellenistic and Roman periods that are unencumbered by the great-artist legacy. However, the study of 'classical' Greek art, that is, of the fifth and fourth centuries BC, long the most conservative, even jealously guarded area of the discipline, has been changing too.[33]

The swift gains of the new approach can be seen in shorter studies of material already well collected and processed in the way described above. For example, more than one thousand Hellenistic and Hellenistic-looking grave reliefs from western Asia Minor were published in two large catalogue volumes by E. Pfuhl and E. Möbius, while a social and political setting for a large group of them has been created in a short study by P. Zanker that looks at the stelai through the lens of civic values in Smyrna in the second century BC.[34]

Some of the best historically based work consists of monographs that combine the new premises with systematic presentation of all the relevant material in a certain category. This is the (unstated) goal of a series titled *Beiträge zur Erschliessung hellenistischer und kaiserzeitlicher Skulptur und Architektur* (*Contributions to the Exploration of Hellenistic and Roman Sculpture and Architecture*). An example of these monographs is R. Neudecker's collection and study of all the provenanced marbles (around 900) that certainly come from Roman villas in Italy.[35] It shows two things little appreciated before: firstly, that a large proportion of the Greek-looking

[33] Important work has been done in this area in very different ways, for example, by N. Himmelmann, T. Hölscher and J. J. Pollitt. See, for example, J. J. Pollitt, *Art and Experience in Classical Greece* (Cambridge 1972); N. Himmelman, *Reading Greek Art: Essays* (ed. W. P. Childs, Princeton 1998); T. Hölscher, 'Die Nike der Messenier und Naupaktier in Olympia', *Jahrbuch des deutschen archäologischen Instituts* 89 (1974) 70–111; id., *Griechische Historienbilder des 5. und 4. Jahrhunderts v. Chr.* (Würzburg 1975); id., *Die unheimliche Klassik der Griechen* (Bamberg 1989); id., 'Immagini dell'identità greca', in S. Settis (ed.), *I Greci* 2.2 (Turin 1997) 191–248; id., 'Images and political identity: the case of Athens', in D. Boedeker and K. A. Raaflaub, *Democracy, Empire, and the Arts in Fifth-Century Athens* (Cambridge, Mass. 1998) 153–83. See also E. La Rocca (ed.), *L'esperimento della perfezione: Arte e società nell'Atena di Pericle* (Milan 1988); R. Osborne, *Archaic and Classical Greek Art* (Oxford 1998).

[34] Pfuhl and Möbius (n. 20); P. Zanker, 'The Hellenistic grave stelai from Smyrna: identity and self-image in the polis', in A. W. Bulloch et al., *Images and Ideologies: Self-Definition in the Hellenistic World* (1993) 212–30. See also S. Schmidt, *Hellenistische Grabreliefs: Typologische und chronologische Beobachtungen* (Cologne 1991); C. Breuer, *Reliefs und Epigramme griechischer Privatgrabmäler: Zeugnisse bürgerlichen Selbstverständnisses vom 4. bis 2. Jahrhundert v. Chr.* (Cologne 1995).

[35] R. Neudecker, *Die Skulpturen-Ausstattung römischer Villen in Italien* (Mainz 1988). The importance of this work is described in a review by the present writer in *Journal of Roman Studies* 82 (1992) 270–3.

marbles argued about for a century by art historians from a purely aesthetic/ artistic point of view should be located within the context of Roman villa culture; and secondly, that the primary motive for the selection of the figures was not to do with artists and art but with thematic relevance to the different parts of a palatial Roman country house. The statues articulated the mental architecture of Roman private leisure culture. The spatial and visual environment of the Roman villa has in general been a very profitable area of recent visual research.[36]

Local context

Some of the most important new ideas and results have come from the historical task of relocating the monuments from their position in an abstract classification or art-sequence into their physical, cultural and mental contexts, as preserved, reconstructed or properly imagined. A simple example: archaic kouros statues have been collected in a famous catalogue, archaic Athenian grave stelai in another, and archaic relief bases are scattered elsewhere.[37] Only recently however have there been studies that use these three separate archaeological categories together to illuminate and interpret the one historical setting in which they often intersected — namely archaic tombs.[38] The stelai marked graves, as often did kouroi, and the relief bases were kouros and stele supports. The relief scenes on the bases functioned as specifying visual commentaries on the images posted above them. The physical and

---

[36] J. R. Clarke, *The Houses of Roman Italy, 100 BC–AD 250: Ritual, Space, and Decoration* (Berkeley 1991); E. K. Gazda, *Roman Art in the Private Sphere: New Perspectives on the Architecture and Decor of the Domus, Villa, and Insula* (Ann Arbor 1991); R. Förtsch, *Archäologischer Kommentar zu den Villenbriefen des jüngeren Plinius* (Mainz 1993); A. Wallace-Hadrill, *Houses and Society in Pompeii and Herculaneum* (Princeton 1994); R. Laurence and A. Wallace-Hadrill (eds.), *Domestic Space in the Roman World: Pompeii and Beyond* (*Journal of Roman Archaeology* Suppl. 22, Providence, RI 1997); P. Zanker, *Pompeii: Public and Private Life* (Cambridge, Mass. 1998).

[37] Archaic kouroi: G. M. A. Richter, *Kouroi: Archaic Greek Youths* (3rd ed., London 1970). Archaic Grave Reliefs: G. M. A. Richter, *Archaic Attic Gravestones* (London 1961). Relief bases: J. Boardman, *Greek Sculpture: the Archaic Period* (London 1978) 164, 247 (with references), figs. 240–3 has the main ones.

[38] See, for example, all with different perspectives: A. M. D'Onofrio, 'Aspetti e problemi del monumento funerario attico arcaico', *Archeologia e Storia Antica, Annali: Istituto Universitario Orientale, Napoli* 10 (1988) 83–96, with references to her several earlier studies on this subject; I. Morris, *Death-Ritual and Social Structure in Classical Antiquity* (Cambridge 1992); C. Sourvinou-Inwood, *'Reading' Greek Death, to the End of the Classical Period* (Oxford 1995); B. D'Agostino, 'La necropoli e rituali delle morte', in S. Settis (ed.), *I Greci* 2.1 (Turin 1996) 435–70.

social–political setting of such images, now for the most part without archaeological context, needs to be creatively imagined. That context was the archaic cemeteries of the Attic countryside where these great marble totems acted as potent markers of aristocratic power; around them were orchestrated the great clan funerals so offensive to demos sentiment in the early fifth century BC that they seem to have been banned by law.[39]

An astonishing new find made this context speak more loudly, when the dazzling statue of a young woman called Phrasykleia was excavated at Merenda (in north-east Attica) in 1972 and was found to fit exactly on to an inscribed base (long known) that gives her sad story:[40]

> Marker (*sēma*) of Phrasykleia. I shall ever be called maiden (*korē*), the gods allotting me this title (*onoma*) instead of marriage. [Aris]tion of Paros made me.

She died an unmarried girl, and her statue was made by the great Aristion of Paros, sculptor to the rich of mid-sixth-century Attica. We know more about this new image of Phrasykleia than about almost any other archaic statue. Dressed in her festival finery, she and others illuminate a whole world of glittering aristocratic ostentation, in the cemetery and sanctuary, at games and festivals.[41] When the festival and funeral music stopped, the statues remained.

Class, level, price

The social class or level at which ancient images operated — both in terms of their customers and their intended audiences — is also an important parameter to be considered closely alongside physical display context. For example, many of the fine 'republican'-looking marble portrait busts that seem to exemplify the accentuated personal identities of the Roman aristocracy in the age of Caesar and Cicero do not in fact belong in that context. Many of the surviving examples represent freedmen of the early imperial period. The basic self-styling is that of the republican aristocracy, but in their right setting the style of such images had come to mean

---

[39] Cicero, *De Legibus* 2.64–6; J. Engels, *Funerum sepulcrorumque magnificentia: Begräbnis- und Grabluxusgesetze in der griechisch-römischen Welt* (Stuttgart 1988) 97–106, with earlier literature.
[40] E. I. Mastrokostas, 'La koré Phrasykleia, oeuvre d'Aristion de Paros et un kouros en marbre', *Athens Annals of Archaeology* 5.2 (1972) 298–324; C. Rolley, *La sculpture grecque I: des origines au milieu du Ve siècle* (Paris 1994) 285, fig. 287.
[41] L. A. Schneider, *Zur sozialen Bedeutung der archaischen Korenstatuen* (Hamburg 1979); B. Fehr, 'Kouroi e korai: formule e tipi dell'arte arcaica come espressione di valori', in S. Settis (ed.), *I Greci* 2.1 (Turin 1996) 785–846.

something rather different—the arrival of loyal and prosperous slaves at the cherished status of *civis Romanus*.[42]

One of the most fundamental and broad-based realisations of historically based work in this area has been that it was not only obviously cheaper, poorly executed images that occupied a proletarian environment, but also a lot of the fine, classical-looking figured marbles that formerly were unreflectively taken to be elite material. A large proportion of the Roman-period portrait statues, busts and sarcophagi surviving from central Italy in modern museums were in fact 'middle-class' products. They attest the penetration of the marble-using classes by the most successful section of the 'middle levels': the wealthy and successful upper levels of the freedman class, for example. It is this phenomenon that explains, partly, the extraordinary quantity of surviving marbles of the early and middle imperial period.

Roman versus Greek art

Another great gain has been the breaking down of the 'Greek art versus Roman art' divide. Connoisseurs of formal essences used to claim to find distinct Greek and Roman formal structures and specialities in art that defined a distinctive 'national' contribution: every great culture, it was felt, should have its own creative and defining visual art forms. Thus had been invented, for example, the distinctive Roman illusionism of Franz Wickoff, or the underlying Italian structures of Guido Kaschnitz von Weinberg.[43] And the search for what is distinctively 'Roman' in the classical-looking marbles ('Roman *Ideal-plastik*') that decorated Italian villas and other structures seems to be based ultimately on the same premise or theory of intrinsic 'national' cultures.[44]

---

[42] Best treatment of these images: V. Kockel, *Porträtreliefs stadtrömischer Grabbauten* (Mainz 1993).

[43] F. Wickhof, *Roman Art: Some of its Principles and their Application to Early Christian Painting* (London 1900); G. von Kaschnitz Weinberg, *Kleine Schriften zur Struktur: Ausgewählte Schriften* 1 (Berlin 1965). On these, see the outstanding intellectual history of the subject by O. Brendel, *Prolegomena to the Study of Roman Art* (New Haven 1979).

[44] Some varied examples: R. Wünsche, 'Der Jüngling vom Magdalensberg: Studie zur römischen Idealplastik', in *Festschrift Luitpold Dussler: 28 Studien zur Archäologie und Kunstgeschichte* (Munich 1972) 45–80, an early and important article in this area; K. Hartswick 'The Ares Borghese reconsidered', *Revue Archéologique* (1990) 227–83; H. Meyer, 'A Roman Masterpiece: the Minneapolis Doryphoros', in W. G. Moon (ed.), *Polykleitos, the Doryphoros, and Tradition* (Madison 1995) 65–75. In this context ('Roman masterpiece'), it depends of course what one means by 'Roman'—surely not simply 'Roman-period', but something more culturally specific, although quite how that might be defined has not been attempted.

The historically based tradition saw a long time ago that a sharp division between Greek and Roman art was misconceived. Italy down to 200 BC was part of a sub-Hellenistic periphery, and from the second century BC Rome became a new (eventually *the*) Hellenistic capital. Visual culture at Rome had some of its own priorities but they were realised within a continuously evolving Hellenistic language. There never was, either later or in an earlier 'native' past, an equivalent of Latin in ancient visual representation.

Late republican art is best understood as an informed appropriation and reformulation of component parts of the Hellenistic repertoire. One of the most recognisably 'Roman' reformulations was the carving out of a distinctive political-moral identity within and beyond late Hellenistic portrait norms.[45] Delos, a main conduit for the transfer of late Hellenistic culture and personnel to Italy, provides superb early examples. Two remarkable new busts from a businessman's house on Delos (the Skardhana House) put on display with full force the aggressive individuality and personal severity that the socially Romanised Italian and Levantine businessmen on Delos had learned from their aristocratic customers in Italy.[46] Without their archaeological context, these two busts would have been identified unhesitatingly as Roman aristocrats and probably dated in the Flavian or Trajanic period. Preliminary reports of their context seem to indicate that they represent Italian bankers and belong between the two sacks of the island in 88 and 69 BC.

Architectural wall-painting and mythological sculptures are cognate reformulations in the sphere of Roman villa decor. The new wall-paintings from the reception rooms of the grand villa at Oplontis (near Herculaneum) and their so-called 'second-style' facade compositions show us the proper monumental use of architectural painting to create palatial, regal-looking

---

[45] L. Giuliani, *Bildnis und Botschaft: Hermeneutische Untersuchungen zur Bildniskunst der römischen Republik* (Frankfurt 1986); with a slightly different perspective (already 'beyond context'), J. Tanner, 'Portraits, power, and patronage in the late Roman Republic', *Journal of Roman Studies* 90 (2000) 18–50, seeking to locate the origin of the style abroad in the relationship of Roman patrons and foreign clients. Generally on late republican visual culture, the best and fullest accounts are: E. La Rocca, 'Linguaggio artistico e ideologia politica a Roma in età repubblicana', in *Roma e l'Italia: Radices Imperii* (Milan 1990) 289–495; and F. Coarelli, *Revixit Ars: Arte e ideologia a Roma. Dai modelli ellenistici alla tradizione repubblicana* (Rome 1996), his collected articles on this subject published between 1969 and 1995.

[46] A. Hermary, P. Jockey and F. Queyrel, *Sculptures déliennes* (Paris 1996) 218, no. 99 (both busts). For some evaluation of the historical context of the house and its Italian owners: N. K. Rauh, *The Sacred Bonds of Commerce: Religion, Economy, and Trade Society at Hellenistic Roman Delos* (Amsterdam 1993) 215–19.

interiors.[47] Formerly, the phenomenon was misunderstood because we looked
at it in the confines of small Pompeian houses and bedrooms where it did not
seem to make sense. This was the grand gilded 'French' interior style of the
Caesarian age, widely imitated by social levels and in contexts, such as
Pompeian bedrooms, beyond its point of origin. It uses an old Hellenistic
painted vocabulary radically reconfigured for its new, constantly changing
Roman domestic contexts.[48]

The remarkable finds in the cave at Sperlonga give us something similar
in the marble register: grandiose Hellenistic-style mythological groups by
the latest names in town (the sculptors of the Laocoon) to decorate a cliff-
side dining installation.[49] There was a colossal 'Ship of Odysseus attacked
by Scylla' for the centre of the pond and a colossal sculptural tableau of
'Odysseus and his Companions blinding Polyphemus' for the back of the
cave — each chosen and crafted with impeccable thematic suitability to the
spaces decorated. Rome was a late Hellenistic capital, and the astonishing
diversity of its images allows us to feel something of the texture of that
vigorously refracted Hellenism.

Afterlife, this life

Another great gain has been the long, slow realisation that funerary images
and tomb narratives in antiquity have little to do with eschatology or the
afterlife and very much to do with the life regretfully left behind. This shift of
course makes these images very much more interesting from a historical point
of view: they move from the fringe zone of mystery religions to the centre of
mainstream social history. Different periods and cultures thus lay out for us in
concentrated emblematic images, which we can try to read, the key things,
persons, ideas and activities that made their lives worth living. The most
afterlife-dominated category of all — Roman mythological sarcophagi — has
recently been shown in various studies to be better understood as providing,

---

[47] A. de Franciscis, *Die pompeianische Wandmalereien in der Villa von Oplontis* (Recklinghausen 1975).

[48] K. Fittschen, 'Zur Herkunft und Entstehungen des 2. Stils: Probleme und Argumente', in *Hellenismus in Mittelitalien* (Göttingen 1976) 539–59; R. A. Tybout, *Aedificiorum Figurae: Untersuchungen zu der Architekturdarstellungen des frühen zweiten Stils* (Amsterdam 1989).

[49] B. Conticello and B. Andreae, *Die Skulpturen von Sperlonga (Antike Plastik* 14, Berlin 1974); N. Himmelmann, *Sperlonga: die homerischen Gruppen und ihre Bildquellen* (Opladen 1995); Ch. Kunze, 'Zur Datierung des Laokoon und der Skyllagruppe aus Sperlonga', *Jahrbuch des deutschen archäologischen Instituts* 111 (1996) 139–223.

with endless variety and changes of emphasis, poetic commentaries on the lives and deaths of the thousands of little local heroes and heroines buried in them.[50] They did great deeds when alive (great, that is, in the eyes of their loved ones) and they have now been cruelly and tragically snatched from this life — as were the heroes and heroines of mythology.

Something similar has been done in the very different visual register of Athenian grave reliefs of the fourth century BC. Instead of asking which of the participants in the scenes depicted is dead or which still living (questions that tended to exclude others in the earlier literature), it has been realised that these are better taken as emblematic scenes of correct civilian family relations — *oikos*-leaders displaying a calm domestic discipline. It has also been shown that in some cases there was no necessary relationship between the participants in the pseudo-narratives figured on the stelai, the names inscribed above the scenes, and the persons buried below.[51]

Imperial representation

Imperial Roman art has naturally been a central focus of historically based visual research. Both imperial portraits and historical narratives have been very well studied. The portrait icons of successive emperors and selected family members have been in large part sorted out by application of an effective, verifiable method that allows an imperial portrait to be

---

[50] P. Blome, 'Zur Umgestaltung griechischer Mythen in der römischen Sepulkralkunst: Alkestis-, Protesilaos-, und Proserpinasarkophage', *Mitteilungen des deutschen archäologischen Instituts: Römische Abteilung* 85 (1978) 435–57; E. D'Ambra, 'A myth for a smith: a Meleager sarcophagus from a tomb in Ostia', *American Journal of Archaeology* 92 (1988) 85–100; L. Giuliani, 'Achill-Sarkophage in Ost und West: Genese einer Ikonographie', *Jahrbuch der Berliner Museen* 31 (1989) 23–39; K. Fittschen, 'Der Tod der Kreusa und der Niobiden: Überlegungen zur Deutung griechischer Mythen auf römischen Sarkophagen', *Studi italiani di filologia classica* 3rd series, 10.1–2 (1992) 1046–60; M. Koortbojian, *Myth, Meaning, and Memory on Roman Sarcophagi* (Berkeley 1995); P. Zanker, 'Phaidras Trauer und Hippolytos' Bildung: Zu einem Sarkophag im Thermenmuseum', in de Angelis and Muth (n. 4) 131–42; R. Turcan, *Messages d'outre-tombe: L'iconographie des sarcophages romains* (Paris 1999).

[51] J. Bergemann, *Demos und Thanatos: Untersuchungen zum Wertsystem der Polis im Spiegel der attischen Grabreliefs des 4. Jahrhunderts v. Chr. und zur Funktion der gleichzeitigen Grabbauten* (Munich 1997); in a similar direction R. E. Leader, 'In death not divided: gender, family, and status on Classical Athenian grave stelae', *American Journal of Archaeology* 101 (1997) 683–99. Contrast N. Himmelman, *Attische Grabreliefs* (Wiesbaden 1999), and, in English, 'Quotations of images of gods and heroes on Attic grave reliefs of the Classical period', in G. R. Tsetskhladze, A. M. Snodgrass and A. J. N. Prag (eds.), *Periplous: Essays for Sir John Boardman* (London and New York 1999) 136–44.

distinguished objectively from that of a private citizen.[52] New material in this area constantly fills out and expands the picture, the best pieces often adding striking impact — for example, a large new gilded bronze portrait head of Nero from the last years of his reign (now in Berlin).[53]

Imperial narratives have been well sited somewhere between two unhelpful old ideas: that they illustrate what really happened, or that they are 'propaganda'. A variety of detailed studies has shown how the huge narrative panels known as 'Roman historical reliefs' were carefully composed pseudo-narratives whose actions epitomised key imperial virtues and exemplary activities in which the emperor was in reality actively involved: expansion of the empire, care of the army, care of the people, proper relations with the gods, proper relations with the senate.[54] Similar ideas are read, for example, in Pliny's *Panegyric*, but their selection and manner of representation in these grand marble pictures gives them a quite different weight and impact. And even where precisely the same themes are represented, they are treated with different emphases according to the needs of the different media and their audiences.[55]

New finds have allowed us to look through the other end of the telescope and to see and study the emperor as viewed from the provinces. Superb new statues and busts illustrate the mechanics of distribution and wilful re-design of the emperor's image in line with local expectations. For example, a new equestrian bronze of Augustus from Greece, from late in his reign, uses a portrait type of the dynast that was current in the 30s BC but still clearly

---

[52] Some important and accessible studies: K. Fittschen, 'Zum angeblichen Bildnis des Lucius Verus im Thermen-Museum', *Jahrbuch des deutschen archäologischen Instituts* 86 (1971) 214–52; M. Bergmann, *Marc Aurel* (Frankfurt 1978); K. Vierneisel and P. Zanker, *Die Bildnisse des Augustus* (Exhibition catalogue, Munich 1979); P. Zanker, *Provinzielle Kaiserporträts: zur Rezeption der Selbstdarstellung des Princeps* (Munich 1983); D. Boschung, *Die Bildnisse des Caligula: das römische Herrscherbild* 1.4 (Berlin 1989); Boschung (n. 5). The importance of this work and its methodology are discussed by the present writer in 'Typology and diversity in the portraits of Augustus', *Journal of Roman Archaeology* 9 (1996) 31–47.

[53] H. Born and K. Stemmer, *Damnatio Memoriae: das Berliner Nero-Porträt* (Mainz 1996).

[54] Some important studies: K. Fittschen, 'Das Bildprogramm des Trajansbogen zu Benevent', *Archäologischer Anzeiger* (1972) 742–89; V. M. Strocka, 'Beobachtungen an den Attikareliefs des severischen Quadrifons von Lepcis Magna', *Antiquités Africaines* 6 (1972) 147–72; M. Torelli, *Typology and Structure of Roman Historical Reliefs* (Ann Arbor 1982); M. Pfanner, *Der Titusbogen* (Mainz 1983); A.-M. Leander Touati, *The Great Trajanic Frieze: the Study of a Monument and of the Mechanisms of Message Transmission in Roman Art* (Stockholm 1987); E. La Rocca, 'Arcus et Arae Claudii', in V. M. Strocka (ed.), *Die Regierungszeit des Kaisers Claudius: Umbruch oder Episode* (Mainz 1994) 267–92; T. Hölscher, *Monumenti statali e pubblico* (Rome 1994), a collection of important earlier studies in Italian translation.

[55] *Cf.* Fittschen (n. 54).

available in this workshop more than a generation later.[56] The image combines the hair pattern of the earlier type with the physiognomy of later Augustus portraits. A pair of superb, dynamically postured new marble busts of Tiberius and Livia from Ephesus provides our most remarkable examples of the *interpretatio Graeca* of the early imperial image (Figs. 4.9–4.10).[57] And a comparable provincial Greek view of the emperor in narrative action is given by the extraordinary new reliefs from a cult centre (Sebasteion) for the Julio-Claudian emperors at Aphrodisias in Caria.[58] There, the reliefs show the emperors as all-conquering Hellenistic saviour-gods in charge of the universe and thoroughly at home among the old gods of the Olympian pantheon represented in adjacent reliefs. This is an astonishing view of the emperor from below and outside, unthinkable on a public monument at the Roman centre where the familiar images of carefully controlled, stately ceremonies prevailed.

Late antiquity

Another great gain has been classical archaeology's renewed interest in late antique visual history, setting it in a centuries-long, backward-looking Greek and Roman tradition within and against which it can be better understood.[59] Study of visual production in the period AD 300–600 was formerly carried out by experts in early Christian art who wrote tendentious stories about the rising of a new abstract aesthetic from the dying embers of the classical tradition. Images with Christian subjects in the fourth and fifth centuries are of course a fascinating body of material, but they make up only one zone of late antique visual production. There were other productive zones, domestic and public, that remained neutral in religious or cultic terms — that is, they displayed images that were neither

[56] E. Touloupa, in *Kaiser Augustus und die verlorene Republik* (Exhibition catalogue, Berlin 1988) 311-13, no. 149; J. Bergemann, *Römische Reiterstatuen: Ehrendenkmäler im öffentlichen Bereich* (Mainz 1990) 57–9, cat. P 5, pls. 14–16.

[57] M. Aurenhammer, 'Römische Porträts aus Ephesos: Neue Funde aus dem Hanghaus 2', *Jahreshefte des österreichischen archäologischen Instituts in Wien* 54 (1983) Beiblatt 104–12; E. Bartman, *Portraits of Livia: Imaging the Imperial Woman in Augustan Rome* (Cambridge 1999) 172–3, cat. 61, fig. 157.

[58] R. R. R. Smith, 'The imperial reliefs from the Sebasteion at Aphrodisias', *Journal of Roman Studies* 77 (1987) 88–138.

[59] See, for example, the fruitful overlap of two general books in the same series: J. Elsner, *Imperial Rome and Christian Triumph: the Art of the Roman Empire AD 100–450* (Oxford 1998); R. Cormack, *Byzantine Art* (Oxford 2000), covering AD 330–1453.

Fig. 4.9. Tiberius in dynamic provincial Greek interpretation. Marble bust (H: 49.5 cm), found in one of the Terrace Houses at Ephesos. AD 14–38. Selçuk Museum.

Christian nor pagan. In this period, new visual ideas and expressive priorities were added alongside a broad band of continuing ones, and for some products — for example, for the more extravagant kinds of marbles — there were simply many fewer customers. We have inverted values

Fig. 4.10. Livia in dynamic provincial Greek interpretation. Marble bust (H: 43 cm), found in one of the Terrace Houses at Ephesos. AD 14–38. Selçuk Museum.

when we take Antonine marble consumption as a norm against which to measure later decline. It was surely second-century hyperactivity in carved marble that requires special explanation.

The temptation to conflate reduced output and reduced technical standards can now be better resisted. Throughout antiquity there had been figured objects of low grade that were perfectly adequate for their purpose, price, customer-level, and audience (otherwise we would not have them) and which, had 'antiquity' ended soon after them, would have been taken as witnesses of decline and looming catastrophe. Decline (like the concept of a 'late' period itself) is a historically abstract idea that explains little, and new finds, for example of fifth- and sixth-century statuary at Aphrodisias and Ephesus, and more generally finds of fourth- to sixth-century silverware and mosaics from all over the Roman East, show now in much more detail for how long the technology and grammar of the classical-Hellenistic visual tradition continued.[60] They remained alive and well for as long as and wherever city life was maintained and with it the customers and audiences for such products.

A general theory?

From all these solid gains, one might think it would now be easy to prepare some general theories of visual history in antiquity. Some outlines have perhaps appeared. Customers, commission and history are prior. Ancient images are active, positive, structured expressions of their customers' aspirations and agendas, not neutral reflectors of reality. That is, in modern media jargon, they can carry heavy spin. As far as we can now see, different styles represent not so much individual originating makers' hands as different self-perceptions of different sections of ancient society, and they are as numerous, variable and changeable as the society was complex and volatile. After the visual revolution of the fifth century BC, changing styles were part of a single broad visual language that lasted through late antiquity, in which new expressive forms were constantly being added without any of the old ones being thrown away—whether metaphorically or literally.

---

[60] New statuary: Inan and Alföldi-Rosenbaum (n. 8) nos. 151–6 (Ephesus), nos. 199–208 (Aphrodisias); R. R. R. Smith, 'Late Roman philosopher portraits from Aphrodisias', *Journal of Roman Studies* 90 (1990) 127–55; id., 'Late antique portraits in a public context: honorific statuary at Aphrodisias in Caria, AD 300–600', *Journal of Roman Studies* 99 (1999) 155–89. For silverware and mosaics, see n. 22 above.

The cities and sanctuaries of antiquity became like huge open-air museums with a prodigal millennium-long acquisition policy.

So far, so good; and perhaps few in the historically based tradition would today disagree with such premises, but to go much further, it simply gets very complicated.[61] One clause in any general theory, to the dismay perhaps of archaeologists of prehistorical periods looking into the rich data-sets of classical archaeology for comparanda, would have to be that all good interpretations depend on some examples of the category under investigation having a meaningful context, that is, not only a physical setting but also some external written documentation attached to them or at least collateral with them. Otherwise we would simply get most things at least half-wrong most of the time. All full-blown theories of ancient visual practice will be brought up against the extraordinarily rich and complicated variety of ancient figured objects and their great range of contexts.

The two approaches that I have sketched have different aims and questions. One asks questions about artists and art which there is usually not enough evidence to answer and which in historical terms may not be well conceived. The other asks about customers, local audiences, and collective expressions and effects. The methods of the two approaches may be used in a complementary way, but their unstated models of explanation in fact propose quite opposed theories of why ancient images look the way they do. The older tradition's real virtue is careful description, observation of detail, formal analysis and useful categorisation. Its real vice has been to leave the matter there. Sometimes it seems to have been assumed, in a lofty manner, that the answers to the historically based questions now posed are self-evident. Alternatively interpretation has been postponed on the grounds that the state of the evidence or the state of research is not yet ready to sustain such grand historical–political inquiry: the moment remains forever unripe. And often it has been assumed that modern descriptions and typologies of figured artefacts (Types A, B and C) correspond unproblematically to historical ancient categories. Modern archaeology may find out that terracottas of Type A were made in central Greece, Type B in Etruria, but did the distinctions between them present themselves to ancient users in this way — as Greek versus Etruscan? Careful description, differentiation and classification are still essential, but they also need to be made sense of in terms of ancient mentalities and perceptions.

---

[61] For such theoretical complexity, see especially T. Hölscher, *Römische Bildsprache als semantisches System* (Heidelberg 1987).

The use of images

Since most convincing interpretations of ancient images seem to depend somewhere on historical information, and may thus be only as good as the historical premises on which they are based, it might be objected: if our interpretations merely repeat back what we know from other sources, what then is the use of images? This question of course implies a very narrow view of what constitutes useful historical information, but it comes to the core of what visual history is all about — for images can indeed in themselves add little or nothing new in terms of 'facts'. They are not concerned with facts — it is simply not their province of expressive competence. Generally ancient images aimed rather to represent in a striking and forceful way a conception of things their viewers shared. At the same time, they could also shape an attitude and a response and make it appear as though the things, persons, ideas, actions or events represented could not be any other way.

The answer to the question then is that even the very best historical interpretation can only *circumscribe* the correct area in which to locate some of the meaning of an ancient image. At the centre of that verbal circumscription lies a visual–aesthetic core, which cannot fully or properly be reduced to words, and which itself shapes, from its position within an evolving visual repertoire and tradition, a striking definition of the kind of person, divinity, idea or action that it represents. Images have remarkable power to define for us whole zones of ancient culture in a way that easily eludes our control — in the sense that we take in visual images instantly and unreflectively in a way that seems to bypass our conscious thought-processes. A good or 'correct' historical interpretation, far from exhausting the historical meaning or 'information' of an image, merely allows us to put ourselves in the right place, on the right waveband, to receive one part of its loud, multi-resonant effect. Since an image could have effect in a number of overlapping spheres (religious, political, domestic, for example), it follows of course that there is not only one good 'correct' historical interpretation possible, but several.

To appreciate in what ways ancient art contains some of the vital texture of ancient history, it is enough to imagine what our conception of classical societies would be like without their images. Whether we are aware of it or not, we have little alternative but to see the men who controlled mid-fifth-century Athens as they are composed 'democratically' on the Parthenon frieze (Fig. 4.1), to see Augustus as shaped in his statues and monuments such as the Ara Pacis as fundamentally different in moral–political character from his aristocratic 'republican' competitors and predecessors (Fig. 4.2), and to see the caravanning Palmyrenes and their wives as they want us to see them in their heavily accoutred grave reliefs and statues (Fig. 4.3): see pp. 61–3 above. These images define in some strange totalising way what their subjects are for us. We cannot see 'behind' the images. The Palmyrene woman represented in Fig. 4.3 is definitively constituted by a striking combination of exaggerated ideal Hellenic beauty and a rich jewellery-encrustation that belongs to pre-classical and local traditions. It is this exclusive character of ancient images, which denies space to other versions (except authorised versions) of how things might have been, that gives them such force. Before we do anything else, we have to try to delineate, with historically informed reconstruction and circumscription, the areas in which their powerfully projected visual agenda should be located.

Style as history

Images were part of ancient life and they are part of the surviving representations or 'evidence' by which we write ancient history. If we ignore them, we miss an important historical dimension. If we take them simply at face value, they risk controlling our view of history in unseen ways, and we risk getting them at least half-wrong. So far from exhausting the historical information contained by ancient images, it is striking how much of their expressive effect is left unmediated by good historical interpretations. In reaction to the self-contained style-studies of the artist-driven tradition, historical explanations of the kinds outlined here have generally eschewed prolonged analysis of the aesthetic effect of ancient images and have concentrated instead on subjects, symbols, narratives and contexts. How much can be left unmediated in this process is clear from the way in which one interpretation can fit images of the same subject, purpose and period, but which are of sometimes strikingly different stylistic effects.

Different examples illustrating this point can be found in densely attested categories of figured monument — for example, among archaic Greek statues or Roman sarcophagi. A single historical meaning may inform grave kouroi of the sixth century BC, but within a single satisfying image type, they also cultivated a meaningful difference of style — both of personal style (hair arrangement, for example) and 'art' style.[62] And on Roman sarcophagi of the second century AD, the same four episodes, for

---

[62] See references at nn. 37 and 41.

example, from the story of Jason, Creusa and Medea, are represented using clearly repeated iconographic schemes or types for each of the four scenes, but the treatment of the same scenes varies from calm and classical (for example, on a sarcophagus in Mantua) to flowing, wild and flamboyant (for example, on a sarcophagus in Basel). These sarcophagi carry the same iconographic story, message, and meaning but with a drastically different style and visual effect, a difference that can hardly be reduced to one merely of chronology.[63]

Apart from resolving some of the epistemological contradictions described above that lie dormant at the heart of the subject's fact-base, it may be an important future challenge for the discipline to elaborate some method and language for analysing the historical significance of different visual stylings and effects, in addition to and in combination with the other procedures of historical interpretation of ancient images. What is represented ('iconography') is being well studied from the perspective described here. How it is represented ('style') remains however largely in the domain of the maker and artist. A challenge might thus be to re-analyse with appropriate language different and changing stylistic formulations as historical expressions.

Under style, stylistic formulation and aesthetic effect, we might under-stand all those aspects of an image not due to what it represents and to its function as an object. In one direction, this quality blurs imperceptibly into the technical handling of a fashioned object and its material, but is something in essence separate from it. The technical character (*technē*), one might say, belongs to the maker, while the informing visual style (*tropos* or *logos* are words sometimes used in this context)[64] belongs to a complex sum of historical factors, both inside and outside the image-making process. In this perspective and with some of the premises outlined above, changing visual styles might be analysed more systematically as parts of ancient societies' changing mentalities, perceptions, and self-perceptions — style as history.

---

[63] H. Sichtermann and G. Koch, *Griechische Mythen auf römischen Sarkophage* (Tübingen 1975) no. 37 (Mantua); M. Schmidt, *Der Basler Medeasarkophag: ein Meisterwerk spätantoninischer Kunst* (Tübingen 1968) pls. 1–22 (Basel).

[64] *Tropos*: W. Dittenberger, *Orientis Graecae Inscriptiones Selectae* (Leipzig 1903) 90, line 39 (the Rosetta Stone): the Egyptian priests of Ptolemy V (204–180 BC) order that the king's statues 'shall be made in the native (or Egyptian) style (*tropos*)'. *Logos*: ibid., 383, line 30: Antiochos I of Commagene (mid-first century BC) orders his statues and reliefs to be made 'according to (the) ancient *logos* of Greeks and Persians — blessed root(s) of my clan'.

Conclusion

This chapter has tried to describe how art and images are embedded in the wider material history of antiquity and can profitably be studied as part of the wider culture of the long distinctive period of Mediterranean history known as classical antiquity. It was argued that two major focuses of scholarly attention in this area of the discipline require careful scrutiny. One has been the emphasis on the artist and the creative process, that sees the essential shaping of ancient images too one-sidedly from the point of view of their makers. The other has been a modern concern with change, progress and cultural evolution that sees ancient image-making in terms of one or more linear developments that can be traced gradually and constantly through time, and can be assumed to have operated even when the evidence does not allow us to see it. These twin assumptions, it was argued, are not well founded and have given rise to acute epistemological problems. The accumulated authority of a conservative discipline has left these problems unacknowledged, and they have driven the subject into a series of dead-ends: either to establish a chronology is enough, or nothing further can usefully be said until the chronology is better established.

More seriously, these assumptions have produced a badly distorted profile of ancient visual history. In some periods and in some categories of image, ancient visual production performed according to the model of perceptible evolution; in other periods and categories (as every field archaeologist knows) there are long and wide tracts of virtually unchanging production. The evidence of ancient images answers *both* to the fast-changing surface of political history (seen, for example, in the political and visual revolution of the fifth century or in the mercurial sequence of imperial portrait styles) *and* to the deep, *longue durée* of social and religious history (attested, for example, in unchanging male clothing styles or in the image styles of the Olympian gods).

Much recent work has brought out the value of looking at the material from the historical perspective of its buyers and viewers, and of its local contexts and functions. This is still a project that is largely untheorised, and the observations offered here have tried to make explicit some of its assumptions and some of its remaining internal contradictions that arise from its incorporation of older but irreconcilable methods. At the same time the subject has been constantly invigorated by extraordinary new finds and a welcome flow of top-class primary publication of both new and older material. There remains much to do. Re-siting dislocated ancient images in their contexts of ancient use, locating the ideas that informed them, and reconstructing the mentalities with which they were approached and understood constitute challenging tasks that classical archaeology has taken up only recently.

None of these things can be arrived at *a priori* simply by looking, and few of them are capable of single correct interpretative answers. And when from a chosen perspective these parameters of local context, controlling ideas and audience expectations have been established, there remains the irreducible aesthetic core which often contains the most potent expressive aspect of an image and which only careful relative description can circumscribe. Riace Bronze A (Fig. 4.6) was not merely a votive bronze statue of a naked warrior hero but one styled in *this* way, with *this* (powerful and specific) impact. And the bust of Livia from Ephesus (Fig. 4.10) was not merely an eastern provincial version of an official icon of the first Roman 'empress' but one done in *this* (extraordinary) way. To describe the styling and impact of such images in historical terms — style as history — thus remains a further challenge. Ancient images are a powerful but volatile section of the historical evidence for the classical world.

5
Ciceronian correspondences: making a book out of letters

Mary Beard

The *Letters* of Cicero are one of the most extraordinary survivals from the ancient world, and a correspondence that ranks with the great letter collections of all time, from Abelard to Virginia Woolf. This chapter is an experiment in reading those *Letters* in a radically old-fashioned way. It poses a (deceptively) simple question: what difference does the order in which we choose to read it make to our literary, cultural and historical understanding of the collection? I shall be ranging from the ancient world to the present day; but my story will start (where so many of the best classical stories do) in the late nineteenth century — with an article written, we shall find, by one of the most influential readers of Cicero ever.

The old school of Classics and the new

In January 1888 readers of the *Fortnightly Review* were treated to a characteristically late-Victorian satire on 'The Old School of Classics and the New'.[1] Set in Hades and cast in the form of a Dialogue of the Dead (educated subscribers to the *Fortnightly* would not have missed the reference to Lucian and *his* 'Dialogues of the Dead'),[2] it featured a predictably unlikely combination of characters: three textual critics (Bentley, Porson and Madvig),

---

[1] *Fortnightly Review* 49, n.s. 43 (1888) 42–59.

[2] Second-century AD Lucian's *Dialogues of the Dead* staged some predictable and unpredictable groups in conversation: Philip of Macedon and his son Alexander the Great; Ajax and Agamemnon; Alexander, Hannibal, Minos and Scipio; and so on. Nineteenth-century England found it a particularly congenial form of satire: see, for example, the series of 'Imaginary Conversations' by W. S. Landor, collected as *Imaginary Conversations* (ed. C. G. Crump, London 1891); H. D. Traill, *The New Lucian: being a Series of Dialogues of the Dead* (London 1884).

Euripides and (with a walk-on part that gave him just enough time to confess to 'small Latin and less Greek') William Shakespeare. For the first few pages, the critics bemoan their lot in the Underworld, and in particular their awkward encounters with the ancient poets whose work they had emended or (depending on your point of view) garbled: as Madvig puts it, 'Hardly had I set foot in the Shades when I was fiercely assailed by Ovid... He wanted to have me consigned at once to the depths of Tartarus for having proposed to introduce into one of his poems *patetur* with the *a* short.'[3] But the old stagers soon change the subject and turn to grilling Madvig ('thou <who> hast come most recent of us to the Shades' — in 1886; Bentley had died in 1742, Porson in 1808) about the current state of classical learning 'in the upper world'.[4]

Madvig has a bleak tale to tell. In Germany, the 'art of emending' no longer reigns supreme; instead men are constantly on the look-out for spurious passages ('the hunt after the *Unecht* is in full cry') or for traces of multiple authorship ('Those Greek masterpieces which Horace told us to thumb so assiduously are now ascertained to be the work of a committee with power to add to their number').[5] In England, things are even worse; for there 'scholarship' (not merely textual criticism, but even grammar) has been

> invaded on every side by archaeology, anthropology, epigraphy and dilettantism. It is more blessed to gush than to construe. To study the works, for instance, of the Greek dramatists is no longer a road to success as a scholar or as a student. No: you must be ready to liken Aeschylus to an Alpine *crevasse*, Sophocles to a fair avenue of elms, and Euripides to an amber-weeping Phaethontid, or a town pump in need of repairing, according to the divined proclivity of the examiner or reader.[6]

---

[3] P. 43. Madvig is referring, as the notes tells us, to his emendation of *Tristia* 3.2.21 in his *Adversaria Critica ad Scriptores Graecos et Latinos* (Copenhagen 1873) vol. 2, 98; though the point is confused by the (deliberate?) misprint *patetur* for *paletur*.

[4] P. 46.

[5] Pp. 46–7. A prime example of the German hunt after the *Unecht* would be O. Ribbeck's assault on the text of Juvenal: *Der echte und der unechte Juvenal* (Berlin 1865); but part of the joke here may also rest on the fact that one of Bentley's most famous contributions to scholarship was his proof of the spuriousness of the letters attributed to Phalaris; see *A Dissertation upon the epistles of Phalaris, with an answer to the objections of the Hon. Charles Boyle* (London 1699).

[6] P. 48. One of the targets here may well have been the extravagant metaphors of John Addington Symonds (see, for example, *Studies in the Greek Poets* (London 1873) 211, which does in fact compare Euripidean poetry to a mountain stream: 'The lyrics of Euripides flow like mountain rivulets, flashing with sunbeams, eddying in cool shady places, rustling through leaves of mint, forget-me-not, marsh-marigold, and dock').

A good example of these deplorable tendencies is a recent edition of Herodotus books 1–3, which is subjected to an unfairly scurrilous attack,[7] before the shades settle down to another long moan about the decline of standards. Archaeologists refuse to learn Latin and Greek properly ('Must a writer on archaeology make good his title to be heard by confounding οἰκίζω and οἰκέω?'); the 'New School' insists on ridiculous principles of transliteration from Greek ('Whosoever will be a scholar before all things it is necessary that he write *Aiskhulos*. Poor Conington restored λέοντος ἶνιν to the poet, but what availed that when he habitually called him *Aeschylus*?'); and in Oxford a distinguished young critic (Housman, though he is not named) has recently failed Greats — presumably 'because he had compared the wrong man to an Alpine *crevasse*, or because he had failed to commit to memory an inscription in which an Assyrian king stated that he had ascended the Kinchinjunga followed by 2,000,000 men on bicycles!'[8] In the end it is all too much for Bentley, who brings the dialogue to a close by stomping off.

So who is the joke on? The New School with their silly fads and sloppy grammar? Or these time-expired shades of the Old School, huffing and puffing about the ills of the modern world — which they don't and won't properly understand? As always, one of the pleasures and teases of satire is its sheer elusiveness; the impossibility of fixing its target. The new fashions in classical scholarship may come off badly here; for who, after all, could prefer 'gushing' to 'reading', or the novice howler to accurate grammar? But, at the same time, who could forget that these carping critics themselves stand on very weak ground; for, as even they must confess, their encounters in the Underworld prove conclusively that their prize emendations — impeccably accurate though they might be — were quite simply *wrong*. And who could not suspect that their account of all this up-to-the-minute late-nineteenth-century theory was a hotch-potch of old-fashioned prejudice and wilful misunderstanding? In 1888, we cannot *really* be on Bentley's side, as the last line of the dialogue reminds us. 'Walker, our hat,' he commands, as he leaves the scene. Expert readers of the *Fortnightly* would have spotted the

---

[7] Unfair, because A. H. Sayce's edition (*The Ancient Empires of the East* (London 1883)) was explicitly written from the point of view of Near Eastern studies (see pp. ix–x); the nitpicking about Greek grammar (intentionally or not) misses the point.

[8] Pp. 52–9. The significance of this support for Housman (in 1888 still toiling away in the Patent Office) is discussed by P. G. Naiditch, *A. E. Housman at University College, London: the Election of 1892* (Leiden 1988) 217–18.

quote (from Alexander Pope's *Dunciad*)[9] and caught the allusion to the final years of Bentley's tyranny over his college (Trinity, Cambridge). The story goes that, in response to the Fellows' campaign to oust him from the Mastership, Bentley secured the election of Dr Richard Walker as his Vice-Master, a devoted poodle (in fact, commonly known as 'Frog') who prevented any move against him — but whom he treated as a personal servant.[10] Nothing has changed in Hades; imperious and insufferable as ever, Bentley would be an unlikely choice if you wanted a balanced view of the state of classical studies at any time — least of all in the modern world.

Our satirist, then, has cleverly captured the ambivalence of academic fashion; and has confronted his readers with the impossibility of understanding even the apparently stark battle lines of late Victorian Classics in terms of simple allegiances. We should not be misled by a narrow reading of the satire's title. It was not so much a matter of competing programmes and priorities of study, but of what was to *count* as '*New* (or *Old*) *Classics*'. The satirist prompts us to see that question as a handy summary of the agenda always at the heart of Classics — now as much as then.

Tyrrell-and-Purser

The satire was written by Robert Yelverton Tyrrell (1844–1914), who was to become in 1901 one of the first 49 Fellows of the brand new British Academy. His career was remarkable even by the more flexible standards of the late nineteenth century: luminary classical scholar of Trinity College, Dublin (he was in turn its Professor of Latin, of Greek and of Ancient History); icon of the so-called 'Dublin School' of Classics (mythologised for its combination of 'deep scholarship ... zest ... critical sanity and ... sense of humour' — and for helping 'to save England from the heavy influences of the German tradition');[11] friend and colleague of the equally charismatic J. P. Mahaffy (between them they launched both Oscar Wilde and William Ridgeway into

---

[9] '"Walker, our hat!" — nor more he deign'd to say / But, stern as Ajax' spectre, strode away', book 4 (London 1742 = *The New Dunciad*) 273–4. Presumably the *Fortnightly* crowd would also have spotted the appropriateness to the satire of the words that followed 'Walker, our hat!'.

[10] See J. H. Monk, *The Life of Richard Bentley* (London 1830) vol. 2, 406–7; R. J. White, *Dr Bentley: a Study in Academic Scarlet* (London 1965) 232–3.

[11] J. Healy, from an obituary notice of L. C. Purser in the *Irish Times*, cited *Proceedings of the British Academy* 18 (1932) 408.

Classics);[12] founder of the would-be weighty Irish classical journal, *Hermathena*, as well as the skittish, and long-ago folded, *Kottabos* (where he produced memorable parodies of Mommsen, Aristotle and contemporary Virgilian criticism);[13] lauded by his admirers as an eminent wit, raconteur, versifier, family man and tennis player (though even his closest associates would admit to 'some loss of old-world erudition').[14] Surprisingly perhaps, as the piece in the *Fortnightly* already hinted, he was also instrumental in the rescue and rehabilitation of the austere A. E. Housman, who had notoriously—and mysteriously—failed Greats in 1881. Tyrrell had noticed and admired Housman's work by the mid 1880s; he 'ghosted' a short note by Housman for the very first volume of the *Classical Review* in 1887 ('Mr A. E. Housman has favoured me with an interesting suggestion, which he permits me to communicate to the *Review* . . .');[15] and by 1892 he was among Housman's sponsors for the Chair of Latin at University College, London. What Housman, with all his crushing erudition, thought of Tyrrell is much harder to ascertain.[16]

For us, however, Robert Yelverton Tyrrell is forever locked in the compound Tyrrell-and-Purser (T.-P.), the familiar shorthand that usually identifies his major contribution to Latin literature and Roman history: *The Correspondence of M. Tullius Cicero, arranged according to its chronological order, with a revision of the text, a commentary and introductory essays on The Life of Cicero, and The Style of His Letters.* This was a multi-volume, collaborative and (more than) lifetime project: though it started to appear under Tyrrell's name alone in 1879, it soon become a joint work; and the carefully hierarchised duo of Tyrrell and Louis Claude Purser (note the flagrantly non-alphabetical order of their names) graced every succeeding title page until the final volume of the second edition appeared in 1933—even though, by then, Tyrrell himself had been dead for almost twenty years and Purser did not

---

[12] For a brief account of the 'Dublin School' and its cast of characters, see R. B. McDowell and D. A. Welsh, *Trinity College Dublin 1592–1952: an Academic History* (Cambridge 1982) 265–8.

[13] *Kottabos* was founded in 1869 and expired in 1895; selections (sadly, not always the most amusing pieces) were published in R. Y. Tyrrell and E. Sullivan (eds.), *Echoes from Kottabos* (Dublin 1906).

[14] This authorised myth of Tyrrell can be found in his memoir (by L. C. Purser), *Proceedings of the British Academy* 7 (1915/16) 533–9 (quotation at 534).

[15] *Classical Review* 1 (1887) 313.

[16] The clearest account of Tyrrell and Housman is that of P. G. Naiditch, (n. 8), and more briefly Naiditch's entry on Housman in W. W. Briggs and W. M. Calder (eds.), *Classical Scholarship: a Biographical Encyclopaedia* (New York and London 1990) 195; even Naiditch (who rarely leaves a stone unturned in his search for such documentation) admits that he has been able to find little trace of Housman's judgement of Tyrrell.

live long enough to see the book off the press.[17] The key to the novelty of *The Correspondence* is blazoned in the wording of the title: ...*arranged according to its chonological order*. This was the first attempt, in the English-speaking world at least (there were, as we shall see, German precedents), to take the different collections of Cicero's letters as they are preserved in the manuscript tradition, to disaggregate them, to attempt to fix a precise date on to each individual letter — and then arrange the whole lot in a new and entirely *chronological order*.

It was a considerably more radical project than that bald summary suggests. This was not so much a matter of dating the letters. True, very many of them are preserved without any exact indication of date (Roman letters were as variable as our own in this respect); and in many places the traditional ordering does not even help by offering a rough *relative* chronology. But assigning dates to individual (or series of) letters had been on the academic agenda for centuries, and Tyrrell-and-Purser had plenty of previous studies to go on.[18] Infinitely more significant was their ruthless dismantling of the traditional letter collections. The surviving letters had been preserved in four distinct groups, going back directly or indirectly to antiquity itself, each with a different history, character and conventions. Most famous were the *Letters to Atticus* (*Epistulae ad Atticum*), 426 letters in 16 books, written by Cicero to his friend Titus Pomponius Atticus between 68 and 44 BC (arranged roughly in date order). The other major group comprised the 435 *Letters to Friends* (*Epistulae ad Familiares*, to give them the Renaissance Latin title — which has stuck) again in 16 books. This collection is quite different from the *Ad Atticum* in a number of important respects: it includes letters not to a single correspondent only, but to more than 80 of Cicero's 'friends' (from political colleagues to his wife Terentia); it also includes some of their letters to him (we have, by contrast, not one word from Atticus); and, as we shall see, it is arranged as much by theme and

---

[17] Volumes 1 and 2 of the first edition (1879 and 1888), and volume 1 of the second edition (1885) went under Tyrrell's name (although he was effectively collaborating with Purser by 1885); all the remaining volumes (vols. 3–6 of the first edition, 1890, 1894, 1897, 1899, plus vol. 7, the index, 1901, vol. 1 of the third edition, 1904, vols. 2–6 of the second edition, 1906, 1914, 1918, 1915 and 1933) were blazoned as joint enterprises. The publication was also a collaboration: between Hodges, Foster and Figgis of Dublin and Longmans, Green and Co. of London (as one of the 'Dublin University Press' series). The full title I have quoted is that of the first edition of volume 1 (from now on abbreviated as T.-P.1[1], 1[2] etc.).

[18] Ranging from as far back as the sixteenth century to the cutting edge of recent scholarship; see, for example, H. Ragazzonius = C. Sigonius, *In epistulas Ciceronis familiares commentarius, in quo brevissime, quo quaeque earum ordine scripta sit, ex ipsa potissimum historia demonstratur* (Venice 1555); J. von Gruber, *Quaestio de tempore atque serie epistolarum Ciceronis* (Sund 1836).

addressee as it is by date. The other two collections are much shorter, and each defined by a single correspondent: the three books of *Letters to his Brother Quintus* (*Ad Quintum Fratrem*), 27 in all, mostly dating between 59 and 54; and the 25 *Letters to Brutus* (*Ad Brutum*), all dating to 43 BC, including letters from Brutus (the assassin of Julius Caesar) to Cicero, plus one from Brutus to Atticus. In taking all these letters together and rearranging them solely on grounds of date (a letter to Quintus sandwiched between two to Atticus if that is what chronology seemed to demand) Tyrrell-and-Purser constructed what was, in effect, a *new book*. Gone were the separate collections, with their classification according to addressee, their book divisions and distinctive referencing system (*Ad Att.*, *Ad Fam.*, *Ad Brut.*, *Ad QF*); in their place a new work, the *Correspondence of Cicero* (Letters 1, 2, 3, 4, 5 etc.... all the way up to 931).

Tyrrell's partner in crime was another Dublin man (Professor of Latin at Trinity College between 1898 and 1904), who was also to become a Fellow of the British Academy (in 1923); but he was of a very different type.[19] The myth of Purser is not of brilliant wit, but of selfless collaboration, of taking the back seat in the service of scholarship, and of single-minded duty to the task in hand: the last time he left his house before his death was, it is said, to visit the press in connection with the final revisions to the second edition of the sixth volume. He will always be best remembered as the partner of Tyrrell (who had been his teacher). But he also stepped in to rescue at least two other major projects (without, on either occasion, getting his name on to the title page): he finished off Arthur Palmer's edition of Ovid's *Heroides*, when Palmer himself sickened some five poems before the end;[20] and later, in 1925, when J. S. Reid became too ill to complete his edition of Cicero's *De Finibus*, Purser came over to Cambridge to add the finishing touches and deal with the publishers.[21] It was a generosity apparently learned early. His memorialist was delighted to discover amongst Purser's papers after his death (all too conveniently we might now suspect) a scrawled note, written — so it appeared — during a translation class, in the distinctive handwriting of Oscar Wilde, his fellow student at Trinity College, Dublin: 'If he

---

[19] The best account of his life is by A. C. Clark, *Proceedings of the British Academy* 18 (1932) 407–21.

[20] A. Palmer, *P. Ovidi Nasonis Heroides* (Oxford 1898). The division of labour is fully explained in Purser's Preface to the volume.

[21] J. S. Reid, *M. Tulli Ciceronis, De Finibus Bonorum et Malorum, Libri I, II* (Cambridge 1925). The Preface in this case is on the reticent side; but the details are given in Clark's memoir (n. 19).

puts me on to construe, I shall say that it is your turn.'[22] Purser, we are asked
to conclude, was always happy to 'construe' for a friend.

Collaboration inevitably raises the question of the division of labour —
and of glory. What does sharing a scholarly enterprise amount to? Who really
did the work? On whose c.v. will the final product count (the most)?[23] In the
case of Tyrrell-and-Purser, it would be tempting — and, in fact, not un-
reasonable — to imagine that Tyrrell was responsible for the style and literary
verve, while Purser did the hard work, the unglamorous behind-the-scenes
scholarship; and increasingly so, as the project progressed. But that was not
necessarily Purser's view: 'I think I may fairly tell you privately,' he wrote to
A. C. Clark in 1894, 'that the section on Caelius . . . and all the Introductions to
vol. IV are solely (excepting a very few verbal corrections) my work. Tyrrell
had nothing to say to their composition. There is no reason why he as "Senior
Partner" should not get all the credit in public, but I should not like you to think
that all that possesses anything of the nature of literary style in our edition
belongs to Tyrrell.'[24] Purser-and-Tyrrell then, as much as Tyrrell-and-Purser;
or so the letter takes care to insinuate.

The late nineteenth century was the best of times and the worst of times
to be attempting an authoritative edition of Cicero's letters. Best, because of
the enormous interest in the collections generated by new work (largely
German) on their manuscripts and transmission; the letters were closer to the
top of the international scholarly agenda than they have ever been, before or
since.[25] Worst, because of the other side of exactly the same coin: it was
almost impossibly hard to keep up with all the new theories and developments. One problem, in particular, dogged the work. When Tyrrell conceived
his edition he assumed (following the traditional orthodoxy) that all
the various manuscripts of the letters were inferior to two manuscripts in

---

[22] We can only guess why Purser kept this scrap. The story is of course about Wilde as much as
himself: the one shirking the task in hand, the other (too) ready to take it over. See Clark (n. 19) 407.

[23] Purser, one cannot help but observe, did not do badly from his self-sacrifice.

[24] Letter written, November 1894, in response to Clark's reference to 'Tyrrell's brilliant article' on
Caelius Rufus (n. 19, 410–11).

[25] Easily confirmed by the contents list of almost any late-nineteenth-century classical periodical or
library catalogue of editions and German dissertations. This work is conveniently summed up in
H. Peter, *Der Brief in der römischen Literatur* (Leipzig 1901) 38–100. The work of L. Gurlitt was
particularly influential (and remains so; see below, n. 48): for example, *De M Tulli Ciceronis
epistulis earumque pristina collectione* (Göttingen 1879); *Nonius Marcellus und die Cicero-Briefe
(Wiss. Beilage zum Progr. Progymn. zu Steglitz* 1888); 'Ciceros Briefschaften und ihre Verbreitung
unter Augustus', *Fleckeisens Jahrbuch* (1894), 209–24; note also F. Bücheler, 'Coniectanea',
Rheinisches Museum 34 (1879) 352–5 (a landmark in the modern debate on the date of the
publication of *Ad Att.*).

Florence, both of which he believed to have been discovered by (and so to bask in the glamour of) Petrarch.[26] No sooner had his first volume appeared in 1879, than it became clear that this was quite simply false. Not only was the manuscript containing the 16 books of the *Letters to Friends* nothing whatsoever to do with Petrarch, as two German studies showed conclusively (also in 1879, and too late for Tyrrell);[27] but even more significantly, there were increasingly powerful arguments that other manuscripts were of first-rate importance, that they were sometimes independent of those favoured by Tyrrell, and that they had a major part to play in establishing the texts of the letters. Tyrrell was not blind to this. In fact, Purser's first task, in what was to become their joint project, was to go to the British Museum and collate two manuscripts of the *Letters to Friends,* both of which now seemed to offer a tradition independent of the manuscript in Florence.[28]

All the same, it was inevitably a matter of 'running to stand still'. The complicated publishing history of Tyrrell-and-Purser, and in particular the changes from volume to volume and edition to edition through the 1880s and 90s, gives some hint of this. Purser delivered a lecture on his collation of one of the British Museum manuscripts, and its implications, to the Royal Irish Academy in June 1885, which later that same year Tyrrell managed to note briefly in the Preface to the second edition of his first volume (confusingly published before any further volumes of the first edition had appeared). The text of the lecture was then printed in full in Volume 2 of the first edition, though it was removed from the second edition in 1906; by that stage the British Museum collation had been included in a long essay (Purser's

---

[26] In detail the manuscript tradition of the *Ad Fam.* is quite separate from the *Ad Att.* (together with *Ad Brut.* and *Ad QF*); but the basic framework of debate, and the challenge to the overriding authority of a single manuscript tradition, follows broadly the same pattern in each case. For a convenient general summary of the current state of play, see R. H. Rouse, in L. D. Reynolds (ed.), *Texts and Transmission: a Survey of the Latin Classics* (Oxford 1983) 135–42 (though for more accurately up-to-the-minute discussions, see P. L. Schmidt, 'Die Rezeption des römischen Freundschaftsbriefes (Cicero-Plinius) im frühen Humanismus (Petrarca-Coluccio Salutati)', in *Der Brief im Zeitalter der Renaissance* (Mitteilung IX der Kommission für Humanismusforschung, Weinheim 1983) 25–59, and M. D. Reeve, 'The rediscovery of classical texts in the renaissance', in O. Pecere (ed.), *Itinerari dei Testi Antichi* (Rome 1991) 115–57, esp. 140–5). The Florentine manuscripts are Medicean 49.9 (*Ad Fam.*) and Medicean 49.18 (*Ad Att.* etc.).

[27] A. Viertel, *Die Wiederauffindung von Ciceros Briefen durch Petrarca* (Konigsberg 1879); G. Voigt, 'Ueber die handschriftliche Ueberlieferung von Ciceros Briefen', *Berichte über die Verhandlungen der sächsischen Gesellschaft der Wissenschaften, Phil.-Hist. Classe* 31 (1879) 41–65. The other manuscript (of the *Ad Att.* etc.) also had a remoter connection with Petrarch than Tyrrell imagined; for Medicean 49.18 has no claim to be (as Tyrrell stated, T.-P. 1[1] lxxxvii, and as was once widely believed) Petrarch's own copy, made from the (now lost) manuscript of *Ad Att.* etc. that he was said to have discovered (see Reeve (n. 26), 141–5).

[28] Harley 2682 and 2773.

work, presumably) in the third edition of Volume 1 (1904), which surveyed a whole range of other recent developments on the text of the letters.

There is, in fact, no better way to get a sense of the revolution in the study of this material over the last quarter of the nineteenth century than to compare Tyrrell's introduction to the first volume in 1879 with its equivalent in the third edition of 1904. For it is not only that the whole manuscript tradition had been rewritten, with new readings and new theories about the history of the collection; in twenty-five years, the range of issues, of controversies and of what counted as important or taken-for-granted, had been transformed. The 1879 version was rooted in the, to us, unfamiliar debates (and certainties) of the mid-1800s: it was a world in which Orelli's theory — now a mad, forgotten fantasy — that Cicero's last three speeches against Catiline were in fact forgeries by his secretary Tiro was still taken seriously (and indeed was used by Tyrrell to bolster his argument that Tiro was the editor of the whole correspondence); a world in which, conversely, the spurious *Commentariolum Petitionis* (*Handbook on Electioneering*) hardly needed to be defended as a *bona fide* letter of Quintus Cicero (number 12 in T.-P., in fact).[29] The edition of 1904, by contrast, is framed in terms that are more or less recognisably our own (and even though the *Commentariolum* is still considered to be 'genuine', it is no longer with the certainty of two decades earlier). As L. Gurlitt remarked in an unexpectedly gracious review of two volumes (1[2] and 2[1]) in the *Berliner philologische Wochenschrift* in 1887, whatever the virtues of the book, it was sadly 'premature' (*verfrüht*) to be producing a complete edition of the text, given the unfinished business with the manuscripts and other changes in the field.[30] Though Tyrrell could hardly have predicted it before he started, as his vast project trundled on, it turned out always to be in danger of getting left behind by the cutting edge of textual (and other Ciceronian) studies.

Most recent critics have tended to treat Tyrrell-and-Purser with some disdain. Ancient historians may still find the notes useful, for want of a better alternative. But textual critics, led very *un*graciously (and in the circumstances

---

[29] As will be the case with our own in due course, the pet theories and collusive fantasies of previous generations are often breathtaking. In the case of Tiro's editorship of the correspondence, Tyrrell argued from a passage of *Ad Att.* 2.1 (T.-P. 27) which he regarded as interpolated (largely because it contained reference to the Catilinarian speeches, which he considered forgeries anyway). In whose interest would such an interpolation have been? Tiro's, of course. And who would have had the opportunity to interpolate? Tiro again, while editing the correspondence. QED (T.-P. 1[1], lx).

[30] 3 September 1887, 1112–15. This review, from one of those most involved in rewriting the manuscript history of the Letters, gives a vivid impression of the excitement (or sheer confusion) of Ciceronian studies at the time.

unfairly) by D. R. Shackleton Bailey, have seen little more than in-competence.[31] When it first appeared, however, reviewers hailed the book as a decisive step forward, largely because of its wholesale re-ordering of the material. Never mind that Tyrrell-and-Purser were not the first to attempt such a restructuring. That distinction goes (so far as I have discovered) to C. M. Wieland, whose *Sämmtliche Briefe*, in German translation, began to appear in 1808, quickly followed — this time in Latin — by C. G. Schütz's *M. T. Ciceronis Epistolae… temporis ordine dispositae* (1809–1812).[32] But they were the first in English — and the first to make much impact on English-speaking Classics.

Tyrrell himself, like Wieland and Schütz before him, was relatively low-key about his new chronological arrangement, as if the arguments were self-evident. It took him no more than a short paragraph in the Preface to Volume 1 to explain that the traditional divisions of the collection (which sometimes had the effect of putting into quite different books two letters written on exactly the same day) made understanding the correspondence needlessly difficult; and even within the traditional books (*Ad Att.*, *Ad Fam.* etc.) the absence of a rigorous chronological order could often lead to confusion: 'For instance, in Att. i. 1, the chances of Cicero in his candidature for the consulship are discussed, and in Att i, 10 we find him anxious about his election to the praetorship which he held three years before his consulship. In the letters to Brutus this confusion is very embarrassing.' But reviewers did not let the (for them) new ordering pass so lightly. A particularly extravagant piece in the *Athenaeum* greeted the first publication of Volume 1, listing (where Tyrrell himself had remained silent) a variety of reasons why the new ordering was superior to the old — including, it must be said, some pretty odd ones: it gave the reader 'far more hold of the political position of the day' to have the letters to Atticus integrated with those to other corres-pondents; the letters that were not worth reading *en bloc* (such as those to Trebatius or Paetus, which dominated whole books of the *Ad Fam.* on the traditional arrangement) could usefully be read if they were 'scattered among more serious matter'; any arrangement that forces the reader to plough through the 'more formal and duller letters, such as those to Lentulus' will help them appreciate (by contrast presumably) the 'great importance of the

---

[31] The only question was whether or not to draw attention to it. 'In my introduction to the Atticus letters, having no good to say of it, at least as a source of guidance and information, I said nothing' (Shackleton Bailey, *Cicero: Epistulae ad Familiares* 1 (Cambridge 1977) 25).

[32] C. M. Wieland, *M. T. Cicero's Sämmtliche Briefe* (Zurich 1808–21); C. G. Schütz, *M. T. Ciceronis Epistolae… temporis ordine dispositae* (Halle 1809–1812), soon followed by I. Billerbeck, *M. T. Ciceronis Epistolae… temporis ordine dispositae* (Hanover 1836).

letters to Atticus'. So obviously was this the 'true' arrangement, hyped the reviewer, ' — indeed the only one which fairly brings out the immense interest of this large and most varied correspondence — that it is strange that editions still appear of the Atticus Letters alone, and sometimes only of a few books of them'.[33]

If this was to be read as a prediction about future directions in studies of the *Letters*, then, to all intents and purposes, it came true. For decades now most of us have taken it for granted that unless our interest was exclusively in the text and its manuscript history, we read the letters chronologically. We would hardly dream of setting ourselves, or our students, to study a single book of the letters as traditionally collected; and the stream of school editions of individual books of (especially) the *Ad Atticum*, that continued up to the early years of the twentieth century, seems to belong to a quaintly foreign world.[34] Almost every modern commentary or selection from the *Letters* uses chronology as its basic principle of ordering; and there is no English translation currently in print which still follows the traditional manuscript order. Even Shackleton Bailey, whose recent edition of the whole correspondence did preserve the identity of the four major collections (*Ad Att.*, *Ad Fam.*, etc.), chose to arrange the letters within them by date, so far as was possible.[35] Hardly a reviewer shed a tear for

---

[33] *Athenaeum* 18 October 1879, 493–5 (the piece was unsigned). Such praise was not universal. We have already noted Gurlitt's objection (n. 30); the reviewer in *The Times* (16 August 1880) wanted more information on how the letters were dated. Underlying Gurlitt's objection to T.-P.'s ordering was the fact that it disaggregated the traditional collections, whose history he was trying to understand; though he conceded its pedagogical usefulness ('die studierende Jugend Englands wird dem Verf. vielfache Anregung und Belehrung danken', 1115).

[34] These were a staple of the Pitt Press and Macmillan series. My particular favourite is M. Alford's edition — with (excellent) commentary — of *Ad Att.* 2 (London 1929): 'This book of Cicero's letters is especially suitable for reading as a whole,' ran its bold start. Margaret Alford was one of J. P. Postgate's Girton girls (Postgate, while a fellow of Trinity, was a stalwart of Girton teaching, social and — though not, so far as we know, with Miss Alford — romantic life); placed in the first division of the first class of Part I of the Cambridge Classical Tripos in 1890 (without the national hullabaloo that greeted Agnata Ramsay's 'first division first' just three years earlier), she lectured at Girton and Westfield College London, and was head of Classics at Bedford College London between 1904 and 1909.

[35] Shackleton Bailey's *Cicero's Letters to Atticus* (Cambridge 1965–1970) (henceforth, SB, *Att.*) is systematically chronological; his *Cicero: Epistulae ad Familiares* (Cambridge 1977) (SB, *Fam.*) is: 'a compromise between chronological order and grouping by correspondents and *genre*'. His Loeb editions of the *Ad Atticum* (and the forthcoming *Ad Familiares*) follow the same scheme, replacing the traditional book divisions in the 'old' Loeb of E. O. Winstedt et al. Chronology also rules the Budé edition, ed. L.-A. Constans et al. (1934–1996). Selections from the letters have always been faced more starkly with the question of ordering. From even before T.-P. (and perhaps a stimulus to their chronological project), many adopted the chronological scheme, which is now universal: from A. Matthiae (Leipzig 1849), through A. Watson (Oxford 1870), D. Stockton (Oxford 1969) to Shackleton Bailey's own selections in both English (Harmondsworth 1986) and Latin (Cambridge

the conventional book divisions of the different collections that were destroyed in the process.[36] This is largely no doubt because the advantages of a chronological ordering have come to seem to us (as to Tyrrell-and-Purser, and their German predecessors before them) so self-evident. For how else could you easily plot the history of the times? Or understand what exactly Cicero was writing about? Or even (more a nineteenth-century preoccupation than our own) make a *judgement* about his character and intentions? As Wieland summed it up in the introduction to his translation, if you want to understand *Cicero als Mensch*, you really do need to study the correspondence in the order in which it was written.[37] If the *Letters* are about life, they need to be arranged in life's order.

The rest of this chapter will wonder whether we have lost as much as we have gained in reading Cicero's *Letters* in this way. Specifically it will ask what difference it could make to our literary and historical understanding of this material if we went *back* to reading the correspondence according to the traditional ordering and divisions of the collection (in that sense, it is an object lesson in what is to count as 'Old' or 'New' approaches in Classics). It will suggest that there is a strong cultural logic in the order of the letters preserved in the manuscripts; and that whoever originally selected and designed the various collections as we have them was engaged in a project quite different from our own — a project whose aims, assumptions and priorities are well worth our attention. There is more than a hint in my argument that modern orthodoxies in interpreting the letters (as a window on to the real Cicero, as privileged evidence for his attitudes, emotions and motivations) are not unconnected with the order in which we have chosen to read the *Letters* and with our assertion of chronology over the more complex traditional structure.

My final section will take one of the traditional books (*Ad Familiares* 16, traditionally seen as one of the most hopelessly jumbled in the whole collection) and try to show how and why it is worth reading it *as a book* — the individual letters taken together *and* in the order in which they are

1980); though the earlier you go, the more variants you find (a selection published in London, 1689, for school use arranges them explicitly in order of difficulty). The traditional arrangement is now preserved only in standard editions where the Latin text (and its manuscript history) is the main focus.

[36] Closest to crying was R. G. M. Nisbet: 'this system suits the historian better than the textual critic' (review in *Phoenix* 32 (1978) 348–50; at 348).

[37] Wieland, *Sämmtliche Briefe* (p. iv, cited from edition of 1840–1841); soon echoed in Latin by Schütz (*qua ratione* [i.e., reading the *Letters*, across all the different collections, in date order] *non solum multis locis, quae sit Ciceronis sententia facilius intelligitur, sed etiam de eius consiliis rectius iudicatur* etc. above, n. 32, pref.).

preserved in the manuscripts. Before that, we need to think briefly about when the different collections were compiled and what general principles of ordering they display. Admirers of the *Letters to Quintus* and *to Brutus* should be warned that from this point on I shall be concentrating almost exclusively on the *Letters to Atticus* and *to Friends*.[38]

Leave the letters till we're dead[39]

It is a powerful tribute to our modern fixation with chronology that we have accepted, with hardly a murmur of objection, the wholesale dismantling and reordering of the traditional collections of *Letters to Atticus* and *to Friends*. For there is clear evidence to suggest that both sets of correspondence, more or less as they are preserved in the manuscripts, were assembled, 'published'[40] and became part of the literary tradition of Rome some time before the end of the first century AD; clear evidence, in other words, that the books whose dismemberment we have witnessed were the product of a Roman editor, or editors, working within a century or so, at most, of Cicero's death.

To summarise briefly. The *Letters to Atticus* were certainly in the public domain by the 60s AD, when Seneca wrote his *Letters to Lucilius*: for two of

---

[38] Though this is largely for reasons of space, I am confident that detailed consideration of the *Ad QF* and *Ad Brut.* (whose manuscript tradition is in many ways tied to the *Ad Att.*) would not introduce a usefully different perspective.

[39] This is the title of the final volume of the *The Letters of Virginia Woolf* (Volume 6, 1936–1941) (edited by N. Nicolson and J. Trautmann, London 1980). It is adapted from a phrase in a letter from Woolf to Ethel Smyth (17 September 1938): 'Let's leave the letters till we're both dead. That's my plan. I don't keep or destroy but collect miscellaneous bundles of odds and ends, and let posterity, if there is one, burn or not.'

[40] I put 'publishing' in inverted commas to signal the difference between modern publishing and its ancient equivalent: '...there was no such thing as publication in anything like the modern sense... [it] was less a matter of formal release to the public than a recognition by the author that his work was now, so to speak, on its own in the world' (E. J. Kenney, in E. J. Kenney and W. V. Clausen (eds.), *The Cambridge History of Classical Literature II: Latin Literature* (Cambridge 1982) 19). In the case of private letters, the process of publication may be even more complicated than for (say) a poem — whose author always had a public audience in mind. As is clear from the notes that follow, all kinds of semi-public (but pre-'publication') existence have been postulated for Cicero's correspondence (for example, as letters gathered together in a private archive that was accessible to the privileged few). While recognising all these complications, I am confident enough that we can show that both the *Ad Att.* and *Ad Fam.* were, in Kenney's terms, 'on their own in the world' before the end of the first century AD.

these contain a verbatim quotation from the collection;[41] while another blazons the claim that Atticus' fame rests not so much on his links with the imperial family (his granddaughter was the first wife of the future emperor Tiberius), but on the renown brought by Cicero's correspondence with him.[42] The division of this collection into its 16 books, and the internal arrangement of their contents, also seems to go back to this date. Or so at least we can infer from the ancient citations: for wherever — and admittedly it is not often — a Roman author attaches a precise reference to a quotation ('as M. Cicero says in the ninth book of his *Letters to Atticus*'[43]), it tallies in each instance with the numbering of 'our' traditional 16-book collection. The same broad picture holds for the *Letters to Friends*. Again we find verbatim quotations in authors of the first century AD, this time going back to the Elder Seneca in the 30s,[44] and references to individual books of the collection that seem to match 'our' books exactly — except for one detail. In antiquity the books were apparently not known by numbers, but by the name of their first addressee ('in M. Tullius' book of letters to Servius Sulpicius', i.e., our *Ad Fam.* 4).[45] These titles may have been simple alternatives to a numerical system of distinguishing the books in the collection; the manuscripts, in fact, use both styles. But it could also be that the books of what we call the *Ad Familiares* circulated individually at first, and were only later

---

[41] 97.3–4 (quoting *Ad Att.* 1.16.5); 118.1–2 (quoting *Ad Att.* 1.12.1 and 4). It is often claimed that 97.3–4 is the earliest quotation to cite a specific book reference: 'It is accepted that the younger Seneca knew them in published form, since he quotes a passage from 16 (1.16) under the heading *Ciceronis epistularum ad Atticum I* in a letter to Lucilius of about A.D. 63' (SB, *Att.* 1.61). In fact, the book reference is a glaring later gloss — as anyone who was not on the search for Ciceronian citations would instantly see.

[42] 21.4 (a predictably self-glorifying claim for a letter-writer to make).

[43] *Itaque M. Cicero in libro epistularum nono ad Atticum*, Aulus Gellius, *Attic Nights* 4.9.6 (citing *Ad Att.* 9.5.2). Written in the late second century AD, this is the earliest citation of an exact book number; given the range and interests of surviving imperial Latin, it is probably no particular cause for suspicion that no other book references are found until the early fourth-century AD grammarian Nonius (see, for example, Nonius 315L, citing *Ad Att.* 2).

[44] *Suasoriae* 1.5.

[45] *In libro M. Tulli epistularum ad Servium Sulpicium*, Aulus Gellius, *Attic Nights* 12.13.21; *cf.* 1.22.19: *in libro epistularum M. Ciceronis ad L. Plancum et in epistula M. Asini Pollionis ad Ciceronem*, 'in M. Cicero's book of letters to L. Plancus, in a letter of M. Asinius Pollio to Cicero' (citing *Ad Fam.* 10.33.5, which is a letter from Pollio to Cicero in a book which opens with a series of letters to Plancus).

(possibly as late as the fourth or fifth century AD) brought together into a unified collection of 16 and numbered accordingly.[46] We cannot be certain.

Many other aspects of the transmission of these letters — that process by which the day-to-day correspondence of Cicero with his friends, colleagues and family became the 'published' collections that have come down to us — remain puzzling. The first citations provide only a *terminus ante quem*, a date *before* which the letters were in the public domain. We do not know how much earlier than that they appeared.[47] Nor do we know who selected, edited and arranged the material for public consumption, though the sooner after Cicero's death we imagine this happening, the more the finger points at Tiro and/or Atticus himself.[48] We have very little idea of how the letters were assembled for 'publication', where they were kept before they were

---

[46] It is for this reason that I am not exploring the articulation of the collection *Ad Fam.* as a whole; though I am not necessarily dismissing the idea that Cicero's secretary Tiro was the editor of *Ad Fam.* and that we should therefore date the collection to the late first century BC/early first century AD.

[47] *How much earlier* has been the main focus of debate — which has turned on the question of whether allusions to, or even quotations from, the letters in early imperial literature are sure signs of the correspondence being in the public domain. So, for example, when Quintilian (*Inst. Or.* 6.3.109) quotes an Augustan poet, Domitius Marsus, apparently quoting from a Ciceronian letter (*Ad Att.* 8.7.2), does this indicate 'publication' of the letters before the end of Augustus' reign? Or could Domitius Marsus have found his quotation in one of the anthologies of Cicero's *bons mots* that were assembled before and after his death? If the latter alternative looks like special pleading, we should bear in mind that the same quotation is also found in Plutarch *Apophthegmata* 205c and Macrobius, *Saturnalia* 2.3.7 — did they get it from the Ciceronian text itself, from each other, or from some handy anthology? Other (yet more complicated) arguments have focused on the apparent ignorance of the content of the letters on the part of writers who could have been expected to have consulted them had they been available! On the hopelessly unresolved question of whether Asconius, the mid-first-century AD commentator on Cicero's speeches, did or did not know the letters, see SB, *Att.* 1.63–73; R. S. Stewart, 'The chronological order of Cicero's earliest Letters to Atticus', *Transactions of the American Philological Association* 93 (1962) 459–70 (esp. 469, n. 17); A. Setaioli, 'On the date of publication of Cicero's Letters to Atticus', *Symbolae Osloenses* 51 (1976) 105–20; B. A. Marshall, *A Historical Commentary on Asconius* (Columbia 1985) 47–50.

[48] The prime piece of evidence here has been *Ad Att.* 16.5.5, which refers to Tiro (in 44 BC) gathering together a collection of 'about 70' (often taken to be what we now know as the 70-something letters of *Ad Fam.* 13 following the suggestion first made by Gurlitt, *De M Tulli Ciceronis epistulis*). This is discussed by W. C. McDermott, 'M. Cicero and M. Tiro', *Historia* 21 (1972) 259–86 (esp. 281–2); though *cf.* J. E. G. Zetzel, 'Emendavi ad Tironem: some notes on scholarship in the 2nd century AD', *Harvard Studies in Classical Philology* 77 (1973) 225–43 (on the invention of Tiro's editorial role). Who edited the letters, and when, partly hangs on how far we imagine that they were treated as literature (and so follow the pattern of so much posthumous literature in the Roman world, where the process of selecting, editing and publishing the *Nachlass* is well known to have fallen to the writer's friends and executors immediately after his death); or how far they were anomalous documentary relics, languishing in an archive until for some reason they were re-discovered.

'published', in what kind of archives, with what kind of filing systems, and under whose control.[49] We can only speculate on the relationship between the material we have and the other lost collections of Ciceronian letters, now preserved only as names or in brief quotations: the *Letters to Caesar*, the *Letters to Pompey, to Q. Axius, to C. Pansa* and so on.[50] Each of these issues has generated intense discussion over the last hundred and fifty years, with opinions veering wildly and unpredictably; and the controversy has not shown classical scholarship off at its most rigorous or best, as anyone who chooses to investigate it will discover.[51] But the crucial fact is that none of the uncertainties or disputes have undermined the status of the 16 books of the *Ad Atticum* and *Ad Familiares* as books edited and assembled before the first century AD was out.[52]

---

[49] The locus classicus of the archival pre-life of the letters to Atticus is an over-interpreted passage of Nepos' *Life of Atticus* (16.3), where Nepos claims that the clearest sign of Cicero's affection for Atticus is the 'eleven rolls of letters that had been sent to Atticus from the time of Cicero's consulship to the very end of his life' (*XI uolumina epistularum, ab consulatu eius usque ad extremum tempus ad Atticum missarum*); 'anyone who were to read them, would almost get a continuous history of that period' (*quae qui legat, non multum desideret historiam contextam eorum temporum*). The implication is that Nepos knows of and has seen (he goes on to discuss the subject matter in greater detail) the letters in some version — archival it is assumed — arranged in 11 (rather than the current 16) rolls. He says nothing about access (note the remote subjunctive of *quae qui legat*), but the passage is often used as a convenient fall-back for those who wish to explain away inconveniently early quotations from the correspondence (. . . the writer in question must have seen the letter in the archive). Obviously an archival stage may well have been important in the selection and ordering of the collection, but we know nothing of it (beyond the mysterious figure 11) — and, in what follows, I have consistently tried to avoid using it as a convenient solution to the inconvenient problems.

[50] For a review of the lost collections, see J. Nicholson, 'The survival of Cicero's Letters', in C. Deroux (ed.), *Studies in Latin Literature and Roman History* 9 (*Collection Latomus* 244, Brussels 1998) 63–105 (76–87); with the full documentation in K. Büchner, RE 7A, 1199–1206.

[51] The most recent discussion, with an excellent bibliography, is Nicholson (n. 50). Nicholson himself follows a path of extreme scepticism to conclude (p. 104) that 'there is no specific evidence that they were ever intentionally published . . . It appears instead that interested scholars were occasionally granted access to the private library of someone who happened to own a copy of the letters . . . and allowed to reproduce what they wanted.' In the course of this argument, he raises a whole range of interesting problems (is it suspicious, for example, that Seneca only quotes from *Ad Att.* 1?). But overall he offers an object lesson in the dangers of having *too* hard a head: of course, almost any quotation *could* be secondary, drawn from an anthology or from a quick snoop in the archive, but the aggregate of references to and about the correspondence, not to mention the simple fact that we now have it, make that position extremely difficult to sustain. On Nicholson's criteria I suspect that it would be hard to show that Ovid 'published' anything either.

[52] We could not rule out some fluidity in the composition of the collections, at least in the early years. Seneca's *De Brevitate Vitae* 5 (40s AD) quotes a short passage from a letter to Atticus that is certainly not in the collection we have. Either this letter has been 'lost' from our version of the text, or (and this tends to be the preferred solution) we should emend the Senecan text to read 'to *Axius*' (one of the lost letter collections) rather than 'to *Atticus*'.

The principle that will guide the rest of this chapter is that the internal ordering of these letter-books deserves to be taken seriously, for two main reasons. The first centres on the very nature of editing a collection of letters, whether in the ancient or modern world. No editor is ideologically neutral; every edition is founded on a series of *choices* (omissions, juxtapositions, emendations and excerptions) that combine to offer a loaded *representation* of the letter-writer and the relationships instantiated in the letters. Even those collections which blazon their own 'completeness' (*The Collected Letters of...*) must rest on a series of decisions about what is to count as a 'letter', or as a letter 'worthy of publication': notes to the butcher, in or out? almost identical letters sent to two correspondents, in once or twice? Dilemmas of just this sort are rehearsed in preface after preface of modern editions, arbitrary exclusions confessed, priorities insinuated: 'when I print an archetypal letter giving directions and trains to Rye...there is no need to print another hundred resembling it' (so exit most of Henry James's notes to the butcher);[53] 'we have tried, therefore, to choose letters...according to quite specific criteria...Above all, the letters must make the reader feel the intensity of the convictions that motivated Forster as a professional and spiritual being' (no random selection here);[54] 'she repeated herself almost as much in writing as speakers ordinarily repeat themselves in the rush of spontaneous speech. To permit such redundancy to remain in the text would, we assumed, have had an adverse effect on the reader; and so it was necessary to delete much of the repetition...' (so Violet Trefusis' characteristic epistolary style falls victim to the editorial blue pencil).[55] The inclusion or exclusion of just a single letter can, in fact, have a powerful effect on a collection as a whole. When, in a parody of editorial dispassion, the editors of Virginia Woolf's correspondence decided to count her suicide note to Leonard as a 'letter' (number 3710, the last in the book), they made their collection at a stroke quite different from the one that would have ended at number 3709 (which discusses future plans to revise the manuscript of her novel *Between the Acts*).[56] They opt, in other words, for finality and narrative

---

[53] L. Edel (ed.), *Henry James Letters*, vol. 1, 1843–1875 (Cambridge, Mass. 1974) xxxii.

[54] M. Lago and P. N. Furbank (eds.), *Selected Letters of E. M. Forster*, vol. 1, 1879–1920 (London 1983) xvi.

[55] M. A. Leaska and J. Phillips (eds.), *Violet to Vita: the Letters of Violet Trefusis to Vita Sackville-West, 1910–1921* (London 1989) x.

[56] The letter is addressed to John Lehmann, and was probably written the day before Woolf's suicide. In a displacement characteristic of epistolary time (see below, pp. 128–9), it was received after her death.

closure — rather than the day-to-day continuity of a writing life, however tragically we, the readers, know it will be interrupted.

The Ciceronian collections contain no editorial prefaces; there is no attempt to explain how or why the letters were selected, arranged or excerpted as they are. It is partly this silence that has encouraged modern commentators to overlook the role of the editor and to treat the correspondence almost as if it were unmediated, 'raw' documentation. In fact, the gap between a series of letters as sent (and received) and a published collection of correspondence is a complex and significant one: even the humblest editorial activity (the division of a collection into books, the omission of a letter here or there, and so on) constitutes intervention; and all editorial choices are, consciously or unconsciously, loaded. This logic alone justifies a closer look at the edited books of Cicero's letters as they have come down to us.

The second reason is more specifically classical. In the last twenty years it has become almost a truism of Latin literary studies that Roman poets regularly took exquisite care in the design of their poetry books. These were not rough assemblages of as many individual poems as it would take to fill up a roll, but carefully crafted collections — in which the order, the juxtaposition of one poem with another, the beginning and ending, telling symmetries, sequences and variations all mattered to the composition as a whole. Reading an ancient poetry book, in other words, was more than reading a series of autonomous units 'separately conceived and written'; at its most developed, 'each piece [was] made for the ensemble and meant to be understood in its position in the order the poet gave.'[57] This emphasis on book design has enormously enhanced our understanding of the poetry collections of the Augustan age, from Virgil's *Eclogues*, through Horace to the elegists,[58] as well as causing us to look again at such ensembles as the poetry of Catullus,

---

[57] J. Van Sickle, 'The book-roll and some conventions of the poetic book', *Arethusa* 13 (1980) 5–42 (quote at 31); Van Sickle rightly stresses the links between the material form of the ancient book roll, the reading practices it encouraged ('The roll imposes linear movement through or back. No skipping around or dipping in. But it also permits gradual change in the field of study') and the literary structure of the book.

[58] There is now an enormous bibliography on this subject. See, for example, the other contributions to Arethusa 13.1 (1980) (especially, on Horace's *Epistles*, J. E. G. Zetzel, 'Horace's *Liber Sermonum:* the structure of ambiguity', 59–77); M. S. Santirocco, *Unity and Design in Horace's Odes* (Chapel Hill and London 1986); G. O. Hutchinson, 'Propertius and the unity of the book', *Journal of Roman Studies* 74 (1984) 99–106, and, coming from (and pointing in) a slightly different direction, D. Fowler, 'First thoughts on closure: problems and prospects', in *Roman Constructions: Readings in Postmodern Latin* (Oxford 2000) 239–83. Beyond Classics, see N. Fraistat, *The Poem and the Book: Interpreting Collections of Romantic Poetry* (Chapel Hill and London 1985).

where we can now detect, in what had sometimes been written off as a ragbag of poems stitched together by a medieval scribe, traces of the design of one or more books).[59] It has also started to make an impact on our reading of prose texts. Greg Woolf has recently explored the design of the letter-books of the Younger Pliny, to show what we gain from reading them *as books* rather than raiding them for particular historical examples.[60] Take book 1, he suggests. If you start at the beginning and read through to letter 24, as the mechanics of the roll demanded,[61] you will have been system-atically introduced, letter by letter, to a particular Plinian version of Rome and its social life and values — which carefully juxtaposes the claims of politics and literary 'leisure', while at the same time repeatedly empha-sising the role of letter-writing itself in fulfilling obligations and servicing friendships. For Woolf, even book 10, the letters between Pliny and the emperor Trajan, often assumed to be the least 'literary' of the whole col-lection, raw archival documents hardly reworked for publication, should be read as a carefully contrived construction *in letters* of the relationship be-tween author and emperor, and of the implications of that relationship for (Pliny's) friends and (Trajan's) subjects alike.

Why then, if no one would now dream of dismantling a book of (say) Ovid's *Tristia*, and rearranging it in its supposed chronological order of composition, are we happy to treat the books of Cicero's *Letters* in exactly that way? The answer is partly because of the disjunction in their case be-tween author and editor. The assumption behind recent analyses of Augustan poetry books is that the poet himself designed and orchestrated the collec-tion — which is thus seen as an integral part of the creative process ('[the poet] went through a second phase of composition, editing and adjusting the text of each poem, to fit the position he wanted it to occupy in his book'[62]). If we

---

[59] W. Fitzgerald reviews the question (and its significance) in *Catullan Provocations: Lyric Poetry and the Drama of Position* (Berkeley etc. 1995) 24–33. For attempts to work through the logic of Catullan order, see M. B. Skinner, *Catullus' Passer: the Arrangement of the Book of Polymetric Poetry* (New York 1981); T. K. Hubbard, 'The Catullan Libellus', *Philologus* 127 (1983) 218–37. Manuscript evidence is discussed by S. J. Heyworth, 'Dividing Poems', in O. Pecere and M. D. Reeve (eds.), *Formative Stages of Classical Traditions: Latin Texts from Antiquity to the Renaissance* (Spoleto 1995) 117–48 (esp. 131–2; he suggests that the collection was originally divided into three books/rolls. On the methodological issue, see T. P. Wiseman, *Catullus and his world* (Cambridge 1985) 265–6.

[60] In a paper given to the Roman Society in London, January 2000; I am very grateful to G. W. for allowing me to consult the unpublished text of this lecture.

[61] Woolf quotes Hutchinson (n. 58) 100: 'Readers were expected to start at the beginning and read through to the end, not to dip at random.'

[62] E. Fantham, *Roman Literary Culture* (Baltimore and London 1996) 63–4.

believed Cicero himself to be the editor of the correspondence, we would surely hesitate before destroying his arrangement (however inconvenient it was); we are much less concerned to preserve the intervention of an editor who was not himself the author, and whose identity (or identities) and exact date we do not know.[63]

But the underlying reason that we are prepared to ride roughshod over the organisation and design of the *Letters to Atticus* and *to Friends* is, I suspect, that we have not taken the collection seriously *as literature*. We may admire the rhetorical power of individual letters; we may choose to stress their varied artistry — with different styles adopted on different occasions and for different functions; we may emphasise (as G. O. Hutchinson does so strongly in his 'literary study' of *Cicero's Correspondence*[64]) the self-conscious, self-proclaiming 'literariness' of the rhythmical prose that characterises some passages; we may gush over their 'picturesque' vocabulary, their charm, delicacy and wit.[65] Nonetheless even the most radical admirers of the letters would not reckon that the collection as a whole added up to more than the sum of its parts. Trapped by their unique distinction of being 'real' letters, and not (for the most part at least) specifically written for publication,[66] they are always victims of their own marginal status *between* documents and literature. Whatever their *literary qualities* (and Hutchinson has amply demonstrated these), they are always liable as a group to be treated as *documents* — cavalierly reordered, excerpted, rearranged to suit our own convenience.

In proposing that we respect the manuscript order of the letter-books, I am suggesting that we respect the work of the Roman editor or editors. The fact that we are not dealing with the design of the author himself does not

---

[63] I should stress that, despite the ingenious and brilliantly unconvincing arguments of B. Kytzler, 'Beobachtungen zu den Matius-Briefen (*Ad Fam.* 11, 27/28)', *Philologus* 104 (1960) 48–62, there are no good grounds for supposing that Cicero himself edited (or oversaw the editing of) any part of the surviving correspondence. Fitzgerald (n. 59) 249, n. 51 recognises just this dilemma in the case of the Catullan collection.

[64] G. O. Hutchinson, *Cicero's Correspondence: a Literary Study* (Oxford 1998); Hutchinson deals effectively with the view that the (individual) letters are transparent documents of self-relevation and not 'literary' at all (esp. 1–24), but he never considers the collections *as books*.

[65] 'Picturesque' is G. B. Conte's adjective in an uncharacteristically off moment of his *Latin Literature: a History* (Baltimore and London 1994) 203 ('It should be emphasised that these are real letters...thus they show us an unofficial Cicero...').

[66] This does not preclude the idea that some of the more aggressively elegant compositions (such as the famous letter of consolation to Servius Sulpicius Rufus, *Ad Fam.* 4.5, which significantly opens the second volume of Shackleton Bailey's Penguin translation of the *Ad Fam.*) were written with more than half an eye on posterity; one or two (notably, *Ad Quintum Fratrem* 1.1, on provincial government) are, to all intents and purposes, mini-treatises.

mean that we are dealing with no design at all. The editors of these collections were assembling and arranging the letters in a literary world in which book organisation was taken seriously; and this is itself a further prompt to treat their editorial work, their selection, division and articulation of the material, as significant — that is, as an important aspect of the literary, cultural and historical construction of Cicero and his circle in the years following his death. I shall be very happy if, in the process, this approach nudges the collections more securely across the boundary that separates them from 'literature'. The boundary between document and literature is inevitably a contested one; and private letters, published or unpublished, are always a challenge to it. In the Roman world, however, Cicero's letters were certainly much less marginal than they have become in our own; they stood at the head of a whole genealogy of literary letter collections (such as the literary letters of Pliny),[67] which would be quite unthinkable without the model of Cicero behind them. Whatever their origin in the day-to-day world of real-life letter writing, through their collection and publication, through the very editorial practices I have been discussing, through their reading and reception, they were progressively reformulated as a *literary collection*.

A sense of order

The search for *order* and *arrangement* in a work of literature is always liable to be self-fulfilling. It is not just that the clever reader can almost always construct a narrative logic out of an arbitrary jumble, but 'no order at all' can always be understood as one particularly loaded form of 'order' — indeed, the negative claim that 'no order exists' can always be turned on its head, to imply intentional or wilful nonchalance, and so 'order' in the most positive sense.[68] In what follows I shall be treading the usual tightrope between two

---

[67] There is no good modern discussion of the dependence of Pliny's *Letters* on their Ciceronian predecessors. At 9.2.1–4, Pliny makes an elaborate (and effusively modest) disclaimer of Cicero's letters as a model for his own. In fact they include a host of clever allusions to the *Ad Fam*. For example, at 9.5, Pliny writes to his own correspondent named Tiro (in fact, a senator, but an obvious prompt for the reader to remember Cicero's manumitted slave secretary Tiro; see below, pp. 130–43); he ends the letter, significantly (as John Henderson has pointed out to me), with a reflection on status-change at Rome (*quae si* [sc. *discrimina ordinum*] *confusa, turbata, permixta sunt, nihil est ipsa aequalitate inaequalius*). It is hard to imagine that Pliny's depiction of *this* Tiro's major role in his province (see 7.16; 23; 32) was entirely 'innocent': it was manumission. For the tribute of the second-century letter-writer Fronto to Cicero, see *Ad Ant. Imp.* 2.4 and 2.5.

[68] Hence, in part, the unresolved debates on Catullan ordering (see n. 59); one person's order is another's disorder.

different but related questions: on the one hand, that of editorial design; on the other, that of the reader's experience (what difference does it make to read the letter-books as they are ordered, and to read that order as significant). But it is worth emphasising that, all those difficulties aside, there are some obvious basic principles of ordering in the collections, principles which operate distinctively differently in the *Ad Atticum* and in the books of the *Ad Familiares*.

The *Letters to Atticus* are arranged broadly in date order, in a main sequence that stretches from AD 61 to 44 BC, with a few preliminary 'strays' from 68–65 BC; the majority of the letters were written in the last six years of Cicero's life (we reach 49 BC by book 7). Within this sequence of progression the divisions between the 16 books are not random: they do not simply break the collection into equal book-roll lengths, but construct an episodic narrative out of the letters. This is particularly clear in the early books: book 2 focuses on the critical year of Caesar's first consulship and its immediate prelude;[69] book 3 consists of a series of letters from Cicero's exile in 58–57 BC; book 4 covers Cicero's period in Italy between his exile and his second 'exile', as governor of Cilicia in 51–50. But some later books also fall into this episodic pattern: book 11 covers the period between Cicero's departure to join Pompey in the Civil War and his meeting with Caesar at Brundisium; book 12 focuses on the death of Cicero's daughter Tullia and his reaction to it.

The divisions between these books are often emphasised by a break in the sequence of letters, so that (for example) there is a gap of seven months between the end of book 3 and the beginning of book 4, more than two years between books 4 and 5, and seven months again between books 10 and 11.[70] The conventional explanation is that there simply was no correspondence in these periods: Cicero and Atticus were together and so did not need to rely on letters to keep in touch; the book divisions, in other words, are direct reflections of the pattern of the letters as they were exchanged, rather than selective editorial constructions. This cannot, in fact, be true — or, at least, not in every case. Granted that the two friends did spend some time in each other's company, and probably did then suspend or restrict their regular correspondence, it is impossible to imagine that they were continuously together in the period between 54 and 51, which separates books 4 and 5; and there is some evidence that they were apart during at least some of the

---

[69] 'Critical year' is Alford's formulation, in the prelude to her edition of book 2 (n. 34) vii.

[70] Though there is not always a gap, especially in the later books: 12 to 13, for example, seem to run directly on, as do 14 to 15 and 15 to 16.

months that separate books 10 and 11, and books 3 and 4.[71] These gaps are equally, if not more, likely to reflect the process of editorial selection and omission.[72]

That certainly is regularly suggested by the choice of letters to start and finish the books. Book 3, for example, opens with a cumbersomely choking sentence that heralds many of the themes — longing, travel and the desire to meet — that will define the rest of the book. Already (somewhere) outside Rome, on his way into exile, Cicero writes:[73]

> cum antea maxime nostra interesse arbitrabar *te esse nobiscum,* tum uero, ut legi rogationem, intellexi ad iter id quod constitui nihil mihi optatius cadere posse quam ut *tu me* quam primum *consequare,* ut, cum ex Italia profecti essemus, siue per Epirum iter esset faciendum tuo tuorumque praesidio uteremur, siue aliud quid agendum esset certum consilium de tua sententia capere possemus. quam ob rem te oro des operam ut me statim consequare; quod eo facilius potes, quoniam de prouincia Macedonia perlata lex est. pluribus uerbis tecum agerem nisi pro me apud te *res ipsa* loqueretur.

> I had been thinking that it was my top priority to have you with me, but when I read the bill, I realised that there was nothing I wanted more for the journey that I've decided on than that you should catch me up as soon as you can, so that when I'd left Italy, if I was to travel through Epirus, I could take advantage of the protection of you and your friends, or if I had to do something else, I could make my mind up on the basis of your advice. So I beg you to try to catch me up straightaway; all the simpler for you, now that the law about the province of Macedonia has gone through. I would use more words to plead with you, if the actual facts didn't speak to you on my behalf.

The book ends in a brief two-liner, which not only amounts to the starkest assertion of the exile's (literal and/or social) death — a perfectly ironic climax to an exile-story, which the readers know will actually culminate in triumphant return to Rome (as indeed the chirpy words of the first letter in the next book underline: 'As soon as I arrived in Rome ...'[74]); but which also offers a reprise of the themes and language of the opening — the

---

[71] For books 10 to 11, see SB, *Att.* 5.265; in the case of books 3 to 4, as Shackleton Bailey points out (*Att.* 2.165), the language of *Ad Att.* 4.1 'reads rather oddly if he and Atticus had been together from February to July'.

[72] Peter (n. 25), on the other hand, blames 'der Unsicherheit der Politik' (which could equally well, one would have thought, have occasioned a whole flurry of letter writing); no less arbitrary is the possibility that letters were exchanged, but for some reason did not end up in the archive.

[73] *Ad Att.* 3.1 (I have quoted the complete letter).

[74] *Ad Att.* 4.1: *cum primum Romam ueni ...*

repeated longing for Atticus' company and the appeal to the facts of the case (*res ipsa*):[75]

> ex tuis litteris et ex *re ipsa* nos funditus perisse uideo. te oro ut quibus in rebus tui mei indigebunt nostris miseriis ne desis. *ego te*, ut scribis, *cito uidebo*.
>
> From your letter and from the actual facts, I see that I am completely finished. I beg you, whatever help my family needs of you, not to let us down in our distress. As your letter says, I shall see you soon.

Within this frame, the narrative of Cicero's banishment is laid out as a story of togetherness deferred. At the very close of the exile-book, Cicero's re-union with Atticus is still emphatically in the future tense; the moment of unity still postponed. In a poetry book we would take such echoes seriously, and grace them with terms of art ('ring-composition' and the like).

Not so in the *Ad Atticum*, where the problem that has most preoccupied critics is the chronological 'disruption' of some parts of the collection: if the sequence of letters is basically in date order, how do you explain the fact that there are some groups of letters that are chronologically muddled? The standard scholarly response is to appeal to the process by which the letters were assembled, and published. Shackleton Bailey is typical in envisaging two stages. The first is the arrangement of the correspondence in Atticus' own private archive, where (so a passage of Atticus' biographer, Cornelius Nepos, suggests) the letters were collected into 11 books (*uolumina*); these were, of course (because they were arranged by Atticus himself), in the 'correct' order. The second stage comes when a later editor prepares the material for formal 'publication'. He finds, we must imagine, further letters from Cicero in Atticus' archive, but not incorporated into the 11 books; he wishes to include these in his edition, in their proper place in the sequence — but without 'Atticus available for consultation' makes numerous blunders. The chronological mistakes, in other words, 'can fairly be regarded as evidence that the letters involved were not in the series assembled by Atticus'; letters out of their proper sequence were additions by the final editor.[76]

Whatever there is to be said in favour of this reconstruction (and in my view there is, frankly, not much), it ignores two vital points which cut across

---

[75] *Ad Att.* 3.27. It is worth emphasising that, although this letter is conventionally dated to February 57, there is no internal dating evidence whatsoever; the 'argument' for its date rests entirely (and with inevitable circularity) on its position in the book.

[76] SB, *Att.* 1.69–72. E. Meyer, *Caesars Monarchie und das Principat des Pompeius* (Stuttgart and Berlin 1918; 2nd ed., 1919), 583–617 even offers a reconstruction of Atticus' archive (in Nepos' 11 rolls) before the addition of the extra material.

any simple appeal to 'correct' chronology. First, where the time sequence *is* disrupted, the disruption does sometimes serve to emphasise an important theme in the letter-books concerned. Again, the first letters in the books are often crucial. For example, the 'hopeless... jumble' of book 12 (which centres, as I have already noted, on the death of Tullia) opens with a Cicero longing 'to run to the embrace' of his daughter[77] — a letter aptly announcing the book's focus. Even more striking is the first letter in the whole published collection, *Ad Atticum* 1.1. These early letters (between 68 and 65 BC) are a classic case of a chronological muddle assumed to derive from the later editor: he obviously tracked down some additional early material to introduce the main sequence, which starts in 61 BC, but did not know its exact date (hence the apparent illogicality of starting with two letters of 65 BC, moving back to 67, on to 66, then back to 68 and so on). Be that as it may, it should not blind us to the fact that, in this muddled arrangement, the very first words of the whole collection are *petitionis nostrae*, 'my campaign for the consulship'. This is a brilliantly appropriate overture to a collection of letters by a Roman whose career was defined (and ultimately ruined) by his tenure of the consulship — and one that is entirely lost when the 'correct' chronological scheme is reinstated: in both Tyrrell-and-Purser and Shackleton Bailey *petitionis nostrae* is buried as the opening to what they make 'Letter 10'. Even if we *are* dealing with the work of a chronologically challenged later editor, he was certainly an editor who knew how to open a letter collection of Rome's most famous consul.[78]

The second point concerns the *temporality* of letters more generally. The exchange of letters always revolves around the temporal distance that separates writing and receipt. In Rome (given the conditions of letter delivery) that distance was inevitably uncertain, sometimes lengthy and almost always unpredictable; as the Ciceronian correspondence itself shows, letters could take weeks to deliver and the order of their receipt did not necessarily match the order of their writing.[79] In their chronological zeal, all recent editors have concentrated exclusively on the moment of writing, without pausing to reflect

---

[77] *Ad* Att. 12.1.: *utinam continuo ad complexum meae Tulliae, ad osculum Atticae possem currere.*

[78] *Ad Att.* 1.1: *petitionis nostrae, quam tibi summae curae esse scio, huius modi ratio est, quod adhuc coniectura prouideri possit.* 'My campaign for the consulship — and I know you're really interested in this — is working on the following strategy; at any rate insofar as it can be projected in advance.' The fact that Nepos (*Life of Atticus* 16.3) described the collection of Cicero's letters to Atticus as starting at his consulship might suggest that the 'rolls' (*uolumina*) which Nepos had seen in fact already started with this letter.

[79] Two classic examples can be found in *Ad Att.* 3 (where Cicero's exile may well have exacerbated the problems of delivery): 3.15 (four letters received on the same day); 3.23 (three letters received on the same day — though written more than three weeks apart).

on the different chronologies that could determine a letter sequence, or on what might count as putting letters in their 'correct' chronological order. In fact, some of the apparent disruptions of the dating sequence pointedly dramatise the disputed temporalities of epistolary genre — as is particularly clear in the extreme case of book 3. The exile is, by definition, completely at the mercy of the shifting temporalities that govern letters and letter-exchange — his life being passed in 'letter-time', radically unsynchronised with the political life in 'real-time' Rome, from which he was forcibly excluded. Where the order of letters is flagrantly inverted (where, for example, the manuscripts place two letters in the 'wrong' chronological order despite being clearly and explicitly dated), a strong reading will encourage us to reflect on the competing chronologies at play; on how far letters and letter collections must, at some level, always be *about time*.[80]

Chronology is not the explicit guiding principle of the books of *Letters to Friends*, which are defined rather by theme or (as the ancient titles suggest) by addressees. The most resoundingly thematic is our book 13, consisting entirely of letters of recommendation by Cicero for his friends, colleagues and clients; and there is an equally strong unifying logic in, for example, book 3 (all letters to Appius Claudius Pulcher, Cicero's predecessor in the province of Cilicia), book 14 (letters to Terentia and his family) and book 16 (letters from Cicero, his brother and his son to — or, in one case, about — Tiro). But others are more closely defined than they might at first appear: book 6, for example, is focused on letters to exiled supporters of Pompey, book 12 comprises correspondence from the civil war years of 44–43, be-tween Cicero and military commanders in the East and Africa. The internal arrangement of these books 'shows more [cohesion] than has been generally recognized', as Shackleton Bailey acknowledges in his preface to the *Ad Familiares*, only a few pages before he proceeds to demolish what cohesion there is. I shall be looking in greater detail at the organisation of book 16 in

---

[80] See, for example, 3.13 and 3.14. Both are dated: number 13 to 5 August; number 14 to 21 July. Both discuss the moves that might be made in Rome on Cicero's behalf, once the elections are over (*secundum comitia*); they attempt to chart and predict the progress of his case by reference to a major public political event. But Cicero in exile can only guess whether that event has taken place (*comitia enim credo esse habita*, 'I suppose that the elections have been held'). He cannot even know whether, or in what order, his letters of enquiry are reaching the city; and *we* cannot know how far a strict chronological order of writing reflects the order in which they were read and received by Atticus, at the centre of the political events they attempt to reconstruct. For other aspects of letter time, see Hutchinson, (n. 64), 139–171; S. Mellet, *L'imparfait de l'indicatif en latin classique: Temps, aspect, modalité* (Paris 1988) 189–206 (on the so-called epistolary imperfect, 'une des curiosités de la syntaxe latine' — whereby the letter writer commonly narrates present time in the imperfect tense, as if seeing events from the time perspective of the recipient; see, for example, *Ad Fam.* 16.10.2).

my final section. For the moment, I would point only to the principles of *association* governing some sections of the arrangement that might appear at first sight muddled or merely arbitrary. Book 1, for example, contains ten letters to Lentulus Spinther, during his governorship of Cilicia, followed by an apparent 'stray' to a certain L. Valerius; in fact this also concerns Lentulus, for it is Cicero's reply to Valerius — who had asked him to write a letter of recommendation to Lentulus. Similarly book 2 is focused on letters sent by Cicero from his province in 51 and 50 BC, but it opens with an apparently unconnected earlier sequence (numbers 1–6) of letters from Cicero to Curio in 53 BC; in fact this series (sent from Rome to Curio while he was in *his* province of Asia) provides the introduction to the main series from Cilicia, the first of which (number 7) was addressed to Curio. Theme, personality, relationship and historical context, rather than chronology, are what count for most in these books.

The consequence is that the *Letters to Friends* come off by far the worse when modern editors attempt to 'restore' chronological order to the correspondence. The *Letters to Atticus* are shuffled slightly, the disruptions ironed out — but, insofar as it is broadly chronological, the overall structure of the collection remains detectable even in the most interventionist editions. Many of the books of the *Ad Familiares*, on the other hand, become almost invisible as soon as date order is imposed, scattered about new collections, losing all touch with their original structure and logic. The remnants of book 7, for example, a loosely integrated collection of 33 private letters between Cicero and a number of Epicurean friends, are now to be found at intervals between numbers 24 and 334 in Shackleton Bailey's edition of the *Ad Fam.*, between 94 and 776 in Tyrrell-and-Purser. It is here that the contrast between our treatment of books of 'literature' and (these) books of letters is at its starkest.

Liberation: *Ad Familiares* book 16

The sixteenth book of the collection of *Letters to Friends* consists of 26 letters from Cicero and other members of the family to his (ex-)slave Tiro; and one letter to Cicero from his brother Quintus, on the subject of Tiro (*de Tirone*, 'About Tiro' it starts — and it continues by expressing Quintus' delight that Cicero had granted Tiro his freedom). Tiro, who is generally referred to as Cicero's 'secretary', has a walk-on part in the political and cultural narrative of the late Republic and early empire, mythologised for his invention of a new system of shorthand and for his longevity (Eusebius'

Chronicle implies his death in 4 BC at the age of 100).[81] In fact, most of what (we think) we know about Tiro is drawn from this book of letters;[82] and it is also this book that has fed the notion (attractive, but unprovable) that Tiro was the editor of the whole collection *Ad Familiares* — Tiro, in other words, paraded his own achievement by signing off with a final collection of letters to, or about, himself.

Ad Fam. 16 is probably the stiffest test that any argument for reading these letter-books *as books* could face — for at first sight, it is not only a chronological jumble, but also a thematic ragbag of often trivial, day-to-day subject matter, linked only by the identity of the addressee. Not that we have much chance of spotting any unity. In both Tyrrell-and-Purser and Shackleton Bailey the 27 individual letters are so widely dispersed that the original book is practically invisible: with letters dating between 53 and 44 BC, it is spread between number 40 and 352 in Shackleton Bailey, and between 285 and 815 in Tyrrell-and-Purser's chronological sequence.[83] In fact the position is even more complicated than it is for the other books of the collection. For the early editors of our printed texts, seeing — from the dates on the letters themselves — that the first letters in the book were 'disrupted', proceeded to 'restore' what they believed to be the 'correct' sequence, and to number the letters accordingly.[84] The result is that even the traditional numbers (16.1, 2, 3 etc.) do not match the order of letters in the manuscripts.[85] In what follows I shall work from the manuscript order; though I shall continue to use the traditional numbering (for it would only add to the confusion to introduce yet another system), I shall be careful to make clear,

---

[81] Eusebius, *Chron.* Olympiad 194; if this is correct, then Tiro was over 50 when he was manumitted (an implication which most critics have been unwilling to accept; they want Tiro manumitted young); McDermott (n. 48) 271–2 debunks the myth of Tiro's shorthand.

[82] With sometimes ludicrous results; see, for example, S. Treggiari, *Roman Freedmen during the Late Republic* (Oxford 1969): 'The career of Tiro perhaps provides one of the better excuses for the institution of slavery and manumission', 263; on p. 261, Treggiari exposes the dangers of assuming that these letters represent a (full) life story: 'His work for Cicero was broken only by periods of ill health, just before his manumission; on the way home from Cilicia, from June 50 to May 49; again in 45.' What she actually means is that book 16 includes correspondence from those three periods, and those three periods only.

[83] Not including 16.10 and 13–16, which they put in their final section of letters that cannot be exactly dated.

[84] The now traditional order was established in Lambinus' edition of Cicero's works (Paris 1565–1566).

[85] The order of letters in the manuscripts runs (using the traditional numbering) 5, 7, 1, 2, 3, 4, 6, 8, 9, 11, 12, 10, 15, 14, 13, 16, 17 etc. Purser lists this manuscript order in his Oxford Classical Text of 1901. There is no trace of it in the most recent Oxford edition by W. S. Watt (1982); you would simply never know that any re-ordering had gone on.

where it matters to my argument, the position of the letter in the manuscripts themselves. My question is simple: is it worth our while to read the letters of this book together as a group, and in their manuscript order?

I shall shortly be returning to the precise ordering of the letters, but let me emphasise now that the book (in its original manuscript order) does have a clear overall structure. First come 11 letters dating to 50–49 BC, largely concerned with Tiro's ill health on his return to Rome from Cicero's province of Cilicia;[86] in the centre are four letters, probably dating to 53 BC, drawn from the run-up to Tiro's manumission — followed immediately by the one, from Quintus to Marcus Cicero, which by celebrating the news of the event announces to the reader that the manumission has taken place.[87] Finally another set of 11 letters, this time from 45–44 BC, and more varied in theme and author:[88] they still return to questions of Tiro's shaky health, but now we see him also in the midst of business with some awkward gardeners, being consulted on big questions of politics, as well as teasingly chastised for some literary solecisms; the longest letter (in this group, and in the whole book) is from Cicero junior, young Marcus, a far from diligent student in Athens — making the usual student claims about regret for past follies and new leaves already turned over.[89]

Even in this brief summary it is hard to miss the significance and impact of the 'manumission letter': the crucial moment in which Tiro became both a human being (in the fullest, social sense of the term) and a Roman citizen is reported by the only letter in the book that was *not* addressed to him — but made him the subject of his masters' dealings amongst themselves. It is worth quoting in full:[90]

> de Tirone, mi Marce, ita te meumque Ciceronem et meam Tulliolam tuumque filium uideam, ut mihi gratissimum fecisti, quom eum indignum illa fortuna ac nobis amicum quam seruum esse maluisti. mihi crede, tuis et illius litteris perlectis exsilui gaudio et tibi et ago gratias et gratulor. si enim mihi Stati fidelitas est tantae uoluptati, quanti esse in isto haec eadem bona debent additis litteris, [et] sermonibus, humanitate, quae sunt his ipsis commodis potiora! amo te omnibus equidem de maximis causis, uerum etiam propter hanc uel quod mihi sic ut debuisti nuntiasti. te totum in litteris uidi. Sabini pueris et promisi omnia et faciam.

[86] 1–11 in the manuscript order (on the traditional numbering: 5, 7, 1, 2, 3, 4, 6, 8, 9, 11, 12).

[87] 12–16 in the manuscript order (on the traditional numbering: 10, 15, 14, 13, 16).

[88] 17–27 in both the manuscript order and traditional numbering.

[89] 16.21; 21.2: *tantum enim mihi dolorem cruciatumque attulerunt errata aetatis meae, ut non solum animus a factis sed aures quoque a commemoratione abhorreant,* 'My youthful mistakes have brought me so much unhappiness and agony that I don't just hate to reflect on what I did, but even hear it referred to.'

[90] 16.16.

On the subject of Tiro, my dear Marcus — as surely as I hope to see you and my
boy Cicero, and my little Tullia, and your son — you have given me cause to be
extremely grateful, when you judged his former rank to be unworthy of him and
preferred to have him as a friend of ours rather than a slave. Believe me I jumped
for joy when I read your letter and his. Not just my gratitude but my
congratulations too! For if Statius' loyalty gives me so much pleasure, how
highly you must value the same qualities in that man of yours, plus his literary
talents and conversation and culture, which outweigh those useful qualities! In
addition to all the reasons I have for loving you, strong ones at that, there is now
this too — that is, the fact that you gave me the news in just the way you should. I
saw you, one hundred percent, in your letter. I have promised Sabinus' slaves
everything, and I shall deliver.

After a series of letters from Cicero to Tiro, apparently referring obliquely to
the forthcoming manumission (*dies promissorum adest*, 'My promise will be
performed on the appointed day'),[91] the occasion itself is presented to us as
an event in the lives of the brothers Cicero, Marcus and Quintus. Whatever
joy there was on Tiro's part, we are not to see it — here congratulations are
extended from master to master; it is they who 'jump for joy'. And their
pleasure in Tiro's change of status (from *seruus* to *amicus*) turns still on the
very language of obligations that defines the relationship between master and
slave. Parading his delight in the *fidelitas* of his own freedman, Statius (the
loyalty of the ex-slave gives pleasure, *uoluptas*, to his master), Quintus turns
to the special qualities of Tiro: *litterae*, *sermones* and (crucially) *humanitas*.

These are qualities not just of literary culture, but more specifically of
the free *person*. In writing to Atticus from exile, Cicero insisted on the
centrality of *sermo* to full civic life (its absence signifying social death);[92]
humanitas, too, regularly signals that side of civilised living, 'humanity', that
could always exclude those who were not free. They are exactly the characteristics you would expect of a 'friend', then, not of a 'slave'; but only up
to a point. For Quintus moves instantly to rank these qualities on a scale of
commoda — the 'advantages' or 'benefits' gained by the master from his
slave. Tiro's *humanitas* is represented as a 'credit', in more senses than one,
to Cicero. William Fitzgerald has recently stressed the importance of slavery
as a political, social and literary institution in offering to the Romans a series

---

[91] 16.14.2 (14 in the manuscript order). There is very little internal or external dating evidence for
this group of letters (as T.-P. recognised) — their date and the references to the forthcoming
manumission are deduced from their position in the book, immediately before 16.16 (as, no doubt,
the editor intended).

[92] See, for example, 3.12.3: *ego etiam nunc eodem in loco iaceo sine sermone ullo, sine cogitatione
ulla.* 'I'm still down in the same gutter with no human interaction, and without a real thought in my
head.'

of models and metaphors for their own culture; in its simplest form, the slave could act as a mirror of the master (and of his aspirations, fantasies and discontents).[93] This letter is a classic instance of this kind of mirroring — and its famous claim, *te totum in litteris uidi*, often cited as if it were proof of the transparency of the correspondence,[94] serves precisely to emphasise that.

Ad Fam. 16 is one of the most important texts on slavery to have survived from the ancient world, consisting as it does of a unique series of letters written by a master to an (ex-)slave. The fact that it has figured so rarely in discussions of slavery in Roman culture or in the Roman literary imagination must be due largely to the fact that we have so rarely read the letters it contains *together*.[95] Seen side by side, strategically juxtaposed, and read *as a book*, they offer a series of reflections on the nature of the relationship between master and (ex-)slave; and they present the ambivalence of the positions of slave, freedman and master yet more emphatically than the 'manumission letter'.

One major strand of the book blazons the possibilities of affection between Tiro and his masters; and it is this aspect, if anything, that has caught the attention of most sympathetic critics, who have tended to be touched by the expressions of love and care of *Ad Fam.* 16, and the emotions apparently underlying it: 'the master's love for his (now ex-)slave is vividly expressed in the letters he wrote when Tiro was dangerously ill with malaria';[96] 'it is likely enough that, Tullia apart, Cicero came to care as much for this young man as for anyone in the world, or more.'[97] The key topos throughout the book is Tiro's illness, which strips away the social difference between the correspondents and reduces their relationship to the zero degree: survival — and love. Letter after letter (and the first editor was right, the exact chronological order is not what counts here) has Cicero making arrangements for his ailing freedman, urging him to rest, look after himself, get proper doctors and recover his

---

[93] W. Fitzgerald, *Slavery and the Roman Literary Imagination* (Cambridge 2000) 11, 69–86.

[94] See D. Stockton, *Thirty-five Letters of Cicero* (Oxford 1969) xxviii; J. Carcopino, *Cicero: the Secrets of his Correspondence* (London 1951) 2; or, as D. R. Shackleton Bailey puts it (*Cicero* (London 1971) xi), 'In Cicero's letters we see a Roman Consular without his toga.'

[95] There is, for example, not a mention of Tiro in M. I. Finley, *Ancient Slavery and Modern Ideology* (London 1980); and only one allusion (to his name, p. 34) in T. Wiedemann, *Greek and Roman Slavery* (London 1981).

[96] Fitzgerald (n. 93) 13 (surprisingly his only reference to *Ad Fam.* 16).

[97] Shackleton Bailey (n. 94) 133; Pliny too thought that Cicero had a special — and specially erotic — relationship with Tiro (*Ep.* 7.4.3–6), a conclusion that has been strenuously resisted by almost every commentator since (see, for example, McDermott, (n. 48) 272–5). Needless to say, there is no evidence either way.

health — despite his own overwhelming desire to see him. So, for example, he signs off one letter, the first in the book, dated 7 November 50, with typical advice:[98]

> ego omnem spem tui diligenter curandi in Curio habeo. nihil potest illo fieri humanius, nihil nostri amantius. ei te totum trade. malo te paulo post ualentem quam statim imbecillum uidere. cura igitur nihil aliud nisi ut ualeas; cetera ego curabo. etiam atque etiam uale. Leucade proficiscens VII Id Nov.
>
> I put all my hopes of you getting proper *care* in *Cur*ius. Nothing could be kinder than he is, nothing more devoted to me. Hand yourself over to him, one hundred percent. I prefer to see you a little later and fit, than straightaway poorly. So *care* for nothing except getting well — I shall *care* for the rest. Goodbye once again. Written on departure from Leucas, 7 November.

And on another occasion (in a letter preceding the manumission), Cicero extends his regret for Tiro's illness into a wry expression of that Catch 22 of Roman slavery: the inevitable symbiosis of master and slave, in this case the symbiosis of their *writing*. Get well, he urges, for without you 'my — sorry, our — *belles-lettres* have missed you so, they've flopped... without you all that is mine is dumb. Get ready to pay your dues to our Muses.' (*litterulae meae siue nostrae tui desiderio oblanguerunt*... [*dixi*] *sine te omnia mea muta esse. tu Musis nostris para ut operas reddas.*)[99] The greatest writer needs his slave. *Litterulae meae siue* nostrae: for Cicero, read Cicero-and-Tiro.

Even when Tiro's illness is not the main item on the agenda, we find repeated expressions of affection for their (ex-)slave from all members of the Cicero family, as well as explicit admiration for his character, talents and qualities. Justly, the first letter in the book heralds this tone. It starts:[100]

> TULLIUS ET CICERO ET Q. Q. TIRONI HUMANISSIMO ET OPTIMO S. P. D.
> uide quanta sit in te suauitas. duas horas Thyrrei fuimus. Xenomenes hospes tam te diligit quam si uixerit tecum.
>
> FROM TULLIUS AND MARCUS AND THE TWO QUINTUSES, TO THE EXCELLENT TIRO, FULL MEMBER OF COMMON HUMANITY, WARMEST GREETINGS.
> See how much charm you have! We spent a couple of hours at Thyrreum, and our host Xenomenes is as fond of you as if you had spent your whole lives together.

---

[98] Letter 1 (= 16.5).

[99] Letter 12 (= 16.10). This dependence of master on slave is an underlying theme of K. Hopkins, 'Novel evidence for Roman slavery', *Past and Present* 138 (1993) 3–27; see also Fitzgerald (n. 93) 24–5.

[100] Letter 1 (= 16.5).

In the overall design of the book, this makes a powerful and appropriate opener. Our first introduction to Tiro casts him already, in the very address of the letter, as a man brimming with the qualities of *humanitas* which define him as free; while the 'charm' (*suauitas*) that this book will take care to document (and which, as we shall soon discover, the very last words of the book echo) is shown not merely to be a figment of those who wrote the letters, or a private passion of one family for their favourite slave. Anyone who meets Tiro will fall for him. Xenomenes was smitten after just a couple of hours.

Yet it is not quite so simple. Those who admire the relationship of love and care between Cicero and Tiro, forged across the boundaries of social status, tend not to point to the language of dependence, hierarchy and servitude which underpins even the most intimate, joking or affectionate passages in these letters. The paradox is that Cicero and his family love their (ex-)slave in the language of slavery itself (or its parodies). One of the clearest cases of this, and where, to many modern sensibilities, it will seem that the correspondence hits rock bottom, is to be found at the very end of the book, in a bantering letter from Quintus; it begins:[101]

> *uerberaui* te cogitationis tacito dumtaxat conuicio, quod fasciculus alter ad me iam sine tuis litteris perlatus est. non potes effugere huius culpae poenam te patrono; Marcus est adhibendus, isque diu et multis lucubrationibus commentata oratione uide ut probare possit te non peccasse.

> I have given you a thrashing, or at least a silent heckling in my head — because a second packet has reached me with no letter from you. You can't escape the penalty for this offence if you take on your own defence. No, Marcus must be wheeled in, and see if he can prove you innocent, with a speech that he's worked on for ages, up late night after night.

Quintus' joke about big brother Cicero burning the midnight oil, to write a speech that would prove the guilty innocent, has probably blinded most modern readers to the language in which Tiro is addressed here. If there was one word in the Latin language that evoked slavery and the bodily vulnerability of the slave to his master it is *uerberare* ('to thrash' or 'to beat'). A slave could almost be defined as a body to be beaten, 'the whip [was] the primary symbol of the master's power over the slave'.[102] Here the letter opens with a word that effectively reasserts the master–slave relationship

---

[101] 16.26 (the penultimate in the book and whole collection).
[102] Fitzgerald (n. 93) 33; see also Finley (n. 95) 93.

between Quintus and Tiro, despite his manumission many years earlier.[103] The (bad) joke is that this mental thrashing has been inflicted for a crime against *friendship* — viz. failing to write a letter — rather than neglecting the duties associated with slave labour; though just a few lines further on Tiro's failure is described as *cessatio* ('laziness'), one of the classic complaints against the slave and one of the most powerful weapons in the slave's armoury of resistance.[104] But this is not the end of it. Quintus continues his banter by saying that Tiro is not going to escape the charges *te patrono* ('if you take on your own defence'); to have any hope of getting off, he will need to engage Cicero in that capacity. Here the sense of *patronus* is what is at stake. It can mean, as my translation has it, an advocate in a court of law — the perfect encapsulation of Cicero, as Catullus uncomfortably put it, *optimus omnium patronus* ('the best advocate of all'/'everyone's advocate').[105] But it is also the term regularly used for the former master of an ex-slave, to whom the ex-slave owed a series of formal and informal obligations.[106] Hence the other side of the joke: Tiro *cannot* be his own *patronus* (*te patrono*) in that sense; for that role belongs to Cicero anyway.

This use of the language of servitude is found, more or less stridently, throughout the book. When Tiro is urged to look after his health, for example, he is simultaneously urged to become a slave again — this time to serve his body: ... *indulge ualetudini tuae; cui quidem tu adhuc, dum mihi deseruis, seruisti non satis* ('... go easy on your health. While you've been a perfect slave for me, you haven't yet slaved enough for that');[107] *omnia depone, corpori* serui ('Drop everything, slave for your body').[108] In the end, Tiro's care for himself in illness — far from transcending the social hierarchies embedded in the relationship between master and (ex-)slave — becomes part of a series of obligations that only serve to reaffirm his dependent status. Just as in the 'manumission letter' Quintus could rank Tiro's civilised qualities among the services a slave could offer, so here Tiro's recovery is a duty (*officium*) that he owes to his (ex-)master. As Cicero

---

[103] Again, the date of this letter (which on internal grounds could be placed in any year) is deduced from its context in the collection, with letters of the mid 40s.

[104] P. A. Cartledge, 'Rebels and Sambos in Classical Greece', in P. A. Cartledge and F. D. Harvey (eds.), *Crux: Essays in Greek History presented to G. E. M. De Ste Croix on his 75th Birthday* (Exeter and London 1985) 16–46 (esp. 28–30), reviews a number of ways the ancient (or modern) slave could resist the demands of a master — this side of rebellion.

[105] Catullus 49; for the delicious ambiguity in the Latin between 'the best advocate of all' and 'the man who'll hire himself out to anyone', see K. Quinn, *Catullus: the Poems* (London 1970) 235.

[106] Treggiari (n. 82) 68–81.

[107] 16.18.1.

[108] Letter 6.4 (= 16.4.4).

himself puts it: *cura ergo potissimum ut ualeas. de tuis innumerabilibus in me* officiis *erit hoc gratissimum* ('Take the utmost care to get well. Of your countless services you have rendered to me, this will give me the most pleasure').[109] Joke or not, it emphatically underlines the status differential inscribed in the correspondence.

On several occasions the juxtaposition of letters serves to highlight precisely the ambivalence of Tiro's position, as a free(d) citizen but forever an (ex-)slave. The (imaginary) thrashing of Tiro by Quintus is picked up in the very next letter — we have no idea how close in date they actually were — where in the first sentence Quintus refers to the 'thrashing' for his 'laziness' which Tiro, so he claims, had given *him*: *mirificam mi* uerberationem cessationis *epistula dedisti* ('You have given me an amazing thrashing for my idleness — by post!').[110] Does this collocation serve to draw the sting of Quintus (mock) aggression against Tiro? Or does it rather emphasise the fact that a (metaphorical) 'thrashing' has very different connotations when applied to ex-slave and a free-born senator? No less strikingly, the letter which follows the manumission letter in the manuscript collection, though it was probably written about eight years later, offers some telling glosses on Tiro's freedom. Starting from a joke that Tiro is now himself planning a collection of his own letters (what better parade of his citizenly status could there be?), Cicero continues by taking issue with him on a tricky point of linguistic usage. But what word is it that Tiro has been misapplying? Inevitably perhaps, it is *fideliter* (faithfully) — when *fides*, of course, was the moral quality that underlay the obligations owed by the freedman to his patron.[111] Sincere affection and care there may have been here; but they do not escape the language of subordination — which stalks (and is shown to stalk) every letter of *Ad Fam.* 16.

So far I have discussed this book as if it were a book 'about' slavery. But this is an oversimplification. At the same time, *Ad Fam.* 16 is a book about Cicero himself, about his political role in the Republic, about the loss of liberty that marked the advent of autocracy at Rome. The Roman

---

[109] Letter 3.3 (= 16.1.3); see also Letter 6.3 (= 16.4.3), Letter 7.1 (= 16.6.1).

[110] 16.27.1.

[111] 16.17.1. *uideo quid agas; tuas quoque epistulas uis referri in uolumina. sed heus tu, qui* κανών *esse meorum scriptorum soles, unde illud tam* ἄκυρον *'ualetudini fideliter inseruiendo'? unde in istum locum 'fideliter' uenit? cui uerbo domicilium est proprium in officio, migrationes in alienum multae,* ' I see what you're up to! You want *your* letters put into rolls too. But hang on, you yardstick as ever of all that I write, where did you pick up such a solecism as 'being a faithful slave to my health'? How does 'faithful' come into this sort of context? That word is properly at home where duty is concerned, but it often takes a trip where it doesn't belong.'

imagination constantly worked *with* slavery as a model and metaphor for other relationships and institutions; Roman slavery was, in the anthropological truism, 'good to think with'. Here we find the fate of the state mapped on to the fate of the slave; and Cicero himself figured as a man who could free his Tiro (to rounds of applause), but was forced to look on while the state itself lost its liberty. Or so we will conclude if we attend carefully to the order of the letters as they are arranged in the manuscripts of this book.

We have already glimpsed some strong principles of arrangement in *Ad Fam.* 16. The manuscript order sets the letters in three groups: a central set of five, focusing on Tiro's manumission, framed by two sets of 11 letters — from 50–49 BC on the one hand, 45–44 on the other. The opening letter highlights the *humanitas* and *suauitas* of Tiro. Equally emphatically the closing letter from Quintus to Tiro sets the freedman centre-stage; the very last words of the book run:[112]

> ego uos a. d. III K. uidebo tuosque oculos, etiam si te ueniens in medio foro uidero, dissauiabor. me ama. uale.

> I shall see the whole family on the 30th and kiss your eyes to bits, even if the first time I catch sight of you is in the middle of the Forum. With love. Take care.

We leave Tiro, in other words, at the heart of Roman political action — though, as ever, there is a sting in the tail. *Dissauiabor* is doing heavy duty. It clearly echoes the *suauitas* of the book's opening; but it also raises the question of what kind of kisses Quintus is anticipating. The Latin language of kissing is often caught on the cusp: evoking *both* the customary and public mode of greeting (*in medio foro*) between elite males, the kisses of male bonding, *and* at the same time the erotic embraces, mouth-to-mouth-to-eyes (*oculos*), that characterise desire for one's love object, male or female.[113] Here we must wonder whether our last glimpse of Tiro is not so much as the politically active citizen in his Forum, greeting and being greeted by Quintus

---

[112] 16.27.2.

[113] The terminology of kissing in Latin is thoroughly discussed by P. Moreau, 'Osculum, basium, suavium', *Revue de philologie* 52 (1978) 87–97 (who clearly demonstrates — even if this is not exactly what he intends — the cultural importance of the erotic ambiguity of the Roman kiss). A classic instance is Catullus 79, on which see M. B. Skinner, 'Pretty Lesbius', *Transactions of the American Philological Association* 112 (1982) 197–208. Quintus' words, in fact, echo Catullus 9 — the greeting to Veranius, *os oculosque suauiabor*. The compound *dissauiabor* is unique in surviving Latin — unless (and this would be a loaded echo) it is to be restored in one of Fronto's letters, *Ad Ant. Imp.* 3.3.

in the time-honoured way, but as the erotic plaything of his master, the *puer delicatus*, the object of desire — conjuring yet another aspect of the subordination of the slave.[114]

But the ordering and selection of the letters in *Ad Fam.* 16 has wider implications than this. Cicero and Tiro did presumably write to each other at other times; Tiro's archive presumably included many more documents than those we have here. Whoever edited the book (Tiro or not) has chosen three groups of correspondence, drawn from three distinct periods, each one of enormous significance in the history and the breakdown of the Republic. The years 45–44 saw the assassination of Caesar in the name of 'liberty' and the slide into the civil war which would finish the 'free' Republic for good; 50–49 marked the onset of the civil war between Julius Caesar and Pompey, and the establishment of Caesar's dictatorship; 53 was a year of anarchy and cataclysmic Roman defeat at the battle of Carrhae (at the moment of Tiro's manumission, the state had no consuls — they were only elected in July of that year, under the threat of Pompey taking sole control of Rome); while Caesar's own grip on Gaul was under threat of widespread revolts, and Vercingetorix was just round the corner. We are surely being asked to reflect on how the private story of slavery and manumission relates to the public crises of the state.

It relates quite explicitly in fact. The first group of 11 letters is largely concerned, as I have noted, with Tiro's illness; though in the last two the focus changes. In the tenth letter[115] the first paragraph contains the characteristic expressions of Cicero's anxiety for Tiro's condition: a certain optimism that his malarial fever is now recurring less frequently; firm instructions not to risk his health on a dangerous sea-crossing. But this moves directly on to a discussion of Roman politics and the 'flame of civil conflict or rather war' which was raging in the city. Now we find that the state is just as sick as Tiro — a point underlined by Cicero's continued use of the language of medicine: *cui* [sc. *flammae ciuilis discordiae*] *cum cuperem* mederi *et, ut arbitror, possem, cupiditates certorum hominum ... impedimento mihi fuerunt.* ('I should have liked to find a remedy for it [sc. the inflammation of civil war], and I reckon I could have, but the lust for power of particular individuals... got in my way').[116] The final letter in this sequence reverses that order: the details of Tiro's recuperation and plans to rejoin Cicero bring

---

[114] See Fitzgerald (n. 93) 51–5; C. Williams, *Roman Homosexuality: Ideologies of Masculinity in Classical Antiquity* (New York and Oxford 1999) 30–8.
[115] On the traditional numbering, 16.11.
[116] 16.11.2.

the letter to its close (*numquam sero te uenisse putabo, si* saluus *ueneris,* 'I shall never think you have come too late, so long as you come safe and sound');[117] but this time the very first sentence launches the concern for the safety (*salus*) of Cicero, his political allies and the state as a whole:[118]

> quo in discrimine uersetur *salus* mea et bonorum omnium atque uniuersae rei p. ex eo scire potes quod domos nostras et patriam ipsam uel diripiendam uel inflammandam reliquimus. in eum locum res deducta est ut, nisi qui deus uel casus aliquis subuenerit, *salui* esse nequeamus.

> Safety is in peril—for me, all patriots and the whole republic; and you can tell that from the fact that we have abandoned our homes and Rome itself for sacking or burning. Things have reached that point where we cannot be safe/saved, unless some god or stroke of luck comes to the rescue.

We are being asked to read, in other words, the sickness of Rome on and against the sickness of Tiro; the body politic against the body of the slave.

Tiro at least can be freed, much to the joy of his masters. The final section of the correspondence sees Tiro operating as a player in the Ciceronian family, through a series of apparently cross-cutting letters addressed to him (there is no pretence of chronological order) from Marcus Cicero, brother Quintus and Cicero junior. Life goes on: young Cicero uses him as a sounding board for his boasts of scholarly progress in Athens, while playfully (or nastily) teasing Tiro's pretensions at becoming a Roman landowner (*rusticus Romanus factus es,* 'well, you've turned into a regular Roman squire');[119] Cicero himself has payments to be settled;[120] there are the inevitable illnesses.[121] But all this is against the background of a state in disintegration. By the very end of the book, we have been sharply reminded that the end of the free Republic will also signal the end of Cicero himself, along with his brother.

The last two letters in the book are both written by Quintus, the one before by Cicero junior: in the characteristic triangulation that defines most letter exchange (*from* x *to* y *about* z), Cicero himself is now neither the writer nor the recipient, but the subject of his son's and brother's letters to Tiro—already either mythologised (as the renowned advocate) or marginalised:[122]

---

[117] On the traditional numbering, 16.12.6.
[118] 16.12.1.
[119] 16.21.7.
[120] 16.24.1.
[121] 16.18.1; 22.1.
[122] 16.27.1.

nam quae parcius frater perscripserat uerecundia uidelicet et properatione, ea tu
sine adsentatione ut erant ad me scripsisti et maxime de coss. designatis.

My brother's account was rather economical, through modesty presumably, and
being in a hurry. In your letter to me you told it as it was, without pandering, most
of all about the consuls designate.

The man who was once the most privileged witness of Roman politics is no
longer the man whose account you want to hear; while the reunion *in medio
foro* that is foretold in the very last lines of the very last letter is a reunion
between Quintus and Tiro, Cicero himself not in sight. But there are yet
more sinister overtones. The central section of the final letter discusses the
consuls for the next year:[123]

quos ego penitus noui libidinum et languoris effeminatissimi animi plenos; qui nisi
a gubernaculis recesserint, maximum ab uniuerso naufragio periculum est.
incredibile est, quae ego illos scio oppositis Gallorum castris in aestiuis fecisse,
quos ille latro, nisi aliquid firmius fuerit, societate uitiorum deleniet.

I know them to the core, saturated with the lusts and lassitude of minds that have
lost all manhood. Unless they leave the bridge, there is every risk of a total
shipwreck. It is unbelievable what I know they did on campaign, when the Gauls
were camped right opposite. Unless a stronger line is taken, that bandit will soften
them up in a partnership of vice.

Of course, as the editor must have known when he chose it to be the last
letter, Quintus' prediction came absolutely true: there was 'a total shipwreck'. But the 'bandit' whose figure lurks at the back of this account was to
have a particular role in the ruin of Cicero. For it can be none other than
Mark Antony, the man who not only ordered the murder of both Cicero and
Quintus, but had Cicero's head and hands pinned to the rostra in the forum;
the man with whom, in a letter placed only a little earlier in the sequence
(compression of chronology here makes a devastating point), Cicero had
vainly claimed never to have exchanged a cross word.[124]

The last letter in the last book of the *Letters to Friends* has already
written Cicero's end — months away though it still was. The only members
of the family displayed before us here who would survive the disintegration
of the state in civil war are Tiro himself and the insufferable (and in-
sufferably naive) Cicero junior. It would not have passed Roman readers by
that Cicero junior would in the end have last laugh over the bandit. When the
news of Antony's defeat at Actium came in 31 BC, it was young Cicero who

[123] 16.27.1.
[124] 16.23.2.

read out the dispatch — at the very rostra, as the historian Appian explicitly reminds us, where his father's head had been nailed.[125]

The new school of Classics and the old

Tyrrell-and-Purser's reading of Cicero's *Letters* was one of the most successful innovations ever in the history of classical scholarship. Of course, you can object to the limitations of their edition, its desperate chase (never quite) to keep up with the cutting-edge of German textual criticism, its slips of Latinity; or you can query, as I have, the whole basis of their approach to the correspondence. For all that, theirs was a bravura project which held out the promise of recreating a man's life history in letters, as well as a day-by-day commentary on the collapse of one of the most influential political regimes ever in western history. In fact, so completely have modern scholars internalised T.-P.'s chronological ordering of the collection and (consequently) the unimportance of the traditional book divisions that they do not even stop to reflect on what makes up a letter-book, and why. In the intense recent interest in the ideology of slavery, for example, no historian has thought to explore the only substantial group of letters we possess between master and (ex-)slave — beyond occasionally admiring their affectionate tone. In all the recent writing on ancient exile, no one has explored how *Ad Atticum* book 3, *as a book*, articulates a powerful version of exile *as a state of (not-)being*, rather than merely a piecemeal commentary on Cicero's own banishment. So completely has the traditional structure of the collection been effaced that there is now no available English translation that still preserves the letter-books as they were transmitted, via the manuscripts, from antiquity itself.

At the same time, it would hardly be an exaggeration to claim that the arrangement of the correspondence in its chronological order underlies the whole of the modern biographical tradition of Cicero, and the myth that he (and he alone in antiquity) is in some sense *knowable* to us. Biographies of Cicero are, to all intents and purposes, Tyrrell-and-Purser expanded; they depend on treating the correspondence as raw, unmediated documents — certainly not as part of an editorial construction, with a particular story to tell, and a particular axe to grind. In suggesting that — for all their undeniable success — we have lost more than we have gained in

---

[125] Appian, *B. Civ.* 4.51.

following Tyrrell-and-Purser so wholeheartedly, I am suggesting that the letters are worth much more than simply the raw material of biography; that we have a lot to learn from attending to the literary and historical story inscribed in the letter-books; and that we are missing out on much of the point of the whole collection, *as a collection* (or series of collections), if we do not take its traditional ordering seriously.

To claim, as I did at the opening of this chapter, that my approach is 'radically old-fashioned' is obviously to raise the question — just as Tyrrell himself did in the *Fortnightly Review* — of what counts as *new* or *old* in Classics. Is it a radical innovation to suggest taking the Ciceronian letter-books as books, and to read them with all the intensity and attention that we might devote to an Augustan poetry book? Or is it a nostalgic return to an old way of reading, a *re*-discovery of a lost tradition? Tyrrell's answer to this would be, I think, much the same as my own: that it is both. For at the heart of his sharp satire lies the idea that classical scholarship is always re-invention as much as invention, that novelty can always be seen in terms of tradition (and vice versa), and that what is to count as new or old is a question that Classics must always face (afresh). To cast Classics as a Dialogue of the Dead was not to consign it once and for all to Hades, but to remind us that an ongoing debate with the past lies at the very heart of Classics as a discipline.

The origins of this chapter go back a long way: to my PhD thesis (1981), supervised by John Crook, which first started me thinking (though on very different lines) about Cicero's letters. The (re-)thoughts offered here have been ably fostered by the other contributors to this volume, and (especially) by Michael Reeve, who read and improved the whole text. I am also grateful to John T(yrrell) Killen for keeping me straight on the Irish connection.

6
Discovery, autopsy and progress: Diocletian's jigsaw puzzles

M. H. Crawford

It is a commonplace that historical enquiry evolves as successive generations ask different questions, in a complex interplay between, on the one hand, the intellectual traditions in which individual historians have grown up, the different traditions that they discover, and the world as a whole in which they move; on the other hand, an ever greater body of knowledge and a wider range of historical tools. What I should like to explore here, by way of the particular example of the edicts of the Emperor Diocletian on maximum prices and on the coinage — the story of the discovery and study of their texts — is the impact on historical enquiry both of chance discoveries and of deliberate autopsy, going to see for oneself something that one does not understand.[1] We cannot, if we work on the ancient world, emulate Thucydides and write about what we have witnessed; but we can explore with our own eyes much of what moulded the societies we study and of what those societies created.

---

[1] Editions and translations of the prices edict: Th. Mommsen, in *CIL* iii.2 (Berlin 1873) pp. 824–41; Th. Mommsen, in *CIL* iii Suppl. 1 (Berlin 1902) pp. 1926–53 (= Th. Mommsen and H. Blümner, *Der Maximaltarif des Diocletian* (Berlin 1893, repr. 1958) 3–50); E. R. Graser, 'The edict of Diocletian on maximum prices', in T. Frank, *Economic Survey of Ancient Rome* vol. 5 (Baltimore 1940) 305–421; S. Lauffer, *Diokletians Preisedikt* (Berlin 1971); R. and F. Naumann, *Der Rundbau in Aezani, mit dem Preisedikt des Diokletian und das Gebäude mit dem Edikt in Stratonikeia* (*Deutsches archäologisches Institut: Istanbuler Mitteilungen* Beiheft 10, Tübingen 1973); M. Giacchero, *Edictum Diocletiani et Collegarum de Pretiis Rerum Venalium* vols. 1–2 (Genoa 1974); C. M. Roueché, with contributions by J. M. Reynolds, *Aphrodisias in Late Antiquity* (London 1989) 265–318.

i

Scholars of the fifteenth and most of the sixteenth century would of course not have been prepared by the literary sources with which they were familiar for anything like the edict on maximum prices of Diocletian, had a fragment of one of the inscribed texts come to light, though we shall see that, when the edict *was* discovered, its impact was independent of any literary association. It was not till 1615 that anyone would have had easy access to the Fasti of Hydatius, with their charming notice that in AD 302 'the emperors ordered there to be cheapness'; and the *Caesars* of Aurelius Victor was published only in 1579, allowing the discovery that 'anxious and careful thought was taken for the supply of the city of Rome and the well-being of those receiving salaries, and by rewarding the well-behaved and on the other hand by punishing all criminals zeal for virtue was encouraged'. A rather different spin was revealed in 1691, with the publication of John Malalas, who has an undated notice that, at Antioch, Diocletian 'gave everyone measures for corn and all other commodities on sale, so that none of the market traders should be intimidated by the soldiers'.[2]

Early scholars might indeed have reflected that they knew of no general attempt to control prices; and they might have remembered the story in the *Golden Ass* of Apuleius, highlighting the different approach to price control at the local level in the Greek and Roman worlds: the hero and narrator of the story, from the Roman colony of Corinth, attempted in a nearby city, whose Greek structures were evidently untouched by Roman rule, to buy some fish; he and the vendor agreed on the price and the fish changed hands; at that point, a local official discovered that the price paid was above that authorised, and to the amazement of the narrator dashed the fish underfoot and returned him his money (1.24). Renaissance lawyers might have thought of texts such as *Digest* 18.1.71, where Antoninus and Verus rule very firmly that the measures and prices of wine are in the power of the parties to a contract. So what was a Roman Emperor up to, attempting to control prices? The answer to that question may remain not altogether satisfactorily answered;[3] but we shall see as the story unfolds that Diocletian made remarkable, if not wholly well directed, efforts to ensure that people knew that he was up to something.

---

[2] Th. Mommsen (ed.), *Chronica Minora* 1 (*Monumenta Germaniae Historica: Auctores Antiquissimi* 9, Berlin 1892) 230; Aurelius Victor, *De Caesaribus* 39, 45; John Malalas 307 (12, 38), trans. E. and M. Jeffreys and R. Scott (Melbourne 1986).

[3] For a preliminary analysis of price control in the ancient world, see M. H. Crawford, *Classical Review* n.s. 25 (1975) 276–9, reviewing S. Lauffer, *Diokletians Preisedikt* (Berlin 1971).

One of the most inveterate explorers of the Greek East and recorders of its inscribed monuments was also the first, Cyriac of Ancona:[4] a sequence of journeys, primarily as a merchant, began with Egypt, Rhodes, Chios, Samos, Icaria, Miletus, Cyprus, Syria, Sicily and Dalmatia in 1412–1413 and ended with the Peloponnese in 1447–1448. In contrast to the Low Countries diplomat Busbecq, to whose travels in the Ottoman Empire Europe perhaps owed its acquaintance with the tulip, and the scholarly world certainly owed its knowledge of the text of the *Res gestae* of Augustus,[5] Cyriac's journeys took him to several of the places from which texts of the prices edict are now known, such as Delphi, Thebes, Athens and Samos. The prices edict is by a comfortable margin not only the longest inscription known from the Greco-Roman world, it is also the best attested, with one part or another of the edict known from between 42 and 44 separate sites.[6] Yet not a single fragment appears in the material transcribed by Cyriac. It is of course always possible that a fragment of the list of prices was seen by him without its catching his eye; and the story of the discovery of the edict might have been very different if any of those who travelled in the Greek East after the publication of Guillaume Budé's *De asse* or Leonardo Porzio's (Leonardus de Portis') *De sestertio*, the former certainly, the latter probably, of 1514, both dealing with Roman monetary practice, had had Cyriac's voracious interest in antiquity.

Nor, when a text was discovered, did it immediately make much impact, despite the fact that the text in question offered, nearly complete, both the

---

[4] E. W. Bodnar, *Cyriacus of Ancona and Athens* (*Collection Latomus* 43, Brussels 1960); E. W. Bodnar and C. Mitchell, *Cyriacus of Ancona's Journeys in the Propontis and the Northern Aegean, 1444–1445* (*Memoirs of the American Philosophical Society* 112, 1976); J. Colin, *Cyriaque d'Ancône* (Paris 1981) 561–99; C. Mitchell and E. W. Bodnar (eds.), *Vita Viri Clarissimi et Famosissimi Kyriaci Anconitani* (*Transactions of the American Philosophical Society* 86, 4, 1996).

[5] *CIL* iii, pp. 769–99; Z. R. W. M. von Martels, *Augerius Gislenius Busbequius. Leven en werk van de Keizerlijke gezant aan het hof van Süleyman de Grote* (1989).

[6] Finds of fragments of the prices edict (from Lauffer (n. 1), unless otherwise indicated): Egypt (nn. 19–21 below). Achaea: Acraephia (*Bulletin de Correspondance Hellénique* 15 (1891) 661: 'très court fragment'; it may be lost or it may be the fragment in the museum in Thebes), Aedepsus (now also in E. J. Doyle, *Hesperia* 45 (1976) 77–97), Aegeira, Argos, Asine, Atalante, Athens, Boiae (*Bull. Ép.* (1974) 247; G. Steinhauer, *Arch. Eph.* 131 (1992) 165–77), Carystus, Cleitor, Corinth (E. Sironen, *Hesperia* 61 (1992) 223–4), Delphi (add J. Bingen, *Bulletin de Correspondance Hellénique* 108 (1984) 543–4), Elatea, Geronthrae, Gytheum (add G. Steinhauer, *Arch. Eph.* 131 (1992) 163–5), Lebadea, Megalopolis, Megara, Oetylus, Pharae, Plataea, Scolus, Tamynae (now also in E. J. Doyle, *Hesperia* 45 (1976) 77–97), Tegea, Thebes, Thelpusa (*Bull. Ép.* (1974) 82), Thespiae, Troezen. Caria and Phrygia: Aezani, Aphrodisias, Bargylia (?), Eumenea, Halicarnassus, Heraclea Salbace, Iasos (G. Pugliese Carratelli, *Parola del Passato* 40 (1985) 381–3; F. Trotta, *Parola del Passato* 56 (2001) 9–14), Mylasa, Sandikli near Eucarpia, Stratonicea, Synnada. Crete: Cnossus, Cnossus or Chersonesus (G. Preuss, *Zeitschrift für Papyrologie und Epigraphik* 80 (1990) 189–202), Hierapytna. Cyrenaica: Ptolemais. For the Pettorano, Samos and Odessus fragments, see n. 27 below.

preface and chapters I–XII of the list of prices, in the current numbering. It was William Sherard who found it, at Stratonicea, near modern Eskihisar in south-west Turkey (Fig. 6.1), inscribed on one of the outside walls of a building which is probably the Bouleuterion, the council-chamber (Fig. 6.2). We shall return both to the extent of the edict covered by the Stratonicea text and to the choice of location for its engraving. William Sherard was British consul in Smyrna, and took advantage of his position to explore Asia Minor, in 1705, twice in 1709, and in 1716;[7] a number of manuscript records of his visits to Stratonicea survive;[8] and the inscription was in due course mentioned briefly by Edmund Chishull, in his *Antiquitates Asiaticae Christianam Aeram Ante-cedentes* of 1728 (p. 165), a work which largely drew on Sherard's copies.[9] But the actual text of the prices edict did not see the light of day, despite the fact that Sherard himself had clearly seen the importance of the inscription:

> This Latin inscription is on an old building at Eskihizar, the first part in the middle, the others on the prices, on the right and left hand. At the foot of the wall, about the midst of it, grows a large elm, which if I return I will get cut down and copy the part it covers and is underground. (BL, Add. MS 10101, f. 140[v])

The discovery generated some excitement outside Great Britain, but even there interest in the end fizzled out. One of William Sherard's correspondents was Gisbert Cuper (Gisbertus Cuperus), an assiduous collector of inscrip-tions, as emerges from his earlier correspondence with Antonio Maglia-becchi. Cuper's early source in Smyrna was Daniel Cosson, about whose discoveries Cuper writes in 1687, 1690 and 1692.[10] But a later source was Sherard, and on 8 March 1712 Cuper wrote to J. J. Scheuchzer:[11]

> I've just this moment received a letter from Smyrna, from the British consul, as he is called, including ... an early inscription, in which there are the prices of goods for sale, and which survives at Stratonicea ...

---

[7] In 1824, Leake gives the date of the first journey, with A. Picenini, as 1709, misunderstanding Chishull; in 1827, he gives the date as 1705, correctly; in 1827, he gives the date of the third journey, with Samuel Lisle, as 1716, correctly, against 1718 of Chishull.

[8] See M. H. Crawford, 'William Sherard and Diocletian's prices edict' (forthcoming).

[9] BL, 584.k.2, is a copy with additional material of Chishull, some already printed; the volume was passed to Lord Sandys, presumably in the hope that he would see to the publication of a revised edition, then to the British Museum on 15 April 1785.

[10] *Clarorum Belgarum ad Ant. Magliabechium ... epistolae* vol. 1 (Florence 1745) 8, 15–16, 26; see also vol. 2, 303–18, for Cosson's letters to Magliabecchi, also including texts of inscriptions; see also *Memoria Cossoniana* (Leiden 1695).

[11] J. G. Schelhorn, 'Sylloge epistolarum mutuarum Jo. Jac. Scheuchzeri et Gisb. Cuperi ...', in *Amoenitates historiae ecclesiasticae et litterariae* vols. 1–2 (Frankfurt and Leipzig 1737–1738) vol. 1, 754–1051, at 987.

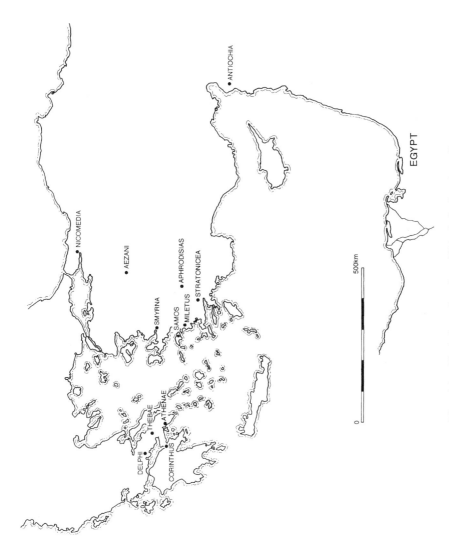

Map 6.1.   Find-sites of copies of Diocletian's price edict.

Cuper goes on to quote the price for a *fasianus pastus* and a *fasiana pasta*; and similar information went on 1 May 1712 to M. Veyssière de la Croze and on 16 April 1712 to Abbé Bignon.[12] We know also from the Sherard manuscripts that on his way home he showed his material to A. M. Salvini in Florence; but I know of no evidence that Salvini diffused the knowledge that he had acquired in commenting on Sherard's material.

Neither Cuper nor anyone else yet made the connection between the inscription and Lactantius, whose *On the Deaths of the Persecutors*, devoted to the horrible ends of Diocletian and the other authors of the Great Persecution (AD 303–311) had been published for the first time in 1679. Reading it attentively, scholars would have noted the following remark (7.6–7):

> Although he himself brought about massive shortages as a result of his various iniquities, he set out to introduce a law on the prices of commodities for sale. So much blood (of all those denounced by informers) was shed because of things that were trivial and cheap, and things for sale disappeared from the market as a result of fear, and the shortages became much worse, until the law was abandoned by the sheer force of events, after many had been killed.

Yet the work had attracted the interest of the young Cuper, who wrote a series of notes, completed in 1689 and published in 1692.[13]

It was not until the rediscovery of the Stratonicea text, apparently by William Richard Hamilton in 1801, that the prices edict became part of scholarly discourse. The period was of course one of intense competition between France and Great Britain for territory and power; competition for antiquities was not far behind in intensity; and scholarly emulation had its part to play too. Hamilton had been in Egypt in 1800, two years after the decisive encounter between Nelson and the French fleet at the Battle of the Nile; the victory in due course brought the Rosetta Stone as war booty to London, instead of to Paris. Undeterred, Napoleon turned his attention to Italy; and nine years later the arrest of Pius VII was followed by the temporary transfer of a large part of his collections, library and archives to Paris.[14]

---

[12] *Lettres de critique ... par feu Monsieur Gisbert Cuper* (Amsterdam 1743) 109 (not 199, as *CIL*) and 286.

[13] *Lucii Caecilii Firmiani Lactantii de mortibus persecutorum* (Utrecht 1692); also in *Lucii Caecilii Firmiani Lactantii opera omnia* vol. 2 (Paris 1748).

[14] Ch. Saunier, 'Les conquêtes artistiques de la révolution et de l'empire et les réponses des alliés en 1815 (8ᵉ et dernier article)', *Gazette des Beaux Arts* 25 (1901) 244–59; C. Gould, *Trophy of Conquest: the Musée Napoleon and the Creation of the Louvre* (London 1965); *Dominique-Vivant Denon* (Paris 1999); M. A. Dupuy, *Vivant Denon ... Correspondance* vols.1–2 (Paris 1999).

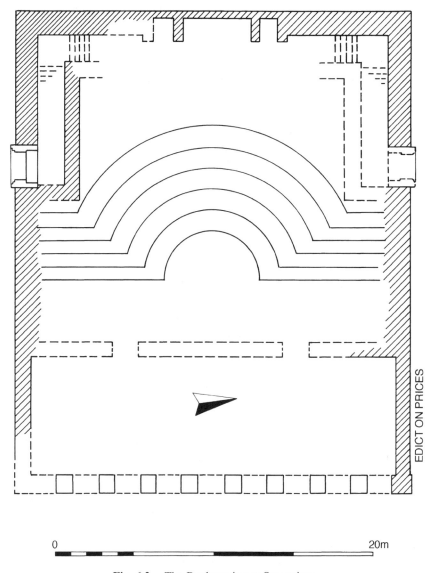

EDICT ON PRICES

0 20m

Fig. 6.2. The Bouleuterion at Stratonicea.

A mystery hangs over the rediscovery of the Stratonicea text. When William M. Leake came in 1824 to publish his *Journal of a Tour in Asia Minor*, containing 'the substance of the memoir in R. Walpole, *Collection of Memoirs on Greece and Asia Minor*,[15] he claimed that 'among modern travellers, two only have yet traversed Asia Minor in various directions for exploratory purposes: Paul Lucas in the years 1705, 1706 and 1715, and Capt. Macdonald Kinneir in the years 1813 and 1814' (p. vi). The failure to mention Sherard, whose work as we shall see was known to Leake, is not surprising, since Sherard did not record the geographical information relevant to the map which Leake included in his book; but Leake depended for his knowledge of Caria precisely on William Richard Hamilton, who is cited but once, for an inscription of Amyzon.[16] And when Leake published the Stratonicea text, he went back to the MS of Sherard (pp. 229–30, 329–38), although he knew that in the meanwhile William Bankes had made a transcription, perhaps better. There was the further problem that the Stratonicea text does not — and perhaps never did — include the imperial titulatures, which led Leake to attribute the edict to Theodosius I.

A partial copy of the Sherard transcription had been acquired in 1822 by Carl Otfried Müller, which was eventually used by Spangenberg in his posthumous publication of Christian Gottlob Haubold's *Antiquitatis Romanae Monumenta Legalia extra Libros Juris Romani sparsa* (Berlin 1830) pp. 268–79, the first such collection of legal sources outside the codification of Justinian since 1583 and the predecessor of the similar handbooks by K. G. Bruns and his successors.[17] Spangenberg also used Leake's *Journal* of 1824, correcting it from Müller's notes, and hence knew about, but did not have access to, the transcription by William Bankes; he also knew about the article of Moreau de Jonnès, to which we shall come in a moment.

The Stratonicea text, then, had been seen and transcribed by Colonel William J. Bankes in 1817, and privately printed as *Facsimile of a Roman tariff fixing a maximum of price for all manner of commodities*, whence it was in due course re-published by L. Cardinali, in *Memorie romane di antichità* 2 (1825) pp. 27–84, 'Intorno al marmo stratonicense', correctly attributing the edict to Diocletian and citing *CIL* vi, 1785, by way of comparison.[18]

But it was a quite different text, from Egypt, that lay behind the early nineteenth-century explosion of interest in the edict. It was bought from Egypt in 1807 by François Sallier, and given to the Museum of Aix in

[15] In fact *Memoirs Relating to European and Asiatic Turkey* vol. 1 (London 1817, 2nd ed. London 1818), vol. 2 (London 1820).

[16] For Hamilton, see, provisionally, L. Robert, *Fouilles d'Amyzon en Carie* vol. 1 (Paris 1983) 44–6, at 44 n. 9: 'Leake n'a pas voyagé en Carie.'

[17] *Briefwechsel zwischen August Boeckh und Karl Otfried Müller* (Leipzig 1883) 71–97; M. H. Crawford (ed.), *Roman Statutes* (London 1996) 2.

[18] Also in *Atti Acc. Romana Arch.* 2 (1825) 681–732 (non vidi).

1822.[19] The stone had apparently already been seen by Gaetano Marini in 1810, and it was noticed after its arrival in the museum by de St-Vincens and then copied by Marcellin de Fonsolocombe; it was also copied by L. Vescovali, in 1824, who furnished transcriptions to Leake and Girolamo Amati. Vescovali also came to London on behalf of Amati, who had heard of the journey of Bankes through Bartolomeo Borghesi, and saw the Harleian MS of William Sherard and the BM copy of the publication by Bankes. All three, de Fonsolocombe, Leake and Amati, then published a composite version of the edict in the same year, 1827 (Amati the preface only).[20] It was Marcellin de Fonsolocombe who first saw the importance of the reference to the edict by Lactantius, then Angelo Mai, deriving his text from Cardinale and Amati, perhaps citing Lactantius independently and also citing *Panegyrici Latini* XI (III) (Mamertini Genethliacus Maximiani Augusti) 15.[21]

The interest aroused provoked and informed further exploration, which in turn generated, relatively speaking, a flood of material. When Mommsen came to publish his first edition in 1851, he was able to draw on the Stratonicea and Egypt texts, but also on transcriptions of fragments from Aezani (chapters VII–X, 8, corresponding to Blocks 1 (part), 2, and 3 (part), in the numeration of R. and F. Naumann), Mylasa, Geronthrae and Carystus; Aezani, Mylasa and Geronthrae had been transcribed by Le Bas, who had also re-transcribed Stratonicea, Carystus by the architect E. Schaubert.[22] When Waddington saw to the posthumous publication of the material transcribed by Le Bas, he was able to add evidence from Megara and Lebadea,

---

[19] O. Cavalier, 'Le cabinet Sallier d'Aix-en-Provence', in M. Fano Santi (ed.), *Le collezioni di antichità nella cultura antiquaria europea* (*Riv. Arch.* Suppl. 21, Rome 1999) 91–9, provides a rather chaotic account of the Egyptian interests of Sallier.

[20] Marcellin de Fonsolocombe, *Recueil de mémoires ... de la Société Académique d'Aix* 3 (1827) 60–150, mentioning the visit of Marini (= *Mémoire sur le préambule d'un édit de l'empereur Dioclétien relatif au prix des denrées dans les provinces de l'Empire Romain* (Paris 1829) (non vidi)); W. M. Leake, 'On an edict of Diocletian fixing a maximum of prices throughout the Roman Empire, AD 303'; *Trans. Roy. Soc. Lit.* 1.1 (1827) 181–204; G. Amati, 'La grande iscrizione di Stratonicea' (preface only), *Giornale Arcadico* 33 (1827), 41–65; note also a report of a lecture to the Institut in Paris by Moreau de Jonnès, in *Morgenblatt für gebildete Stände* 21, 99 (1827) 394–5; 100 (1827) 399. For Amati, see M. Buonocore, *Codices Vaticani Latini 9734–9782. Codices Amatiani* (Vatican City 1988); G. Bevilacqua, *Antiche iscrizioni augurali e magiche dai codici di Girolamo Amati* (Rome 1991); for Vescovali, see Bevilacqua, 10–11; I should like to thank Marco Buonocore for assuring me that the edict has left no trace in Marini's epigraphic MSS.

[21] A. Mai, *Scriptorum veterum nova collectio* vol. 5 (Rome 1831) 296–315.

[22] *Ber. Sächs. Ges. Wiss.* Phil.-Hist. Kl. 3 (1851) 1–62 = (in part) 'Über das Edict Diokletians de pretiis rerum venalium vom Jahre 301', *Gesammelte Schriften* 2 (1905) 292–311; 383–400 = 'Nachtrag zu dem Edict Diocletians de pretiis rerum venalium', 312–22.

both from transcriptions by François Lenormant.[23] For his second edition, in the third volume of the *Corpus Inscriptionum Latinarum* of 1873, Mommsen used also material from Thebes, transcribed by a local schoolmaster, A. Mustoxydis (Moustoxydes), and from Gytheum, transcribed by Paul Foucart.

By this time, nineteen chapters were known, as opposed to the 35 plus one of the edition by Siegfried Lauffer of 1971, just under a century later. By now also, certain patterns had become clear: the preface was always in Latin, the prices from the province of Achaea were in Greek, from elsewhere in Latin; and there were no texts that had been inscribed in the West. It was also clear that every new text that turned up might improve or supplement what was already known, and the concern for the next century was essentially with building up as complete a composite version of the edict as possible, as well as — of course — with translating, understanding and using the evidence that it provided. This process rapidly showed that Lactantius was wrong to claim that the edict covered only things that were trivial and cheap: it covered purple, gold, silk, lions for the games and much more besides.

ii

In 1970, an earthquake struck Aezani and neighbouring regions of the Anatolian plateau. It brought down the mosque, which had been built conveniently on the foundation of the Roman Macellum (meat-market), on the outside of which the edict had been inscribed, and in the wall of which Le Bas had been able to see part of the text (Fig. 6.3). The German team already working at Aezani set out to reconstruct the Macellum, publishing also the text which adorned it, promptly, but with a knowledge both of Latin epigraphy and of Diocletian that was unfortunately limited. Their text was taken over without further investigation by Marta Giacchero, including such curious phrases as *denarium numeticus* (= *denarium unum et uictus*).[24] Their publication also included an imperfect transcription of a second text, at the end of the edict, in Greek, in an area where all the texts, including the Aezani text itself, were entirely in Latin.

A spot of autopsy seemed called for, undertaken in and after 1974 — though if Joyce Reynolds and I had realised the privations involved, we

---

[23] *Voyage archéologique en Grèce et en Asie Mineure*, Inscriptions, Tome III (Paris 1870, repr. Hildesheim and New York 1972), vol. 1, 167–82, no. 535; vol. 2, 145–85, no. 535.

[24] See M. H. Crawford, *Classical Review* n.s. 27 (1977) 316, reviewing M. Giacchero (n. 1).

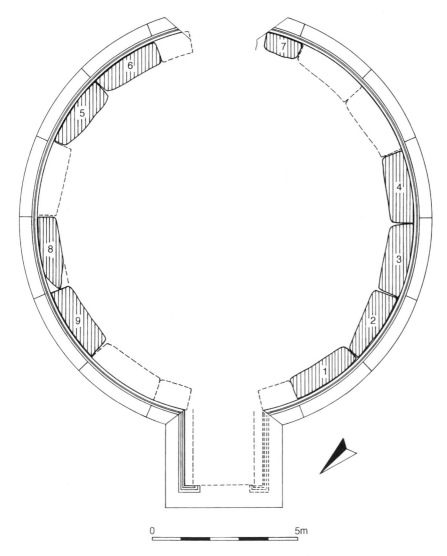

Fig. 6.3. The Macellum at Aezani.

might have had second thoughts: on the Anatolian plateau in late September, where the temperature dropped dramatically as soon as the sun went down; during Ramadan in a tiny village, where not even a cup of tea was available until that same moment of sunset.

The Greek text was established as an edict of a governor, Fulvius Asticus, who now turned out to have been governor of both Phrygia and

Caria.[25] This fact provoked further reflection on the pattern of occurrence of texts of the edict on stone: the forty or so texts known turned out to have been put up in the provinces of just five men, the governors of Egypt, Caria and Phrygia combined, Achaea, Crete and Cyrenaica.[26] Not only a mere five men, but all of them in the East. Of them, only the governor of Achaea had had the bright idea of translating the list of prices into the language of his charges, though Fulvius Asticus had explained in Greek what he thought the edict was about, capturing rather well at any rate some of the themes of the preface.

The pattern now revealed threw into sharper focus the evidence of Lactantius, based as he was in Nicomedia in Bithynia. No friend of the Tetrarchs he may have been (see p. 150 above), but it would be excessively sceptical to doubt his testimony that the edict was published and enforced in Nicomedia. Not a single inscribed text, however, has yet turned up there or anywhere else in Bithynia.[27]

The Aezani text also provided a second case, alongside Stratonicea, of the edict having been inscribed on an existing monument, and there was soon to be a third.[28] Aphrodisias in Caria had been known as one of the sites where the edict had been inscribed since the journey of (J.) W. Kubitschek and W. Reichel in 1893, with further fragments discovered by the expedition of Giulio Jacopi in 1937; but it was the excavations undertaken by Kenan Erim from 1961 that generated a flood of material which hoisted Aphrodisias to the same level as Stratonicea, Egypt and Aezani in terms of amount of

---

[25] J. M. Reynolds and M. H. Crawford, 'The publication of the prices edict: a new inscription from Aezani', *Journal of Roman Studies* 65 (1975) 160–3; 'The Aezani copy of the prices edict', *Zeitschrift für Papyrologie und Epigraphik* 26 (1977) 125–51; 34 (1979) 163–210.

[26] I have not seen the stone in Aix since becoming interested in these problems; but Marcellin de Fonsolocombe claimed that it was similar to 'des bas-reliefs égyptiens que possède M. Sallier'. The copy from Cyrenaica is from Ptolemais, the capital of the province known after Diocletian as Libya Superior; it remains possible that although Libya Superior was clearly intended to be separate from Crete, the two happened to be united under one man in AD 301.

[27] For the view that the Pettorano fragment is *verschleppt* from Greece, see M. H. Crawford, 'The Pettorano fragment of the prices edict', *Athenaeum* n.s. 62 (1984) 315; the reply by M. Guarducci, 'Ancora una volta sul frammento dell'*edictum de pretiis* di Diocleziano trovato a Pettorano sul Gizio', *Athenaeum*, n.s. 63 (1985) 491–4, revealed that the attribution of the fragment to Carrara marble was based on sight of a diminutive splinter, hence worthless. Marco Buonocore informs me of the view of Patrizio Pensabene, endorsing that of Lucos Cozza and Amanda Claridge, that the marble is Greek. See Addendum, p. 163 below. The fragments from Odessus and Samos may similarly be regarded as having wandered from their original homes: S. Corcoran, *The Empire of the Tetrarchs* (2nd ed., Oxford 2000) 229–30.

[28] The Macellum of Aezani was idiosyncratically reconstructed by R. and F. Naumann, and the blocks numbered, in an order other than that of the text on them.

preserved text. The Aphrodisias text also often made intelligible passages which were wrongly engraved in other texts. And it was Aphrodisias that produced what is so far the only text of the Diocletianic currency revaluation edit (or rather edicts, as further discovery has established).[29]

Aphrodisias and Aezani between them also made it clear that we possess the end of the edict: a chapter on transport prices at Aezani is followed by the edict of Fulvius Asticus; and the same chapter at Aphrodisias is followed by *FELICITER MVLTIS ANNIS*, the Roman equivalent of 'Long live our noble Queen.'[30] There is then at Aphrodisias a revised chapter on transport prices, the initial letters of the lines of which are on the extreme right edge of the last preserved block at Aezani. By way of contrast, we possess only the first block of the Egypt text; and at Stratonicea, lassitude seems to have set in half-way through chapter XII, *De materiis*, 'On wood': after line 11, *materiae fraxineae*, 'Ash wood', the text just stops, although there was a great deal of empty wall still available.

We now have, then, what the advisers of Diocletian and his colleagues thought should be the maxima in the case of some 1,500 commodities in AD 301. It is not, however, with the importance of these prices for the economic history of the Roman world that I am here concerned, nor with the question of whether the edict 'worked';[31] rather with the reflections provoked by the interplay between the process of attempting to understand the publication and engraving of the edict and the progress of discovery and exploration.

What was the text engraved on at Aphrodisias? Leaving aside pieces rather obviously re-used, for instance in converting the Temple of Aphrodite into a church, it was early apparent that there was a concentration of find-spots in front of the Basilica; and Charlotte Roueché formulated the hypothesis that the text had been inscribed on its façade. Unfortunately, the enthusiasm of the excavators for uncovering ever more of the city and its monuments was not matched (except in the case of sculpture) by an interest in understanding what had been discovered. And the engraving of the edict at Aphrodisias is precisely a case where the monument cannot be fully understood without the text, or the text without the monument.

The blocks on which the text is inscribed have what appears at first sight to be an exuberant variety of mouldings; and, in consequence, the correct

---

[29] S. Corcoran (n. 24) 134–5, 177–8, 346.

[30] C. M. Roueché, with contributions by J. M. Reynolds, *Aphrodisias in Late Antiquity* (London 1989) 305.

[31] See, provisionally, J. Ermatinger, *The Economic Reforms of Diocletian* (St Katharinen 1996), *discutibile*, as my Italian friends say.

solution was excluded in exchange for the view that 'the inscribed panels ... were part of a balustrade in front of a large basilica which was probably used by the governor of Phrygia/Caria', with the smooth backs of the panels visible from behind the balustrade, rather than from within the Basilica.[32] The correct interpretation would have been impossible without the concern of Bert Smith and Chris Ratté for every aspect of the Basilica, which they are preparing to publish (Fig. 6.4). The mouldings turn out to be just what one would expect for the different levels of such a building: the dado blocks have mouldings at top and bottom only, the upper and lower panels of the middle range have mouldings all round, as do the panels at the attic level; in the middle range, pilasters divide two of the intercolumniations vertically; at the attic level, the moulding is inset at the top around the capitals of the col-umns; the upper panels of the middle range are thinner than the lower, except at each end of the façade. Against this background, gratitude for the work of the century from 1873 to 1971 in creating a composite version of the edict is appropriate, since almost every fragment from Aphrodisias can be placed in sequence and hence in place on the façade of the Basilica.

The interplay is in fact between a monument of known type, with some idiosyncrasies, and of known size, with some gaps, and a text whose content and order are largely established, but where there are some lacunae. And the process of reconstruction in tandem of façade and text not only shows that, apart from a few lines, there is now nothing missing of the edict; it also forces us back to reflection on patterns of diffusion and display.

iii

What then are the consequences of the story of the interplay between dis-covery and autopsy that I have tried to trace?

1. It is apparent that the engravers at Aphrodisias were fairly relaxed about the layout of the text until they arrived at or just before the central door (see Fig. 6.5). At the beginning, they used only the lower half of the middle range, continuing at this level as far as the third intercolumniation. Here, however, they seem to have become alarmed: although the third inter-columniation is only slightly wider than the second — 2.3 metres as opposed to 1.9 metres — when they reached the dado, they used it for four columns

---

[32] J. M. Reynolds, 'Diocletian's prices edict: new fragments of the copy at Aphrodisias', in R. Frei-Stolba and M. A. Speidel (eds.), *Römische Inschriften: Neufunde, Neulesungen und Neuinterpre-tationen. Festschrift für Hans Lieb* (Basle 1995) 17–28, at 18.

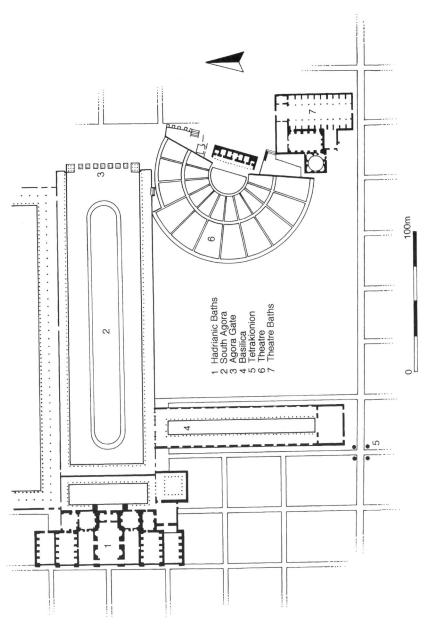

1 Hadrianic Baths
2 South Agora
3 Agora Gate
4 Basilica
5 Tetrakionion
6 Theatre
7 Theatre Baths

0   100m

Fig. 6.4.   The location of the Basilica at Aphrodisias.

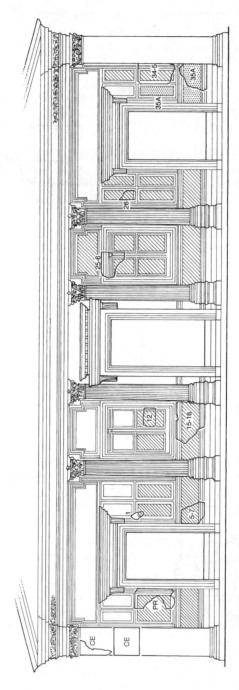

Fig. 6.5.   The façade of the Aphrodisias Basilica: the diagonal lines indicate the area covered by the main body of the prices edict, the dots the appendix on water transport.

rather than three, with evident overcrowding of very long lines: the fourth column was squeezed into half the space occupied by the others. What is more, to the right of the central door, they went up not simply to the upper half of the middle range, but actually to the attic level, the top of which is some five metres above ground level. By the time they got down to the dado at this point, in the fourth intercolumniation, they were becoming relaxed once again, using it for only one column. They used the upper and lower halves of the middle range in the fifth intercolumniation, but placed only one column on the dado. In the sixth and final intercolumniation, they used only the right-hand panels of the middle range, at any rate to begin with.

The text will not have been an easy one to lay out, for reasons that make its reconstruction also a fiddly business: there will perhaps not have been much point in counting the lines in the papyrus text which was presumably what was circulated by Fulvius Asticus; and a count by items will have provided only a rough indication, since items are of extremely variable length. A count by chapters would have been even more misleading.

Did the text arrive in more than one instalment? There is perhaps an indication that it did: the point at which the engravers at Aphrodisias seem to have realised that they had a space problem is close to the point at which the engravers at Stratonicea stopped their work altogether, or inscription was replaced by painting.[33] Perhaps the next instalment never arrived; or, if it did, the quantity of text was so dispiriting that they just gave up. The engravers of Aphrodisias were made of sterner stuff, or perhaps rather they were more under the eye of the governor: they got out their ladders and carried on.

Within their changing sense of the availability of space, however, their work reveals considerable attention to aesthetic considerations: they occupied at least a bit of the dado of the fifth intercolumniation; and they decided that it would look better if the last engraved panels were those immediately adjacent to the right-hand pilaster of the whole building, using the upper and lower right-hand panels of the middle range of the sixth and last intercolumniation. In the end, the whole thing looked better than they could have dreamed, because of the arrival of a revised chapter on transport prices. One might suppose anyway *a priori* that such a revised chapter — the principal difference is in the inclusion of rules for *onera fiscalia*, state levies of goods — was despatched after the text as a whole had been engraved; but Aphrodisias provides formal proof, since the engravers went *backwards* to the lower left-hand panel of the middle range and then down to the dado.

---

[33] I owe thanks to Francesca Fontanella and René Rebuffat for discussion here, and to Benet Salway for much happy sharing of fragment-hunting.

2. As we have seen, visibility will not have been the most obvious characteristic of substantial parts of the text of the prices edict, with some of it as much as five metres above the eye-level of the bystander; and the coinage edicts began at the same level, at the very top of the left-hand pilaster of the whole building. In passing, I am not sure what this implies for the order of engraving of the two texts: one might think it logical to begin at the left of a façade; but I find it very hard to suppose that the authorities at Aphrodisias would really have put the two currency edicts where they did, if the façade as a whole had still been at their disposal.

In any case, it is fashionable to claim that the function of engraved texts was largely symbolic; and I should not wish to deny this aspect. In the case of the prices edict at Aphrodisias, it is readily apparent: rather than using the two lower panels of the middle range one after the other for the imperial titles and the beginning of the preface, our engravers chiselled away the mouldings of each panel where they abutted, so as to create a longer line both for the titles and for the preface; the titles are also in larger letters, as is the beginning of the list of prices.

But a correctly engraved text may also be seen as the ultimate guarantee of an edict: forgery of documents was all too easy in the ancient world, as is abundantly attested. A change to an epigraphic text, whether in stone or bronze, is usually rather evident; and there the text is to be checked as a last resort. How many people who wanted to sell anything from chickpeas to a lion for more than the authorised price would have had the nerve to climb up a ladder on the façade of the governor's offices to achieve their end, with the risk that their handiwork would have been only too evident to someone else with a ladder?

3. Finally, the location chosen for the various texts of the edict: at Aphrodisias, Aezani and Stratonicea, the location was the wall of an existing building; and the Egypt block, 1.475 metres long by 0.405 metres high, looks like part of a pretty solid structure. The fragments from elsewhere are mostly smaller and all found in a secondary context; but while Plataea II is a stele with pediment, Aegeira I, Megara II and Ptolemais (n. 6 above) look pretty monumental. We have already seen that engraving on stone seems to have depended to a considerable degree on gubernatorial initiative; I leave it to others to decide whether the initiative they showed was also a manifestation of common sense, with the preface always in Latin, the prices in Greek only in Achaea, despite the fact that the overwhelming majority of all the populations were Greek-speaking; also whether five enthusiastic governors is more or fewer than one would expect in the Roman Empire as renewed by Diocletian. But it may be that initiative was not all that was needed — a large building with a lot of empty wall space, and a willingness to use it, may also have been necessary.

I should like to thank seminar audiences in Belfast, Florence and Paris for their comments on earlier versions, as well as the other contributors to this volume, and Peter Wiseman for his patience with a wayward contributor. To Joyce Reynolds I owe not only comments on this piece, but also my involvement with the edict on maximum prices of Diocletian in the first place, and immeasurably more besides.

Addendum to n. 27. I have just seen A. Mattiocco, 'Il frammento di Pettorano sul Gizio dell' *edictum de pretiis* di Diocleziano', *Bull. Dep. Abr. St. Pat.* 111, n.s. 89 (1999) 59–103, which publishes for the first time analyses of the Pettorano fragment and observes their compatibility with Carrara marble; but the author compares the analyses with only one out of the 27 or 28 places in Achaea from which the fragment may have originated.

7
The 'long' late antiquity:
a late twentieth-century model

Averil Cameron

The last generation has seen what one scholar has called an 'explosion' in the study of late antiquity.[1] Whereas in the 1950s the gaze of an editor planning a compendium on classical scholarship did not extend to the inclusion of a chapter covering the period from the reign of Constantine to, say, the Arab conquests, now, half a century later, no equivalent volume could appear without it. The original edition of the *Cambridge Ancient History* (1923–1939) ended at AD 324, the date at which Constantine became sole emperor. It thus neatly avoided having to cover the Christian empire, or even indeed the foundation of Constantinople. But its recently published successor volumes take the concept of 'ancient history' as far as AD 600.[2] Whether we call it 'the later Roman empire' or 'late antiquity', the term now in much more common use in English, this period has become enormously popular with professional historians and students alike. Curricula in ancient history which formerly ended at some date in the high empire now commonly include this later period, and it generates great enthusiasm with students. Handbooks are rapidly appearing to help their teachers meet this demand, and they too express the current understanding of what is to be

---

[1] See A. Giardina, 'Esplosione di tardoantico', *Studi Storici* 40 (1999) 157–80.

[2] Averil Cameron and Peter Garnsey (eds.), *Cambridge Ancient History* 13. *The Late Empire, AD 337–435* (Cambridge 1998); Averil Cameron, Bryan Ward-Perkins and Michael Whitby (eds.), *Cambridge Ancient History* 14. *Late Antiquity: Empire and Successors, AD 425–600* (Cambridge 2000). On volume 13, and the changing conceptions of the period see Arnaldo Marcone, 'La tarda antichità e le sue periodizzazioni', *Rivista Storica Italiana* 112 (2000) 318–34. Naturally (*pace* Fergus Millar, *Journal of Roman Archaeology* 13 (2000) 754–5, a review of vol. 13 written without benefit of having seen vol. 14) the chronological divisions between volumes in such a series tend to be somewhat arbitrary: in this case, vol. 13 (Cambridge 1997) covers AD 337–425 and 14 (Cambridge 2000) AD 425–600.

included.[3] As I shall argue, a particular model for the study of this period has come to have a strong influence on students and scholars alike, and this chapter will ask how and why this is so, and what implications there are for the future study of the subject. Andrea Giardina, the same scholar who referred to the 'explosion' of late antiquity, has called this a particularly Anglo-centric phenomenon,[4] and that too deserves discussion, as does the question whether 'late antiquity', as understood in this particular way, is likely to survive as a distinct discipline.

i

A new phase in English-speaking scholarship in the period was begun with the publication in 1964 of A. H. M. Jones's great two-volume work *The Later Roman Empire, AD 284–602: a Social, Economic and Administrative Survey*. This was and remains a monumental achievement, and it is still the fundamental study for the topics it covers. After more than 300 pages of narrative, Jones's 'descriptive' chapters dealt with the following subjects: government, administration, finance, justice, senators, the civil service, the army, Rome and Constantinople, the cities, the land, industry, trade and transport, the church, religion and morals, education and culture, and 'the decline of the empire'.[5] However, it was Peter Brown's small but highly influential book, *The World of Late Antiquity* (London 1971), following only a few years after that of Jones, that set study of the period in a new direction, and which popularised the term 'late antiquity'. This book has been endlessly discussed, especially in the context of the twenty-fifth anniversary of its publication,[6] and through his publication series for the University of California Press and his influence on a younger generation of scholars,

---

[3] E.g. Michael Maas (ed.), *Readings in Late Antiquity: a Sourcebook* (London 2000) and A. D. Lee (ed.), *Pagans and Christians in Late Antiquity: a Sourcebook* (London 2000), both from the same publisher; R. Valantasis (ed.), *Religions of Late Antiquity in Practice* (Princeton 2000). Other guides and introductions are published or in production.

[4] Giardina (n. 1) 167, n. 35.

[5] See on Jones, Peter Brown, *Religion and Society in the Age of Saint Augustine* (London 1972) 46–73; J. H. W. G. Liebeschuetz, 'A. H. M. Jones and the *Later Roman Empire*', *University College London, Institute of Archaeology Bulletin* 29 (1992) 2–8.

[6] See particularly the debate, 'The world of late antiquity revisited', *Symbolae Osloenses* 72 (1997) 5–90.

many of whom were his pupils,[7] Brown's conception of late antiquity has become an extremely powerful model.

The World of Late Antiquity presented the period to the reader in the form of an exciting, if at times breathless, panorama, extending chronologically from the third century to the seventh, and geographically from the western provinces to Sasanian Iran. This was not a classical world in decline, or a Roman empire that 'fell' in AD 476 when the last emperor in the West was deposed. Rather, it was an exciting time of change, a period of variety and creativity, which is reflected in its vigorous visual arts and cultural production. Nor was it the straightforwardly Christian empire assumed by theologians or patristic scholars, for in this model due weight was also given to the many forms of late polytheism, including Neoplatonism, as well as to the varied religious experience of the eastern borders of the Roman empire. In the same year Brown also produced what was to prove a seminal article on what he called 'holy men', a convenient term which could embrace both Christian saints and Neoplatonist ascetics. This too stimulated a huge amount of interest in saints, asceticism and religious experience in late antiquity, though it would also be fair to say that by the 1980s at least, these topics were also being energetically pursued by scholars in related disciplines, and that this provided a great impetus to the reception of Brown's work.[8]

More traditional work of course continued to be produced. Jones's *Later Roman Empire*, a work of enormous and exceptional scholarship, had provided the essential framework on which Brown's *World of Late Antiquity* could rest, and the *Prosopography of the Later Roman Empire*, which Jones himself initiated, began publication in 1971, covering the period AD 260–641 and reaching completion in 1992.[9] Nor was Brown by any means

---

[7] The series is entitled *The Transformation of the Classical Heritage* and now extends to many volumes. Brown's influence has been most perceptibly felt in North America, where he has taught since the 1970s at Berkeley and Princeton.

[8] 'The rise and function of the holy man in late antiquity', *Journal of Roman Studies* 61 (1971) 80–101; on this article and its influence see the papers in the *Journal of Early Christian Studies* 6 (1998), and James Howard-Johnston and Paul Heywood (eds.), *The Cult of the Saints in Late Antiquity and the Early Middle Ages* (Oxford 1999). Brown himself turned to the study of the importance of relics in *The Cult of the Saints: its Rise and Function in Latin Christianity* (Chicago 1981). Something of the early impact of Brown's article on the holy man can be seen reflected in several of the papers in S. Hackel (ed.), *The Byzantine Saint* (Birmingham 1981).

[9] A. H. M. Jones, J. R. Martindale and J. Morris (eds.), *The Prosopography of the Later Roman Empire* vol. 1, AD 260–395 (Cambridge 1971); J. R. Martindale (ed.), vol. 2, AD 395–527 (Cambridge 1980); vol. 3, AD 527–641 (Cambridge 1992). Christian prosopographies have also appeared: A. Mandouze (ed.), *Prosopographie de l'Afrique chrétienne (303–533)* (Paris 1982); Charles Pietri and Luce Pietri, (eds.), *Prosopographie de l'Italie chrétienne (313–604)*, 2 vols. (Rome 1999).

the first to see late antiquity in positive terms or to question the older view of the period as marking a steady decline from Gibbon's famous delineation of the Antonine age at the beginning of his *History of the Decline and Fall of the Roman Empire* as the peak of classical civilization.[10] Yet Brown's work of the early 1970s undoubtedly provoked in English-speaking scholarship on the period a major shift towards cultural history, and was very influential in establishing the conception of a 'long late antiquity', with forms of continuity lasting far beyond the traditional date for the fall of the western empire in AD 476. Several books have subsequently extended this still further, in the East until the Abbasid period, in the eighth and ninth centuries, with the implication that the early Islamic world was in many senses a continuation of the Mediterranean world of late antiquity.[11]

In the 1960s, when Brown's ideas were taking shape, the so-called 'Pirenne controversy', arising from the views of Henri Pirenne,[12] was still a lively one. Pirenne argued that it was not the Germanic invasions but the Arab conquest that was responsible for a break in continuity in Mediterranean civilisation. This gave rise to a vigorous debate, which still continues, as to the extent of Mediterranean trade and production during the fifth to seventh centuries. Much of the evidence comes from pottery, and given the technical sophistication of the argument as it is now conducted, it is hard to realise that the fundamental work which established a means of dating the main forms of late Roman pottery was not published until 1972.[13] The debate continues as to how far long-distance trade, and therefore complex economic life, continued after the Vandal conquest of

---

[10] Brown's predecessors included the Italian and French historians Santo Mazzarino and H.-I. Marrou; see Giardina, (n. 1) 157–9. The collection of essays edited by Arnaldo Momigliano, *The Conflict between Paganism and Christianity in the Fourth Century* (Oxford 1963), was also an influential predecessor.

[11] For this see Garth Fowden, *From Empire to Commonwealth: the Consequences of Monotheism in Late Antiquity* (Princeton 1993). G. W. Bowersock, Peter Brown and Oleg Grabar (eds.), *Late Antiquity: a Guide to the Post-Classical World* (Cambridge, Mass. 1999) starts from a similar perspective, and the recent European Science Foundation project on The Transformation of the Roman World, whose main emphasis was on the western empire, took the period AD 400–900 as its frame.

[12] H. Pirenne, *Mahommed and Charlemagne* (Eng. trans., London 1939). See for example Brown's references to Pirenne and Rostovtzeff in his discussion of W. H. C. Frend, *The Donatist Church* (Oxford 1952), Brown (n. 5) 237–59, esp. 240–1.

[13] John Hayes, *Late Roman Pottery* (London 1972). For the debates about ceramic evidence and long-distance trade see for instance the papers in A. Giardina (ed.), *Società romana e impero tardoantico* vol. 3, *Le merci, gli insediamenti* (Milan 1986); *Hommes et richesses dans l'empire byzantin* vol. 1, *IVe–VIIe siècle* (Paris 1989).

North Africa in the early fifth century,[14] but on the whole a 'long' late antiquity prevails.

Certainly this overall model is not without challenges. The issue of periodisation is again on the agenda. Historians of the eastern empire who are mindful of the many signs of continuity in the eastern Mediterranean provinces and wish to extend late antiquity into the Arab period have to contend with those historians of the early medieval West who would still argue for rupture as a result of the barbarian invasions in the fifth century.[15] However, the nature and impact of barbarian infiltration in the western empire is also currently a contested area. Historians here are divided as between models of migration or gradualism ('seepage'). The idea of the arrival of the barbarians in terms of the migration of peoples has been challenged on many fronts. It lends itself on the one hand to illicit backward projections of modern nationalist assumptions,[16] and on the other to simplistic interpretation of the archaeological evidence.[17] Cultural change does not necessarily show itself clearly in material culture, and arguments from material objects to the identity of the user can be very dangerous.[18] There was certainly no simple or clear-cut divide of 'nationality'. Many barbarians were already serving in the Roman army in the fourth century, and Romans in turn took service with emergent barbarian rulers.[19]

Yet even if the traditional image of waves of 'barbarian invasions' no longer holds, one must admit that there was still violence and rupture.[20] One may also point to a notable recent output of books and papers on military history, the social impact of warfare and the study of armies, with particular

---

[14] This is complicated by the realisation in the current literature of the striking prosperity of the eastern provinces in late antiquity, especially Syria and Palestine, in contrast with the western parts of the empire. See for example M. Whittow, 'Ruling the Late Roman and early Byzantine city: a continuous history', *Past and Present* 129 (1990) 3–29.

[15] Nor is Whittow's emphasis on continuity in the East universally shared: see for example H. Kennedy, 'The last century of Byzantine Syria: a reinterpretation', *Byzantinische Forschungen* 10 (1985) 141–83.

[16] Contrast W. Pohl, 'The barbarian successor states', in Leslie Webster and Michelle Brown (eds.), *The Transformation of the Roman World. AD 400–900* (London 1997) 33–47, at 46. 'The ethnogenesis of early medieval peoples, therefore, was not a matter of blood, but of shared traditions and institutions.'

[17] For recent discussion see Ellen Swift, *The End of the Western Roman Empire: an Archaeological Investigation* (Stroud 2000) and individual essays in Webster and Brown (n. 16).

[18] Thus Pohl, (n. 16) 45: 'the distinction between Byzantine imports, local production in Roman tradition and the work of barbarian artisans is rather blurred.'

[19] For the former see J. H. W. G. Liebeschuetz, *Barbarians and Bishops: Army, Church and State in the Age of Arcadius and Chrysostom* (Oxford 1990).

[20] See Brent Shaw, 'War and violence', in Bowersock, Brown and Grabar, (n. 11) 130–69.

relevance to the western empire; some of these purvey a more dramatic model of the change.[21] Furthermore, historians differ in their view of the effectiveness, and even the overall size, of the late Roman army itself, in comparison with the military forces and equipment of the various barbarian groups.

A not dissimilar debate exists in relation to the East at a somewhat later date, in the context of the wars against the Persians under Heraclius, and the Arab conquest of Syria and Palestine.[22] In the effort to understand the complexities of the late antique and early Byzantine military system — which also entails understanding how it was financed — there are more outstanding issues than some recent publications suggest. One of them concerns the level of credence that can be placed on the relatively few actual numbers found in ancient sources, and the kind of calculation that can be based on them, whether in relation to the barbarian immigrants or the Arab invaders, or to the Roman military forces themselves.[23]

Yet for many scholars working on these issues of arrival and assimilation the problem has shifted away from the older and clear-cut divisions between chronological periods towards the attempt to find a more nuanced interpretation of the nature of the change perceptible in the archaeological record. Such a shift of emphasis lies behind the sense of dissolving boundaries and new ways of assimilation that is evident in many recent publications.[24] It is by no means always clear who is barbarian and who is Roman, or in which direction the transfer takes place. Indeed, the very category 'barbarian' has proved deceptive. Applied as a value term rather than a description in late Roman writers, the term itself has in the past contributed to the view of the Roman West as having been 'overrun' by invading Germanic peoples, with the concomitant debate as to whether the Roman empire in the West 'fell',

---

[21] E.g. H. Elton, *Warfare in Roman Europe 350–425* (Oxford 1966) 130–69; J.-M. Carrié and S. Janniard offer a critical analysis of some of the recent publications on the late Roman army and late Roman warfare in *Antiquité tardive* 8 (2000) 321–41. The difficult balance between warfare and treaty-making is a central theme in e.g. Peter Heather, *Goths and Romans 332–489* (Oxford 1991).

[22] See the essays in Averil Cameron (ed.), *The Byzantine and Early Islamic Near East* vol. 3: *States, Resources and Armies* (Princeton 1995).

[23] W. Treadgold, *Byzantium and its Army 284–1081* (Stanford 1985), is an example of calculations based on the numbers given in ancient sources, as well as of the idea that Byzantium begins with Diocletian (see below, p. 190); for a different approach see John Haldon, *Warfare, State and Society in the Byzantine World 565–1204* (London 1999).

[24] Another recent volume on late antiquity is entitled *Shifting Frontiers*, edited by R. Mathisen and H. Sivan (Aldershot 1996); the frontiers in question are conceptual as well as territorial.

through its own internal decline, or 'was pushed' by the impact of these outsiders.[25]

So far has opinion changed on this classic historical problem that it was possible for Glen Bowersock to write that 'Now, in 1995, it is probably fair to say that no responsible historian of the ancient or medieval world would want to address or acknowledge the fall of Rome as either fact or paradigm.'[26] As Andrea Giardina remarks,[27] this collapsing of what were hitherto regarded as great events into a more or less continuous cultural history has been one of the most noticeable features of the scholarship of the recent generation. It is a model which is able to emphasise small-scale continuous change over rupture precisely because it turns aside from institutional, administrative and economic history. To that extent it was also a model for the late twentieth century, which saw the fall of communism and a consequent rapid decline in acceptability of the broadly Marxist economic models of explanation for late antiquity and the early Middle Ages which had influenced an earlier generation, and which continued to be influential in Italian scholarship.[28]

That decline, and the concomitant rise in cultural history, have been striking features of most, even if not all, English-speaking scholarship. I suspect however that Giardina is right to argue that the result has been to produce an over-benign and certainly a one-sided view. As can be seen in Peter Brown's own work, it is a view which privileges culture, and places a strong emphasis on religion as part of the overall cultural pattern, but which is very low in the amount of attention it gives to economic and institutional change, the role of the state or indeed such traditional questions as the role of

---

[25] For the 'internal' explanation see G. E. M. de Ste. Croix, *The Class Struggle in the Ancient Greek World from Archaic Greece to the Arab Conquests* (London 1981). There has been a recent attempt to rehabilitate the idea of decline: see J. H. W. G. Liebeschuetz, 'The uses and abuse of the concept of 'decline' in later Roman history, or, Was Gibbon politically incorrect?', in L. Lavan (ed.), *Recent Research in Late-Antique Urbanism, JRA* Suppl. series 42 (Portsmouth, RI 2001) 233–8, and see his book, *The Decline and Fall of the Late Roman City* (Oxford 2001). The shorter version of Jones's *Later Roman Empire* was published as *The Decline of the Ancient World* (New York 1966).

[26] Glen W. Bowersock, 'The vanishing paradigm of the fall of Rome', *Bulletin of the American Academy of Arts and Sciences* 49 (1996) 29–43, at 42.

[27] Giardina (n. 1) 172–3.

[28] Expressed for example in Perry Anderson, *Passages from Antiquity to Feudalism* (London 1974); *cf.* C. Wickham, 'The other transition: from the ancient world to feudalism', *Past and Present* 103 (1984) 3–36. Against the trends I am discussing, John Haldon, *The State and the Tributary Mode of Production* (London 1993) offers an analysis of the late Roman and Byzantine state from a post-Marxist, historical materialist perspective.

slavery, class or or landholding in the transition from the Roman empire to the medieval world.

ii

A renewed consciousness in the late twentieth century of the need to explain what constitutes Europe and the European heritage has invited many scholars to reflect on questions of ethnicity and identity in late antiquity. Thus it is argued that through their contact with and entry into the Roman empire the barbarian groups themselves underwent a process of ethnic formation, an 'ethnogenesis', rather than bursting upon it fully formed and distinct.[29] The great debates that raged around the 'Pirenne thesis' as to what events, or which invaders, brought about the break between the ancient world and the Middle Ages have taken a new form, with the definition of identity at its heart. Out of some twenty contributions to a recent volume entitled *Ethnicity and Culture in Late Antiquity*,[30] six have the word 'identity' in their titles and most address issues of definition or self-definition in a changing environment. The editors had asked participants to 'explore the ways in which individuals and communities sought to establish their identities between AD 300–600, with reference to ethnicity, religious allegiances and cultural traditions, and the ways in which such identities were perceived'.[31] Another recent volume has the title *Constructing Identities in Late Antiquity*.[32] A heightened regional consciousness is also very apparent in recent work, though it is not the same as the regionalism of the past. Instead of accepting 'local cultures' in an essentialist way as something out there to be inspected, though usually the domain of the specialist, and an object for remark if they seem to be becoming more visible at any one period,[33] historians have more

---

[29] See e.g. H. Wolfram and A. Schwarcz (eds.), *Anerkennung und Integration: zu den wirtschaftlichen Grundlagen der Völkerwanderungszeit 400–600* (Vienna 1988); W. Pohl (ed.), *Kingdoms of the Empire: the Integration of Barbarians in Late Antiquity* (Leiden 1997); W. Pohl and H. Reinitz (eds.), *Strategies of Distinction: the Construction of Ethnic Communities, 300–600* (Leiden 1998), and contributions by Peter Heather to that volume and to R. Miles (ed.), *Constructing Identities in Late Antiquity* (London 1999).

[30] Edited by Stephen Mitchell and Geoffrey Greatrex (London 2000).

[31] Mitchell and Greatrex (n. 30) xi.

[32] See n. 29.

[33] It used to be a given that the third century AD saw a 'rise of local cultures' as an index of imperial crisis: this idea, reminiscent of Rostovzeff, is still evident in the conception behind F. Millar, *The Roman Empire and its Neighbours*, (2nd ed., London 1981). Millar (n. 2) 761–2 takes *CAH* vol. 13 to task for insufficient regional emphasis, but for this see vol. 14.

recently attempted to address issues such as assimilation and acculturation, and to give full weight to the complexities of changing situations.[34]

As already suggested, along with this more or less multicultural view, awareness of the non-Greek-speaking cultures of the eastern Mediterranean has increased enormously in the literature, as has the importance which is now attached to them.[35] Not only the Arabs and Islam but also Jews and Judaism have become far more visible in historical studies of late antiquity, in both cases being the subjects of debates about identity and development parallel to those surrounding the term 'barbarian'. As we recognise the project of the contemporary texts to 'separate' and render distinct from each other the religions of the period, current scholarship tends to look for their common features and similarities. We tend to forget that their ability to maintain their distinctiveness was also constantly threatened by daily social intercourse.[36] In the East, the nature of the Arab conquest in the early seventh century has been questioned in a revisionist historiography which plays down the idea of rupture, emphasises continuity over change and sees the full development of Islam as a product rather than a cause of the invasions.[37] As with the barbarian West, this debate focuses in part on the size of the Arab armies and the degree of central control or planning in the campaigns — that is, how far this was indeed a 'conquest' in the usual sense of the term. In this context historians have begun to question a further favourite explanation for the conquests, the supposed disaffection of the local population from the central government in Constantinople.[38]

---

[34] See for instance for an earlier period G. Woolf, *Becoming Roman: the Origins of Provincial Civilisation in Gaul* (Cambridge 1998), with P. Amory, *People and Identity in Ostrogothic Italy, 489–554* (Cambridge 1997).

[35] For example Fowden (n. 11); Glen Bowersock, *Hellenism in Late Antiquity* (Ann Arbor 1990) and papers in Mitchell and Greatrex (n. 30). The role of Jews and Judaism in late antiquity is also now a well-worked theme, and one can also point to the greatly increased interest among Roman and Byzantine historians of the antecedents and development of Islam, exemplified for example in Bowersock, Brown and Grabar (n. 11).

[36] G. Fowden, 'Religious communities', in Bowersock, Brown and Grabar (n. 11) 97.

[37] See n. 22, and see Giardina (n. 1) 176–7. Dealing with cultural identity in a later period, Paul Langford, *Englishness Identified: Manners and Character 1650–1850* (Oxford 2000), remarks on the change from the time not so long ago when it was still possible to argue that nation states were rooted in ethnic or racial origins to the present assumption (p. 14) that 'national character is a construct, an artifice'.

[38] W. E. Kaegi Jr., *Byzantium and the Early Islamic Conquests* (Cambridge 1992) argues for the continued effectiveness of the Byzantine army and believes that its defeats were attributable to mistakes in strategy; at ch. 9 he debates the degree to which there was 'anxiety' or 'confidence' among the Christian population of the eastern provinces.

As for the presentation of Jews and Judaism in late antique Christian sources, a variety of historians have recognised that this needs to be read with special care, in that the topics of Jews and Judaism are so often turned by Christian writers to tendentious purposes. It is not only in obvious religious writings such as homilies that such a reading is necessary, but also in histories and chronicles. How necessary this is can easily be seen when it is recognised just how much taking such Christian accounts at face value has affected modern discussions of the role of the Jews in supposedly helping the Persian invaders of Palestine and Jerusalem in the early seventh century; the effect can be paralleled in much the same way in Christian accounts of the Arab invasions (though the very fact that these are so few in comparison is an indicator of the immense ideological importance of references to the Jews for contemporary Christian writers).[39] Just as in the case of the barbarian West, therefore, when the eastern provinces also succumbed to external forces, albeit at a somewhat later period, recent accounts have tended to redraw the traditional contours of conflict, and to dissolve the issues into an examination of terminology, focusing in particular on questions of identity.

All these questions took on a new relevance in the light of the changes resulting from the end of communism in eastern Europe,[40] a set of events which stimulated much discussion not only about their causes but also about the shape and indeed the borders of many eastern European states, and particularly about the definition and future of Europe itself.[41] The earlier history of some of these states and regions has emerged as relevant to their contemporary problems, and their recent history has also contributed to a sharper awareness of the power of colonial narratives in history and the nature of the post-imperial or post-colonial situation.

Edward Said's book *Orientalism* appeared in 1978. It provoked criticism of some aspects of its exposure of the condemnatory attitudes to the East

---

[39] *Cf.* Averil Cameron, 'Byzantines and Jews: some recent work on early Byzantium', *Byzantine and Modern Greek Studies* 20 (1996) 249–74.

[40] See also Averil Cameron, 'The perception of crisis', in *Morfologie sociali e culturali in Europa fra tarda antichità e alto medioevo, 3–9 aprile 1997* (*Settimane di Studio del Centro italiano di Studi sull'alto Medioevo* 45, Spoleto 1998) 9–31.

[41] This is sometimes made quite explicit, for example in the case of a new European Science Foundation programme focusing on the early modern period, which claims to examine 'how Europe's distinctive cultural patterns were reshaped during its transition from a medieval phase, when its primary self-definition as "Latin Christendom" overemphasised (*sic*) its uniformity, to its more modern nationalist phase, whose individual units overstressed their cultural differentiation' (*ESF Newsletter*, August 2000).

which pervade so much western literature,[42] but it also played an important role in stimulating the development of a wide-ranging awareness of the strategies and techniques employed in colonial and post-colonial discourse.[43] Said's ideas deserve to be applied to the study of Byzantium, which has been notoriously characterised until recently by adverse stereotypes. They are also relevant to late antiquity, in that both contemporaries and modern historians have been apt to impose categories and terminology that are imperial and classicising in perspective. Two forms of *altérité* are thus at work: Byzantium suffers from a 'western' and 'enlightened' perspective, while both Byzantium and late antiquity suffer from adverse comparison with classical antiquity.

Not only Byzantium, but also 'the later Roman empire', have traditionally been seen through classical spectacles and found wanting, and the same is true for the peoples and cultures that were seen as bringing the ancient world to an end. In its current usage among English-speaking scholars, the term 'late antiquity' attempts to subvert these value judgements, and the kaleidoscopic conception of the late antique world presented by Peter Brown consciously aimed at breaking down the conceptual barriers of cultural imperialism erected by old-fashioned classicists. Brown's book antedated Said's *Orientalism*, and it was of course a very different project, yet both were subversive of existing assumptions.

The concept of 'late antiquity' as it is commonly understood today owes a great deal to this sense of overturning traditional categories, and I would argue that the collapse of the Soviet regimes since 1989 is a factor which may influence the agendas and the questions which historians bring to the period, and which can be regarded as a powerful stimulus to the preoccupation with cultural and ethnic identity.[44] Far from marking the 'end of

---

[42] For the debate and for some criticisms see for instance John M. MacKenzie, *Orientalism: History, Theory and the Arts* (Manchester 1995). See also Edward Said, *Culture and Imperialism* (New York 1993).

[43] 'Post-colonial discourse', a phenomenon identified following Said in the context of the historiography of modern India, could have much to say about late antiquity, and especially Byzantium. See for example Robert Young, *Colonial Desire: Hybridity in Theory, Culture and Race* (London 1995).

[44] Western writing about the Balkans is equally replete with stereotypes. In contrast, Mark Mazower, *The Balkans* (London 2000), argues against the 'Balkan character', and contends that nationalism in the Balkans is a product of the weakening of the Ottoman empire, not its cause.

history', as claimed by some,[45] the fall of communism and the opening of modern boundaries in Europe and elsewhere have disturbed old certainties and caused historians to focus on aspects of late antiquity where they think they can detect a similar fluidity. Mitchell and Greatrex observe that 'issues of ethnicity [despite the fact that this word is a twentieth-century coinage], culture and communal identity are particularly important in the period from 300 to 600'.[46] Few scholars nowadays would disagree with this formulation, and yet it is a way of seeing late antiquity that is wholly different from how it was perceived half a century ago.

iii

Perhaps it is true that each age gets the history it deserves. At any rate I am willing to defend the idea that history itself is perceived in the mirror of the present, and that historians bring their perceptions of the present to their view of the past. Let us take another example.

In the age of globalisation one of the most discussed issues is that of communication, and this too is a subject for the historian of late antiquity.[47] The imagination, memory and emotion are beginning to surface as possible subjects for the historian,[48] and travel, forms of popular culture, the communication of ideas make this period peculiarly appealing to modern, and indeed postmodern, writers. It was, after all, in the Brownian late-twentieth-century view, a time when frontiers were shifting, when ideas were changing, when unexpected juxtapositions were always liable to surprise. Narrative history was a natural casualty of such an approach. The thematic

---

[45] F. Fukuyama, *The End of History and the Last Man* (London 1992), taking up ideas expressed by him in an essay published already in 1989. Other kinds of 'end of history' have been announced, and Fukuyama attacked, from the opposite end of the intellectual spectrum: see Stuart Sim, *Derrida and the End of History* (Duxford 1999).

[46] Mitchell and Greatrex (n. 30) xi.

[47] Especially in relation to pilgrimage, e.g. David Frankfurter, *Pilgrimage and Holy Space in Late Antique Egypt* (Leiden 1998); S. Coleman and J. Elsner (eds.), *Pilgrimage, Past and Present, in the World Religions* (Cambridge 1995). Communication of ideas: Averil Cameron, 'Christianity and communication in the fourth century: the problem of diffusion', in H. W. Pleket and A. M. F. W. Verhoogt (eds.), *Aspects of the Fourth Century AD* (Leiden 1997) 23–42; Ian Wood, 'The transmission of ideas', in Webster and Brown (n. 16) 111–27.

[48] Thus Georgia Frank, *The Memory of the Eyes: Pilgrims to Living Saints in Christian Late Antiquity* (*The Transformation of the Classical Heritage* 32, Berkeley and Los Angeles 2000), aims to explore the religious sensibilities of pilgrims by examining 'the poetics of pilgrims' writings' (pp. 2–3).

approach has been much more favoured in recent scholarship than narrative, and indeed the new *Cambridge Ancient History* has been criticised as 'old-fashioned' precisely because it does include narrative chapters.[49] Perhaps this is in part a function of the smaller amount of surviving source material from antiquity when compared with the modern period. But a deeper reason is to be found in the fact that narrative, especially political narrative, is antipathetic to the fluidity inherent in the contemporary project of late antiquity.

The model that I have been describing undoubtedly owes much to the intellectual climate of the late twentieth century. Central to traditional ways of seeing the late empire and Byzantium, I have implied, was the idea of classical antiquity as representative of stable cultural values, as the very foundation of the 'western canon'.[50] A willingness to envisage antiquity as not only embracing the Christian empire but extending chronologically into periods formerly labelled as medieval or Byzantine fits well with the kind of postmodern eclecticism that we see in other forms of contemporary cultural criticism. The older notion of a strong dividing line between 'classical' and 'medieval' or 'Byzantine', on the other hand, implies a confident ability to apply moral and aesthetic judgements, and an authoritarian stance on the part of the historian, and this has not fitted well with the permissive and multi-culturalist stance of the late twentieth century.

It is noticeable that while there has not been as yet the same degree of change in the study of Byzantium as in that of late antiquity, a growing number of Byzantinists are now preoccupied with trying to overturn the negative reception of Byzantium among modern historians.[51] Yet as we have seen, older conceptions of the late Roman empire as a period of decline are not dead. We are still apt to encounter the idea of a decline into sterility during the later Roman period, facilitating the transition towards medie-valdom, even if it is rarely nowadays so strongly expressed as in Aldo

---

[49] So Millar (n. 2). This contrasts with historiography on more modern periods: *cf.* Dominic Lieven, *Empire: the Russian Empire and its Rivals* (Cambridge 2000) xx: 'Narrative is back in fashion with historians.'

[50] For the idea that the classical 'canon' is itself changing, *cf.* Chapter 2 above. Harold Bloom, *The Western Canon* (New York 1994) lists largely the classic works of English literature, but the ancient, especially Greek, foundations of a civilising education in the humanities are fundamental to Allan Bloom's book, *The Closing of the American Mind* (New York 1987), a book which aroused passionate acclaim but also abuse from literary theorists.

[51] For a recent discussion of earlier historiography see Jean-Michel Spieser, 'Du Cange and Byzantium', in Robin Cormack and Elizabeth Jeffreys (eds.), *Through the Looking Glass: Byzantium through British Eyes* (Aldershot 2000) 199–210.

Schiavone's *The End of the Past: Ancient Rome and the Modern West.*[52] He writes in highly emotive language of late antiquity that 'the losing fork of the road was selected. . . . What remained was an indelible imprint of the material and mental limits that had been reached: the shadow of a missed opportunity, surviving in a world that had denied it existence.'[53]

As currently formulated, the debate about the passage from late antiquity to the medieval world is a matter of perception, the gaze of the historian.[54] To be sure, emphasis on the historian's gaze can be characterised as a species of relativism, in that it avoids value judgements.[55] At the same time, it makes of history a moral enterprise, expressive of the influences which drive the individual author. In the historiography in English on later periods we are currently witnessing something of a reaction against the thematic and the theoretical in favour of a traditional political narrative.[56] But with its juxtapositions and its continual change, late antiquity has lent itself ideally to the other kind of approach. Not least, it seems modern, and therefore accessible and sympathetic.[57] Such a protean subject is inimical to the traditional forms of historical explanation. It can be seen almost as requiring the very Brownian technique of empathy and evocation that is employed to such powerful effect in *The World of Late Antiquity*.

Historiography has inevitably shared in the intellectual movements by which since the 1950s and 1960s an assault has been launched from a number of different directions on the assumption that there are fixed truths to be discovered. In the terminology of Clifford Geertz, one of the anthropologists whose work has been very influential on ancient historians,[58] 'local knowledge' and 'thick description' are better aims for historians to pursue than the continued hunt for universals which had dominated historical inquiry since the Enlightenment. Similarly, an emphasis on the detail of ordinary life and

---

[52] Eng. trans., Cambridge, Mass. 2000.

[53] P. 203. Another writer who purveys decline, but from a different perspective, is Ramsay MacMullen, e.g. in his *Corruption and the Decline of Rome* (New Haven 1988).

[54] The concept of the 'gaze', and recognition of the centrality of representation, owes a great deal to John Berger, *Ways of Seeing* (Harmondsworth 1972).

[55] For the positive, see *Cambridge Ancient History* 14 (Cambridge 2000), Epilogue. Peter Brown's *The Rise of Western Christendom: Triumph and Diversity, AD 200–1000* (Oxford 1996) also conspicuously avoids the language of comparison inherent in traditional views.

[56] For a good survey of the argument see R. J. Evans, *In Defence of History*, (rev. ed., London 2000).

[57] Giardina (n. 1), 158–9.

[58] Clifford Geertz, *Local Knowledge* (New York 1983), and *cf.* his earlier book *The Interpretation of Cultures* (New York 1973). By 'thick description', Geertz meant the detailed contextual analysis of phenomena against their own background rather than ours, as exemplified in his famous study of cockfighting in Balinese culture.

the so-called *longue durée* — those factors in history like physical environment in which change takes place over centuries rather than as the result of specific events — were also features imported into the historiography of late antiquity and which broke down the existing dominance of political narrative.[59] But there was a far broader context also. It was not only in history but in the human sciences generally that ideas were changing. In philosophy, for example, Richard Rorty and others addressed the question of the kind of knowledge that could be achieved by science, history or philosophy,[60] and the highly controversial book by Jean-François Lyotard, *The Postmodern Condition*, as is suggested by its sub-title, *A Report on Knowledge*,[61] in fact followed this already established tendency in questioning the status of scientific knowledge. The effects of these movements are well known, especially in relation to the 'linguistic turn', the powerful combination of structuralism and literary theory in the last generation of scholarship, and the field of late antiquity has been deeply affected by them.

iv

So late antiquity has become a popular and growing field. Why should this be so? We can point first to a rather mundane reason. For many scholars, especially those who came from a classical background, late antiquity offered an unprecedented amount of written and visual evidence, much of it still relatively unexplored. Classicists have discovered the rich literature of the patristic period. The Christian literature of late antiquity — saints' lives, exegesis, homiletic, letters — offered wide and exciting vistas for scholarly exploitation. At the same time the period still suffered under stereotypes of decline which were clearly due for revision. It therefore offered plenty of scope. For these reasons, and also because of the breaking down of

[59] The influence of works such as Philippe Ariès, *Centuries of Childhood* (Paris 1960), Emmanuel le Roy Ladurie, *The Peasants of Languedoc* (Paris 1966) and Fernand Braudel, *The Structures of Everyday Life* (Paris 1967) can be seen to have influenced the study of late antiquity, for example, in the first volume edited by Paul Veyne in the series under the general editorship of Philippe Ariès and Georges Duby, *The History of Private Life* (Eng. trans., Cambridge, Mass. 1976). Evelyne Patlagean's important book *Pauvreté économique et pauvreté sociale à Byzance, 4e–7e siècles* (Paris 1977), applied similar principles, though she would reject the notion of belonging to an 'Annales school'.

[60] Richard Rorty, *Philosophy and the Mirror of Nature* (Oxford 1980); *Objectivity, Relativism and Truth* (Cambridge 1991).

[61] Manchester 1984; the bibliography is immense, and of course not univocal, *cf.* for example Terry Eagleton, *The Illusions of Postmodernism* (Oxford 1996).

boundaries between academic disciplines, many young scholars have been attracted into this field from other disciplines, notably art history, medieval history or religious studies. In most cases these practitioners have not had the traditional training in ancient history and are as unlikely to be interested in or technically competent to specialise in institutional, administrative or economic history as they are to be influenced by a post-Marxist or historical materialist concern for social structures. They approach late antiquity from the point of view of cultural history and the history of ideas, thus confirming Giardina's general observation about the comparative lack of institutional history currently being written in English. At the same time, given this profile of current scholarship, the confessionalism of older patristic studies has been challenged. Texts and subject matter once the realm of the isolated specialist have increasingly attracted an academic enterprise based on social history and literary analysis rather than the traditional editing of texts.

Barriers of content as well as chronology have been broken down. Once the gaze no longer rested on traditional problems, but could range more widely, there was a vast amount of source material and subject matter to be explored. In addition to these advantages for the young scholar, late antiquity has offered a chance to explore some of the favourite agendas of the past generation. A list would include topics such as the body,[62] gender, asceticism, power, performance, spectacle and the construction of the self ('self-fashioning'). In the early 1980s very influential books by Michel Foucault and Aline Rousselle drew on the enormous range of late antique texts, and the sheer quantity, as well as the type, of available material, much of it Christian, has acted as a great stimulus for theoreticians and others.[63]

Perhaps the single greatest change has been the colonisation of early Christianity by classicists and others from outside the tradition of theology or patristics. In Anglo-Saxon scholarship since the nineteenth century, study of the classics had largely excluded Christianity and relegated the early Church to a different range of disciplines altogether — New Testament studies, ecclesiastical history or patristics. Alternatively, as in Gibbon's *History of the Decline and Fall*, Christianity might feature as a regrettable development which was itself identified as a factor in 'decline'. Christian writers were studied within the context of theology or according to confessional interests, and the study of the Fathers was left to specialists. Now, in contrast,

---

[62] *Cf.* Ann Hanson, in a review of a recent volume of collected essays, *Journal of Roman Archaeology* 12 (1999) 593: 'problematizing the ancient body has become an important project'.
[63] Michel Foucault, *History of Sexuality*, (Eng. trans., New York 1979–1988); Aline Rousselle, *Porneia* (Paris 1983).

Christianity and Christian writing in the Roman empire have benefited from a quite different and non-confessional approach, and this in itself made available a literally vast amount of material hitherto largely passed over. Peter Brown's original approach, especially in his article on the holy man, owed most to the methods of social anthropology, although the dominant influence came from social history. But more recently, and especially in North American scholarship, its place has been taken by literary theory.[64] One no longer has to be a Christian to give Christianity an important place in the history of late antiquity. Indeed, for a historian nowadays to leave out Christian evidence, or the issues posed by religion in late antique culture, would be regarded as quixotic to a degree.

This 'takeover' over of Christian texts by historians of late antiquity has had a further result, in that it has given far greater space to religion. It has for example been a feature of the last generation not only that biographical studies of educated and powerful bishops like Augustine of Hippo and Ambrose of Milan have found wide audiences,[65] but also that there has been a surge of curiosity focused on the ample material relating to the lives of saints and the role of asceticism.[66] Why did so many men and women apparently choose to give up their familiar lifestyles and take to lives of renunciation and denial? Part of the appeal for modern students lies in their seeming exoticism, the sheer strangeness of the phenomena whereby women disguised themselves as men and men stood on pillars for years on end. But there are also deeper and contemporary reasons: the pull of changing life-styles, a desire to study popular as well as élite culture, the rhetorical con-struction in the texts of new models of conduct and the construction of the self.[67] Many of these texts give conspicuous attention to matters of gender,

---

[64] This is very apparent in the consciously interdisciplinary nature of the *Journal of Early Christian Studies,* still less than a decade old, a large proportion of whose contributions lie in the field of late antiquity. One of the most influential figures here is Elizabeth Clark, whose book *Reading Renunciation: Asceticism and Scripture in Early Christianity* (Princeton 1999) offers a striking examination of the rhetorical techniques by which ascetic writers used Scriptural texts to promote their agendas.

[65] Peter Brown, *Augustine of Hippo* (London 1967, rev. ed. 2000); Neil McLynn, *Ambrose of Milan: Church and Court in a Christian Capital* (Berkeley and Los Angeles 1994).

[66] A good instance of the varied and interdisciplinary nature of this interest can be found in the volume edited by V. Wimbush and R. Valantasis, *Asceticism* (New York 1995).

[67] For biography in the period see Thomas Hägg and Philip Rousseau (eds.), *Greek Biography and Panegyric in Late Antiquity* (Berkeley and Los Angeles 2000); Patricia Cox Miller, *Biography in Late Antiquity* (Berkeley and Los Angeles 1983); an attractive introduction to two key pagan philosophical biographies can be found in Mark Edwards, *Neoplatonic Saints: the Lives of Plotinus and Proclus by their Students*, translation with introduction (Liverpool 2000).

to the preoccupation with the human body as metaphor and to questions of display and performance.

Late antiquity was an age in which biography flourished and in which pagan and Christian writers vied with each other to establish authoritative models. The pagan *Life* of the first-century sage Apollonius of Tyana by Philostratus was taken seriously enough as a challenge to the model of Jesus for Eusebius of Caesarea to have taken some pains to refute it in his own apologetic writing. Late antiquity offers a particularly rich collection of such subject matter in a variety of languages and cultural settings, and the available writings invite analysis from the point of view of psychology as well as religious history and rhetorical criticism.[68]

The same set of evidence offered great scope for the study of gender. Augustine's mother Monica is just one example of a female historical figure whose representation in the text (Augustine's *Confessions*) has been repeatedly studied, but we need to ask not only how these women are presented but also why they are now allowed to occupy so much space in male texts.[69] The 'male gaze' still prevails in the literature of late antiquity, but it seems nonetheless, at least in some cases, to allow women a legitimacy they did not hitherto enjoy. Many scholars have therefore wondered whether women in late antiquity really had more freedom or more opportunities, or whether they merely occupy more textual space for rhetorical and ideological reasons — as objectifications of ascetic values, for example.[70] Why for instance did St Jerome devote so much attention to the Hebrew studies of his women friends and patrons? Can we find convincing earlier parallels for Melania the Elder or her granddaughter Melania the Younger, both great Christian ladies from the Roman aristocracy of the late fourth and early fifth centuries, and if not, what has changed? What are the sexual politics behind representations of repentant prostitutes who become Christian saints, or indeed behind the representation of the Virgin Mary? The briefest look

---

[68] The classic topic of martyrdom, for example, has become a subject illustrating sexual politics rather than a heroic narrative of the early church persecuted; *cf.* for example Gillian Clark, 'Bodies and blood: the late antique debate on martyrdom, virginity and resurrection', in D. Montserrat (ed.), *Changing Bodies, Changing Meanings: Studies on the Human Body in Antiquity* (London 1998), 99–115.

[69] See Elizabeth A. Clark, 'Rewriting early Christian history: Augustine's representation of Monica', in Jan Willem Drijvers and John W. Watt (eds.), *Portraits of Spiritual Authority: Religious Power in Early Christianity, Byzantium and the Christian Orient* (Leiden 1999) 3–23 (with remarks about the 'what is history' debate).

[70] See particularly Elizabeth A. Clark, *Ascetic Attitudes and Women's Faith: Essays on Late Ancient Christianity* (Lewiston 1986); Gillian Clark, *Women in Late Antiquity: Pagan and Christian Lifestyles* (Oxford 1993).

through the bibliography of late antiquity over the last generation will reveal how much study has been devoted to questions of gender, a field which in the 1950s and even the 1960s was at only a very rudimentary stage of development. In this, the period has shared in a general trend, and the change is not to be attributed solely or even mainly to the agendas of Christianity and Christianisation.[71]

Why then does religion occupy so much space in contemporary accounts of late antiquity? In most cases it is not because scholars want to debate again the traditional questions of conversion and Christianisation but because religion is the carrier of culture and because religious texts offer such rich material for a critic. In particular, the late antique debates about celibacy and virginity, in which pagans as well as Christians took part, offer to scholars a remarkable amount of material for analysis and explanation. Much of this ground was covered in another important book by Peter Brown, *The Body and Society: Men, Women and Sexual Renunciation in Early Christianity,*[72] but the discussion has since been taken further by others, with a particular concentration on the rhetorical strategies employed in the texts.[73]

Another area which has benefited from this realisation of the power of texts is the study of late Roman law, or more properly, the law codes. Formerly taken as proof of the repressiveness of late Roman government, the great collections of late Roman law known to us as the Theodosian and Justinianic Codes have been re-read as compilations of rhetoric, filled with repeated pronouncements often issued more from hope than from the assurance that they would be put into practice.[74] Matching the documented

---

[71] And now in common with work on other periods, collective volumes have moved on from studying women to studying men, or more often, 'masculinity': see for instance Lin Foxhall and John Salmon (eds.), *Thinking Men: Masculinity and its Self-Representation in the Classical Tradition* (London 1998); *When Men were Men: Masculinity, Power, and Identity in Classical Antiquity* (London 1998). Maud Gleason's *Making Men: Sophists and Self-Presentation in Ancient Rome* (Princeton 1995), dealing with the early imperial period, is an influential book which was early in this field. Compare also Liz James (ed.), *Women, Men and Eunuchs: Gender in Byzantium* (London 1993). The first 'modern' book in English about ancient women, Sarah Pomeroy's *Goddesses, Whores, Wives and Slaves: Women in Classical Antiquity* (New York), came out as late as 1975 and did not cover late antiquity.

[72] New York 1988.

[73] Patricia Cox Miller is a scholar who has produced particularly interesting work in this area: see for instance 'The blazing body: ascetic desire in Jerome's Letter to Eustochium', *Journal of Early Christian Studies* 1 (1993) 21–45.

[74] Ramsay MacMullen pointed out in a classic article of the 1960s that repetition of laws over a long period suggests not that they were put into practice by an authoritarian regime but rather that they were unknown or ignored: 'Social mobility and the Theodosian Code', *Journal of Roman Studies* 54 (1964) 49–53.

laws with other evidence often leads to the conclusion that the gap between pronouncement and practice was wide. Moreover while these are not our only sources of knowledge of individual laws, the complex histories of the surviving collections mean that our main evidence has been shaped by editorial and bureaucratic agendas which themselves need to be explored in detail before the evidence is safe to use as a basis for generalisation.[75] But once it has been fully recognised that the legal evidence is not to be taken simply at face value, a much more complex relationship emerges between the texts and actual practice.

This is particularly exemplified by the very difficult problems inherent in understanding the late Roman 'colonate' — that is, assessing the meaning of the countless legal regulations surrounding the social and legal position of *coloni*, tenants on the land, whose own financial position might in fact range from the relatively rich to the 'servile poor'. Despite the centrality of this group to modern theories of tied labour and incipient feudalism, or to the older view of the Later Roman Empire as rigidly repressive in its attempts to control labour and ensure the collection of taxes, it is now recognised that their actual status varied very greatly, and there seems to have been no overall legislation governing them. Debate has also focused on the likely gap between text (the laws themselves) and actuality (how or whether they were implemented in practice).[76] Another case in point is provided by the legal pronouncements of the tetrarchs, from the early part of the period, recently studied by Simon Corcoran in a work which reminds us of the gaps in our evidence and the frequent difficulty of reconstructing even the authentic texts themselves.[77] It is striking to find that late Roman law is now no longer seen only as the specialist preserve of Roman lawyers. The study of late Roman legislation is inseparable from an understanding of late Roman society, and is no more immune from general intellectual currents than any other issue in the period.[78]

---

[75] For the Theodosian Code see now Jill Harries and Ian Wood (eds.), *The Theodosian Code* (London 1993); more generally Jill Harries, *Law and Empire in Late Antiquity* (Cambridge 1999); the Code and legal activity of Justinian have been discussed by Tony Honoré, *Tribonian* (London 1981).

[76] C. R. Whittaker, in Bowersock, Brown and Grabar (n. 11) 385–6, and see the revisionist approach of J.-M. Carrié, 'Le "colonat du bas-empire": un mythe historiographique', *Opus* 1 (1982) 351–70.

[77] S. Corcoran, *The Empire of the Tetrarchs: Imperial Pronouncements and Government AD 284–324* (Oxford 1996).

[78] One field which demands this more sophisticated understanding of late Roman legal thinking and process is that of religious persecution, whether of Manichaeans or Christian heretics, and this too is being addressed, for instance in forthcoming work by Caroline Humfress, and see Richard Lim, *Public Disputation, Power and Social order in Late Antiquity* (Berkeley and Los Angeles 1995).

V

Finally, and perhaps even more than in earlier periods of ancient history, the study of late antiquity is now inseparable from consideration of material culture. Indeed, it would be fair to say that the arena in which the current argument over decline or continuity is most conspicuously being played out is in the debates largely conducted by archaeologists as to the fate or transformation of the late antique city. Nowadays the importance of material culture to historians may seem too obvious to remark, yet though A. H. M. Jones himself had had considerable archaeological experience, and had travelled in the Roman provinces of the eastern Mediterranean,[79] his *Later Roman Empire* is based largely on textual and documentary sources. In contrast Peter Brown's *The World of Late Antiquity* was attractively illustrated and written with a strong consciousness of the material background. Late antique archaeology as such had not been much developed when Jones wrote, and archaeology was still dominated by the search for the classical; but subsequently, and especially after the publication of Hayes's *Late Roman Pottery*, late antique archaeology grew as a field in its own right alongside the early medieval archaeology which focused on the transition to the barbarian West. The excavations conducted at Carthage in the 1970s marked an important stage in this development, producing a large body of material relevant to late antique urban history, and it is largely the archaeological research over the last decades in Syria, Israel and Jordan which has completely transformed our picture of the eastern provinces in the period. But art historians have also been quick to grasp the implications of the new theories of representation, and especially to exploit the possibilities offered by the study of early Christian art.

From the point of view of late antiquity the visual evidence is arguably even more critical in that it has long been interpreted as the index of cultural change. *The Age of Spirituality* was the title given to a major exhibition of the art of the fourth to seventh centuries organised in the late 1970s at the Metropolitan Museum in New York by the late Kurt Weitzmann, and an influential book by Ernst Kitzinger published in 1977 covering much the same period was called *Byzantine Art in the Making*.[80] The idea behind both was that of an increased religiosity, a more spiritual age, deducible from the surviving art. It is of course an interpretation bound in with the notion of a transition from

[79] See Liebeschuetz (n. 5).
[80] See K. Weitzmann (ed.), *The Age of Spirituality: Late Antique and Early Christian Art, Third to Seventh Century* (New York 1979); E. Kitzinger, *Byzantine Art in the Making: Main Lines of Stylistic Development in Mediterranean Art, 3rd–7th Century* (Cambridge, Mass. 1977).

a Roman to a medieval mentality and belongs inherently with a triumphalist view of the rise of Christianity.

The debate centred on issues of style, and proceeded particularly in Kitzinger's case from the assumption that the more elongated and two-dimensional features which he saw in some late antique Christian art (Fig. 7.1) derived from 'a new religious atmosphere', far removed from the classical ideal of the human form.[81] The successive periods from the fourth to the sixth century and later are seen in terms of 'regeneration', 'conflicts', 'polarization' and 'synthesis', in a linear progression from classical to Christian, culminating in a 'major stylistic shift' around the year AD 550 exemplified in the sixth-century apse mosaic of the Transfiguration in the Justinianic monastery now known as St Catherine's at the foot of Mount Sinai and the near-contemporary apse mosaic in S. Apollinare in Classe at Ravenna (Fig. 7.2).[82] He was not the only scholar to have detected a similarly 'spiritual' quality in secular portrait sculpture,[83] and in the case of the Christian examples the change was further linked by Kitzinger with his view of the increased documentation of religious images from the second half of the sixth century onwards as indicative of a new popular spirituality.[84] Of the apse mosaics of S. Apollinare in Classe (sixth century) and S. Agnese in Rome (seventh century), Kitzinger writes that 'one associates such still and lonely figures — gaunt and remote, timeless and supremely authoritative — with Byzantine art in its mature state in the centuries after Iconoclasm'.[85] Underlying this stylistic judgement, therefore, though not explicitly stated, is a deeper assumption about the nature of the transition from the 'classical' to the 'Byzantine'.

The development of Christian art has also traditionally been seen as deeply influenced in its techniques and iconography by imperial art.[86] On the one hand the artists employed on Christian commissions will often have had experience in the techniques and iconography of imperial art, and on the other the Christian view of salvation encouraged a hierarchical model to which the motifs of imperial art lent themselves well.[87]

---

[81] Kitzinger (n. 80) 104–5.

[82] Kitzinger (n. 80) 99–103.

[83] Kitzinger (n. 80) 80; *cf.* A. Grabar, *Byzantium: From the Death of Theodosius to the Rise of Islam* (London 1966) 226.

[84] See E. Kitzinger, 'The cult of images in the age before Iconoclasm', *Dumbarton Oaks Papers* 8 (1954) 83–150.

[85] Kitzinger, (n. 80) 104.

[86] See A. Grabar, *L'empereur dans l'art byzantin* (Paris 1936, repr. London 1971).

[87] For some of the issues, and the varying attempts at adaptation, see Jas Elsner, *Imperial Rome and Christian Triumph* (Oxford 1998).

Fig. 7.1.   Bust of Eutropius from Aphrodisias.

Fig. 7.2.   Apse mosaic, S. Apollinare in Classe, Ravenna.

Both these views of the development of Christian art are closely linked with the problem of 'transition' to a Christian medieval world, and both have recently been challenged. Recent reactions against the first assumption have focused on the technicalities of production and the material record itself rather than its supposed interpretation, and have argued that this so-called 'spirituality' is neither new nor specifically Christian; rather, the explanation for the changes that have been interpreted in this way lies within the complex domain of Roman imperial art itself.[88] In the second case a controversial book by Thomas Mathews has offered a vigorous attack on the 'imperial' model of early Christian art, arguing for a bottom-up rather than a top-down process of development.[89] Mathews sees in Christian art 'a radically new imagery of extraordinary power', and against the great public compositions, stresses the miracle imagery in which 'Christ stepped into a void which none of the gods of the ancient world had managed to fill. He showed himself a god of the "little man", a genuine "grass-roots" god'.[90]

Such a view — even if over-stated — rightly draws attention to the important role played by visual art in indicating to the historian something of the communication of ideas within the given society.[91] It is of course central to the notion of the 'gaze' and the problem of representation. It is therefore interesting to note in this context that while Giardina's call for a move away from the Anglo-centric late antiquity does highlight some of the latter's deficiencies, he makes no allusion to the highly influential theme of change as seen in visual art, or to the interesting work currently being done by historians within the school which he is criticising on the interconnections between art and text.[92]

---

[88] So Jas Elsner, *Art and the Roman Viewer* (Cambridge 1995); for the Sinai mosaic see 100–24. For the argument in relation to late antique sculpture see R. R. R. Smith, 'Late antique portraits in a public context: honorific statuary at Aphrodisias in Caria, AD 300–600', *Journal of Roman Studies* 89 (1999) 155–89, who argues that these depictions have more to do with accepted ideas of official deportment than with 'inner spirituality'. Similarly in the later part of the period Robin Cormack's book *Writing in Gold* (London 1985) rejected the 'spiritual' interpretation of religious icons and explained their popularity in terms of social function.

[89] Thomas F. Mathews, *The Clash of Gods: a Reinterpretation of Early Christian Art* (Princeton 1993, rev. ed. 1999); Mathews' first chapter is entitled 'The mistake of the emperor mystique'.

[90] Mathews (n. 89) 92.

[91] Late antique historians have been much influenced by a book about the early Roman empire: Paul Zanker, *The Power of Images in the Age of Augustus* (Ann Arbor 1988).

[92] Giardina (n. 1) and *cf.* e.g. J. Elsner (ed.), *Art and Text in Roman Culture* (Cambridge 1996).

vi

How long will the Brownian model of late antiquity remain with us? I have argued that it was particularly suited to the context of the late twentieth century, and indeed that in many respects it grew out of that context. This should not be surprising, of course. Nor should it be surprising if more conservative voices are calling for some return to traditional topics and methodologies. Thus even while deploring narrative, Fergus Millar advocates government, law and state finance as being among essential subjects to be covered.[93] Giardina has pointed to the overvaluing of the cultural in comparison with the institutional, and Liebeschuetz wishes to reinstate decline as a useful explanatory concept, while other scholars clearly find the recent strong emphasis on ethnogenesis and the smooth assimilation of barbarians into the western Roman empire overdone.[94]

However, the kind of history that is written depends also on the intellectual and educational context in which it is produced. It has been rightly pointed out that the 'long late antiquity', with its strong emphasis on cultural history, is an Anglo-centric phenomenon. It flourished most when there was a sense of optimism about the contemporary world, and when for a brief time the barriers seemed to be coming down. This was a view that found favour in North America, and which resonated particularly with the dominance of the 'linguistic turn'. Ideas of conquest and invasion did not fit well with this perception. Perhaps as its over-hasty optimism begins to recede we shall begin to see a real return to an emphasis on conflict and rupture, and a shorter late antiquity.

Meanwhile the issue of periodisation seems to be returning as a major preoccupation. It is appropriate to conclude therefore with some observations on a 'boundary' that has attracted somewhat less attention than that between the Later Roman Empire and the medieval West. When, therefore, is Byzantium deemed to have begun — with Constantine and the foundation of Constantinople, or later, perhaps sometime in the sixth or seventh century? Again, there are different views, partly dictated by the intellectual traditions of differing academic disciplines. The *Oxford Dictionary of Byzantium* starts with late antiquity, defining its chronological range as stretching from the fourth to the fifteenth century.[95] Where there is a Greek or Orthodox connection, the Byzantine period begins unequivocally with Constantine and

---

[93] Millar, *Journal of Roman Archaeology* 13 (2000) 757–79.
[94] See Giardina (n. 1) 167, n. 35; 173; 179; for Liebeschuetz see n. 25 above.
[95] A. P. Kazhdan (ed.), *Oxford Dictionary of Byzantium*, 3 vols. (New York 1991).

Constantinople. Other scholars favour a seventh-century or later start, coinciding with the Arab conquests and the drastic urban change in Asia Minor that accompanied it, or with the wholesale reorganisation of the Byzantine state apparatus that was under way in the eighth century.[96] In contrast the 'long late antiquity' flowed into Byzantium and emphasised the elements of survival from the late Roman period.

As in the case of late antiquity, scholars coming from different backgrounds and with different kinds of training bring differing perspectives and agendas to the same problems. But it does leave us with a question relevant to the topic of this chapter, namely, whether late antiquity can really stand alone as an academic field. It has done so for some decades, I have suggested, not least because this fitted so well with wider intellectual agendas in our own contemporary world, and this may not of course always be the case. We may see a return to institutional history, as called for by Andrea Giardina, and the political agendas which have been in eclipse may be waiting to be revived. But in the meantime this heyday of late antique studies has disrupted the old certainties about our own historical development. It has substituted new questions for old ones and subverted traditional assumptions about the classical and medieval worlds. Even while giving so central a place to religion as a cultural factor, it has answered to a post-Christian suspicion of the supposed 'triumph' of Christianity and subjected the role of the post-Constantinian church to a new critical scrutiny. These developments will certainly stay with us for a long time to come. So will the sheer excitement and energy felt by many scholars, young and more experienced, in opening up a vast new range of subject matter, and that perhaps will be the most memorable of all the aspects of this discovery in the late twentieth century of a long late antiquity.

[96] To give only two examples out of many, Mark Whittow, *The Making of Orthodox Byzantium 600–1025* (London 1996), chooses 600 as the start of early medieval Byzantium, though not because he sees it as marking rupture or decline (p. 428); John Haldon, *Byzantium: a History* (Stroud 2000), effectively starts with the death of Leo III in AD 741, having earlier presented the seventh century as a time of transition in historical materialist terms in *Byzantium in the Seventh Century: the Transformation of a Culture* (Cambridge 1990).

8
Recolonising Egypt

Alan Bowman

Prologue

> This country is a palimpsest in which the Bible is written over Herodotus and
> the Koran over that. In the towns the Koran is most visible, in the country
> Herodotus.[1]

The palimpsest which this Victorian lady observed in the mid-nineteenth
century was the result of the numerous occasions during its long history on
which the land of Egypt was captured or claimed by peoples or cultures
regarded as non-natives, foreigners, or outsiders, from the Hyksos to the
British. As well as physical occupation, there is also a long series of historiographical captures by those who lay claim to being part of Egypt's
history or who write it for themselves in and from their own perspective(s).[2]
The two phenomena are, of course closely and organically linked, but not
completely coextensive.

  The subject is a rich and fascinating one for classical scholars, especially
in view of the current interest in constructing accounts which weave ta-
pestries of 'little narratives' based more on ephemeral documentary sources

---

[1] Lucie Duff Gordon, *Letters from Egypt* (3rd ed., repr., London 1983) 67–8. In what follows editions
of papyri are cited according to the abbreviations in J. F. Oates et al., *Checklist of Editions of Greek
Papyri and Ostraka* (Atlanta 1992; new electronic version at http://scriptorium.lib.duke.edu/papyrus/
texts/clist.html).

[2] The title adopted for this chapter is an intentional (and complimentary) reference to T. Mitchell,
Colonising Egypt (Berkeley 1991). It was drafted and delivered in a somewhat different form at the
University of Tel-Aviv in May 2000. Shortly thereafter, 80 papers for a conference at University
College London (December 2000) on various aspects of the subject were temporarily posted on the
Worldwide Web (http://www.ucl.ac.uk/archaeology/general/enco). Many of these were informative
and relevant to my discussion and I have cited the electronic versions with the tag 'Encounters 2000'.
Some, but perhaps not all, of these will eventually be published in the volume(s) of conference
proceedings (University of Pennsylvania Press, forthcoming; I am indebted to Professor John Tait for
this information).

than grand themes of political history.[3] Egypt as a historical subject has never lacked attention in the field of international political history but it is also almost uniquely fruitful as a source of evidence for little narratives and as a historiographical battlefield, as the controversial works of Martin Bernal and Edward Said have so vividly demonstrated in recent years.[4] Lucie Duff Gordon's perception of Egypt, derived not from a fleeting visit, but from a long period of residence near Luxor, emphasises, despite its chronological imprecision, at least two of the key elements which determined the way in which the European mind constructed Egyptian history: the classical tradition and the Judaeo-Christian Bible. Nevertheless her perception was not divorced from the Islamic present, but an integral part of it, as her remarks about religion illustrate:[5]

> The Christianity and the Islam of this country are full of the ancient worship and the sacred animals have all taken service with the Muslim saints. At Minieh one reigns over crocodiles; higher up I saw the hole of Aesculapius' serpent . . . and I fed the birds, as did Herodotus . . . Bubastis' cats are still fed at the Cadi's court at public expense in Cairo and behave with singular decorum when the 'servant of the cats' serves them their dinner. Among gods, Amun-Ra, the sun-god and serpent-killer calls himself Mar Girgis (St George) and is worshipped by Christians and Muslims in the same churches, and Osiris holds his festivals as riotously as ever at Tanta in the Delta, under the name of Seyd al Bedawee. The fellah women offer sacrifices to the Nile, and walk around ancient statues in order to have children. The ceremonies at births and burials are not Muslim, but ancient Egyptian.

With a simple transposition of context and references, we might almost be reading an invocation of Isis, written some 1500 years earlier:

> . . . at Sais ruler, perfect; at Iseum Isis; at Sebennytus inventiveness, mistress, Hera, holy; at Hermopolis Aphrodite, queen, holy; . . . at Pelusium bringer to harbour; in the Casian district, Tachnepsis; at the outlet Isis, preserver; in Arabia great, goddess, in the Island giver of victory in the sacred games; in Lycia Leto; at Myra in Lycia sage, freedom; . . . you who also interpret first of all in the fifteen commandments, ruler of the world; guardian and guide, lady of the mouths of seas and rivers; skilled in writing and calculation and understanding . . .

---

[3] P. Horden and N. Purcell, *The Corrupting Sea: a Study of Mediterranean History* (Oxford 2000) 9–10; J. H. Sibal, review of C. Haas, *Alexandria in Late Antiquity* (Baltimore 1997), in *Journal of the American Research Center in Egypt* 36 (1999) 171.

[4] M. Bernal, *Black Athena: the Afroasiatic Roots of Classical Civilisation*, vol. 1: *The Fabrication of Ancient Greece, 1785–1985* (London 1987); E. Said, *Orientalism* (repr., London 1995).

[5] Gordon (n. 1) 56–7.

and so on for almost 300 lines of text.[6]

What follows is in the nature of an essay, an attempt, inevitably far from comprehensive or in any way definitive, to describe and explain, from an explicitly classical perspective, aspects of the relationship between some ancient and some modern perceptions of Egypt and the role which 'history in' and 'history of' the classical world has played and continues to play in shaping those perceptions.

Greeks in Egypt

In AD 130/1 when Hadrian, the most travelled of Roman emperors, was in Egypt, his young male lover Antinous was drowned in the Nile. There were several consequences, some of them quite literally far-reaching. Antinous received cult which spread throughout the empire and became, Roman emperors excepted, the most frequently sculpted human in classical antiquity. The great majority of the portrayals and the best-known, many of them extremely fine, are sculptures in the classical Greek style, but there is one from Hadrian's villa at Tivoli which represents him strikingly in the Egyptian style, as the god Osiris.[7]

Another result of this tragic event was the foundation of a 'Greek city' named after him at the place of the drowning — Antinoopolis, situated on the east bank of the Nile, almost opposite the great metropolis of Hermopolis and at the point where the *via Hadriana*, coming from the Red Sea coast, reaches the river. The foundation date, 30 October 130, must have been close to the time at which Hadrian inaugurated that great symbol of Greek cultural unity, the Attic Panhellenion; Athens was its epicentre and its membership ranged far and wide, but neither Antinoopolis nor, more significantly, the far greater 'Greek city' of Alexandria belonged.[8] From the time of the original foundation under Hadrian, the Antinoites as a citizen body were overtly much more privileged and accorded greater status distinctions than citizens of the nome-capitals (*mētropoleis*) of Egypt. They were divided into tribes

---

[6] *POxy* XI 1380. The combination of deities is not syncretism but the reverse, as A. D. Nock observed, *Gnomon* 30 (1958) 294.

[7] For examples see *Antinoe cent'anni dopo: catalogo della mostra: Firenze, Palazzo Medici Riccardi, 1998* (Florence 1998).

[8] Antinoopolis: *Antinoe* (n. 7), E. Kühn, *Antinoopolis: ein Beitrag zur Geschichte des Hellenismus im römischen Ägypten* (Göttingen 1913) 7–8 for the foundation date. The Panhellenion: A. J. Spawforth and S.Walker, 'The World of the Panhellenion I: Athens and Eleusis', *Journal of Roman Studies* 75 (1985) 78–104.

Fig. 8.1. Antinoopolis: the colonnaded street, as drawn by members of the Napoleonic expedition.

and demes with Greek names; afforded tax privileges and exemption from liturgical service in other towns; and the city was allowed to have a council (*boulē*) which Alexandria did not obtain until the reign of Septimius Severus, 70 years later.[9]

Had the documentary evidence for all this been available to the members of the Napoleonic expedition in 1798–1799, they would not have been surprised when they came upon the ruins of the Greek style buildings and colonnaded streets at El Sheikh Abadah, the site of ancient Antinoopolis (Fig. 8.1). One thing they would not have seen, as far as we can tell from their drawings, was the splendour of the circular gymnasium in which the roof of the colonnades and entrances was extensively repaired with the use of gold leaf in AD 263. Nor would they have been aware of the fact that the site of this foundation was also a palimpsest, containing remains of earlier Egyptian buildings.[10]

It is worth dwelling on the content and significance of 'Greek' status both for communities and individuals in Ptolemaic and Roman Egypt. As an example, a nome capital or metropolis such as Oxyrhynchus, with a population perhaps in excess of 20,000, was officially called πόλις by the second century AD. The metropoleis had an elite class, defined by membership of the gymnasium and obtained by admission to the ephebate through the process of *epikrisis*, an innovation which goes back to the Augustan period and to original lists drawn up in AD 4/5.[11] By the third century AD (somewhat later than elsewhere in the Roman East) the metropoleis of Egypt self-consciously display their Greek 'civic' status, with town councils created in 200/1, magistrates, an association of elders (*gerousia*), Capitoline Games, public pensions for athletes, a public *grammatikos* and so on.[12]

---

[9] Kühn (n. 8); M. Zahrnt, 'Antinoopolis in Ägypten: die hadrianische Gründung und ihre Privilegien in der neueren Forschung', *Aufstieg und Niedergang der römischen Welt* 2.10.1 (Berlin 1988) 669–706; the council: A. K. Bowman, *The Town Councils of Roman Egypt* (*American Studies in Papyrology* 11, Toronto and New Haven 1971) 14–15; H. Braunert, 'Griechische und römische Komponenten im Stadtrecht von Antinoopolis', *Journal of Juristic Papyrology* 14 (1962) 73–88 stresses similarities to the government of Roman *municipia*.

[10] *Description de l'Égypte* IV, Plates 53–9; gymnasium: *PKöln* I 53; Egyptian buildings: A. Gayet, 'L'exploration des ruines de Antinoé et la découverte d'un temple de Ramses II enclos dans l'enceinte de la ville d'Hadrien', *Annales du Musée Guimet* 26.3 (1897) 1–62.

[11] A. K. Bowman and D. W. Rathbone, 'Cities and Administration in Roman Egypt', *Journal of Roman Studies* 82 (1992) 120–5.

[12] A. K. Bowman, 'Urbanization in Roman Egypt', in E. Fentress (ed.), *Romanization and the City: Creation, Transformations and Failures* (*Journal of Roman Archaeology*, Supplement 38, 2000) 183, with further bibliography.

But the picture at Antinoopolis is in fact more complex, not just because there are remains of earlier Egyptian buildings on the site. A papyrus of the second century shows that the Antinoites were officially allowed by Hadrian to intermarry with Egyptians, that is, presumably without diminution or loss of status and privileges. Even more interesting, this was a privilege 'which the Naukratites, whose laws we employ, do not have'.[13] It is noteworthy that Naukratis, a somewhat special case, was chosen as the source of Antinoopolis' *nomoi*. Alexandria drew upon Athens for its laws.[14]

The Antinoites were officially addressed as *Neoi Hellēnes*, for example by the emperors Antoninus Pius and Gordian III. Many of the citizens of the new city were drawn from the privileged class of the 6,475 ἄνδρες Ἕλληνες living in the Fayyum — that is the term by which the gymnasial class of the metropolis of the Arsinoite Nome was known. M. Lucretius Diogenes, whose archive, including his will, survives in the British Museum, is one example; many of these Antinoite citizens were certainly Roman veteran soldiers and we may legitimately wonder whether many of them had residence at Antinoopolis or, indeed, ever went there.[15] It is also worth emphasising that the term Ἕλλην on its own is not generally or widely used in the metropoleis of Roman Egypt to refer to the gymnasial class. It is relatively rare and complex, carrying status and cultural, but not ethnic or geographical (in the modern sense) connotations — the 'Hellenes' are in fact the upper stratum of those whom Roman legal sources describe as *Aiguptioi*, a term which itself acquired a new meaning with the advent of Roman rule.[16] The study of the antecedents, the so-called 'ethnics' in Ptolemaic Egypt, reveals a situation of great cultural and terminological complexity in which there were both genuine and fictitious ethnic designations, the latter indicators of fiscal or legal status.[17]

What about other cultural indicators? The literary papyri found at Antinoopolis and assignable to the second and third centuries offer a range of Greek literature comparable to that at Oxyrhynchus, with due allowance for quantity and scale: Aristophanes, Chrysippus, Dinarchus, Isocrates,

---

[13] *WChr*.27.20-24, ἥνπερ οὐκ ἔχουσι Ναυκρατεῖται ὧν τοῖς νόμοις χρώμεθα.

[14] *POxy* XVIII 2177 I.i.13–15.

[15] 'New Hellenes': F. Hoogendijk and P. Van Minnen, 'Drei Kaiserbriefe Gordians III an die Bürger von Antinoopolis', *Tyche* 2 (1987) 41–74; the 6,475, *Jur.Pap.* 48: Bowman and Rathbone (n. 11) 121; M. Lucretius Diogenes: P. Schubert, *Les archives de Marcus Lucretius Diogenes* (*Papyrologische Texte und Abhandlungen* 39, Bonn 1990).

[16] J. Mélèze-Modrzejewski, *Droit impérial et traditions locales dans l'Égypte romaine* (Aldershot 1990), chs.1 and 9.

[17] C. La'da, 'Encounters with ancient Egypt: the Hellenistic Greek experience' (Encounters 2000), counts 184 different genuine ethnic labels and argues that there was no institutionalised ethnic discrimination (in favour of 'Greeks' and against 'Egyptians') in the Ptolemaic state.

Menander, Pindar, though Homer is noticeably thin on the ground.[18] There are a good number of so-called mummy portraits, funerary masks and shrouds, comparable to those found in the Fayyum. In cases where the portraits carry names they are generally Greek but the portraits themselves have often been classified as 'Graeco-Egyptian'. This material has attracted much recent attention which has not adopted the perspective of the French archaeologist Guimet, who characterised their purpose as 'pour renforcer le pouvoir romain en Moyenne Égypte, superposée à une société encore très proche du monde pharaonique'.[19] There are clear traces of traditional Egyptian deities such as the familiar statuettes of the household god Bes and at Antinoopolis its eponymous hero is firmly linked to Osiris.[20] In short, this is very much a cultural mix.[21]

From both the ancient and the modern perspective, 'being Greek' and identified as such in Ptolemaic and Roman Egypt goes beyond terminology, is far from a simple matter, and has a relevance beyond the 'Greek cities' of Alexandria, Ptolemais and Antinoopolis. Two of many possible illustrations will suffice. The first is a passage from the editors' introduction to a relatively recently discovered archive of the fourth century AD, describing the principal figures:[22]

> . . . [the] fourth century advocate . . . of Panopolis, a well-educated lawyer who professes and exhibits interest in rhetoric and philosophy . . . [his] half-brother . . . who styled himself *sophistēs dēmosios*, was at times a member of the imperial comitatus declaiming panegyrics in honour of the emperors, meanwhile serving as curator and procurator of the principal cities of Greece.

The name of the first person described is Aurelius Ammon Scholasticus, his brother is Aurelius Harpocration and they were the sons of Petearbeschinis

---

[18] Location list of papyri in R. A. Pack, *The Greek and Latin Literary Texts from Greco-Roman Egypt* (2nd ed., Ann Arbor 1965) is given by K. A. Worp, 'A note on the provenances of some Greek literary papyri', *Journal of Juristic Papyrology* 28 (1998) 209. Compare also the catalogue for the Fayyum villages by P. Van Minnen, 'Boorish or bookish? Literature in Egyptian villages in the Fayum in the Graeco-Roman period', *JJP* 28 (1998) 99–184.

[19] *Antinoe* (n.7) 45–7; S. Walker and M. Bierbrier, *Ancient Faces* (London 1997) 24, S. Walker, 'Mummy portraits in their Roman context', in M. L. Bierbrier (ed.), *Portraits and Masks: Burial Customs in Roman Egypt* (London 1997) 1–6; E. Guimet, *Les portraits d'Antinoe au Musée Guimet* (Paris 1912) v.

[20] Bes: *Antinoe* (n.7) no. 28; note Ἀντίνοος ὁ καὶ Ἀρεώτης Φιλαντινόιδος Ὥρου παστόφορος Ὀσειραντινόου θεοῦ μεγίστου, *PLond* 1164 g.20 (III, p. 163).

[21] P. Cauderlier, 'Sciences pures et sciences appliquées dans l'Égypte romaine: Essai d'inventaire Antinoite', *Recherches sur les artes à Rome, Troisième siècle, Dijon, Octobre 1978* (Dijon 1979) 48: 'bien plus redevables à la couture égyptienne que leur phraséologie officielle de "nouveau grecs" . . . ne le laisse entendre'.

[22] *PAmmon*, pp. 1–2.

Fig. 8.2. The Ptolemagrius Monument from Panopolis.

and Senpetechensis also called Nike, hereditary priests of the god Min, a wealthy Egyptian family of high status in Panopolis at the time when Christianity was well on its way to predominance (*c.* AD 340).

Min was the Egyptian god whom the Greeks identified as Pan; Panopolis is Herodotus' floating island of Chemmis, modern Achmim, which was to become a centre of Greek literary activity (notably poetical) in late antiquity.[23] It was also the site of the garden of Ptolemagrius which has produced my second illustration, one of the most striking monuments of the Roman period in Egypt (Fig. 8.2). On each of the four faces of the stela there is carved at the top a bust of a Greek deity or religious personification, some of which are identified by lines of Homer; below them are Egyptian-style carvings of Canopic jars representing 14 Egyptian deities, and below that texts of hexameter verses of which the context is unmistakeably Homeric. The begetter of this monument, of the second or third century AD, appears to be a Roman veteran and towards the end of the text he memorialises his public benefactions in a context which juxtaposes Greek and Egyptian religious elements:[24]

> Agrius feasts twice yearly the entire people of Pan the mountain dwelling god at the solemn banquets of Phoebus, calling two men, *archontes*, from each *ethnos*; and is accustomed to honour the priests of the *ethnos* and helpers for the libations to the number of 100, likewise twice a year.

The form which Greek identity, ethnic or cultural, took in Egypt is heavily conditioned by an evolving ancestral memory vested in immigrant groups of diverse origin; 'being Greek' will not have meant exactly the same to a member of one of these groups in the third century BC, to a descendant under Augustus, and to another in the fourth century AD.[25] That is, so to speak, one layer of 'text' on the palimpsest that is Egypt.

---

[23] A. Cameron, 'Wandering poets: a literary movement in Byzantine Egypt', *Historia* 14 (1965) 470–509.

[24] O. Guéraud, 'Le monument d'Agrios', *Annales du Service des Antiquités d'Égypte* 39 (1939) 279–303; C. B. Welles, 'The Garden of Ptolemagrius at Panopolis', *Transactions of the American Philological Association* 77 (1946) 192–206; E. Bernand, *Inscriptions Métriques de l'Égypte gréco-romaine* (Paris 1969) 114–15; L. Criscuolo, 'Nuove reflessioni sul monumento di Ptolemaios Agrios a Panopolis', G. Paci (ed.), *EPIGRAFAI: Miscellanea epigrafica in onore di Lidio Gasperini* (Rome 2000) 275–90; I am very grateful to Lucia Criscuolo for providing the photograph reproduced in Fig. 8.2 and for her permission to use it.

[25] See W. Clarysse, 'Ethnic diversity and dialect among the Greeks of Hellenistic Egypt', in A. M. F. W. Verhoogt and S. P. Vleeming (eds.), *The two faces of Graeco-Roman Egypt: Greek and Demotic and Greek-Demotic Texts and Studies Presented to P. W. Pestman* (*Papyrologica Lugduno-Batava* 30, Leiden 1998) 1–13, and on ancestral memory, D. L. Selden, 'Alibis', *Classical Antiquity* 17 (1998) 289–300.

Perceptions of Egypt

But there is more to it than that. The inhabitants of the classical Mediterranean world both inside and outside Egypt, had a variety of perceptions and perspectives on a land which had a very high profile. For them, as for their modern descendants, there were many different, interleaved Egypts, or aspects of Egypt, to be appealed to and captured, some more metaphysical than others, in which the separation of 'history', 'geography', 'language' and 'culture' in the modern sense or senses cannot adequately represent the reality of what was happening — a dynamic evolution over several millennia, the nature of which may be fundamentally misrepresented as soon as one makes a distinction between history and geography, or attempts to convey meaning and cultural connotation in the process of translating Greek and Egyptian languages.[26] In trying to describe some of these ancient Egypts I can see no way of avoiding the pitfalls of classifying and characterising discretely. It will not escape notice that almost every example used in any particular heading could equally pertinently be used in one or more of the others.

1. Egypt is prominent as the romanticised or idealised setting for ancient **fiction**, as it continues to be for modern authors, many of whom manipulate the historical time frame to move between past and present.[27] Of the many ancient authors who use Egyptian settings, Achilles Tatius and Heliodorus are perhaps the most widely studied. Heliodorus' *Aithiopika* opens with a scene involving band of Egyptian brigands — swarthy and unkempt — in the Delta, precisely located at the Heracleotic mouth of the Nile, in the course of which the author proceeds to an apparently realistic description of the area called the Boukolia:[28]

> . . . the home of the entire bandit community of Egypt, some of them building huts on what little land there is above water, others living on boats that serve them as both transport and dwelling. On these boats their womenfolk work at their weaving; on these boats their children are born. Any child born there is fed at first on its mother's milk, later on fish from the lake dried in the sun. If they see a child trying to crawl, they tie a cord to its ankles just long enough to allow it to reach the edge of the boat or the door of the hut.

[26] K. J. Clarke, *Between Geography and History* (Oxford 1999), S. Clackson, 'Who was who in late antique Egypt: modern appropriations of cultural perspective' (Encounters 2000). On translation see below, p. 204.

[27] E.g. Amitav Ghosh, *In an Antique Land* (London 1992); Ahdaf Soueif, *The Map of Love* (London 1999).

[28] *Aithiopika* 1.5, trans. J. R. Morgan in B. P. Reardon (ed.), *Collected Ancient Greek Novels* (Berkeley 1989) 357.

There are echoes here of Herodotus' description of the Paeonian lake-dwellers (5.16), as well as thematic links to an earlier work of fiction, the *Phoinikika* of Lollianus, in the context of which modern scholars have evoked the possible historical reality underlying such descriptions, for we are told of a serious revolt of the Boukoloi in the Egyptian Delta in the year AD 172.[29]

It is, of course, easy to imagine how this identifying mark might have been attached to actual incidents of revolt or local unrest but less easy to see whether disruptive elements in the population were actually pastoralists (or, on another interpretation, priests!). In any event, this example invites us to consider the relationship between fiction and reality in cases where the historical setting of fictionalised real events leads us along a path on which, at some point which cannot precisely be identified, we move from one to the other, retaining, as we move seamlessly into the explicit fiction, the 'reality' of the lawlessness of the region.[30]

2. The statement that the classical world, from Herodotus onwards, identified 'native' Egyptian **religion** as the prime source of ancient wisdom and ritual stands in need of no lengthy justification — Egyptian cult and religious ritual was generally believed to be the oldest. During the millennium from Alexander to the Arab conquest, Egypt came to accommodate a huge variety of cults and religious groups, Egyptian, Greek, Roman, Jewish and Christian. Within this heterogeneous array there are bodies of religious literature and practice very different from each other (and from the modern), co-existing in bewilderingly complex patterns, which accommodate separate, parallel and interlocking development and growth.[31] A vivid demonstration of the subtle interplay of the different elements and traditions is provided by the contents and character of the so-called *Corpus Hermeticum*, brilliantly evoked by Garth Fowden: a heterogeneous corpus of technical and philosophical treatises betraying Egyptian, Greek and Jewish traditions (with no provable influence of Christianity), and propounding in the Graeco-Egyptian milieu of the Egyptian Hermes Trismegistos (where Greek Hermes is equated with Egyptian Thoth) a prophetic and Egyptocentric religious attitude.[32] Set beside

---

[29] On Lollianus see J. Winkler, 'Lollianus and the desperadoes', *Journal of Hellenic Studies* 100 (1980) 155–81; on the revolt of the Boukoloi, R. Alston, 'The revolt of the Boukoloi: geography, history and myth', in K. Hopwood (ed.), *Organised Crime in Antiquity* (London 1999) 129–53.

[30] For discussion of this in relation to the lack of solid documentary evidence for banditry see B. McGing, 'Bandits, real and imagined in Greco-Roman Egypt', *Bulletin of the American Society of Papyrologists* 35 (1998) 158–83.

[31] See D. Frankfurter, *Religion in Roman Egypt* (Princeton 1998).

[32] My understanding, such as it is, of this complex material is essentially derived from G. Fowden, *Egyptian Hermes* (2nd ed., Cambridge 1993), far superior to the account of M. Bernal (n. 4) ch. 2.

that (for example), the temple of Jupiter Capitolinus at Arsinoe, metropolis of the Arsinoite Nome (Fayyum) in the early third century AD, adorned with a colossal statue of the emperor Caracalla.[33]

If it is hard to provide a neat characterisation of this agglomeration, it is almost as hard to offer a simple description of the way in which Greek observers understood it and reacted to it, a matter of considerable interest. Without going into details of liturgy, practice or belief, it is on one level relatively easy to understand what Herodotus tells us about the priestly records he claims to have seen and to have had interpreted for him.[34] It is also possible, on the face of it, to understand what Plutarch is doing when he tells us about Isis and Osiris in the linguistic and conceptual framework of the Greek language and lore (though it proves harder when modern commentators try to match it empirically or positivistically to an Egyptian framework).[35] There is a huge amount of evidence which places Isis and her associated legends and rituals very much at the interface of contact between Egyptian and Graeco-Roman religion. With that one can contrast the evidence for an uncomprehending and contemptuous stock attitude on the part of the Greeks to Egyptian animal cult.[36]

Perhaps all this merely illustrates the difficulty of describing idiosyncratic features of one culture in the language of another, as the *Corpus Hermeticum* shows:[37]

> those who read my books will think that they are very simply and clearly written, when in fact, on the contrary, they are unclear and hide the meaning of the words, and will become completely obscure when later on the Greeks want to translate our language into their own, which will bring about a complete distortion and obfuscation of the text.

But it did not stop them trying, as Greek translations of Egyptian ritual texts show.[38] One of the most intriguing attempts was that made in the first century AD by a certain Chaeremon, an Egyptian priest and Stoic philosopher — a good combination — to explain the organisation, regime and behaviour of the Egyptian priesthood, also proffering translations and explanations of the

---

[33] *BGU* II 362.vi.4–6 (= *WChr.* 96).

[34] 2.44.2, 2.54.1 etc.

[35] E.g. J. G. Griffiths, *Plutarch's De Iside et Osiride* (University of Wales Press 1970).

[36] E.g. Lucian, *Deorum concilium* 10–11.

[37] *CH* XVI, quoted and translated by Fowden (n. 32), 37.

[38] R. Merkelbach, 'Ein Ägyptischer Priestereid', *Zeitschrift für Papyrologie und Epigraphik* 2 (1968) 5–30.

'sacred symbols'.[39] This was a process followed by later exegetes, including the translation of the text on the Lateran obelisk by Hermapion and the later work of Horapollo.[40] The process of demystifying Egyptian hieroglyphs has an intriguing and highly successful modern manifestation too.[41]

A less explicit mode of expressing the relationship between Egyptian religion and Greek understanding is abundantly illustrated in the innumerable examples of the 'twinning' of deities, especially the *Aretalogies* or *Invocations of Isis*,[42] which also incidentally emphasise the extremely high degree of regional variation in Egyptian religion, a phenomenon which is not confined to religion and a feature which it shares with Greek. Nor should it be assumed that these equivalences were fixed and standardised.[43]

3. Closely connected is the perception of Egypt as an object of pilgrimage or tourism and a **repository of ancient culture**. From Hecataeus and Herodotus onwards, Egypt was a great attraction to tourists who went to visit religious monuments and other sights. A Roman senator named L. Mummius visited the Fayyum towards the end of the second century BC and observed the sacred crocodiles being fed. Strabo journeyed up the Nile in the company of his friend Aelius Gallus, the prefect of Egypt. The graffiti in the Memnoneion at Abydos and in the tombs of the Valley of the Kings, the poems and other texts inscribed on the statue of Amenhotep III in the Theban plain (the 'Colossus of Memnon') by those who came to hear it 'sing' when struck by the rays of the morning sun are testimony to the many visitors, from emperors down, who recorded their presence in inscriptions and graffiti in a variety of scripts and dialects (Fig. 8.3), from original verses to simple formulae like εἶδον καὶ ἐθαύμασα ('I saw and I wondered').[44]

[39] P. W. Van der Horst, *Chaeremon: Egyptian Priest and Stoic Philosopher* (*Études Préliminaires aux religions orientales dans l'empire romain* 101, Leiden 1984), *fr.* 12 (hieroglyphs).

[40] Hermapion: Ammianus Marcellinus 17.4; Horapollo: F. Sbordone, *Hori Apollinis Hieroglyphica* (Napoli 1940); G. Boas, *The Hieroglyphics of Horapollo* (New York 1950), who assembles other ancient testimonia on hieroglyphs.

[41] M. Collier and W. Manley, *How to Read Egyptian Hieroglyphs* (London 1998).

[42] See above, p. 194.

[43] See the doubts about the identity of Bes in a graffito from the Memnoneion at Abydos (P. Perdrizet and G. Lefebvre (eds.), *Inscriptiones Graecae Aegypti* Vol. 3 (Paris 1919) 498), discussed by I. Rutherford, 'Pilgrimage in Greco-Roman Egypt: new perspectives on graffiti from the Memnonion at Abydos' (Encounters 2000).

[44] Herodotus 2.143; Mummius: *PTeb* I 33 (?112 BC); Strabo: J. Yoyotte, P. Charvet and S. Gompertz, *Strabon, Le voyage en Égypte: un regard romain* (Paris 1997); Memnoneion: Perdrizet and Lefebvre (n. 43), Rutherford (n. 43); tombs: J. Baillet, *Inscriptions grecques et latines des Tombeaux des Rois ou Syringes* (*Mémoires de l'Institut français d'archéologie orientale* 42, Cairo 1920–1926); 'Colossus of Memnon': A. and E. Bernand, *Les Inscriptions grecques et latines du Colosse de Memnon* (*IFAO, Bibl. D'Étude* XXXI, Paris/Cairo 1960).

Fig 8.3. Statue of Amenhotep (the 'Colossus of Memnon') in the Theban plain; inscriptions commemorating the visits of tourists.

Visiting the relics of an ancient civilisation is one thing, capturing it another. The inhabitants of the classical world did both, although the later European notion of a museum, in which one can capture and 'objectivise' the essence of a civilisation and make it static in a room or a series of tableaux or cabinets is very different, I think, from any ancient *mentalité*.[45] But there are some distant analogues suggesting a pervasive classical form of Egyptomania, many in familiar objects.

The roster of Egyptian and Egyptianising monuments in imperial Rome is a long and impressive one (even if one discounts buildings such as Temples of Isis as being not merely ornamental but functional). The pyramid of Caius Cestius is prominent in the urban landscape of Rome, as was the horologium of Augustus. Hadrian's villa at Tivoli, which contained

---

[45] See M. Beard, 'Casts and cast-offs: the origins of the museum of Classical Archaeology', *Proceedings of the Cambridge Philological Society* 39 (1993) 1–29; M. Beard and J. Henderson, 'Please don't touch the ceiling: museums and the culture of appropriation', *New Research in Museum Studies* 4 (1993); P. Connor, 'Cast-collecting in the nineteenth century: scholarship, aesthetics, connoisseurship', in G. W. Clarke (ed.), *Rediscovering Hellenism* (Cambridge 1989) 187–235.

obelisks, was itself an Egyptianising monument, and there is also the obelisk on the Lateran, described and interpreted by Ammianus Marcellinus (above, n. 40). Of Egyptian themes in the plastic arts, the Palestrina mosaic is merely the most prominent example among very many in Italy.[46] It may be misleading to think that this is simply an Italian or Roman imperial fashion, for monuments were moved within Egypt (just as many visitors to Egyptian sites were themselves from other parts of Egypt). The recent discoveries of relics of buildings in the harbour of Alexandria have rescued a very surprising number of blocks from Egyptian monuments: were the Ptolemies (and the Roman prefects) creating an 'Egyptian museum' in the Greek capital, Greek Alexandria once again 'capturing' Egyptian Memphis?[47]

4. As for **anthropology and ecology**, the legacy of Herodotus, in method and perspective, was a major determinant for the ancients and continued to be influential into the nineteenth century, as exemplified in major works on the 'Manners and Customs' of both the ancient and the 'modern' Egyptians. Here, hard and fast distinctions between anthropology, geography and history cannot be sustained. Ancient authors continued to be fascinated by the flora and fauna, the physical characteristics of the land and its people. The papyri reveal works of anonymous authors dealing with the customs of barbarian peoples and ethnographic ὀνόμαστα καὶ ἀξιόλογα, perhaps in Arabia or India.[48] Diodorus, Strabo and Pliny the Elder stand, among others, in direct succession to Herodotus. The famous surviving digression of Ammianus may serve as an illustration:

> Now the men of Egypt are, as a rule, somewhat swarthy and dark of complexion, and rather gloomy-looking, slender and hardy, excitable in all their movements,

---

[46] On all this, A. Roullet, *The Egyptian and Egyptianising Monuments of Imperial Rome* (*Études préliminaires aux religions orientales dans l'empire romain* 20, 1972); The Horologium: *Cambridge Ancient History* 10 (new ed. 1996) 789; Palestrina mosaic, most recently F. Burkhalter, 'La mosaïque nilotique de Palestrina et les *Pharaonica* d'Alexandrie', *Topoi* 9 (1999) 229–60 and S. Walker, 'Carry-on at Canopus: the Nilotic mosaic from Palestrina and Roman attitudes to Egypt' (Encounters 2000).

[47] For the much-publicised harbour excavations see F. Goddio, *Alexandria, the Submerged Royal Quarters* (London 1998), J.-Y. Empereur, *Alexandrie Redécouverte* (Paris 1998) and *cf.* D. J. Thompson, 'Alexandria: the city by the sea', *Bulletin de la Société d'archéologie d'Alexandrie* 46 (2001) (Alexandrian Studies in Honour of Mostafa el Abbadi) 77. For the contrast of Greek Alexandria with Egyptian Memphis, see the discussion of the Oracle of the Potter by L. Koenen, 'The prophecies of a potter: a prophecy of world renewal becomes an apocalypse', *Proceeedings of the XII International Congress of Papyrology* (*American Studies in Papyrology* 7), 249–54 and *cf.* Thompson, above.

[48] *POxy* II 218, *PHib* II 185 (*c.*280–250 BC).

quarrelsome and most persistent duns. Any one of them would blush if he did not, in consequence of refusing tribute, show many stripes on his body; and as yet it has been possible to find no torture cruel enough to compel a hardened robber of that region against his will to reveal his own name.[49]

In ancient, as in modern Egypt, such sociological observations determined the way in which the inhabitants were treated, as in the letter of the emperor Caracalla expelling 'Egyptians' from Alexandria in AD 215:[50]

> For true Egyptians can easily be recognised among the linen-weavers by their speech, which proves them to have assumed the dress and appearance of another class; moreover the mode of life, their far from civilised manners, reveal them to be Egyptian country-folk.

It is worth noting that here the distinction is not made on the basis of their facial appearance or the colour of their skin, although it is clearly one element in Ammianus' description.

5. The **history and historiography** of Egypt before the arrival of Alexander is a complex matter. Modern Egyptologists have been until recently apt to state that much of the original source material on which it has to be based is in some sense fundamentally ahistorical:

> It is difficult . . . to escape from simply describing the various theological facets of kingship in the Egyptians' own terms . . . The source material is so slight that narrative history may be considered an inappropriate literary form, particularly if one begins to suspect that the impressive façade of uniformity and continuity presented by inscriptions and monuments designed to propound the theology of divine kingship hides a complex and changing political scene.

---

[49] 22.16.3 (trans. J. C. Rolfe): *Homines autem Aegyptii plerique subfusculi sunt et atrati, magisque maestiores, gracilenti et aridi, ad singulos motus excandescentes, controversi et reposcones acerrimi. erubescit apud eos siqui non infitiando tributa, plurimas in corpore vibices ostendat. et nulla tormentorum vis inveniri adhuc potuit, quae obdurato illius tractus latroni invito elicere potuit, ut nomen proprium dicat.* A comparison with E. W. Lane, *An Account of the Manners and Customs of the Modern Egyptians* (repr., London 1954), writing about modern Egyptians in 1836, is instructive: 'The natural or innate character of the modern Egyptians is altered in a remarkable degree by their religion, laws and government, as well as by the climate and other causes . . . they are endowed, in a higher degree than most other people, with some of the more important mental qualities, particularly quickness of apprehension, a ready wit and a retentive memory (277). . . . The generality of the Egyptians are easily excited to quarrel, particularly those of the lower orders who when enraged curse each other's fathers, mothers, beards etc.; and lavish upon each other a variety of opprobrious epithets such as "son of the dog, pimp, pig"' (307). The moral content of nineteenth-century attitudes towards the Egyptians, particularly their 'indolence' is very striking, *cf.* Mitchell (n. 2) 106–8.
[50] *PGiss* 40.ii.

This is a complex statement, ripe with implicit historiographical assumptions and frustrations.[51] The character of the slight source material which is thought to provide the basis for the more remote periods of Egyptian history may be in part appreciated by looking at the some of the selections presented in the third edition of a standard compendium, J. B. Pritchard's *Ancient Near Eastern Texts Relating to the Old Testament* (3rd ed., Princeton 1969). Not only do the Egyptian 'historical texts' sit oddly with modern notions of what history is, but the title of the work itself suggests a conceptual framework and an aim which might seem to marry genres which are fundamentally incompatible; implicit in it is the search for historical 'proof' of what is to be found in the scriptures. Even a glance at the later material in the standard compendium of Egyptian literary texts reveals the absence of history in a narrative framework. Romances and 'myth' supplement evidence of king-lists and the like which broadly fall into Collingwood's category of 'theocratic' history.[52] This statement is, of course, not intended to deny the existence of real historical figures in Egyptian history but to underline the difficulty of extracting from these records what heirs of the classical tradition regard as 'real' history.[53]

The earliest prominent example of an Egyptian account in which historical events are set in a narrative framework seems to be the *Demotic Chronicle*, a propagandistic compilation whose 'nationalistic' overtones are now regarded as more clearly anti-Persian than anti-Greek. The date of composition, or of the redaction which we have, seems likely to be early Ptolemaic (or possibly Second Persian occupation).[54] This suggests that the

---

[51] B. F. Trigger, B. J. Kemp, D. O'Connor and A. B. Lloyd, *Ancient Egypt: a Social History* (Cambridge 1983) 73. For a more enterprising attempt see A. Kuhrt, *The Ancient Near East c.3000–300 BC* (London 1995) 1, chs. 3–4, although she too recognises the impossibility of constructing a proper narrative history for some periods (p. 137) and laments the absence of a counterpart of Herodotus as a source for social history (p. 7).

[52] M. Lichtheim, *Ancient Egyptian Literature* vol. 3 (Berkeley 1980); R. G. Collingwood, *The Idea of History* (Oxford 1946) 14–17.

[53] The point is neatly illustrated by the argument of J. Assman, *Moses the Egyptian: the Memory of Egypt in Western Monotheism* (Cambridge, Mass. 1997) 24, that until the nineteenth century there was virtually no memory of Akhenaten, who was a real historical figure, whereas the reverse is the case with Moses, of whose existence no historical trace remains; this leading to the (unanswerable) question of whether Akhenaten was the Egyptian Moses and the 'biblical image of Moses was a mnemonic transformation of the forgotten pharaoh'. There is an interesting comparison to be made here with Josephus, *Contra Apionem*, 1.279–87, discussing the Egyptian claim that Moses was one of the priests expelled from Heliopolis for leprosy.

[54] See J. H. Johnson, 'The Demotic Chronicle as an historical source', *Enchoria* 4 (1974) 1–19; 'The Demotic Chronicle as a statement of a theory of kingship', *Journal of the Society for the Study of Egyptian Antiquities* 13 (1983) 61–72; 'Is the Demotic Chronicle an anti-Greek tract?' in H.-J. Thissen and K.-Th. Zauzich (eds.), *Demotika Grammata: Festschrift für E. Lüddeckens* (Würzburg 1984) 107–24.

introduction of what modern historians recognise as narratological history of Egypt more or less coincides with the imposition of Macedonian–Greek dominance in Egypt.

It hardly needs saying that the Greeks had earlier fitted Egyptian 'historical' events into their own chronological narrative scheme, which accommodated, for example, Solon's visit to Egypt, where he heard about Atlantis.[55] But early in the Ptolemaic period an internal Egyptian chronological 'narrative' was constructed, was used by classical historians such as Diodorus, and is still used, as is too rarely explicitly stated, as the basis of the modern chronology of dynastic Egypt. This was created in the third century BC in the ambience of the Ptolemaic court by an Egyptian priest of Isis, Manetho of Sebennytos (in the Delta), writing in Greek, who alone 'represents a complete and systematic version of the Egyptian tradition.'[56] Egyptian history was thus captured or re-invented within a classicising historiographical framework possibly with the encouragement, if not instruction, of Ptolemy II Philadelphus, the monarch who founded that factory of classical scholarship, the Alexandrian Museum.

The history and culture of one civilisation were described and explained in the language of another. It is hardly necessary to labour the striking parallels: the work of Berossus, the Letter of Aristeas and the Septuagint.[57] Manetho, of course, uses earlier Egyptian source material but, as far as I am aware, none of this is self-reflexive or historiographically conscious; that is, it never asks itself whether what it is saying is correct or plausible. The key difference is that Manetho and his material become part of a historiographical tradition, in which he debates with and criticises Herodotus and is in turn criticised by Josephus.[58]

---

[55] J. G. Griffiths, 'Atlantis and Egypt', *Journal of the Society for the Study of Egyptian Antiquities* 13 (1983) 10–28.

[56] G. P. Verbrugghe and J. M. Wickersham, *Berossos and Manetho* (Michigan 1996) 120, and more recently J. Dillery, 'The first Egyptian narrative history: Manetho and Greek historiography', *Zeitschrift für Papyrologie und Epigraphik* 127 (1999) 93–116. I am oversimplifying a complex issue here: as Verbrugghe and Wickersham note (p. 119) there is no evidence for the view that this was history written to order for Ptolemy Philadelphus. Dillery (pp. 112–13) characterises it as 'a narrative history of Egypt constructed out of a traditional method of preserving the past that had existed for millennia (the King List)', and one that 'also contained narratives that offered another way to present the history of Egypt, one that concerned both the past and the future and which privileged the role of the native priest'; he concludes that 'the incentive to write the work, indeed perhaps the model itself of the combined King List and narrative, evidently came from the Greek world.'

[57] Berossus: Verbrugghe and Wickersham (n. 56); letter of Aristeas etc.: most recently E. Gruen, *Heritage and Hellenism: the Reinvention of Jewish Tradition* (Berkeley 1998) ch. 6.

[58] Josephus, *Contra Apionem* 1.227–87. On Greek attitudes to Egyptian history see also Selden (n. 25) 319–54.

Inventing Egyptology

As far as the European consciousness and understanding of Egyptian history is concerned, it is perhaps not too much of a travesty to say that that was how matters stood for a couple of millennia. Before the end of the nineteenth century there were of course a good number of Europeans who visited Egypt,[59] but it is important to remember that they were faced with hugely impressive monuments carrying inscriptions which they could not understand, even though some such as Athanasius Kircher had made serious, unsuccessful but by no means ludicrous attempts to decipher the hieroglyphs.[60] So the landscape of 'classical' Alexandria and 'Greek' Antinoopolis might not have seemed so anomalous to them and to the Napoleonic savants as they did, and to some extent still do, to later generations. The perspective of one such early traveller, the Frenchman C.-F. Volney, who visited Syria and Egypt in 1783–1785 and published his account of the 'spectacle des moeurs et des Nations' in 1787, is instructive:[61]

> C'est en ces contrées . . . que sont nées la plupart des opinions qui nous gouvernent; c'est de là que sont sorties ces idées religieuses qui sont influé si puissament sur notre morale publique et particulière, sur nos lois, sur tout notre état social.

Equally striking and paradoxical are some of the paintings by Cassas which accompanied Volney's account of this visit, showing the ancient state of native Egyptian temples populated by figures wearing classical dress.[62]

All that was to change with the visit of the Napoleonic expedition and, twenty years later, the decipherment of hieroglyphs, forever associated with Champollion and the Rosetta Stone, which had come to rest in the British Museum in 1802. Champollion's achievement has been described in lyrical terms and in France he achieved a popular recognition which Emmanuel Le Roy Ladurie has compared with that accorded to Louis Pasteur, which is interesting from various points of view.[63] There are several important fea-

---

[59] Of the English travellers, the best known is perhaps Richard Pococke, sometime Canon of Christ Church (*A Description of the East, and Some other Countries* (London 1743–1745)). See also A. Siliotti, *Egypt Lost and Found: Explorers and Travellers on the Nile* (London 1998) and P. and J. Starkey, *Travellers in Egypt* (London 1998) chs. 3–4.

[60] H. Whitehouse, 'Towards a kind of Egyptology: the graphic documentation of ancient Egypt', in E. Cropper, G. Perini and F. Solinas (eds.), *Documentary Culture: Florence and Rome from Grand-Duke Ferdinand to Pope Alexander VII* (Bologna 1992) 63–79.

[61] C.-F. Volney, *Voyage en Syrie et en Égypte pendant les années 1783, 1784 et 1785* (Paris 1787) vi.

[62] For examples see Siliotti (n. 59), plates 60–71.

[63] *Mémoires d'Égypte: Hommage de l'Europe à Champollion* (Strasbourg 1990) 1.

tures of the Rosetta story, some of which have been well brought out by Parkinson.[64] One is that it was a gradual process. Not only did others apart from Champollion, notably Thomas Young, also play a part, but the importance of earlier work on the scripts (by Kircher in particular) and the knowledge of the Coptic language in the medieval Arabic period were crucial to Champollion's success. Another is that the structure and format of the text, which has tended to attract less attention than the object itself, shows clearly that the original decree relating to the Egyptian priesthood in 196 BC was written in Greek and translated into Egyptian, as some early commentators had argued. That is a salutary reminder of one of the facts of history *in* Egypt — the primacy of the language and culture of the politically dominant power.[65]

The major consequence of this was, of course, the creation of the subject of Egyptology. When a superficially scientific title ('-ology') is attached to a subject area, it often has a connotation which is not entirely neutral. Many '-ologies' are protected by their practitioners as enclosed subjects, whose designation warns the rest of us that they are clearly defined, enclosed and in many cases inward-looking disciplines to which only the chosen few have direct access: consider Assyriology, or even Mycenology, papyrology and philology — whereas we notably do not have 'Hellenology' or 'Romanology'.[66] The development of Egyptology was perhaps assisted in its exclusivity by the fact that the language when deciphered was widely (though not accurately) believed to have very few etymological links to other known languages of the region.[67]

Much early study (and not a little subsequently) was directed towards the language, and many Egyptologists have been linguists rather than historians in the conventional European sense, this despite the fact that many of them, such as John Gardner Wilkinson, were classically educated.[68] Only very recently has there been a noticeable move away from the tendency to see the Rosetta stone, for example, as 'a deeply strange, if wonderful, product of an

---

[64] R. B. Parkinson, *Cracking Codes: the Rosetta Stone and Decipherment* (London 1999).

[65] See C. Onasch, 'Zur Königsideologie der Ptolemäer in den Dekreten von Kanopus und Memphis (Rosettana)', *Archiv für Papyrusforschung* 24/5 (1976) 140, 148.

[66] I am suggesting only a tendency, not a universal truth; archaeology, to name only the most obvious, would be a counterexample to such a generalisation.

[67] A. H. Gardiner, *Egyptian Grammar* (3rd ed., Oxford 1957) 2, notes links to Semitic languages and Berber. See also F. Haikal, 'Egypt's past regenerated by its own people' (Encounters 2000).

[68] J. Thompson, *Sir Gardner Wilkinson and his Circle* (Austin, Tex. 1992) 146; '"Purveyor-General to the Hieroglyphics": Sir William Gell and the development of Egyptology' (Encounters 2000).

incomprehensible civilisation.'[69] For reasons already explained, for the conventional history of Egypt the early Egyptologists tended to fall back on what they found in the classical authors from Herodotus onwards. For classicists, too, there was (and still is) an attraction in subjects which were clearly delimited and no longer 'alive' — all the evidence could be encompassed and controlled: in the Griffith Institute in Oxford, the whole subject was in essence (until 1999) contained in three small rooms and two book-lined corridors!

In more recent times, the preoccupation with the *longue durée* has characterised much serious historical writing, and there has also been a less helpful tendency to evoke the timelessness of Egyptian history through the image of the peasant or *fellah* toiling with primitive tools over the cultivation of a small plot on the banks of the Nile. For European Egyptologists of the nineteenth century, pharaonic civilisation was dead and remote: what links there were with the present were more impressionistic than historical. Although many were very well connected, often in high governmental and diplomatic circles, they were not unfailingly sensitive to the politics and culture of the Egyptian present in which they found themselves. One striking of symptom of both their intense curiosity and their self-confident control was the fly-on-the-wall practice of infiltrating the 'native' culture in 'oriental' garb and re-importing the understanding thus gained into their own anthropological construct.[70]

The context in which early European Egyptology developed was therefore a complex, interwoven consciousness of the classical past, the ancient 'oriental' past and the Islamic present, but it might be argued that the developing discipline of Egyptology was deliberately isolated from all of these, as a more or less conscious tactic of cultural imperialism. The two latter were not always clearly distinguished in the minds of the Europeans, nor is the attitude of the culturally Arabised nineteenth-century Egyptians to their past a simple matter. There is some tendency in modern times to evoke a 'nationalist' theme by linking the Egyptian present with the pharaonic past, ignoring the millennium of Greek and Roman rule as an aberration, but

---

[69] J. Katz, review of Parkinson (n. 64) in *Bryn Mawr Classical Review* 00.03.13, 1 (2000) 1. Note also the exceptional appeal of Collier and Manley (n. 41) in demystifying hieroglyphs (also noted by Katz, above, 4).

[70] There are many well-known examples (apart from Sir Richard Burton), see Mitchell (n. 2) 26–7. But there is some uncertainty arising from the fact that many Europeans, including Gardner Wilkinson, simply adopted oriental dress for comfort and convenience and not for purposes of 'espionage'; see J. Rodenbeck, 'Edward Said and Edward William Lane', in P. and J. Starkey (n. 59) 233–43. It is also a popular theme in novels, e.g. Ahdaf Soueif (n. 27).

Arabic historiography of the eighteenth and nineteenth centuries had no trouble in distinguishing between an 'oriental' past and an Islamic present when reformulating Egypt's history. It is often claimed, however, that Arabic historians of Egypt tended to regard the pagan pre-Islamic civilisation with contempt. In the case of Al-Tahtawi, in the mid-nineteenth century, it is significant that his ideas of ancient Egypt were derived from contact with orientalist scholars in France.[71] Nevertheless, it may be the case that nine-teenth-century European scholars consciously excluded Egyptians from the discipline and ignored or did not know the medieval Arabic evidence for knowledge of pre-Islamic Egypt.[72] As an instructive parallel it can be noted that European historians of Egypt have tended to ascribe changes in the crop regime, the commoditisation of land and the stratification of rural society in Egyptian agriculture of the eighteenth and nineteenth centuries to contact with Europe, a view which has recently been emphatically challenged by Kenneth Cuno.[73]

At the same time, the nineteenth century saw, advancing *pari passu* with the increasing knowledge of the Egyptian language, the rediscovery and collection of antiquities and the development of archaeology. This was a sort of dismemberment of Egypt by the Europeans, the physical counterpart of the intellectual capture of the ancient civilisation. The process of collection of Egyptian antiquities and their dispersal among the public spaces, mu-seums, cities and aristocratic houses of Europe and North America needs no detailed documentation here. The museum mentality, in which a subject, a culture, a discipline can be collected, classified and objectivised in a series of rooms or cabinets, is a central feature of nineteenth-century intellectual history, and the parallels between this phenomenon, the study and classifi-cation of oriental languages and the development of scientific method have been appositely noted.[74]

There are almost innumerable books dealing with the 'rape' or 'redis-covery' of Egypt in the nineteenth century. Biographies of Egyptologists,

---

[71] A. Hourani, *Arabic Thought in the Liberal Age 1798–1939* (Cambridge 1962) 70, cf. Mitchell (n. 2) 107.

[72] Haikal (n. 67). O. El Daly, 'Ancient Egypt in medieval Arabic writings' (Encounters 2000) discusses the medieval Arabic evidence.

[73] K. Cuno, *The Pasha's Peasants: Land, Society and Economy in Lower Egypt 1740–1858* (Cambridge 1992) 198; cf. in general A. K. Bowman and E. Rogan, *Agriculture in Egypt from Pharaonic to Modern Times* (Oxford 1999).

[74] Mitchell (n. 2) 139. Despite the possible examples of Hadrian's villa at Tivoli and the Alexandria harbour discoveries (above, n. 47) as proto-museums, the phenomenon does not seem to be widespread in classical antiquity.

books about the pillage of the antiquities, the colonisation of Egypt, visitors to Egypt, women's writings about Egypt and 'the orient' continue to flood on to the shelves.[75] Alongside this we have witnessed a preoccupation with the documentation of 'Egyptomania' in the nineteenth and early twentieth centuries, which has its counterpart in classical times and in the very recent past.[76] Among the most influential events of the past in formulating the European view of ancient Egypt have been Verdi's *Aida*[77] and the Paris exhibitions of 1867, 1878 and 1889. A key point is brought out by Timothy Mitchell in his *Colonising Egypt*, the best modern analysis of the self-reinforcing and cyclical process of the European capture, understanding and appropriation of Egyptian culture and civilisation, and in particular its dependence on the understanding of the language as the basis of ordering and constructing its physical shape and its *mentalité*:[78]

> Exhibitions, museums and other spectacles were not just reflections of this [European political] certainty, however, but the means of its production, by their technique of rendering history, progress, culture and empire in an 'objective' form. They were occasions for making sure of such objective truths . . .

As I have tried to show, this statement could equally well be footnoted by reference to Greek and Roman sources, and the cycle continues: all this and more was documented and re-created in Paris in the magnificent 1994 Louvre exhibition entitled 'Egyptomania: L'Égypte dans l'art occidental, 1730–1930', by which time the entrance of the Louvre itself boasted its very own pyramid.[79]

Towards the end of the nineteenth century, 'serious archaeology' developed in Egypt, associated with the magisterial figure of Flinders Petrie, whose activities were by no means confined to Egypt. Petrie's influence in terms of developing scientific methods of excavating and recording was enormous, as was his range, which effectively touched on all the major

---

[75] The bibliography is enormous (much of it can be found in bibliographies of the papers given at the conference referred to in n. 2 above). Examples include M. S. Drower, *Flinders Petrie: a Life in Archaeology* (London 1985), T. G. H. James, *Egypt Revealed: Artists–Travellers in an Antique Land* (London 1997), Mitchell (n. 2), P. and J. Starkey (n. 59), Thompson (n. 68) and Siliotti (n. 59).

[76] J. S. Curl, *Egyptomania: the Egyptian Revival, a Recurring Theme in the History of Taste* (Manchester 1994), *cf.* Haikal (n. 67).

[77] It is instructive to compare and contrast *The Magic Flute*, written before the Napoleonic expedition and the decipherment of the Rosetta Stone; particularly the religious/mystical theme of Mozart, contrasted with the underlying political theme in Verdi (*cf.* P. Frandsen, 'Aida and Edward Said: attitudes and images of ancient Egypt and Egyptology' (Encounters 2000)).

[78] Mitchell (n. 2) 7.

[79] *Egyptomania: L'Égypte dans l'art occidentale, 1730–1930* (Paris 1994).

periods of Egyptian archaeology, and his breadth of approach, which is surely one of the founts of archaeological anthropology (even if some of the assumptions about racial typology do not suit modern taste or political attitudes). Petrie was a key figure as much for what he found as for what he thought it meant. Much of his activity took place away from the major 'Egyptological' sites, and this too was important. He excavated extensively in the Fayyum where he found less that was pharaonic and more that was Graeco-Roman, including the famous mummy-portraits.[80] This feature, along with his personal influence and that of his supporter Amelia Edwards in the somewhat fraught history of the Egypt Exploration Fund in this period, was no doubt important in the organisation of its research and publication into the Egyptological and the Graeco-Roman branch of what eventually became the Egypt Exploration Society.[81]

The contents of the Petrie Museum in University College, London give a fair idea of the range and richness of the finds of this important period of Egyptian archaeology, but in many other places the relics of the Graeco-Roman era have been forgotten, neglected or confined to the dustier corners of museums. Despite being treated as poor relations to the pharaonic monuments in catalogues and exhibitions, they are still very much part of that same continuing process of dismemberment and dispersion. There is no little irony in this, in view of the fact that many of the major Egyptian religious sites and monuments on which our knowledge of pharaonic Egypt is based were actually built, in whole or in part, during the Ptolemaic and Roman periods: the Temples of Horus at Edfu, Isis at Philae and the Temple of Esna, for example. The rituals associated with the voyage of Horus down the Nile to Denderah and his marriage to Hathor at her temple there are known in detail only from reliefs carved long after the pharaonic period when, on the conventional view, Egyptian religion was declining or moribund.[82]

The other important element in this archaeological activity, in which Petrie was also deeply involved, was the discovery of large quantities of papyri which burgeoned in the 1890s. The expeditions of Grenfell and Hunt

[80] See most recently Walker and Bierbrier (n. 19).
[81] See the excellent biography by Drower (n. 75). For an interesting but little-known archaeological predecessor see D. Jeffreys, 'Ahead of his time: the experience of Joseph Hekekyan' (Encounters 2000).
[82] Esna: S. Sauneron, *Les Fêtes religieuses d'Esna aux derniers siècles du paganisme* (*Esna* 5, Cairo 1962); Dendera: F. Daumas, *Dendera et le Temple d'Hathor* (*Recherches d'Archéologie, de Philologie et d'Histoire* 29, Cairo 1969). See Frankfurter (n. 31) for an attempt to analyse the complex patterns of religion in the Roman period.

to Oxyrhynchus and the villages of the Fayyum were typical and very productive examples. The exciting discovery of new works of classical literature, theological texts and great quantities of administrative documents, almost all written in Greek, proved more immediately attractive to classical scholars than to Egyptologists. Classicists concentrated their enthusiasm on the written texts and, on the whole, put the analysis of the physical circumstances of discovery in second place: 'the evidence of archaeology fully prepares us for accepting the general account of the Fayum given by Herodotus' wrote Grenfell and Hunt in their introduction to *Fayum Towns and their Papyri* (1900).

The impact of the papyri on various fields of study in classical antiquity has been nothing short of revolutionary. For much of the first hundred years of papyrology the fields of study which have been most heavily affected have tended to remain somewhat discrete: literature, New Testament theology, the history of Ptolemaic and Roman Egypt, the latter in particular traditionally seen as standing somewhat apart from the rest of the Roman Empire.[83] The papyri, perhaps to an even greater extent than the archaeological remains, have been taken out of their context and dispersed. This is partly the result of the circumstances of discovery. Much of the excavated material was removed from Egypt and distributed to many dozens of musems, universities, libraries and private collections. Much was also acquired through the antiquities market, with no acknowledged provenance: we still do not know for example, exactly where the great Zenon archive of the third century BC and the even larger Heroninus archive of the third century AD were found, and attempts to reconstruct them are relatively recent and still incomplete.[84]

Another effect of the concentration on Greek papyri has been that the large numbers of demotic Egyptian papyri of the Ptolemaic and early Roman periods have lain relatively ignored and are much underrepresented in the

---

[83] See Parsons, Chapter 3 above; P. Van Minnen, 'The century of papyrology (1892–1992)', *Bulletin of the American Society of Papyrologists* 30 (1993) 5–18.

[84] Zenon: P. W. Pestman et al., *Guide to the Zenon Archive* (*Papyrologica Lugduno-Batava* 21, Leiden 1981); Heroninus: D. W. Rathbone, *Economic Rationalism and Rural Society in Third-century AD Egypt* (Cambridge 1991). Maurice Nahman, a dealer in Cairo, was prominent in this trade and his customers included a cartel of European and North American institutions, among which was the British Museum represented by H. I. Bell. There is a good deal of underexploited documentation in the form of notebooks, letters and diaries of excavators in the 1890s and 1900s, see for example D. Montserrat, '"No papyrus and no portraits": Hogarth, Grenfell and the first season in the Fayum, 1895–1896', *Bulletin of the American Society of Papyrologists* 33 (1996) and A. Martin, 'The Oxyrhynchus Papyri and the antiquities market (in the light of the "Deutches Papyruskartell")', in A. K. Bowman, R. A. Coles, D. Obbink and P. J. Parsons (eds.), *Oxyrhynchus: a City and its Texts* (London forthcoming).

published corpus; the relatively numerous classicists capable of reading the Greek papyri and the relatively small number of Egyptologists capable of reading demotic papyri (and within Egyptology the minority of scholars interested in this late material) has accentuated the divide. Many scholars familiar with the Oxyrhynchus papyri may well be unaware, for example, that the collection contains not only Greek and Latin texts, but small numbers of demotic, Syriac and Hebrew papyri as well.[85]

Crossing boundaries

At the beginning of the twenty-first century, with the consciousness of cultural plurality stronger than it has ever been, we are more inclined to cross than to defend boundaries, to approach the classicist's subject-matter in a more Herodotean spirit, even if that leads us to venture views and to make judgements in areas where we do not all command all the necessary technical skills. Among the boundaries which are more readily being permeated are those between 'popular' and 'serious' study, between the various branches and periods of classical scholarship and, perhaps most controversially and most significantly, between the 'classical' and the 'oriental'.

In the popular imagination, Egypt may still be primarily the land of pyramids and pharaohs, which connects to the 'western' or Judaeo-Christian experience mainly via the Bible,[86] but scholars of the late twentieth and early twenty-first centuries are much more alert to the importance, as well as to the 'romance' of Graeco-Roman Egypt, writing of the 'renaissance' of the study of Egypt in the Graeco-Roman period (now less frequently designated by this portmanteau term).[87] A reviewer of Haas's recent book on Alexandria, while noting the traditional dogma that 'the Graeco-Roman periods are a purgatory considered neither quite fit for the Classicist nor the Egyptologist,' wrote that 'Only Egypt . . . provides the necessary and ample documentation for multicultural concerns of subjectivity, perspective and what postmodern theorists call "little narratives".'[88]

---

[85] Bowman et al. (n. 84).

[86] This is both reflected and created in the modern film industry, on which see S. Serafy, 'Egypt in Hollywood: pharaohs of the fifties' and 'Egypt in Hollywood: enter Cleopatra' (Encounters 2000). Particularly significant are the two versions of Cecil B. de Mille's *The Ten Commandments*: the later version (1956), generally considered inferior as a film, carries a strong contemporary political message.

[87] Montserrat (n. 84). More common now are Ptolemaic, Roman and Late Antique Egypt.

[88] Sibal (n. 3).

This new attitude and interest has found its reflection in the public arena too, going well beyond the perennial and superficial fascination with Cleopatra VII.[89] Graeco-Roman Egypt is taken seriously in the arts. Tony Harrison's *Trackers of Oxyrhynchus* brought Grenfell and Hunt on to the West End stage, evoking the heady excitement of the early days of discovery of unknown fragments of classical literature in the papyri. William Golding wrote of the rich harvest to be reaped from the remains of this period:[90]

> It was, after all, a kind of challenge to see what would arise in an unusual juxtapostion of two cultures and two wildly differing sets of experience. As the scrap of papyrus says . . . 'Sailors who skim deep waters, Tritons of the salt sea, and you Riders of the Nile who sail in happy course upon the smiling waters, tell us, friends, the comparison of the ocean with the fruitful Nile.

The British Museum's exhibition of *Ancient Faces* had a considerable impact, not least because of the humanity and immediacy of the so-called Fayyum portraits (which occur only in the Roman period and are by no means confined to the Fayyum).[91] Academic classicists who ignore these manifestations or refuse to take them seriously do so at their peril, although they need always to be alert to the transition from 'true' to 'false' history or to fiction masquerading as history.[92]

In response to the growing consciousness of the effects of dismemberment of artefacts and documents in the past two hundred years, there is a noticeable desire to repair the ill effects by putting them back together again in their proper context, particularly in bringing the documentary evidence into a closer relationship with the archaeological, a process which modern information technology makes possible on an unprecedented scale. Reassembling artefacts and documents in exhibitions and publications has advanced and stimulated

---

[89] Mainly manifested on celluloid (see Serafy (n. 86) but now also the recent exhibition, and the excitement caused by the discovery of a possible example of her subscription on a late Ptolemaic papyrus, P. Van Minnen, 'An official act of Cleopatra (with a subscription in her own hand)', *Ancient Society* 30 (2000) 29–34.

[90] William Golding, *An Egyptian Journal* (London 1985) 207, quoting *POxy* III 425 (= Page, *Greek Literary Papyri*, no. 97, E. G. Turner, *Greek Manuscripts of the Ancient World* (2nd ed.= *BICS* Suppl. 46, 1987), no. 5): [ν]αῦται βαθοκυμα[τ]οδρόμοι ἁλίων Τρίτωνες ὑδάτων καὶ Νειλῶται γλυκυδρόμοι πλέοντες ὑδάτη τὴν συνκρισιν εἴπατε φίλοι πελάγους καὶ Νείλου τε γονίμου. As Page notes, 'the poem is an invitation to these two groups of men to compete with each other in song or play, the subject of the competition being the "comparison (or rather contrast) of ocean and Nile".'

[91] Walker and Bierbrier (n. 19) For examples from Antinoopolis see n. 19 above.

[92] For subtle denunciation of Marguerite Yourcenar's novel *Memoirs of Hadrian* in this vein see R. Syme, 'Fictional history, old and new: Hadrian', *Roman Papers 6*, (Oxford 1991) 155–81. For classical novels on Egypt, see above, pp. 202–3. Amitav Ghosh's novel *In an Antique Land* scrupulously uses as a basis documents from the Cairo Geniza.

interest, and given the objects of study a higher profile. The mummy portraits are put into context with shrouds and masks and other examples of funerary art, their dates are reassessed and an attempt is made to map them on to social history. Are they Egyptian, Greek, neither or both? Can we identify the subjects of these portraits in the documentary record?[93] The records of discovery of the monuments of the Ptolemaic and Roman periods are re-evaluated, fragments of 'classical architecture' are re-examined, and much material discovered a century ago proves to be a sound basis for reconstructing the physical development of a nome-capital like Hermopolis, settlement patterns in the Fayyum or the relationship between Greek architecture in Alexandria and in the towns of the *chora*.[94]

The actual physical context of the discovery of papyri and other objects can be to some extent reconstructed on a house-to-house basis in the Fayyum village of Karanis, a site whose archaeology and documentation still invites detailed reconstruction — it will never be the Montaillou of the ancient world but it may be the closest we can get.[95] For Karanis, as for other towns and villages, we can reconstitute the roster of literary works found, hitherto listed in the standard catalogue by author or genre.[96] This eventually may help us to understand how a scribe at Karanis in the second century AD could translate an Egyptian name in a tax-list by an extremely rare Greek word which he can only have known from having read Callimachus and could not have used correctly without understanding the etymology of the Egyptian name as well.[97]

That example perhaps suggests the need for alertness to the issues of multiculturalism and cultural contact in all periods. As J. W. B. Barns emphasised in 1966:[98]

> For those in particular who are interested in the interplay of Greek and oriental civilisations there is no better documented field than Egypt; it is to be hoped that a closer synthesis of classical and Egyptological study will help us to a better

---

[93] Walker and Bierbrier (n. 19).

[94] D. M. Bailey, 'Classical architecture in Roman Egypt', in M. Henig (ed.), *Architecture and Architectural Sculpture in the Roman Empire* (Oxford University Committee for Archaeology, Monograph 29, 1990), 121–37; id., *Excavations at El-Ashmunein IV: Hermopolis Magna: Buildings of the Roman Period* (London 1991); D. W. Rathbone, 'Towards a historical topography of the Fayum', in D. M. Bailey (ed.), *Archaeological Research in Roman Egypt* (*Journal of Roman Archaeology* Suppl. 19, 1996) 50–6; J. McKenzie, 'Alexandria and the origins of baroque architecture', *Alexandria and Alexandrianism* (Malibu 1996) 109–25.

[95] P. Van Minnen, 'House-to-house enquiries: an interdisciplinary approach to Roman Karanis', *Zeitschrift für Papyrologie und Epigraphik* 100 (1994) 227–51.

[96] Van Minnen (n. 95), Worp (n. 18).

[97] H. C. Youtie, 'Callimachus in the tax rolls', *Scriptiunculae 2* (1973), 1035–41.

[98] J. W. B. Barns, *Egyptians and Greeks* (Oxford 1973).

understanding of a thousand and more years actual synthesis of two of the greatest civilisations in history.

It is difficult to make cultural comparisons without resorting to mere description, wholesale syncretism or romanticisation. But much has been achieved in recent years: attempts at new readings of Egyptian art, particularly funerary, in the Roman and Byzantine periods, not least because of the attraction of the unique mummy portraits; re-evaluations of the history of religion and cult, juxtaposed in a culture where Egyptian, Greek, Roman and Christian are at once both distinct and interrelated; the physical development of towns which brought classical elements into Egyptian architecture and layout; numerous studies of ethnicity; and, fundamental to all studies of cultural contact, the difficult questions of bilingualism and language contact (where few are truly qualified to analyse and understand the processes at work and to appreciate what is involved in 'translation'), along with studies which do actually mobilise both Greek and demotic documents for social history.[99] To such studies the processes of reassembling the *disiecta membra* are central.

Finally, there is the formidably controversial issue of the classical and the oriental. Of the Roman Near East (though he omits specific treatment of Egypt) Fergus Millar has written:[100]

> The social and cultural history of the Near East in this period is no simple matter of a conflict between 'Classical' and 'Oriental'. The various local cultures could find expression in ways which were strikingly different one from another . . . [W]hatever metaphor we use for the interplay of cultures in this region, every aspect of society and culture was influenced both by Greek civilisation and by the progressive extension of Roman rule. When we have examined the different sub-regions of the Near East in comparison with each other, it will be necessary to ask whether the region as a whole should be seen as part of the 'Orient' or as part of the wider Graeco-Roman world.

In directing this question towards the study of ancient and modern Egypt it is impossible to avoid mentioning Edward Said's *Orientalism* and Martin Bernal's *Black Athena*, both of which have evoked passionate criticism,

---

[99] For an illustrative analysis of the difficulties of conveying meaning across linguistic boundaries and the impossibility of achieving completely 'objective' translation, see Mitchell (n. 2) 142–50. The same point is made in a slightly different way in the passage from the Corpus Hermeticum quoted on p. 204 above. Greek and demotic: C. La'da, 'One stone two messages (CG 50044)', *Proceedings of the XX International Congress of Papyrology* (Copenhagen 1994) 160–4.

[100] F. Millar, *The Roman Near East 31 BC– AD 337* (Cambridge, Mass. 1993) 235.

often amounting to fierce denunciation, from some quarters.[101] In general, positive reactions to these authors have tended to focus more on their analyses of modern approaches to the history of the orient and the classical world ('history of') than on the actual history of these regions ('history in'), where they have been accused of misunderstanding or misrepresenting the evidence for what actually happened. This carries a salutary lesson for the future of the study of Egypt.

We have seen how the nineteenth-century European consciousness, with its classical heritage, objectivised Egypt and Egyptian history, capturing it in a particular frame of reference which served to reinforce and create its present and to ensure, by contact with Europe and by the promotion of various technologies, principally literate education, that the 'objective' view and the frame of reference were adopted and reinforced by the Egyptians themselves. However much modern sensibilities wish to condemn this, its actual occurrence cannot just be dismissed as an aberration or a 'derivative' phenomenon. So too, classicists should be prepared to insist on the importance of the fact that Egypt was effectively dominated by a Greek-speaking culture for a millennium, without complete obliteration of other cultural elements. If we fail to do this we run the risk of underplaying, for example, the decisive effect which Alexandria had on the cultural, social and economic history of the Mediterranean world and its role as a link between Egypt and that wider world; or of creating a deeply damaging rift between its history before the Arab conquest and after it (when, after all, both Greek and Coptic language and culture did survive, now in a subordinate rather than a dominant role).

Conversely, we should be prepared to re-examine, re-evaluate and perhaps abandon some of our prejudice and dogma, especially in the light of recent debate about 'orientalism' and the relations between the history of the classical world and that of the ancient Near East. The difficulty appears to lie in an inability to accommodate the Near East to a classicising, Eurocentric historicism without being patronising or simply dismissing it as 'alien'. We might be well advised to adopt a more Herodotean perspective and consider how the non-classical *logoi* might help us to more of a polycultural understanding. For example, a contemporary historian of the ancient Near East, Marc Van de Mieroop, has written an account of the ancient Mesopotamian city in which he seeks to question and undermine the perspective of classical historians who 'often continue to see the origin of the city as a Greek phenomenon, and either

---

[101] Said and Bernal (both n. 4).

deny the existence of the Near Eastern city, or see it as inconsequential for later urbanism . . . ', which involves ' . . . perpetuating some old prejudices such as the idea of Oriental Despotism'.[102]

Few contemporary classical historians would accept such an idea without qualification, but there are relatively few areas, accessible to both classical and Near Eastern historians, in which a better understanding can be constructed. Egypt surely offers the greatest potential, and the ways in which it is now treated by significant numbers of scholars in the various periods of its history should and surely will play a leading role in undermining that implicit antithesis between the classical and the oriental, and enhance the study of cultural relationships in both the ancient and the modern world.

For help and advice I am indebted to the other contributors to this volume, to Professor Fergus Millar, Professor Bert Smith, Professor Peter Parsons, Dr. Eugene Rogan and Professor Ian Christie.

---

[102] M. Van de Mieroop, *The Ancient Mesopotamian City* (Oxford 1997) 4–5.

9
Greek history: a discipline in transformation

John K. Davies

i. Introduction

From their predecessors, who had created and adorned the heroic age of historical scholarship on the history of ancient Greece, those who had survived the First World War inherited a discipline already characterised by a multiplicity of formats, interests, and specialised sub-sets. Thenceforward for a generation or more, though there were innovations (such as the 'historical commentary'), and though there were technical advances (such as the new standard of epigraphical reportage and accessibility set and maintained by *Hesperia* from 1932), the shape and the main agendas of the discipline remained largely stable. In contrast, those of us who have been active as historians of ancient Greece since 1960 or so have lived through, and contributed to, a series of remarkable shifts and enlargements of scholarly focus, many of which have been heavily influenced by ideas and debates which have developed in other disciplines.

The task of this chapter has therefore to be to describe those innovations as lucidly and as dispassionately as possible, while not devaluing much other work which has kept alive and viable a well-embedded traditional understanding of 'Greek history' as a largely autonomous discipline with a trajectory of its own. Though the names of individual scholars will inevitably and rightly figure in these pages, the chapter will not follow the biographical approach which has characterised much recent work on the historiography of Greek history. That is not to belittle the value of the detailed biographical studies, especially those of Momigliano and Christ,[1] which provide an

---

[1] *Cf.* especially Conrad Bursian, *Geschichte der classischen Philologie in Deutschland, von den Anfängen bis zur Gegenwart* (Oldenbourg, Munich and Leipzig 1883); (Sir) J. Edwin Sandys,

invaluable conspectus of individuals' activity, intellectual influences and publications in the field. However, studies of individual scholars — even of those as influential as Rostovtzeff or Finley — cannot by themselves plot the changing conceptions of Greek history: the growth of institutions such as learned societies and archaeologically oriented Schools in Classical lands, the changing patterns of school and university teaching,[2] the interests of the wider reading public, the reading of the present into the past, and the growing complexities and interpenetrations of older and newer academic fields of study, have all helped to transform what is denoted by 'Greek history'.

What follows here, therefore, will largely eschew personalities in favour of formats and themes. Part ii surveys the main genres of scholarship historically, Part iii attempts to identify the main directions and problems which preoccupy scholars at present, while Part iv presents four case-studies of new material.

ii. The genres of scholarship

1. Multi-volume narrative histories

It may be useful to begin by reviewing briefly the main formats within which Greek historical scholarship had crystallised by 1914, for their inheritance is still influential today.[3] First and foremost come the classic multi-volume narrative histories, above all those of Meyer, Busolt and Beloch, the latter indeed still in progress in 1914 since the final volume of its second edition

---

A History of Classical Scholarship, 1–3 (Cambridge 1903–1908; vol.1, 2nd ed. 1906, 3rd ed. 1921); Arnaldo Momigliano, *Studies in Historiography* (London 1966); Karl Christ, *Von Gibbon zu Rostovtzeff* (Darmstadt 1972; 2nd ed. 1979); A. Momigliano, *Essays in Ancient and Modern Historiography* (Oxford 1977); K. Christ, *Neue Profile der alten Geschichte* (Darmstadt 1990); A. Momigliano, *The Classical Foundations of Modern Historiography* (Berkeley, Los Angeles and Oxford 1990); A. Momigliano, in G. W. Bowersock and T. J. Cornell (eds.), *Studies on Modern Scholarship* (Berkeley, Los Angeles and Oxford 1994); K. Christ, *Griechische Geschichte und Wissenschaftsgeschichte* (Stuttgart 1996).

[2] *Cf.* Dankward Vollmer et al., *Alte Geschichte in Studium und Unterricht* (Stuttgart 1994); Christopher Stray, *Classics Transformed: School, Universities, and Society in England, 1830–1960* (Oxford 1998).

[3] For more detailed surveys of the earlier stages of such scholarship see Carmine Ampolo, *Storie greche: la formazione della moderna storiografia sugli antichi Greci* (Turin 1997), and Davies, *Neue Pauly* 14 (2000) 188–98.

was not published until 1927.[4] These *Geschichten*, each the masterpiece products of single minds, represented the culmination of the multi-volume monograph tradition. As a genre, they went back through several heroic generations of mostly German-language scholarship to the work of the Anglo-Scottish quartet of Mitford, Gillies, Niebuhr's emulator Thirlwall, and above all George Grote,[5] whose twelve volumes both defined the subject chronologically and set the agenda of debate for over fifty years. Since the focus of the present chapter is on more recent developments, and since much attention has already been devoted to many of the scholars who contributed to this genre, it is enough here to note briefly that the multi-volume narrative 'History of Greece' was the first literary form within the discipline to treat its source-material critically, to interact with contemporary political themes and social developments, and to wield influence internationally in wider intellectual circles.

More relevant is to understand why after 1918 it ceased to be, as it had been for over a century, the backbone of the subject. Largely, it was a matter of practicality, for the general post-1918 response was to recognise that the growth of knowledge and the proliferation of published scholarship made it impossible to sustain Busolt's ideal of perfection, viz. to cite every text and contribution relevant to the topic under discussion. Practice developed instead in three alternative directions. One was the summary monograph, of one or two volumes.[6] A second was to adlect collaborators, as Glotz did in the 1920s and 1930s,[7] or, more adventurously, to create a new art form of

[4] In chronological order of first publication, (a) the Greek volumes of Eduard Meyer, *Geschichte des Altertums* 1–4 (Stuttgart 1884–1902; 2nd ed. 1907–1939), with William M. Calder III and Alexander Demandt (eds.), *Eduard Meyer: Leben und Leistung eines Universalhistorikers* (Leiden 1990), and Momigliano 1994 (n. 1) 209–22; (b) Georg Busolt, *Griechische Geschichte bis zur Schlacht bei Chaeronea* 1–3.2 (Gotha 1885–1888, 2nd ed. 1893–1904), with Mortimer H. Chambers, *Georg Busolt: his Career in his Letters* (Leiden 1990); and (c) Karl Julius Beloch, *Griechische Geschichte* 1.1–4.2, (Strassburg 1893–1904; 2nd ed. 1912–1927), with Momigliano 1994 (n. 1) 97–120.

[5] W. Mitford, *The History of Greece* 1–5 (London 1784–1810); John Gillies, *The History of Ancient Greece, its Colonies, and Conquests; from the Earliest Accounts till the Division of the Macedonian Empire in the East* 1–2 (London 1786); Connop Thirlwall, *A History of Greece* 1–8 (London 1835–1847); George Grote, *A History of Greece* 1–12 (London 1846–1856), with Momigliano 1994 (n. 1) 15–31.

[6] E.g. (Sir) J. B. Bury, *A History of Greece to the Death of Alexander the Great* (London 1900, 2nd ed. 1913, 3rd ed. 1951 (rev. R. Meiggs), 4th ed. 1975); Helmut Berve, *Griechische Geschichte* 1–2 (Freiburg im Breisgau 1931–1933); Gaetano De Sanctis, *Storia dei Greci, dalle origini alla fine del secolo V* 1–2 (Florence 1939); Hermann Bengtson, *Griechische Geschichte von den Anfängen bis in die römische Kaiserzeit* (Munich 1950, 5th ed. 1977); Wolfgang Schuller, *Griechische Geschichte* (Oldenbourg and Munich 1980, 3rd ed. 1990 [1991]); and others.

[7] Gustav Glotz, Robert Cohen, and P. Roussel, *Histoire grecque*, 1–4.1 (Paris 1925–1938).

collective history, where an editorial team commissioned chapters from individual specialists to fit within a still largely diachronic format: the *Cambridge Ancient History* led the way, followed more recently by *Storia e Civiltà dei Greci, Hellenische Poleis* and *I Greci*.[8] Third, more recent, has been the growth of monograph series such as those of Methuen, Nouvelle Clio, and Fontana/dtv, each breaking up 'Greek history' into periodised sections.

Since the pros and cons of such narrative history formats have long been debated, it is needless to do more here than signal them as they apply to this particular segment of human history. The overwhelming concentration of the Greeks' own historiographical tradition on political and military affairs did indeed provide modern Greek historiography with a usable diachronic backbone from *c*.550 BC onwards until the Roman period, though an intractable hiatus of uncertainty between *c*.280 and *c*.230 BC is only now being bridged by the detective work of generations of epigraphically based scholarship. However, that very concentration made it hard for scholars to integrate the narrative of often fast-changing political and military events in the public domain with consideration of those features of life which changed more slowly, or changed in a different rhythm, or involved the excluded and the nameless. Moreover, Greek history, unfolding as it did via a multitude of regional and civic microhistories most of which were only spasmodically documented if at all, presented — as Roman history did not — the acute technical problem of interweaving different narratives in different theatres in such a way as to show both their independence and their degrees of inter-locking. That in turn set the challenge of balancing the affairs and agendas of the bigger players (Athens above all, but also Sparta and Macedon and Syracuse) on the one hand against those of the small fry, and on the other against the looming presence of the Achaimenid Persian empire, its pre-decessors, and its successors. Indeed, but for the powerful influence of the Hellenocentric cultural tradition, it would be tempting — and indeed more rational — to write most Greek politico-military history as a subset of Persian history.

A brief glance at recently published volumes within the various series cited above shows how the solutions to such technical challenges can differ.

---

[8] The Greek volumes (3 to 7) of the first edition of the *Cambridge Ancient History* were published in 1925–1928: those of the second edition (volumes 3.1 to 7.1) came out in 1982–1984. More recent are R. Bianchi Bandinelli (ed.), *Storia e Civiltà dei Greci*, 1–10 (Milan 1977–1989), Elisabeth C. Welskopf (ed.), *Hellenische Poleis* 1–4 (Berlin 1974) and Salvatore Settis (ed.), *I Greci*, 1–2.3 to date (Turin, 1996–).

Part 2 of *I Greci*, for example, confines narrative to a few chapters, widely scattered through its three volumes, and otherwise articulates itself via regional or thematic studies, descriptions of institutions, and essays on the meanings of culturally complex words. In contrast, the Greek volumes of the new edition of the *Cambridge Ancient History* range from linear, unified narrative (most of IV and V, pp. 1–208 of VI, much of VII, Part 1) and chapter-length sketches of separate regional trajectories within the sixth (III, Part 3) and fifth/fourth centuries BC (the rest of VI) to a concentrated section on the cultural history of the fifth century (pp. 171–369 of V).

Intrinsic to any diachronic format is the barely avoidable expedient of periodisation, which has had very ambivalent effects. Grote's influential decision to treat pre-776 material as unhistorical made the subject manageable but created a barrier which has become a handicap now that 'narratives' based on the evidence of sites and artefacts are being seen as appropriate as much for the 'Archaic' period as for Bronze Age or Early Iron Age Greece. Likewise, Grote's decision to end in 301 BC typified a growing consensus to focus only on the Greece of the 'free' states: Beloch alone went on till 217, De Sanctis not even continuing past 404. Indeed, the history of the Greece of the Successor kingdoms had already become a separate subgenre with Gillies' later book of 1807.[9] It received definitive form with Droysen's new term 'Hellenismus' of 1836[10] and has generated a distinguished sequence of monographs ever since.[11] In this way the split between 'Classical' and 'Hellenistic', later mirrored by the emergence of 'Archaic' as a third category, has deeply influenced the profile of the subject. It has perpetuated notions of rise, zenith and decadence, has hindered wider views of Greece as part of the Balkan–Mediterranean Iron Age, and has left entrenched the prejudice that military power and the quality of art and literature are what define 'central' periods.

[9] John Gillies, *The History of Ancient Greece from the Reign of Alexander to that of Augustus . . .* 1–2 (London 1807).

[10] Gustav Droysen, *Geschichte des Hellenismus,* (1–2, Hamburg 1836–1843; 1–3, 2nd ed. 1877–1878), with Reinhold Bichler, *Hellenismus: Geschichte und Problematik eines Epochenbegriffs* (Darmstadt 1983) and Momigliano 1994 (n. 1) 147–61.

[11] E.g. G. F. Hertzberg, *Die Geschichte Griechenlands unter der Herrschaft der Römer* 1–4 (Halle 1866–1875); Benedikt Niese, *Geschichte der griechischen und makedonischen Staaten seit der Schlacht bei Chaeronea* 1–3 (Gotha 1893–1903); Julius Kaerst, *Geschichte des Hellenismus,* (Leipzig and Berlin, vol. 1, 3rd ed. 1927; vol. 2, 2nd ed. 1926); Éduard Will, *Histoire politique du monde hellenistique* 1–2 (Nancy 1966–1967; 2nd ed. 1979–1982); Carl Schneider, *Kulturgeschichte des Hellenismus,* 1–2 (Munich 1967–1969); Claire Préaux, *Le monde héllenistique: la Grèce et l'Orient de la mort d'Alexandre à la conquête romaine de la Grèce* 1–2 (Paris 1978); and Graham Shipley, *The Greek World after Alexander* (London 2000).

2. 'Altertumswissenschaft'

The second genre of scholarship to emerge was that of a systematic syn-
chronic description of the public and private antiquities of ancient Greece.
First formulated by Wolf from the 1780s onwards, and first committed to
print in 1807,[12] it crystallised in May 1817 with Boeckh's *Staatshaushaltung
der Athener*.[13] Dedicated to Niebuhr, but owing its title as much to Hume as
to Wolf, its publication, together with his later work on Greek inscriptions,
made him, with Grote, the other founding father of Greek history, by
demonstrating in practice his vision of what could be done with the source
material. A generation later his vision had become an organised and generalised reality, represented above all via the common format of the volumes
of K. F. Hermann's *Lehrbuch*, in its various editions. They came to include
Staats-, Rechts-, Kriegs-, Bühnen- and Privat-Altertümer, and were in their
turn succeeded by the *Handbuch der Altertumswissenschaft*, which has
continued to flourish to the present day under its successive editors. For the
Handbuch and for its all-embracing structure, 'Greek history' is simply one
topic or volume among many, within a context of codified scholarship which
embraces but separates 'history' and 'Staatskunde'.[14]

Yet, even the *Lehrbuch/Handbuch* format did not include everything.
Work on the topography and geography of Greece, stimulated by the
Napoleonic wars, has remained a largely separate activity. So, regrettably,
have numismatic study and papyrology. So, above all, has the study of Greek
inscriptions. Boeckh led the way with his *Corpus Inscriptionum Graecarum*,
as much by energy and organising ability as by specifically epigraphical
acumen, creating a format which has been followed but much expanded
by *Inscriptiones Graecae* and *Supplementum Epigraphicum Graecum* and by
a steady stream of specific titles. The emergence of these specialist areas
presents a paradox within the sociology of knowledge. As will be
exemplified in Part iv below, they — particularly epigraphy — have become
the prime source of new evidence for the political, administrative, social
and cultic history of ancient Greece. Yet, in part because inscriptions and

---

[12] Wilfried Nippel (ed.), *Über das Studium der Alten Geschichte*, (Munich 1993) 76–103.

[13] August Boeckh, *Die Staatshaushaltung der Athener*, 1–2 (Berlin 1817; 2nd ed. 1851; 3rd ed.
1886), with Max Hoffmann, *August Boeckh, Lebensbeschreibung und Auswahl aus seinem
wissenschaftlichen Briefwechsel* (Leipzig 1901).

[14] K. F. Hermann (ed.), *Lehrbuch der griechischen Antiquitäten*, 1–4 (Heidelberg, 1831–1852);
Georg Busolt, *Griechische Staatskunde*, vol. 1, 3rd ed.: *Allgemeine Darstellung des griechischen
Staates* (Munich 1920) and vol. 2, 3rd ed. (ed. H. Swoboda): *Darstellung einzelner Staaten und der
zwischenstaatlichen Beziehungen* (Munich 1926).

documentary papyri rarely provide narratives and more usually offer fragmentary snapshots, whose evaluation requires specialised knowledge and whose understanding presupposes much contextualisation, those who are attuned to the literary narrative tradition, whether in texts or in textbooks, still find them, as a bridge into a new and untidy semantic world, hard to cross.

3. Cultural history

As a form of reception, the *Handbuch* format was an extreme form of professionalisation, systematising knowledge within an outward uniformity at the cost of fragmentation, impersonality, and a forbidding level of detail. Its necessary complement was a response which resurrected the individual person of Greek antiquity and attempted to reconstruct his values and his psychological world within a static or slow-changing environment of rituals, institutions and representations. This was cultural history. Though already foreshadowed in Boeckh's unwritten *Hellen* and named by 1857–1858 in Hermann's *Lehrbuch*, it owes its centrality, and the basic distinction between it and the history of customs, to two pioneers, Fustel de Coulanges and Burckhardt. Fustel's *La cité antique*[15] was one of a number of works of the 1850s and 1860s which reflected the discovery of Indo-Europeans and of collective property-ownership. It offered a complex interwoven reading of the origins, via the *gens/genos* and the cult of the dead, of society, property and the state. It lost none of its influence for being simplistically linear, not being finally dismantled until the 1970s.[16] It stimulated a distinguished tradition of (largely French) scholarship which has run through Durkheim, Mauss, Gernet and Jeanmaire to Vernant and the present day,[17] both owing and contributing much to general historical sociology and social anthropology.

---

[15] Numa–Denis Fustel de Coulanges, *La cité antique* (Paris 1864), with Moses I. Finley, 'The ancient city: from Fustel de Coulanges to Max Weber and beyond', *CSSH* 19 (1977) 305–27; Momigliano 1994 (n. 1) 162–78 and 236–51; Christ 1996 (n. 1) 114–22.

[16] Its insoluble contradictions were set out in detail by Felix Bourriot, *Recherches sur la nature du génos. Étude d'histoire sociale athénienne: périodes archaique et classique* (Lille 1976) and by Denis Roussel, *Tribu et cité* (Paris 1976). For a brief summary of the debate, *cf.* John K. Davies, 'Strutture e suddivisioni delle poleis arcaiche: le repartizioni minori', in Settis (n. 8) 2.1, 599–652, at 628–34.

[17] *Cf.* S. C. Humphreys, *Anthropology and the Greeks* (London 1978) 76–106.

The lectures which posthumously became Burckhardt's *Griechische Kulturgeschichte* of 1898[18] complemented the work of Fustel de Coulanges by 'reading' Greek society through its representations and the *mentalités* which they consciously or unconsciously reflected. By exploring conflicts of values and the relationships between politics, religion and culture, it showed how the evidence of Greek literary and philosophical texts could be constructively used in a non-narrative, non-antiquarian way. Its influence, though slow, diffuse and indirect, has made the study of the cultural history of Greece into a very broad church, in part untheoretical but also warmly receptive to interpretative approaches drawn from a variety of newer disciplines. These have ranged from Freudian psychoanalysis through legal sociology and Lévi-Straussian structural anthropology to the deconstructionism of current literary criticism: Foucault and Ariès can fairly be seen as inheritors of the tradition.[19]

iii. Current trends and themes

Any sketch under this heading runs the risk of gross over-simplification, for the variety is endless. It is affected in complex ways by culturally significant choices which may, for example, reflect teaching needs[20] (which are themselves a complex cultural construct), or the investment made over many years in national prestige projects of excavation at major sites. Some activity, such as that devoted to editions of texts or the historiographical work surveyed by Griffith in the precursor to the present volume,[21] is as much philological as historical, but even so it reflects selectively differentiated levels of perceived importance: thus, for example, Athenian inscriptions attract continuous attention while those of Boiotia are neglected, and the orators have until recently attracted far less attention than the historians. However, in the decades since Griffith compiled his survey one notable novelty, the emergence to full maturity of the genre of the *historical*

[18] Jacob Burckhardt, *Griechische Kulturgeschichte* (Berlin and Stuttgart 1898). Abridged translation by S. Stern as *The Greeks and Greek Civilization* (ed. O. Murray, London 1998).

[19] For various aspects of this paragraph *cf.* Momigliano 1994 (n. 1) 44–53; Humphreys (n. 17); Robin Osborne, 'Law in action in Classical Athens', *Journal of Hellenic Studies* 105 (1985) 40–58; Wilfried Nippel, *Griechen, Barbaren, und 'Wilde': Alte Geschichte und Anthropologie* (Frankfurt 1990); and Murray in Burckhardt, *The Greeks* (n. 18) xi–xliv.

[20] See Vollmer and Stray (n. 2).

[21] Guy T. Griffith, 'The Greek historians', in M. Platnauer (ed.), *Fifty Years of Classical Scholarship* (Oxford 1954) 150–92.

commentary, has transformed access to the main historical writers. Pioneered long ago by How and Wells's work on Herodotos,[22] but developed into a fundamental instrument of scholarship above all by Gomme's work on Thucydides,[23] it has extended its scope much more widely while remaining (for reasons far from clear) a largely Anglophone or Italophone activity and defining itself by concentrating on the reconstruction of events, on the incorporation of collateral evidence, and on the evaluation of the author's reliability rather than on textual or stylistic matters. Besides Thucydides and Herodotos, the genre now embraces the Aristotelian *Constitution of the Athenians*, much of Arrian's *Anabasis*, two books of Diodoros, the *Hellenica Oxyrhynchia*, most of Plutarch's Greek Lives, and Polybios.[24] However, Herodotos and Xenophon have eluded full-scale recent commentary (apart from Herodotos' book 2 on Egypt),[25] scholars seemingly preferring to map the complexities of their texts through interpretative monographs. Whether the narratological approach through which Hornblower is currently revisiting Thucydides[26] presages a second generation of commentaries on more 'literary' lines remains to be seen.

Other genres may be surveyed more briefly. Conceptually straightforward is *chronology*, a core service to scholars from Scaliger and Clinton onwards, transformed by the intricate reconstructions of archon-lists which epigraphical finds have made possible, and far more demanding in the polycentric Greek context than in the Roman.[27] Equally intricate is the making of *collections of fragments* (notably that of Jacoby and his

---

[22] W. W. How and J. Wells, *A Commentary on Herodotus*, 1–2 (Oxford 1912).

[23] A. W. Gomme, A. Andrewes and K. J. Dover, *A Historical Commentary on Thucydides*, 1–5 (Oxford 1945–1981).

[24] In alphabetical order of author (as in the text): Peter J. Rhodes, *A Commentary on the Aristotelian Athenaion Politeia* (Oxford 1981: re-issued with Addenda, Oxford 1993); A. B. Bosworth, *A Historical commentary on Arrian's History of Alexander* 1–2 (Oxford 1980–1995; vol. 3 is in preparation); Anne Burton, *Diodorus Siculus, Book I: a commentary* (Leiden 1972); Marta Sordi, *Diodori Siculi Bibliothecae liber sextus decimus* (Florence 1969), and E. I. McQueen, *Diodorus Siculus: the Reign of Philip II* (Bristol and London 1995); I. A. F. Bruce, *An Historical Commentary on the Hellenica Oxyrhynchia* (Cambridge 1967); Luigi Piccirilli et al., editions of individual pairs of Plutarch's *Lives* under the auspices of the Fondazione Lorenzo Valla (Milan, in progress); F. W. Walbank, *A Historical Commentary on Polybius*, 1–3 (Oxford 1957–1979).

[25] Alan B. Lloyd, *Herodotus, Book II*, 1–3 (Leiden 1975–1988).

[26] Simon Hornblower, *A Commentary on Thucydides*, in progress (1–2 so far, Oxford 1991–).

[27] Here and in the following notes full bibliographies are beyond the scope of the chapter. Minimal references are: in general Alan E. Samuel, *Greek and Roman Chronology* (Munich 1972); for Athens, B. D. Meritt, 'Athenian archons 347/6–48/7 BC', *Historia* 26 (1977) 161–91, and for Delphi, Georges Daux, *Fouilles de Delphes, 3: Epigraphie: Chronologie delphique* (Paris 1943).

continuators),[28] which alone have allowed some estimate of lost historians, orators and biographers. A third is *biography* itself, not just of major individuals but also of elite groups such as the Athenian cavalry, Alexander's commanders,[29] or even, as *prosopography*, of whole societies. *Histories of individual states and regions* have been ubiquitous, more obviously of Sparta and of less prominent polities than of Athens, whose history tends to be seen as coterminous with that of Greece. Likewise, *military history* has always been a core component, along with its close relation *topography*.

Yet other genres are more ideologically complex. Throughout the twentieth century *social and economic history*, exemplified at its most ambitious by Rostovtzeff,[30] has been a prime battleground for the reception and reconciliation of competing ideas, ranging from neo-classical economics through the concept of 'embeddedness' which Polanyi and Finley developed[31] to the geographers' concept of locational analysis. Even *historiography*, once a matter primarily of the identification of sources, has come to embrace genre-analysis and narratology as well as the classic 'Historical Commentary' discussed above. Work on *Greek law*, long conditioned (or hampered) by the categories of Roman law, by the mirage of a Greek *Staatsrecht*, and by the comparative uniformity of law in Ptolemaic Egypt,[32] has had not only to acknowledge the kaleidoscopic range of Greek legal systems but also to grapple with notions of 'pre-law' and of law as discourse rather than as a system of statutes and precedents.[33] A similar complex shift is affecting work on *Greek religion*, at one stage pursued as a quasi-autonomous study through traditions such as the Scandinavian school magisterially represented by Nilsson, but now

---

[28] F. Jacoby et al., *Die Fragmente der griechischen Historiker*, in progress (Berlin, subsequently Leiden, 1922–).

[29] *Cf.* Glenn R. Bugh, *The Horsemen of Athens* (Princeton 1988) and Waldemar Heckel, *The Marshals of Alexander's Empire* (London and New York 1992).

[30] M. I. Rostovtzeff, *The Social and Economic History of the Hellenistic World* 1–3 (Oxford 1941; 2nd ed. 1953), with Zofia Archibald, 'Away from Rostovtzeff: a new SEHHW', in Zofia H. Archibald et al. (eds.), *Hellenistic Economies* (London and New York 2000) 379–88.

[31] Karl Polanyi, Conrad M. Arensberg and Harry W. Pearson (eds.), *Trade and Market in the early Empires* (Glencoe, Ill. 1957); Moses I. Finley, *The Ancient Economy* (London 1973, 2nd ed. 1985); Moses I. Finley, in Brent D. Shaw and Richard P. Saller (eds.), *Economy and Society in Ancient Greece* (London 1981).

[32] *Cf.* H. J. Wolff, *Das Recht des griechischen Papyri Ägyptens in der Zeit der Ptolemäer und des Prinzipats, 2: Organisation und Kontrolle des privaten Rechtsverkehrs* (Munich 1978).

[33] Respectively, Moses I. Finley, 'The problem of the unity of Greek law', in *La storia del diritto nel quadro delle scienze storiche: Atti del 1° congresso internazionale della Società Italiana di storia di diritto* (Florence 1966) 129–142; Louis Gernet, *Anthropologie de la Grèce antique* (Paris 1968) 175–321; Osborne (n. 19).

increasingly being steered by Durkheim's insistence that religious practice is above all a social act into rejoining the mainstream as an aspect of cultural history.[34] More complex still is *site excavation and publication*, where conceptual or institutional boundary disputes with Classical Archaeology interact with common-sense perceptions that if Greek History is not also about the history of Delos or Olympia or the Athenian *Agora*, it loses half its *raison d'être*. Most complex of all is *the history of political ideas* and of their relationship with events and institutions. Not only has it proved exceptionally difficult to challenge the assumption that Greek political philosophy affected the course of Greek political and constitutional history, but also the further assumption, that Greek political ideas can and should influence current political and social discourse, continues to be live and influential, above all among scholars in the USA.[35]

Certain other themes can be defined in terms of *boundaries*. Topographically, the explosion of recent work on Thessaly, Epeiros and Makedonia has extended the Greek 'third world'[36] still further north, and in particular is allowing Makedonia to be seen from the inside rather than through a Demosthenic distorting mirror. Even more dramatically, Louis Robert's lifetime work on Asia Minor, plus the growing accessibility of the epigraphical harvest from the same area, are allowing an Anatolian Greek 'fourth world' to take shape and to repay increasingly detailed attention.[37] Further east still, ever more intensive work on the Achaimenid Empire, on Perso-Greek relations, and on the Seleukid Empire is at last replacing a Hellenocentric image of autonomous Greek development by a more realistic discourse which treats Greek and Eastern Mediterranean history as a continuum and thereby begins to dissolve the intrinsically racist distinction

---

[34] Martin Nilsson, *Geschichte der griechischen Religion* 1–2 (Munich 1941–1950); Walter Burkert, *Greek Religion* (Oxford 1985); Christiane Sourvinou-Inwood, *'Reading' Greek culture: Texts and Images, Rituals and Myths* (Oxford 1991); Jan N. Bremmer, *Greek Religion* (*Greece and Rome* New Surveys in the Classics 24, Oxford 1994); Robin Hägg (ed.), *Ancient Greek Cult Practice from the Epigraphical Evidence* (Stockholm 1994); Robert Parker, *Athenian Religion: a History* (Oxford 1996).

[35] *Cf.* Paul A. Rahe, *Republics Ancient and Modern: Classical Republicanism and the American Revolution* (Chapel Hill NC and London 1992); Pierre Vidal-Naquet, *Politics Ancient and Modern* (Cambridge 1995); Josiah Ober and Charles Hedrick (eds.), *Demokratia: a Conversation on Democracies, Ancient and Modern* (Princeton 1996).

[36] *Cf.* the title of Hans-Joachim Gehrke, *Jenseits von Athen und Sparta: das dritte Griechenland und sein Staatenwelt* (Munich 1986) and the papers recently published in Roger Brock and Stephen Hodkinson (eds.), *Alternatives to Athens: Varieties of Political Organization and Community in Ancient Greece* (Oxford 2000).

[37] Louis Robert, *Hellenica* 1–13 (Paris 1940–1965).

between 'Greek' and 'Oriental'.[38] To the south, in contrast, in proportion as more demotic documents are deciphered and as more is understood about Egypt, both pre- and post-Alexander, the less abnormal, the less uniformly governed, and the less Greek it appears: Egypt is becoming a prime example of the decolonisation of 'Greek' history.[39] Lastly, the Greek presence in Sicily, south Italy, and the western Mediterranean, once seen in Greek terms as classically colonial, is re-emerging from the Taranto *Convegni* and the rapid progress of Italian and Spanish archaeology as a contributor to a very complex cultural interpenetration which is only now being properly mapped.[40]

Professional subject boundaries are also under pressure. The decipherment of Linear B as Greek both turned much pre-history into 'Greek history' and helped to make the so-called Dark Ages into territory contested between classical archaeologists, with their own (by now autonomous) agendas of social action,[41] and Greek historians who sought therein the roots of their own 'Archaic Greece'. Greek history is therefore not merely located between the two stools of *Altertumswissenschaft* and history, as it has been described,[42] but even more awkwardly in the midst of a triangle of competing and incompatible styles of analysis. Since information from intensive surface surveys is impinging on other periods and areas too, this contestation will undoubtedly spread.

Lastly, four ideological issues are live and urgent. The first stems precisely from the activity which has gone into such surface surveys.[43] It is

---

[38] Amélie Kuhrt and Susan Sherwin-White (eds.), *Hellenism in the East: the Interaction of Greek and non-Greek Civilizations from Syria to Central Asia after Alexander* (London 1987); Susan Sherwin-White and Amélie Kuhrt, *From Samarkhand to Sardis: a New Approach to the Seleucid Empire* (London 1993); Pierre Briant, *Histoire de l'Empire Perse* (Paris 1996); Maria Brosius, *The Persian Empire from Cyrus II to Artaxerxes I* (*London Association of Classical Teachers Original Records* 16, London 2000).

[39] *Cf.* Alan Lloyd, 'Egypt 404–332 BC', *CAH* 6 (2nd ed., 1994) 337–60.

[40] For a conspectus *Cf.* Jean-Paul Descoeudres (ed.), *Greek Colonists and Native Populations* (Festschrift Trendall, Oxford 1998).

[41] *Cf.* Ian Morris (ed.), *Classical Greece: Ancient Histories and Modern Archaeologies* (Cambridge 1994).

[42] By H.-J. Gehrke in 'Zwischen Altertumswissenschaft und Geschichte: zur Standortbestimmung der alten Geschichte am Ende des 20. Jahrhunderts', in Ernst-Richard Schwinge (ed.), *Die Wissenschaften vom Altertum am Ende des 2. Jahrtausends n. Chr.* (Stuttgart and Leipzig 1995) 160–196.

[43] For a conspectus of such surveys *cf.* Susan Alcock, *Graecia Capta: the Landscapes of Roman Greece* (Cambridge 1993) 33–92, and 'Breaking up the Hellenistic world: survey and society', in Morris (n. 41) 171–90. The resultant shift of gaze towards microregions is taken further by Peregrine Horden and Nicholas Purcell, *The Corrupting Sea: a Study of Mediterranean History* (Oxford 2000).

not just that they have helped to give work on rural settlement, land-use, crop-yields, demography and land-ownership a much enhanced role in analysing social action. It is also that such work tends to ignore political boundaries and to direct attention to the countryside rather than the town. It has thereby reinforced the post-war concern, inspired in part by Marxist or feminist approaches, to re-orientate scholarship round the invisible and the dispossessed — metics, women, slaves, serfs or peasants.

Second, and closely linked thereto, is the '*polis*-debate'. Nineteenth-century historiography treated Athens, Sparta, Thebes, and so on straight-forwardly as 'states', even if interest concentrated on the unified urbanised states, not the poorly attested rural cantons and leagues. However, the twentieth-century tendency has been, with Aristotle but against recent scepticism, to see the *polis* as a specific constitutional species and as a precise juridical category.[44] The unresolved issues are whether historians of Greece must follow the analytical terminology used by the Greeks them-selves or should devise their own, and whether study of the trajectory of Greek *polis* development can be separated from that of other regions of Mediterranean urbanisation.

A third issue involves *alterité*, a term of complex paternity[45] now used to emphasise the immense distance — especially in values, mind-sets, and ra-tionality — between Ancient Greece and ourselves, and thereby to challenge cosy emotional identifications. Fourthly, the very word 'Greek' itself, to-gether with other ethnic identifiers such as 'Dorian' or 'Pelasgian' and with group-labels such as 'tribe', is caught up in a debate about ethnicity and ethnogenesis, the argument being that 'Dorians', 'Geleontes', and so on de-noted not primordial human groups but recent, artificial, fluid social con-structs.[46] It is too early to judge what effect these two last issues will have.

iv. Case-studies

However, not all the intellectual movement within the discipline since 1950 or so has stemmed from the transplantation of ideas or from a refocusing

---

[44] Contrast Wilfried Gawantka, *Die sogennante Polis* (Stuttgart 1985) (sceptical) with the approach of the Copenhagen Polis Project as exemplified in Mogens H. Hansen (ed.), *The Ancient Greek City-state: Symposium on the Occasion of the 250th Anniversary of the Royal Danish Academy, July 1992* (Copenhagen 1993).

[45] *Cf.* Paul Cartledge, *The Greeks: a Portrait of Self and Others* (Oxford 1993) 2–7.

[46] *Cf.* Davies (n. 16) 612–19; Jonathan M. Hall, *Ethnic Identity in Greek Antiquity* (Cambridge 1997).

of interest on hitherto neglected areas, aspects or groups: some has been stimulated by new information. The final section of this chapter sketches four examples of such new information. Unsurprisingly, they are epigraphical, for throughout the twentieth century inscriptions have been far and away the richest source of new material.

The first example is a bronze plate, attributed to the Lyttos area of central Crete and dated *c.*500 BC (Fig. 9.1). Its text, written on both sides, is brief enough to be cited in full.[47] Side A begins intelligibly:

> Gods. It seemed good to Dataleis, and we the polis, from the tribes five from each, pledged to Spensithios maintenance and exemption from all dues, to him and to his descendance, on terms that he is to be Writer and Remembrancer for the city of public matters, both divine and human: to be Writer and Remembrancer for the city of public matters, neither divine nor human, is no other person save Spensith[i]os himself and his descendance, unless Spensithios himself or his descendance, the majority (of) so many as may be adult of his sons, may induce or bid. To give as pay of the year to the Writer fifty measures of must and [(*unintelligible*)] of twenty drachmai or fruits, and to give the must from the (public?) part(?) however he may choose to take (it). If one should not give the must, [(*the rest of side A yields no safely restorable text*)].

Side B:

> The Writer is to have the equal share, and the Writer also is to be present and is to take part in sacred and in secular matters on all occasions where the Kosmos is also, and for whichever god a priest is not (specifically appointed?), the Writer is to make the public sacrifices and is to have the precinct-(dues?), nor is there to be seizure(?), nor is the Writer to take pledge, and lawsuit [(*unintelligible*)]. As dues to the men's mess he shall give ten axes of meats, if the others also give tithes, and the yearly offering, and shall (?collect the portion?), but nothing else is to be compulsory if he does not wish to give. The sacred matters are to be to t[he eld?]est (son?).

Though some details in this telegraphic document remain open to debate, its impact has spread far outside the specialist areas of Cretan custom and dialect: as so often in Greek history, a substantial new document proves to be a piece which fits several fragmentary jigsaws. First is the actual substance

---

[47] First publication in Lilian H. Jeffery and Anna Morpurgo-Davies, '*Poinikastas* and *poinikazen*: BM 1969.4–2.1, a new archaic inscription from Crete', *Kadmos* 9 (1970) 118–54, and much discussed since: main references summarised in *SEG* xxvii.631 and in Henri Van Effenterre and Françoise Ruzé, *Nomima: Recueil d'inscriptions politiques et juridiques de l'archaisme grec* 1 (Rome 1994) no. 22.

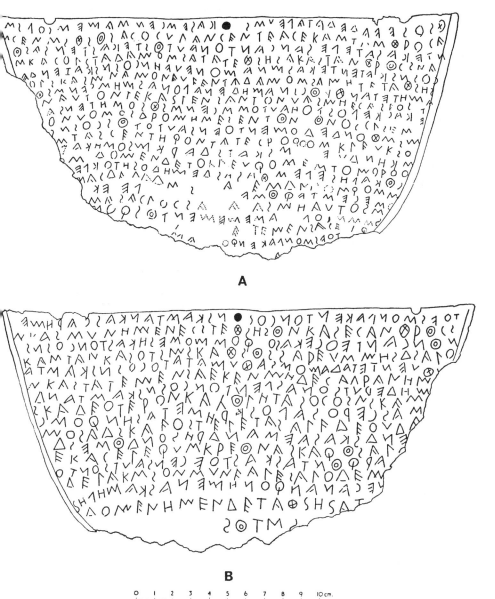

Fig. 9.1. Bronze plate with inscription, central Crete, *c.*500 BC.

of the decree, for, as the first editors noted,[48] 'this is the earliest surviving full record of the creation of a high technical office in a Greek city': the fact that it was intended to be hereditary and to have priestly functions assimilates the office to a priesthood, a status all the more remarkable since it remains unclear whether Spensithios was a citizen of the community in question or not. Barely second in importance is the title of the post, for the word here translated with Scottish resonances as Writer, *poinikastas*, and the corresponding verb *poinikazein*, both hitherto unattested, must reflect the tradition known to Herodotos (5.58) that the alphabet was brought to Greece by Kadmos the Phoenician. Perhaps third is the sense of impenetrable strangeness, as one glimpses the miniature world of this tiny Iron Age Cretan community, proudly calling itself *polis* yet comprising a bare handful of participants: one thinks of the miniature *agora*, 40 m by 20 m, of the hilltop town of Dreros some 25 km to the east. Last but not least is the light which it throws on the changing balance between oral and written record, on questions of record-keeping and archives,[49] and on the comparable appointments which the other *poleis* of Crete must have made in order to create their tremendous outpouring of legal texts from the late sixth century BC until the mid-fourth century.

A second example, endlessly discussed since its first publication in 1960,[50] is the so-called Themistokles Decree. The stone in question, inscribed and set up at Troizen in the early third century BC some two centuries after its dramatic date in 480, presents in its 47 surviving lines the text of an Athenian decree proposed by Themistokles which makes detailed provisions for the evacuation of Attika, the mobilisation and manning of a fleet of 200 ships, and the recall of 'those who had withdrawn for the ten years'. While all agree that the document echoes decisions recorded at various junctures by Herodotos (7.144.3 and 8.41), agreement ceases thereafter, for the basic initial problem, of reconciling the testimony of the literary sources (Herodotos, Plutarch and others) who all place the

---

[48] Lilian H. Jeffery and Anna Morpurgo-Davies, 'An archaic Greek inscription from Crete', *British Museum Quarterly* 36 (1971–1972) 27.

[49] *Cf.* Rosalind Thomas, 'Written in stone? Liberty, equality, orality, and the codification of law', *Bulletin of the Institute of Classical Studies* 40 (1995) 59–74 (also in Lin Foxhall and A. D. E. Lewis (eds.), *Greek Law in its Political Setting: Justifications, not Justice* (Oxford 1996) 9–31); W. Kendrick Pritchett, *Greek Archives, Cults, and Topography* (Amsterdam 1996) 17–18; James P. Sickinger, *Public Records and Archives in Classical Athens* (Chapel Hill NC and London 1999).

[50] Michael H. Jameson, 'A decree of Themistokles from Troizen', *Hesperia* 29 (1960) 198–223; summary of the debate in R. Meiggs and D. M. Lewis, *A Selection of Greek Historical Inscriptions* (Oxford 1969) 48–52, no. 23.

evacuation of Attika *after* the Greek defeats at Artemision and Thermopylai, with its placing *before* Artemision in the document and in one literary source (Nepos, *Them.* 2.6–8 and 3.1), has remained insoluble. Instead, it rapidly became a meta-problem, i.e. that of deciding what sort of problem scholars had on their hands, and the ramifications of that debate have been extensive.

One way out was to suspect that Herodotos had got it wrong, a route which led at one stage to a ferocious assault on his veracity and to what has been called the 'Liar School of Herodotos'.[51] That approach has now been replaced by a series of ever more sophisticated studies of what Herodotos was doing with his material and of the intellectual influences which moulded his compositional methods;[52] a series in which the decree has receded from view. A second expedient was to infer, from the citation of 'the decree of Themistokles' by Athenian orators from 348 onwards (Dem. 29.303, etc.), that the document as we have it represents the fruit of subsequent re-editing and modernisation. That inference in turn poses questions both about patterns of collective memory, which have been fruitfully explored in detail,[53] and (as with the Cretan document discussed above) about the transmission of public documents and the growth of archive systems in Athens and elsewhere.[54] A third way out, formulated in an epoch-making article by Christian Habicht written immediately after the first publication,[55] has proved more far-reaching still. It argues that this decree, and many others which begin to be cited by orators and historians from *c*.350 onwards, are forgeries, or more kindly (as perhaps here) 'imaginative expansions' of earlier references or memories, created in order to feed Athenian self-esteem. If that view is right (and the evidence is increasingly persuasive), it challenges the usability of the whole fabric of much Greek history, at least insofar as later authors such as Diodoros and Plutarch were content to use 'documents' plucked from what now looks more and more like a dangerously contaminated tradition. In this way the publication of the Themistokles decree

---

[51] Detlev Fehling, *Die Quellenangaben bei Herodot* (Berlin and New York 1971), trans. J. G. Howie as *Herodotus and his 'Sources': Citation, Invention and Narrative Art* (Leeds 1989); W. Kendrick Pritchett, *The Liar School of Herodotos* (Amsterdam 1993).

[52] Two recent contributions are Lesley Kurke, *Coins, Bodies, Games, and Gold: the Politics of Meaning in Archaic Greece* (Princeton 1999) and Rosalind Thomas, *Herodotus in Context: Ethnography, Science and the Art of Persuasion* (Cambridge 2000).

[53] Rosalind Thomas, *Oral Tradition and Written Record in Classical Athens* (Cambridge 1989) and *Literacy and Orality in Ancient Greece* (Cambridge 1992); Kevin Robb, *Literacy and Paideia in Ancient Greece* (New York and Oxford 1994).

[54] *Cf.* especially Sickinger (n. 49).

[55] Christian Habicht, 'Falsche Urkunden zur Geschichte Athens im Zeitalter der Perserkriege', *Hermes* 89 (1961) 1–35.

has had far-reaching consequences, which are still to be fully assessed: at the extreme, it may end by deconstructing much of what we thought we knew.

It is a relief to turn to two much more reliable Athenian documents, Nikophon's coinage law of 375/4 and Agyrrhios' grain-tax law of 374/3. The first[56] sets out criteria, which public Testers sitting in Athens and Peiraieus are to apply, for the acceptability of silver coins, with detailed rules for procedures and penalties if the law is infringed. The second[57] sets out in 61 meticulous lines how the tax of one-twelfth levied *en nature* on the grain grown on the three Athenian-held Aegean islands of Lemnos, Imbros and Skyros is to be transported to Athens by the buyers of the tax, how it is to be stored and weighed out and sold, and how all concerned are to render account and dispose of the proceeds.

At first sight these laws might appear to be no more than dry administrative measures, devised by politicians of a prosaic age. Maybe so, but their virtue lies precisely in their detail. In part that detail is procedural, for they show how lawmaking worked in practice after the tightening-up which had been deemed necessary after the debacles of 411 and 404/3. In part it is substantive and deeply political, in that they reflect basic Athenian public priorities in eliminating counterfeit or impure coins or in assuring the city an adequate corn supply. However, there is more to them than that. They both reveal the workings of sophisticated minds, accustomed to thinking an administrative-political problem through, devising a tightly defined step-by-step procedure to deal with it, driving it through the political process, and buttressing the new procedure with appropriate sanctions to make sure it is effectively carried out. Indeed Agyrrhios, the proposer of the 374/3 law, was poacher turned gamekeeper, for he had been a tax-farmer himself as a young man (And. 1.133–4), and when we find his nephew Kallistratos, in exile after 361, helping Methone in Makedonia to increase its revenues from harbour dues,[58] or Kallistratos' associate Chabrias recommending to his Egyptian employer Tachos in 360 ingenious and far-reaching taxation measures for the sake of paying his mercenaries,[59] we can be sure that

---

[56] First publication by Ronald S. Stroud, 'An Athenian law on silver coinage', *Hesperia* 43 (1974) 158–88, whence *SEG* xxvi.72: subsequent discussions cited in *SEG* xxviii.49, xxix.87, xxx.59, xxxi.63, xxxii.55, xxxiii.77, xxxiv.62, xxxv.57, xxxvi.145, xxxvii.69, xli.41, xlii.88. This is not the place to enter the lively debate whether the law is directed at debased coins or at coins not minted at the Athenian mint (but not necessarily of inferior weight or purity).

[57] First publication by Ronald S. Stroud, *The Athenian Grain-Tax Law of 374/3 BC* (*Hesperia*, Suppl. 29) (Princeton 1998).

[58] [Dem.] 50.46; [Arist.] *Oikon.* 2.2, 22, 1350a.

[59] [Arist.] *Oikon.* 2.2, 25a–b, 1350b–1351a, and 37, 1353a; Polyainos 3. 11.5.

our laws are two more products of that remarkable strand of Athenian expertise in public finance and administration which runs right through the classical period, from Perikles to Lykourgos and beyond, to be tapped and developed by the Hellenistic kings. It is a privilege to be given, by these two laws, a better insight into the extreme constructive professionalism which the Athenian political elite could deploy.

No sketch of important new Greek historical material can be adequate without moving beyond Alexander into the Hellenistic period, for it was in that period above all that what has come to be called 'the epigraphic habit', i.e. that of inscribing major public documents for public display, spread out beyond Athens and the major sanctuaries to take root in the ever widening area of Greek speech and culture. Of especial interest and importance has been a series of newly published documents, mostly dating from the third century BC and emanating from the southern and western coasts of Asia Minor. They are too numerous to permit individual review:[60] one must serve as an example.[61] This, like many others from the same period and areas, is a dossier reflecting a complex situation which was hitherto unknown.[62] To summarise it very briefly, probably in the 260s a Ptolemaic governor, Aetos of Aspendos, founded a new city, named Arsinoe, in western Kilikia on the southern coast of Asia Minor on land hitherto belonging to a Samian colony, Nagidos. After the area had then been lost to the Seleukids but regained after the 240s, the two towns evidently fell into dispute over land ownership and boundaries, so that (we are now somewhere after 238 BC) the Arsinoeis sent a delegation to Aetos' son Thraseas, by now himself Ptolemaic governor of the area. Thraseas evidently prevailed upon the Nagideis to accede to his request to vacate and delimit the disputed territories, upon which Nagidos passed a decree to give effect to that request and to recognise the Arsinoeis as *isopolitai* of the Nagideis but also as their own colonists (lines 19–56), a copy of which Thraseas transmitted to Arsinoe with instructions to comply (lines 1–18).

Many themes intersect here. One is the Greek/non-Greek boundary, for Aetos founded Arsinoe by 'expelling the barbarians who were encroaching on

---

[60] Notable examples have been Peter Herrmann, 'Antiochos der Grosse und Teos', *Anadolu* 9 (1965 [1967]) 29–159, and the numerous detailed studies published by Michael Wörrle in *Chiron* from the 1970s onwards.

[61] Christopher P. Jones and Christian Habicht, 'A Hellenistic inscription from Arsinoe in Cilicia', *Phoenix* 43 (1989) 317–46, whence *SEG* xxxix.1426. I am grateful to Katja Mueller for fruitful discussion of this text.

[62] *Cf.* Roger S. Bagnall, *The Administration of the Ptolemaic Possessions outside Egypt* (Leiden 1976) 159–175 for what was known till the mid-1970s.

(the land)' (lines 23–4). Another, age-old, that of neighbours quarrelling over boundaries, interrelates with a third, the sometimes constructive intervention of a suzerain power in order to defuse such quarrels, and thence with a fourth, the creation of pseudo-filiations between 'mother-city' and 'daughter-city' in order to generate amicable relationships. Another is the contrast between the unwillingness of the Ptolemies to create formal 'cities' in Egypt and their eagerness to do so overseas, even if (as here) 'Arsinoe' has by now virtually become the generic name for a harbour strategically sited to serve as a staging post for naval movement between Egypt and Ptolemaic bases in the Aegean.[63] Another again is royal revenue, for Thraseas enjoins upon the Arsinoeis 'to work and plant all of (the land), so that you yourselves may enjoy prosperity and that the revenues which you contribute to the king may be more than those that were produced previously' (lines 6–9). Yet another is the language of diplomacy, wherein Thraseas observes the courtesies though leaving no doubt where power lies, while he himself, son of one Ptolemaic governor and father of two others, citizen of Aspendos but also of Alexandria and Athens,[64] spectacularly illustrates the pivotal role and long-distance connections of the able and ambitious men whose services — as court officers, as provincial governors, as military commanders — were crucial in turning the Hellenistic monarchies into going concerns.

Yet, even when all those themes are identified and interwoven, this flood of new documentation has wider implications still. As Christian Marek has noted,[65] southern and western Asia Minor were above all others the areas within which all the Hellenistic powers — Ptolemies, Seleukids, Antigonids, Attalids and Rhodians — competed for influence and control. This was partly because the area offered an unusually rich array of the assets of men, materials and revenue which were seen as legitimate prey by kings who were, as Cato caustically observed, by nature predatory animals, partly because it was in this area above all that the fields of influence of the kingdoms, ever weakening as distances from their respective capitals hampered the effective deployment of force, met, dissipated and cancelled each other out. Such decrees therefore, and the boundaries of influence which they reveal, are an invaluable way of mapping the balance of power throughout the third century and beyond: each new one fills in another corner of this complex map of interaction.

---

[63] Jones and Habicht (n. 61) 333, citing Louis Robert, *Hellenica* 11/12 (1960) 132–76, at 146–56.

[64] Evidence and details are set out by Habicht in Jones and Habicht (n. 61) 337–46.

[65] Christian Marek, 'Ein ptolemaischer Strategos in Karien', *Chiron* 12 (1982) 119–123, at 119.

v. Envoi and prospect

'Greek history provides little pleasure,' Goethe is reported to have commented bleakly in November 1824.[66] Uttered just when the subject was emerging into its first maturity, his remark may have lacked prescience, but had substance insofar as Greek history, unlike its older brother Roman history, has always had to live in the shadow of the great creations of classical Greek art, literature and philosophy, and could even be seen, by those of a historicist turn of mind, as recording a brilliant but short-lived trajectory of emergence, flowering and decay. Indeed that shadow took long to lift: as late as 1954, for the planners of this volume's predecessor, the corresponding chapter[67] bore as a title not 'Greek history' but 'Greek historians', as if the history did not exist and there was nothing beyond the texts.

For two reasons we must now see things differently. First, the sociology of the subject cannot be ignored. For over 200 years 'Greek history' has had a life of its own as an intellectual construct, generated by an ever changing field of interaction between data and human minds. Throughout that period, there have been four principal components: first, the ancient texts themselves, supplemented with increasing urgency by inscriptions and papyri and by the analysis of landscapes and artefacts; second, a small international network of professional scholars; third, a fragmented clientele of students and the interested public; and finally, the general world-wide flux of ideas, issues and values. Though, as sketched in the foregoing pages, the focuses of attention have moved continually, the components have remained stable, anchored within a specific land- and seascape and within a generally acknowledged timespan from the sub-Mycenaean period until the final Roman conquest of the entire Mediterranean seaboard in 30 BC.

The second reason, by contrast, stems from a more recent shift in the scholarly agenda, namely an increasing acceptance that the business of the subject must be not only with politico-military narrative and institutions but also, and perhaps above all, with that land- and seascape, with the people who populated it, and with the ways in which they made a living from it within the constraints of available technologies. In part, that shift has been stimulated by the continuous flow of newly published inscriptions, which

---

[66] 'Die griechische Geschichte bietet wenig erfreuliches.' Quoted by H. E. Stier, *Grundlagen und Sinn der griechischen Geschichte* (Stuttgart 1945) 4, but I have been unable to verify the citation in any of the standard Goethe editions.
[67] Griffith (n. 21).

shed light on communities hitherto barely known and reveal new names by the thousand;[68] one cannot encounter the text of the name on a newly published gravestone, whether in *Supplementum Epigraphicum Graecum* or elsewhere, without occasionally speculating what that person's lifetime experience had been. In part, too, it has stemmed from survey activity, from awareness of the work of Fernand Braudel on later periods of Mediterranean history, and from increased sensitivity to the economic and ecological factors[69] which at all times left *poleis* as towns subject to processes unfolding in the economically primary countryside.

Such shifts have amounted to nothing less than a wholesale renewal of the subject. Whereas in 1952 there was an uncomfortable degree of truth in Momigliano's comment, in his London inaugural lecture, that 'all students of ancient history know in their heart that Greek history is passing though a crisis',[70] no one, I think, could say that today. On the contrary, my sense is that all forms of scholarship in Greek history — monographs, journal papers, colloquia, site publications, editions and commentaries, and the rest — currently reflect a sense of confidence and innovative expansion.

I thank the publishers of *Neue Pauly* for permission to reproduce material originally published as part of the entry 'Griechische Geschichte' in *Neue Pauly* 14 (2000) 188–98 (© 2000 J. B. Metzlersche Verlagsbuchhandlung and Carl Ernst Poeschel Verlag GmbH in Stuttgart). For help towards tracing the owner of the copyright for Fig. 9.1 I thank Professor Anna Morpurgo Davies, the Department of Greek and Roman Antiquities of the British Museum, and Messrs Willans of Cheltenham, executors of the estate of Mrs. J. Neufville Taylor as heir of Dr. L. H. Jeffery. I owe renewed thanks to the Leverhulme Trust, whose provision of thinking time allowed this paper to crystallise. My thanks also to other contributors to this volume for helpful suggestions, to John Hind for fruitful discussion, to Peter Wiseman for editorial guidance, and to participants in my Liverpool seminar on 'Seven types of Antiquity' in 1998, especially to Zosia Archibald, Phil Freeman and Graham Oliver.

---

[68] That flow has in turn generated a major project to compile and publish a *Lexicon of Greek Personal Names* (Oxford 1987–).

[69] *Cf.* for example Tom Gallant, *Risk and Survival in Ancient Greece: Reconstructing the Rural Domestic Economy* (Stanford 1991) and Robert Sallares, *The Ecology of the Ancient Greek World* (London 1991), among much other work in the same vein.

[70] Most accessible in Momigliano 1994 (n. 1) 16.

10
Greek civilisation and slavery

Paul Cartledge

> Ideologies matter, not so much as guides to history, but as vehicles for belief and political action.
>
> M. Mazower, *The Dark Continent: Europe's Twentieth Century* (London 1998) xii

i

At the beginning of a millennium, it is not a bad idea to look back to the ancient world with a view to going forward better. It may not be pleasant at such a potentially hopeful juncture to contemplate the topic of slavery, but the institution still flourishes, alas, in too many parts of the world, and its potent legacy affects, afflicts or infects even those societies which have long ago legally abolished it and publicly denounce it as a contradiction of their governing ideal of freedom or liberty.[1]

More parochially, the very existence of slavery in ancient Greece constitutes a problem for those who wish to regard that society, or rather their idea of it, as in some sense paradigmatically admirable — a moral problem, that is, as well as a purely technical or professional one.[2] The version that I have chosen to focus on here is something like David Brion Davis' 'problem of slavery in western culture':[3] that is, what is the nature of the connection

---

[1] K. Bales, *Disposable People: New Slavery in the Global Economy* (Berkeley 1999). Slavery's poison: D. B. Davis, 'Slavery and the post-World War II historians', *Daedalus* 103 (Spring 1974) 1–16, at 11.

[2] 'A significant problem in writing about slavery lies in the anxiety and moral apprehension every historian of slavery feels toward the institution' (R. C.-H. Shell, *Children of Bondage: a Social History of the Slave Society at the Cape of Good Hope, 1652–1838* (Princeton 1994) xix). Classicists: P. Cartledge, '"Like a worm i' the bud"? A heterology of classical Greek slavery', *Greece and Rome* 40 (1993) 163–80.

[3] D. B. Davis, *The Problem of Slavery in Western Culture* (Ithaca 1966, rev. ed. New York 1988).

between the prevalence of slavery as an institution in ancient Greece and the concurrent emergence there of an ideology of freedom, and vice versa? Or, to put that in its starkest and most oxymoronic terms, was Greek civilisation based on slavery?

The silence of classicists on the subject should not surprise us. Classical scholarship is a desperately conservative affair, on the whole, as a recent authoritative analysis of the work recorded in *L'Année philologique* has demonstrated quantitatively;[4] and Eric Hobsbawm's lament in 1972 that work on slavery in Greece and Rome was apparently 'in recession' by comparison with the work being done on other slave cultures and societies of the past has found a disturbing reprise in Kurt Raaflaub's 1997 survey of recent research in ancient, especially archaic, Greek history.[5]

In what follows I shall limit myself to Anglo-American scholarship, in an attempt to achieve a manageable focus (though of course a great deal of the last half-century's work on ancient Greek slavery has been written in French and German);[6] my strategy will be to select for special attention one work from each of the decades from 1950 to 2000 that seems to me of unusual relevance to my chosen problematic because of either the nature or the handling of the topic discussed. That four of my selections are Americans, one admittedly based at the English Cambridge but formed intellectually on the other side of the Atlantic, is no coincidence. The coercions of the times have always pressed harder on American historians of slavery than on their British counterparts.[7]

First, a couple of methodological preliminaries, beginning with some definition of terms. For the purposes of this chapter, 'the ancient Greek world' will be taken as meaning the world of the *polis*, from about 700 to 300, excluding both the pre-political and the Hellenistic worlds. The term

---

[4] W. Scheidel, 'Continuity and change in classical scholarship: a quantitative survey', *Ancient Society* 28 (1997) 265–89.

[5] E. J. Hobsbawm, 'Social history to the history of society', *Daedalus* 100 (1971) 20–45, at 42; K. A. Raaflaub, 'Greece', in C. G. Thomas (ed.), *Ancient History: Recent Work and New Directions* (Claremont, Calif. 1997), 1–35, esp. 29 and n. 104 ('work on slavery . . . continues').

[6] Bibliography: H. Klees, *Sklavenleben im klassischen Griechenland* (*Forschungen zur antiken Sklaverei* 30, Stuttgart 1999) 448–73; E. Herrmann and N. Brockmeyer, *Bibliographie zur antiken Sklaverei* (2nd ed., Bochum 1983); J. C. Miller (ed.), *Slavery and Slaving in World History: a Bibliography 1900–1991* (Charlottesville, Va. 1993, Suppl. 1998). The names of Yvon Garlan and Joseph Vogt come immediately to mind, not least because they represent almost opposite poles of interpretation, respectively the hard and the soft; see for instance Y. Garlan, *Slavery in Ancient Greece* (Ithaca 1988, French original 1982), and J. Vogt, *Ancient Slavery and the Ideal of Man* (Oxford 1974, German original 1972, 1983).

[7] Davis (n. 1).

'Greek' should not be allowed to disguise the fact that by 300 BC there were well over a thousand separate, usually fiercely independent, Greek political communities scattered from the western end of the Mediterranean to the eastern end of the Black Sea.[8] Of only two, however, Athens and Sparta, do we know enough to be able to talk in any detail about their slave systems, despite laudable attempts to do justice to the 'third Greece' beyond them.[9]

By the same token, however, we also know enough to be able to establish that the slave systems of those two in many ways exceptional polities were of different kinds. 'Slavery', that is, may cover (and cover up) very different types of unfreedom,[10] and it is essential to distinguish between, for example, the chattel slave system of Athens and the helotage that was the predominant form of servitude practised by Sparta (however precisely the latter should be classified).[11] Whether slaves, especially chattel slaves, are to be seen principally as living property or as socially dead outsiders evokes further, no less contested, levels of definition.[12] 'Civilisation' too is susceptible of more than one determination. For the purposes of this chapter it will be taken to mean something more than just a bare mode of existence and something less than high culture, since the moral force of our problematic lies precisely in the awkward juxtaposition of something intrinsically negative with something intrinsically positive.[13]

Finally, a word on the nature of the available evidence. That 'we do not possess a single work composed by a slave while in slavery' has rightly been

---

[8] The full evidence will be published in due course by the Copenhagen Polis Centre under the direction of Mogens Herman Hansen; meanwhile see M. H. Hansen, *Polis and City-State: an Ancient Concept and its Modern Equivalent* (Copenhagen 1998), with my review in *Classical Review* 49 (1999) 465–9. *Cf.* Raaflaub (n. 5) 12, where the statistics are already out of date.

[9] H. J. Gehrke, *Jenseits von Athen und Sparta: das 'dritte' Griechenland* (Stuttgart 1986).

[10] S. Engerman, 'Slavery, serfdom and other forms of coerced labour: similarities and differences', in M. L. Bush (ed.), *Serfdom and Slavery: Studies in Legal Bondage* (London 1996) 18–41. On the variety of servile statuses in Greece, see M. I. Finley, *Economy and Society in Ancient Greece* (ed. B. D. Shaw and R. P. Saller, London 1981) 116–66.

[11] J. Ducat, *Les Hilotes* (*Bulletin de Correspondance Hellénique* Suppl. 20, Paris 1990). P. Cartledge, 'Rebels and *sambos* in Classical Greece', in Cartledge and F. D. Harvey (eds.), *CRUX: Essays in Greek History Presented to G. E. M. de Ste. Croix* (Exeter and London 1985), 16–46 (= Cartledge, *Spartan Reflections* (London and California 2001) ch. 11).

[12] See below, on G. E. M. de Ste. Croix' *The Class Struggle in the Ancient Greek World* (London 1981, corr. impr. 1983).

[13] A. Barnard and J. Spencer, 'Culture', in Barnard and Spencer (eds.), *Routledge Encyclopedia of Social and Cultural Anthropology* (London 1996) 136–43.

called tragic and horrifying;[14] it entails also that for our knowledge and understanding of the attitudes and beliefs and behaviour of slaves in ancient Greece we are largely dependent on the extant evidence of their masters or of spokesmen for their masters.[15] We are, on the other hand, relatively well endowed with evidence for the attitudes and beliefs of the masters themselves, both their implicitly held and habitually acted-upon moral norms or received views and their — much rarer — conscious and explicit declarations of theory or ideology.[16] Comparison with other servile systems, delicate though it is in application, may help to explain or account for the evidence we have, but may not, indeed must not, be used as a substitute for that which we have not.[17]

ii

First, back to the 1950s. Linn Westermann's general survey of Greek and Roman slave systems, published in 1955, might reasonably be expected to provide my obvious jumping-off point.[18] But that was in essence only an update of his article 'Sklaverei' for the standard classical encyclopaedia 'Pauly-Wissowa', published in 1935, and was rightly found very unsatisfactory by many of its distinguished reviewers.[19] A fresh start was needed. It was definitively provided by a former Columbia graduate student whom Westermann had vitally influenced, and whose own circumstances were formative for a historian of freedom and its opposite.

[14] D. Daube, 'Three footnotes on civil disobedience in antiquity', *Humanities in Society* 2 (1979) 69–82, at 69; Ste. Croix (n. 12) 643 n. 11; Cartledge (n. 11) 24–5.

[15] General discussion of Greek written sources: Klees (n. 6); P. Vidal-Naquet, *The Black Hunter: Forms of Thought and Forms of Society in the Greek World* (trans. A. Szegedy-Maszak, Baltimore 1986) 168–88. Greek historiography of slaves in war: P. Hunt, *Slaves, Warfare and Ideology in the Greek Historians* (Cambridge 1998), on which see further below.

[16] (Non-philosophical) attitudes: R. Schlaifer, 'Greek theories of slavery from Homer to Aristotle', *Harvard Studies in Classical Philology* 47 (1936) 165–204, reprinted in M. I. Finley (ed.), *Slavery in Classical Antiquity* (Cambridge 1960, 2nd ed. 1968) 93–132. Theories: P. Garnsey, *Ideas of Slavery from Aristotle to Augustine* (Cambridge 1996). Mixture of the two: Cartledge (n. 2); *The Greeks: a Portrait of Self and Others* (Oxford 1997) ch. 6; and 'Historiography and ancient Greek self-definition,' in M. Bentley (ed.), *Routledge Companion to Historiography* (London 1997) 23–42.

[17] M. I. Finley, *Ancient Slavery and Modern Ideology* (London 1980, new edition ed. B. D. Shaw Princeton 1998), 285–308; Cartledge (n. 14); *cf.* S. Drescher and S. Engerman (eds.), *A Historical Guide to World Slavery* (New York 1998).

[18] W. L. Westermann, *The Slave Systems of Greek and Roman Antiquity* (Philadelphia 1955).

[19] They included G. E. M. de Ste. Croix and P. A. Brunt: see the Bibliographical Essay attached to Finley (n. 16).

Moses Finley was dismissed from his post at Rutgers in 1953 for refusing to incriminate himself before the Senate Committee on Internal Security; from 1957, after two years as a lecturer, he was a Fellow of Jesus College, Cambridge. Between 1959 and 1965 Finley produced an unrivalled series of five articles on various aspects of ancient Greek slavery and unfreedom, and a sixth of which the subtext was also slavery-related, namely the vexed question of slavery's likely responsibility for the relative lack of both technical innovation and economic progress in antiquity.[20] It is the earliest of these six, deservedly much reprinted, that I select for discussion here, since its problematic conforms very closely to the overall interpretative framework of my survey: 'Was Greek civilisation based on slave labour?'

What was Finley's answer to his own question? Look to the end, Herodotus' Solon sagely advised his Croesus, and we might well do likewise. Probably the most strikingly memorable, certainly the most quoted, passage in Finley's article is its final sentence: 'One aspect of Greek history, in short, is the advance, hand in hand, of freedom *and* slavery.' I have suggested elsewhere that Nathan Huggins' metaphor of slavery and freedom being joined at the hip is a more apt image.[21] One might prefer to say 'shackled together at the ankle' — but what matters, first and foremost, is that Finley saw Greek slavery and Greek civilisation as inseparably linked, causally as well as functionally, even if he did not spell out in detail the precise nature of the causal connection.

Nor did he attempt to define 'civilisation', though he did make clear, in a typically comparative way, where he thought the essence of that concept lay, in freedom in some defining sense.[22] Just before that final sentence, he wrote: 'The pre-Greek world — the world of the Sumerians, Babylonians, Egyptians, and Assyrians; and I cannot refrain from adding the Mycenaeans — was, in a very profound sense, a world without free men, in the sense in which the west has come to understand the concept.'[23]

---

[20] The sextet of articles is conveniently collected in Finley (n. 10): 'Was Greek civilisation based on slave labour' (1959) 97–115; 'Between slavery and freedom' (1964) 116–32; 'The servile statuses of ancient Greece' (1960) 133–49; 'Debt-bondage and the problem of slavery' (1965) 150–66; 'The slave trade in antiquity: the Black Sea and Danubian regions' (1962) 167–75; 'Technical innovation and economic progress in the ancient world' (1965) 176–95.

[21] Cartledge (n. 2).

[22] *Cf.* Finley, 'The freedom of the citizen in the Greek world' (1976) (n. 10) 77–94.

[23] Compare the more recent pattern of Orlando Patterson's work, in which the cultural history *Freedom in the Making of Western Culture* (Cambridge, Mass. 1991) followed on from his important work of comparative historical sociology, *Slavery and Social Death: a Comparative Study* (Cambridge, Mass. 1982).

Also important, and revealing of its time, was that Finley in 1959 treated slavery as an institution from a fundamentally materialist point of view.[24] Numbers of slaves, though unknowable, mattered to him. So too did the types of work in which they featured. But what he was concerned to discover, above all, was their social location: that is, the relationship between their labour and the wealth of those whom he called the elite, typically a landholding elite, the economically dominant movers and shakers of the Greek world. Finley was subsequently involved in a long-running standoff with Geoffrey de Ste. Croix for his preference for 'status' over 'class' as an explanatory tool. (Finley's *Ancient Economy* was published in 1973, the same year that Ste. Croix delivered the Cambridge lectures on which his 1981 book on the class struggle was based.) But here in 1959, Finley's concept of a 'spectrum of statuses' running from the freest of the free to the most enslaved of the unfree was not allowed to occlude the relationship of exploitation between rich citizen masters and their slaves which is the kernel of Ste. Croix's book.[25]

Not that ideology was ignored in Finley's paper; far from it. But he does not do much more than simply register 'how completely the Greeks always took slavery for granted'. One of his supporting illustrations, plausibly enough, was the extraordinarily large number of words the Greeks had for 'unfree' people: about a dozen in all, some of which, especially *andrapodon* (formed on analogy with one of the Greek words for animal, *tetrapodon*), could be far more expressive than the standard-issue term *doulos*, which was used much too imprecisely to our way of thinking.[26]

It was only later that Finley was especially concerned with the ideology of slavery, and then significantly what he chose to study most was ancient slavery (how ancient slavery actually was, so to speak) and *modern* ideology. Indeed, when reviewing David Davis' book *The Problem of Slavery in*

---

[24] For a useful recent overview of research on slavery in the Old South from a primarily economic viewpoint, see M. M. Smith, *Debating Slavery: Economy and Society in the Antebellum American South* (Cambridge 1998).

[25] This was a struggle which in Finley's as well as Ste. Croix's view centrally involved agricultural slaves — another issue that was to explode later in controversy, especially between Michael Jameson and Ellen Wood (n. 34).

[26] Terminology: F. Gschnitzer, *Studien zur griechischen Terminologie der Sklaverei* (Wiesbaden 1963 and 1976). *Andrapodon* and its cognates *andrapodizein* and *andrapodistēs* were applied especially to the process of enslavement through warfare. The implied 'animalisation' trope would have been especially useful at a time when the chief source of Greek slaves was other Greeks — that is, before non-Greek barbarians became widely and easily available on the slave market, and *a fortiori* before barbarians were universally debited with naturally slavish characteristics (Schlaifer, n. 16).

Western Culture (1966), Finley complained that for all its brilliance as an exercise in the history of ideas it failed to place them within their structural context, since ideas about slavery 'have to be examined structurally too'.[27]

iii

Davis' work is my selected contribution from the 1960s. Nowadays, for a thoroughgoing, up-to-date technical examination of 'ideas of slavery from Aristotle to Augustine' we turn to Garnsey's 1996 book of that title (which deals also with precursors of Aristotle). But Davis' account remains a landmark work, chiefly because it forms the first part of a tripartite study culminating in an attempt to answer one of the biggest historical questions of our modern times. Why was slavery at last abolished, when and where it was, whereas until shortly before that conjuncture it had hardly been even so much as questioned, and 'pro-slavery' had been not so much an intellectual position as a habit of mind?

Most of Davis' first volume concerns slavery after the classical Greek era. But that does not disqualify it from our attention, for two reasons: first, because his wide comparative reading convinced him that norms of institutional arrangements and attitudes regarding slavery are common to many societies;[28] and second, specifically, because 'there was more institutional continuity between ancient and modern slavery than has been generally supposed'.[29] So far as Aristotle's troubled explorations of the issue are concerned, Davis rightly emphasised one of his less contentious contentions, that it would be best if Greeks were to acquire their agricultural slaves from 'a race lacking the Hellenic spirit of liberty'. And he most acutely put his finger on Aristotle's worry about free children being corrupted by their too frequent or too intimate association with slaves.[30]

However, Davis' searching for 'a pattern of thought that gave rise to the first explicit questioning of slavery' led him to give perhaps undue weight to

[27] M. I. Finley, *New York Review of Books* 26 January 1967, reprinted in A. Weinstein and F. O. Gatell (eds.), *American Negro Slavery: a Modern Reader* (2nd ed., New York 1973) 394–400.
[28] *Cf.* Cartledge (n. 14) 21.
[29] Davis (n. 3) 31, in a chapter entitled 'Patterns of continuity in the history of servitude'. For Davis' discussions of Greek slavery, see ch. 3 'Slavery and sin: the ancient legacy', at 66–8 (Plato), 69–72 (Aristotle), 72–8 (Sophists to Stoics); also index s.v. 'Plato' and (especially) 'Aristotle'.
[30] Davis (n. 3) 72, 77 n. 43 — though one wonders whether the use in his translation of the loaded American term 'liberty' might not be culturally overdetermined.

Aristotle's anonymous opponents;[31] and his comparatism — citing Calvinism, the Hebrew concept of deliverance, bohemians and beatniks, and seeing the Christian idea of slavery as 'part of the grand scheme of divine order' anticipated by Plato — was perhaps too often of the kind that homogenises rather than differentiates.[32] Nevertheless, the book does mark an epoch, not least because it presents an analysis of the ideology more than the sociology of slavery, a standpoint that was well ahead of the general historiographical trend of its time.

iv

My next illustration, Michael Jameson's 1977 article on agriculture and slavery, had its origins 'in a desire to understand the ways in which the Greek countryside has been used and changed over the centuries', and thus reverted to Finley's materialist framework of 1959.[33] But it did so the better to tackle a 'problem' comparably central to that of Davis within the rather more parochial beat of ancient Greek history. In so far as the modern world still likes to think that in some sense the Greeks invented a form of democracy that is ancestral to ours, the issue of how precisely that ancient democracy came into being, and what sustained it materially and spiritually, remains a live and contemporary one.

   Jameson started with the entirely reasonable assumptions that classical Greece was primarily an agricultural society (or rather, as we have noted, a collection of agricultural societies), and that even in relatively urbanised and industrialised Athens the large role slavery played cannot be separated from agriculture. What interested him especially was the relationship between slaveholding and the ordinary (poor) Greek farmer's capacity to be 'fully a citizen' — that is, in the case of classical Athens, a democratic citizen.[34]

[31] Davis (n. 3) 74, on Arist. *Pol.* 1253b20–3, 1255a3–12. *Cf.* G. Cambiano, 'Aristotle and the anonymous opponents of slavery', in M. I. Finley (ed.), *Classical Slavery* (London 1987, repr. 1999) 21–41; Garnsey (n. 16) 75–8.

[32] Davis (n. 3), 70, 72, 73, 88. On the 'sin' of homogenisation, *cf.* Cartledge (n. 14) 24 and n. 26.

[33] M. H. Jameson, 'Agriculture and slavery in classical Athens', *Classical Journal* 73 (1977–1978), 122–45, quotation from 122 n. 1. It appeared shortly after E. D. Genovese's *The Slave Economies* (New York 1973); *cf.* also S. Engerman and E. D. Genovese, *Race and Slavery in the Western Hemisphere: Quantitative Studies* (Princeton 1975), and the works discussed by Smith (n. 24).

[34] On the relationship of slavery and citizenship see further E. M. Wood, *Peasant-Citizen and Slave: the Foundations of the Athenian Democracy* (London 1988); R. Osborne, 'The economics and politics of slavery at Athens', in A. Powell (ed.), *The Greek World* (London 1995) 27–43; Cartledge, *The Greeks* (n. 16) ch. 6.

Bringing to bear his unrivalled familiarity with the full range of ancient evidence, together with first-hand knowledge of the Mediterranean agricultural regime, Jameson argued that at least in the conditions of the classical period, the addition of some slave help to the farmer's own capacity was essential for all but the richest, who would not work at all personally, and the poorest, who lacked the land to work in the first place. Yet he constantly found himself stumbling up against the objection to this hypothesis, the difficulty of identifying the specifically farm slave, as opposed to the mining, industrial, or urban–domestic slave. To which he replied, devastatingly: 'If we have trouble identifying "agricultural slaves" in Athens it may be in part because they are everywhere.'[35]

Jameson has revisited the scene of his article more than once, both in print and in unpublished work, partly in response to a variety of different attacks.[36] He has modified his original position, somewhat unnecessarily in my view, by suggesting that for classical Athens 'it is not the slave working on the land that needs to be found but the small subsistence farmer, primarily dependent on the land'.[37] But he has continued to maintain that slave-owning was advantageous in the kind of intensive agriculture practised in situations of high population density like classical Athens by citizens of middling and higher status, and the title of his latest published contribution, 'Class in the ancient Greek countryside', is more than just a gesture of interpretative solidarity with my next selection, Geoffrey de Ste. Croix.[38]

V

Definition of slavery has been a live issue within the study of ancient societies, as within that of other slave systems, and for obvious reasons one of interest and concern especially to comparativists. Is the essence of the slave that he or she is property, a thing, or rather that he or she is an outsider? Or is the slave best

---

[35] Jameson (n. 33) 137.

[36] E.g. Ste. Croix (n. 12) 506; Wood (n. 34) ch. 3.

[37] M. H. Jameson, 'Agricultural labor in ancient Greece', in B. Wells (ed.), *Agriculture in Ancient Greece* (Stockholm 1992) 135–46.

[38] M. H. Jameson, in P. N. Doukellis and L. G. Mendoni (eds.), *Structures rurales et sociétés antiques* (Paris 1994) 55–63, esp. 60 n. 29; *cf.* P. Cartledge, 'The economy (economies) of ancient Greece', *Dialogos* 5 (1998) 4–24, at 10–12.

defined, with Orlando Patterson, as a natally excluded, socially dead human being?[39]

In his great book *The Class Struggle in the Ancient Greek World*, published in 1981, Ste. Croix adopted the not entirely satisfactory solution of citing and following a 1926 League of Nations convention on slavery that offered a definition in terms of property and ownership: 'the status or condition of a person over whom any or all of the powers attaching to the right of ownership are exercised'.[40] This accorded well with his primarily economic approach, and gave rise to his later distinction between slavery and 'other forms of unfree labour',[41] but it simply left to one side the issues implied by Finley's outsider-status and Patterson's social-death conceptualisations.

Ste. Croix was emphatic that his book was about class. Indeed, he spent many pages trying to rescue Karl Marx from the self-contradiction, or at best vagueness, of which he had sadly been guilty, in order to be in a legitimate position thereafter to apply his own dynamic definition to the understanding and explanation of the ancient Greek world. Some of Ste. Croix's critics, however, denied that any definition of class is applicable to the ancient world, and claimed that what Ste. Croix was really discussing was exploitation, of the weak by the strong or the poor by the rich; in their view invoking class merely confused the issue.[42] But for Ste. Croix exploitation was at the heart of class, as his definition shows: 'Class (essentially a relationship) is the collective social expression of the fact of exploitation, the way in which exploitation is embodied in a social structure.'[43]

It therefore mattered very much to Ste. Croix to make absolutely clear the distinction between the relationship of free and slave on the one hand and that of slave–owner and slave on the other. Whereas the former was a matter of status, and not necessarily a relationship of opposition, let alone exploitation, the latter was a dynamic and inevitably more or less antagonistic relationship of class exploitation. Indeed, as for Finley in 1959, though Finley himself had theorised it very differently, it was the essence or foundation of what made the ancient Greek world the way it was.[44]

[39] Patterson 1982 (n. 23).

[40] Ste. Croix (n. 12) 135.

[41] Ste. Croix (n. 12) 133–74; G. E. M. de Ste. Croix, 'Slavery and other forms of unfree labour', in L. Archer (ed.), *Slavery and Other Forms of Unfree Labour* (London 1988) 19–32.

[42] Major reviews of Ste. Croix are listed at Cartledge and Harvey (n. 14) xi.

[43] Ste. Croix (n. 12) 43.

[44] Ste. Croix (n. 12) 63–5 (slaves as a class). *Contra*: Vidal-Naquet (n. 15) 159–67.

Slavery occupies explicitly three sections and two appendices of *The Class Struggle*, and is integral to other parts of the book. But *caveat lector*! The 'Greek world' the dynamics of which Ste. Croix was most keen not merely to explore but to explain was not the classical Greek world of the fifth and fourth centuries BC, but the Greek-speaking half of the Roman empire in late antiquity. His problem, in other words, was not Davis' or Jameson's, but Edward Gibbon's: the problem of what Gibbon framed as decline and fall, and which moderns would rather envisage as the transformation of the Roman world between, say, the third and sixth centuries of our era.

Ste. Croix's explanation, offered under the rubric of class struggle, was couched chiefly in terms of the reduction of free peasant farmers to the status and function of effectively servile labourers; the once free *coloni* of the Republic and early Empire had become collectively the colonate of the late Empire. Their exceptional, and exceptionally important, status baffled even the Roman lawyers, for though *de facto* servile they remained technically free. Hence the compromise that defined them, or at any rate labelled them, as 'slaves of the earth itself'. Ste. Croix had no difficulty in establishing that this was precisely an ideological formulation, a product of false consciousness on the part of a ruling class engaged, successfully, in an unremitting 'class struggle on the ideological plane'.[45] Old-style slavery of course continued, and indeed continued to flourish, alongside the development of the colonate, but in Ste. Croix's picture it was the latter that made the difference, that accounted for the difference of culture and civilisation between the 'high' Roman empire and the late antique world.

There is still plenty of room for doubt and disagreement over the definition of the status, and interpretation of the historical function, of the colonate, if indeed it is not just a modern myth.[46] More generally, however, as an attempt at a global sociological history of ancient Greek servitude, given that it was just a part of its problematic, Ste. Croix's *Class Struggle* is still without an equal.

vi

Within slave studies, the comparative sociology of Orlando Patterson (*Slavery and Social Death*, 1982) marks the shift in emphasis from economics,

---

[45] The title of Ste. Croix's chapter 7.
[46] Surely an extreme view: B. D. Shaw, in the second edition of Finley (n. 17) 31–7.

the material basis, to social-psychological superstructure that was to typify the historical enterprise as a whole.[47] By the late 1990s that shift, or flight, had become a rout: we're all historians of consciousness now, aren't we? At any rate, my representative selection for the final decade of the century entirely fits into the modern paradigm.

Peter Hunt's *Slaves, Warfare and Ideology in the Greek Historians* is one of the most important books in all ancient Greek historiography since Ste. Croix's behemoth. What it shows is how the silences of the ancient literary sources can be turned to modern historiographical advantage, provided the historian has an ear as acutely sensitive as his. It is no accident, as they say, that Hunt is a graduate pupil of Michael Jameson.

The historians who provide his principal subject-matter are those three who between them invented history (i.e., history-writing) in something like at least one of that protean term's many and contested contemporary western senses. Herodotus, Thucydides and Xenophon aimed to tell a true story about a significant political past without obviously displaying, let alone giving rein to, an excess of anger or partisanship; and they did so not merely to relate, but also to explain, those verifiably significant past phenomena. Thucydides indeed famously claimed that his account of the Peloponnesian War would be so accurate and penetrating that it would prove a useful guide to understanding *any* relevantly similar future conflicts.[48] But if those were their conscious and explicit aims and claims, we must now add, following Hunt, that that is *all* they were. For it is his thesis, or rather his case (in the forensic sense), that the big three classical Greek historians were also guilty of a massive conspiracy of silence, a cover-up of systemic and (by ancient Greek standards) global proportions.

To be precise, the fact about which they were wholly or partly silent, understandably enough but inexcusably, was the decisive contribution made by unfree people to the waging of war during the high classical period. According to Hunt, slaves or 'serfs' played a far larger role in the Peloponnesian and many other wars than the contemporary historians were willing to acknowledge. It is here that the 'ideology' of his title begins to bite. For his explanation of this silence about, or silencing of, slaves in

---

[47] Cartledge (n. 38); and see now R. J. Evans, *In Defence of History* (London 1997).

[48] The literature on the historian's historian Thucydides continues to grow apace, but K. J. Dover, *Thucydides* (*Greece* and *Rome* New Surveys in the Classics 7, Oxford 1973), remains as good a short introduction as any; there is a useful bibliographical update by S. Hornblower in *The Oxford Classical Dictionary* (3rd ed., 1996) 1520–1.

classical Greek warfare is fundamentally cultural, or as he prefers, ideological.[49]

On the one hand, war was in Herakleitos' words 'father and king of all ... some he has made slaves, others free' (*fr.* 53 Diehl); or as we might put it, war was one of the major sources of the thousands of men and women, mainly non-Greek 'barbarians', held in servitude in Greece. On the other hand, making war was literally men's work: it not only separated the men from the boys (*paides*, which could also mean 'slaves'), but also the men from the women (the Greek for courage or pugnacity was literally 'virility', *andreia*), and especially the free citizen men from all the rest, above all, or rather below all, the slaves.[50] A brave slave would have been in ancient Greek no less an oxymoron than a brave woman.

Hence, according to Hunt's entirely cogent and well-developed argument, Greek writers who by their selection and shaping of past narratives were helping to forge and maintain a national or local identity and sense of self-worth for their hearers or readers, simply could not afford to allow slaves their due place of honour. Hence too arises the temptation, which Hunt does not seriously resist, to argue that slaves' real role in war must have been far greater than actually recorded, or indeed absolutely crucial — precisely because of the historians' studied reticence. But here the logic is neither so firmly supported by, nor so straightforwardly compatible with, the extant evidence. These are, to employ a suitably nautical metaphor, dangerous waters, littered with sub-merged rocks and permeated by tricky currents.

Consider just two test cases. No one in antiquity or today has denied that the Spartans' helots had a military role.[51] That in itself constituted a huge breach in the Greek military code of citizen solidarity. But not quite so huge a breach as one might at first think, since the helots were themselves Greeks, and more than half of them, the Messenians, were precisely politically motivated men, keen to re-establish their own independent *polis* or city. The question is therefore what

---

[49] Hunt (n. 15) 19–25, a helpful survey of the sometimes confusingly wide range of meaning of 'ideology'. He himself opts for a less exclusive definition than Ste. Croix's Marxist version: 'a system of intellectual beliefs and emotional judgements that make up a model of the world according to which raw experience is interpreted' (19–20).

[50] Cartledge, *The Greeks* (n. 16) ch. 4, and 'The machismo of the Athenian empire — or the reign of the *phaulus*?', in L. Foxhall and J. Salmon (eds.), *When Men Were Men: Masculinity, Power and Identity in Classical Antiquity* (London 1999) 54–67; S. Murnaghan and S. Joshel (eds.), *Women and Slavery in Greek Culture* (London 1998); M. H. Jameson, 'Women and democracy in fourth-century Athens', in P. Brulé and J. Poulhen (eds.), *Esclavage, guerre et économie en Grèce ancienne: Hommages à Yvon Garlan* (Paris 1998) 97–107. On the ambiguity of *pais*, see M. Golden, '*Pais*, Child and Slave', *L'Antiquité classique* 54 (1985) 91–104.

[51] Garlan (n. 6) 40–8; K.-W. Welwei, *Unfreie im antiken Kriegsdienst*, vol. 1 (Wiesbaden 1974).

sort of a military role, and how significant a military role, did the Spartans grant to or require of the helots in their foreign wars? Hunt, it seems to me, is too anxious too often to allot them a front-line fighting function.

As for the slaves who rowed, or helped to row, the Athenian navies, the problem here starts at first base, with the inadequacy of the extant primary evidence. We simply do not begin to have the requisite serial data to calculate, for example, what proportion of the twenty thousand or so rowers of a fleet of a hundred trireme warships would typically consist of slaves, whether rowing on the same ships as their masters or independently of them.[52] But in the context of this chapter's problematic, a great deal hangs on our answer to such a question. For it was Athens' navy, as its principal fighting arm, which contributed crucially to the development of democracy at Athens, and so indirectly in the Aegean Greek world as well. At least we may safely observe that the presence of slave rowers, in whatever numbers, did not necessarily impair naval efficiency, and that is interesting enough in itself.

But we may surely go further, and state that, if as a matter of fact Athenian or Athenian-led fleets were significantly crewed by slaves, then Athenian democracy was significantly dependent on slave labour. In a way, that would not be such a startling statement. The functioning of the democracy, like that of the Athenians' empire in the fifth century, was also significantly dependent on the silver ore extracted from the soil of Attica by the labour almost entirely of slaves. Nevertheless, it would inflict a pretty sizeable dent in the ancient Athenian self-image of the free democratic citizen at war, which in its Periklean version at least liked to emphasise that even (or especially) poor citizens had a decisive democratic role to play on as well as off the field, or sea, of battle. It would also dent the otherwise suggestive modern notion of the trireme as a sort of capsule of democratic egalitarianism.[53]

On that, the jury is still out. What is not in dispute is the enormous sophistication and aplomb, as well as sheer scholarly endeavour, with which Hunt's monograph embraces and embodies the current secular turn away from straight economic and social history, from Finley's characteristic question of 1959 to the history of ideological and cultural representations. It is a book to be re-read, and not only by historians of ancient Greek slavery.

---

[52] Further evidence in A. J. Graham, 'Thucydides 7.13.2 and the crews of Athenian triremes: an addendum', *Transactions of the American Philological Association* 128 (1998) 89–114.

[53] B. S. Strauss, 'The Athenian trireme, school of democracy', in J. Ober and C. Hedrick (eds.), *Demokratia: a Conversation on Democracies Ancient and Modern* (Princeton 1996) 313–25; but see Cartledge in Foxhall and Salmon (n. 50).

vii

One way of re-posing the question 'Was Greek civilisation based on slavery?' is to ask what Greek civilisation would have been like without it. To put it even more starkly, would there have been any Greek civilisation worth transmitting, inheriting or studying, but for slavery? An answer may emerge if we consider how the Greeks themselves 'thought' slavery within their own collective and individual frameworks of cultural self-definition and self-identification. Did *they* believe their civilisation was based on slavery?

Retrospective myth, prospective imaginings and hard-headed presentism all gave the same unequivocally positive answer. Once upon a time, before the Greeks had slaves, it was women and children who mythically performed the equivalent servile functions on behalf of men.[54] Looking forward, to the world of semi-realistic Utopia, no matter how hard they tried to view things otherwise, the Greeks could not quite envisage a slaveless future.[55] The only alternative to slave labour that they could imagine was a world of automatic life (*automatos bios*), in which the necessities were constantly available without human labour, on tap as it were, and craft goods were produced or moved by automation.[56]

The inescapable inference is that the Greeks could conceive of no practical alternative to slavery. That is especially clear from the work of Aristotle, whose school inaugurated the systematic science of mechanics but eschewed its practical applications.[57] The prophet of things as they are, Aristotle spoke for all free Greeks when he associated slavery with *praxis* not *poiesis*: with living the good life, not securing or continuing mere material life. The proverb he quoted, 'No leisure for slaves,' was at one level a statement of fact; more significantly, leisure (*skholē*) was what distinguished the truly free man (*eleutheros*) and the truly 'liberal' lifestyle (*eleutherios*).[58]

The claim has even been made that it was 'the growth of slavery in the archaic period [that] prompted the Greeks to invent politics'.[59] That may be

---

[54] M. M. Austin and P. Vidal-Naquet, *Economic and Social History of Ancient Greece: an Introduction* (London 1977) 184–6, no. 15.

[55] 'Slaveless societies': Garlan (n. 6) 126–38. On Greek utopias generally, see D. Dawson, *Cities of the Gods* (New York 1992).

[56] Arist. *Pol.* 1253b33–54a; *cf.* Ste. Croix (n. 12) 113.

[57] Finley (n. 10) 180.

[58] Arist. *Pol.* 1334a20–1 (proverb). On Aristotle's 'natural slavery' doctrine (*Pol.* 1253b–55b30), see for instance Ste. Croix (n. 12) 416–18; N. Smith, in D. Keyt and F. Miller (eds.), *A Companion to Aristotle's 'Politics'* (Oxford 1991) 142–55; Cartledge, *The Greeks* (n. 16) 122–6; and especially Garnsey (n. 16), 105–27, *cf.* 11–14, who notes that it appears only in the *Politics*, and nowhere else in Aristotle's preserved *oeuvre*.

[59] T. E. Rihll, in Bush (n. 10) 111.

going too far; but some such connection seems required, to make sense not only of Greek actuality but also of the way they themselves conceived and interpreted that actuality.

Moses Finley, as we have seen, did not give a direct, unequivocal answer to his own question. The nearest he came to it, with consciously appropriate imagery, was this: 'If we could emancipate ourselves from the despotism of extraneous moral, intellectual and political pressures, we would conclude, without hesitation, that slavery was a basic element in Greek civilisation.'[60] If we could... Granted that we cannot, should we even try?

I would like to end by returning to my starting point, morality, and by quoting some wise words of Keith Bradley which I entirely endorse:[61]

> The kinds of impact on slaves made by the traffic in human merchandise that I have posited are symptomatic of what in contemporary affairs we should now call violations of fundamental human rights. If the current sensitivity to that concept sharpens perception and understanding of the past, then that to my mind marks a true historical advance. It does not follow that what is admirable from the past is any the less admirable; it simply means that the price of the admirable — an incalculable degree of human misery and suffering — is given its full historical due. It is in this sense, accordingly, that one might assert that the best history is very much contemporary history.

To put the same point emblematically: 1959 was the year not only of Finley's epoch-making article but also of the death of Billie Holiday. Both, it seems to me, have a place within the study and understanding of ancient Greek slavery. They remind us, rather uncomfortably, just how deeply the whole western tradition of freedom is implicated, at its source and in the ever flowing current, with a history of unfreedom.[62]

I am indebted above all, for help of various kinds, to Keith Bradley, Stan Engerman, Joe Miller and Walter Scheidel.

---

[60] Finley (n. 10) 111 ('without hesitation' a Gibbonian reminiscence?).

[61] K. R. Bradley, '"The regular daily traffic in slaves": Roman history and contemporary history', *Classical Journal* 87 (1992) 125–36, at 136.

[62] Patterson, *Freedom* (n. 23); E. Foner, *The Story of American Freedom* (New York 1999).

11
Socrates on trial in the USA

Malcolm Schofield

i

For the last thirty years or more publications on Socrates have become a major growth industry. Its centre is the USA; and much of it has been occasioned by engagement with the work of Gregory Vlastos, conceivably the single most influential writer on ancient Greek philosophy in the English-speaking world in the twentieth century. Vlastos devoted most of the energies of his last 15 years to working on Socrates, not just in his publications, but in lectures, seminars, and correspondence, and not least in the summer schools for younger scholars (funded by the National Endowment for the Humanities) which he led on more than one occasion. In a footnote in the Introduction to his book on Socrates he suggested himself that 'more work on Socrates is now appearing in a single year than in a decade during the thirties, forties or fifties'.[1] Of course, something similar is probably true of many subjects in most academic disciplines, for a variety of reasons. But the development of interest in Socrates remains striking, and Vlastos' own role in it has been central.

Socrates has one or two apparent drawbacks as candidate for all-American hero. Around the time of the Vietnam War, and of the widespread practice of civil disobedience of various forms in relation to US policy in general and the draft in particular, Plato's *Crito* started to attract attention, containing as it does Socrates' apparent blanket endorsement, on paternalist grounds, of the thesis that 'on the battlefield, in the lawcourt, everywhere, one must do as one's city and fatherland commands' (51b–c). Eventually in 1984 there appeared one of the finest recent contributions to Socratic studies, a book by Vlastos' pupil Richard Kraut entirely devoted to the *Crito*, entitled

---

[1] *Socrates: Ironist and Moral Philosopher* (Cambridge 1991) 19 n. 71.

Socrates and the State.[2] The most distinctive claim of *Socrates and the State* related precisely to the issue of civil disobedience.

Kraut pointed out that what is said about obedience is a bit more nuanced than the quotation above might suggest. For it continues with the enunciation of an alternative: 'or persuade the city what justice consists in'. In the disjunction 'persuade or obey' Kraut saw an opening for a less authoritarian, more liberal interpretation of Socrates' position. 'Persuade', said Kraut, is better translated '*try* to persuade'. On this reading, endorsed by Vlastos,[3] disobedience is permitted provided a citizen endeavours to persuade the established authority that an order is unjust or otherwise faulty. But many scholars were *not* persuaded, and arguments about the *Crito* continue, as we shall be seeing when we engage with the dialogue in more detail later.

Another tricky area for citizens of the world's greatest contemporary democracy is Socrates' political stance. Probably there would be fairly wide agreement among scholars that the principal motive behind the prosecution which led to Socrates' death in 399 BC was political animus against someone who had had close associations with Critias, leading member of the junta which overthrew the Athenian democracy in 403 BC. The assumption underpinning the formal charges brought against him will have been that Socrates was guilty by association, even if he had not engaged in political *activity* himself. But did he hold *views* which lent credibility to the prosecution? Did he articulate a more or less anti-democratic *position*? On this question passions have run high; and I shall begin this article by looking at a particular debate about Socrates' relationship — theoretical and practical — to democracy in which Vlastos took up a stance antithetical to that championed by the radical journalist I. F. Stone in his book *The Trial of Socrates.*[4]

ii

I. F. Stone (1907–1989) was an independent investigative journalist (or as he put it himself, an 'old Washington muckraker'), committed to a succession of left-wing causes, from Spain to Cuba, and to the defence of civil liberties, notably during the periods of the McCarthy witchhunts and of the Vietnam

---

[2] *Socrates and the State* (Princeton 1984).

[3] 'The historical Socrates and Athenian democracy', in his *Socratic Studies* (Cambridge 1994) 107 n. 34.

[4] *The Trial of Socrates* (Boston and London 1988). References are to the London edition.

War. He is perhaps most famous for *I. F. Stone's Weekly*, which he edited from 1953 until his retirement from full-time journalism in 1971 at the age of 63. By then the *Times Literary Supplement* had compared him to Diogenes the Cynic and Jeremiah, while Henry Steele Commager had described him in the *New York Review of Books* as 'a modern Tom Paine, celebrating Common Sense and the Rights of Man, hammering away at tyranny, injustice, exploitation, deception and chicanery'.[5] In his retirement Stone decided to write 'a study of freedom of thought in human history', with 'a liberating synthesis of Marx and Jefferson' as its goal.[6] The enquiry led him back to ancient Athens, 'the earliest society where freedom of thought and its expression flourished on a scale never known before, and rarely equalled since'. Stone found himself enticed into exploring Greek literature and indeed — at the age of 70 — into learning Greek. Aeschylus seems to have been a particular love of his, and above all the *Oresteia*, whose 'ultimate hero', he wrote, 'is Athenian democracy'. Its 'climactic political message' is delivered when Athena 'pays tribute for her victory over the Furies to two "gods of the city" peculiar to Athens. They are Peitho, or persuasion personified as a goddess, and the Zeus Agoraios, or the Zeus of the assembly, the tutelary divinity of its free debates. They embodied the democratic institutions of Athens.' If Socrates did not honour them, so much the worse — Stone was to decide — for Socrates.

Stone never wrote his general historical essay. In the concluding words of his Preface to *The Trial of Socrates* he said:[7]

> The more I fell in love with the Greeks, the more agonizing grew the spectacle of Socrates before his judges. It horrified me as a civil libertarian. It shook my Jeffersonian faith in the common man. It was a black mark for Athens and the freedom it symbolized. How could the trial of Socrates have happened in so free a society? How could Athens have been so untrue to itself?
>
> This book is the fruit of that torment. I set out to discover how it could have happened. I could not defend the verdict when I started and I cannot defend it now. But I wanted to find out what Plato does not tell us, to give the Athenian side of the story, to mitigate the city's crime and thereby remove some of the stigma the trial left on democracy and on Athens.

---

[5] This — like virtually all my knowledge about Stone — is taken from R. C. Cottrell, *Izzy: A Biography of I. F. Stone (Rutgers 1992); these quotations at 266.*

[6] Information and quotations here and in the remainder of this paragraph come from the Preface to Stone (n. 4) ix–xi.

[7] Stone (n. 4) xi.

The book was published in 1988, one year before Stone's death at the age of 81. It was a popular success. Reviews appeared in many of the quality papers, daily, weekly and monthly, in the UK and the USA. Extravagant praise in some quarters was matched by equally extravagant denunciation in others.

Looked at one way, Stone's attempt to do something to get Athens off the hook is — as he himself intimates — what one might expect of an investigative journalist. Plato in the *Apology* paints Socrates as a martyr; and his version of what was at stake in the trial of Socrates has become something like an official version. All Stone's professional and radical instincts made him distrust the official version of *any* story. No wonder, therefore, that he started reading other sources, other authors, to discover 'what Plato does not tell us'.

From another point of view it is rather more difficult to see why Stone should have gone in the direction he describes here: of seeking to exculpate — in some degree — the Athenians' judicial murder of Socrates. Were it not for phenomena such as his love affair with Castro's Cuba, we might have expected Stone to have perceived Socrates as a kindred spirit: a fiercely independent member of the awkward squad, a voice society and the dominant forces within it found uncomfortable and decided to silence if they could. The trial of Socrates could then have pointed a moral about the fragility of civil liberties in any place and time. And with his rhetoric of agony and horror Stone makes it clear that he was well aware of that expectation.

In fact his major line of argument turns precisely on a point about the conditions under which civil liberties are best secured. The general idea is that you can't make an omelette without breaking eggs. More specifically, for Stone Athens' identity as a society rested on its democratic recognition of freedom of speech for all its citizens. But it could only sustain that identity by remaining a *democracy*. And if it was to remain a democracy it was only to be expected that it should take steps to forestall any attempt at a third oligarchic coup like those of 411 and 403 BC. In this connection the silencing of Socrates could well have been intended to send a salutary message to oligarchic sympathisers, letting them know that the democracy would take no chances in the matter — even if his elimination involved an isolated suspension of the ordinary tolerance of free speech and thought which was at the heart of democratic ideology and the democratic way of life. So Athens should get the benefit of the doubt. Socrates' execution was a crime; but not a crime which need shake our fundamental admiration for Athenian constancy in upholding democratic freedoms.

iii

Stone's defence of Athens has a number of different strands, but the one I want to single out is his argument that the trial of Socrates was conceived as a shot across the bows against oligarchic sympathisers. Stone holds not merely that Socrates was reasonably enough *perceived* as a close associate of leading oligarchs. More than that, Socrates actually championed anti-democratic views, and took a pretty minimalist attitude to his practical responsibilities as a citizen of a democracy — which may have encouraged more committed democrats to see him as one who, not being for us, must be against us. They will have been the more inclined to see him that way because of a prevailing climate of fear that the democracy might be again under threat. Here Stone reminds us that as late as 401 there is evidence of another attempt by the defeated oligarchic party to deploy a mercenary force from their base at Eleusis against the democracy. But we may also recall with the distinguished Greek historian Mogens Herman Hansen that the period 400–399 bristled with trials for impiety and lawsuits concerning religious offences: most famously the case brought against Andocides for profaning the mysteries back in 415, clearly a matter of settling old scores.[8] The political anxiety diagnosed by Stone no doubt fuelled and exploited religious anxiety.

Nobody questions Stone's first point: that Socrates was perceived as someone much involved with Critias, leading member of the regime of thirty tyrants, in particular. In a forensic speech delivered half a century after the event, the orator Aeschines could say apparently without fear of contradiction (*Against Timarchus* 173): 'Men of Athens, you executed Socrates the sophist because he was shown to have educated Critias, one of the Thirty who put down the democracy'. In Xenophon's list of the accusations made against him, we are told (*Memorabilia* 1.2.12): 'But the accuser said that Critias and Alcibiades, having associated with Socrates, did great evil to the city'. Hansen proposes that the reference is to Anytus, one of the three Athenians who laid charges against Socrates and so precipitated the trial. Hansen notes that the amnesty agreed at the restoration of democracy meant that association with Critias or Alcibiades could not figure among the formal charges, but argues, drawing attention to Lysias' *Against Nicomachus* as

---

[8] M. H. Hansen, 'The trial of Sokrates — from the Athenian point of view', *Historisk-filosofiske Meddelelser* 71 (Royal Danish Academy of Sciences and Letters, Copenhagen 1995).

a parallel, that it does not follow that 'a prosecutor was prevented from mentioning Socrates' earlier relations with those two sinister figures'.[9]

The star text for the ascription of anti-democratic views to Socrates himself is again from Xenophon's list of charges (*Memorabilia* 1.2.9):

> But by Zeus, said the accuser, he made his associates despise the established laws, saying it was silly to appoint the city's magistrates by lot, when no one would want to use a lot-selected pilot or builder or flute-player or anyone else for work in which mistakes are far less disastrous than those which concern the city.

Prima facie this passage counts strongly in Stone's favour.

As to Socrates' conduct as a citizen, Stone is not thinking primarily of his well-known decision to avoid political activity as much as he could, but more specifically of his behaviour at the time of Critias' oligarchic putsch in 404. Many committed democrats left the city; great numbers of poorer citizens were driven out. It was the regrouping of the democrats and their capture of the hilltop border stronghold of Phyle which precipitated the overthrow of the junta in 403. Socrates was evidently not one of those who left the city: he stayed behind. What Stone points out is that 'when democracy was restored, to have "stayed in the city" became a badge of dishonour', as attested by Lysias and other orators.[10] 'The odium' such people incurred 'was often utilised to influence the courts',[11] as witness for example the title of a speech of Lysias (from which only a fragment survives): *In defence of Eryximachus, who remained in the city.*

I think Stone is persuasive in his suggestion that Socrates might well have been regarded as tarred with this brush. It is noteworthy that in Plato's *Apology* he goes out of his way to deny that he is a 'quiet Athenian' — that is, the sort of person castigated by Pericles in the funeral speech as good for nothing, not as minding his own business in admirable fashion. This suggests that Socrates (or Plato on his behalf) was sensitive to the implication that what might be perceived as his minimalist interpretation of the duties of a citizen was undemocratic.

Here we uncover the root of Stone's palpable antipathy to Socrates. When the chips were down, Socrates did not leave the city and stand up to be counted with the democrats out at Phyle, but 'simply went home' (as Plato makes him say in the *Apology* with regard to the Leon of Salamis incident he

---

[9] Hansen (n. 8) 7–15; quotation at 11.
[10] Stone (n. 4) 153.
[11] Ibid.

retails there).[12] Stone found this hard to take; Myles Burnyeat commented in his review of the book that the right to pass such a judgment (rightly or not) was one Stone had earned.[13]

iv

Vlastos, like Stone born in 1907, allowed himself a number of rejoinders to Stone's book, although he refused invitations to review it and declined Stone's suggestion of a public debate between the two of them.[14] I have counted two explicit responses, one implicit one, and a curious echo, on which more anon.

Stone's book makes a number of generous tributes to Vlastos and his work. In his acknowledgements he says: 'I treasure encouraging words at the beginnings of my autodidactic labours from Professor Gregory Vlastos, retired, of Princeton'. There is an approving reference to Vlastos' observation that 'while Jesus wept for Jerusalem, Socrates never shed a tear for Athens', as the utterance of 'one of the foremost Platonists of our time'. And Stone calls the paper on political obedience and disobedience by 'the great American classicist Gregory Vlastos' a 'brilliant effort' to resolve the difficulties it tackles.[15] On the other hand, Stone does not mention at all Vlastos' papers in *Political Theory* 1979 and 1983, the one explicitly and the other implicitly critical of his views.

Vlastos' reaction to Stone is rather more intriguing. The short 1979 article in *Political Theory*[16] responded urbanely to a preliminary statement of his views published by Stone in the *New York Times* magazine section of 8 April 1979. After admiring remarks about Stone's record during the McCarthy era and his work with *Stone's Weekly*, he turned to criticism. Among various points he made were the following:

(a) Plato's *Apology* puts on trial *not* (as Stone suggests) Athenian democracy and its protection of free speech, *but* the 'preposterous judicial system' institutionalised at Athens.

---

[12] Stone (n. 4) ch. 8; quotation at 114.

[13] M. F. Burnyeat, 'Cracking the Socrates case', *New York Review of Books* 35 no. 5, 31 March 1988, 12–15; comment from p. 13 (top).

[14] Information about the declined invitations and suggestion is from a letter from Vlastos to Burnyeat dated 25 August 1988 kindly copied to me by Myles Burnyeat.

[15] Stone (n. 4) 269, 146, 256 n. 16.

[16] 'On "The Socrates Story"', *Political Theory* 7 (1979) 533–6.

(b) Stone's argument that Socrates' 'staying in the city' could well have been seen as evidence of oligarchic sympathy is unconvincing.

(c) Stone overdoes the political dimension of the case against Socrates. Here Vlastos allows that the judges will indeed have allowed political considerations to affect them. As well as noting Socrates' association with Critias and Alcibiades, Vlastos says:[17]

> From even what Plato and Xenophon say elsewhere in their writings it is abundantly clear that their hero is sharply critical of his city's constitution: he makes no secret of his view that it prescribes government of the ignorant by the ignorant for the ignorant. It would be known that he questioned the principles of majority rule, election by lot, pay for public office.

Some points to note here: (a) It might strike one as difficult to combine admiration for Athenian democracy with dislike of its jury system. How could one have one without the other? Did Vlastos want Athens to be a modern liberal democracy? (b) Vlastos' reply took no account of evidence Stone was later to produce from Lysias (and cited also by Hansen) — which swayed Myles Burnyeat from siding with Vlastos on the issue to agreeing with Stone.[18] (c) Vlastos (i) allowed Socrates anti-democratic views and (ii) treated Plato and Xenophon as equal authorities on this point at least — but was subsequently (in fact as soon as 1983) to abandon both positions, and later showed particular irritation with Stone's assumption of the propriety of (ii).

Vlastos commented on Stone's book, when it appeared, on at least two occasions. First, in a letter to the *TLS* (4–10 November 1988, 1227), he reiterated his admiration for Stone's record as journalist and political activist, but warned readers not 'to treat indulgently the false view of Socrates presently propagated by his book'. He made two specific points: Stone suffers from 'abysmal innocence of Quellenkritik', and in particular treats the evidence of Xenophon and Plato on a par; and Stone is 'blatantly philistine' in his comprehension of philosophy. Second, in a review of Brickhouse and Smith's *Socrates on Trial* published in the *TLS* the following year (15 December 1989, 1393), and after Stone's death, his tone became more feline: 'Readers who have been swept off their feet by the late I. F. Stone's bestseller on the same topic will find here facts from which an honest effort to get at the truth should start'.

It is hard to avoid the suspicion that Stone's book had got under the skin of 'one of the foremost Platonists of our time' — who was yet to publish his

---

[17] Vlastos (n. 16) 534.
[18] Burnyeat (n. 13) 12.

own book on Socrates, of course. Here is a curious parallel which might support that verdict. Stone's book begins with a Preface entitled 'How this book came to be written'. In three compelling pages it tells the story I have already recounted of how retirement in 1971 from *I. F. Stone's Weekly* and a writing project on freedom of thought eventually led Stone the autodidact to the writing of a book on Socrates and Athens. When three years later Vlastos published his *Socrates: Ironist and Moral Philosopher*, *it* carried an Introduction entitled: 'How this book came to be', and running to no less than 20 pages. 'Well, he's a great figure in the subject, but this is a bit much,' I thought to myself when I first read the book, and not on account of its length alone. What Vlastos presents is a partial intellectual autobiography, which discloses that *his* attempts to write on Socrates went back as far as 1953. It paints the picture of a heroic struggle to get Socrates right, conducted for the best part of forty years, assisted at every turn by dialogue with many of the leading younger scholars of the age, and fortified by the inspiration of great teachers of Vlastos' youth like Cornford and Whitehead.[19] The contrast with Stone's late, amateur, and comparatively brief solo venture into the field could not be more marked.

V

Vlastos' article of 1983 entitled 'The historical Socrates and Athenian democracy'[20] does not refer to Stone at any point. But in the Introduction to *Socrates* its author says: 'I would pit [the paper] against the picture of Socrates as a crypto-oligarchic ideologue lately given currency in Stone's popular book.'[21] His Socrates had indeed become the complete opposite of

---

[19] 'An *introduction* should get the reader interested in the subject of the book by briefly describing it, praising its author and providing a fascinating curriculum vitae without necessarily explaining or parsing the work. The introduction is an extended blurb, a barker's spiel, and hence it is like an old-fashioned *advertisement*, and may concern itself with the personal history of the author. It permits reminiscence and gossip. Both preface and introduction can apologise for the public's past neglect of the work. The author may write his own blurb but this is definitely bad form. He will pretend to be introducing his book to the reader, which is a little like introducing his dog. Ideally it should be by another writer of fame if not distinction, because an introduction is an endorsement. Introductions are usually a lot of baloney. And there are far too many of them'. William Gass, 'Flattery and whining', *London Review of Books* (5 October 2000) 9.

[20] *Political Theory* 11 (1983) 495–516; here cited in the version reprinted as ch. 4 of *Socratic Studies* (Cambridge 1994).

[21] Vlastos (n. 1) 18.

Stone's—except as far as concerns political quietism, a topic not broached in the paper about democracy. For on Vlastos' account, in contrast with Stone's, Socrates holds *no* political theory of any kind. On the other hand, and in striking opposition to his own statements in the 1979 article (never mentioned in its successor of 1983), Vlastos now argues that despite his association with the likes of Critias, Socrates has in practice a profound attachment to Athens and its democratic institutions.

The core of Vlastos' interpretation is his reading of a passage from Plato's *Crito*, in which Socrates imagines the laws of Athens as addressing him as follows (52b–c):

> O Socrates, we have strong proof that both we and the city have been pleasing to you. For you would not have been, above other Athenians, exceedingly constant in your residence in the city, if it were not exceedingly pleasing to you. Not even for a festival did you ever go out of Athens, except once to the Isthmian games—nowhere else, except on military service; nor did you make any out-of-town visits, like other folk, nor did the desire ever seize you to know some other city, some other laws: you have been satisfied with us and our city. So intensely did you prefer us and agree to conduct your civic life in accordance with us that, among other things, you had children in it [sc. the city], which shows that the city pleased you.

The way Vlastos announces the importance of the passage — 'one of the most familiar, yet least heeded, ... in the Platonic corpus'[22]—which (as he subsequently admits)[23] constitutes his sole positive evidence for Socrates' democratic views, strongly suggests that it was re-reading this bit of text which converted him from the interpretation he had adopted in the 1979 article (where, as we saw, he represented the Socratic verdict on democracy as 'government of the ignorant by the ignorant for the ignorant'). On the basis of *Crito* 52b–c he construes Socrates as by his own avowal an Athenophile, and in particular as someone who is effectively saying that he preferred the Athenian democratic constitution to any other known to him, given that its democratic cast was the salient feature which distinguished it from other cities whose *eunomia* or cultivation of law he admired, notably at Sparta and in Crete.

What it is about Athenian democracy that Socrates found so congenial is not thereby determined. And Vlastos' position on the question verges on the quixotic. It seems to consist of two elements:[24] (i) the Platonic Socrates has not even the glimmerings of a theoretical justification for his preference;

[22] Vlastos (n. 3) 90.
[23] Vlastos (n. 3) 104.
[24] Vlastos (n. 3) 104–5.

(ii) his conception of the 'royal art' (see further below) implies a moral vision of a society in which everyone, not a favoured elite, pursues the 'examined life' — but Vlastos at once points out that the actual Athens was *not* that society. This seems to leave the preference for Athenian democracy he ascribes to Socrates pretty much a mystery. He prefers to call Socrates' attitude 'demophilic',[25] to register its untheorised status, but one might feel this is just whistling in the dark.

In developing his thesis Vlastos evidently makes a number of hermeneutic assumptions. He takes it that (a) the views attributed in the *Crito* to the laws of Athens are the Platonic Socrates' own opinions;[26] (b) the Platonic Socrates of early dialogues such as the *Crito* is an accurate representation of the historical Socrates;[27] (c) the historical Socrates actually voiced these opinions on the occasion Plato depicts: 'He tells his friend in the privacy of his prison cell, where he could have no motive for dissembling, that he prefers the laws of Athens to those of any other state known to him'.[28]

This is evidently an extreme or naive realist reading of the *Crito*. Each element in it is and was highly contestable. Much of the work on the *Crito* produced in the last five years, in particular, adduces strong reasons for rejecting (a).[29] In a postmodernist climate in literary studies it is not surprising that (b) is a position less popular than once it was;[30] and Vlastos' own attempt to establish its truth in his *Socrates* met with powerful criticism in some of the extended reviews of the book.[31] Finally, (c) seems to imply at any rate qualification of the virtually universal view among scholars — elsewhere endorsed by Vlastos himself[32] — that Platonic dialogues are generally works of fiction, not pretending historical accuracy (one can hardly believe that Vlastos himself really thought that Plato constructed the *Crito*

---

[25] Vlastos (n. 3) 105.

[26] Vlastos (n. 3) 90 and n. 8.

[27] Argued at length in Vlastos (n. 1) chs. 2 and 3.

[28] Vlastos (n. 3) 107.

[29] See for example the studies cited in nn. 43 and 44 below.

[30] Note for example the judicious remarks on Plato's Socrates and the historical Socrates in John Cooper's authoritative introduction to *Plato: Complete Works* (Indianapolis 1997), xii–xviii. 'There was a time', says M. M. McCabe (p. 363 below), 'when to read Plato was to do away with reading'; and as she implies, nobody was more influentially a non-reading reader of that kind and that era than Vlastos.

[31] Notably C. H. Kahn, 'Vlastos's Socrates', *Phronesis* 37 (1992) 233–58; J. Beversluis, 'Vlastos's quest for the historical Socrates', *Ancient Philosophy* 13 (1993) 293–312.

[32] Vlastos (n. 1) 50–3.

more or less exclusively from notes on what Crito said or wrote about his conversation with Socrates on the occasion described in the dialogue).[33]

Having set out his reading of the *Crito* Vlastos asks whether the resulting view of Socrates is contradicted by (i) other evidence in Plato or (ii) evidence in Xenophon. On question (i) his answer is 'No'; on question (ii) he answers 'Yes', and produces lots of passages to support it. Xenophon and Plato are therefore incompatible sources. In Vlastos' opinion we simply have to opt for one or the other. He leaves us in no doubt which way his own vote goes.

In finding no contradiction between the *Crito* and other evidence in Plato, Vlastos allows that in the *Apology* and the *Gorgias* Plato's Socrates is fiercely critical of Athenian political life and the conduct of those prominent in it. But it is one thing to reject a city's laws, another to attack those who conduct their lives within the framework of those laws. And after making this point Vlastos moves on to question (ii), the conflict between Plato and Xenophon. Here much space is devoted to their differing interpretations of the Socratic idea of the 'political' or 'royal' art or expertise, as articulated by Xenophon above all at *Mem.* 3.9.10 and by Plato at *Euthydemus* 291b–292e. Vlastos sums these up as follows:[34]

> For Xenophon's Socrates the royal art is statecraft — mastery of the great instrumentalities of civic happiness: wealth, military supremacy, good external relations, harmonious internal relations. For Plato's Socrates the royal art is nothing of that sort. It has no more to do with the art of fiscal prudence, of military science, of shrewd diplomacy, of persuasive oratory, than with the art of making us immortal or of turning stones into gold. Needless to say, we cannot run a city without economists, generals, ambassadors, orators, and other masters of the instrumentalities: public doctors, architects, engineers, and so forth. But all these specialists should do their job under the direction of the royal art, whose sole competence is moral knowledge: expertise in determining how the instrumentalities can be used best in the interest of moral perfection.

It follows that whereas Xenophon's Socrates does indeed have an anti-democratic political theory, Plato's has no political theory at all — only a moral transformation of political theory. For the Platonic Socrates, the 'doctrine' of the royal art 'defines only the moral dimension of the

---

[33] Indeed in *Socrates*, 50 n. 17, he specifically dissociates himself from any position of this sort relative both to the *Crito* and to a number of other dialogues where Socrates converses with a single interlocutor. Nonetheless in that work he remains confident that Socrates' deep attachment to Athens and its laws as attested by *Crito* 52c–e is one of the authentic personalia disclosed by Plato in the early dialogues: ibid. 252.

[34] Vlastos (n. 3) 102–3.

statesman's vocation'.[35] The more important contrast Vlastos draws in this context for the main question which concerns him and us, however, is the following:[36]

> This wisdom cannot be monopolized by members of the city's upper crust, as it has to be for Xenophon's Socrates, for if it were, moral virtue could only belong to few, while for Plato's Socrates it must belong to everyone.

There are three considerable difficulties with this sequence of argument. First is one which may well strike anyone who reads M. M. McCabe's chapter in this volume. Whether or not one accepts (as I do) her view of the *Euthydemus* as a middle period or latish dialogue exhibiting affinities with the *Republic*, and constituting *inter alia* a 'reading' of the earlier *Meno*, it would be widely agreed nowadays that it is dangerous to try to use it as transparent testimony about the 'doctrines'[37] of 'the Platonic Socrates' of the early dialogues. More particularly, the passage of the *Euthydemus* about the royal art is a particularly teasing stretch of text. It begins with Socrates remarking that 'when we got to the royal art and were giving it a thorough inspection to see whether it might be the one which both provided and created happiness, just there we got into a sort of labyrinth' (291b). Then the labyrinth is described (no hint of any of this in Vlastos): briefly, if the royal art is to make people happy, it will do so by making them wise and thereby good; but the only form of wisdom which appears to meet the bill is the royal art itself— 'so it must convey a knowledge which is none other than itself', and of which we can apparently say nothing except that anyone in possession of it will convey it to others in turn, making them good too in some way which remains endlessly elusive. 'Mercy on us, Socrates,' says Crito (interlocutor at this point, 292e), 'you seem to have got yourselves into a lot of puzzlement (*aporia*)'. As his comment nicely emphasises, Socrates appears much less clear than Vlastos about what the royal art is and whether it has the makings of a viable idea.

Second, we might provisionally agree that for the Socrates of Plato's early dialogues, moral virtue in general is simply 'knowledge of ends', having nothing to do with 'knowledge of the instrumentalities of the good life'. But the specific form of moral knowledge Vlastos associates with the royal art— 'expertise in determining how the instrumentalities can be used

---

[35] Vlastos (n. 3) 104.

[36] Vlastos (n. 3) 103.

[37] In the case of the royal art Vlastos' talk of doctrines reflects an explicit interpretative commitment: 'Plato's Socrates most certainly has a doctrine of the "royal art"' (101).

best in the interest of moral perfection' — looks as though it has after all an essentially political concern with 'instrumentalities' (that is, the means as well as the end), and is likely to require of its practitioner an intellectual grip not obviously attainable by every citizen. So even if one concedes some truth in the contrast between a moral and a political interpretation of the royal art, it is not clear that the one has different implications from the other for a verdict on the merits of democracy. The royal art in Plato, at any rate as conceived by Vlastos, may well be accessible to just as small an intellectual elite as in Xenophon.

Third, Vlastos' confident claim that for Plato's Socrates moral virtue is a form of knowledge which 'must belong to everyone', even if true, is therefore not to the point. But is it true? There is something to be said for the view that Socrates' habit of engaging all-comers in moral enquiry involves the presupposition that in some sense everyone is potentially capable of virtue. And in the opening discussion of the *Meno* (71–3) he argues memorably that there is not a different virtue for a man from a woman, or for a free person from a slave, or for a child from someone who is elderly. But the implication of the general upshot of the enquiries made by the Platonic Socrates is a pessimistic one: nobody except Socrates himself is *actually* virtuous, for wherever he probes he finds only ignorance or conceit of knowledge about moral truth — a state of affairs hardly laying much foundation for confidence in the merits of democracy.

Yet the key question is (as Vlastos concedes): what did the historical Socrates think of the actual Athenian democracy and its central institutions?[38] And here again the positive answer he extracts from the *Crito* looks decidedly shaky. From Plato and for democratic convictions Vlastos produces (1) a statement within a hypothetical discourse by an imagined personification in what most scholars would count a fiction, claiming that Socrates prefers the laws of Athens (*Crito* 52b–c), and (2) an *argumentum ex silentio*: apart from his attack on pay for public office in the *Gorgias* (515e), Plato's Socrates never criticises election by lot or any other Athenian democratic practice. From Xenophon and with anti-democratic implications there is (1) the accuser's charge that Socrates attacked the appointment of magistrates by lot and so made his associates despise the established laws (*Memorabilia* 1.2.9) — the one charge Xenophon mentions which, as Vlastos notes,[39] he does not attempt to rebut; and against the background of

---

[38] For what follows see Vlastos (n. 3) 105–8.
[39] Vlastos (n. 3) 89.

(2) the ascription to Socrates of a political version of the idea of a royal art elsewhere in the *Memorabilia* (3.9.10; *cf.* 4.6.14). There seem to be fewer difficulties in supposing that point (1) in Xenophon transmits a historical truth about Socrates' views than with any of the other items.

Moreover Vlastos' account of Plato's evidence may need supplementation requiring a different conclusion from the one he reaches about it. In *Socrates and the State* Richard Kraut reviewed a sequence of passages (some from earlier in the *Crito* itself, and most not mentioned by Vlastos), in which Plato represents Socrates as attacking 'the many'.[40] For taking decisions on any matter of importance their views should be disregarded; they have no relevant expertise — that is the province of 'the one'. And Kraut noted that this was entirely consistent with Xenophon's evidence that at his trial Socrates was accused of criticising election by lot (Xenophon point (1) above). He concluded that for Socrates the basis and consequent procedures of democracy were radically and irremediably flawed.[41] Of course, it would not necessarily follow that Socrates could identify any better system of rule that was actually practicable. But the issue for the present is what he thought of Athenian democratic institutions. And Kraut's diagnosis of a negative verdict looks better supported than Vlastos' conviction that he approved of them.[42]

vi

Perhaps Vlastos chose the wrong ground for a fight with Stone over his picture of Socrates the crypto-oligarch. The case he put for holding that

---

[40] Kraut (n. 2) ch. 7.

[41] But Kraut, though not a realist interpreter of the *Crito*, holds that the ideas in the speech of the laws of Athens are 'worthy of Socrates' endorsement', and 'are completely consistent with the philosophy he expounds throughout Plato's early dialogues': (n. 2) 41. In line with this approach, he tries to identify a sense in which Socrates *does* approve of the Athenian democratic system (as the laws claim he does), and proposes that while he rejects the principle of rule by the many, he values the freedom of enquiry permitted or even encouraged by democratic institutions. The argument for the positive element in the proposal is inevitably pretty speculative. But in any case the negative element constitutes a fatal drawback: the laws' speech contains no suggestion that Socrates is *selective* in his strong preference for them; and the possibility that he might be would scupper the argument they are making at this point — that he has made an implicit contract with them, and so must in justice abide by the decision of the court (which was of course a majority vote of the many).

[42] At the same time we need not deny that Socrates' actual political *behaviour* was such that a committed democrat like Lysias was prepared to write his own *Apology* for him, in reply to a pamphlet attacking Socrates composed a few years after his death by the Athenian *rhētōr* Polycrates (schol. in Aristidem 3.480 Dindorf), as Vlastos (n. 3, 108) and Hansen (n. 8, 29 n. 130) agree.

Socrates held democratic or demophilic views and not anti-democratic ones has crumbled when subjected to scrutiny. And what Vlastos took to be the key passage from the speech of the laws of Athens in the *Crito* can be given a reading quite different from that favoured by him. For example, Roslyn Weiss in her 1998 book on the dialogue[43] and Verity Harte in an article of 1999[44] suggest that what the *Crito* does is dramatise the incommensurability of two different value systems: Crito's traditional ethic, oriented towards family and friends, and Socratic ethics, focused on the health of the soul. The fiction of the personified laws of Athens is then introduced to indicate how one might get to the Socratic conclusion that it would be wrong to try to escape the hemlock, but from premises and by trains of thought a Crito might be prevailed upon to accept. On this reading, the laws' speech is to be seen not as a presentation of the arguments which decided Socrates, but as considerations designed to enable unphilosophical adherents of traditional Greek ethics to make sense of Socrates' decision, and sway them to acceptance of it. Hence the paternalism of the conception of city and laws which is such a notable feature of the speech. Hence the shift from Socratic conversation to rhetoric.

One consideration in support of an alternative reading of the dialogue on these lines might be drawn from other indications about why Socrates went to his death that are supplied in Plato and Xenophon. Plato's *Apology* and Xenophon's *Apology* alike suggest simply that he had decided the time for him to die had arrived (because his *daimonion* or 'divine voice' had fallen silent), and indeed thought of his impending death as a divine blessing.[45] This implication is also consistent with the introduction and epilogue which frame the *Crito* itself: in dying as the Athenians have determined, Socrates will be following the course the god has pointed out (54e; as most recently verified by a prophetic dream he recounts to Crito, 44a–b). As for the laws' arguments, they are compared with the noise of flutes ringing in the ears of corybants, and deafening Socrates to 'the others' (54d): a warning to readers — if ever there was one — about the status we should assign to them.

So for Vlastos' purposes use of the *Crito* was best avoided. On the other hand his argument that the Platonic Socrates is a moral, not (in any straightforward sense) a political thinker, radically transforming the language of politics for ethical purposes, seems at first blush rather more promising. It

[43] R. Weiss, *Socrates Dissatisfied: an Analysis of Plato's Crito* (Oxford 1998).

[44] V. Harte, 'Conflicting values in Plato's *Crito*', *Archiv für Geschichte der Philosophie* 81 (1999) 117–47.

[45] See Pl. *Ap.* 39e–40c, Xen. *Ap.* 4–9, 22–3.

points us to the *Apology* again, and to the terms in which Socrates there denies that he is a quietist — the issue so crucial to Stone's disillusionment with him.[46]

There are two key passages to be considered, the first at 30a–32e. Here Socrates makes his notorious claim that he is a benefit bestowed by the god on the citizens of Athens, viz. in virtue of his ceaseless questioning of the Athenians for the good of their own souls. This is clearly tantamount to maintaining that his conduct *is* in a sense political. But Socrates goes on to explain just how it is and is not. He says he has always abstained from political activity (*politika pragmata*) or public affairs (*dēmosiai*) in favour of the private sphere (*idiai*). This is because his *daimonion* opposed any political involvement — felicitously, since trying to assist what is just and opposing what is unjust on the public stage, as a good man would, is just too dangerous in a democracy. He has therefore been active (*polupragmonein*) in giving advice to the extent of neglecting his own affairs — all marks of a politically engaged citizen — but in the private domain.

In the speech after the verdict (35e–38b), his opportunity to make a counter-proposal about the penalty, this theme now dominates Socrates' discourse. He begins (36b) with a reiteration of the claim that he has never been a quietist (*hēsuchian agein*), but has neglected everything else in order to persuade everyone and anyone to care for their own good and for that of the city itself before all else. At the end (37e) he insists that he *cannot* be a quietist. His innovatory conception of quietism and activity poses a radical challenge to Athens: as he makes clear (38a), he proposes a distinctive gadfly conception of the route to achieving virtue and wisdom, viz. moral and intellectual examination of people's lives.

None of this cut much ice with Stone. But Myles Burnyeat in reviewing Stone suggested that Socrates appears here not as apolitical, but as the advocate and practitioner of a reorientation of politics for moral ends, not in the least lacking in passion or public concern.[47] One might have supposed that Vlastos would have wanted to appeal to these passages to argue that this Socratic politics simply transcends the conventional categories of oligarchy and democracy. In fact he made no use of them. I suspect this was at bottom for two simple but troubling and contrary reasons: Vlastos could not bring

---

[46] For what follows I am indebted to some brief discussion in M. F. Burnyeat (n. 13) 13, and C. D. C. Reeve, *Socrates in the Apology* (Indianapolis 1989), 155–60; and there is stimulating and thoughtful material on Socratic quietism in J. Ober, *Political Dissent in Democratic Athens* (Princeton 1998), ch. 4.

[47] Bunyeat (n. 13) 13.

himself to think that Socrates had no special attachment to democracy as such, despite his difficulties in articulating what it might have consisted in; and yet he was no more convinced than Stone that there was any way of avoiding the conclusion that Socrates *was* a quietist — and a lesser human being on that account. The evidence for Vlastos' adherence to this conclusion involves another curious coincidence.

When Burnyeat edited Vlastos' posthumously published collection *Socratic Studies*, he included as epilogue a graduation address delivered in May 1987 under the title 'Socrates and Vietnam'. Vlastos' address is a homily on the obligations an intellectual or a philosopher has to become *engagé* — to join 'the corporate struggle for justice'. His message is that, confronted with the enormity of an event like the Vietnam War, Socrates' retreat to the private sphere will not do. This verdict might already put us in mind of Stone's similar assessment of Socrates. It gets a special interest from the two examples of Socratic 'silence' Vlastos instances in illustrating Socrates' quietism and its moral drawbacks. They are drawn from crucial moments in Athenian history.

One was Socrates' failure to speak on the side of Diodotus in the debate of 428 BC over Mytilene and the Athenian decision to put to death all Mytilenean males. The other was his failure a few years later (in 415) to speak out against the disastrous naval expedition to Sicily. Vlastos quotes in explanation Socrates' words in the *Apology* (31d):[48] 'You know that if I had tried to do politics long ago I would have perished long ago and done no good to you or to myself'. Of course, we do not know for sure that Socrates was silent (if present) on these two occasions, but if he *had* spoken out Plato would presumably have been likely to have him tell us so in the *Apology*; and his claim there that that he had never ascended the rostrum to address the assembly would not have been made.

We now turn to Stone's *The Trial of Socrates*, and *his* discussion of Socrates' quietism in chapter 8. Here we find exactly the same two examples (along with the Melian massacre), with the Mytilene case given pride of place (as in Vlastos), and capped by a different quotation from the same part of the *Apology* in explanation. Stone's report of the two examples is much fuller and more circumstantial than Vlastos'. In particular, he repeats an interesting story from Plutarch (*Nicias* 13.6), according to which Socrates let it be known to his intimates, who then spread it about widely, that his *daimonion* had a message about the Sicilian expedition: it would make for

---

[48] Vlastos (n. 3) 129.

the ruin of Athens. *Ben trovato*, no doubt: had Socrates said anything on the subject, whether publicly or in private, we would have heard about it from Xenophon or Plato, as Stone argues.

Were Vlastos' and Stone's pretty well simultaneous decisions to deploy these two examples of Socratic silence, introduced to illustrate the same complaint about his quietism, entirely independent of each other? Thucydides says nothing about Socrates in either context, nor is Socrates' inferred silence a commonly discussed topic in modern scholarship, so far as I am aware. So one might conjecture borrowing by one from the other. But again, so far as I am aware there is no evidence to support the conjecture.

vii

What does emerge from the material we have been exploring in this paper is the difficulty of being dispassionate in assessing Socrates' stance on democracy. Both Stone and Vlastos were well aware that their fascination with the problem derived much of its power from contemporary attempts to grapple with the intellectual's political responsibilities. Both were however committed to models of investigation which were designed to enable its practitioners to achieve a high degree of historical objectivity, transcending the limitations of contemporary concerns. And in a volume celebrating the foundation of an academy designed to foster scholarship, one would like to be in a position to report that they had had some success in doing just that.

But Socrates is not just one more figure in the cast of thousands who fill the pages of histories of ancient Greece and Rome. He is still alive. Let me illustrate the point with a couple of anecdotes. When I was a graduate student in Oxford in the mid-sixties, I was present at the meeting of the University's Socratic Club at which the philosopher Peter Geach presented his famous paper on Plato's *Euthyphro*,[49] arguing that the Socratic method as applied in that dialogue to questions of religion and morality is philosophically confused, misguided, and sometimes sophistical, and also potentially destructive of sound moral conviction and practice. In the audience was a professor from (as I recall) Princeton Theological Seminary who was outraged by Geach's proposal. Was not Socrates, he asked, the founding father of the Western liberal tradition in ethics and religion? Did he not die for the practice of what he preached? Did not Geach's reassessment defame his

---

[49] P. T. Geach, 'Plato's *Euthyphro*: an analysis and commentary', *The Monist* 50 (1966) 369–82.

memory and threaten the whole basis of free intellectual enquiry? The atmosphere became highly charged, and the chair had to call a relatively early halt to the proceedings. Moving on a few decades I hear — also from Oxford — that when during the University's institutional audit in the early 1990s the visiting team of assessors met the philosophers, they asked them what innovations in teaching methods had been developed over the last two or three years. It is reported that the stunned silence which followed was broken by Christopher Peacocke, then Waynflete Professor of Metaphysics, who observed that Socrates had discovered the right way to teach philosophy 2,500 years ago, and nobody had ever been able to make any significant improvements to it since.

Nor has the Greek invention of democracy ever subsequently been a topic of exclusively antiquarian interest. Cultural historians have recently been charting the mixed fortunes of Athenian democracy as it has been reflected in centuries of Western political thought, for much of the time dyspeptically 'as a foil the better to set off the virtues of governments that accorded far less power to the untutored masses'.[50] The tide began to turn in the nineteenth century, especially with the publication of Grote's *History of Greece*. Frank Turner was able to begin his chapter on the Athenian constitution in *The Greek Heritage in Victorian Britain* as follows:[51]

> In 1915 when it became apparent that the war with Germany would involve a prolonged conflict, new posters appeared in the advertising slots on London buses. The placards displayed excerpts from the funeral oration Pericles had delivered in 431 B.C. over the bodies of Athenian soldiers who had fallen during the first year of the Peloponnesian War. To the university-trained civil servants charged with the propaganda effort, the call of Pericles for steadfastness against Sparta seemed to provide appropriate inspiration for modern citizens of a liberal, commercial nation engaged in a struggle with a largely absolutist, militarist state. The spirit and values of the ancient Athenian polis so memorably set forth by Pericles symbolized in the minds of many educated people the social and political solidarity to which the modern British democracy should aspire.

Discussion of Athenian democracy by contemporary ancient historians is more nuanced than that, but not less *engagé*. In the introduction to the proceedings of a conference timed to mark the twenty-fifth centenary of Cleisthenes' reform of the Athenian constitution in 508–507 BC,[52] the

---

[50] J. T. Roberts, *Athens on Trial: the Anti-democratic Tradition in Western Thought* (Princeton, NJ 1994), xi–xii.

[51] F. M. Turner, *The Greek Heritage in Victorian Britain* (Yale 1981), 187.

[52] J. Ober and C. Hedrick, (eds.), *Dēmokratia: a Conversation on Democracies, Ancient and Modern* (Princeton 1996); quotations at 3–4.

editors inform us that 'the essays presented here are united by the conviction that the political experience of classical Athens is not only interesting in itself but also an important tool for rethinking contemporary political dilemmas'. Some of their authors regard classical democratic citizenship as 'so deeply flawed as to be useful to modern democrats only as a negative example', whereas others find it 'truly admirable and worthy of emulation'. I think they probably include in the latter category Mogens Herman Hansen, whose writings on Athenian democracy are shot through with enthusiasm for his subject matter. In his contribution to their volume he deprecates the fashion for emphasising the distance between ancient and modern conceptions of liberty, and advocates 'a swing of the pendulum': in his view, 'the undeniable differences are overshadowed by the striking similarities'. He says: 'My paper must therefore be read as a plea, not as an attempt to present a so-called "objective" or "balanced" view of the problem.'[53]

So if in each of the two cases we have been examining one comes away with a sense that the scholarly project was driven by an antecedent agenda (Stone's the more brutal, Vlastos' the more tortuous), then that may be inevitable where two such explosive subjects as Socrates and democracy are played off against each other. The idea that scholarship in this area could or should be 'neutral' is perhaps a mirage; and experience suggests that whatever advocates of 'scientific history' might claim, in practice it would have to be something of a novelty. But incautious selectivity and overenthusiasm in the handling of evidence are the obvious consequent dangers; and I fear that it was Vlastos, the professional academic, who succumbed the more damagingly and less warily to temptation, not Stone, the professional student of politics, despite some animus on his part against Socrates and — rather crudely — against philosophy itself. There must be a moral in that somewhere.

A first version of this chapter was delivered as a talk to a seminar in Cambridge on Socrates and democracy organised in Lent Term 1997 by myself and (mainly) Paul Cartledge, to whom therefore much thanks. This version is an expanded form of a paper published in *Apeiron* 34 (2000) under the title 'I. F. Stone and Gregory Vlastos on Socrates and democracy'. I am grateful to Myles Burnyeat for supplying me with copies of Stone's *New York Times* magazine article of 1979 and his own review of Stone in the *New York Review of Books* of 1988, as well as for showing me copies of letters to himself from Vlastos and for commenting on them. Finally, I thank M. M. McCabe and Peter Wiseman for helpful remarks on my draft.

[53] M. H. Hansen, 'The ancient Athenian and modern liberal view of liberty as a democratic ideal', in Ober and Hedrick (n. 52) 91–104, quotation at 91.

12
Roman history and the ideological vacuum

T. P. Wiseman

i

For the twentieth century, the political history of Athens was essentially ideological, involving great issues of freedom and tyranny, while that of the Roman Republic was merely a struggle for power, with no significant ideological content. 'Roman politicians', we are told, 'did not normally divide on matters of principle.'[1]

Why should that be? The Romans were perfectly familiar with the concepts and terminology of Greek political philosophy, and used them to describe their own politics. Cicero, writing in 56 BC, put it as clearly as anyone could wish: in the Roman republic, he said, there have always been two sorts of politician, by name and by nature respectively *populares* and *optimates*; the former speak and act for the *multitudo*, the latter for the elite.[2] The terms translate directly into Greek political language. The *populus* (whence *populares*) is the *dēmos*, and the *multi* (whence *multitudo*) are the *polloi*; the *optimi* (whence *optimates*) are the *aristoi*, and Cicero's 'elite', whom less friendly critics called 'the few' (*pauci*), are the *oligoi*.[3]

---

[1] Erich S. Gruen, *The Last Generation of the Roman Republic* (Berkeley 1974) 50.

[2] Cic. *Sest.* 96: 'duo genera semper in hac ciuitate fuerunt eorum qui uersari in re publica atque in ea se excellentius gerere studuerunt; quibus ex generibus alteri se populares, alteri optimates et haberi et esse uoluerunt. qui ea quae faciebant quaeque dicebant multitudini iucunda uolebant esse, populares, qui autem ita se gerebant ut sua consilia optimo cuique probarent, optimates habebantur.'

[3] *Optimates* as *pauci*: Cic. *Rep.* 1.51–2, 55. *Factio* and/or *potentia paucorum*: Caes. *B. Civ.* 1.22.5, Hirtius [Caes.] *B. Gall.* 8.50.2; Sall. *Cat.* 20.9 (Catiline speech), 39.1, 58.11 (Catiline speech), *Iug.* 3.4, 27.2, 31.19 (Memmius speech), *Hist.* 1.12M, 3.48.27–8 (Macer speech); Livy 10.24.9 (P. Decius speech).

Not surprisingly, Greek authors who dealt with Roman politics used the concepts of democracy and oligarchy, the rule of the many or the rule of the best, without any sense that it was an inappropriate idiom.[4] So too the eighteenth- and nineteenth-century historians of Rome found it natural to refer to 'the popular side', 'the aristocratical faction', 'the democratic party', 'the oligarchs', and so on. Or it could be described in the language of Sallust and Tacitus, as a struggle between the Senate and the people.[5] The people's champion eventually won, but the result was the end of the Republic and a return to monarchy.[6]

'Men generally look to this period of Roman history for arguments for or against monarchy, aristocracy, or democracy.'[7] So wrote Edward Freeman in 1859, summing up a long tradition: from Machiavelli to Mommsen, the history of the Roman Republic was above all ideological. But twentieth-century scholarship turned its back on all that. Here is a representative assessment by a very distinguished historian:

> How does one analyze the politics of the period? It can be argued that they were very much as they had always been. The great families continued to maintain control through interlocking marriages and adoptions, a whole network of relationships and *amicitiae* which formed the principal branches of the oligarchy. Behind the more publicized activities of military conquerors and demagogic tribunes lay the subtle manipulations of senatorial factions ...

Erich Gruen explicitly rejects the 'older scholarship', which 'reduced Roman politics to a contest between the "senatorial party" and the "popular party". Such labels obscure rather than enlighten understanding.'[8]

Of course the word 'party' is anachronistic, if it is taken to mean the disciplined political organisations made necessary by modern mass suffrage. But the 'older scholarship' didn't mean that; it meant what Livy meant when in a highly ideological context — the opposition to the tyrannical Decemvirs — he used *partes* with reference to *optimates* and *populares*. *Partes* is normal Latin for a political or ideological

---

[4] Especially (but not solely) Plutarch, whose sources for late-republican politics included Sulla's memoirs and the *History* of Asinius Pollio. See C. B. R. Pelling, 'Plutarch and Roman Politics', in I. S. Moxon, J. D. Smart and A. J. Woodman (eds.), *Past Perpectives: Studies in Greek and Roman Historical Writing* (Cambridge 1986) 159–87.

[5] E.g. Sall. *Cat.* 38.3, *Iug.* 41.2–5, *Hist.* 1.11M; Tac. *Dial.* 36.3, *Hist.* 2.38.1, *Ann.* 4.33.1–2. It is the basis of Appian's history of the civil wars: App. *B. Civ.* 1.1.

[6] E.g. Plut. *Brut.* 47.7; App. pref. 6, *B. Civ.* 1.6; Dio 52.1.1, 53.11.4–5.

[7] Edward A. Freeman, *Historical Essays, Second Series* (2nd ed., London 1880) 314: reprinted from *National Review* (April 1859).

[8] Gruen (n. 1) 48 and 50.

grouping;[9] granted that its modern derivative is now misleading, is that any reason to deny the history of the Roman Republic its entire ideological dimension? How can this view be squared with what Cicero says?

Cicero's analysis was not at all dispassionate. On the contrary, it was the tendentious self-justification of a controversial politician at the crisis of his career — the best sort of evidence, and at the same time the most difficult to use. To understand it properly, I think we have to look again at a familiar story, one that had begun two generations before Cicero wrote.

ii

Tiberius Gracchus' agrarian bill in 133 BC was a measure in favour of the poor against the rich and powerful (Plutarch and Appian are explicit about that), but it soon became a power struggle between the people's tribune and the Senate. Our sources claim that previously Senate and people had been in harmony;[10] what that means, and how long it had lasted, is a question to which we shall return, but certainly Gracchus put an end to it. Inconvenient tribunician proposals could usually be checked by getting one of the other tribunes to interpose a veto, and then waiting for the end of the would-be legislator's term of office. Gracchus countered that, firstly by getting the assembly to depose the vetoer on the grounds that he was acting against the people's will,[11] and secondly by standing for election to a second year's tribunate himself.

The effect on the Senate was dramatic. When the consul declined to take executive action, the *pontifex maximus* announced 'Then let those who want to save the Republic follow me,' and led out a large group of senators and their supporters to beat Gracchus to death.[12] In their view, by going against the unwritten rules of the Republic as they understood it, he was aiming at tyranny and therefore justly killed. 'Thus perish whoso else may do such deeds,' commented the great Scipio Aemilianus, quoting Homer.[13]

[9] Livy 3.39.9 (M. Horatius speech): *cuius illi partis essent, rogitare. populares?... optimates? Partes* in general: e.g., Cic. *Rosc. Am.* 137, *Quinct.* 69–70, *Verr.* 2.1.35, *Cat.* 4.13, *Att.* 1.13.2; Sall. *Cat.* 4.2, *Iug.* 40.2–3, 73.4; Vell. 2.28.1, 2.62.6, 2.72.1; Suet. *Caes.* 1.3. See H. Strasburger, *RE* 18.1 (1939) 784–8.

[10] Sall. *Iug.* 41 (until 146), Dion. Hal. *Ant. Rom.* 2.11.2–3 (until 123), Plut. *Ti. Gracch.* 20.1.

[11] Plut. *Ti. Gracch.* 11.3, 15.2; App. *B. Civ.* 1.12.51.

[12] Val. Max. 3.2.17, Vell. Pat. 2.3.1–2, Plut. *Ti. Gracch.* 19.3–6, App. *B. Civ.* 1.16.68–70.

[13] Plut. *Ti. Gracch.* 21.4 (Hom. *Od.* 1.47); *cf.* Vell. Pat. 2.4.4 (*iure caesum*).

And perish they did, beginning with Gaius Gracchus in 121. Against him, as against others in later years, the Senate formalised its position with a decree that the consul 'should see to it that the Republic be not harmed'.[14] Once again, it was a particular definition of the Republic that prevailed: mobilising the citizen body to pass laws in its own interest was interpreted as tyranny.

Tiberius Gracchus' *lex agraria* was for dividing public land among the citizens; Gaius Gracchus' *lex frumentaria* was for using public money to subsidise a guaranteed corn supply for the urban poor. On the one hand:[15]

> quid tam iustum enim quam recipere plebem sua a patribus, ne populus gentium uictor orbisque possessor extorris aris ac focis ageret? quid tam aequum quam inopem populum uiuere ex aerario suo?

> What could be so just as the commons getting back its own property from the senators, so that a world-conquering people should not live banished from its altars and hearths? What could be so fair as the treasury supporting a people that had no resources of its own?

On the other hand:[16]

> multis in rebus multitudinis studium ac populi commodum ab utilitate rei publicae discrepabat.

> In various matters the desire of the many and the advantage of the people were not consistent with the good of the Republic.

Here were two rival ideologies, two mutually incompatible understandings of what the Republic was. That is surely what Cicero and Sallust mean when they say that the Gracchan crisis split the state into two *partes*; the Greek philosopher Posidonius put it that Gaius Gracchus wanted to abolish *aristokratia* and establish *dēmokratia*.[17] Those are different formulations of the same phenomenon — an ideological conflict between 'parties', identified as aristocratic (*optimates*) and democratic (*populares*), which would last until the Republic itself collapsed.

In his history of the Jugurthine War, Sallust describes Opimius' destruction of Gaius Gracchus and his followers as the victory of the *nobilitas* over the *plebs*.[18] (He consistently uses *nobilitas* for the dominant oligarchy,

---

[14] Cic. *Cat.* 1.4, *Phil.* 8.14; Plut. *Ti. Gracch.* 14.3; Andrew Lintott, *The Constitution of the Roman Republic* (Oxford 1999) 89–93.

[15] Florus 2.1.2–3 (from Livy?).

[16] Cic. *Sest.* 103.

[17] Cic. *Rep.* 1.31; Sall. *Iug.* 41.5, 42.1; Diod. Sic. 34/35.25.1 (Posidonius *FGrH* 87 F111b). On C. Gracchus, *cf.* App. *B. Civ.* 1.22.93 (destroying the Senate's power), Plut. *C. Gracch.* 5.3 (changing the constitution ἐκ τῆς ἀριστοκρατίας εἰς τὴν δημοκρατίαν).

[18] Sall. *Iug.* 16.2, 42.1–4; *cf.* Plut. *C. Gracch.* 11.2, 14.2 on Opimius and his allies as ὀλιγαρχικοί.

varying it occasionally with *pauci* or *senatus*.) The reversal of that victory, he tells us, was one of his reasons for choosing the subject:[19]

> ... quia tunc primum superbiae nobilitatis obuiam itum est; quae contentio diuina et humana cuncta permiscuit eoque uecordiae processit ut studiis ciuilibus bellum atque uastitas Italiae finem faceret.

> ... because at that time the arrogance of the nobility was first challenged, a conflict which threw into confusion everything human and divine, and reached such a level of madness that through political conflict it ended in war and the devastation of Italy.

That was probably written at the time of the civil war of 41–40 BC, which resulted in the destruction of Perusia. So Sallust's book will show how the ideological conflict developed from the 'struggles of Senate and people', as Tacitus later phrased it,[20] into the sequence of full-scale civil wars that still continued in his own time. Two of the protagonists of Sallust's story are the people's hero Marius (whose election as consul is the main 'challenge to the nobility') and the aristocratic Sulla, each introduced with a character-sketch that hints at future events.[21] His readers didn't need to be told what resulted from their rivalry.

The earliest contemporary evidence for the people's point of view comes from the mid-eighties BC, in the examples from a rhetorician's manual. Here, for instance, the fate of the people's champions is used to illustrate the figure *paronomasia*:[22]

> Tiberium Graccum rem publicam administrantem prohibuit indigna nex diutius in eo commorari. Gaio Gracco similis occasio est oblata, quae uirum rei publicae amantissimum subito de sinu ciuitatis eripuit. Saturninum fide captum malorum perfidia per scelus uita priuauit. tuus, o Druse, sanguis domesticos parietes et uultum parentis aspersit. Sulpicio, cui paulo ante omnia concedebant, eum breui spatio non modo uiuere sed etiam sepeliri prohibuerunt.

> Tiberius Gracchus was a statesman, but an unworthy killing prevented him from continuing in that role. To Gaius Gracchus came a similar fate, which snatched away a great patriot from the embrace of the citizen body. Saturninus, betrayed by trust, the treachery of wicked men deprived of life. Drusus, your blood spattered the walls of your house and the face of your mother. For Sulpicius, to whom at first they conceded everything, soon they allowed neither life nor burial.

---

[19] Sall. *Iug.* 5.1–2; *cf.* 31.2 (Memmius' speech) on the *superbia paucorum*.

[20] Tac. *Dial.* 36.3, *assidua senatus aduersus plebem certamina*; *Ann.* 4.32.1, *plebis et optimatium certamina*.

[21] Sall. *Iug.* 63.1–6, 95.4. The final sentence (114.4) is equally pregnant.

[22] [Cic.] *Rhet. Her.* 4.31 (*cf.* 4.68 on the martyrdom of Ti. Gracchus).

It was a great tradition of Gracchan martyrs.[23] What did for Saturninus in 100 BC was again the Senate's decree and 'whoever wants to save the Republic...';[24] for Drusus in 91 an assassin's knife was enough, while Sulpicius in 88 was hunted down at the orders of a consul who had just taken the city by military force. All of them had been duly elected as tribunes of the people, and passed their legislation by due process in the assembly. But Sulla regarded the tribunes' powers as tyrannical.[25]

His own tyranny was described at the time (here too we now have contemporary evidence) as the victory of the *nobilitas*.[26] The lower orders had fought their betters, and lost; now everyone knew his place again.[27] The Republic would be ruled by the Senate's authority, as it had been before the 'struggle of the orders', and the tribunes and popular assembly would have no power.[28] As for opposition, the proscriptions would see to that; the final total of dead was 4,700.[29] The counter-revolution was meant to be permanent.

But the result of the Senate's rule was a spectacularly corrupt oligarchy, resulting in a reform movement that demanded, and in 70 BC eventually obtained, the full restoration of the tribunes' powers. Cicero, prosecuting one of the worst culprits, had this to say to the senators on the jury:

> tulit haec ciuitas quoad potuit, quoad necesse fuit, regiam istam uestram dominationem in iudiciis et in omni re publica tulit; sed quo die populo Romano tribuni plebi restituti sunt, omnia ista uobis, si forte nondum intellegitis, adempta atque erepta sunt.

> As long as it could and as long as it had to, the Republic put up with that monarchical domination of yours in the courts, and in the whole of public life. But in case you don't yet realise it, all that was snatched from you and taken away on the day the tribunes were restored to the Roman people.

---

[23] Saturninus and the memory of Ti. Gracchus: App. *B. Civ.* 1.32.141; *cf.* Cic. *Rab. perd.* 20, Val. Max. 9.7.1. Livius Drusus *per Gracchana uestigia*: Sen. *Cons. Marc.* 16.4; *cf.* Florus 2.5.6. Sulpicius in the Gracchan tradition: Cic. *Corn.* ap. Asc. 80C.

[24] Cic. *Rab. perd.* 20, auct. *De uir. ill.* 73.10.

[25] App. *B. Civ.* 1.59.267 (*cf.* 1.57.253, his reason for the march on Rome).

[26] Cic. *Rosc. Am.* 138, 141–2, 149.

[27] Cic. *Rosc. Am.* 136: 'quis enim erat qui non uideret *humilitatem cum dignitate* de amplitudine contendere? quo in certamine perditi ciuis erat non se ad eos iungere quibus incolumibus et domi dignitas et foris auctoritas retineretur. quae perfecta esse et *suum cuique honorem et gradum redditum* gaudeo, iudices, uehementerque laetor, eaque omnia deorum uoluntate, studio populi Romani, consilio et imperio et felicitate L. Sullae gesta esse intellego.'

[28] App. *B. Civ.* 1.59.266–7; on *patrum auctoritas* (Livy 8.12.15, Cic. *Rep.* 2.56), see S. P. Oakley, *A Commentary on Livy Books VI–X*, vol. 2 (Oxford 1998) 525–7.

[29] Val. Max. 9.2.1; Florus 2.9.25 (from Livy?) gives 2,000 senators and *equites*.

Is it really true, as Erich Gruen assumes, that Romans wouldn't understand the phrase 'senatorial party'?[30]

Cicero the *popularis* was an ambitious young senator with no inherited connections, making his way on talent alone and using it for the currently powerful cause. Seven years later, when he was consul, the reformers had lost the moral high ground. There was serious hardship among the poor; the tribunes attacked the Senate, and vainly brought in proposals for land distribution and debt relief. But the self-styled 'standard-bearer of the oppressed' was Catiline, a patrician playboy with a record of murder and extortion.[31] Cicero could plausibly claim for himself the status of a *popularis*, complete with honorific references to the Gracchi, while now defending the Senate's authority.[32]

In October 63, alarmed by reports of an armed uprising in Etruria and a planned *coup d'état* in Rome, the Senate passed the same emergency decree that had authorised the killing of Gaius Gracchus in 121 and of Saturninus in 100.[33] Catiline left Rome to take command of the rebel army; five of his associates were arrested, and on 5 December Cicero had them executed without trial. Once again, Roman politics were ideologically polarised.

On the one hand, Cicero had acted like a tyrant. That was the view of the tribunes of 62, and of Caesar, now in his praetorship and a conspicuous *popularis*; Cicero knew that it was only by allying himself with Caesar that he could have 'peace with the multitude'.[34] It was also the view of Clodius, another patrician playboy, who now emerged as leader of the demand that Cicero should be put on trial before the people, or otherwise summarily dealt with.[35]

On the other hand, Cicero was the saviour of the Republic, hailed as 'father of his country' by Catulus, the leading figure in the Senate and (what comes to the same thing) the quintessential optimate.[36] Cicero's own

---

[30] Cic. *Verr.* 2.5.175; *cf. Cluent.* 136, *cum inuidia flagraret ordo senatorius.* Gruen (n. 1) 50.

[31] Hardship: Sall. *Cat.* 33 (C. Manlius). Tribunes: Cic. *Leg. agr.*, Dio 37.25.4; Cic. *Rab. perd.* 20 (*hos patres conscriptos qui nunc sunt in inuidiam uocatis*). Catiline: Cic. *Mur.* 50–1, *cf.* Sall. *Cat.* 20.2–21.2 (programme speech). For the politics of the sixties BC, see T. P. Wiseman in *CAH*² vol. 9 (Cambridge 1994) 327–67.

[32] Cic. *Leg. agr.* 2.6–10, *Rab. perd.* 11–15: speeches delivered before the people early in 63 BC, but revised for publication in 60 (Cic. *Att.* 2.1.3).

[33] Cic. *Cat.* 1.4, *Phil.* 8.14–15; *cf. Sull.* 21, *Pis.* 14, *Mil.* 8, *Phil.* 2.18 (Senate's responsibility).

[34] Plut. *Cic.* 23.2 (δυναστεία), *cf.* Cic. *Sull.* 21 (*regnum*); Cic. *Cat.* 4.9 on Caesar, *in re p. uiam quae popularis habetur secutus. Multitudo*: Cic. *Att.* 2.3.4 (60 BC), *cf.* Suet. *Caes.* 16 on their rioting in support of Caesar in 62.

[35] Cic. *Att.* 1.16.10 (*rex*); *Att.* 2.22.1, *Q. Fr.* 1.2.16, *Flac.* 96–7, *Sest.* 40.

[36] Cic. *Pis.* 6: *me Q. Catulus, princeps huius ordinis et auctor publici consili, frequentissimo senatu parentem patriae nominauit.* Catulus as *optimas*: Cic. *Att.* 1.20.3, *Sest.* 101. *Res p. conseruata*: Cic. *Fam.* 5.2.7 (January 62), *Pis.* 6, etc.

accounts of his consulship emphasised *aristokratia*, and one of them no doubt lies behind Plutarch's account of the climactic moment (the translation is by John and William Langhorne, 1770):[37]

καὶ πρῶτον ἐκ Παλατίου παραλαβὼν τὸν Λέντλον ἦγε διὰ τῆς ἱερᾶς ὁδοῦ καί τῆς ἀγορᾶς μέσης, τῶν μὲν ἡγεμονικωτάτων ἀνδρῶν κύκλῳ περιεσπειραμένων καὶ διαφορούντων, τοῦ δὲ δήμου φρίττοντος τὰ δρώμενα καὶ παριόντος σιωπῇ, μάλιστα δὲ τῶν νέων, ὥσπερ ἱεροῖς τισι πατρίοις ἀριστοκρατικῆς τινος ἐξουσίας τελεῖσθαι μετὰ φόβου καὶ θάμβους δοκούντων.

First he took Lentulus from the Palatine hill, and led him down the Via Sacra, and through the middle of the Forum. The principal persons in Rome attended the consul on all sides, like a guard; the people stood silent at the horror of the scene; and the youth looked on with fear and astonishment, as if they were initiated that day in some awful ceremonies of aristocratic power.

The Greek idiom came naturally in the politics of the time. 'He spoke like an aristocrat' was Cicero's private (and bilingual) comment when Pompey, addressing the people after his return from the East, praised the Senate's authority to the disgust of the *populares*.[38]

At first, the people's view prevailed. The triumph of the *populares* came in 59–58 BC, Caesar's consulship followed by the tribunate of Clodius. There was a rush of reform legislation, including Gracchan land laws and a Gracchan corn law; Cicero was exiled by popular vote, his house torn down and a shrine of Liberty erected on the site;[39] the Senate was quite explicitly excluded from the political process.[40] But then the pendulum swung back. The consuls of 57 got Cicero recalled by the centuriate assembly, in which the votes of the wealthy predominated.[41] The site of his house was restored to him, the shrine deconsecrated. There were protest demonstrations round the Senate-house ('protect the people's Liberty!'), and Cicero was even attacked by an armed mob in the street. But he had his own security guards, and the people were denied their vengeance.[42]

That is the context of Cicero's disquisition on *optimates* and *populares*, the passage with which this chapter begins. He stitched it into the text of a

---

[37] Plut. *Cic.* 22.1, probably from Cicero's Greek monograph περὶ ὑπατείας: C. B. R. Pelling, *Hermes* 113 (1985), 313–6.

[38] Cic. *Att.* 1.14.2 (μαλ' ἀριστοκρατικῶς); 1.14.6 for the reaction.

[39] Cic. *Att.* 3.15.5 on his exile: *legem illam in qua popularia multa sunt. Libertas*: Cic. *Dom.* 110–12, Plut. *Cic.* 33.1, Dio 38.17.6.

[40] Dio 38.4.1, App. *B. Civ.* 2.10 (Caesar in 59). Cic. *Sest.* 28 (Gabinius in 58): *errare homines si etiam tum senatum aliquid in re publica posse arbitrarentur.*

[41] App. *B. Civ.* 1.59.266 (οἱ ἐν περιουσίᾳ καὶ εὐβουλίᾳ) — 'the Roman people' by Sulla's definition.

[42] Cic. *Att.* 4.1.6, 4.2.3, 4.3.3 (*clamor, lapides, fustes, gladii*).

speech given in early March 56 BC, when he had successfully defended, on a political charge, one of the optimate tribunes of the previous year who had helped to bring about his return. At the time of writing, still in his post-recall euphoria, Cicero was attacking the legality of Caesar's land laws — the very citadel, as he put it, of the *popularis* cause.[43]

What matters is the premise of his argument, not the content of it. We don't have to share his view that all patriotic citizens are by definition *optimates*, and that *populares* can only be criminal, bankrupt or insane. But we do, I think, have to accept the assumption on which it is based, that the Republic was divided into two rival ideological camps — two *partes*, as he put it in a speech to the Senate — and that this rivalry had been fundamental in Roman politics since the time of the Gracchi.[44] That is, our most explicit evidence comes from within the conflict itself; it is in the highest degree tendentious, but it cannot simply be waved away as an anachronism.

The story can be briefly concluded. Cicero backed down, knowing that he was a marked man unless he made his peace with Caesar.[45] The *optimates* were determined that neither Caesar nor Clodius should hold legislative office again. When Clodius stood for the praetorship in 52, with a predictably radical programme, he was murdered in a brawl on the Appian Way. His body was brought to Rome and given an impromptu funeral in the Forum; the Roman people burned down the Senate-house as his funeral pyre.[46] Caesar in 49 planned to return from Gaul to a second consulship, with *popularis* tribunes urging his cause. As against Gaius Gracchus in 121, Saturninus in 100 and the Catilinarians in 63, the Senate passed its decree 'that the consuls should see to it that the Republic be not harmed'. Rather than wait for the fate of their predecessors, the tribunes fled to Caesar, who marched on Rome 'to free the people from the tyranny of the few'.[47]

Although the outbreak of civil war retrospectively overshadowed them, the events of 52 BC symbolised the struggle and its outcome. One of the

---

[43] Cic. *Q. Fr.* 2.6.1 (noisy Senate meeting, 5 April), *Fam.* 1.9.8 (*in arcem illius causae inuadere*); cf. *Att.* 1.19.2 and 20.4 for the 'triumvirs' as *populares*.

[44] Cic. *Sest.* 96 (*duo genera*), 97–9 (tendentious definitions), 103–5 (history of rival ideologies); *Red. sen.* 33 (*duae partes*).

[45] Cic. *Att.* 4.5.1–3 (his 'palinode'); 8.11d.7 (*cf.* 8.3.5) on *popularis* threats against him.

[46] Programme: Cic. *Mil.* 33, 87, 89; *Scholia Bobiensia* 173St. Pyre: Cic. *Mil.* 90, Asconius 33C, Dio 40.49.3.

[47] Caes. *B. Civ.* 1.5.3 (decree), 1.22.5 (*ut se et populum Romanum factione paucorum oppressum in libertatem uindicaret*).

popularis tribunes of that year, who must have been present at the burning of the Senate-house, was Sallust.[48]

Ejected from the Senate by an optimate censor, restored and rewarded by the victorious Caesar, Sallust then retired from politics to become a historian. By the time he had written his monographs on Catiline and on the post-Gracchan 'challenge to the nobility', he had seen Caesar become permanent dictator by vote of the popular assembly; he had seen outraged senators assassinate the man they saw as a tyrant; he had seen Cicero trying to guide a restored Republic by resuming optimate politics; he had seen Caesar's son and two of his political heirs become joint dictators by vote of the popular assembly; and he had seen Cicero's head and hands nailed up on the Rostra. When Sallust described Roman politics as a struggle between the people and the Senate (*plebs* and *patres*), he knew what he was talking about.[49]

But that wasn't how it seemed to the greatest Roman historian of the twentieth century. Sir Ronald Syme blamed Sallust for giving rise to a false doctrine, 'namely the belief that Rome had a regular two-party system, Optimates and Populares'. But that 'regular system', like the 'organised Popular Party' referred to a sentence or two later, is a mere straw man (Sallust says no such thing); and when in the same passage Syme refers to *nobiles* who were 'advocates of the People's cause', he has tacitly conceded the very case he attacks.[50]

Syme's interests lay elsewhere, as a more famous passage shows:[51]

> In all ages, whatever the form and name of government, be it monarchy, republic, or democracy, an oligarchy lurks behind the façade; and Roman history, Republican or Imperial, is the history of the governing class ...
>
> The political life of the Roman Republic was stamped and swayed, not by parties and programmes of a modern and parliamentary character, not by the ostensible opposition between Senate and People, *Optimates* and *Populares*, *nobiles* and *novi homines*, but by the strife for power, wealth and glory. The contestants were the *nobiles* themselves, as individuals or in groups, open in the elections and in the courts of law, or masked by secret intrigue.

---

[48] Asconius 37C, 49C.

[49] For the people granting power to Caesar and the Triumvirs (and to Augustus), see Lintott (n. 14) 40: 'they were in theory permitted to abolish the Republic by legislation.' Sallust on *plebes/patres*: e.g., *Cat.* 33.3, 38.1; *Iug.* 27.3, 30.1, 84.3; *Hist.* 1.11, 3.48.1.

[50] Ronald Syme, *Sallust* (*Sather Classical Lectures* 33, Berkeley 1964) 17–18, citing Strasburger (n. 97), and 'for the social basis of Roman political life', Gelzer, Münzer and Taylor (nn. 93, 95 and 103 below).

[51] Ronald Syme, *The Roman Revolution* (Oxford 1939) 7 and 11. *Cf.* 152: 'the realities of Roman politics were overlaid with a double coating of deceit, democratic and aristocratic.'

One can't help feeling that that doesn't quite encompass the Gracchi, or even Cicero. For Syme, the strife was for power, wealth and glory; for Sallust, it was for '*liberty*, glory or domination'.[52] The difference is not insignificant.

iii

After the Tarquins were expelled, the new Republic enjoyed internal harmony for as long as there was a danger that they might return. Once that danger was past, wrote Sallust in the introduction to his *Histories*,[53]

> seruili imperio patres plebem exercere, de uita atque tergo regio more consulere, agro pellere et ceteris expertis soli in imperio agere. quibus saeuitiis at maxume faenore oppressa plebes, quom adsiduis bellis tributum et militiam simul toleraret, armata montem sacrum atque Auentinum insedit tumque tribunos plebis et alia iura sibi parauit. discordiarum et certaminis utrimque finis fuit secundum bellum Punicum.

> the patricians reduced the plebeians to the condition of slavery; they disposed of the lives and persons of the *plebs* in the manner of kings; they drove men from their lands; and with the rest of the people disenfranchised, they alone wielded supreme power. Oppressed by such harsh treatment, and especially by the load of debt, the plebeians, after enduring the simultaneous burden of tribute and military service in continual wars, at length armed themselves and took up a position on the Mons Sacer and the Aventine; thus they gained for themselves the tribunes of the *plebs* and other rights. The Second Punic War brought an end to the strife and rivalry between the two sides.

Those events — the armed plebeians forcing concessions from a tyrannical oligarchy — are constantly appealed to by the late-republican *populares* portrayed by Sallust. In the next generation, the historians of early Rome found it natural to portray the 'struggle of the orders' in terms of *optimates* and *populares* (in Livy's Latin) or *dēmotikoi* and *aristokratikoi* (in Dionysius' Greek).[54] The sense of continuity is unmistakable: as Cicero said, there had *always* been those two sorts of politician in the Republic.[55]

---

[52] Sall. *Hist.* 1.7M: *nobis primae dissensiones uitio humani ingenii euenere, quod inquies atque indomitum semper* in certamine libertatis aut gloriae aut dominationis *agit*.

[53] Sall. *Hist.* 1.11M (Augustine *De civ. D.* 2.18); translation by Henry Bettenson (Penguin Classics), except that his final phrase is '...between the two *parties*'. Livy (2.21.5–6) tacitly follows Sallust's sequence of events.

[54] Sall. *Cat.* 33.3 (C. Manlius), *Iug.* 31.6 and 17 (C. Memmius), *Hist.* 1.55.23 (M. Lepidus), 3.48.1 (Macer). Livy: see n. 9 above; Robin Seager, '"Populares" in Livy and the Livian tradition', *Classical Quarterly* 27 (1977) 377–90. Dionysius: e.g. *Ant. Rom.* 7.65.1, 7.66.2, 7.67.1 (on 'the first *stasis*', 7.66.1).

[55] Cic. *Sest.* 96 (n. 2 above).

It is possible that that was true. The Republic may well have been in constant tension between the respective interests of the many and the few. Sallust's periodisation is schematic (harmony requires fear of an external enemy, so conflict continued until the Hannibalic War), but he may still be essentially right; the 'period of concord' broken by Tiberius Gracchus' legislative programme may well have been untypical and comparatively short-lived.[56] But no one can now be certain, because of the absence of contemporary evidence.

What *is* clear, on the other hand, is that some of the second- and first-century historians whom Livy and Dionysius used as sources must have interpreted and elaborated the old stories in ways that would be exemplary for their own times.[57] As one instance out of many, take the case of Spurius Maelius, who in 439 BC supplied corn to the people and was suspected of aiming at tyranny. He was killed by Servilius Ahala at the order of the dictator Cincinnatus. There was no trial, just a summary execution like that of Tiberius Gracchus, with which it was often compared. In Dionysius, Maelius is an innocent man cut down 'like an animal' before the eyes of the horrified populace; in Livy, Ahala is congratulated for saving the Republic.[58] Both ideologies were represented in the tradition — and they had an impact. Marcus Brutus was inspired by the example of Ahala, from whom he was descended on his mother's side, to 'save the Republic' by killing Caesar.[59]

Here too, however, the presuppositions of twentieth-century scholarship have been an obstacle to understanding.

In the narratives of both Livy and Dionysius, the first act of the 'struggle of the orders' begins when a dreadful figure stumbles into the Roman Forum. Filthy, emaciated, his back a mass of recent scars, he tells his story to the people. He is a Roman citizen, a veteran of the Republic's wars who fell into debt when his farm was destroyed by the Sabines; after all he owned had gone to pay the interest, he himself was seized by the creditor and subjected to a regime of hard labour, imprisonment and frequent floggings.[60] Popular

[56] On popular issues in the period between the 'struggle of the orders' and the Gracchi, see Andrew Lintott, 'Democracy in the Middle Republic', *Zeitschrift der Savigny-Stiftung* 104 (1987) 34–52; on *libertas* throughout the Republic, see T. P. Wiseman, 'Liber: myth, drama and ideology in the Roman Republic', *Acta Instituti Romani Finlandiae* 23 (2000) 265–99.

[57] For a convenient selection, see Dagmar Gutberlet, *Die erste Dekade des Livius als Quelle zur gracchischen und sullanischen Zeit* (*Beiträge zur Altertumswissenschaft* 4, Hildesheim 1985).

[58] Dion. Hal. *Ant. Rom.* 12.4.7–8, Livy 4.13.3–7. Gracchan parallel: Cic. *Cat.* 1.3, *Mil.* 72, *Rep.* 2.49, *Amic.* 36–7.

[59] Cic. *Att.* 2.24.3, 13.40.1, *Phil.* 2.26; Plut. *Brut.* 1.3. Ahala on Brutus' coin-issue in 54 BC: Michael H. Crawford, *Roman Republican Coinage* (Cambridge 1974), 455–6.

[60] Livy 2.23.1–9, Dion. Hal. *Ant. Rom.* 6.26.1–2.

indignation and senatorial intransigence leads to the secession of the *plebs* the following year (494 BC), which in turn results in the establishment of the tribunate.

The main recurring economic themes of the 'struggle of the orders' were corn supply, land distribution and debt. The first two were Gracchan issues, no doubt elaborated in contemporary terms by historians of the post-Gracchan period like the optimate Piso.[61] But debt — particularly debt as a result of war in Italy, debt as suffered by old soldiers — was an issue that became acute in 89 BC, and lasted as an ongoing problem at least until the late sixties.[62] An influential historian who wrote in that period was Licinius Macer; he was tribune in 73 BC, and according to Sallust he took an outspoken part in the *popularis* campaign to get the powers of the tribunate restored after Sulla's legislation.[63]

We know one thing for certain about Macer as a historian: he conspicuously praised his ancestors, the Licinii of the fourth century BC.[64] Prominent among his heroes was surely Licinius Stolo, one of the two determined tribunes who pressed home the plebeian demands for debt relief, land reform and the sharing of the consulship, supposedly for ten successive years. Macer may well be responsible for the version of events, not followed by Livy, which alleged a secession of the *plebs* on that occasion, and the election of Licinius Stolo as the first plebeian consul.[65] Similarly, it was surely Macer who named two Licinii among the founding college of tribunes in 493.[66]

Sallust, narrating Macer's tribunate in the third book of his *Histories*, gave him a splendid speech. It begins like this:[67]

> si, Quirites, parum existumaretis quid inter ius a maioribus relictum uobis et hoc a Sulla paratum seruitium interesset, multis mihi disserundum fuit docendique quas

[61] Piso's politics: Cic. *Font.* 39, *Tusc.* 3.48; *Scholia Bobiensia* 96St. Text, translation and commentary in Gary Forsythe, *The Historian L. Calpurnius Piso Frugi and the Roman Annalistic Tradition* (Lanham, Md. 1994).

[62] App. *B. Civ.* 1.54.232–9, Val. Max. 9.7.4, Livy *Per.* 74 (89 BC); Festus 516L (88 BC); Vell. Pat. 2.32.2 (86 BC); Cic. *Off.* 2.84, *Cat.* 2.8, Dio 37.25.4 (63 BC). Veterans: Cic. *Cat.* 2.20, Sall. *Cat.* 16.4.

[63] Sall. *Hist.* 3.48M. Text and commentary in Walt (n. 78 below).

[64] Livy 7.9.5 (on C. Licinius Calvus *cos.* 361): *quaesita ea propriae familiae laus leuiorem auctorem Licinium facit.*

[65] Livy 6.34–42 ('376–367 BC'); detailed discussion in Oakley (n. 28) vol. 1 (1997) 645–61. Secession: Ampelius 25.4, Ovid *Fasti* 1.643–4 (*cf.* Livy 6.4.10 *prope secessionem*). Stolo first consul: auct. *De uir. ill.* 20.2.

[66] Dion. Hal. *Ant. Rom.* 6.89.1 (contrast Asconius 77C); 'Licinius Macer must be the one ultimately responsible' (Forsythe (n. 61) 292).

[67] Sall. *Hist.* 3.48.1–2; Bruce W. Frier, *Transactions of the American Philological Association* 105 (1975) 94–5.

ob iniurias et quotiens a patribus armata plebes secessisset utique uindices
parauisset omnis iuris sui tribunos plebis; nunc hortari modo relicuom est et ire
primum uia qua capessundam arbitror libertatem.

'Romans: if you didn't understand what the difference is between the rights
bequeathed to you by your ancestors and this slavery devised by Sulla, I would
have to go on at length and explain how often, and because of what injustices, the
plebeians in arms seceded from the patricians, and how they achieved tribunes of
the *plebs* as defenders of all their rights. As it is, all I need to do is encourage and
go before you on the road I believe we must take to win liberty.'

There is no point wondering whether the real Licinius Macer said this in 73
BC. It is Sallust writing nearly forty years later, and he and his readers knew
Macer's *History*. When one historian gives a speech to another (as Tacitus
did with Cremutius Cordus), it can hardly be innocent of intertextual allusion. Here, the hint is unmistakable: the imagined *Quirites*, like Sallust's
readers, don't need telling about the heroic plebeians of the past, because it's
all in Macer's history — including the secession of 367 BC that other historians didn't have.[68]

At the end of his speech, Sallust's Macer is scathing about the low
expectations of his present-day audience:

...abunde libertatem rati, scilicet quia tergis abstinetur at huc ire licet et illuc,
munera ditium dominorum. atque haec eadem non sunt agrestibus, sed caeduntur
inter potentium inimicitias donoque dantur in prouincias magistratibus.

'You think you have liberty in abundance just because your backs are spared and
you're allowed to move around — gifts from your masters, the rich. And country
people don't even have that: they are flogged when the men of power quarrel, and
sent as gifts to magistrates in the provinces.'

Enslavement for debt was forbidden by the *lex Poetelia*, the flogging of
Roman citizens by the *lex Porcia* — but enforcement of those laws depended
on the protective power of the tribunes.[69] Their *ius auxilii*, the one power
Sulla had left them, applied only in the city and for a mile outside the walls.
Beyond that, there was no defence if magistrates allowed such abuses to
happen. And they did.

---

[68] See n. 65 above. Implicit at 3.48.1 (*quotiens*) and at 3.48.15: *ne uos ad uirilia illa uocem, quo
tribunos plebei, modo patricium magistratum, libera ab auctoribus patriciis suffragia maiores uostri
parauere. Virilia illa* were the secessions ('Be men today, Quirites,...'), and the *patricius
magistratus* was the consulship, won in 367 BC.

[69] Sall. *Hist.* 3.48.26–7; Livy 8.28 (*lex Poetelia*), Sall. *Cat.* 51.21 (*lex Porcia*).

Again, Sallust gives the evidence. Ten years after Macer's tribunate the peasants rose in revolt. Their leader was an old soldier, Gaius Manlius, to whom Sallust attributes this message to the Roman commander:[70]

> deos hominesque testamur, imperator, nos arma neque contra patriam cepisse neque quo periculum aliis faceremus, sed uti corpora nostra ab iniuria tuta forent, qui miseri egentes, uiolentia atque crudelitate faeneratorum plerique patriae, sed omnes fama atque fortunis expertes sumus. neque quoiquam nostrum licuit more maiorum lege uti neque amisso patrimonio liberum corpus habere: tanta saeuitia faeneratorum atque praetoris fuit.

> 'We call gods and men to witness, Imperator, that we have taken up arms not against our country or to endanger others, but in order that our bodies may be safe from abuse. We are poor and wretched. Thanks to the violence and cruelty of the money-lenders, many of us have been deprived of our native land, all of us of our good name and possessions. Not one of us was allowed the traditional protection of the law, or to keep our bodies free when our inheritance was lost. Such has been the savagery of the money-lenders and the magistrate.'

For Sallust, the issues that sparked the 'struggle of the orders' were still unresolved after four centuries. In this passage of *Catiline*, in the preface to the *Histories* (p. 295 above) and in the speech of Macer in book 3, the theme and phraseology are the same: freedom and slavery, cruelty and arrogance, the physical maltreatment of the poor by the rich and powerful. And if, as it surely must, the speech of Macer reflects Macer's history, then we may with some confidence infer the nature of that history — an ideologically committed narrative presenting the plebeians' achievement of freedom and the tribunate in the light of Sulla's attempt to reverse those gains.[71]

That in turn allows the hypothesis — by its nature unprovable, but plausibly explaining the phenomena — that passages in Livy or Dionysius that betray a particular sympathy for the oppressed plebeians and their tribune champions may be influenced by, or even recast versions of, Licinius Macer's tendentious narrative.[72] One likely example is the scene with which the whole

---

[70] Sall. *Cat.* 33.1 (*cf.* 33.3, *saepe ipsa plebs... armata a patribus secessit*). Manlius an ex-centurion: Dio 37.30.5.

[71] Macer's interest in the origin of the dictatorship was probably because of Sulla: Dion. Hal. *Ant. Rom.* 5.74.4 and 77.4, with Emilio Gabba, *Dionysius and the History of Archaic Rome* (*Sather Classical Lectures* 56, Berkeley 1991) 142.

[72] To deny this possibility *a priori* — as do T. J. Luce, *Livy: the Composition of his History* (Princeton 1977) 165–9, and T. J. Cornell, *The Beginnings of Rome: Italy and Rome from the Bronze Age to the Punic Wars (c.1000–264 BC)* (London 1995) 4–5 — seems to me to misplace the burden of proof.

long story begins, that scarred and haggard figure telling his tale in the Forum in 495 BC.

It is important to remember that this hypothesis depends entirely on Sallust's treatment of Macer and his themes. Sallust's own historical *persona* was politically neutral, as befitted one who had retired from the conflict before he began to write.[73] But he had been a *popularis* tribune in his time, and he knew what could cause the Roman people to burn down the Senate-house. As for Macer, who never reached the serenity of retirement, his history was written during a life of active politics.[74] From the interaction of the two we can gain some idea of how *populares* saw Roman history, a necessary corrective to the Ciceronian attitudes which otherwise dominate our view of the late Republic. Indeed, the very existence, and importance, of Macer's version of the political history of early Rome may be the reason why in his *De republica* Cicero devoted a whole book to a liberal-optimate narrative of his own.[75]

I have dealt with Macer's ideological position at what may seem un-necessary length, since literary scholars, discussing Livy's sources, have lar-gely taken it for granted that this 'vehement supporter of the Popular party... is undoubtedly responsible for much of the pro-plebeian element in the early books of the *Ab Urbe Condita*'.[76] That was Mommsen's view as well — but late twentieth-century historians have reacted against it, and even against the idea that *anything* useful can be said about the lost historians of the Roman Republic. See for instance the firmly expressed opinion of Tim Cornell:[77]

> Even if it were possible to distinguish with certainty between those parts of Livy and Dionysius that derive from (e.g.) Licinius Macer and those that come from Valerius Antias, we should gain little, partly because of our general ignorance of those writers, but more particularly because their contributions are unlikely to have had a decisive effect on the character of the tradition.

For Macer at least, that seems to me a very difficult position to maintain.

---

[73] Sall. *Cat.* 4.1–2; *cf.* 38.3–4, *Iug.* 40.3, 41.5, *Hist.* 1.12M.

[74] He committed suicide in 66 BC, two years after his praetorship (Cic. *Att.* 1.4.2, Val. Max. 9.12.7, Plut. *Cic.* 9.1–2). The history was probably unfinished, since there are no surviving fragments after 299 BC (Livy 10.9.10).

[75] Cic. *Rep.* 2.3 (Scipio): *nostram rem publicam uobis et nascentem et crescentem et adultam at iam firmam atque robustam ostendero.*

[76] P. G. Walsh, *Livy: his Historical Aims and Methods* (Cambridge 1961) 122–3. See also (e.g.) R. M. Ogilvie, *A Commentary on Livy Books 1–5* (Oxford 1965) 7–12; John Briscoe, in T. A. Dorey (ed.), *Livy* (London 1971) 9–10; Oakley (n. 28), vol. 1 (1997) 92.

[77] T. J. Cornell, 'The foundation of the historical tradition of early Rome', in Moxon, Smart and Woodman (n. 4) 67–86, at 86.

There is now at last a thorough and scholarly edition of, and commentary on, the 'fragments' of Licinius Macer. Siri Walt begins her long and detailed introduction by pointing out how much, in fact, we know about the author.[78] That offers a valuable corrective to Cornell's allegation of general ignorance — and yet Walt ends up expressing a series of agnosticisms even more explicit than his.

First, we are not to suppose that the *popularis* politics of the late Republic were in any sense ideological: there was no 'popular party', just individual politicians choosing the *popularis ratio* as a political strategy to achieve their own particular ends.[79] Second, we are not to suppose that the speech Sallust gave Macer has anything to do with what a tribune of 73 BC might really have said, or with the actual issues of the time: it is just free invention based on what Sallust thought appropriate to Macer's great ancestor Licinius Stolo in the fourth century BC.[80] Third, we are not to suppose that Macer in particular had any influence on the politically tendentious presentation of historical episodes in Livy and Dionysius: Mommsen's *Tendenzthese*, like the work of the nineteenth-century *Quellenforscher* that depended on it, is not valid.[81] And finally, we are not to suppose that 'political propaganda' had any place in late-Republican life or literature: Macer was a politician operating within the conventions of an aristocratic system, and a historian whose creative reconstructions had no distinguishable ideological content.[82]

---

[78] Siri Walt, *Der Historiker C. Licinius Macer: Einleitung, Fragmente, Kommentar* (*Beiträge zur Altertumskunde* 103, Stuttgart 1997) 1: 'Im Gegensatz zu vielen anderen...sind wir über die Biographie des C. Licinius Macer relativ gut unterrichtet.'

[79] Walt (n. 78) 10–11, 21–28. 'Die Verknüpfung der popularen Methode mit der Volksversammlung und der Gegensatz *populares/optimates* könnte nun die Vorstellung erwecken, es habe sich bei den Popularen um eine demokratische Partei gehandelt. Dies ist aber von der modernen Popularenforschung widerlegt worden' (10). 'Die moderne Popularenforschung hat gezeigt, dass die *popularis ratio* nicht das beistehende System in Frage gestellt habe, sondern ein Mittel gewesen sei, um innerhalb des Systems Einfluss zu gewinnen' (25). The reference is to Gelzer and Strasburger (nn. 93 and 97 below).

[80] Walt (n. 78) 11–28, esp. 13f. But if it was 'eine Konstruktion Sallusts, der sich inspirieren liess von Macers Darstellung der Ständekämpfe in dessen *annales*' (13, after Syme (n. 50) 200 and 207), surely that invalidates the third point? The inconsistency reappears at Walt (n. 78) 104 (third and fourth paragraphs).

[81] Walt (n. 78) 47–50, 102–5; *cf.* 72–5, grouping all the 'late annalists' together without distinction. 'Das Bild, das man von den Annalisten hat, steht schon vor der eigentlichen Quellenforschung fest und beruht auf *aüsserlichen und sachfremden* Kriterien wie der demokratischen Einstellung Macers' (49, my italics).

[82] Walt (n. 78) 104: 'Wir können nun in der Kritik noch einen Schritt weitergehen und uns fragen, ob politische Propaganda in diesem Sinne in Rom überhaupt denkbar ist... Auch die populare Methode war ein Mittel der Nobilitätspolitik, die die Herrschaft der Aristokratie nie ernsthaft in Frage stellte.'

In the light of the evidence presented above, I think it is fair to describe all these propositions as deeply paradoxical. They are based, quite explicitly, on *neuer Forschung*,[83] a twentieth-century way of thinking about Roman politics with the ideology taken out. It is time to look at this phenomenon in its historical context.

iv

> MENENIUS   Alack,
>   You are transported by calamity
>   Thither where more attends you, and you slander
>   The helms o' th' state, who care for you like fathers,
>   When you curse them as enemies.
>
> FIRST CITIZEN Care for us? True indeed! They ne'er cared for us yet. Suffer us to famish, and their store-houses crammed with grain; make edicts for usury, to support usurers; repeal daily any wholesome act established against the rich, and provide more piercing statutes daily to chain up and restrain the poor. If the wars eat us not up, they will; and there's all the love they bear us.
>
> William Shakespeare, *Coriolanus*, Act 1, Scene 1 (produced probably in 1608, the year after the Levellers' riots in the English Midlands)

> GRACCHUS Détruisez, renversez ces abus sacrilèges,
>   Tous ces vols décorés du nom de privilèges.
>   Jusqu'ici, peu jaloux de votre dignité,
>   Vous avez adoré le nom de liberté:
>   Elle n'existe point dans les remparts de Rome,
>   Partout où l'homme enfin n'est point égal à l'homme.
>   Mais la fin de vos maux est en votre pouvoir;
>   Et punir ses tyrans c'est remplir un devoir.
>
> LE PEUPLE Jusqu'au fond de nos coeurs sa voix se fait entendre;
>   C'est la voix de son frère.
>
> Marie-Joseph de Chénier, *Caïus Gracchus*, Act 1, Scene 4 (produced in February 1792, six months before the establishment of the French Republic)

105: 'Die Anachronismen der römischen Annalisten sind folglich nicht politisch bedingt. Bei der Vorstellung, Macer habe ein "populares Geschichtwerk" verfasst, handelt es sich um ein modernes Konstrukt, das sich nicht beweisen lässt.'

[83] Walt (n. 78) 104: 'Dieses Schema [aristocratic v. democratic parties] ist aber von der neueren Forschung widerlegt worden.' See n. 79 above.

Ye good men of the Commons, with loving hearts and true,
Who stand by the bold tribunes that still have stood by you,
Come, make a circle round me, and mark my tale with care,
A tale of what Rome once hath borne, of what Rome yet may bear.

> . . .

'Now, by your children's cradles, now, by your fathers' graves,
Be men today, Quirites, or be for ever slaves!'

> Thomas Babington Macaulay, *Lays of Ancient Rome*, 'Virginia' (published in 1842, the year the petition for the People's Charter was presented to Parliament)

Throughout the long history of radical politics, the struggles for the liberty of the Roman people have been an example and an inspiration.[84] Even in papal Rome itself, for five months in 1849 those ideals prevailed over autocracy: 'La forma del Governo dello Stato Romano sarà la Democrazia pura, e prenderà il glorioso nome di Repubblica Romana.'[85]

One of the incidental effects of the revolutionary fervour in Europe in 1848–1849, and of the reaction that followed it, was the dismissal of the young Theodor Mommsen from his post as Professor in Roman Law at Leipzig. An active liberal, Mommsen took refuge for two years in Zürich, where he wrote the classic Roman history of the nineteenth century.[86]

Mommsen believed that the establishment of the Republic was the result not of popular enthusiasm for liberty, 'as the pitiful and deeply falsified accounts of it represent', but of two political parties uniting for a moment in the face of a common danger, like the Whigs and Tories in 1688.[87] (It is sobering to remember that Mommsen was almost as close in time to 1688 as we are to him.) However, 'every aristocratic government of itself calls forth a corresponding opposition party.' In Rome's case, the effect of the struggle

---

[84] See for instance Markku Peltonen, *Classical Humanism and Republicanism in English Political Thought 1570–1640* (Cambridge 1995); David Norbrook, *Writing the English Revolution: Poetry, Rhetoric and Politics 1627–1660* (Cambridge 1999); Carl J. Richard, *The Founders and the Classics: Greece, Rome, and the American Enlightenment* (Harvard 1994); Harold T. Parker, *The Cult of Antiquity and the French Revolutionaries: a Study in the Development of the Revolutionary Spirit* (Chicago 1937). 'On ne peut jamais quitter les Romains' (Montesquieu, *L'esprit des lois*, 1748).

[85] *House of Commons Parliamentary Papers* 1851.lvii.156: item 3 of the decree passed by the 'Roman Constituent Assembly' on the night of 8–9 February 1849.

[86] Thomas Wiedemann, 'Mommsen, Rome and the German *Kaiserreich*', in Theodor Mommsen, *A History of Rome under the Emperors* (trans. Clara Krojzl, London 1996) 36–47. The *Römische Geschichte* was published in 1854–1856: I cite it below from the most widely available edition of the English translation.

[87] Theodor Mommsen, *History of Rome* (trans. W. P. Dickson, Everyman's Library, London n.d. [1910]) vol. 1, 257.

of the orders, and the resulting admission of the plebeians to government, was the creation of 'a new aristocratic and a new democratic party':

> The formation of these new parties began in the fifth century [i.e. 353–254 BC], but they assumed their definite shape only in the century which followed. The development of this change is, as it were, drowned amidst the noise of the great wars and victories, and the process of formation is in this case more concealed from our view than in any other in Roman history. Like a crust of ice gathering imperceptibly over the surface of a stream and imperceptibly confining it more and more, this new Roman aristocracy silently arose; and not less imperceptibly, like the concealed current slowly swelling beneath, there arose in opposition to it the new party of progress.

The breaking of the ice came with the Gracchi, and the 'democratico-monarchical revolution' that followed.[88]

Mommsen believed that the 'party names' of Optimates and Populares had become meaningless. 'Both parties contended alike for shadows'; the Roman revolution arose not out of 'paltry political conflict' but out of the economic and social conditions which the Roman government had allowed to develop; it was 'a great conflict between labour and capital'.[89] Nevertheless, Mommsen constantly uses the 'party names', in translation, as he describes the politics of the revolutionary period as the struggle of the democrats against the aristocracy.

Mommsen's *History* was hugely influential: it won him the Nobel Prize for Literature as late as 1902. The English translation, by W. P. Dickson, appeared in 1862–1875, but in England Mommsen had a rival. Charles Merivale's *History of the Romans under the Empire* (1850–1864) and *The Fall of the Roman Republic* (1853) were expanded into *A General History of Rome from the Foundation of the City* (1875). Its final manifestation was as the *History of Rome to the Reign of Trajan* (Everyman's Library, 1911), designed to form a continuous narrative with Gibbon's *Decline and Fall*. Throughout Merivale's work, Roman politics were disputed between the popular and senatorial parties.

From Mommsen and Merivale alike, the educated public of the late nineteenth and early twentieth centuries understood that the Roman Republic was in near-constant tension between democracy and oligarchy, reform and reaction, the people and the Senate.[90] Nor was it an illusion: the evidence

---

[88] Mommsen (n. 87) vol. 1, 304, 305; vol. 2, 295, 339.

[89] Mommsen (n. 87) vol. 3, 71, 72, 73.

[90] See for instance Charles Merivale, *History of Rome to the Reign of Trajan* (Everyman's Library, London 1911) 215, on Gaius Gracchus: '"Caius made the republic double-headed," was the shrewd remark of antiquity; but in fact the powers of the Roman state, the consuls and the tribunes, the

was there, in Cicero, Sallust, Livy and Dionysius. What *was* an illusion was the old idea that the issues applied straightforwardly to the modern world. In the age of Marx, Nietzsche and Freud, all such simple certainties were under attack.

Mass suffrage had made necessary, and mass literacy had made possible, a different sort of politics and a new concept of what a political party must be. As early as 1852, Marx himself noted the difference:[91]

> Camille Desmoulins, Danton, Robespierre, Saint-Just, Napoleon, the heroes as well as the parties and the masses of the old French Revolution, performed the task of their time in Roman costume and with Roman phrases, the task of unchaining and setting up modern *bourgeois* society....The new social formation once established, the antediluvian colossi disappeared and with them resurrected Romanity — the Brutuses, Gracchi, Publicolas, the tribunes, the senators and Caesar himself. Bourgeois society in its sober reality... no longer comprehended that ghosts from the days of Rome had watched over its cradle.

However, Marx was wrong about Caesar. Now that the great powers aspired to empire, Caesar's name was appealed to more than ever. It usefully symbolised two glamorous topical themes, imperial conquest and populist autocracy.[92] The Roman paradigm was now not the Republic but the man who destroyed the Republic.

It was against that background that the first 'modernist' interpretation of Roman republican politics, the 26-year-old Matthias Gelzer's *Die Nobilität der römischen Republik*, appeared in 1912. Ideological issues had no place in his analysis. For Gelzer, political life was the pursuit of power — that is, election to office — by the exploitation of personal and patronal relationships (*Nah- und Treuverhältnisse*). There were no parties, and 'factions' were just *ad hoc* combinations to secure election. When standing for the consulship, the candidate 'should avoid taking up a position on any political question, whether in the senate or in the assembly, so that every man will expect him to intervene in his interest'.[93]

Senate and the people, were always arrayed with co-ordinate powers one against the other, and Caius only introduced a fresh element of discord where there existed already others which could never long be held in equilibrium together.'

[91] Karl Marx and Frederick Engels, *Collected Works*, vol. 11 (London 1979) 104, from 'Der 18te Brumaire des Louis Napoleon', *Die Revolution* 1 (1852).

[92] 'On Caesarism', see now Peter Baehr, *Caesar and the Fading of the Roman World: a Study in Republicanism and Caesarism* (New Brunswick, NJ 1998), esp. 186–90 (Max Weber on modern parties).

Gelzer took that piece of advice from Quintus Cicero's essay to his brother about electoral strategy, the *Commentariolum petitionis*. But Quintus was writing very specifically for the election campaign of a 'new man' who needed all the support he could get; it didn't necessarily apply in general. Besides, what he actually said is a bit different from Gelzer's paraphrase:[94]

> atque etiam in hac petitione maxime uidendum est ut spes rei publicae bona de te sit et honesta opinio; nec tamen in petendo res publica capessenda est neque in senatu neque in contione. sed haec tibi sunt retinenda: ut senatus te existimet ex eo quod ita uixeris defensorem auctoritatis suae fore, equites R. et uiri boni ac locupletes ex uita acta te studiosum oti ac rerum tranquillarum, multitudo ex eo quod dumtaxat oratione in contionibus ac iudicio popularis fuisti te a suis commodis non alienum futurum.

> Also, the main thing to be sure of in this campaign is that politically people should have high hopes and a good opinion of you. But while you're campaigning you mustn't take any political position, either in the Senate or in the assembly. This is what you must take care of: that the Senate should think from your way of life that you'll be a defender of its authority; that the Roman knights and the rich and respectable should think from your career that you'll be in favour of peace and quiet; and that the many should think that since you've been a *popularis*, at least in your speeches in the assembly and the courts, you won't be hostile to their interests.

No hint in Gelzer of the Senate and the *multitudo* — or of *popularis* speeches. This, I think, is the moment when the ideological vacuum was created.

In 1920 appeared Friedrich Münzer's *Römische Adelsparteien und Adelsfamilien*, a brilliantly original reading of the political history of the Republic according to the patterns of names in the consular *fasti* (magistrate lists). Münzer certainly didn't reject the ideological; indeed, the editor of the English translation has to explain away his use of 'democracy' and 'democratic'. But since the aristocratic 'parties' of his title were essentially electoral alliances, the book could be seen as a history of Roman politics in Gelzerian terms.[95] So the two names are cited very frequently together, as

---

[93] Matthias Gelzer, *Die Nobilität der römischen Republik* (Berlin 1912) 45 = *Kleine Schriften* vol. 1 (Wiesbaden 1962) 64 = *The Roman Nobility* (trans. Robin Seager, Oxford 1969) 56.

[94] Q. Cic. *Comm. pet.* 53; *cf.* 5, ... *persuadendumque est iis nos semper cum optimatibus de re publica sensisse, minime popularis fuisse.*

[95] Frierich Münzer, *Römische Adelsparteien und Adelsfamilien* (Stuttgart 1920) = *Roman Aristocratic Parties and Families* (trans. Thérèse Ridley, Baltimore 1999), with R. T. Ridley at xxv-xxvi on 'democratic'. E.g. Münzer, 422–3 (= 358) on the Gracchan movement, 'this great antagonism between the democratic party and the nobility' and its effect on noble families: 'Torn

joint founders of the modern view, in works of Roman history published in the mid-twentieth century.[96]

That view was established as orthodoxy by Hermann Strasburger's Pauly-Wissowa article on *optimates*, which appeared in 1939. Yes, Cicero says *duo genera semper in hac ciuitate fuerunt*, but it is anachronistic to infer two political groupings of government and opposition. The idea of 'parties' was borrowed from seventeenth-century England and used for Rome without any serious thought. Mommsen's whole approach was vitiated by this assumption, but Gelzer's pathbreaking work, completed and confirmed by Münzer, has corrected the misunderstanding. The whole history of the late Republic needs rethinking, with the misleading evidence discounted; Greek authors used inappropriate Greek concepts (democracy, aristocracy), while Latin authors of the imperial period could not understand what was for them no longer a living reality.[97] As for the contemporary sources, Strasburger was too honest a scholar to conceal the evidence that counted against his view, but he argued it away with the confidence of a true believer.[98] There was no democracy in Rome; the *populares* were individuals using the masses as a tool to achieve their own political ends; none of their proposals would have changed the self-evident leadership of the nobility.[99]

By the time Christian Meier's article on *populares* appeared in Pauly-Wissowa in 1965, all this was accepted doctrine. It was stated without argument, and with no sense of paradox, that the *popularis ratio* was a political method, as it were a career choice for achieving one's own ambitions.[100] One might have thought that the deaths of Tiberius and Gaius Gracchus, Saturninus, Livius Drusus, Sulpicius and Clodius were *prima facie* evidence that being a radical tribune was not likely to bring you to

between revolutionary and reactionary movements, the sons of these families could no longer follow a middle course as their ancestors had done; they perished in futile struggles with the superior strength of the right and left.' See also 15–20 (= 20–4) on Licinius Macer, 'a vehement democrat and enemy of the aristocracy'.

[96] Most explicitly in E. Badian, *Foreign Clientelae (264–70 BC)* (Oxford 1958) vii: '... Gelzer and Münzer, who revolutionized the approach to the study of this period'. *Cf.* among others Syme (n. 50) 17 n. 3; E. S. Gruen, *Roman Politics and the Criminal Courts, 149–78 BC* (Harvard 1968) 2 n. 2; H. H. Scullard, *From the Gracchi to Nero: a History of Rome from 133 BC to AD 68* (3rd ed., London 1970) 381–2 nn. 4–5.

[97] Strasburger, 'Optimates', *RE* 18.1 (1939) 773–98, at 774–82 (esp. 779 on Gelzer and Münzer).

[98] Strasburger (n. 97) 782–4 (*populares*), 784–8 (*partes*), 788–90 (*factio*).

[99] Strasburger (n. 97) 790–7; *cf.* 782 ('*Popularis* wird ein Politiker genannt, der ... einer bezeichnenden staatsrechtlichen Taktik bedient').

[100] Christian Meier, 'Populares', *RE* Suppl. vol. 10 (1965) 549–615, at 549–68 (esp. 553–4 on Gelzer and Strasburger). Already in Taylor (n. 103 below) 13–15, though she thought Strasburger's attack on Mommsen had 'gone too far'.

the consulship; but perhaps these were just epiphenomena, not affecting the essential pattern.[101]

Meanwhile, in the English-speaking world the nature of Roman politics had been subjected to cold scrutiny in Ronald Syme's great book *The Roman Revolution*. Basing himself explicitly on Münzer's method, and clearly influenced by the rise of Stalin, Mussolini and Hitler (the book was published the week after the invasion of Poland in September 1939), Syme kept his eye firmly fixed on *Machtpolitik*:[102]

> The rule of Augustus brought manifold blessings to Rome, Italy and the provinces. Yet the new dispensation, or 'novus status', was the work of fraud and bloodshed, based upon the seizure of power and redistribution of property by a revolutionary leader ...
>
> One thing was clear. Monarchy was already there and would subsist, whatever principle was invoked in the struggle, whatever name the victor chose to give to his rule, because it was for monarchy that the rival Caesarian leaders contended.

When Syme used the word 'party', it was with all the overtones of Europe in the 1930s. Power for its own sake was his subject.

Less overwhelming, but also influential in its way, was Lily Ross Taylor's *Party Politics in the Age of Caesar* (1949). Like Gelzer, she took Quintus Cicero's advice to his brother as a general rule, not just for the particular circumstances of a new man in 64 BC; her analogy for Roman politics was the American system of party conventions in a Presidential election year, when the Republican and Democrat hopefuls relied on their personalities for success and kept quiet about political issues.[103]

So Gelzer gave you the norm, aristocrats exploiting connections and patronage to get their consulships, and Syme gave you the crisis, as power was usurped by a 'chill and mature terrorist'.[104] Either way, you were not to suppose that there were causes that men would die for. And so you could end up as Siri Walt has done, unable to recognise a radical activist, the historian of the Roman people, because you had been taught to believe that such men did not exist.

---

[101] For an extreme version of that view, see Gruen (n. 1) 4–5: 'Civil war need not be read as a token of the Republic's collapse.'

[102] Syme (n. 51) 2, 258; *cf.* viii, on 'the supreme example and guidance of Münzer'. On Syme and *The Roman Revolution*, see Kurt A. Raaflaub and Mark Toher (eds.), *Between Republic and Empire: Interpretations of Augustus and his Principate* (Berkeley 1990).

[103] Lily Ross Taylor, *Party Politics in the Age of Caesar* (*Sather Classical Lectures* 22, Berkeley 1949) 8; the system of 'primaries' has evolved somewhat since then. See nn. 93–4 above for Gelzer and Q. Cicero.

[104] Syme (n. 51) 191, on Octavian in 43 BC.

V

Of course there have been notable dissenting voices — Wirszubski on *libertas*, Brunt on social conflicts, Ste. Croix on the class struggle, Millar on the urban crowd — but these independent-minded historians have had to argue against a prevalent orthodoxy.[105] Much more characteristic of twentieth-century assumptions is the recent biography of Publius Clodius, which in a 31-page introductory chapter on 'politics and popularity in the late Roman Republic' never once refers to the fact that the People's champions had been assassinated. 'The explosive careers of the Gracchi,' we are told, 'truncated and inconclusive, lent and lend themselves to varying interpretations.' As for Clodius, in pursuing his own career he showed 'how the *via popularis* could safely, even triumphantly, be trod'.[106] But it was no safer for him than it had been for his martyred predecessors.

Even after three generations, the sheer inertia of the Gelzer model seems to prevent the ideological content of republican politics, amply attested in contemporary sources, from being accepted as a given. Evidently historians still feel nervous about discussing *optimates* and *populares* as if the terms had a real meaning.

No doubt it would be unjust to attribute to modern scholarship what was said in 1866 about 'the credulous unphilosophical spirit, the ignorance of practical politics, the conservative tone of mind, and the literary *esprit de corps* too common among historians'. E. S. Beesly's complaint was not that his colleagues ignored ideology, but that they sympathised with the wrong side.[107] It is true, though, that twentieth-century academics have been less involved in real politics than, for instance, Mommsen was; and it may even be that university life predisposes one to think that cliques, patronage and the pursuit of office are all that count. But I think there is a more general reason too.

---

[105] Ch. Wirszubski, *Libertas as a Political Idea at Rome during the Late Republic and Early Principate* (Cambridge 1950); P. A. Brunt, *Social Conflicts in the Roman Republic* (London 1971), and '*Libertas* in the Republic', in *The Fall of the Roman Republic and Related Essays* (Oxford 1988), 281–350; G. E. M. de Ste. Croix, *The Class Struggle in the Ancient Greek World from the Archaic Age to the Arab Conquests* (London 1981) 332–72; Fergus Millar, *The Crowd in Rome in the Late Republic* (*Jerome Lectures* 22, Ann Arbor 1998).

[106] Jeffrey Tatum, *The Patrician Tribune: Publius Clodius Pulcher* (Chapel Hill 1999) 12, 238; 'it is perverse to question the aristocratic locus of political initiative and activity in Rome' (10).

[107] E. S. Beesly, *Fortnightly Review* 5.4 (1 July 1866) 421 (= *Catiline, Clodius, and Tiberius* (London 1878) 40). For Beesly, see T. P. Wiseman, *Roman Drama and Roman History* (Exeter 1998) 121–34.

Although it is unlikely that the Roman paradigm will ever lose its significance in Western culture, what it signifies varies from one age to the next. For the last four or five generations we have thought of Rome as the imperial power. Our Roman myths have been *Quo Vadis*, *I, Claudius* and *Gladiator*; in the idiom of television, 'Rome' means a triumphal arch or marching legionaries, with horns and drums and a portentous voice-over. If we need a radical reading, it has to be *Spartacus*.

But now the modern empires have gone (including the one that laid claim to Spartacus), and popular sovereignty is a real political issue. The Roman Republic is becoming interesting again. If we are to understand it, we need to hear all its voices. In 121 BC, with the consul's Cretan archers closing in and his own followers deserting him, Gaius Gracchus fled for sanctuary to the temple of Diana on the Aventine. On his knees, arms outstretched, he prayed aloud to the goddess: 'For this ingratitude and treachery, may the Roman people be slaves for ever!'[108] Whether he really did so hardly matters: the story was told, for a Roman audience, and that fact itself shows us what the Republic was like.

---

[108] Plut. *C. Gracch.* 16.5 (λέγεται). *Cf.* Sallust's Licinius Macer (*Hist.* 3.48.13 and 26) on the people's *ignauia*.

13
Look your last on lyric: Horace, *Odes* 4.15

Jasper Griffin

Phoebus uolentem proelia me loqui
uictas et urbis increpuit lyra,
 ne parua Tyrrhenum per aequor
  uela darem: tua, Caesar, aetas

fruges et agris rettulit uberes   5
et signa nostro restituit Ioui
 derepta Parthorum superbis
  postibus et uacuum duellis

Ianum Quirini clausit et ordinem
rectum euaganti frena licentiae   10
 iniecit emouitque culpas
  et ueteres reuocauit artis,

per quas Latinum nomen et Italae
creuere uires, famaque et imperi
 porrecta maiestas ad ortus   15
  solis ab Hesperio cubili.

custode rerum Caesare non furor
ciuilis aut uis exiget otium,
 non ira, quae procudit enses
  et miseras inimicat urbis: 20

non qui profundum Danuuium bibunt
edicta rumpent Iulia, non Getae,
 non Seres infidique Persae,
  non Tanain prope flumen orti:

nosque et profestis lucibus et sacris   25
inter iocosi munera Liberi
 cum prole matronisque nostris
  rite deos prius apprecati

uirtute functos more patrum duces
Lydis remixto carmine tibiis   30
    Troiamque et Anchisen et almae
    progeniem Veneris canemus.

My wish was to tell of battles and the conquest of cities, but Phoebus checked me
with his lyre, so that I should not set out on the Tyrrhenian Sea with such tiny sails.
Your age, Caesar, has brought back rich harvests to the fields and has also restored
to Jupiter, our own god, the legionary standards torn down from the haughty
temples of Parthia; it has closed the temple of Janus Quirinus, free from wars,
tightened the reins on licentiousness which was straying beyond good order, taken
away crime, and brought back the arts which made the Latin name and the power
of Italy grow great, the fame and majesty of the Empire spreading all the way from
the rising of the sun to his couch in the west. So long as Caesar is guardian of the
world no madness of civil strife, no act of violence, shall chase away our peace; no
fit of anger, which forges armaments and sets unlucky cities at strife. Not those
who drink of the deep Danube, not the Getae, not the Seres or the treacherous
Persians, no, nor those who are born near the river Tanais: none shall break the
Julian laws. As for us, both on working days and on festivals, amid the delights of
the playful god of wine, and surrounded by our wives and children, we shall first
duly worship the gods, then sing, mingling our song with the Etruscan flute, of the
chieftains who practised the ancestral virtues, and of Troy, and of Anchises, and of
the offspring of kindly Venus.

i

Quintus Horatius Flaccus brought his first three books of *Odes* before the
public in 23 BC. They came with impressive sponsors. The first ode was
addressed to Maecenas, the second to the Princeps himself, the fourth to
L. Sestius, consul of the year, and the sixth to the second man in the Empire,
M. Agrippa. Such grandees as L. Munatius Plancus (consul in 42), C. Asinius Pollio (consul in 40 and *triumphator* in 39), and C. Sallustius Crispus,
the successor to Maecenas in the inmost counsels of Augustus, also received
prominently placed dedications (*Odes* 1.7, 2.1, 2.2).

Horace did not repeat, in books 1 to 3, the bold stroke of directly addressing the Princeps; that was reserved for book 4, odes 5 and 15. What was
his relation to Augustus, and what was the relation of his poetry to the
imperial propaganda? What we call 'Augustan poetry' is so intimately
connected with our estimate of the crucial event in Roman history, the
change from Republic to Empire, that both historians and literary scholars
find the question fascinating. Over the years very different answers have

been given.[1] In 1939, cynical era of the European dictators, the great Roman historian Ronald Syme spoke of 'the organization of opinion', and of Maecenas as Augustus' Minister of Propaganda.[2] But in 1957, in contrast, the great literary scholar Eduard Fraenkel declared: 'To the loyalty and admiration for Rome's leader which [Horace] had long felt there was now added a strong element of personal affection...'.[3]

In the 1990s postmodern attitudes asserted themselves. Thus D. F. Kennedy asserts the Foucauldian view that 'every utterance, whether those involved realise it or not, enacts a relationship of power', so that even an apparently impertinent gibe by Ovid (*Ars* 1.637, 'It is expedient that the gods should exist, and as it's expedient, let's suppose they do'), really 'helps to render legitimate the moral and religious programme of Augustus'. That is a state of affairs all the gloomier, as 'the power of Augustus was a collective invention, the symbolic embodiment of the conflicting desires of the Romans, the instrumental expression of a complex network of dependency, repression, and fear.'[4] This dark *a priori* view, dogmatically stated, rules out, of course, any such possibilities as hope, trust, or gratitude; and a subjective view, the opposite of Fraenkel's, assumes the stage armour of theoretical rigour.

Purely subjective pronouncements have indeed proved hard to resist. Thus D. Little argues that: 'If we are to believe what the poets say, Augustus seemed divine to them. Face to face, they found that his mien and character answered to his deeds, and promised greater...'.[5] But in another volume of the same publication, and in comical contrast, P. Connor asserts that 'it is clear from a number of passages that Horace did not stand in awe of Augustus.'[6] The flatness of such disagreements suggests that the right questions are not being asked.

---

[1] It is not possible here to give an exhaustive bibliography. See P. White, *Promised Verse: Poets in the Society of Augustan Rome* (Harvard 1993), and A. Powell (ed.), *Roman Poetry and Propaganda in the Age of Augustus* (Bristol 1992). O. Lyne, *Horace: Behind the Public Poetry* (Yale 1995) gives a nuanced discussion of the relations of the Princeps and Horace. On the question of 'Augustan' literature, see recently P. J. Davis, 'Ovid's *Amores*: a political reading', *Classical Philology* 94 (1999) 431–49.

[2] R. Syme, *The Roman Revolution* (Oxford 1939) ch. 30.

[3] E. Fraenkel, *Horace* (Oxford 1957) 438: 'Being the sincere man he was...'.

[4] D. F. Kennedy, '"Augustan" and "Anti-Augustan": reflections on terms of reference,' in Powell (n. 1) 26–59: quotations from pp. 29, 45, 35.

[5] D. Little, 'Politics in Augustan Poetry', in W. Haase (ed.), *Aufstieg und Niedergang der römischen Welt* 30.1 (Berlin 1982) 254–370, at 281–2.

[6] P. Connor, 'The actual quality of experience: an appraisal of the nature of Horace's "Odes", in Haase (n. 5) 31.3 (Berlin 1981) 1612–39, at 1623. There are those, too, who think the poet was

It is not easy to tell what a tricky customer like Horace 'really' felt on such a subject, even if it was true that his feelings about Augustus were always the same.[7] Some have preferred to argue that Horace actually played a part in creating the propaganda of Augustus.[8] Those who like to believe in Horace's committed sincerity[9] may care to ponder the passages in Cicero's speech *Pro Marcello* where he proclaims in splendid prose his conviction that without Caesar a decent life would be impossible for anyone:

> quis est qui non intellegat tua salute contineri suam, et ex unius uita pendere omnium?... nisi te, Caesar, saluo... salui esse non possumus.

> Surely everyone understands that his own security depends on yours, and that it is on your single life that all our lives depend.... Our only hope of security is conditional upon your being secure.

But Cicero's reaction to Caesar's murder was, of course, unmixed delight.[10]

Let us try to distinguish more closely. It is clear from the intimate and jokey tone of Augustus' letters to him that the Princeps was prepared to talk to Horace, in private, as a kind of equal, not without mildly dirty jokes;[11] but both knew he was not an equal; and such egalitarian informality is very far from the tone in which Horace treats him in his public poetry. It is clear that the poets found it very hard to know how to address Augustus. In *Odes* 1.2 he is addressed as a god, perhaps an avatar of Mercury. In 3.5 Horace proclaims his future apotheosis. When he presents a copy of his First Book of *Epistles*, he is in a flurry of nervous jokes (*Epist.* 1.13): don't make out

unwilling to support the regime and did so without conviction: so W. R. Johnson, *The Idea of Lyric* (Berkeley 1982) 137–8, who speaks of 'some ironic victory songs' in *Odes* 4 and concludes 'The praise that Horace offers Augustus consists more in warning than in laudation.'

[7] 'There is no point in questioning Horace's sincerity: *fides* to Maecenas required co-operation, there was no alternative to the regime, and everybody likes to participate in important causes': R. G. M. Nisbet and M. Hubbard, *Commentary on Horace, Odes i* (Oxford 1970) xviii.

[8] M. Santirocco, 'Horace and Augustan ideology', *Arethusa* 28 (1995) 225–44: 'The extensive coincidence of detail and strategy between the earlier lyrics and later inscription [sc. the *Res Gestae*] at least suggests that what we have come to think of as Augustan ideology was a long time in the making, and that its creation was not so much the imposition of ideas from on high as it was an interactive process in which the poet Horace, the patron Maecenas, and the *princeps* Augustus all had a hand' (231); 'Horace retains his independence by co-opting Augustus to his own agenda' (243). Discounted in advance and *a priori* by Nisbet and Hubbard (n. 7), xviii: 'Some scholars even think that Horace gave advice to the regime, as if the opinions of poets could ever be of the slightest consequence to Roman society.'

[9] 'Das Bekenntnis eines grossen Dichters zu einem grossen Herrscher': E. Doblhofer, *Die Augustuspanegyrik des Horaz in formalhistorischer Sicht* (Heidelberg 1966) 162.

[10] Cicero, *Marc.* 22, 32. Useful bibliography, and some perceptive discussions, in White (n. 1).

[11] Quoted in Suetonius' *Life of Horace*: *Imperatoris Caesaris Augusti operum fragmenta* (ed. H. Malcovati, 5th ed., Turin 1969) 22–4.

that it's inconveniently heavy to carry—don't present it at the wrong moment—don't drop it and break it. When he braces himself to write Augustus
himself a poetic letter, he begins with a most uncharacteristic flutter of
modest hesitation: it would be unpardonable if he were to trespass long on
the precious time of the man who in every imaginable sphere is restoring the
Roman Empire, and to whom in his lifetime we all pay the heartfelt honours
for which Hercules and the Dioscuri had to wait until they were dead.[12] Even
Virgil, when he must address Augustus directly, falls into a baroque vein of
exaggeration which surely suggests unease.[13] How *did* one address such a
man? Better, surely, to address Maecenas instead; or to leave him in the
respectful distance of the third person; or, in the *Aeneid*, in the still safer
distance of prophecies about the remote future.[14]

No less suggestive than the prominence of the grandees is the fact that
the greatest poet of the age, too, is addressed by Horace in terms of close
friendship, in *Odes* 1.3 and 1.24.[15] The ability to boast of potent and cred-
itable supporters meant a lot to Horace. He had allowed it to be seen, at the
end of the First Book of his *Satires*, that he attached importance to having the
big names on his side.[16] His opponents there are backed only by obscure
hacks, professional writers of no distinction or standing. Horace's associates
fall into two groups: there are the great poets, Virgil among them, and also
men of the highest social rank, including Pollio, Messalla, and his brother
L. Gellius Poplicola (consul in 36). In the Second Book (2.1.76) he is even
more explicit: detraction itself will have to admit that he has lived in the
company of the great! In the *Epistles* he generalises, in a list of commonly
accepted virtues: 'to please the great is not the lowest of distinctions.'[17] And
when he comes to give a description of himself, at the end of that book, what

---

[12] *Epist.* 2.1.1–17. The comparison of Augustus to mythical heroes being apotheosised after death
turns out to be capable of a yet more flattering twist: he gets *more* honour than they did!

[13] *Georgics* 1.24–42.

[14] *Aen.* 1.286–96, 6.791–807, 8.675–728.

[15] *Odes* 4.12, to a Vergilius, is surely not addressed to the poet. Virgil was dead by the time this
poem was published. Is it possible to believe that Horace would have addressed his dead friend, the
author of the epic which can be seen to have impressed and influenced him so much, as 'the client of
young aristocrats', made no mention of his poetry, and told him not to worry so much about money?
'Impossibile', in fact, is the verdict of the judicious A. La Penna, *Orazio e l'ideologia del principato*
(Turin 1963) 146. The point would not be worth hammering, were not the other view championed by
R. G. M. Nisbet (*Classical Review* 18 (1968) 56), D. M. Porter (*Latomus* 31 (1972) 71–87), and
F. Cairns (*Generic Composition in Greek and Roman Poetry* (Edinburgh 1972) 244).

[16] *Serm.* 1.10.78–92. *Cf.* R. Syme, *The Augustan Aristocracy* (Oxford 1986) 205–6: these men have
'a Republican and Antonian nexus'.

[17] *Epist.* 1.17.35, *principibus placuisse uiris non ultima laus est.*

he tells us is that he has found favour with the highest men in Rome, both in war and peace.[18]

It is natural to connect that repeated emphasis with the poet's anxiety about his humble origins. The two points are put immediately together in *Epistles* 1.20, where it takes first place among his 'virtues':[19]

> me libertino natum patre et in tenui re
> maiores pennas nido extendisse loqueris,
> ut quantum generi demas uirtutibus addas:
> me primis Vrbis belli placuisse domique...

> You will declare of me that, born the son of a freedman with a modest inheritance, I stretched my wings too wide for my nest; the more you deny me the advantages of birth, the more you will add to my personal merits. You will say that I found favour with the first men in Rome, both in war and at home...

But despite such exalted backing, Horace seems to express dissatisfaction with the reception accorded to his very unusual publication of 23 BC, which contained three books of *Odes*, each with its own intricate architecture but all forming part of the even more elaborate structure of the whole. *Epistles* 1.19 is rather a sour poem. He is much imitated, but he is also treated with ingratitude and injustice: 'you would like to know why the ungrateful reader praises my work and admires it in private, but runs it down in public — I do not deign to go in for the literary log-rolling that secures success.'[20]

It may be conjectured that it was the commission for the *Carmen sae-culare* in 17 (*Carmen composuit Q. Horatius Flaccus*),[21] a signal mark of public acceptance, that chiefly encouraged Horace to compose his Fourth

---

[18] *Epist.* 1.20.23. It may be added that *placere*, being liked, is a key word with Horace: cf. *Odes* 4.3.24, with E. Doblhofer, in Haase (n. 5) 31.3 (Berlin 1981), 1983–6. That too looks like insecurity.

[19] *Epist.* 1.20.20–3. The passage is one in which Horace applies to himself the phrase *libertino patre natum*, not merely as the reported malice of other people. It therefore tells against the interesting view of G. Williams, in S. J. Harrison (ed.), *Homage to Horace* (Oxford 1995) 296–313, that Horace was not really the son of a freedman at all, except in the sense that his father, a doughty fighter for the Italian side in the Social war and a man of good social position, was among those forced to surrender at the fall of Asculum in 89 and so briefly in servitude. This passage seems inescapably to say more than that.

[20] *Epist.* 1.19.35–6: *scire uelis mea cur ingratus opuscula lector / laudet ametque domi, premat extra limen iniquus....*

[21] From the great inscription recording the Secular Games, *CIL* vi.32323.149. It is worth observing, for the intoxicating quality of this occasion for Horace, that the very next lines of the inscription read *XVuir. adfuerunt Imp. Caesar, M. Agrippa, Q. Lepidus, Potitus Messalla, C. Stolo, C. Scaevola*, and so on. The poet is on public record in the exclusive company of the grandest men in Rome, rather as he is in *Odes* 4 (Paullus Fabius Maximus, Iullus Antonius, Tiberius and Drusus, Marcius Censorinus, Lollius, and the Princeps himself).

Book. As he says in 4.3, he is being recognised now as a lyric poet, and is *less* gnawed by the tooth of envy (*et iam dente minus mordeor inuido*, line 16). There was also pressure from Very High Places. Suetonius tells us, perhaps rather crudely, that Augustus 'forced' Horace to add a Fourth Book, to glorify the conquest of the Vindelici by Tiberius and Drusus.[22]

A request from Augustus was not, of course, like a request from an ordinary person: it contained an element of something like compulsion.[23] Yet it is surely exaggerated to say that 'if Augustus requests, there is no possibility of refusal.'[24] That epic poem on his own *res gestae*, so urgently pressed for — Quis *sibi res gestas Augusti scribere sumit?* asked Horace in comic desperation at the end of the twenties BC: *who* is writing up Augustus' achievements, immortalising his deeds of war and peace? (*bella quis et paces longum diffundit in aeuum?*)[25] — for all Augustus' requests, that epic never did get written.

There are other possibilities between instant compliance on the one hand and blank refusal on the other.[26] The existence of the *Aeneid* itself illustrates one of them. In the end Augustus had to write up his career himself, the extraordinary *Res gestae* which no subsequent emperor presumed to emulate; but we should remember his failure and his response when we laugh at Cicero for failing to find a panegyrist to immortalise his consulship, and for having in the end to write the poem himself.[27]

ii

The Fourth Book of the *Odes* has a character of its own. Pindar, rather than Alcaeus, is in the ascendant, and his name is the first word in 4.2. Pindar's style, as Horace conceived it, is described in that poem, and it is exemplified in the two long poems on the warlike exploits of the stepsons of the Princeps, 4.4 and 4.14. Horace shows that he too is one who did not flinch from

---

[22] Suet. *Vita Horati* 9: *eumque coegerit propter hoc tribus carminum libris ex longo interuallo quartum addere*. Acute discussion in Lyne (n. 1) 194–5.

[23] J. Griffin, 'Caesar qui cogere posset: Augustus and the Poets', in F. Millar and E. Segal (eds.), *Caesar Augustus: Seven Aspects* (Oxford 1984) 189–208.

[24] G. Williams, in K. A. Raaflaub and M. Toher (eds.), *Between Republic and Empire: Interpretations of Augustus and his Principate* (Berkeley 1990) 269.

[25] *Epist.* 1.3.8–9.

[26] One is reminded of Tacitus' insistence (*Annals* 4.20.3) that there existed for senators a middle way between *deforme obsequium* and *abrupta contumacia*.

[27] See now E. Courtney, *The Fragmentary Latin Poets* (Oxford 1993) 156–73.

a draught of the Pindaric fountain.[28] But each of those grandiose narrative compositions, themselves not to everyone's taste,[29] is followed by a shorter and more personal poem, at least ostensibly simpler, addressed to Augustus himself.[30]

It was inferred long ago that 4.15 was connected with the voting of the Ara Pacis Augustae in the summer of 13 BC.[31] Augustus returned to Rome in July of that year from a three-year absence in Spain and Gaul; 4.5 presents Rome as yearning for him like a mother for her adventurous absent son. Janus was closed. All was well with the Roman world. In January of 12 BC Augustus succeeded, at last, as Pontifex Maximus, and he had himself represented in that role on the Ara Pacis. In 13–12 he began to lay out the titanic sundial which went with his mausoleum and which, in its size and its astrological significance, placed him in a category beyond comparison with other mortals.[32] The planning of the Augustan Forum was going ahead, with its grandiose scheme of patriotic decoration, centring on the family and person of the Princeps.[33]

When we think of Horace as pressed to compose patriotic and encomiastic verse, it should be remembered that not all pressure comes from outside. There is also the desire to share the mood of the time. On the one hand, that means behaving as if one shared it, and saying acceptable things. But on the other there is also the more subtle pressure: the wish to believe, to accept that the nightmares of civil war, proscriptions and insecurity are finally over; that great things are afoot, and that Augustus really is inaugurating a new and splendid age (*tua, Caesar, aetas* . . .).[34]

---

[28] *Epist.* 1.3.10, *Pindarici fontis qui non expalluit haustus* . . .

[29] Horace's Pindaric encomia are frigid: that is the verdict of La Penna (n. 15) 118.

[30] *Odes* 4.5, 4.15. That repeated and emphatic pairing is one reason for withholding credence from the suggestion of O. Murray (in N. Rudd (ed.), *Horace 2000: a Celebration* (London 1993) 91) that 4.15 was originally intended as a preface and only later replaced by 4.1. *Cf.* also the arguments of Lyne (n. 1), 38 n. 15. *Odes* 4.5 and 4.15 form, in fact, an artfully contrasted pair. In the former, Augustus is addressed emotionally, as a darling son; in the latter, more formally, as Commander in Chief and moral authority. Horace wants both sides represented, and in a way that produces a full and complex effect.

[31] See Heinze ad loc., and Fraenkel (n. 3) 449.

[32] E. Buchner, *Die Sonnenuhr des Augustus* (Mainz 1982).

[33] Well discussed and illustrated by K. Galinsky, *Augustan Culture* (Princeton 1996); the excited mood of the time, and the contemporary outburst of astrological symbolism, are well brought out by G. W. Bowersock, 'The Pontificate of Augustus', in Raaflaub and Toher (n. 24) 381–94.

[34] That wish is expressed with inimitable dryness by Nisbet and Hubbard (n. 7): 'Everybody likes to participate in important causes.'

Each of the first three Books of the *Odes* closed with a poem about Horace himself and his aesthetic ideals and poetical claims. They add up to a complex picture. The keynote of 1.38 was understatement: brevity, simplicity, avoidance of the opulent and the elaborate. *Odes* 2.20 is very different. The poet will attain immortality, assume the form of the bird sacred to Apollo, and be known all over the world. *Odes* 3.30 makes an even stronger claim, in a style less whimsical and more classical. His monument will outlast brass and stone; his fame, the gift of the Muse, will endure as long as Rome herself. The total statement of the three is large and subtle. Horace is not untrue to the standards of Callimachus, to simplicity, irony, plainness; but he does take his art seriously, and while at moments he may be pleased to phrase his claims in terms which are picturesque and far-fetched, those claims are none the less ambitious and elevated.

Now he comes to close his Fourth Book, having made it clear that he expects it to be his last. Even the invitation to Phyllis to share a bottle of good wine tells her sombrely that she will be the last of his amours, meaning not (of course) that he will be faithful to her, but that now he is practically past it. *Non enim posthac alia calebo / femina*; if she will kindly sing to him, that will keep black Care at bay (4.11.31–6). An elderly gentleman in love is of course a touching and wistful theme, quite different from that object of disgust, an amorous old woman (4.13). Evidently, no more love poems are to be looked for. How is Horace to find a form for signing off, not only this book but his whole career as a lyric poet?

The Fourth Book has had a strong encomiastic element. But Horace has been anxious not to allow that to extinguish the other sides of his carefully burnished poetic persona. He has included erotic poems, one of which is an invitation;[35] a hymn to Apollo (4.6), complete with allusion to the *Carmen saeculare*; a poem which opens with a bow to Callimachus and discusses the poet's high sense of his own vocation (4.3); and even a final exercise in that (to him) strangely alluring form, the attack on the lecherous ageing woman— 'die Vetulaskoptik', in the fastidious phrase of modern scholars.

That poem (4.13) can be seen as standing in the same relation to *Epistles* 2, the other book on which Horace was at work at this time, as the encomiastic odes stand to the opening of *Epistles* 2.1. The theme of ageing, and of renouncing betimes the pleasures unbecoming to grey hair, recurs in *Epistle* 2.2 in a moralised form, free from any aggressive attack on any

---

[35] 4.1.32–6, 4.10, 4.11.

individual (or mention of a female), at lines 55–6, 142–3, and most memorably at 213–5:

> *lusisti* satis, edisti satis atque *bibisti*;
> tempus abire tibi est...

You have played enough, eaten enough, drunk enough; it's time for you to be gone.

Compare *Odes* 4.13.2–4:

> fis anus, et tamen
> uis formosa uideri,
> *ludisque* et *bibis* impudens...

You are growing old, yet you still want to look glamorous; you play and drink without shame.

The same material, but a different ethos; typically of the poet's skill, and of his economy, in rehandling and varying an essentially limited range.

iii

The last poem of the book opens with a witty flourish (4.15.1–4). It certainly is a surprise that a closing poem should begin with a *recusatio* in the tradition established by Virgil in his sixth *Eclogue*,[36] that of echoing the opening of Callimachus' *Aetia*: Apollo forbade me to attempt one kind of poetry and told me to stick to another kind, less massive, less apparently ambitious.

More specifically, it seems clear that certain recent passages of Propertius are in play. In 3.3 Propertius presented himself as planning to sing of Roman history in epic verse when *Phoebus* checked him, leaning on his golden *lyre*.[37] Six poems later he asked Maecenas why he was urging him to the composition of historic epic, including the career of Augustus. 'Why are you sending me out into so vast a *sea* of material? Great big *sails* are not right for my little boat.'[38] All four elements reappear in Horace's first stanza.

The true connoisseur will have heard also an echo of the opening of the *Aeneid* in line 3: '*gens inimica mihi* Tyrrhenum *nauigat* aequor' (*Aen.* 1.67,

---

[36] The word *proelia* in line 1 echoes *Eclogues* 4.1, *cum canerem reges et proelia*... Horace has both Propertius and Virgil in mind, as he takes his leave of ambitious poetry.

[37] Prop. 3.3.1–6 and 13–14.

[38] Prop. 3.9.3–4: *quid me scribendi tam uastum mittis in* aequor? / *non sunt apta meae grandia* uela *rati.*

'a people I hate is sailing over the Tyrrhenian Sea'). Horace's new coined verb *inimicat* at line 20 (*fictum uerbum est*, Porphyrio) may also contain an echo of that line. Virgil thus makes an appearance at the beginning as well as the end of this closing poem: a most notable tribute. *Furor*, too (line 17), immediately following the closing of Janus, has an echo of another early passage of the *Aeneid* (1.294–6):

> claudentur Belli portae; Furor impius intus
> saeua sedens super arma et centum uinctus aenis
> post tergum nodis fremet horridus ore cruento.

The gates of War shall be shut; wicked Madness shall sit within on the cruel weapons, his arms tied behind his back with a hundred links of bronze, and rage furiously with bloody mouth.

It is evident how closely Horace keeps to Propertius,[39] while turning the elegiac cliché in new directions. Apollo's speech of instruction is not reported but compressed to the shortest possible space; and, more wittily, the opposite of encomiastic military verse is now not the purely personal poetry of the elegist, the lover, or the scholar, but actually encomium of the Princeps — only in a different ethos and for different things: not for war, but for peace.[40]

The circle is thus squared, and what had seemed to Propertius, as it would continue to seem to Ovid, to be an irreconcilable opposition of public versus private, martial versus personal, turns out to be no opposition at all. The most Callimachean poet can praise Our Leader, in a short poem, for having established the reality of peace. And it will appear in the end that we are to continue to be mindful of the heroes of Roman history, *uirtute functos*. Most of them, a moment's reflection will remind us, will have been of the type glorified in the parade of Rome's unborn heroes in *Aeneid* 6.777–853, warriors and conquerors — though Horace does not say so, leaving that implication, as we reach the end of the poem, to resonate in the mind.

That trumps Propertius, a poet never congenial to Horace. More important, it allows Horace to speak the praise of Augustus in a way that chimes well with his own persona as a poet of private life and pleasure. There have been points in Horace's poetical production when tension has been felt between that persona, whose literary ancestor is Alcaeus, and the committed encomiast of the emperor. Thus: eastern conquest is splendid —

---

[39] F. Solmsen, 'Propertius and Horace', *Classical Philology* 43 (1948) 105–9 (= *Kleine Schriften* (Hildesheim 1968) 2.278–83); M. C. J. Putnam, *Artifices of Eternity: Studies in Horace Odes IV* (Cornell 1986) 266–70.
[40] C. Becker, *Das Spätwerk des Horaz* (Göttingen 1963) 171.

but can Iccius really be planning to sell his books and go off on a get-rich-quick military expedition to the East? He gave promise of better things! Adulterous love shames our virtuous ancestors and threatens the ruin of the state, and the penalty should be death, as it is among the Scythians; but even if you were married to a Scythian husband, Lyce, you should have had pity on me and let me in.[41] And so on.

Horace has often tried to bridge that gap by exploiting the motif of wine and vinous celebration. Wine is the hallmark of the lyric poet. The defeat of Cleopatra is the occasion for a party at which he will get as drunk as Alcaeus did at the death of Myrsilus, his personal enemy. The return home of Augustus from Spain in 24 is the occasion for a party, with old wine and a young woman. Maecenas spends too much anxious thought on the state of Rome; but all her enemies are defeated, it is time to relax, and I have a bottle of wine.[42]

In Book Four he has already tried a new variant on this trusty motif. *Odes* 4.5 has followed the ambitious Pindaric manner of 4.4 with something more personal. At the end the poem turns to the drinking theme, telling of men all over Italy drinking the health of the Princeps, the guarantor of stability and prosperity, in potations, morning and evening. Not 'I' this time, but 'we'. That will be the turn at the end of this poem, too. Every day, on holidays and ordinary days alike, we shall over our cups sing of the offspring of Venus, a title which fits both Aeneas and Augustus; our wives and children shall join in (lines 25–32). With extraordinary skill Horace has converted the regular motif of 'the poet turning away at the end of the poem to his own pleasures'[43] into one which endorses the attitudes and civic responsibilities of the collectivity, and in making the motif of 'the lyric poet as toper' into a statement of loyalty to the regime.

iv

These things cannot, of course, be achieved entirely without cost. In 4.5 we read that 'every man sees the sun go down on his own hills', and trains his own vines.[44] What, *every* man? 'This year pashmina stoles are everywhere...'. Rather a lot of people were excluded from that 'everyone': not only the *faex Romuli* (of course) in Rome, but those more poetical figures, the dispossessed

---

[41] *Odes* 1.29, 3.6, 3.24, 3.10.

[42] *Odes* 1.37, 3.14, 3.29.

[43] E.g., the endings of *Odes* 1.5, 1.6, 2.1, 2.7, 2.16, 3.14.

[44] *Odes* 4.5.29, *condit quisque diem collibus in suis.*

of the first and ninth *Eclogues*, driven out from their homes and without re-course or champion.[45] They are as invisible now, both in literature and in history, as the followers of Catiline or of the Gracchi. We might add that these country people, so obediently celebrating both in 4.5 and in 4.15, are hardly the sturdy old Republican Romans glorified in the 'Roman Odes'; rather, they are grateful subjects, happy to live an unpolitical life under a benevolent autocrat. *Non his iuuentus orta parentibus ...* [46]

In 4.15 it is a different point that Momus could find vulnerable. We are to celebrate *cum prole matronisque nostris*, with our wives and children (line 27). Now, it is not merely that we happen to know from some scurrilous gossip-monger that Horace never married. At *Odes* 3.7 he made a point of telling us so, and basing a charming poem on the fact: *Martiis caelebs quid agam Kalendis?* Why is he, though unmarried, celebrating the day of the Matronalia?[47]

As so often with this poet, it will not do to allow one poem to remain in the mind as we read another. Each poem is separate. Do they contradict each other? Very well then, they contradict each other ... But there is a price to be paid for that, too. Our acceptance of each poem is to some extent less convinced, less unconditional, because (after all) we have a continuous ex-istence and continuous memory outside them, and so the last one does not simply disappear and leave a *tabula rasa* when the poet implies that it should.[48] And Horace tempts us in just that way: he is, pre-eminently, a poet who leaves in the mind of his admirers an enduring image of himself as a familiar personality.[49]

---

[45] 'Liberty was gone, but property, respected and secure, was mounting in value': Syme (n. 2) 304.

[46] 'It was not the offspring of parents like these who defeated Hannibal' (*Odes* 3.6.33). See H.-P. Syndikus, 'Die Einheit des horazischen Lebenswerks', in *Entretiens Hardt* 39 (1993) 207–47, at 241.

[47] 'The author of the most eloquent commendations of rustic virtue and plain living was himself a bachelor of Epicurean tastes, a man of property, and an absentee landlord': Syme (n. 2) 452.

[48] A rather similar view is reached, by a different route, by D. P. Fowler, in Harrison (n. 19) 254. I do not, however, agree that 'the contradictions in the traditions which are drawn upon in Horace's works make panegyric of Augustus an impossibility' (250), or that 'a poet like Horace, in his historical situation, cannot successfully praise a dictator like Augustus' (successfully for whom?). That is to insist that a definite kind of analytical reading is the only valid one. *Contra*, perhaps with a certain naiveté, but perhaps also truer to the experience of reading, Fraenkel (n. 3) 445: 'However, considerations like these need not impair our delight in Horace's picture.'

[49] I imagine Persius had something not wholly dissimilar in mind when he wrote of Horace that he *admissus circum praecordia ludit* (*Satires* 1.117). 'Against the current critical consensus we must set the reports of so many readers over the centuries that in Horace's poems they have encountered a unique individual, even a kind of friend', admits Martindale in C. Martindale and D. Hopkins (eds.), *Horace Made New* (Cambridge 1993) 11. Cf. H. Krasser and E. A. Schmidt (eds.), *Zeitgenosse Horaz: der Dichter und seine Leser seit zwei Jahrtausenden* (Tübingen 1996).

So, Horace really wanted to tell of battles and the capture of cities, had not Phoebus intervened. Again the existence of *Epistles* 2 is relevant. Writing at just this time, the poet there informs the Princeps that it is only a sense of his inadequate powers that restrains him from transcending the humble style of his *sermones* and versifying the *res gestae* of Augustus himself: the topography of his campaigns, the rivers, the mountain strongholds, the barbarian kingdoms, and the happy conclusion of wars throughout the world: the temple of Janus closed, and Rome respected by the Parthians. But, alas, his abilities are insufficient, and a decent modesty inhibits him from tackling a task beyond his strength.[50] The Princeps was still anxiously looking for his epic encomiast. In the *Epistle* Horace was content to say, quite conventionally, that he wasn't up to it; but in this final ode of all, a most prominent position, he has found something more striking.

The heroic theme and the god's prohibition are both dispatched in less than one complete stanza. In line 4 Horace makes an abrupt turn: *tua, Caesar, aetas...* The mannerism, overriding the division of stanzas for a striking transition, is a Pindaric one, which Horace affects when composing in his highest lyric style.[51]

The phrase *tua aetas* is devised with subtlety. One spoke naturally of *nostra aetas*, 'our time'; it was also perfectly natural to speak of 'X's period'. Thus Cicero talks of *Romuli, Solonis, Alexandri, Homeri aetas*; it meant no more than 'in the days of...'. The age of Demochares, or that of Sulpicius and Cotta, could be so used as markers of time.[52] One could say *tua aetas*, meaning 'of your time, contemporary with you',[53] or *ante meam aetatem*, 'before my time'. But Horace's deft phrase conveys more than that. He has already ventured *tuae patriae* (*Odes* 4.5.5) and *tuus populus* (*Epist.* 2.1.18). This, after all, is being said to a man who has given his name to one of the months.

Tua aetas: the age belongs to Caesar, is his [Augustan] age. The flattery is delicate, because it does not depart from possible idiomatic speech, and yet it conveys something new and amazing. It is a morsel fit for the palate of an emperor; especially in a time more than usually alert to chronological and astrological nuances, which had read and remembered the fourth

---

[50] *Epist.* 2.1.250–9.
[51] E.g., Pindar, *Olympian* 8.21–2, 9.28–9, 9.84–5, *Pythian* 2.73–4, 4.138–9, 4.161–2, 4.184–5; Horace, *Odes* 1.37.12, 4.2.27–8, 4.14.9.
[52] Cicero, *Brutus* 286, 301; *TLL* 1.1136.25–50.
[53] Cicero, *Fam.* 6.6.9.

Eclogue of Virgil and meditated the meaning of the last age of the Sibyl's song: *ultima Cumaei uenit iam carminis aetas...* We are told that at Augustus' death it was actually proposed in the Senate that *saeculum Augusti* should be adopted as an official name for the period of his whole life-time.[54]

Augustus' age has restored the crops (line 5): a theme of Horace's earlier poetry is reversed.[55] At the level of common sense, that meant that it had brought the peace which allowed agriculture to flourish again, but perhaps it is right to hear also an echo of more magical, or more religious, beliefs: that with a righteous ruler the earth is more fertile. The idea was as old as the *Iliad*, as Philodemus had recently pointed out.[56] Here for the first time Horace speaks of Augustus' achievements in the perfect tense,[57] and scholars rightly point to the sequence of verbs with the restoring prefix *re-*: *rettulit, restituit, reuocauit*. All has been put right at last, and we see the meaning of *res publica restituta*, completed before our eyes.

The standards lost to the Parthians by Crassus in 53 have been got back and dedicated to 'our Iuppiter' (line 6). Elsewhere Horace had said they were restored 'to the temples' (*Epist.* 1.18.56). '*Our* Iuppiter' is bolder, more interesting. It is perhaps an echo of a memorable line of Propertius, also in his Third Book, about Cleopatra, who presumed to set the barking dog Anubis aginst our Iuppiter: *ausa* Ioui nostro *latrantem opponere Anubim* (3.11.41). Propertius says in that same book, of the standards returned by the Parthians, that they will become familiar objects to Latin Iuppiter: *assuescent* Latio *Partha tropaea* Ioui (3.4.6). Horace has studied Propertius 3 with close attention; closer, perhaps, than he would want the reader to recognise. The standards have been torn down, *derepta* (line 7), from the presumptuous Parthian shrines. As usual in Augustan propaganda, the

---

[54] Suetonius, *Aug.* 100.3 (*...et ita in fastos referretur*). It would be interesting to know whether Augustus recalled Horace's phrase when he wrote in his *Res gestae* the phrase *ad memoriam aetatis meae* (16.2); I suspect that he did not.

[55] On the ruin of agriculture, cf. *Odes* 2.15, 2.18.26–40, and the end of Virgil, *Georgic* 1. Its restoration has been praised at 4.5.17–18, and fertility of vegetation is a great theme of *Odes* 4: 2.53–60, 3.10–11, 4.13–14, 6.38–40, 7.11, 11.1–5, 12.9–10, 14.27–8; *cf.* also the end of *Epistles* 1.12, and Vell. Pat. 2.89.4.

[56] Homer, *Iliad* 16.384–8; Philodemus, *On the Good King According to Homer* (ed. Dorandi 1982). Galinsky (n. 33) 119, points out the relevance for Horace of that, and of passages in which Cicero implies that in his exile the fields of Rome were barren (*Red. Sen.* 34, *Red. Quir.* 19, *Mecum etiam frugum ubertas... afuit*).

[57] M. Lowrie, *Horace's Narrative Odes* (Oxford 1997) 344.

prosaic reality of successful pressure is camouflaged as something more heroic.[58]

But war in the East is only hinted at, and Horace goes on at once to proclaim Rome at peace.[59] The great sentence runs on to the centre of the poem (line 16).[60] It lists the greatest achievements of the Princeps in the various spheres. Uppermost is the bringing of peace, but what goes with it is no less emphasised: moral reformation. Vice has been reined in, crime removed, and the *artes* recalled which made Rome great. It need hardly be said that they are not the fine arts, but the rigour of moral self-command and military discipline which Anchises commends to Aeneas at a climactic moment of the *Aeneid*: *hae tibi erunt artes.* Horace uses the verb *reuocare* in line 12; Augustus himself uses *reducere* in the same context in the *Res gestae*.[61] We see how close Horace — the Horace of *Odes* 3.6 and 3.24 — is here to the imperial thinking. He arranges a neat crescendo, which reflects the order of Rome's growth: first Latium, then Italy, then the whole world. It culminates in the grandiose rhetoric, ancient already when it was adopted by the Great Kings of Persia, of an empire on which the sun never sets.[62]

The second long period, and the second half of the poem, opens immediately with Augustus: while he is in charge of the world, our *otium* is safe. *Custos* (line 17) is a useful word. Essentially unofficial, it was sometimes used quasi-officially: a loyal decree of the decurions of Pisa in AD 4 described Augustus as *custos imperi Romani* and protector of the whole

---

[58] Cf. *Res gestae* 29.2, and the central scene on the cuirass of the Prima Porta statue of Augustus: the Parthian on his knees. 'In the East, prestige was his object, diplomacy his method... the threat of force was enough': Syme (n. 2) 388. 'In the East generally Augustus affected war but practiced diplomacy': E. Gruen, in Raaflaub and Toher (n. 24) 397.

[59] *Ianus Quirinus* seems to have been the the god's official title in this temple (*cf.* Heinze ad loc.), and Passerat in consequence conjectured *Ianum Quirinum* at line 9; but the poet prefers to avoid the *kurion onoma* in favour of something more exquisite. This short poem contains three words which appear to be Horace's own coinages, *apprecati, inimicat, remixti*; and another, *aeternare*, which is 'preternaturally rare' (Bowersock, in Raaflaub and Toher (n. 24) 389). *Edicta Iulia*, too, for *leges Iuliae*, is very choice.

[60] I think it probable that Horace thought of his poem as falling into two long periods, each exactly half the length of the whole: punctuate lightly, with a colon after *darem* in line 4, and colons, not full stops, after lines 20 and 24.

[61] *Aeneid* 4.852; *Res gestae* 8.5, *multa exempla maiorum exolescentia iam ex nostro saeculo reduxi.*

[62] Cf. Fraenkel (n. 3) 451 and n. 4: 'A claim in which from time immemorial the masters of one great empire after another seem to have rejoiced, and which never lost the mark of its origin in oriental magniloquence.' He traces it back to Lugal-zagassi, conqueror of Sumer in the early third millennium BC.

world.[63] Cicero, writing anxiously to his choleric brother, had used it of a good provincial governor; Horace uses it of Iuppiter, *gentis humanae pater atque custos*.[64] It had the poetical and emotional resonance of a celebrated passage of Ennius, on the death of Romulus:[65]

> o Romule, Romule die,
> qualem te patriae *custodem* di genuerunt!

> O Romulus, Romulus, what a guardian for our country the gods created in you!

The theme of security under the emperor is one to which Horace responds with warmth. In *Odes* 3.14 he evoked the memory of the bad old days, the Social War and the war with Spartacus, observing in comfortable contrast, 'I shall have no fear of death from riot or from violence, so long as Caesar rules the world': *ego nec tumultum / nec mori per uim metuam, tenente / Caesare terras*. It receives full statement at 4.5.25–8: who can fear the Parthian or the gelid Scyth, the shaggy scions of Germany or war with fierce Iberia, as long as Caesar is safe and sound?

We recognise the slight but cunning adaptation which this master of the deft adjustment has made to one of his favourite themes, seamlessly combining Epicurean self-indulgence with panegyric of a victorious leader.[66] Stop worrying about the warlike barbarians; they are safely on the other side of the Adriatic. Why not stretch out in the shade, have a few drinks, and send for a pretty girl? Stop worrying about questions of policy: the Dacians have collapsed, the Orientals are fighting each other, Spain and Scythia offer no danger; enjoy the moment and my good wine! And I could not care less about Tiridates—all I care for is poetry.[67]

In book 4 the motif, hitherto predominantly Epicurean, wears a more respectably patriotic and encomiastic look. Lines 21–4 list some of the vanquished peoples from whom we need fear no ill; that had just been done in 4.14, too (41–52). In 4.15 we find a reassuring litany of negatives: not

---

[63] *ILS* 140.7–9: *Augusti patris patriae pontif. maxsumi custodis imperi Romani totiusque orbis terrarum praesi[dis]. Cf.* the *feriale Cumanum* (A. Degrassi, *Inscriptiones Italiae* xiii.2 (Rome 1963) 278–80) on a public holiday between 16 January and 6 March, possibly 30 January, dedication day of the Ara Pacis: *supplicatio imperio Caesaris Augusti custo[dis . . .]*.

[64] Cicero, *Q Fr.* 1.1.9, *cum urbs custodem non tyrannum . . . recepisse uideatur*; *Odes* 1.12.49.

[65] *Annales* 106–7Sk, with Skutsch's note.

[66] D. P. Fowler, in Harrison (n. 19) 258, does not allow for the possibility that sufficient skill on the poet's part can make such strategies succeed; he insists that 'we cannot praise a ruler, because we can't (as Epicureans) admire one.' But that is an unduly Puritanical demand to make, both on poet and on reader. If such a life is, for the Epicurean, good, and Augustus guarantees it, then to withhold recognition from him on dogmatic grounds is self-defeating.

[67] *Odes* 3.11, 3.8, 1.26; so too 3.29.

furor, not violence, not anger; not Dacians, not Getae, not Parthians: emphatically, Caesar has everything under control. So much so, in fact, that the most exotic barbarians will scrupulously observe the laws of Rome (lines 21–2) — or, more specifically, the pronouncements of Augustus, *edicta Iulia*.

The whole world is imagined as under Roman control,[68] and Augustus can lay down the law like a magistrate entering office. *Leges Iuliae* would presumably have suggested specifically those that already existed under that title; *edicta Iulia*, a stranger phrase, and welcome on that account, was perhaps less limited in its scope, more flattering to an autocrat whose will was, in fact, often expressed without reference to law-making procedures.[69] Most prominent among actual legislation, no doubt, in the light of lines 9–11, is the *lex Iulia* of 18 BC laying down rules for marriage. There is indeed an implication, too *outré* to be fully spelled out, that as we cluster our wives and children about us (line 27), so the barbarians, too, will all live model bourgeois lives. The Empire of Augustus will anticipate that of Queen Victoria.

From the outside and the absence of causes for anxiety we turn (line 25) to the inside and the occasions for rejoicing. Day by day our whole families shall pray to the gods, drink and pour libations, and sing of the great Romans of old.[70] A striking contrast with the last poem of book 1 and its Epicurean vision of the poet sipping his wine in solitary enjoyment (1.38): not *ego* but *nos*.[71] In the contemporary *Epistle to Augustus* Horace imagines the simple festivals of Italian rustics in days gone by. The farmer feasted with his wife and children, and Fescennine songs were sung: gibes at individuals, but innocent and good-humoured, until with the passage of time the satire became vicious and had to be repressed; and the verses, in that age before Greek refinement, were stylistically very crude (*Epist.* 2.1.139–63). That was all very well in a hexameter poem, its stylistic level only medium; but

---

[68] Cf. *Epist.* 2.1.254, *totum confecta duella per orbem*; Virgil, *Aeneid* 1.278–90 (the prophecy of Iuppiter), 8.722–8 (a conquered world queues to pay tribute); La Penna (n. 15) 68–9; P. A. Brunt, *Journal of Roman Studies* 53 (1963) 170. Syme (*History in Ovid* (Oxford 1978) 203) speaks of our present passage as 'forced or frivolous hyperbole', with some justice; but what, in that case, are we to call a passage like *Aeneid* 6.791–7, where Augustus will conquer regions which lie beyond the zodiac?

[69] We find an *edictum imp. Caesaris Augusti* on the water supply of Venafrum, *CIL* x.4842; cf. *CIL* v.5050 on the status of the Anauni, from the reign of Claudius.

[70] *Cf.* Cicero, *In Catilinam* 3.23: *celebratote illos dies cum coniugibus ac liberis uestris.*

[71] The frequent pattern in the *Odes* of ending with a turn by the poet to 'me' is discussed by D. Essen, *Untersuchungen zu den Odenschlüssen bei Horaz* (*Beiträge zur klassischen Philologie* 77, Meisenheim 1976) ch. 1: 'Der Ich-Schluss'. She has little to say about the end of 4.15, however.

here, in an ode, and at the very end of Horace's production in that kind, something more elevated, more elevating, was in place.

In the last stanza, though, we confront a problem. Do the words *more patrum* go with *uirtute functos* — we shall sing of leaders who exhibited moral excellence in the manner of the ancestors; or do they go with *canemus* — we shall sing in the manner of the ancestors about leaders who exhibited moral excellence?[72] The latter view seems to bring in the doctrine of Varro about the old-time heroic songs which the elder Cato alleged were sung at dinner in Italy, long before his own period.[73] To revive them would have been a hopeless dream: the songs, if they ever existed, had vanished without trace. 'Die Menschen fehlten, die Lieder fehlten.'[74]

The order of words, it must be said, favours the first reading. It has been suggested that the gap between the words *more patrum* and the verb *canemus* finds a parallel in the *Carmen saeculare*:[75]

> cui per ardentem *sine fraude* Troiam
> castus Aeneas patriae superstes
> liberum *muniuit* iter, daturus
> > plura relictis;

> Those for whom the virtuous Aeneas, surviving his country but without fault, built a path from burning Troy to freedom, to give them more than they had left behind.

But a vital difference surely is that in this passage the words make nonsense if taken with *ardentem Troiam*, whereas at line 29 of our poem *uirtute functos more patrum duces* makes perfect sense, and the reader has no warning that the phrase is really hanging in the air for another three lines before it finds its verb.

---

[72] The latter is the view of H. Dahlmann, 'Die letzte Ode des Horaz', *Gymnasium* 65 (1968) 340–55, and 'Zur Überlieferung über die "altrömischen Tafellieder"', *Kleine Schriften* (Hildesheim 1970) 23–34; Becker (n. 40) 174; Murray (n. 30) 91–2; A. D. Momigliano, 'Perizonius, Niebuhr and the character of early Roman tradition', *Journal of Roman Studies* 47 (1957) 110 and n. 40) is notably non-committal. *Contra*, R. D. Williams, 'The pictures on Dido's Temple (*Aeneid* i.450–93)', *Classical Quarterly* 10 (1960) 6; H.-P. Syndikus, *Die Lyrik des Horaz: eine Interpretation der Oden* (Darmstadt 1972–1973), ad loc. Putnam (n. 39) 271, ingeniously suggests that *more patrum* goes with both phrases; it is hard to believe that a reader uninformed of the existence of this scholarly debate would possibly think that.

[73] Cicero, *Brutus* 75. I. Du Quesnay, in Harrison (n. 19) 184–5, argues that 4.5 was composed to be performed by a chorus as part of the celebrations of Augustus' return to Rome.

[74] Dahlmann (1968) (n. 72) 347. Heinze's surprising reply to the point is that these songs are yet to be written, and that Horace 'with his last words sets a new and worthy subject to the poets of Rome'.

[75] *Carm. saec.* 41–4; Becker (n. 40) 174 n. 15.

That said, the ode also makes far better sense if the poetry in question here is not some antiquarian reconstruction which may possibly come into existence but, on the contrary, the great poems of its own time. Surely it is natural to think of the sort of ode which Horace has just exemplified in 4.4 and 4.14, on Romans of our own day, the equals of the heroes of the Roman past, the stepsons of the Princeps; and also, in first place, of the object of Horace's admiration, the epic of national patriotism, the *Aeneid* of his dear friend Virgil.[76] We are in the realm of fantasy, as we were at the end of 4.5, with every man seeing the sun set over his own vine-clad hills. In that realm, we shall all be singing songs which resemble *Odes* 4.4 and 4.14, and, above all, the *Aeneid*. So there is nothing to suggest those Varronian *carmina*, and the *Odes* close, as they began (1.2 and 3), with Augustus and Virgil.

Venus opened the book, appearing in 4.1.1 in her cruel guise, *saeua*; she closes it as Venus the kindly, *alma*, the motherly origin of her race. Her offspring, as Troy and Anchises have just been mentioned, must primarily suggest the *Aeneid* and Aeneas; but the language allows, or encourages, the reader also to think of that scion of the Julian house, Augustus.[77]

The poem closely relates to the programme of Augustus. That can be worked out in detail: compare lines 6–8 with *Res gestae* 29.2, lines 8–9 with *RG* 13, line 12 with *RG* 8.5, lines 21–4 with *RG* 26.4, 29.2 and 31.1. It is close too to the *Carmen saeculare*: compare lines 13–16 with *CS* 17–20, lines 21–4 with *CS* 53–6, lines 31–2 with *CS* 50. The poem is also easily brought into relation with the visual propaganda of the time of its production, especially the Ara Pacis Augustae.[78] *Felix opportunitate mortis*, Horace did not live to see the souring of the hopes of that period and the dark ending of Augustus' reign, with Ovid in exile, the two Julias disgraced, and a disappointed Princeps bereft of his intended heirs and forced to fall back on a resentful and unpopular Tiberius.

---

[76] The end of the poem is 'eine feine Reverenz, wohl auch vor Augustus, mehr aber vor dem verstorben Freunde Vergil': so, rightly, Doblhofer (n. 9) 105. That the ode itself was intended to be sung as part of the celebrations at Augustus' return to Rome, is argued by Du Quesnay in Harrison (n. 19) 184.

[77] At *Carm. saec.* 50, *clarus Anchisae Venerisque sanguis* means 'the Romans'; but some will have felt a second sense, 'Augustus'.

[78] J. M. Benario, 'The Fourth Book of Horace's *Odes*: Augustan propaganda', *Transactions of the American Philological Association* 91 (1960) 339–52; Putnam (n. 39) 327–38; Bowersock (n. 33) 388–91; Galinsky (n. 33) 260–1.

V

What, finally, of the poem? There are those who dislike it. 'My flesh crawls whenever I read *Odes* 4.15,' writes M. Lowrie, 'with its statement that the public has taken over the role of aesthetics in Augustan Rome.' The point is that 'the public sphere edges out the personal', and that in consequence there is 'no room for the independent artist'.[79] Ellen Oliensis similarly finds that

> The pointed contrast between *me* at line 1 and *tua* at line 4 effectively casts the emperor himself as the alternative poet ... to whose superior merits the poet here modestly defers. The fourth book of the odes concludes, accordingly, with *edicta Iulia*, not Horace's poetic *dicta*. What is completed here is the labor of the imperial artist, who has closed his text (*clausit*, 9), curbed its excesses (*frena licentiae iniecit*, 10–11), and edited out its faults (*emouitque culpas*, 11)...

Thus Horace ends the Book 'with an act of self-obliteration that leaves Caesar in sole possession of the poem.... The emperor usurps the place of the poet, and the empire overwhelms the poem...'. It is an 'ultimate extinction of authorial identity'.[80]

''Twere to consider too curiously to consider so' — or too romantically, as Horatio might have said. The language used of Augustus does not really suggest that what he is doing is working on a text. What he closes is the temple of Janus, which has doors and can, notoriously and significantly, be shut.[81] The Fourth Book of the *Odes* concludes not with the Julian edicts but with festivals of song inspired by the mighty poem of Virgil. To insist that 'the public sphere edges out the personal' is, as the bizarre boldness of the image itself perhaps suggests, a highly Romantic notion, which denies what Horace asserts: the possibility that the two can be one, that public events can be the subject of genuine emotions, and that the artist does not inevitably lose his independence when he makes himself the spokesman of those emotions.

We live, especially in the English-speaking world, in a late Romantic period, and such Romantic ideas are natural to us. In Germany quite different ideas are natural. 'A worthy closing poem', says E. Lefèvre, quoting Dahlmann on the poem's 'monumental simplicity' and 'majestic greatness'.[82]

---

[79] Lowrie (n. 57), quotations from 351, 349, 350.

[80] E. Oliensis, *Horace and the Rhetoric of Authority* (Cambridge 1998) 151–2.

[81] *Res gestae* 13: *Ianum Quirinum, quem* claussum *esse maiores nostri uoluerunt ... ter me principe senatus* claudendum *esse censuit.*

[82] E. Lefèvre, *Horaz, Dichter im augusteischen Rom* (Munich 1993) 291.

Horace proclaims the opposite of the late-Romantic consensus of the Anglo-Saxons. At certain moments the artist can have a part to play, and a vital one, in helping the community to find its own highest potential and achieve greatness. 'Learn from me what you are, and live it,' said Pindar to his patron, a Sicilian tyrant.[83] Let me show you what you can potentially be, and live up to it! The visual arts were hard at work in Rome, transforming the city and working out the plans of the Princeps.[84] There was a time when we greatly admired the Augustan poets but were cool about the architects and sculptors of Augustus' Rome (not truly classical, not Greek). Now the visual artists have come back into their own; but we begin to find the poets more difficult to accept.

Odes 4.5 is 'Horace's most fascist poem', says Fowler,[85] leaving it unclear how many other *Odes* must be similarly condemned by the politically fastidious. Perhaps we should be less prompt to condemn the artists of the past for differing from our own proudly held opinions. Perhaps we should not refuse to admit what are, after all, evident facts. Great art has often been produced in response to pressures partly external in origin, to which the artist's own mind responded with a degree of enthusiasm or of ambivalence which we cannot hope to control; and there have been moments when the artist was not exclusively concerned with his own independence and his own integrity, but was willing to find and to play a public role in his society.

This chapter was written in the Elysian surroundings of the Institute for Advanced Study at Princeton. *Beatus ille qui procul negotiis...*

---

[83] Pindar, *Pythian* 2.72, γένοι' οἷος ἐσσὶ μαθών: not an easy phrase to translate into English, or any other language.

[84] P. Zanker, *The Power of Images in Augustan Rome* (Ann Arbor 1988).

[85] D. P. Fowler, in Harrison (n. 19) 258.

14
Another look at Virgil's Ganymede

Philip Hardie

> ipsis praecipuos ductoribus addit honores:
> uictori chlamydem auratam, quam plurima circum
> purpura maeandro duplici Meliboea cucurrit,
> intextusque puer frondosa regius Ida
> uelocis iaculo ceruos cursuque fatigat
> acer, anhelanti similis, quem praepes ab Ida
> sublimem pedibus rapuit Iouis armiger uncis;
> longaeui palmas nequiquam ad sidera tendunt
> custodes, saeuitque canum latratus in auras.
>
> *Aeneid* 5.249–57

In addition the captains were singled out for special honours. The victor received a cloak embroidered with gold round which there ran a broad double meander of Meliboean purple, and woven into it was the royal prince running with his javelin and wearying the swift stags on the leafy slopes of Mount Ida. There he was, eager and breathless, so it seemed, and down from Ida plunged the bird that carries the thunderbolt of Jupiter and carried him off in its hooked talons high into the heavens while the old men who were there as his guards stretched their hands in vain towards the stars and the dogs barked furiously up into the air.[1]

i

The twentieth century was marked by an accelerating intensity of critical attention to Virgil, triggered initially by a revaluation of the merits of Latin literature in comparison to its Greek models, and subsequently fuelled by an often heated debate over the political tendencies of the Virgilian poems,

---

[1] Translations of longer passages from the *Aeneid* are taken from David West's translation (Harmondsworth 1990).

revealing the continuing power of these texts to reflect on and themselves to be coloured by the politics of the reader's own age. The poems also proved ideal subjects for close readings of various kinds: highly wrought urns that rewarded New Critical readings for imagistic and thematic structures, and gratifyingly full of ambivalence and ambiguity, but also the densely laboured works of a scholar-poet in the Alexandrian tradition, packed with cunning references to the whole range of Greco-Roman cultural and textual traditions, to be read for their allusivity and (latterly) intertextuality.

This chapter takes a short passage of the *Aeneid*, what might appear little more than a vignette, and offers a reading both intensive in its detailed teasing out of the text, and extensive in the networks of allusion and meaning in which this passage is caught. The footnotes reveal my debts to a wide range of the scholarship and criticism of the last century. In particular I draw on some of the reader-response approaches which developed in the later part of that century and which continue to generate new perspectives, with attention especially to the interpretation of ecphrasis and to the phenomenon of the 'reader in the text'.

In recent years much attention has been paid to the narrative and rhetorical device of ecphrasis, the verbal 'description' of something seen, and more specifically the literary description of a visual work of art. Once regarded as an adventitious ornament bolted on to a narrative text, ecphrasis is now privileged by critics and theorists as the place where texts, through an evocation of the non-textual, come to a sharp self-awareness of the conditions of their own production and reception. The paradoxical use of words to conjure up before the reader's eyes the vision of a painting or statue is an extreme example of the text's ambition of using linguistic signs to create the illusion of a world that exists prior to and independent of texts. On the other hand the description of a work of art, as opposed to any other kind of visual object, offers the possibility of an analogy between the linguistic and the visual artefact. Framed within the text, and often the object of attention of viewers and interpreters within the text, the ecphrasis functions as a *mise en abyme* of the text itself; the demand for response and interpretation that an ecphrastic work of art places on internal viewers is continuous with the call to the reader to interpret — in the first instance to interpret the ecphrasis itself (does the reader share, fall short of, or rise superior to the perspectives and interpretative powers of the characters?), and beyond that to interpret the textual object as a whole.[2]

---

[2] See B. W. Boyd, '*Non enarrabile textum*: ecphrastic trespass and narrative ambiguity in the *Aeneid*', *Vergilius* 41 (1995) 71–90, at 74–6, on the authority of interpretation and on the 'explicit multiplicity of viewers/readers/audiences' for an ecphrasis as 'a model for reading and interpreting

Ecphrasis originates in epic. Virgil, in keeping with his project of becoming the Roman Homer, includes six ecphrases in the *Aeneid*. The largest, the Shield of Aeneas (*Aen.* 8.625–731), modelled on the great ancestor of all ancient ecphrases, the Iliadic Shield of Achilles, is the vehicle for the grandest prophetic vision of Rome's epic future. Near the beginning of the poem scenes of the Trojan War viewed by Aeneas in the temple of Juno in Carthage (*Aen.* 1.455–93) call up for the hero his epic past, and for the reader the epic tradition that precedes Virgil's own essay in that tradition. Liminal in other ways are the scenes sculpted by Daedalus on the doors of the Temple of Apollo at Cumae (*Aen.* 6.20–33), viewed by Aeneas when he first arrives in the Bay of Naples at the beginning of the book which will lead him into the Underworld and to a vision of a parade of future Roman heroes. The fact that the Sibyl calls the hero away from gazing at the sculptures to more urgent business merely provokes the reader to pry more deeply into the significance for Aeneas' story of Daedalus' uncompleted masterwork. Briefer are the descriptions of two other pieces of armour: the Shield of Turnus (*Aen.* 7.789–92), with an image of Io's metamorphosis into a cow, both memorialising the Argive origins of Turnus' family, and suggestive of the figurative bestialisation of Turnus by the Fury Allecto earlier in the book; and the sword-belt of Pallas, chased with the Danaids' slaughter on their wedding night of their bridegrooms, the sons of Aegyptus (*Aen.* 10.496–9). This is an object fraught with significance, for it is the sight of the sword-belt worn by Turnus, the killer of Pallas, that precipitates Aeneas' rage against his enemy and thus brings the *Aeneid* to its swift close. Recent critics have elaborated on the relevance of the mythological scene on the sword-belt for its bearers and their fates.

The sixth formal ecphrasis in the poem is our passage. Both by its location within the narrative and by the subject-matter of the artwork described, it seems a more casual ornament of the text, and has correspondingly exerted less pressure on modern readers to interpret. As first prize in the ship-race, the first of the contests at the games in Sicily celebrating the anniversary of Anchises' death, Aeneas awards Cloanthus a *chlamys* (a Greek cloak) on which are woven two, it would seem, scenes from the story of Ganymede: firstly, the young Trojan prince hunting deer on Mount Ida; and secondly the rape of Ganymede by Jupiter's eagle, his dis-

---

the *Aeneid* on a larger scale'. The bibliography on ecphrasis expands rapidly: for an excellent introduction both in general and to ancient ecphrasis in particular, with extensive bibliography, see D. Fowler, 'Narrate and describe: the problem of ekphrasis', in *Roman Constructions: Readings in Postmodern Latin* (Oxford 2000) 64–85.

appearance skyward watched by his distraught guardians, stretching up their hands in vain, and by his dogs, barking at thin air.

Richard Heinze, in many ways the father of modern Virgilian criticism, thought that this ecphrasis had a general relevance to the content of the framing narrative, as being 'a famous scene from the earlier history of Troy', but that otherwise, and in contrast to the poem's other ecphrases, its purpose was merely to create a vivid visual effect.[3] Only recently has a sustained attempt been made to find meaning in the Ganymede ecphrasis, in Michael Putnam's *Virgil's Epic Designs*, a subtle and insightful study of all the ecphrases in the poem.[4]

Putnam's reading is my own immediate provocation to reinterpret this scene, but I shall try to show that the wider context of *Aeneid* 5 offers further stimuli to the work of interpretation. The reader trying to make sense of the ecphrasis replicates the attempts of Aeneas to understand things that he sees through a glass darkly. Putnam in his interpretation lays emphasis on elements that are suppressed in this description of the Ganymede story: Jupiter's erotic delight in his human prey, and the triumphant elevation of the boy to immortality on Olympus.[5] But that which is suppressed is hidden, not annihilated. The gaps in this version of Ganymede invite supplementation from those who know the rest of the story, and this work of supplementation may then tempt the reader beyond the narrow frame of the (complete) myth of Ganymede into wider structures of significance.

ii

Putnam focuses his reading on the 'earthbound dissatisfaction' (57) and loss portrayed in the scenes, foreshadowing the series of youths dead before their time in the rest of the poem. The wider meaning of the *chlamys* is thus comparable to a now standard reading of the sword-belt of Pallas, whose scene of the slaughter of the sons of Aegyptus by the Danaids on their wedding night ominously foreshadows the premature death, *acerba mors*, suffered by the belt's wearers, first Pallas and then Turnus. Putnam shares

---

[3] R. Heinze, *Virgils epische Technik* (3rd ed., Leipzig and Berlin 1915) 400 (= *Virgil's Epic Technique* (trans. H. and D. Harvey and F. Robertson, Bristol 1993) 313).

[4] M. C. J. Putnam, *Virgil's Epic Designs: Ekphrasis in the Aeneid* (New Haven and London 1998) ch. 2 (revised version of *American Journal of Philology* 116 (1995) 419–40).

[5] See esp. Putnam (n. 4) 60. Of the two post-Virgilian reworkings of the ecphrasis, Stat. *Theb.* 1.548–51 also omits mention of Ganymede's celestial destination, while Val. Flacc. *Argon.* 2.409–17 shows us the boy as the happy cupbearer of Jupiter.

this perspective on the rape of Ganymede with the onlookers depicted within the work of art itself, the aged guardians who stretch their hands skyward in vain, *nequiquam*, and the hunting dogs, baying impotently after the vanishing eagle and its prey.

The reaction of the *longauei custodes* is described with a pathos, typical of many Virgilian scenes of loss or futility, that enlists the reader's sympathy. *Nequiquam* is a favourite Virgilian adverb, used for example in the final disappearance of Eurydice in *Georgics* 4, a passage that bears other verbal similarities (emphasised) to the rape of Ganymede (*Geo.* 4.497–502):[6]

> 'iamque uale: feror ingenti circumdata nocte
> inualidasque tibi *tendens,* heu non tua, *palmas.*'[7]
> dixit et ex oculis subito, ceu fumus *in auras*
> commixtus tenuis, fugit diuersa, neque illum
> prensantem *nequiquam* umbras et multa uolentem
> dicere praeterea uidit.[8]

'And now farewell; I am carried off, wrapped in vast night and stretching out to you my feeble hands, alas no longer yours.' So she spoke, and suddenly, like smoke mingling into thin air, she fled from his sight in the opposite direction; nor did she see him grasping at the shadows in vain, wanting to say many more things.

But the educated Augustan reader's perspective cannot simply coincide with that of the *longaeui custodes.* As viewers within an ecphrasis the latter are very different, for example, from the Augustus portrayed on the Shield of Aeneas 'reviewing', or 'recognising', the gifts of the nations of the earth, (8.721 *dona recognoscit populorum*), 'both the central figure on and the ideal spectator of the shield',[9] the perfectly informed viewer of the political artefact of which he himself is the maker. Virgil's reader knows that Ganymede is not an example of a youth taken tragically before his time. We know that he is elevated to heaven, to become the perpetually young cupbearer of Jupiter. It is only from the limited perspective of those present

---

[6] The parallel is noted by Putnam (n. 4) 67.

[7] Putnam (n. 4) 65 points acutely to the echo in 5.256 of 233, *ni palmas ponto tendens utrasque Cloanthus*, but sees a contrast between the 'world of game-playing', where 'ordinary animal sacrifice brings the goodwill of the gods', and the 'human victimization and loss' brought by victory in 'the larger sphere of the realities of epic endeavor'.

[8] The first subject of Ovid's Song of Orpheus is the Rape of Ganymede (*Met.* 10.155–61), snatched from earth to heaven, an inverted parallel to Orpheus' initial success in bringing Eurydice from one world-division, the underworld, to another, earth, and a contrast to Orpheus' final inability to secure the lasting presence of his beloved.

[9] A. Barchiesi, 'Virgilian narrative: ecphrasis', in C. Martindale (ed.), *The Cambridge Companion to Virgil* (Cambridge 1997) 271–81, at 276.

on earth at the time that the boy seems to have become the hapless prey of a marauding eagle, like the Trojan Lycus caught by Turnus in the simile at 9.563–4: 'like the eagle, the armour-bearer of Jupiter, seizing in his hooked talons a hare or the white body of a swan and soaring into the air with it' (*qualis ubi aut leporem aut candenti corpore cycnum / sustulit alta petens pedibus Iouis armiger uncis*); it is only from their perspective that Ganymede seems to fit the tragic paradigm of the hunter hunted.[10]

Putnam's error lies in his one-sided assessment of a defining characteristic of the figure of Ganymede in the ecphrasis. As Putnam says, the *puer* is engaged in hunting, 'a youthful pursuit that in an adolescent's ordinary experience would lead to the responsibilities of manhood'.[11] This is all the more striking, given that Ganymede is rarely represented as a hunter.[12] The risky passage from boyhood to adulthood is a central theme of the *Aeneid*, and the failure successfully to achieve that transition results in all those tragic deaths of young men (and a young woman, the *uenatrix* 'huntress' Camilla who fails to survive as *bellatrix* 'warrior woman'), that have so haunted modern Virgilian criticism. The importance of hunting as an activity preparatory for manhood, achieved through the transition from *uenator* to *bellator*, is focused above all in *Aeneid* 9, in the figures of Nisus and Euryalus, and Ascanius. Virgil's use of hunting in narratives of the passage from boyhood to adulthood is reminiscent of the symbolic structures of the Greek *ephebeia*, in which hunting and night are associated with the passage of the adolescent to the status of male hoplite, structures that are explored and tested in Attic tragedy, a genre on which Virgil draws extensively in his epic poem.[13]

---

[10] So Putnam (n. 4) 56, comparing also, 221 n. 3, *Aen.* 11.751–6, the simile of an eagle snatching up a snake. The unenlightened guardians of Ganymede might feel a community of loss with Acoetes, the aged companion of Pallas who accompanies his funeral procession in *Aen.* 11 (30, 85).

[11] Putnam (n. 4) 58.

[12] See E. K. Gazda, 'A marble group of Ganymede and the eagle from the age of Augustine', in J. H. Humphrey (ed.), *Excavations at Carthage 1977 conducted by the University of Michigan* 6 (Ann Arbor 1981) 125–78, at 174 n. 91; P. Friedlaender, *RE* 7.1, 741. Ganymede more commonly is a shepherd, and it is from the still recognisably pastoral landscape of 'leafy Ida' that Virgil's hunting boy is snatched. The juxtaposition of royalty and pastoral setting in *frondosa regius Ida* may be paralleled in the phrase *purpura Meliboea*, a Lucretian collocation (*De rer. nat.* 2.500–1) referring to the Thessalian town Meliboea, but in its Virgilian use possibly punning on Meliboeus, the name of the dispossessed herdsman in *Eclogue* 1. This then is a 'bucolic purple'; for a comparable effect see the riddle at *Ecl.* 3.106–7, flowers inscribed with the names of kings. Ganymede like Meliboeus is removed from a pastoral landscape. The *Aeneid* repeats the first *Eclogue's* tale of forcible expulsion from home into exile, but replaces Meliboeus' prospect of exile to the ends of the earth with a kind of 'homecoming' to Italy. Ganymede's fate is closer to that of Daphnis in *Eclogue* 5, seemingly lost through death to the pastoral world, but elevated to Olympus.

[13] See P. Hardie, *Virgil Aeneid. Book IX* (Cambridge 1994) 15–16; id., 'Virgil and tragedy', in Martindale (n. 9) 312–26, at 320–1.

Nisus and Euryalus are examples of young men or boys who do not survive to manhood, hunters who are themselves hunted down and killed. There are indeed points of contact between Ganymede and Nisus and Euryalus. As Alessandro Barchiesi points out, 'the eroticism of the story of Jupiter and Ganymede prompts an association with the main love story of the poem, that of Nisus and Euryalus (5.294 ff., a few lines after the ecphrasis).'[14] Furthermore Nisus' mother Ida (9.177) shares her name with the mountain on which Ganymede is raped (5.252, 254).

On the other hand, in *Aeneid* 9 Ascanius, in contrast to Nisus and Euryalus, succeeds in his first use of his hunting bow to kill a man in war, and lives to tell the tale. As a *regius puer* ('royal boy', 5.252) Ganymede is more like Ascanius than he is like Nisus and Euryalus; the collocation *regius puer* is used of Ascanius at 1.677–8;[15] and in the previous book we had seen Ascanius exulting in the hunt (4.156–9). The erotic content of the story of Ganymede has relevance for Ascanius, as well as for Nisus and Euryalus: Ascanius is given a highly eroticised charge in the passage already alluded to at *Aeneid* 1.677–94, where the *regius puer* is Venus' 'greatest care' (*maxima cura*), and is the victim of a kind of temporary rape, lifted up to the heights of the Idalian grove, to be supplanted on earth by Cupid himself in the likeness of Ascanius. The use of *cura* here is at home in the language of love poetry, as also at 10.132, in another eroticised image of Ascanius, 'justly Venus' greatest care' (*Veneris iustissima cura*), his gem-like beauty blazing amidst the turmoil of war.[16]

Like Ganymede, Ascanius has a celestial destination. After he has killed Numanus Remulus, Apollo promises him at 9.641–2: 'This is the way that leads to the stars. You are born of the gods and will live to be the father of gods' (*sic itur ad astra, / dis genite et geniture deos*). Ascanius' skyward journey is figurative and prospective, looking forward to the distant elevation of Roman kings and emperors to the heavens, an elevation that will be foreshadowed in the more immediate future in the deification of Ascanius' father, as promised to Venus by Jupiter at Aeneid 1.259–60: 'You will take greathearted Aeneas up to the stars of heaven' (*sublimemque feres ad sidera caeli / magnanimum Aenean*), as the eagle snatches up Ganymede *sublimem* in the

---

[14] Barchiesi (n. 9) 280.

[15] At 5.296–7 the elements of the phrase *regius puer* are distributed over two doomed boys: *Nisus amore pio* pueri; *quos deinde secutus* / regius *egregia Priami de stirpe Diores*. The boy Diores is killed by Turnus at 12.509 ff.

[16] S. J. Harrison, *Vergil Aeneid 10* (Oxford 1991), on *Aen.* 10.132: '*iustissima* indicates the doubly appropriate nature of Venus' care for Ascanius: he is both her grandson and a good-looking boy.'

ecphrasis (5.255).[17] In this passage Jupiter 'remembers' the promise that he had made to Mars concerning the apotheosis of Romulus in Ennius' *Annals*, 54–5 Skutsch, 'There will be one man whom you will raise to the blue spaces of the heavens' (*unus erit quem tu tolles in caerula caeli / templa*). The stars to which Ganymede's guardians stretch their hands suggest the celestial destination of Ganymede, and may even hint at the version in which Ganymede undergoes catasterism into the constellation Aquarius.[18]

Ascanius' success in *Aeneid* 9 also has an element in common with the success of the recipient of the Ganymede *chlamys*, Cloanthus, whose victory, like that of Ascanius, follows the vow of a bull, in Cloanthus' case to the gods of the sea, in Ascanius' case to Jupiter (5.237 'I will place before your altars', *constituam ante aras*: cf. 9.627 *et statuam ante aras*). I will return later to the issue of the appropriateness for the victor of the Ganymede *chlamys*.

Putnam is right, then, to focus on the liminal quality of Ganymede, which he shares with the likes of Nisus and Euryalus, Pallas, and Lausus, but wrong to see an analogy between 'the eros of the omnipotent king of the gods' and 'the fatal eris of war' (66). For Nisus and Euryalus the transition to full adulthood is replaced by the passage from life to death; for Ganymede, as the reader knows, that transition is replaced by the passage from mortality to immortality. The passage from human to god, as we have seen, is another central theme of the *Aeneid*. Ganymede's career collapses into one movement two stages in the Virgilian thematics of liminality, firstly from boy to adult man, and secondly from human to divine. Ganymede passes from hunting boy to apotheosed Trojan in one leap, omitting the rest of the earthly career. The beginning and end of this journey, from Ida to Olympus, coincide with the wider trajectory of the *Aeneid* as a whole, an epic which sees the survivors of the sack of Troy set off in a fleet built from the trees of Mount Ida, and whose ultimate *telos* might be described as a journey to the stars. Putnam may then be right that in the Ganymede ecphrasis, as in the grander ecphrases, 'Virgil is offering a paradigm for his poem as a whole' (55), but there is more than one way of reading the 'poem as a whole'. Putnam is one of the most distinguished Virgilians of

---

[17] In itself *sublimis* is neutral between salvific and destructive elevation: for the former e.g. *Ecl.* 9.27–9, *Vare, tuum nomen . . . / cantantes sublime ferent ad sidera cycni*; for the latter e.g. *Aen.* 11.721–2 *sacer ales ab alto / consequitur pennis sublimem in nube columbam*.

[18] Catasterism of Ganymede: J. Engemann, *RAC* 8 (1972) 1036–7; Friedlaender, *RE* 7.1, 740; Bömer on Ov. *Fasti* 2.145. The description of Ganymede at Horace *Odes* 3.20.15–16 as *aquosa raptus ad Ida* perhaps hints at his transformation into Aquarius (M. Grazia Iodice di Martino, in *Enciclopedia oraziana* (Rome 1997) vol. 2, 382).

what has become known as the 'Harvard school',[19] which stresses the pessimistic and even anti-Augustan qualities of the poem. As a result Putnam sees in the Ganymede ecphrasis what he always sees in the *Aeneid* as a whole, a 'story of loss, prayer, and rage' (74).

iii

Why then the emphasis in the ecphrasis on the futile yearning of the vanished boy's human and animal companions? One answer is that grief at the disappearance of Ganymede is a key component in the most substantial of the early Greek narratives of the story, the *Homeric Hymn to Aphrodite* 202–17. Here the boy's father Tros is stricken with inconsolable grief for his son, until Zeus takes pity on him, gives him some wonderful horses in compensation, and tells Tros that Ganymede is now immortal and ageless — whereupon the father's grief turns to joy. But, as we have seen, explicit mention of Ganymede's glorious fate is withheld in the Virgilian text. Although the informed reader can fill in the dots, a trace lingers of the sense of loss felt by the internal audience composed of the boy's guardians.

Grief at the loss of a young person is the central experience in what was to become a common consolatory use of the Ganymede myth in later imperial Roman funerary symbolism. The frequent appearance of Ganymede on sarcophagi and other monuments is plausibly interpreted as expressive of a belief or hope in the ascent of the dead person's soul to a celestial immortality.[20] The growth of a fashion for 'private apotheosis' of this kind was probably encouraged by the model of imperial apotheosis.[21] My next move seeks to recuperate the typically Virgilian, and apparently private, pathos of the scene of the lost Ganymede for the Roman, public, themes of the poem. Apotheosis replaces death for Ganymede; but for the Trojan and Roman heroes whose celestial elevation Ganymede foreshadows, apotheosis is consequent on, rather than a substitute for, death. Grief for the dead leader or ruler is not so lightly to be converted to joy at the thought of his divinisation. The most

---

[19] For an account of twentieth-century movements in the criticism of Virgil see S. J. Harrison 'Introduction', in id. (ed.), *Oxford Readings in Vergil's Aeneid* (Oxford and New York 1990).

[20] See J. Engemann, *Untersuchungen zur Sepulchralsymbolik der späteren römischen Kaiserzeit* (*Jhrb. f. Antike u. Christentum*, Ergänzungsbd. 2, Münster 1973) chs. 1–2; id., *RAC* 8 (1972) 1037–46 'Ganymed als Jenseitssymbol'; P. Boyancé, '*Funus acerbum*', *Revue des études anciennes* 54 (1952) 275–89, at 283; F. Cumont, *Recherches sur le symbolisme funéraire des romains* (Paris 1966 (1942)) 97–8.

[21] Engemann 1973 (n. 20) 31.

famous account in Latin literature of the grief for a dead ruler is Ennius' description of the desire felt by the Romans for the vanished Romulus, at *Annals* 105–9 Skutsch, a fragment quoted by Cicero to illustrate the longing felt by a people 'bereaved' (*orbatus*) of a just king (*De republica* 1.64):

> pectora . . . tenet desiderium; simul inter
> sese sic memorant: 'o Romule, Romule die,
> qualem te patriae custodem[22] di genuerunt!
> o pater, o genitor, o sanguen dis oriundum![23]
> tu produxisti nos intra luminis oras.'

> Desire filled their breasts, and at the same time they spoke among themselves thus: 'O Romulus, godlike Romulus, what a guardian of the fatherland did the gods beget in you! O father, O parent, O blood sprung from the gods. You brought us forth into the shores of light.'

Ennius figures the relationship between Roman people and king as one of children to father, and given Cicero's use of *orbatus*, it is possible, as Ian DuQuesnay suggests, that Ennius explicitly compared the Roman people's loss to that of an orphaned child (the reverse of Tros's loss of his son).[24]

The Ennian passage is the object of dense allusion in the first four stanzas of Horace *Odes* 4.5, a panegyric of Augustus, where the Roman people's desire for their absent ruler repeats their desire, long ago, for the vanished Romulus. In the third and fourth stanzas Horace compares this desire to that of a mother for her absent son, in lines that seem to echo a lost, possibly Hellenistic, work describing the yearning of parted lovers,[25] and a trace of the erotic survives in the Horatian transformation into a mother–son relationship. Erotic elements are in fact quite at home in panegyric of this kind, as DuQuesnay shows by reference to passages in Menander Rhetor that

---

[22] On Virgil's *chlamys* the *longaeui custodes* strain after the *regius puer*. This may be pointed, in the light of Cicero's comment on the Ennian lines at *Rep.*1.64, *iusto quidem rege cum est populus orbatus*, '*pectora' diu 'tenet desiderium', sicut ait Ennius post optimi regis obitum, 'simul . . . oriundum'. non eros nec dominos appellabant eos quibus iuste paruerant, denique ne reges quidem, sed patriae* custodes, *sed patres, sed deos*. If Ganymede foreshadows Romulus, this should not be pushed to the point of identity: Ganymede did belong to a society with kings, and he was only a boy who needed looking after. On the differing versions of the apotheosis of Romulus see R. M. Ogilvie, *A Commentary on Livy Books 1–5* (Oxford 1965) 84–5.

[23] With *di genuerunt* and *sanguen dis oriundum* cf. *Aen*. 9.642, *dis genite*; Ascanius overbids Romulus with *et geniture deos*.

[24] I. Le M. DuQuesnay 'Horace *Odes* 4.5: *Pro Reditu Imperatoris Caesaris Diui Filii Augusti*', in S. J. Harrison (ed.), *Homage to Horace: a Bimillenary Celebration* (Oxford 1995) 128–87, at 162–4.

[25] DuQuesnay (n. 24) 159 on the possibility of a lost Hellenistic classic describing the yearning of parted lovers, here transferred to a filial relationship.

prescribe reference to the desire (πόθος) and love of a people for its ruler.[26] This tradition goes some way to providing a context, at least, for the erotic elements in both the Virgilian Ganymede ecphrasis, if it is correct to see in it allusion to the relationship between a people and its lost ruler, and the description in *Aeneid* 10 of the glamorous young prince Ascanius.

But the reader needs a more precise cue than I have so far provided if he is to suspect specific allusion in Virgil's description of the rape of Ganymede to Ennius' account of the disappearance of Romulus.[27] This is to be found at the beginning of the ship-race. As is well known, Virgil reworks the Homeric chariot race in *Iliad* 23, a model thrust before the reader by the simile at *Aeneid* 5.144–7 comparing the forwards rush of the ships to the start of a chariot race. But at the Virgilian starting-line we also find allusion to another epic chariot race, this time another chariot race in a simile, in Ennius' account of the auspice-taking of Romulus and Remus at *Annals* 78–83 Skutsch:

> omnibus cura uiris uter esset induperator.
> expectant ueluti consul quom mittere signum
> uolt, omnes auidi spectant ad carceris oras
> quam mox emittat pictos e faucibus currus:
> sic expectabat populus atque ore timebat
> rebus utri magni uictoria sit data regni.[28]

All men's concern was as to which would be ruler. They waited, just as, when the consul is about to give the signal, all eyes greedily watch the starting barriers, to see how soon he will send the painted chariots from the gates. So the people waited, anxiety in their faces, to see which of the two had been granted the victory of the great rule.

Compare *Aeneid* 5.137–47 (detailed parallels emphasised):

> intenti *exspectant signum*, exsultantiaque haurit
> corda *pauor* pulsans laudumque arrecta cupido.
> inde ubi clara dedit sonitum tuba, finibus omnes,

---

[26] DuQuesnay (n. 24), citing Men. Rhet. 428.19–26 (*klētikon*); 384.28–31 (*epibatērion*); 395.31–2 (*propemptikon*) and Martial (7.5.1–3, *desiderium* for Domitian). DuQuesnay also points to the etymology at Paul. Fest. 75 *desiderare... sideribus dici certum est*, implying the derivation *desiderium quod sidus abest*. The ruler is conventionally compared to a sun or star; in one version Ganymede will end up as the constellation Aquarius (see n. 18).

[27] I note here further parallels between the traditions of Romulus and Ganymede. In one version Romulus is torn to pieces, and the story of his elevation to heaven is a cover-up (Livy 1.16.4); there is also a version of the Ganymede story in which he was torn to pieces by wild beasts during a hunt (ΣT *Iliad* 20.234; Friedlaender (n. 18) 740); both were said to have been snatched up by a storm-wind (*Hymn. Hom. Ven.* 208; Livy 1.16.2, *sublimem raptum procella*); in yet another version Minos raped Ganymede, who then threw himself off a cliff, whereupon Minos buried him and invented the story that he had been snatched to heaven in a storm-cloud (Dosiadas, *FGrHist.* 458 F5).

[28] For further allusion to this passage of Ennius in the *Aeneid* see n. 38 below.

haud mora, prosiluere suis; ferit aethera clamor
nauticus, adductis spumant freta uersa lacertis.

. . . .

non tam praecipites biiugo certamine campum
corripuere ruuntque effusi *carcere currus,*
nec sic immissis aurigae undantia lora
concussere iugis pronique in uerbera pendent.[29]

> They strained their ears to hear the starting signal. They were shuddering with fear
> and their hearts were leaping and pumping the blood for the sheer love of glory.
> When the shrill trumpet sounded, in that one instant the ships all surged forward
> from the line and the shouting of the sailors rose and struck the heavens. Their
> arms drew the oars back and the water was churned to foam . . . They were swifter
> than two-horse chariots streaming full-pelt from the starting gates and racing over
> the ground, swifter than charioteers at full gallop cracking the rippling reins on
> their horses' backs and hanging forward over them with the whip.

The nervous anticipation of the starting signal is transferred from the spectators
to the contestants. In Ennius the figurative chariot race ends with Romulus'
victory in the contest of auspices. Cloanthus' figurative chariot race ends with
his victory in the ship-race, as he steers his ship to the finishing line. He has also
figuratively run the course of life, spanning the time between Romulus'
recognition as ruler of Rome and his death and deification, alluded to in the
Ganymede ecphrasis.[30] His ship 'buried itself in the depths of the harbour'
(*Aen.* 5.243, *portu se condidit alto*). Escape from sea into harbour is a very
common (and ancient) funerary image, that is close to the surface in Jupiter's
promise to the Magna Mater that the Trojan ships, built from trees that grew on
her sacred mountain, Ida, will not come to an undignified end (9.98–102):[31]

immo, ubi defunctae finem portusque tenebunt
Ausonios olim, quaecumque euaserit undis
Dardaniumque ducem Laurentia uexerit arua,
mortalem eripiam formam magnique iubebo
aequoris esse deas.

> But when the ships have done their duty, when in due course they reach the end of
> their voyaging and are safe in harbour in Ausonia, each one to survive the sea and
> reach the Laurentine fields with the Trojan leader will lose its mortal shape. I shall
> order them all to become goddesses of the great ocean.

---

[29] The simile goes back ultimately to the comparison of the departure of the Phaeacian ship to the
start of a chariot race at *Od.* 13.81–3.

[30] A. Feldherr, 'Ships of state: *Aeneid* 5 and Augustan circus spectacle', *Classical Antiquity* (1995)
245–65, at 255–6, notes that the boat race is also an image in miniature of another larger trajectory,
'the entire Trojan mission as a voyage toward the Roman future, as well as away from the Trojan
past'.

[31] See Hardie (n. 13) ad loc.

Here, in keeping with Virgil's tendency to personify ships, the language hints at the apotheosis of human beings whose life has run its course.[32]

Aeneas' ships share in the careers of himself and of his illustrious descendants: after a storm-tossed and heroic passage the ships too will come to safe harbour and be rewarded with divinity, as Jupiter in *Aeneid* 1 had promised another female relative, Venus, that Aeneas would be deified after his labours. That divinity is the conclusion to a journey that had begun on Ida, the mountain on which grew the trees from which Aeneas shaped his ships and from which Ganymede was snatched to heaven.[33]

The eagle that snatches Ganymede is *praepes* (5.254).[34] The word has the general sense 'swift' but is originally a technical term of augury, applied to a bird, or quarter of the sky, of good omen. The meaning of *praepes* was disputed in antiquity; Aulus Gellius, *Noctes Atticae* 7.6, reports that Julius Hyginus, librarian of the Palatine under Augustus, criticised Virgil's use of it at *Aeneid* 6.15 in a non-augural context. The word itself, then, triggers questions of interpretation, and a sense that it is properly at home in a context of divination may act as a provocation to find hidden meaning in the Ganymede ecphrasis. For Ganymede the appearance of the eagle is a good omen, if correctly read, since it forebodes his elevation to Olympus. *Praepes* is used twice in the Ennian account of Romulus' auspice-taking (*Ann.* 86–9):

> et simul ex alto longe pulcerrima praepes
> laeua uolauit auis. simul aureus exoritur sol
> cedunt de caelo ter quattuor corpora sancta
> auium, *praepetibus* sese pulcrisque locis dant.

> At the same time a bird flew on the left from on high, by far the happiest of omens. As soon as the golden sun rose, twelve sacred birds came from the sky, and alighted in places of good and happy omen.

---

[32] *Defunctus* may mean 'dead'. There are a number of parallels between this passage and Ovid's account of the apotheosis of the murdered Julius Caesar at the end of *Met.* 15: *rapio, eripio* is used of Venus' snatching away to heaven of Julius' soul (*Met.* 15.840, 845); both the ships and Julius have completed their fated span: *Aen.* 9.107–8, *tempora Parcae / debita complerant*; *Met.* 15.816–17, *hic sua compleuit . . . tempora, perfectis, quos terrae debuit, annis*; Cybele's concern for her nurslings, and Jupiter's reminder that she should not seek to alter fate, are mirrored in Venus' concern and Jupiter's reply, now to his daughter not his mother, at *Met.* 15.803 ff.: with *Aen.* 9.94 *o genetrix, quo fata uocas?* cf. *Met.* 15.807–8 *talibus hanc genitor: 'sola insuperabile fatum, / nata, mouere paras?'*

[33] The Magna Mater is kinder to these nurslings of hers than she was to another protegé, Attis. Putnam (n. 4) 60, 65–6 sees in *Aen.* 5.254 *anhelanti similis* an echo of Cat. 63.31 (of Attis) *simul anhelans*, also located on *uiridis Ida* (Cat. 63.30: cf. *Aen.* 5.252 *frondosa . . . Ida*). Attis' self-castration is another substitute for the passage from childhood to adulthood, here a passage from male to female.

[34] See Norden and Austin on 6.15 for full discussions and further references; Skutsch on Enn. *Ann.* 86.

Thus in the Virgilian ship-race elements of the Ennian scene of the Romulean auspices are divided between inaugural simile and concluding ecphrasis, two different kinds of image that frame the narrative of the legendary ship-race within Roman historical allusion.[35]

Romulean allusion continues, and is reinforced, in the later part of *Aeneid* 5. Cloanthus' safe and victorious arrival in port is an image of other successful journeys, both literal and figurative, made by the Trojans and their descendants. Immediately it is mirrored in the safe passage from Sicily to Italy at the end of book 5 and beginning of book 6. In this case the sea-journey is not itself an image of death and deification, but is rather made possible by an event that itself alludes to the Ennian narrative of the apotheosis of Romulus, the death of Palinurus, as Bill Nicoll has convincingly argued.[36] Neptune tells Venus that one man must die for the safe journey of the rest of the Trojans (5.814), 'there will be just one man whom you will miss, lost at sea' (*unus erit tantum amissum quem gurgite quaeres*); his words echo, not for the first time in the *Aeneid,* the Ennian Jupiter's promise to Mars of Romulus' apotheosis, *unus erit quem tu tolles in caerula caeli/templa.* The emphatic *unus* suggests that in Ennius the deification of the one twin was balanced against the death of the other, Remus; Virgil's Neptune uses *unus erit...quem* to single out Palinurus, helmsman and, in senses shown by Nicoll, 'twin' of Aeneas, for a quasi-sacrificial death which will guarantee the future of Aeneas and his people, but for which no blame can attach to Aeneas.

Taking a broader view, the Romulean allusions in book 5 fit into a pattern that extends from the first to the last books of the poem. A bird omen in the first book of the *Aeneid* (1.393–400) had foretold a safe arrival in harbour. Here, in the interpretation of the omen offered to her son Aeneas by Venus, the twelve swans symbolise the twelve Trojan ships thought lost in the storm, (399–400), 'just so your ships and your warriors are either already in port or crossing the bar in full sail' (*haud aliter puppesque tuae pubesque tuorum/ aut portum tenet aut pleno subit ostia uelo*). I have argued elsewhere[37] that the wider significance of the swans omen lies in a reference to the future

---

[35] The beginning and end of Romulus' career are alluded to, in reverse order, in the Parade of Heroes at *Aen.* 6.780–1, *et pater ipse suo superum iam signat honore?/en huius, nate, auspiciis illa incluta Roma...* (if 780 is taken to refer to the apotheosis of Romulus). With *honore* at line-end in 780 *cf.* 1.28, *rapti Ganymedis honores.* For another example of ecphrasis and simile conjoined as frame to an event in the main narrative see *Aen.* 1.490–502 (ecphrasis of Penthesilea — entry of Dido — Diana simile).

[36] W. S. M. Nicoll, 'The sacrifice of Palinurus', *Classical Quarterly* 38 (1988) 459–72, at 466–70; see id., 'The death of Turnus', *Classical Quarterly* 51 (2001) 190–200, at 197–8.

[37] P. R. Hardie, 'Aeneas and the omen of the swans (Verg. *Aen.* 1.393–400)', *Classical Philology* 82 (1987) 145–50, supporting Housman's emendation of 1.395 *terras* to *stellas.*

heavenly destiny of Aeneas and the Roman race. The swans have escaped from the 'bird of Jupiter', *Iouis ales,* and now make their way to the heavens; in the previous scene Jupiter had reassured Venus that, with his blessing, she would raise Aeneas to the stars (1.259–60), in words that echo the Ennian Jupiter's promise to Mars that the latter would raise Romulus to the heavens (see p. 340 above). 'In the light of this one may understand the *augurium* as a kind of foundation omen, comparable ultimately to the twelve ... birds that announced to Romulus his throne in Ennius.'[38] This wider significance is of course lost on Aeneas, from whom in book 1 so much is hidden that is revealed to the reader. Here too there is an analogy with the disparity between perspectives on the rape of Ganymede, between the point of view of the *longaeui custodes* who were there, that of the artist and consumers of the Trojan *chlamys* that depicts the event, and that of Virgil's readers.

iv

I have argued that Virgil's figurative inscription of the career of Romulus within the ship race in *Aeneid* 5 extends from the augural appointment of Romulus as city-founder to his final disappearance skywards. Certain details in the Ganymede ecphrasis point to a symmetry that links the end of Romulus' earthly existence with its very beginning.[39] Mars snatches his son from earth to heaven, an event alluded to by the rape of Ganymede; the child was born of Mars' rape of Ilia. Ennius indirectly narrated this event in Ilia's account to her sister of a dream in which she foresaw her rape (Enn. *Ann.* 34–50 Skutsch). In her vision she is 'dragged' (*raptare,* a frequentative form of *rapere* which often means 'rape') through pleasant woods by a river. Thereafter Ilia sees herself wandering alone in a trackless waste, searching in vain for her sister.

---

[38] Hardie (n. 37) 149. Virgil returns to the Ennian auspice-taking in a darker key at the end of the *Aeneid*, in the simile comparing Aeneas and Turnus to two bulls duelling for lordship over the herd, with an audience of cows anxiously expectant of the outcome, *Aen.* 12.718–19: *stat pecus omne metu mutum, mussantque iuuencae / quis nemori imperitet, quem tota armenta sequantur;* the Ennian intertext is highlighted by Ovid in his imitation of the Virgilian passage at *Met.* 9.48–9, *spectant armenta pauentque / nescia, quem maneat tanti uictoria regni,* where the last three words verbally echo Enn. *Ann.* 83 Skutsch, *rebus utri magni uictoria sit data regni.* This is a reminder that the decision over rule made ritually by the auspices will be made again with murderous violence in the death of Remus. The Ennian Jupiter's promise to Mars of Romulus' apotheosis is echoed again in Jupiter's reminder to Juno at *Aen.* 12.794–5 of Aeneas' heavenly destination.

[39] My thanks to Alessandro Barchiesi for pointing out to me the relevance of Ennius' account of the dream of Ilia for my argument. Rape recurs in the middle of Romulus' career, in the Rape of the Sabine Women, without which the newly founded city would not have survived its first generation of inhabitants. Rape is recurrently built into the Roman foundation legends.

Ilia's father, Aeneas, then appears and prophesies that after further hardships, her fortunes will be restored from a river, an allusion to the miraculous rescue from the swollen river Tiber of the exposed twins, which will lead in time to the foundation of Rome. Aeneas then disappears (*Ann.* 47–9):

> nec sese dedit in conspectum corde cupitus,
> quamquam multa manus ad caeli caerula templa
> tendebam lacrumans et blanda uoce uocabam.

> Though my heart longed for him, he did not show himself, although I kept on stretching my hands towards the blue spaces of the sky, weeping, and called on him with tender voice.

The dream starts in an idyllic rustic setting, and ends in a landscape that has turned into a scene of loss, as a figure stretches out her hands — in vain — to the heavens. It is not known whether Ennius told the story of how Aeneas became a *deus indiges* (local god); the sky is the destination of the deified Aeneas both in Virgil (*Aen.* 1.259–60) and Tibullus (2.5.43–4) 'there [in Italy] you will be sanctified, when the sacred waters of the Numicus have sent you to the sky as a *deus indiges*'.[40] But the words *ad caeli caerula templa* are repeated in Jupiter's promise to Mars of the future apotheosis of his son Romulus, in a council of the gods that may have followed immediately on the account of Ilia's dream, at *Annals* 54–5: 'there will be one man whom you will raise up to the blue spaces of the sky' (*unus erit quem tu tolles in caerula caeli/templa*). Ilia thus unwittingly reaches towards the final home of the child whose conception has, in her dream, just taken place.

Nita Krevans places the Ennian dream of Ilia within a tradition of 'seduction-dreams' in epic and tragedy, in which '[t]he dynasties and foundations conceived through these divine encounters are in fact held out to [the] heroines as consolation for their rape and subsequent exile.'[41] The elements of anxiety and lamentation in Ilia's dream derive from a tragic tradition of dreams of foreboding, producing a dual role for Ilia as 'both tragic heroine and mother of Romulus'.[42] The Virgilian Ganymede ecphrasis likewise contains both tragedy (the guardians' loss) and, for those in the know, the consolation of apotheosis. In the wider story of the *Aeneid* Ganymede's elevation is also a symbol of the ultimate success of the exiled Trojans, fleeing from a sacked city on a journey that will lead to

---

[40] On this point see O. Skutsch, *The Annals of Quintus Ennius* (Oxford 1985) 261.

[41] N. Krevans, 'Ilia's dream: Ennius, Virgil, and the mythology of seduction', *Harvard Studies in Classical Philology* 95 (1993) 257–71, at 264 (with specific reference to the dreams of Io in Aesch. *PV* 645–9 and of Europa in Moschus *Europa* 1–17).

[42] Krevans (n. 41) 265.

the foundation of Rome. Virgil alludes more overtly to Ilia's dream in the nightmare at *Aeneid* 4.465–8, in which Dido sees herself pursued by a hostile Aeneas, alone on a journey without end, searching for her fellow Tyrians in a deserted land. As Krevans points out, this inverts the pattern of Ilia's dream: Dido is a city-founder cast out of her city.[43]

Ovid, in his account of the apotheosis of Romulus in the *Metamorphoses*, uses the violent word *rapina* for what Mars does to his son (14.818). That the god of war is set not just on 'plunder', but on what might be thought of as a figurative 'rape' is suggested by a parallel with the narrative of the rape of Ganymede with which Orpheus begins his song in book 10: both Romulus and Ganymede are designated by the uncommon *Iliades,* meaning 'son of Ilia' of the former and 'Trojan' of the latter, in both cases the object of a compound verb in *ab-* at line-beginning (10.160 *abripit Iliaden*; 14.824 *abstulit Iliaden*). In a couple of footnotes (nn. 32, 38) I have already used Ovid as an implicit commentator on allusive patterns in Virgil. Here is evidence that at least one Augustan reader of Virgil saw a connection between Ganymede and Romulus, a connection that Ovid also makes at *Fasti* 2.119–48. Elevated epic praise of Augustus as *pater patriae* builds up to a formal comparison of Augustus and Romulus, to the advantage of the former; among other things 'you (Romulus) rape wives, he bids them be chaste under his rule' (139). This solemn day, February 5th, also sees the rising of a constellation (144–6):[44]

> caelestem fecit te pater, ille patrem.
> iam puer Idaeus media tenus eminet aluo
> et liquidas mixto nectare fundit aquas.

> Your father made you a god, he made his father a god. And now the Trojan boy is visible down to the waist, and pours out flowing water mixed with nectar.

The reader in a comparative frame of mind will be intrigued by the parallel between the apotheoses of Roman rulers and of the Trojan boy. Byron Harries takes this as a deliberate and provocative Ovidian juxtaposition, whose intention is to deflate 'heroic pomposity'.[45] By contrast Alessandro Barchiesi raises the possibility of an encomiastic reading ('political *laudes* and playfulness are [not] mutually incompatible'), or of taking Jupiter's love affair as

---

[43] Krevans (n. 41) 266–71.

[44] In fact 5 February falls between the 'true' and 'apparent' morning risings of Aquarius, and seems to have been chosen by Ovid precisely to allow the synchronisation with the day on which Augustus was given the title *pater patriae*: B. Harries, 'Causation and the authority of the poet in Ovid's *Fasti*', *Classical Quarterly* 38 (1989) 164–85, at 166–7.

[45] Harries (n. 44) 166–7.

'a manifestation of omnipotence'.[46] The rising of Aquarius–Ganymede can be taken as astronomical confirmation of the path to heaven open to descendants of the royal house of Troy; alternatively we may reflect that the naming of constellations is an arbitrary human activity, particularly in the case of Aquarius, whose identification with Ganymede is not a constant in antiquity.

The irreverent Ovid, however, can appeal not only to Virgil, but also to Horace as precedent for the inclusion of the pretty boy Ganymede within an Augustan panegyric. Alessandro Barchiesi compares with the *Fasti* passage Horace's Pindaric ode in praise of the emperor's stepson Drusus, with its combination of 'Jove, Augustus, Augustus' military campaigns, Jove's eagle, and Jove's passion for the beautiful boy'[47] in its opening simile comparing Drusus to an eagle (*Odes* 4.4.1–4)

> qualem ministrum fulminis alitem,
> cui rex deorum regnum in auis uagas
>   permisit expertus fidelem
>   Iuppiter in Ganymede flauo...

Just like the bird who bears the thunderbolt, to whom king Jupiter granted rule over the wandering birds, after he tested his loyalty with fair-haired Ganymede...

Odes 4.4 and 4.5 cohere within the structure of their book as two grand imperial panegyrics; 4.5, as we have seen, opens with an address to the absent Augustus modelled on the Ennian *desiderium* for the dead Romulus. Here is another juxtaposition of Ganymede and Romulus. Note further the combination at the beginning of both odes of weighty Roman themes with potentially unsettling erotic elements, the first presented through predominantly Pindaric, the second through predominantly Ennian allusion.

V

In *Odes* 4 Horace draws on both the Republican epicist Ennius and the Greek epinician Pindar in the construction of a triumphalist Augustan poetic language.[48] Many years before, Virgil had already skilfully woven together

---

[46] A. Barchiesi, *The Poet and the Prince: Ovid and Augustan Discourse* (Berkeley, Los Angeles, London 1997) 81–3.

[47] Barchiesi (n. 46) 83.

[48] On Virgil's use of Pindar see R. F. Thomas, 'Virgil's Pindar?', in P. Knox and C. Foss (eds.), *Style and Tradition: Studies in Honor of Wendell Clausen* (*Beiträge zur Altertumskunde* 92, Stuttgart and Leipzig 1998) 99–120, with further bibliography.

motifs of Ennian triumph and Pindaric victory in the advertisement of his powers as a panegyrist in the proem to the third *Georgic.* The sequence of an image of Ganymede within a Pindaric context at the beginning of *Odes* 4.4 followed by the evocation of an Ennian *desiderium* for an absent ruler at the beginning of *Odes* 4.5 may also reflect Horace's response to the combination of the Pindaric and the Ennian in the Ganymede ecphrasis in *Aeneid* 5, and I turn now to consideration of epinician, and specifically Pindaric, elements in the Ganymede ecphrasis.

The focus is on the decorum that links the subject-matter of the *chlamys,* first prize in the ship-race, to the person of the victor himself, the Pindaric *laudandus.*[49] A number of interpretative frames, or points of view, are operative: firstly, the understanding of the Trojan actors as to what might be an appropriate prize within their own culture; secondly, the awareness of the hellenised Augustan audience of the conventions of the genre of Pindaric epinician; and thirdly, the Roman reader's knowledge of their own culture's symbols of political and military success. Reading Ganymede takes us on a kind of journey through a cultural history from Troy to Rome, a miniature exemplification, naturally, of what the *Aeneid* as a whole achieves. Furthermore the agonistic spirit aroused between Trojan ancestors of Roman aristocratic families by the sporting contest in remote legendary times, for which the Ganymede *chlamys* is first prize, functions as a kind of *aition* for the competitive spirit, the *certamen honoris* between upper-class Romans, that Romans believed had fuelled the glorious achievements of the Republic.[50]

Ships and seafaring are the bearers of a variety of symbolic meanings in antiquity. I have already exploited the funerary symbolism of the sea-journey. Cloanthus' successful race can also be read in the common image of the good governance of the ship of state, in contrast to one of the other competitors Sergestus, ancestor of the *gens Sergia,* who runs his ship aground in his impatient *furor,* as his descendant Catiline had nearly brought Rome to shipwreck. For this Cloanthus is appropriately rewarded with a garment in royal purple and gold, and bearing the image of a royal Trojan. Servius points to another correspondence between victory and prize. Cloanthus' ship is finally propelled into harbour with a push from Portunus, in answer to his

---

[49] Offering my own answers to the question posed by Putnam (n. 4) at 65 '...what does it mean for a victor to carry with him such an ominous image as the ekphrasis conveys?' I read rather different omens into the *chlamys.*

[50] I owe this point to Alessandro Barchiesi, who notes 'it almost looks like the Trojans need an aristocracy to emerge and be baited into competition'. The language of competition in the episode is remarkably strong: *Aen.* 5.138, *laudumque arrecta cupido,* and especially 229–30, *hi proprium decus et partum indignantur honorem/ni teneant, uitamque uolunt pro laude pacisci.*

prayer to the gods of the sea: 'Cloanthus had won with the support of the gods, and appropriate prizes are awarded; Cloanthus is given a *chlamys* containing a story about the gods.'[51] We may develop Servius' *aperçu:* as Cloanthus reaches the desired haven with the helping hand of Portunus, so Ganymede is given a passage to Olympus in the talons of Jupiter's eagle.

The parallel between the glorious achievement of the victor Cloanthus and the elevation of the boy Ganymede, beloved of Jupiter, has Pindaric precedent in the first Olympian ode. Here the career of Pelops matches that of the *laudandus,* Hieron, not only in their shared prowess as chariot-racers, but also in the hint that victory in the games figuratively raises the victor to the skies. As Horace puts it with some irony at *Odes* 1.1.4–6, 'by skimming the turning-post with burning wheels and winning the glorious palm, as lords of the earth they are raised up to the gods' (*metaque feruidis / euitata rotis palmaque nobilis / terrarum dominos euehit ad deos*). In the first *Olympian* Pindar reports that Ganymede followed after Pelops to the house of Zeus; Pindar innovates by modelling his story of the abduction of Pelops by Poseidon on the rape of Ganymede by Zeus.[52] Tros's grief at the disappearance of his son is reworked as the vain search of the mother of Pelops for her son, (*Ol.* 1.46–7 immediately after the Ganymede comparison): 'when you disappeared, and despite searching far and wide men did not bring you back to your mother' ὡς δ' ἄφαντος ἔπελες, οὐδὲ / ματρὶ πολλὰ μαιόμενοι φῶτες ἄγαγον. In the light of this the erotic tinge of the simile of the mother yearning for her son at Horace Odes 4.5.9–14 might now be seen as a Pindaric touch.[53]

Virgil had alluded to the first *Olympian* in the catalogue of hackneyed subjects at the beginning of the third *Georgic,* the last of which is (7–8) 'Pelops distinguished by his ivory shoulder, an energetic horseman' (*umeroque Pelops insignis eburno, / acer equis; cf.* Pind. *Ol.* 1.27, ἐλέφαντι φαίδιμον ὦμον κεκαδμένον 'adorned with ivory on his shining shoulder'). The Pindaric allusion signals Virgil's own transition to a Roman version of epinician,[54] which is presented as Virgil's own attempt to strike out on a

---

[51] Servius ad *Aen.* 5.258.

[52] On the relation of Pelops to Ganymede see J. T. Kakridis, 'Die Pelopssage bei Pindar', *Philologus* 85 (1930) 463–77 (= W. M. Calder and J. Stern (eds.), *Pindaros und Bakchylides* (Darmstadt 1970) 175–90); of Pelops to Achilles see T. Krischer, 'Die Pelopsgestalt in der ersten Olympischen Ode Pindars', *Grazer Beiträge* 10 (1981) 69–75.

[53] On the erotic in the ethos of the games and in Pindaric epinician, see D. S. Carne-Ross, *Pindar* (New Haven and London 1985) 29; F. Cairns, *Virgil's Augustan Epic* (Cambridge 1989) 221–2 with n. 43.

[54] See R. F. Thomas, *Virgil: Georgics,* vol. 2: Books III–IV (Cambridge 1988) on *Geo.* 3.7–8.

skyward journey (8–9, 'I must attempt a path by which I too can raise myself from the ground' *temptanda uia est, qua me quoque possim/tollere humo*).[55]

In the proem to the third *Georgic* Virgil presents his own poetic success as a figurative parallel to the triple triumph of Octavian in 29 BC: victory in the Greek games is reconfigured as Roman triumph, in a passage that celebrates Roman 'conquest' of Greek culture. The *chlamys* awarded to Cloanthus is a Greek cloak, and its costly materials, purple and gold, already proudly sported by the captains of the ships before the race begins (*Aen.* 5.132–3), might arouse in the right-thinking Roman reader a sense of alienation from the oriental luxury of his foreign Trojan ancestors. Yet the purple and gold may also hint at the materials of the *uestis triumphalis,* worn by the Roman *triumphator,* arguably a relic from Rome's own regal period.[56] If so, the chlamys as object prefigures the clothing of the most powerful representative of Roman conquest, as the scenes that it bears prefigure founding moments of Roman history. But from another point of view the *chlamys* is an 'anti-toga',[57] a reminder of the distance still to be travelled between Troy and Rome, home of the *gens togata* (*Aen.* 1.282).

But the triumph, ultimate celebration of Roman victory, is also a ritual in which Roman identity is put under strain: the *triumphator* is in danger of overstepping the boundary between mortal and immortal, between Republican and regal, between Roman and un-Roman. The more extravagantly self-advertising Roman emperors will be tempted into triumphal pageants that, to a hostile eye at least, confuse Roman and Greek in unacceptable ways. Caligula's bridging of the bay of Baiae was both symbolic Roman triumph and *imitatio* of Alexander the Great, and he wore a purple silk *chlamys* with gold embroidery (Suet. *Calig.* 19.2; Dio 59.17.3; *Epit.* 3.9).[58] When Nero entered Rome in 'triumph' to celebrate his victories in the Greek

---

[55] *Acer* at line-beginning (*Geo.* 3.8) is shared with Pelops by Ganymede (*Aen.* 5.254). Virgil's ambition of flight at *Geo.* 3.8–9 is modelled immediately on Ennius' epitaph for himself, Enn. *Epigr.* 18V, but is also echoed in the racing chariots 'taking off' at *Geo.* 3.108–9 *iamque humiles iamque elati sublime uidentur/aëra per uacuum ferri atque adsurgere in auras* (in a description of a chariot-race echoed at various points in the ship-race of *Aen.* 5).

[56] *Vestis triumphalis*: H. S. Versnel, *Triumphus: an Inquiry into the Origin, Development and Meaning of the Roman Triumph* (Leiden 1970) 56. According to Appian *Lib.* 56 the *triumphator*'s *toga picta* was embroidered with gold stars: are the stars on the Ganymede *chlamys* (*Aen.* 5.256) meant to remind us of this too?

[57] I owe this felicitous formulation to Alessandro Barchiesi.

[58] See S. J. V. Malloch, 'Gaius' bridge at Baiae and Alexander-*imitatio*', *Classical Quarterly* 51 (2001) 206–17, at 210. Dictionaries perpetuate the claim that the chlamys is 'often equated with the Roman PALVDAMENTVM' (*OLD* s.v. *chlamys*), but at least in late Republican and early imperial times the chlamys is strongly marked as an un-Roman garment: Cic. *Rab. Post.* 27; Val. Max. 3.6.2–3.

games, he rode in Augustus' triumphal chariot, wearing a purple *chlamys* adorned with golden stars, and garlanded with an Olympic wreath (Suet. *Nero* 25.1) — perhaps a deliberately provocative confusion of the implicit cultural history articulated in the poetry of Virgil and Horace.

vi

Ganymede takes allusive flight from a Trojan past into a glorious future invisible to those who were there on the ground at the time. *Aeneid* 5 as a whole is poised between past and future.[59] Aeneas returns to Sicily from Carthage, to commemorate the first anniversary of the death of his father. After the backsliding of the previous book, he now displays the leadership qualities that will allow the Trojans to progress to Italy, where Aeneas himself will make another journey back in time through the Underworld, arriving finally at a reunion with the soul of his dead father, who will reveal to his son the whole forward reach of Roman history. Andrew Feldherr observes that the anniversary games themselves form 'a bridge...between the heroic past and Augustan present':[60] the Homeric models are reworked in such a way as to foreshadow the spectacles of contemporary Rome, and in particular the games for the dead Julius Caesar and Augustus' Actian games.

Ganymede functions as a central symbol for the passage from Trojan past to Roman future. He is also crucial to the motivation of that passage, since 'the honours paid to Ganymede on his rape' (1.28 *rapti Ganymedis honores*),[61] together with her defeat in the Judgement of Paris, are the two deep-seated causes of the 'anger and fierce pain' (1.25) which Juno feels against the 'hated race' (1.28 *genus inuisum*) of the Trojans, the anger which supplies the motive force for the whole of the *Aeneid*.[62] Alessandro Barchiesi notes that 'Trojan mythology is linked to the central preoccupation of book 5, continuity

[59] See G. K. Galinsky, '*Aeneid* 5 and the *Aeneid*', *American Journal of Philology* 89 (1968) 157–85, at 165–6 repr. in P. Hardie (ed.), *Virgil: Critical Assessments of Classical Authors* (London and New York 1999) 4, 182–206, at 187–8; P. Holt, '*Aeneid* V: past and future', *Classical Journal* 75 (1979/80) 110–21.

[60] Feldherr (n. 30) 246.

[61] L. Barkan, *Transuming Passion: Ganymede and the Erotics of Humanism* (Stanford 1991) 19–20 sees a connection between *honores* at 5.249 and 1.28 *rapti Ganymedis honores*: 'These *honores* are translated into a less ambiguous form...when they become the *honores*, or first prize, that Aeneas hands out...'.

[62] *Cf.* Germanicus *Aratea* 316–20, *habet miracula nulla,/si caelum ascendit Iouis armiger. hic tamen aptum/unguibus innocuis Phrygium rapuit Ganymeden/et telo appositus custos quo Iuppiter arsit/in puero, luit excidio quem Troia furorem.*

with the past',[63] and this is true as far as it goes. If we stopped there, we might be inclined to view the presentation of the *chlamys* as being as ominous as the gifts to Dido and to Latinus of heirlooms from the Trojan past (1.647–55; 7.243–8).[64] We might also reflect on Juno's partially successful attempt towards the end of book 5 to burn the Trojan ships, presumably including those that had taken part in the ship-race, a repetition of her attempt to blast the same ships with thunder and lightning at the beginning of the first book. A verbal echo might even hint that the four ships destroyed were the same as the figurative bearers of a Roman future in the ship-race.[65]

But the Ganymede story is not only a cause of Juno's anger, but also the type for that series of skywards journeys by Trojans and Trojan descendants which seals the ultimate success of the Trojan race, Juno's anger finally appeased. Horace dramatises this change of heart through the goddess's acceptance on to Olympus of the once hated Romulus (*Odes* 3.3.30–6):

> . . . protinus et grauis
> iras et inuisum[66] nepotem,
>   Troica quem peperit sacerdos,

> Marti redonabo; illum ego lucidas
> inire sedes, ducere nectaris
>   sucos et adscribi quietis
>   ordinibus patiar deorum.

> Henceforth I shall give up my heavy anger, and forgive Mars for the hated grandson, to whom the Trojan priestess gave birth; I will allow him to enter the realms of light, to drink the juice of nectar, and to be enrolled in the calm ranks of the gods.

Romulus' distant cousin Ganymede presumably pours out the nectar. In the third Roman Ode Romulus is the focus for the conversion of divine anger to approbation. In *Odes* 4.4 Ganymede performs this role: he is introduced at

---

[63] Barchiesi (n. 9) 280.

[64] On the tendency of epic gift-giving in the Aeneid to carry an ominous freight from the past see E. Henry, *The Vigour of Prophecy: A Study of Virgil's Aeneid* (Bristol 1989) 31–9. As an object the *chlamys* also tends to have a negative association, occurring in the following places: 3.484 (*Phrygiam*, gift of Andromache to Ascanius); 4.137 (*Sidoniam*, worn by Dido); 8.167 (*auro intertextam*, given to Evander by Anchises); 8.588 (worn by Pallas); 9.582 (worn by the doomed *Arcentis filius*); 11.775 (worn by Chloreus). Putnam (n. 4) 222 n. 14 notes that the *chlamys* is associated with 'figures . . . observed as they, or those associated closely with them, undergo a crucial moment of change which is always ominous and in three instances betokens death'.

[65] 5.115 quattuor *ex omni delectae classe* carinae; 5.698–9 *omnes* / quattuor *amissis seruatae a peste* carinae.

[66] Cf. *Aen.* 1.28, *et genus* inuisum *et rapti Ganymedis honores*.

the beginning of this highly Pindarizing poem in the context of the successful maturation and military initiation of young Roman nobles, but he also primes the reader for the thoughts about the sack of Troy that pass through Hannibal's mind (53–6). Troy, the reader knows, was punished for the rape of Ganymede, but this was a *felix culpa,* leading to miraculous regeneration, firstly of Rome from the felled stump of Troy, and secondly of Roman fortunes from the devastations of Hannibal.

As figurative anticipation of future Trojan and Roman apotheoses the Ganymede ecphrasis forms part of a wider pattern within *Aeneid* 5. The games are immediately preceded by libations at the tomb of Anchises, the occasion for the amazing appearance from the shrine of a huge serpent, which Aeneas is uncertain whether to take as a *genius loci* or the attendant spirit of his father (*famulus parentis*). Indeed the exact status of the dead Anchises isn't entirely clear to modern readers either. Cyril Bailey suggests that Virgil combines traditional Roman ideas about the *manes* with elements of a Greek hero-cult: 'Anchises is not quite thought of as deified, but as having attained in death to the sanctity of a hero. This idea is brought out by the twice-repeated description of the altars at the tomb as *altaria,* a word used, according to Servius, only of altars to the *di superi.*'[67] Bailey goes on to surmise that Aeneas' worship of his father may be intended to suggest Augustus' cult of the Divus Iulius. This would then correct Aeneas' pessimistic invocation at 80–1, 'Hail, ashes of the father whom I rescued in vain, hail, spirit and ghost of my father' (*saluete, recepti/nequiquam cineres animaeque umbraeque paternae*). Whatever the exact meaning of the disputed phrase *recepti cineres* (the translation offers one possibility), *nequiquam,* 'in vain', registers a mistaken sense of futility on Aeneas' part regarding his piety towards his dead father, comparable to the short-sighted despair of the guardians of Ganymede, who strain their arms skywards *nequiquam* (*Aen.* 5.256).

This opening *monstrum* is answered in the last competitive event of the games, the archery contest, by the even more amazing omen of the ignition of Acestes' skywards-soaring arrow (5.522–8), now very clearly a foreshadowing of the Julian Star, the comet that appeared at the funeral games of Julius Caesar in 44 BC, and was taken as a sign of his apotheosis.[68] A further consequence is that the first contest, the ship-race,

---

[67] C. Bailey, *Religion in Virgil* (Oxford 1935) 291–5, at 293.

[68] See D. West, 'On serial narration and on the Julian star', *Proceedings of the Virgilian Society* 21 (1993) 1–16. It was only Heinze's (n. 3 (1993) 133–4) reluctance to accept this interpretation that prevented its more general acceptance. But note that Aeneas (hardly surprisingly) also fails to realise its full import, taking it simply as a sign that Jupiter wishes to single out Acestes for special *honores* (5.533–4).

and the last, the archery contest, each conclude with riddling allusion to Trojan/Roman apotheosis.[69] Acestes' flaming arrow has a close imagistic connection with the omen of the shooting star that buries itself in the *Idaea silua* at *Aeneid* 2.696, signposting the way to the future to Aeneas and his family, and which in turn has its antitype in the omen that accompanies Ascanius' successful first bowshot in war at *Aeneid* 9.621–37. Mount Ida is the starting-point of Trojan narratives, her timber the material for journeys into the future.

How far into the future does the Ganymede ecphrasis point? How far from that remote hunt on Mount Ida should the reader let himself be carried on the wings of interpretation? The apotheosis of Romulus was of course one of the traditional models for imperial apotheosis, including the apotheosis of Julius Caesar.[70] If Ganymede's elevation alludes to the apotheosis of Romulus, is there any connection between the instrument of his apotheosis, Jupiter's eagle, and the reported flights of eagles from the funeral pyres of Roman emperors? This is a hazardous area: Dio 56.42.3 reports that an eagle was released from the pyre of Augustus, but this is often taken as an anachronistic retrojection by Dio of a practice established only in the second century. Other pieces of evidence have been brought to bear, some in order to argue that the eagle was already associated with the apotheosis of Julius Caesar.[71] What it may be safe to conclude is that, whenever the practice of releasing eagles at imperial funerals was first instituted, it arose out of a network of funerary and royal, or imperial, associations of eagles that certainly goes back to Virgil's time, and to which the Virgilian Ganymede ecphrasis may indeed itself contribute.

vii

As regards the Ganymede *chlamys* we might assume that the actors within the text, the Trojans, are clear about the meaning that they ascribe to the artwork, both within their culture generally (since it is a domestic product), and within the specific context of a prize in the games (since it has been

---

[69] Feldherr (n. 30) 262–3 notes that Ganymede's skyward journey anticipates the ignition of Acestes' arrow.

[70] S. Price, 'From noble funeral to divine cult: the consecration of Roman Emperors', in D. Cannadine and S. Price (eds.), *Rituals of Royalty: Power and Ceremonial in Traditional Societies* (Cambridge 1987) 56–105, at 73–4.

[71] For full discussion, and reference to earlier treatments, see J. Arce, *Funus imperatorium: los funerales de los emperadores romanos* (Madrid 1988) 131–40, 'El águila'.

chosen to be suitable as a prize). But even here there is a doubt: for the Trojans is the *chlamys* a memorial to a golden Trojan prince lost before his time, or a proud reminder of a special relationship between the Trojan royal family and Jupiter? Aeneas, for one, might know the truth of the matter, if Anchises had told him what he had learned from Aphrodite on the subject in the *Homeric Hymn to Aphrodite* (202–17). But Virgil chooses not to tell us how the Trojans within his narrative respond to the work of art. Instead the reader is shown only the response of viewers within the artwork itself, the *longaeui custodes,* and that, as we have seen, is a response based on only part of the evidence: dismay at the boy's disappearance, unmitigated by any awareness of Ganymede's Olympian destination. The partial perspective of these wise old guardians of the coming generation from Troy's past is analogous to the difficulties experienced in *Aeneid* 5 by the current guardian of the Trojan future, Aeneas, in reading signs and omens. In this respect Aeneas may seem not to have advanced far from his persistent misreading of signs in *Aeneid* 2 and 3.

The reaction of Ganymede's *custodes* to the supposed loss of the *regius puer* is as misguided as had been the panic inspired in Aeneas and Creusa by the omen of the flame around the head of their young son Ascanius at *Aeneid* 2.679–86, an omen correctly interpreted by Anchises as a sign of divine protection of Troy, rather than as foreboding a repetition of the loss of the sons of Laocoon. In *Aeneid* 5 there is no father-figure to whom Aeneas can turn in the hope of authoritative readings of omens.[72] As the hero attempts to lay hold of a course to the future, he is repeatedly thrown into situations of interpretative doubt.

More particularly, this uncertainty has to do with interpreting the circumstances and consequences of death, an uncertainty that will make both Aeneas and the reader all the more eager to learn of the (apparent) certainties of the afterlife revealed in the next book.[73] Book 5 opens with Aeneas' and the Trojans' guilty doubt as to the meaning of the flames lighting up the walls of Troy. They suspect, but cannot (or do not wish to) be sure, that

---

[72] Even Anchises does not always get it right, notoriously at *Aen.* 3.102–20.

[73] But there may be limits even to the prophetic reach of Anchises as he expounds the Parade of Heroes to his son. Philip Hills suggests to me that 'the reaction of Anchises and Aeneas to Marcellus' early death [may be] comparable in partial-sightedness to that of the *longaeui custodes* in the Ganymede ecphrasis', and asks whether the 'empty offering' (*Aen.* 6.885–6 *inani/munere*) to Marcellus is empty not because it will not bring back the dead, but in the sense that Marcellus is not really dead (as Horace, certain of his poetic immortality, bids (*Odes* 2.20.21) *absint inani funere neniae*). Propertius, at least, confidently announces that Marcellus has gone to the stars, 3.18.33–4 *quo Siculae uictor telluris Claudius et quo/Caesar, ab humana cessit in astra uia.*

Dido has died; the ultimate meaning of the ominous sign (7, *triste...
augurium*) will certainly elude them, for the death of Dido is the *aition*[74] of
the Hannibalic War, the greatest future threat to the Roman state.

In the immediate sequel Aeneas falls in with Palinurus' reasonable, if not
certain, response to weather signs. There is no answer to the question of why
the storm clouds are collecting, what Neptune has in mind (13–14), and
Palinurus can only suggest 'following Fortune' (22), a Stoic-sounding piece
of advice. *Fortuna* is how *fatum* appears to mortals who cannot see into the
mind of a providential god. At the very end of book 5 Aeneas will take over
as helmsman of the 'ship of state' from Palinurus, but this act of
statesmanship is accompanied not by uncertainty, but by a radical misprision
of the circumstances of Palinurus' death (870–1), that will only be corrected
in the next book.[75] Furthermore, as we have seen, the death of Palinurus
bears meanings pertinent to the future history of Rome that lie far beyond
any powers of interpretation that Aeneas could possibly have.

Within this frame of opening and closing deaths misunderstood there are
the uncertainties or misinterpretations, already discussed, that attend the
anniversary celebrations of the death of Anchises: the uncertainty as to the
meaning of the serpent that emerges from the shrine of Anchises, and
Aeneas' confident, but at best partial, interpretation of Acestes' flaming
arrow. In this case reference to death and apotheosis (of Julius Caesar) is
totally concealed from Aeneas.[76]

In the night after the games, and after the burning of the ships by the
Trojan women, Aeneas is visited in a dream by his father. Anchises, coming
on the order of Jupiter, instructs his son to descend to the Underworld, in
order to learn of his future people and city. But Aeneas is unable at this stage
to reach out to the promise of a glorious future, and instead clutches in vain
at the disappearing ghost, as the guardians of Ganymede feel only the loss of
their charge as he vanishes skywards. Here too there may be Romulean

---

[74] Does 5.5, *causa*, hint that what is hidden is this *aition*, as well as, immediately, the 'cause' of the
flames?

[75] On the Lucretian colouring of Aeneas' mental error at the end of *Aen.* 5 see P. Hardie, *Virgil*
(*Greece and Rome*, New Surveys in the Classics 28, Oxford 1998) 113–14. There is the further
complication that Palinurus' account of his own death does not square with that of the narrator in
Aen. 5.

[76] In the light of these repeated failures to interpret clearly, there may be a hermeneutic hint in the
simile applied to the last event of all in the anniversary celebrations, the *lusus Troiae*, at 588–91, *ut
quondam Creta fertur Labyrinthus in alta/parietibus textum caecis iter ancipitemque/mille uiis
habuisse dolum, qua signa sequendi/frangeret indeprensus et inremeabilis error.* Compare the
maeandro duplici (5.251) that runs round the Ganymede ecphrasis, in which Putnam (n. 4) 62, sees a
'mazelike moment not dissimilar to labyrinth', 'a moment of duplicity'.

allusion: with *Aeneid* 5.722–3, 'then the shape of his father Anchises seemed to glide down from the sky' (*uisa dehinc caelo facies delapsa parentis/ Anchisae*), compare Livy's account of the apparition to Proculus Iulius of the vanished Romulus, with the message that it is the gods' will that Rome should rule the world (1.16.6), 'Romans, at first light today Romulus, father of this city, suddenly glided down from the sky and showed himself to me' (*Romulus, . . . Quirites, parens urbis huius, prima hodierna luce caelo repente delapsus se mihi obuium dedit*).[77]

The reader faced with the problem of interpreting the Ganymede ecphrasis may, as I have suggested, reflect on Aeneas' difficulty in understanding the omen of the eagle and swans in *Aeneid* 1, a difficulty at least partly resolved by Venus' clear exegesis of one of the meanings of the omen. That omen has a pendant in the last book of the poem, in the sign of the eagle which fails to carry away a swan that it has snatched, an omen sent by Turnus' sister Iuturna in order to spur the Latins to break the truce, and seized upon, but totally misinterpreted, by the Italian augur Tolumnius as a sure sign that the Trojans will flee from Italy (12.244–65).[78] This 'rape' of a swan by an eagle (12.250 *cycnum excellentem pedibus rapuit improbus uncis*, 'he seized a noble swan in his pitiless talons': cf. 5.255 (Ganymede) *sublimem* pedibus rapuit *Iouis armiger uncis*,) is a supernaturally motivated event, but not an omen. By contrast the rape of Ganymede might appear to those who were there to be a natural event, but in fact is the immediate realisation, rather than merely an omen, of the elevation of Ganymede to Olympus by a god.

Nor can the modern critic adopt an Olympian stance of interpretative certainty. There is no absolute boundary between our work of making sense of a complex and elliptical text, and the work of the characters in making sense of the complicated world in which they find themselves.[79] The two tasks coincide when a character has to make sense of a work of art, paradigmatically in

---

[77] My attention was drawn to the apparition of Anchises in this context by Andrew Feldherr, who also notes the following verbal parallels between this passage and the Ganymede ecphrasis: 254 *anhelanti*, 739 *anhelis*; 257 *saeuit*, 739 *saeuus*; 257, 740 *in auras*.

[78] On the connection between the two omens see Hardie (n. 37) 150.

[79] On the mirroring within the text of the work of the reader see J. J. O'Hara, 'Dido as "interpreting character" at *Aeneid* 4.56–66', *Arethusa* 26 (1993) 99–114, drawing on N. Schor, 'Fiction as interpretation/interpretation as fiction', in S. R. Suleiman and I. Crosman (eds.), *The Reader in the Text: Essays on Audience and Interpretation* (Princeton 1980) 165–82. In Chaucer's *House of Fame* the fictionalised author figure 'Geffrey' is confronted with the need to interpret signs based on a rewriting of the *Aeneid*, in a scene in which Geffrey is placed in the role of Aeneas in the temple of Juno: both Geffrey and Aeneas are 'hermeneutic heroes', in the formulation of C. Baswell, *Virgil in Medieval England: Figuring the Aeneid from the Twelfth Century to Chaucer* (Cambridge 1995) 223–30.

Aeneas' viewing of the scenes of the Trojan war in the temple of Juno at Carthage in *Aeneid* 1. In one sense Aeneas must be the ideally knowledgeable reader of scenes from his own past history, *noster labor* (1.460); but in another sense he is a very fallible reader, given that he knows little of the producers of the artworks, the Carthaginians, and may therefore stray in delimiting the possible range of meanings of such representations in such a place. Further, for Aeneas, making sense of the appearance of artistic representations of his own past in this strange land is all a part of the wider task of 'reading' the Carthaginians and their ruler Dido.[80] Both the significance of the scenes in the temple of Juno and the moral judgement of Dido and her Carthaginians continue to provoke differing interpretations.

Uncertainties cluster around both the iconographical details of the Ganymede ecphrasis and around the wider meanings of the image(s). Are we looking at one scene or two — or even three?[81] In some versions of the story the eagle is Jupiter himself metamorphosed:[82] if Virgil's phrase *Iouis armiger* is focalised through the eyes of the *longaeui custodes,* can we be sure that this eagle is not Jupiter himself in disguise? Or is *Iouis armiger* simply a poetic expression for 'eagle', any old eagle? Does *praepes* just mean 'swift', or 'of good omen'? Are the stars to which the *custodes* stretch their arms just a poetic expression for 'sky', or a hint of the catasterism of Ganymede?

At the level of the wider significance of the ecphrasis within the poem I might be accused of reading private fantasies out of the thin air into which Ganymede disappears. I could defend myself by saying that the urge to interpret is one that I share not just with other professional Latinists, but with the characters in the *Aeneid* itself. The poem certainly warns of the dangers of over-confidence in interpretation, but more pressing still is its insistence on the need to interpret if progress is to be made.

For comments on earlier drafts of this essay I am grateful to Alessandro Barchiesi, Andrew Feldherr, and Philip Hills.

---

[80] A sizeable literature has grown up around the disputed question of whether Aeneas is correct to see a sign of Carthaginian humanity in the scenes of the Trojan War. The proliferating levels of reception of these scenes are skilfully teased apart by A. Barchiesi, 'Rappresentazioni del dolore e interpretazione nell'Eneide', *Antike und Abendland* 40 (1994) 109–24 (trans. in Hardie (n. 59) 3, 324–44).

[81] See Boyd (n. 2) 86.

[82] E.g. [Theocr.] 20.41; Lucian *Dial. deorum* 10.1; Prop. 2.30.30; Ov. *Met.* 10.155–61. Note esp. *Anth. Pal.* 12.64 (Alcaeus), on an Olympic victor whom the poet hopes will not be taken by Jupiter as another Ganymede.

15
Indifference readings: Plato and the Stoa on Socratic ethics

Mary Margaret McCabe

i

There was a time when to read Plato was to do away with reading.[1] Instead, philosophers sought to analyse Plato's arguments, to discover within the infinite variety of his prose the single sense,[2] to find out 'what Plato meant' and how he meant us to believe it, too.[3] This approach has been replaced, more recently, by something more inclusive. The objective, for sure, is still to find out what Plato meant, but it is no longer supposed that this can be encapsulated in the abstract formalisation of those parts of the dialogues that might be designated 'arguments', in contrast to those parts which were once thought to be merely literary, and so philosophically dispensable. Consequently, nowadays greater attention is paid to the way in which we should read the dialogues — reading them as a whole, and without prejudice as to which bits matter and which do not.[4]

But this is a dangerous business, and one in which the boundaries between sense and nonsense may be difficult to determine. Is this approach going to take us so far away from the concerns of analysis that there is no common ground

---

[1] This time may itself be a legend; but there have been recent masters of the analytic method: G. E. L. Owen, outstandingly.

[2] This highly analytic approach is what we find at the very beginnings of the analytic tradition of philosophy, e.g., in Gottlob Frege, 'Der Gedanke' (1918–1919), trans. by Geach and Stoothof as 'Thought' in M. Beaney (ed.), *The Frege Reader* (Oxford 1997).

[3] This point is made, for the *Euthydemus*, by R. K. Sprague, *Plato's Use of Fallacy* (London 1962) 10, who argues that Socrates' interest in 'the things denoted by words' is indicated by his 'freedom in the use of synonyms'.

[4] Examples are now too numerous to list, but mention should be made at least of Myles Burnyeat's *The Theaetetus of Plato*, Introduction with translation by M. J. Levett (Indianapolis 1990).

between the old practices and the new? Are we to say — for example — that any reading of a dialogue may legitimately be described as 'what Plato meant'? In what follows I offer a case study. I shall suggest that Plato himself may be used as a guide to reading Plato, and that such a guide does indeed lead to a philosophical destination of which the analytic tradition might approve. For a comparison of two short and markedly different passages, one from the *Meno* and the other from the *Euthydemus*, shows us, I shall argue, the second 'reading' the first.

One explanation, of course, of differences between different dialogues might be a developmental one. Here we might invoke a contrast between Socrates and Plato. The historical Socrates — it is commonly thought[5] — may be represented in Plato's earlier, so-called 'Socratic' dialogues:[6] dialogues in which the ethical theorising coheres around the denial of weakness of the will and the insistence that virtue is knowledge. By contrast, this view maintains, Plato's middle-period ethical theory moves away from this by posing a new and complex moral psychology, which allows for ethical conflict and denies any simple equivalence between virtue and knowledge. Corresponding to these chronological contrasts, the difference I shall find between the *Meno* and the *Euthydemus* may be one between a Socratic view (the *Meno*), and its Platonic replacement in the *Euthydemus*.[7]

This account, however, seems not to meet the present case: in particular because both my two passages are significantly indeterminate. The indeterminacy of the *Meno*, I shall argue, is teased out by the *Euthydemus*; it is this feature which, I suggest, should encourage us to see the latter as a 'reading' of the former.[8]

---

[5] See here, for example, Gregory Vlastos, 'The Socratic elenchus', *Oxford Studies in Ancient Philosophy* 1 (1983) 27–58, 71–4, and *Socrates: Ironist and Moral Philosopher* (Cambridge 1991).

[6] The view that there is a significant difference, even amounting to an inconsistency, between dialogues characterised as early or middle or late is coming increasingly under attack: *cf.* e.g. C. H. Kahn, *Plato and the Socratic Dialogue* (Cambridge 1996); C. J. Rowe, introduction to *Plato: Statesman* (Warminster 1995); Julia Annas, *Platonic Ethics, Old and New* (Ithaca 1999). I confess myself, however, an inveterate developmentalist: I find it entirely congenial to suppose that Plato changed his mind as he thought about a given issue more deeply, and that different dialogues allow us to see these changes of mind. This is compatible with a different claim, upon which I focus here: that dialogues may be related in other, more complex and reflective ways.

[7] Without prejudice to the question of Plato's development, many would deny that there is a significant chronological difference between the *Meno* and the *Euthydemus*. In what follows I shall at least claim that the *Euthydemus* shows affinities with the *Republic* — although I think it was written, or fits best with, dialogues that are later still. I shall also, however, insist that in terms of the passage I discuss, the earlier dialogue may not be obviously Socratic after all — merely indeterminate. (A strong developmentalist view would agree that the *Meno* is not Socratic, but transitional.)

[8] Even that thought, of course, makes a developmental claim: that the *Euthydemus* is in some sense 'after' the *Meno*.

This invites us to a rich conception of 'reading'. Consider, first of all, a single Platonic dialogue. An impoverished read would run straight through from beginning to end, once and for all (this gives a view of the Platonic dialogue as detective fiction: once you know who did it you don't need to read it again; once you know the answer to the question, there is no need to re-read). This, of course, would be a silly way to read a philosophical work. But on a richer conception, reading is something you do again and again, a business which attends closely to allusion, to anticipation and to echo.[9] Now if some later passage in a Platonic dialogue alters one's view of an earlier one in the same dialogue, this alteration is itself a part of understanding the earlier passage. So to read Plato we read him again and again, and no less back to front than front to back (this is to treat the dialogues as complex wholes). And we may want to say something similar about the relations between dialogues,[10] or between comparable passages in different dialogues: these may not be the simple relations between, for example, earlier and later, but instead something more reflective. I shall argue that we should understand my two passages in terms of one reading the other. This allows us to see how the view apparently put forward in the *Meno* might successfully be criticised, and how the unclarities of the *Meno* might be resolved in a quite different way than at first appears possible.

This process, moreover, is a dialectical one. For the *Euthydemus* itself offers a conclusion that is vague. This vagueness proved fruitful for Plato's ancient interpreters, themselves engaged in the project of reading Plato. Once again, recent scholarship has enlarged earlier strategies: this time by turning its attention decisively towards the later tradition of ancient philosophy.[11] As a consequence considerable attention has been paid to the ways in which later philosophers used their predecessors. After all, a great deal of the philosophical business of the post-Aristotelian period was taken up with interpretation — whether as a matter of philosophical engagement with earlier thought or as a matter of preserving the canon, especially of the Socratic tradition. For

---

[9] Of course, to those close to an oral tradition this sort of reading will be congenial; compare here e.g., E. A. Havelock, *A Preface to Plato* (Oxford 1963).

[10] This is a view put quite generally by Kahn's (n. 6) 'proleptic' account of the development of Plato's thought. I am not convinced that this view, which seems to invite us to a strongly unitarian account of Plato's work, does justice to Plato's talent for self-criticism (and his ability to change his mind): see M. M. McCabe, 'Developing the good itself by itself: critical strategies in the *Euthydemus*', *Plato: Online Journal of the International Plato Society* 2 (2001). But Kahn is surely right to insist that the relation between dialogues is not merely one of linear development.

[11] This process has been made much easier by A. A. Long and D. N. Sedley, *The Hellenistic Philosophers* (Cambridge 1987).

the figure of Socrates looms large in later antiquity, both as a philosopher and as the exemplar of how philosophy consoles us for mortality — of how the philosophical life should be lived. As such, he was of particular interest to the Stoics; so here I pursue one strand of early Stoic ethics, which itself provides us with a reading of my two Platonic passages. The complex interplay which develops between Socrates and Plato, Zeno and Aristo, provides a view of how a detailed reading of the original texts may bear philosophical fruit.

ii

> They [sc. the Stoics] say that goods are the virtues, intelligence, justice, courage, moderation and the rest; evils are their opposites: folly, injustice and the rest. Neither good nor evil are the things which neither benefit nor harm, such as life, health, pleasure, beauty, strength, reputation, noble birth; and their opposites death, sickness, pain, shame, weakness, poverty, lack of reputation, low birth and the things related to those...these[12] are not goods, but indifferents of the class of 'preferred'. (Diogenes Laertius 7.102)

> Accordingly, after it had been satisfactorily established that only what is right is good[13], and only what is wrong is bad, they [the Stoics] wanted there still to be some difference between those things which were of no importance to the happy life nor the miserable one, so that of these some had positive value, some negative, and some neither. (Cicero, *De finibus* 3.50)

When the early Stoics formulated their theory of ἀδιάφορα, ethical in-differents, they had, it seems, been reading Plato.[14] In particular, they seem

---

[12] Does Diogenes' 'these' refer back to the list of apparent *goods* — i.e., life, health, pleasure, beauty, strength, reputation, noble birth? Or does 'these' describe the whole list, life, health, pleasure, beauty, strength, reputation, noble birth *and* death, sickness, pain, shame, weakness, poverty, lack of reputation, low birth, etc.? His suggestion that 'these' are *preferred* indifferents suggests the former; but I shall argue that the version of the Stoic theory which was directly influenced by Plato should allow anything on the whole list to be a preferred indifferent, depending on the value it derives from wisdom.

[13] I use 'right' here to translate *honestum* (compare Rackham's 'morality') in order to pick up the influence of this sort of theory in modern neo-Kantian accounts; compare e.g. J. Rawls, *A Theory of Justice* (Oxford 1972). My argument will suggest, however, that not all the early Stoics were proto-Kantians. See here J. M. Cooper, 'Eudaimonism, the appeal to nature, and "moral duty" in Stoicism' and J. B. Schneewind, 'Kant and Stoic Ethics', both in S. Engstrom and J. Whiting (eds.), *Aristotle, Kant and the Stoics: Rethinking Happiness and Duty* (Cambridge 1996) 261–84, 285–302.

[14] This chapter was in part provoked by reading A. A. Long, 'Socrates and Hellenistic philosophy', in Long, *Stoic Studies* (Cambridge 1996), who treats the *Euthydemus* as an important antecedent of the Zenonian theory of the indifferents. My account of the history of the *Euthydemus* passage differs from Long's in two vital respects: firstly in terms of the analysis of Socrates' conclusion; and secondly in the way in which Zeno took that conclusion up. In part this paper was also inspired by hearing Bernard Williams on Plato on the intrinsic good at a Keeling lecture which I hope will shortly be published.

to have been reading the *Euthydemus* and the *Meno*.[15] So we might compare the following two passages:

> *Socrates*: Health, we say, and strength and beauty and wealth, indeed. For surely we say that these things and things like them are beneficial?
> *Meno*: Yes.
> *Socrates*: But we sometimes say that the very same things[16] do harm, too — or would you disagree?
> *Meno*: I would not.
> *Socrates*: Consider, then, what is it that when it leads these things, they benefit us, and when it does not, they harm us?[17] Isn't it the case that when correct use leads them they benefit, when it does not, they harm?[18]
> *Meno*: Certainly.
> *Socrates*: Now, let us also consider the qualities of the soul.[19] You say, don't you, that there is such a thing as self-control, and justice, and courage, and quickness to learn, and memory, and magnificence and everything like that?[20]
> *Meno*: I do.
> *Socrates*: Consider, then — if you suppose any one of these not to be knowledge, but to be other than knowledge, surely it sometimes harms and sometimes benefits?[21] Courage, for example, if courage is not wisdom but some sort of recklessness — surely whenever a man is reckless without intelligence he is harmed, and whenever with intelligence, he is benefited?
> *Meno*: Yes.

---

[15] This is frequently pointed out; see e.g Long (n. 14); J. Annas, 'Virtue as the use of other goods', in T. Irwin and M. Nussbaum (eds.), *Virtue, Love and Form* (Edmonton 1994); and Gisela Striker's suggestive analysis of the Stoics as readers of Plato with a wider scope than merely the Socratic material, 'Plato's Socrates and the Stoics', in Striker, *Essays on Hellenistic Epistemology and Ethics* (Cambridge 1996) 316–324.

[16] Back here to an old controversy: here presumably 'the same things' are the same types, not the same tokens. This contrasts with other passages in Plato where he argues from the compresence of opposites in some token (this stick, for example, is equal to that one, unequal to some stone; *Phaedo* 74a–c) to the existence of a form which does not suffer compresence (equality itself is never inequality).

[17] Socrates makes two assumptions: first that there must be some account to be given of when the same things harm and when they benefit; and second that this account is to be given in terms of what 'leads' them. The vocabulary of 'leading' will become important.

[18] It is unclear whether the leader makes health *nice*; or whether it makes it *productive*.

[19] This translation of τὰ κατὰ τὴν ψυχὴν is warranted by the realistic cast of the next sentence.

[20] 'You say that there is such a thing as . . .' makes no claim for the transcendence of these qualities of soul (as is claimed for a similar remark at *Phaedo* 74), merely for their reality. The symmetry of this remark with the opening of the argument, 87e5, suggests that at this stage self-control, etc. are treated as analogous to health and wealth.

[21] Socrates shifts here from supposing that correct use should *lead* health, etc. (so that correct use and health, etc. are non-identical) to wondering whether self-control, etc. should be *identical with* knowledge. In the thought-experiment that follows, non-identity is assumed, so that the next sentences revert (ostentatiously?) to a more instrumental account: courage *with* intelligence and courage *without* it.

Socrates: And isn't the same true of self-control and quickness to learn — whatever is learned and organised with intelligence is beneficial, whatever without intelligence, harmful?

Meno: Absolutely.

Socrates: In short, all the endeavours of the soul and all its endurances end in happiness[22] when wisdom is the leader, but the reverse when ignorance is the leader.[23]

Meno: It seems so.

Socrates: Therefore if virtue is one of the qualities of soul, and if virtue is necessarily beneficial, then virtue must *be* wisdom, since all these qualities of the soul are not beneficial nor harmful in themselves, but they become harmful or beneficial depending on whether wisdom or folly is added to them.[24] And according to this argument, since virtue is indeed beneficial,[25] it must be some kind of wisdom. (*Meno* 87e6–88d3)

'So, by Zeus, is there any benefit in our other possessions without reason and wisdom?[26] Does it profit a man to have many possessions and to do many things[27] if he has no intelligence, or rather to have and do fewer things, but with intelligence?[28] Consider the matter thus. Surely if he were to do less, he would

---

[22] This is a strikingly consequential claim: wisdom *leads* the sort of 'endeavours of the soul' which *end* in happiness. The thought seems to be that happiness is a consequence which is other than the means to securing it; this thought is often allied with the view that there is nothing morally or ethically significant about just these means (if there were some other, more economical way of getting happiness than being led by wisdom, that would be preferable). So I shall characterise *consequentialism* as the view that moral/ethical value is conferred by the end pursued, and not by any features of the pursuit itself. It is worth noticing that on some accounts of consequentialism this treats the end as having intrinsic worth, and thence value as residing principally in states of affairs. See here Bernard Williams, *Ethics and the Limits of Philosophy* (London 1985) 76. Myles Burnyeat suggests to me in conversation that here 'ending in' should be construed inclusively, as 'the endeavours of the soul when accompanied by wisdom *are actually* happy' (compare, perhaps, *Theaetetus* 173b, where boys end up as men). If, as I suggest below, the *Euthydemus* passage provides us with a reading of the *Meno*, then we may be intended to rethink the implications of τελευτᾶν.

[23] Socrates returns to the metaphor of 'leading': but now the suggestion seems to be that what is led is not one of the virtues, but the effects of the virtues (virtuous behaviour, perhaps, or its results).

[24] Here Socrates allies the identity claim about virtue and wisdom to a consequential claim about the ethical quality of the ends. Nothing so far suggests that the quality is determined by the virtue which produces the ends.

[25] That virtue is *good* was conceded at 87d. The emphatic 'virtue is *indeed* beneficial', like the earlier 'virtue is *necessarily* beneficial' (88c5) contrasts the case of virtue with the supposition about self-control in the thought-experiment, that it may be both beneficial and harmful.

[26] There has been an earlier discussion of the relation between wisdom and good fortune which has affinities with the *Meno*; Socrates has concluded at 280a6 that wisdom makes men lucky because wisdom cannot make mistakes.

[27] 'To be busy', perhaps: the expression does not imply that there are specific products of this activity.

[28] Reading ἢ μᾶλλον ὀλίγα νοῦν ἔχων with BT, and resisting Iamblichus' deletion of νοῦν ἔχων (*Protrepticus* 5.26.1 Pistelli). For Iamblichus' paraphrase of the Euthydemus argument is designed to show us the instrumental value of wisdom; so he rewrites Plato's words thus: 'what use is it to

make fewer mistakes, and if he were to make fewer mistakes he would do less badly; and if he were to do less badly he would be less wretched?' 'Certainly,' he said. 'Would a man be more likely to do fewer things when he is poor or when he is rich?' 'When he is poor.' 'When he is weak or when he is strong?' 'When he is weak.' 'When he is respected or when he is without respect?' 'When he is without respect.' Would he do fewer things when he is brave and self-controlled[29] or when he is cowardly?' 'When he is cowardly.'[30] 'And when he is lazy more than when he is busy?' He agreed. 'And when he is slow rather than fast, and short-sighted and dull of hearing rather than sharp-sighted and sharp-eared?' We agreed all these things with each other. 'In short, Cleinias,' I said, 'it seems probable that as for all the things which we said at first were goods,[31] the argument[32] is not about this — how they are by nature goods themselves by themselves — but it seems that matters stand thus: if ignorance leads them, they are greater evils[33] than their opposites, to the extent that they are better able to serve a bad leader; but if intelligence and wisdom lead them, they are greater goods; but themselves by

possess many things and do many things, rather than a few, if it is without intelligence?' Iamblichus thus reorders the first three words of the phrase as μᾶλλον ἢ ὀλίγα. The MS tradition of the Platonic text, however, reads ἢ μᾶλλον ὀλίγα and invites the concluding participial νοῦν ἔχων, symmetrically with the previous clause. E. H. Gifford, *The Euthydemus of Plato* (Oxford 1905) 24 ad loc., following Iamblichus, is wrong to maintain that 'in the following argument there is no place for an antithesis between νοῦν ἔχων and νοῦν μὴ ἔχων but only between πολλὰ and ὀλίγα.' Were this to be the case, Socrates would have no warrant for his conclusion about wisdom itself, only for some kind of claim about its necessity for success: and on any account of what follows he needs at least to show wisdom to be both necessary and sufficient for success or happiness. The next stage of the argument, it is true, focuses on the case of the ignorant man, for it is designed to show that none of the putative goods is a good at all, without intelligence, but that with intelligence, the goods we may have are greater, more good than they would otherwise have been. So in the argument that follows, the contrast is repeatedly made between different (the one apparently negative, the other apparently positive) characters or situations of the agent (wealth/poverty, strength/weakness, etc.). The conclusion is that only the intelligence of the agent is significant. R. S. W. Hawtrey, *Commentary on Plato's Euthydemus* (Philadelphia 1981) 85 claims that the addition of νοῦν ἔχων would 'merely add an extra complication'. F. D. Caizzi, *Platone Eutidemo* (Milan 1996) does not discuss the issue, but follows Burnet. Terence Irwin, *Plato's Ethics* (Oxford 1995) 362 n. 12 also follows the MS.

[29] Here, as earlier in the discussion, the virtues are treated on a par with other states of a person which might be initially thought of as unqualifiedly good (health, wealth, sharp sight). Despite the parallel with the *Meno*, C. Badham (*Platonis Euthydemus et Laches*) (Jena 1865) and Gifford (n. 28) delete καὶ σώφρων. Hawtrey (n. 28) retains.

[30] Cleinias seems to have been betrayed by the sequence of argument here: why should the cowardly person be more quietist than the brave?

[31] Socrates alludes here to various lists in the argument that has gone before: first, wealth, health, beauty, good reputation and power, self-control, justice and courage, wisdom and good luck (279a–c); and then in the argument immediately preceding my quotation, wealth, strength, reputation, courage and self-control, business, quickness of foot and eye, sharpness of hearing (281b–d). There is something strange about both lists, in comparison to the *Meno* list, as I shall suggest further.

[32] R. K. Sprague's reading of λόγος here is 'correct account': translation of the *Euthydemus* in J. M. Cooper (ed.), *Plato: Complete Works* (Indianapolis 1997); cf. Hawtrey (n. 28) 89.

[33] The comparatives here emphasise the relativity of these values; relative, that is, to the context or the character of the agent. This gives rise to the compresence of opposites claim; see further below.

themselves neither sort of thing is worth anything.' 'It seems to be exactly as you say,' he said. 'So what follows for us from what has been said? Surely it is that nothing else is either good or bad, but these things alone are so — wisdom is good and ignorance is bad.' (*Euthydemus* 281b–e).

The *Euthydemus* passage is usually construed as a variant of the *Meno*, on the grounds that both passages seem to argue for the view that wisdom (knowledge) is necessary and sufficient for happiness: 'whatever is done with intelligence is beneficial, whatever without it, harmful.'[34]

One view of the argument common to both passages would take Socrates to be asking about wisdom's utility. Wisdom itself seems to be a good because it is instrumental to the goodness of all the other goods: hence the conclusion of the *Meno* that wisdom is 'the beneficial' (89a2). For it seems obvious, in the first place, that health, wealth and so on are both beneficial and harmful. If correct use 'leads them' they are beneficial; if not, they are harmful. Next, allow that self-control, justice and so on, are qualities of soul. Suppose that some quality of soul (courage, say) is not knowledge: in that case, it both harms and benefits. For it harms when it operates without wisdom, benefits when it operates with it. So for all the endeavours of soul, if wisdom is the leader they end in happiness, if ignorance is the leader they end in the reverse. Qualities of soul, therefore, are not beneficial in themselves, but if and only if wisdom leads them. But virtue must be beneficial; so (contrary to our earlier supposition that some quality of the soul not be knowledge) virtue must be knowledge.

Socrates reaches his conclusion, apparently, by supposing that all the other putative goods considered will harm or benefit according to whether they are 'led' by wisdom or ignorance: thus, for example, the reckless person rushing towards danger in ignorance will come to grief (88b4). So throughout the *Meno* passage value seems to be construed in terms of whether something has good or bad results, and harm and benefit are construed in terms of consequential goods, in terms of whether they 'end in happiness'. Accordingly, knowledge will be both necessary and sufficient for happiness in a purely instrumental sense: if and only if we are knowledgeable, we shall end up happy. How might that conclusion be plausible? Perhaps knowledge is sufficient for good results because whenever we know what will be a good result, we always pursue it (and, if knowledge has executive skill, we get it, too).[35] And perhaps knowledge is necessary for good results because

---

[34] Assuming, simplistically, of course, that benefit and harm are exclusive and exhaustive.

[35] On the assumption, perhaps, that akrasia is impossible.

ignorance reliably results in disaster (ignorance completely lacks executive skill). And that thought may be reflected in the positive conclusion of the *Euthydemus* passage, that wisdom is the only good, ignorance the only evil.

So if wisdom is a good thing just because it produces good things or just because it has excellent, happy results, wisdom is instrumentally good. The value it has, therefore, derives from its consequences, which are understood to be desirable in themselves (whatever they might be: many theories of this kind need some kind of hedonism to make it clear that there are consequences of this sort[36]). Suppose, now, that something other than wisdom turned out to be an equally reliable instrument to those same ends (having a fairy godmother, perhaps, or being attached to a well-oiled pleasure-machine): in that case, there would be nothing to choose between one's own wisdom and the convenient interventions of one's fairy godmother or the switch gear of the machine. There would, that is to say, be no condition on the best outcome that it should be achieved through one's own efforts or endeavours, just so long as an equally efficient means to the end turns up. If wisdom is instrumental in this sense, Socrates' argument is classically consequentialist.[37]

Yet the *Meno* argument, albeit clear in structure, is murky in sense. What is it to 'end in happiness'? Does this describe some extrinsic result of some process, the cheerful counterpart of its ending in tears? Or might the end be somehow internal to the process — as Aristotle would, after all, allow?[38] What is it for something to be 'beneficial'? Does what is beneficial have good results, extrinsic to itself, or may it simply be valuable, in itself? When Socrates asks whether there can be a good separated from knowledge, then supposes that courage may be other than knowledge, and concludes that virtue must *be* knowledge, what does he mean? Does he mean that we are virtuous if and only if we are knowledgeable, so that virtue and knowledge are coextensive? Or is there a stronger metaphysics here: does he mean that

---

[36] See the many utilitarian appeals to hedonism, most famously of all in Bentham.

[37] See here e.g., S. Scheffler, *The Rejection of Consequentialism* (Oxford 1982) ch. 1.

[38] Compare and contrast: I go to the dentist in order to have healthy teeth; the good of having healthy teeth is extrinsic to, independent of, the nasty business of going to the dentist, even if having healthy teeth demands dentistry (could I achieve the teeth without the dentist, I would). But the good of learning about Plato is intrinsic to, inseparable from, the process of reading him: I cannot do one without the other, nor would I want to. Compare here e.g., G. E. Moore, *Principia Ethica* (Cambridge 1903); C. Korsgaard, 'Two distinctions in goodness', *Philosophical Review* 92 (1983) 169–95; W. Rabinowicz and T. Ronnow-Rasmussen, 'A distinction in value: intrinsic and for its own sake' *Proceedings of the Aristotelian Society* 100 (2000) 33–52.

somehow virtue *is the same thing* as knowledge?[39] What is it, further, for wisdom to 'lead' the endeavours of soul? Perhaps Socrates' point is that somehow wisdom or knowledge controls the means to some good end: so the process of leading is, again, to be construed instrumentally; but is the metaphor of 'leading' as simple as that? We might demand a re-read: the *Meno* may not be a safe seat for the consequentialist, after all.[40]

The *Euthydemus*, at first glance, might reassure. For that seems, too, to deploy a consequentialist analysis: wisdom is exactly what produces success, ignorance is exactly what produces failure; and their value derives from what they produce or fail to produce.[41] So both texts seem to attempt an answer to a question such as 'what makes us happy'? — where the notion of 'what *makes* us...' seems to be an instrumental one. What is more, the two texts are remarkably alike, both verbally and structurally. The *Meno* first suggests that it is the leadership of correct use which produces benefit, and then argues that if the qualities of soul are not knowledge ($\epsilon\pi\iota\sigma\tau\eta\mu\eta$, 88b2) or reason ($\phi\rho\delta\nu\eta\sigma\iota\varsigma$, 88b4) then benefit turns up just when intelligence ($\nu o\hat{\upsilon}\varsigma$) is present (88b5).[42] Then, 88c2, 'when reason ($\phi\rho\delta\nu\eta\sigma\iota\varsigma$) leads', it ends in happiness. This is taken to imply that virtue is reason, and that 'the things of the soul' are not beneficial in themselves, unless reason is added (88c). It is, thus, the leadership of reason that makes things beneficial (i.e., that makes things end in goods). So 'for a man everything else needs to be connected to the soul; and everything in his soul itself needs to be connected to reason, if he is going to get goods;[43] and on that argument reason is the beneficial' (88e). The *Euthydemus*, too, makes its point via a discussion of correct use, and it has a similarly catholic vocabulary. Wisdom ($\sigma o\phi\iota a$) either makes people lucky, or makes good luck unnecessary (280a6, b2–3); correct use is explained in terms of knowledge ($\epsilon\pi\iota\sigma\tau\eta\mu\eta$, 281a3), so that it is knowledge

---

[39] Evidently this would need to claim that virtue is more than (some entity over and above?) the collection of virtuous people, and likewise for knowledge.

[40] We may note that what follows, 88d4–89a3, is also indeterminate: does it claim that the soul is the best guide to what is good, or the source of its goodness? As we shall see, the 'leading/guiding' metaphor is a complex one.

[41] On Platonic consequentialism in general, see Irwin (n. 28). If my hypothesis — that the *Meno* is re-read by the *Euthydemus* — is correct, then the *Meno* may be less consequentialist than it seems.

[42] Is the point of the rather elaborate set-up to make us contrast an instrumental view (I did it with a blunt instrument) with something more internal (I did it with malice aforethought)?

[43] This clause is ambiguous: it may mean that if everything is connected in this way, then they will be good; or it may mean (taking $\tau\hat{\omega}$ $\dot{a}\nu\theta\rho\dot{\omega}\pi\omega$ with this clause) that everything must be connected in this way if goods are going to belong to him (an analogous expression is to be found at *Euthydemus* 279a3). I shall suggest below that the indeterminacy of this point is part of the focus of the *Euthydemus* passage.

that produces good luck as well as faring well (281b3); no possession is any use without reason and wisdom (φρόνησις, σοφία, 281b6); men can do no good without intelligence (νοῦς 281b7); and the conclusion is phrased in terms of a contrast between wisdom (σοφία) and ignorance (ἀμαθία 281e5). The *Meno* relies heavily on the metaphor of 'leading', whether the leader is knowledge or correct use (88a3, 88c2, 88e1); so too does the *Euthydemus* (281b1, 281d6, d7[44]). But both passages amplify this metaphor by talk of the possession or the presence of wisdom, reason, or intelligence (*Meno* 88b7–8, c7, *Euthydemus* 280b2, 281b7). In each the terminology of value attends heavily to 'the beneficial and the harmful'. And both passages conclude with some reflection on what fails to be good itself by itself (although the *Euthydemus*, notably, goes further in making a claim about what succeeds).

So perhaps we should see both passages as variants of each other, expressing roughly the same point (about the instrumental use of knowledge or wisdom) in roughly the same language. The similarity between the two passages is to be explained by the thought that there is a basic thesis that underlies them both;[45] and this thesis just happens to be phrased in similar terminology in each case. What Plato lacks in technical vocabulary — we might suppose — he makes up for in metaphor.

Perhaps, in that case, we should see both passages as expressions of a 'Socratic' account of the relation between knowledge and happiness. Knowledge is the only reliable instrument to happiness (however happiness is explicated[46]) and happiness only arises when we have the reliable instrument to it: knowledge is necessary and sufficient for happiness. Just so, it might be said, Socrates recommends the 'measuring art' in the *Protagoras* (352–7):[47] for it is exactly the art that can measure pleasure. So — to return to the *Euthydemus* and the *Meno* — we might suppose that their similarity is a mark of this Socratism, of a body of ethical views represented in the arguments of Plato's early dialogues.[48]

---

[44] Here the metaphor is made richer by talk of the servants of the leader.

[45] So Hawtrey (n. 28) 88: 'the unity of ἀρέτη and its identity with knowledge or wisdom'.

[46] Again, questions of the relation between hedonism and eudaimonism intrude here when we think in consequential mode.

[47] Of course this passage of the *Protagoras* may need re-reading, too — as many of those puzzled by its hedonism have allowed.

[48] See Vlastos (1991) (n. 5). This account of the influence of Socrates on Plato has, of course, been vividly contested recently, notably by Kahn and Annas (n. 6).

iii

Two thoughts about the *Euthydemus* might make a *prima facie* case against such an account, an account that supposes that the literary connection between the passages merely emphasises some doctrine that they are thought to hold in common. If, first, there is a doctrine about the relation between virtue and knowledge lurking behind both passages, it is a doctrine which we might most easily associate with a Socratic view of action and motivation (such as we seem to find in the *Protagoras*). But the view of the conflicted soul to be found in the *Republic* — standardly thought to be characteristically Platonic — tells a more complicated story, both about the nature of motivation, and about the relation between knowledge and the ends we in fact pursue. So if the *Euthydemus* has any affinity with the *Republic*,[49] or with dialogues later than the *Republic*,[50] then its use of the *Meno*'s material is hardly likely to be straightforward. In the second place, the *Euthydemus* itself invites scepticism about facile consequentialism. In the later, companion piece to our passage (288d–293a)[51] Socrates and his companions[52] find themselves trying to specify what science it is that makes its possessor happy, and are caught in a regress. Every science they suggest shows us how to get goods, but not how to use them: and it is only proper use that will give us happiness. In the end, Socrates announces that they have been on a wild-goose chase — or running through a labyrinth where each time they think they have reached the end of their journey, they find themselves back at the beginning again (291b–c).[53] But the regress affecting their reasoning comes about because they are unable to specify the object of their search, to say what it is that

---

[49] *Cf.* e.g. M. Narcy, *Le philosophe et son double: un commentaire de l' Euthydème de Platon* (Paris 1984) 183; M. F. Burnyeat, 'Plato on how to speak what is not: *Euthydemus* 283a–288a', in M. Canto-Sperber and P. Pellegrin (eds.), *Festschrift for Jacques Brunschwig* (Paris 2002) n. 46; also Hawtrey (n. 28) 127–8.

[50] As I have argued, 'Silencing the Sophists', *Proceedings of the Boston Area Colloquium in Ancient Philosophy* (1998) 139–168. But see the more conventional view of Hawtrey (n. 28) 3–11.

[51] The companion piece is the other Socratic episode of the dialogue; each of the Socratic passages is flanked by two sophistic episodes, giving five episodes of argument altogether.

[52] There is considerable by-play about just which companion says what, 291a; this enhances the irony of the Socratic episodes considered as a pair.

[53] The complaints of regress or circularity commonly beset consequentialist reasoning: if you suppose that goods of some specified set, or type, are just good, just desirable, in themselves, what makes them so? An appeal to virtue, or character, of function is designed to pre-empt those complaints by focusing on a richer account of the agent, rather than on setting his ends independently (see here e.g., G. E. M. Anscombe, 'Modern Moral Philosophy', *Philosophy* (1958) 1–19; P. Foot, *Virtues and Vices* (Los Angeles 1978). The danger is that 'virtue ethics' often seems rather vague

provides and brings about happiness (291b6). This failure, in turn, is not so much an ignorance of the means, but a failure to understand just what happiness is. If, then, the earlier passage is a reprise of the *Meno*, and if the *Meno* argument is construed in a consequentialist manner, then the later Socratic episode of the *Euthydemus* directly undercuts the earlier, and in so doing undermines its predecessor in the *Meno*.[54] Yet my two passages have remarkable similarities. So what then is the relation between them after all?

The *Euthydemus* passage is set in an elaborate context, introduced by a heavily ironised account of what we might hold to be goods,[55] by whose presence we count ourselves to be doing well (278e–280a). It proceeds to the claim that wisdom (σοφία) includes good luck, because wisdom protects us from making mistakes, and then suggests ('we reached the conclusion, I know not how' 280b1) that if you have wisdom, you don't need good luck anyway. The argument then restarts at 280b, with exactly the *Meno*'s point: goods that are merely 'present to us' are useless unless they are actually beneficial; and they will not be beneficial without correct use (280b–281b). So knowledge (ἐπιστήμη) does not just provide good luck, it provides doing well (εὐπραγία), for none of our possessions are of any use without reason and wisdom. There follows a short argument about relative benefits and harms (281b–c). Then Socrates concludes with our passage: none of the putative goods is worth anything in itself; but wisdom is the good, ignorance the bad. On a cursory reading, we might indeed conclude that the two arguments are the same.

This apparent congruence of the two passages, however, may mask a more complex relation. If the *Meno* asks 'what makes us happy?' we could read the question instrumentally: what promotes this end, happiness?[56] Or the question may be differently understood: suppose we treat 'happiness' as a place-holder for whatever we shall take to be valuable in a life,[57] then 'what makes us happy' may inquire into the nature, and the source, of value

---

(although see R. Hursthouse, *Virtue Ethics* (Oxford 1999)). Here Socrates points up the worry about specifying the end of our endeavours by showing that the same kind of regressive feature besets arguments about such endeavours.

[54] Point taken by Annas (n. 15). *Cf.* here Striker (n. 15) 318, who takes the two Socratic episodes to be roughly continuous. I think this is not so and that the second episode treats some of the assumptions of the first in different, and critical, ways.

[55] Notice, for example, the cagey way in which the virtues are introduced at 279b4 ff., or the alacrity with which Socrates — Socrates? — suggests that wealth is universally acknowledged to be a good, without himself endorsing the universal view, 279a7.

[56] This seems to be how Sprague takes the passage (n. 3) 9–10.

[57] Ancient eudaimonism is especially about lives: how best to live? See Williams (n. 22).

itself: what is happiness, how is it constituted?[58] If we ask the *Meno* this different question: 'what makes something valuable?' we might expect two different kinds of answer. On the one hand, something may be instrumentally valuable, because it produces happiness; on the other, something may be non-instrumentally valuable — because it is the end to which the instrumental values lead. The argument itself seems to sustain the view that wisdom is instrumentally valuable (and since it is both necessary and sufficient for happiness, wisdom may be the only instrumental value) but not that it is non-instrumentally valuable (there is nothing here, for example, to show that wisdom is in fact constitutive of happiness, nor to show that it is valuable anyway, irrespective of its relation to happiness). The value of wisdom, on that account, is *derivative from its consequences*, and in this sense is a consequential value.

What is more, although this argument seems to show that the *possession* of those consequences requires wisdom, it seems to do nothing to show that the *value* of those consequences derives from wisdom (for while health and wealth do in fact convey benefit because of wisdom, the value of the benefit they convey derives from their consequences). In this respect, therefore, the *Meno* seems again to have affinities with modern consequentialist arguments, which explain the good in terms of states of affairs, and are (or are in their simpler forms[59]) indifferent to how those states of affairs are brought about, just so long as they are brought about in the most efficient and most prolific way. There is nothing, on such an account, to choose between two different means to some desired end except by virtue of their efficiency. So, for the *Meno* argument, were it to turn out false that wisdom is good at producing the right kind of outcome, there would be no residual reason to be wise. What is more, and considerations of efficiency aside, the *Meno* should be indifferent in particular to whether those states of affairs are brought about by the agent who enjoys them, or not brought about by him, but merely enjoyed by him. If it were to turn out that being born at the rising of the dog-star is a more efficient way of getting happiness than being wise, then we should desert the philosophy schools altogether. Consequentialism is not, as the modern debates put it, *agent-relative*. According to the consequentialist, I should value wisdom because it is good at producing the desired consequences, not because there is something important about the fact that this wisdom belongs to me, nor because there is something pertinent to my

---

[58] This point is taken by M. Canto, *L' intrigue philosophique: Essai sur l' Euthydème de Platon* (Paris 1987) 132 and 276 n. 88.

[59] But notice here modern attempts to patch consequentialism up: e.g., Scheffler (n. 37).

happiness in the fact that I myself am its instrument.[60] So a consequentialist view is inclined towards instrumentalism, too: any instrument is valuable just insofar as it produces the consequences we desire.

So what makes the goods which constitute success valuable? That question invites an answer, not about the means to success, nor even about the necessary and sufficient conditions of happiness, but rather about the source of value itself.[61] (If I want to play at Robinson Crusoe, and this aeroplane is both necessary and sufficient to get me to the requisite tropical island, the aeroplane has value derivative from the value of the consequences that it provides. When I arrive at my island, only to be smitten with a grim sense of the meaninglessness of this desert existence, my misery will not be explained by virtue of the aeroplane which got me there, nor merely by virtue of the fact that the aeroplane has flown away.) And that question presses on the consequentialist, who needs to provide a robust account of the goods that constitute our ends (which is why he often finds hedonism so attractive). The *Euthydemus'* argument suggests that this question, 'what makes these goods valuable?', is the one we should ask.[62]

Consider, first, an argument that appears in the *Euthydemus* without any counterpart in the *Meno*. At 280e6 Socrates suggests that if someone uses something badly, he is worse off than if he had left it alone. This introduces a relative consideration, which is amplified at 281b–c. Is someone better off with more possessions but no wisdom, or with wisdom and few goods? The sequence of argument that follows seems to espouse a kind of quietism: we are better off doing less if we are stupid, because we can make fewer mistakes, and the fewer mistakes we make the less wretched we shall be. So far, so consequential. It then follows that the person who lacks the putative goods (wealth, strength, reputation, even courage) will do better than the person who has them, but no wisdom. It is taken to follow from this that 'if ignorance leads them, they are greater evils than their opposites, to the extent that they are better able to serve a bad leader; but if intelligence and wisdom lead them, they are greater goods; but themselves by themselves neither sort of thing is worth anything' (281d). Now the focus of attention seems to have changed. For we are not now thinking about how beneficial or harmful these things are

---

[60] To make this point we need to distinguish between whether I am the agent of my own happiness and whether I am its patient. The consequentialist view does not, of course, insist that the happiness is not enjoyed by the person in question: but this is merely, if you like, a locative claim.

[61] *Cf.* Korsgaard (n. 38).

[62] Indeed, the puzzle of the second 'Socratic' episode — the labyrinthine way in which the ends of our actions recede from us as we pursue them — makes this point too.

(things which we originally thought were uncontroversial goods), nor how far they will reliably issue in the happiness which we pursue. Instead, we are asked to consider their value in themselves: and Socrates insists that they have none, but that their value is derivative from what leads them: if that be wisdom, they are good, if that be ignorance, evil.

How might this be thought to follow from the case of the blind man who is saved from the consequences of his own folly by being unable to see what he is doing (281d1)? The argument does its work, as the conclusion makes clear, by inviting a comparison between the wise man who has access to few assets,[63] and the foolish one who has access to many. How are we to assess, or to compute, the relative value of the two situations (the question of such computation is one that the consequentialist keenly asks, as Plato himself knew, cf. *Protagoras* 351 ff.)? After all, even if the foolish man squanders most of his wealth, there might be enough in his pocket to weigh against the small change of the wise man. Even if he squanders it all, is he any worse off than the wise man who started with nothing and ends with the same amount? If wisdom is valuable instrumentally, and has no scope for action, it will be no more and no less valuable than folly, which is instrumentally useless. Why then should wisdom and folly make the difference in cases like this? The answer Socrates supplies only follows if wisdom and folly are now conceived, not as the instruments to maximising our enjoyment of goods, but as themselves the source of their value, *and* also as valuable in themselves. Then if the foolish man has no matter how much more loot than the wise one, but the very goodness of the loot depends on the wise man's wisdom, its evil on the foolish man's folly, then no matter how little he has, even nothing at all, the wise man comes off best.

The *Euthydemus* alerts us to this conclusion by the way it began its inquiry into the nature of 'doing well'. It is absurd, Socrates suggests, to ask whether all men want to 'do well' — for of course everyone wants that. Socrates' use of the famously opaque expression 'doing well' sets the agenda

---

[63] Rejecting Iamblichus' reading of 281b7; see n. 29 above. Annas (n. 6) 40 ff. follows Iamblichus, but reads the point as 'that without wisdom you are actually better off with conventional evils', since you will be less able to abuse what you have, less able wrongly to exploit what are conventionally thought of as advantages. Consequently, the value of putative goods is dependent on the life into which they are incorporated. I find Annas' overall interpretation sympathetic, as will become clear. However, Iamblichus' reading allows the conclusion that the problem is merely an executive one — of being properly guided in correct use. This is too weak to support the further conclusion that there is something — wisdom — which is good 'itself by itself'. Contrariwise, the thought that the wise man is better off with nothing than the ignorant man with a great deal does give warrant to the conclusion: as, I shall suggest, the Stoic readers of this passage saw.

for what follows, not by telling us just what it means, but rather by suggesting some scepticism about what it might be taken to mean. For if we all want to do well, *how exactly* will this happen? Is it by having many goods? This question is even more absurd, Socrates says, for it is obviously so. Now Socrates offers a list of putative goods, starting with wealth, health and beautiful bodies, continuing to good birth and political power, including more dubiously self-control, justice and courage, then wisdom and finally, after a long flourish, good luck. The list should give us pause.[64] Is this Socrates, his old disreputable self (notice the repeated issue of Socrates' aged obstinacy, e.g. at 272c, 287b), who is extolling the importance of wealth? Or Socrates, who turns some of his best irony on the importance of an impressive genealogy (here of Cleinias at 275a–b, in the same breath as describing the fear lest he be corrupted), advocating the best life of the elite? Or Socrates who thinks that the importance of wisdom is the way it secures good luck?[65]

Consider the conclusion again. Socrates claims, first, that the value of the items on his original list depends on the value of what 'leads' them (that claim, of course, is compatible with a consequentialist analysis, that they are only valuable, for example, in this particular assemblage, intelligently arranged): so they are not valuable 'themselves by themselves'. So far, so compatible with the *Meno*, and so far in the *Meno*'s words. But he suggests, second, that the items on the original list *have no value*, while wisdom, which 'leads them' is *the only good*. This claim seems markedly different from the *Meno*'s offering: that 'all the qualities of the soul are neither beneficial nor harmful in themselves' (88c6), and that wisdom is 'the beneficial' (89a1–2). For the *Meno* still allows for a consequentialist account, still may be asking the instrumental question: 'how can we do best?' The *Euthydemus*, by contrast, in asking 'which things are goods (after all)?' undermines the list of putative goods,[66] and attacks the consequentialist view that our ends can easily be specified. As a result, it shifts our attention to the deeper — metaphysical — question: 'what is the source of value'?

---

[64] Even as we read it for the first time; of course the conclusion of the first phase of the argument at 2801d–e justifies our unease.

[65] Here, 280a, we might suppose that Socrates' interlocutors mean something rather different by the connection between good luck and wisdom than Socrates does. Once again the text is ironical, in the sense that it invites the reader to see the gap between what Socrates says and what his interlocutors understand.

[66] Both by the ironical way in which they are discussed, and through the accusation of circularity of the second Socratic episode.

iv

So does the *Euthydemus*, so far from confirming the consequentialist view of the *Meno*, actually make a quite different point? And if it does, why does Plato choose later to reuse the *Meno*'s terminology and argumentative structure? Had he just run out of new ideas — was he forced thus to recycle the old? On the contrary, I suggest that the similarity between the two passages has a direct philosophical purpose. After all, the *Meno* passage is short and condensed; and it is a matter of interpretation to elicit from it the consequentialist view I have outlined: for example, by construing the assumption that virtue must be beneficial instrumentally in order to generate the conclusion that virtue is knowledge; or, as I suggested above, in taking the relation between virtue and knowledge as a material equivalence rather than as some stronger identity claim.[67] In reading the *Meno* passage, that is to say, we need a bit more help than the bare text gives us. That help is forthcoming, I suggest, from the *Euthydemus*, which invites us to rethink the instrumental account of the *Meno*, and to think in a different way about the nature of value. To invite this re-reading, Plato uses similar vocabulary and argumentative structure: but not from either intellectual poverty nor from parsimony, but as an explicit reflection of one passage on the other. This kind of reflectiveness is itself a mark of a philosophical approach: if, in re-reading each passage, we compare them and contrast, we may by that very process be brought to ask the higher-order question: 'How are we to think about the source of value?'

Even so, the *Euthydemus*' conclusion is vague.[68] It could mean one of two things:[69]

[67] Consider the following, permitted within a consequentialist analysis. Suppose that virtue is maximising pleasure for myself. Knowledge is necessary and sufficient for virtue just because whenever I know what will be pleasant, I grab it; and because I can only grab a pleasure (pleasures being the elusive things they are) when I know what it is. So I am virtuous if and only if I am knowledgeable — but what it is to be virtuous is defined in terms of grabbing, even of enjoying pleasures; what it is to be knowledgeable in terms of spotting the pleasures that are out there to be grabbed. Knowledge and virtue are here materially equivalent. Contrariwise, I might think that virtue is, not so much a felicific maximiser, but a state of soul, some quality of the person who has it over and above its executive advantages. In that case, I might suppose, for example, that virtue has the same psychological dimensions as knowledge, so that virtue and knowledge are in fact two different descriptions of the same thing: the best state of soul. In that case, my identity claim is stronger than a material equivalence.

[68] In my opinion, deliberately so.

[69] See Vlastos 1991 (n. 5). Vlastos, however, takes the view that the text is both determinate in its meaning (which I deny, since I suppose that the ellipse is deliberate) and moderate in its sentiment (and thus compatible with the *Meno*'s view).

(a) Nothing has any value at all except wisdom. Wisdom is the only valuable thing. (I shall call this the *exclusive* view.)[70]

(b) Wisdom is the only thing that has value 'itself by itself'; all the other valuable items are so derivatively from wisdom. (I shall call this the *derivative* view.)[71]

Either goes beyond any sort of consequentialist or instrumentalist account. (a) takes Socrates' remark at *Euthydemus* 281e4–5 literally (as 'nothing is good or bad at all except wisdom and ignorance'). (b) takes it to be an ellipse (for 'nothing else is either good or bad in itself except wisdom and ignorance, which are good and bad themselves by themselves', which allows for the possibility that other things may be good, but not themselves by themselves).[72] In both cases Socrates' claim is not the negative one that we find in the *Meno* ('nothing on the list is good or bad on its own', which neither implies that wisdom is the *only* good, nor even that wisdom is good itself by itself;[73] after all, there may be nothing which is just good), but rather a positive claim about what value really is: wisdom is the *only good* (*itself by itself*).[74]

This conclusion is derived from the thought that things other than wisdom — the putative goods, wealth, health and so forth — may be characterised in opposite ways, since they may either harm or benefit. In general these putative goods suffer from what is often described as the 'compresence of opposites': because an individual case of wealth may harm or benefit,

---

[70] This could be expressed, although it is not apparently so in this passage, as a contrast between an objective view (wisdom is the only thing which is really, genuinely, valuable) and a subjective one (all the other things seem valuable, but in fact they are not). That contrast could be emphasised by the way in which the putative list is set up in terms of who believes such and such an item to be valuable (although I myself think that Socrates' strategy there is quite different).

[71] This view is entirely compatible with an objectivist account of value: both what is valuable itself by itself and what is valuable derivatively from it may be objectively so.

[72] *Cf.* here Vlastos' remarks (1991, n. 5), and Long's disagreement (n. 14) 26.

[73] What may be an identity claim at 89a1, 'according to this argument wisdom would be the beneficial', does not imply that either. The beneficial nature of wisdom here may be its being a necessary and even sufficient condition for all other valuables — this still allows for the possibility that its value may derive from its relation to them.

[74] What should we say about the unclarity, or the elliptical nature, of Socrates' conclusion? In the context of the elaborate composition of the *Euthydemus*, and especially with a view to the critique of some of the assumptions of the first Socratic episode in the second, I am of the view that the unclarity is deliberate: in order to expose, as the argument progresses, the different assumptions which we must make along the way.

wealth in general both harms and benefits.[75] This may then prompt us to look for what is valuable in itself—or 'itself by itself', as Plato often expresses it.[76] Why would we embark on that search? We may be driven to find what is valuable in itself because we suppose that wealth, and the other putative goods, because they both harm and benefit, lose their claim to being truly, properly, good. If that is why we search for what is good in itself, we may incline towards an exclusive view of this argument (we may be searching, that is to say, for perfection). Or we may suppose that the fact that wealth, health and the others suffer from the compresence of opposites implies that they do not explain, by themselves, why we value them. In that case we may search for an explanation, or a source, of their value: and this will incline us towards the derivative view of this argument.

But in either case, what is required from knowledge or wisdom is not so much a calculus of what to do in some particular situation (as the consequentialist reading of the *Meno* suggests) but rather an account of what it is for any of the objects of choice to be valuable at all. If wisdom is what is good itself by itself, then — whether exclusively or derivatively — it explains value. It does that, as the final argument of the *Euthydemus* makes clear, not pragmatically[77] (by merely allowing us to understand the messy chaos of the world and its values), but in reality, by being the source of the value itself. For only thus could Plato justify the argument which so puzzled Iamblichus.

> Does it profit a man to have many possessions and to do many things if he has no intelligence, or rather to have and do fewer things, but with intelligence? Consider the matter thus. Surely if he were to do less, he would make fewer mistakes, and if he were to make fewer mistakes he would do less badly; and if he were to do less badly he would be less wretched? (*Euthydemus* 281b)

Consider what is happening here. One construal of this suggests that the argument turns on the idea that the stupid man makes mistakes, reliably and predictably, by virtue of his stupidity. Making mistakes is a bad thing, because it is harmful; and so it results in the stupid man doing badly and being unhappy.

---

[75] This argument form is familiar from elsewhere in Plato. It is worth noting that in the case of value Plato moves from the claim that ethical tokens may be either valuable or harmful to the claim that the type is both valuable and harmful. For other examples, such as relations, he suggests that the token suffers from compresence directly: Cebes is taller than Socrates, smaller than Simmias, so Cebes is both tall and small (Plato does not, of course, make the mistake of supposing this to be a contradiction). *Cf.* here e.g. *Phaedo* 102b ff.

[76] E.g. *Phaedo* 78d.

[77] See D. H. Ruben, *Explaining Explanation* (London 1991).

So we are to compare the idiot millionaire who has huge opportunities for following his misguided principles with the ignorant pauper who has none; just because the millionaire has executive capacity, he has the scope to make a lifetime of mistakes, from which poverty protects his counterpart. The wise man is a pauper, too; he too has few assets, but the wisdom to use them well: so he is in for a lifetime of doing well, and better off than either of his ignorant counterparts. But of course the assets that each of these characters is using or abusing are themselves members of the list of putative goods. So we are to imagine each character with their putative goods: the millionaire has a million units of wealth; the pauper and the wise man only one. The millionaire will abuse all million; the ignorant pauper will abuse his one; and the wise man will benefit from his singularity. The millionaire, then, has an immense capacity to make mistakes, the pauper hardly any. But why then should we prefer to be one rather than the other? If a mistake is simply a failure to get an asset (as the consequential view suggests), there is nothing to choose between them; but if a mistake is itself a harm, then clearly the millionaire is by far the worse off. Likewise if the choice between the millionaire and the wise man is simply that the millionaire repeatedly fails to get things right, where the wise man does get things right, but only on his one, singular occasion, we might not suppose that the wise man is markedly better off than the millionaire. If, on the other hand, the mistakes are themselves harms (rather than mere failures to get goods) then the choice is an easy one: the millionaire is the worst off, the pauper next and the wise man is the best off of all. But this will only be the result of the calculation if the mistakes are themselves items of value or the reverse; and this in turn will only be a reasonable assumption if we suppose, not that wisdom confers executive power, but that it confers value itself. By virtue of a man's rational capacities, that is to say, his actions are valued: wisdom is a good itself by itself because it is the source of value.

Why then should we say that the stupid man is better off with fewer assets because he has 'fewer servants of a wicked leader'? What exactly are we to make of the metaphor of leadership? The consequential view is made tempting by what we might call the *executive* image: the leader is the chap who gives the orders, the designer of the plan, the artificer of the cunning scheme which he hands down to his subordinates to secure those goods which are already and independently valued. But there is a different image of leadership, which we might call *regal*. The king organises his court, decides who shall be in favour and who shall be cast into the outer darkness; it is the king who appoints one courtier to be master of the bedchamber, and denies another any access to his royal person at all. There are no independent goods, on this view: the value is all within the structure of the court. We may imagine here, also, two different images of a mistake. A mistake, on the executive model, may be simply a bust machine, a broken instrument for achieving the ends set before the leader, an incompetent executive in the owner's employ. Still on this view the ends are pre-set; the instruments are valuable insofar as they achieve them. Or, on the regal model, we may imagine the disappointment of the old career courtier whose value becomes less and less as he is passed over for the younger and more ambitious men. Here the ends are inextricable from the value conferred by the king himself: the courtier's life depends for its value on the king, and not on the ends it achieves.

The conclusion of the *Euthydemus* turns away from the executive, and favours the regal model of leadership. And in doing so, it shifts away from consequentialism. It still insists, however, that the source of the value of other things (what 'leads them') — not now construed as the end of some action, independently specified — is itself valuable. And that value is intrinsic: that is to say, its value is not dependent on anything else.[78] That might allow two further claims for the *Euthydemus* argument:

(c)   what explains value is the source of value;[79]

(d)   what is the source of value is intrinsically valuable,

claims, once again, which are missing from the apparently consequentialist account of the *Meno*.[80] One purpose of the similarities and the differences between the two passages may be to invite reflection on just this point.

In the *Meno*, Socrates' argument can go through on the basis of two sorts of consideration: of extrinsic value, which is dependent on something else (hence, for example, the implication at 87d that no good is separate from

---

[78] Again, it seems to be a commonplace of Plato's account of explanation that what is extrinsically thus and so is explained by what is intrinsically thus and so, especially when it comes to evaluative properties (see Moore, Korsgaard n. 38). So intrinsic value will be independent, extrinsic value dependent on something else for its value; and intrinsic value will thus be, at least from the explanatory point of view, prior. The same pattern seems to be urged for other cases where Plato postulates a form; see here the claims about the 'separation' of forms at *Parmenides* 129a ff.

[79] Just as what explains equality is the source of equality, and the same for largeness, etc.: see *Phaedo* 100d. As elsewhere in Plato, this is a realist account of explanation: the point made in the *Euthydemus* is not about how we see value, but rather about the way value is actually constructed and derived, out there in the world.

[80] Again, one may see this by reflecting on the conclusion of the *Meno*'s argument. If the argument shows that wisdom is the beneficial, it seems to have done so by showing that all other benefits depend on it; but its beneficial nature may equally depend on them, since its beneficial nature derives from its capacity to collect other goods together. This mutual dependency is not vicious; but it does rule out the claim that wisdom is intrinsically valuable. The *Euthydemus*, on the other hand, is committed to the claim that wisdom alone is valuable itself by itself. In doing so it takes wisdom to be intrinsically valuable; and then its value cannot be derivative from the consequences that it may contrive.

knowledge: a claim which does not imply that knowledge is separately, that is intrinsically, good); and of instrumental value, value which is derived from the achievement of something else valuable. These considerations are not the same. Take, for example, health: in order to achieve, or to use in the most effective way, a healthy constitution, we need wisdom: health, therefore, is actually valuable for us only in the presence of something else, namely wisdom; health is extrinsically valuable.[81] But wisdom, conversely, may be valuable because of this instrumental contribution it makes to something else: the wisdom which provides health and makes it useful is itself valuable by virtue of the good thing it provides — namely health. In the *Euthydemus* the situation is different: here (if I read the conclusion aright) the contrast is between items of extrinsic value, derivative from something else, and intrinsic value, a solitary item which is valuable in itself. And here the extrinsically valuable depends for its value on the intrinsically valuable; but the intrinsically valuable is valuable itself by itself.

This conclusion has two important consequences for the account of value to be found in these pages of the *Euthydemus*. First, the relation between what is valuable itself by itself and what is valuable by virtue of it is an *explanatory* relation between two real things. This explanatory relation supports an answer to the question 'why do we value this?' Second, at least on the derivative view, goods are thus arranged hierarchically: what is intrinsically good is so absolutely, what is extrinsically good is so relatively to the intrinsic good.[82] But — because the one explains the other — they are valuable *on the same scale*. In cases such as this, therefore, the expression 'good' is not used ambiguously: these are goods of the same sort, even when one transcends the other. This will be true whichever account of the conclusion of the *Euthydemus'* argument we take. On the exclusive reading, since nothing else than wisdom is intrinsically good, nothing else is good (in the same sense) at all; on the derivative reading, wisdom is intrinsically good, the other things good (in the same sense, but) relative to it.[83]

So, I suggest, the *Euthydemus* prompts us to re-read, or to rethink, the equivalent argument in the *Meno*, specifically by the linguistic and argumentative similarities between the two passages. The purpose of the

---

[81] Of course, that there are extrinsic values (values dependent on something else to be valuable) does not imply that there are intrinsic ones: there may be nothing that is independently valuable; instead everything may be meshed together in mutual dependence.

[82] This relativity does not make the extrinsic good subjective, even if the intrinsic good is somehow cognitive, like wisdom or knowledge.

[83] Relativity does not introduce equivocation.

Euthydemus' complex allusiveness may merely be to re-examine the condensed argument of the *Meno*. Or it may be to provide a Platonic revision of
a Socratic account of wisdom and happiness. But, if my analysis of the
differences between the appearances of the *Meno* and the account of the
good to be found in the *Euthydemus* is accurate, then the point of the allusion
is to invite a deeper consideration of the problems of consequentialism. The
Meno lacks a good account of just how value is to be located in the agent,
and remains unclear about whether this importance of the agent in ethical
theory is itself merely executive. The *Euthydemus*, by contrast, invites us to
think of the agent as central to the account of the intrinsic good, just because
it is the agent who is wise or knowledgeable, and because wisdom and
knowledge are the sources of value itself. The difference between them may
express, not so much the inadequacy of the earlier text and its later revision,
but the opacity of the *Meno*, elucidated in the *Euthydemus*. Consequently the
re-reading of the *Meno* by the *Euthydemus* may be not so much a corrective,
as a provocation to reflect.

V

Recall, now, the Stoic theory of the ethical indifferents (p. 366 above). This
theory may indeed have Socratic antecedents — but it is the Socrates of the
Euthydemus who provides them. For it is the *Euthydemus'* account of the
intrinsic good (rather than the theory which seems to be presented in the
Meno) which seems to lie behind the Stoic contrast between virtue and the
indifferents. Only the *Euthydemus* directly makes a strong claim about what
is good itself by itself (compare Cicero's report, 'only what is right is good').
But now here is the problem. If this passage is what influenced the Stoics, it
appears to be, after all, inconsistent with what they claimed about the relation between what is good and what is indifferent. For that relation is often
construed as one between two quite different sorts of value: moral value, on
the one hand — virtue — and the non-moral value of health, wealth and reputation on the other. I shall call this *evaluative dualism*.

> They expressed this thesis by restricting 'good' to what is morally excellent and
> 'bad' to the opposite of this, and termed everything which makes no difference to
> happiness or unhappiness 'indifferent'.[84]

---

[84] Long and Sedley (n. 11), vol. 1, 357.

This is often compared to the Kantian distinction[85] between those actions that are categorically enjoined, and those that are pressed on us by mere hypothetical imperatives: the former are *unconditioned*, the latter *conditional* on our desires for their result. And the dualism of this distinction is reflected in the difference between the sources of the two values: on the one hand the hypothetical imperative is derived from the practicality of desire, and on the other

> ...there is an imperative which, without being based on, and conditioned by, any further purpose to be attained by a certain line of conduct, enjoins this conduct immediately. This imperative is categorical. It is concerned, not with the matter of the action and its presumed results, but with its form and with the principles from which it follows; and what is essentially good in the action consists in the mental disposition, let the consequences be what they may. This imperative may be called the imperative of morality. (Kant, *Groundwork of the Metaphysic of Morals*, 4: 416/43)[86]

One way of understanding this contrast may be in terms of what we want to do, and what we feel we ought to do. And this contrast itself is often glossed in terms of two quite different psychological drives — on the one hand egoism, the demands of the greedy self, and on the other altruism, the demands of others upon us.[87] Even if we leave on one side the question whether this contrast is itself spurious or grossly simplistic[88] we may find ourselves dubious about its ancient antecedents.[89]

First of all, it is not to be found in whatever the relation is between what is good 'itself by itself' and the putative good, in either the *Meno* or the *Euthydemus*. For whether we have here an exclusive theory (what is good itself by itself is the only good) or a derivative one (all other goods are derivative from what is good itself by itself), the good itself by itself and the putative goods, if they are good at all, must be good in the same sense — if there is, after all, to be some explanatory relation between the two.

Secondly, and consequently, if the Stoic theory is dualist — if the Stoics are committed to an account of value which quite separates the values attached to virtue and morality from the prudential values associated with common lists of goods — then should we say either that the *Euthydemus* is not what influenced them; or that they misread the arguments they found in

---

[85] Kant himself was apparently heavily influenced by the Stoics, *cf.* here Schneewind (n. 13).

[86] Trans. H. J. Paton (New York 1964).

[87] Kant himself is not so crude; see e.g. *Critique of Practical Reason* and compare Korsgaard's defence of Kant, *The Sources of Normativity* (Cambridge 1996).

[88] This issue, of course, is a central one in ethics, and the literature too massive to cite in detail here.

[89] Consider here A. MacIntyre, *After Virtue* (London 1981).

the Platonic text? I shall argue that we should prefer a third option: that the earliest Stoics were indeed influenced by Plato, but that they were not evaluative dualists at all.[90]

It is undeniable that the earliest Stoics were readers of Plato. Zeno was a pupil of both Crates the Cynic and the leaders of the Academy, Xenocrates and Polemo (Diog. Laert. 7.1); and Aristo was a pupil of Zeno, until he became heretical.[91] What is more, the influence of the *Euthydemus* itself hangs heavy on the later doxographical tradition. Diogenes Laertius cites the *Euthydemus'* hostility to the 'sticky arguments' (γλισχρολογία) of the sophists (2.30) and later (2.32) mentions Socrates' late learning of the lyre — an activity of which Socrates makes a great deal in the *Euthydemus*.[92] In between he outlines what he takes to be Socrates' ethical principles; and the context, once again, suggests that these principles are taken from the *Euthydemus*:

> He said, too, that there is only one good, knowledge (ἐπιστήμη), and only one evil, ignorance (ἀμαθία). Wealth and noble birth have nothing high-and-mighty about them,[93] but quite the reverse, evil. (2.31).

Just as Socrates' influence is characterised by Diogenes in Euthydeman mode, we may see, I suggest, the same influence at work on Zeno, and on Aristo as he espoused the heresy which caused the split between him and his master. The issue throughout is the theory of indifferents.

---

[90] Here *contra* Long's explicit claim (n. 14) 32. It may be that later Stoicism, more concerned with an account of the nature of the physical world, could arrive at some kind of dualism by separating the imperatives derived from nature as a whole, and those derived from human needs and drives. Such an account, however, would run the risk of imposing on the Stoics a psychological dualism to which they were opposed. The strength of the connection between developed Stoic ethics and Stoic physics is downplayed by Annas, *The Morality of Happiness* (Oxford 1993), but not by Striker, 'Following nature: a study in Stoic ethics', in *Essays on Hellenistic Epistemology and Ethics* (Cambridge 1996) 221–80. See also M. Frede, 'On the Stoic conception of the good', in K. Ierodiakonou, (ed.) *Topics in Stoic Philosophy* (Oxford 1999) 71–94.

[91] See here M. Schofield, 'Ariston of Chios and the unity of virtue', *Ancient Philosophy* 4 (1984) 83–96, on the question from whom the schism was made.

[92] Diogenes misses its ironic significance, however. At 272c Socrates mentions his lessons with Connus and suggests that they are liable to make both him and his teacher ridiculous. Diogenes, however, reports that Socrates declared there to be nothing absurd in someone learning what they do not know. He evidently garbles Socrates' music lessons with the first sophistic episode; but that he is thinking of the *Euthydemus* is undeniable.

[93] Diogenes uses the word σεμνὸν here to describe what wealth lacks: I take it that it is no coincidence that the inclusion of wealth in the list of goods at 279b6 is something that it doesn't need a high-and-mighty person (σεμνὸς ἀνήρ) to provide. It is easy to see how Diogenes, reading the conclusion of the argument back into the disingenuous list, would come up with the claim he makes about wealth. That he uses the same word signifies, once again, that his account is derived from the *Euthydemus*, and not from the *Meno*; contrast the bland terminology of *Meno* 87e.

First of all, there is some dispute about the origin of the theory: Diogenes suggests (7.37) that Aristo 'brought in indifference'. But both Cicero (*De finibus* 3.51) and Stobaeus attribute the coinage of the contrast between 'preferred' and 'dispreferred' indifferents to Zeno; and Sextus (*Math.* 11.64) suggests that Aristo's heresy was to reject Zeno's contrast. That evidence might suggest that it was Zeno who first suggested the contrast between goods and indifferents, but that he qualified the indifferents in a way rejected by his breakaway pupil Aristo. But there are two separate issues here: first the postulate that what seems to the common view to be an item of value is in fact indifferent; second, the attitude that we should therefore cultivate towards these items — indifference. It is this attitude of indifference which Aristo recommends, and in this sense that he 'brought in indifference'. Now he could not do that without subscribing to a strong account of the indifferents, that is, that they are strictly indifferent (hence Diogenes' report, 'for without exception things indifferent as between virtue and vice have no difference at all' (trans. Long and Sedley)).[94] But his objective seems to have been more prescriptive, to claim that the end is living 'indifferently disposed towards the things which are in between virtue and vice' (Diog. Laert. 7.160). This may have been a recommendation to live haphazardly, doing whatever occurred (*cf.* Cicero *Fin.* 4.79); or it may have been an account of what virtue in fact is.[95] A different account of what the sources give us would be, not that Aristo identified indifference and virtue,[96] but that he had a twofold account of the end: we should live virtuously; and as far as indifferent things are concerned, we should cultivate indifference towards them. Such an attitude towards indifferent things, indeed, might be a part of what it is to be virtuous, or even a consequence of the intrinsic goodness of virtue; but what it is to be virtuous is independently explained — as the intrinsic good of wisdom.[97] If that is right, Aristo is exempt from the charge of vicious circularity, because he supposes that the account of virtue is primary and that virtue is the

---

[94] Supposing, realistically, that it is the nature of the things out there that determines our attitudes to them: hence, if indifference is appropriate, that must be because the indifferents are indifferent. This sort of realism is commonplace, of course, in ancient ethical theory.

[95] Here *cf.* Striker (n. 90), who sees this as the focus of Plutarch's objection (*Comm. not.* 1071f–1072a) that Aristo's theory is viciously circular.

[96] Cicero seems to suggest both that Aristo said that the highest good was living indifferently, (e.g. at *Acad.* 2.130) and that he said that living virtuously was the end (*Fin.* 4.43) without drawing Plutarch's conclusion, that he identified living indifferently and living virtuously.

[97] My suspicion is that the doxographers conflated these two aspects of the end just because they did not always acknowledge that Aristo's heterodoxy was not his theory of value, but his recommendation to cultivate indifference.

primary good. But because he takes this primary good to be the solitary good, too, then there are no extrinsic goods dependent upon it. In that case, the attitude of indifference *is* how we should live, in consequence of the nature of virtue.

If this was Aristo's view, it fits well the exclusive reading of the *Euthydemus* argument (p. 381 above): (a) nothing has any value at all except wisdom; wisdom is the only valuable thing. Aristo's argument to that conclusion (reported by Sextus, *Math.* 11.64–7) is based on the thought that any 'preferred indifferent' may, under different circumstances, turn out to be dispreferred — so that nothing is unconditionally preferred. He infers that nothing is preferred at all.[98] And this argument may be what we find in the *Euthydemus*: for on the exclusive view Socrates argues that if none of his list of putative goods are valuable unconditionally, then they are not valuable at all (compare Cicero, *Academica* 2.130).

But all the same it is not obvious that Aristo's position is well founded. If nothing but virtue is unconditionally good, he seems to suggest, then everything but virtue is indifferent, and should be treated with indifference.[99] The best life, therefore, will be the life of indifference towards 'everything which is in between virtue and vice' (Diog. Laert. 7.160) on the grounds that these in-between things have no distinction between them, but are exactly on a par with each other. We might complain that the notion of what is 'in between' merely indicates that such things are context-relative. It neither implies that what is in between has no value at all, nor suggests that the appropriate attitude to these items is indifference. But Cicero (*Fin.* 4.69) suggests that Aristo's focus of attention was on the practical issues involved in dealing with things which are only valuable in some contexts. And if what we pursue is thus variable, Cicero has Aristo suggest, our choices should be made haphazard, with no expectation of the fixity of value of what we choose.[100] And this suggestion too has its Platonic origins: if whatever is not good itself by itself is unknowable, dangerously unreliable from the point of view of cognition, perhaps there is no reasonable approach to adopt towards the practical life but the throwing up of hands. It

---

[98] Hence the objection of the orthodox Stoics that this makes life unliveable, Cicero *Fin.* 3.50. It is significant that this argument turns, as will Zeno's and as did Socrates', on how we treat the compresence of opposites in cases of value: any indifferent is no more preferred (in some circumstances) than it is dispreferred. The dispute between the contributors to the debate concerns what they suppose to follow from this.

[99] *Cf.* Cic. *Acad.* 2.130; this confirms the suggestion that Aristo's coinage was not the category of indifferents, but his description of the attitude that he recommends towards them, ἀδιαφορία.

[100] *Cf.* A. M. Ioppolo, *Aristone di Chio e lo stoicismo antico* (Naples 1980).

is to answer that question (once again, a question provoked by the Platonic background), I suggest, that Zeno developed the theory of preferred and dispreferred indifferents.

Zeno proposes that while there is a contrast between what is good and what is indifferent, there are still grounds for preference among the indifferents (that is to say, the practical conduct of our lives still has some scope, contrary to Aristo's view). Consider two passages, Cicero *De finibus* 3.51 (a passage which follows the citation at the beginning of this chapter) and Diogenes Laertius 7.102–3.

> But among those things which are valuable, in some cases there is *sufficient cause* why we should prefer them to other things (as in the case of health, unimpaired perception, freedom from pain, glory, wealth and other such like[101]) and in other cases not so;[102] and likewise among those things which are not worthy of value, in some cases there is *sufficient reason* why we should reject them, and in some cases not so.

> These things [sc. e.g. health and wealth] are not goods, but indifferents of the class of preferred: for just as it is the special quality (ἴδιον) of what is hot to heat, not to chill, so it is the special quality of the good to benefit, not to harm. But neither wealth nor health benefits any more than it harms; therefore they are not good.[103]

The first passage is directly associated with Zeno (it precedes Cicero's account of Zeno's coinage of 'preferred' and 'dispreferred'). The second has the air of a definition (hence the expression 'of the class of', κατ᾽εἶδος), and so may belong to the originator of the theory of indifferents — and so perhaps to Zeno himself. And we may notice that there is some similarity between the two passages: for both speak of the theory of indifferents in terms of an issue about causation or explanation. Cicero suggests that there is some cause, or perhaps justification, of the preferability of some indifferents; Diogenes points to the contrast between things which do have causal efficacy (the hot heats) and those which do not (health does not [sc. necessarily] benefit). And in this respect the argument is true to the strategy adopted by Socrates in the *Euthydemus*, on the derivative reading (b) (p. 381 above):

---

[101] This strategy of rejecting, or qualifying, a list of putative goods is true to *Euthyd.* 278e ff.

[102] There is a danger of both over- and under-translation here: Rackham gives 'while others are not of this nature', which pushes the interpreter towards evaluative dualism. I have under-translated: better might be 'other things are not like this'. The point may be to remind us of the account of two different sorts of indifferent, *cf.* Diog. Laert. 7.104–5, and thus to tell us about what is preferred by nature (this tends towards dualism); or to suggest that the grounds for preference may vary (which tends towards the derivative view which, I shall shortly suggest, should be attributed to Zeno).

[103] Notice here another version of the argument from the compresence of opposites.

wisdom is the only thing that has value itself by itself; all the other valuable items are so derivatively from wisdom.

If Socrates' conclusion is that wisdom alone is the good itself by itself, he reaches that conclusion on the basis of an argument to show that wisdom alone is the source of value. Since everything other than wisdom no more harms than benefits, wisdom is the cause of the value of anything else. The same point may be made by the Stoic analogy with the hot heating. At first reading, the Diogenes passage may simply insist on the thought that the good must be unconditioned: so what is good always has beneficial effects. But that is, I suggest, to make too little of the point about special qualities (ἴδια) and their causal properties. If the special quality of the hot is to heat (and never to chill), then anything which may either heat or chill is not the hot; likewise whatever may either benefit or harm cannot be the good (so that wealth, for example, cannot be the good). But the good is what makes other things good (it is what has that special quality), just as the hot makes other things hot; so whatever is made good by the good is not in itself such as to make other things good; therefore it is not the good. Now that account of the causal powers of the good bears some resemblance to the causal powers of what is good itself by itself in the *Euthydemus* (and the resemblance is marked by the reappearance of an argument from the compresence of opposites). It gives Zeno an argument, not about two sorts of value, but rather about the explanatory relations between what is good itself by itself and whatever derives its goodness from that. Zeno makes, in short, a *derivative* reading of the *Euthydemus'* conclusion.

That may be confirmed by a feature of the theory of indifferents that is unquestionably Zenonian. If among indifferent things there are distinctions of value, these are to be described in terms of the distinction between what is 'preferred'[104] (προηγμένον) and what is 'dispreferred'[105] (ἀποπροηγμένον). It was Zeno who coined the expressions προηγμένον and ἀποπροηγμένον, as Cicero elaborately explains:

> For, he said, just as no one says that in a court the king himself has been *promoted* to his rank ('promoted' is the translation of προηγμένον) but rather [they say it of] those who are in some honour whose rank comes close to the primacy of the kings, so that it is second; just so in life it is not those things which are of the first rank but

---

[104] This translation, which is now standard, is appropriate to the Zenonian origin of this theory, but only, as I shall suggest, if we take the expression 'preferred' to allude, not to some aspect of choice, but to the notion of promotion. Zeno concerns himself, not with our desires and preferences, but with the arrangement or hierarchy of value. 'Preference' is thus a slight archaism, but entirely appropriate to the origins of the metaphor.

[105] Long and Sedley's translation (n. 11) captures what I take to be the rebarbative features of Zeno's coinage.

those which take the second place which are called 'preferred', that is, 'promoted'.[106]

Why does Zeno settle on this coinage in particular?[107] If Aristo is right, as Cicero dryly observes, the whole of life would be thrown into confusion (exactly, I suppose, what Aristo intended) (*Fin.* 3.50). So there must be some way of making choice rational, and avoiding Aristo's conclusion (that *neque ullum sapientiae munus aut opus inueniretur, cum inter res eas quae ad uitam degendam pertinerent nihil omnino interesset neque ullum dilectum adhiberi oporteret*[108]). It is this objective, according to Cicero, which provoked the Zenonian theory of what is preferred and what is dispreferred.[109] But once again, this needs to be carefully understood if it is not to miss entirely the point of Cato's objection to Aristo, as Cicero presents it. If Aristo's heresy can be understood as a reading of the *Euthydemus*, then he takes Socrates' point to be that only wisdom has value; and he misses the possibility that the intrinsic value of wisdom may explain the extrinsic value of everything else. But then there had better be something about Zeno's response which counters the thought that non-absolute value is arbitrarily disposed, or else non-existent. And — to re-read the *Euthydemus* — Zeno needs to do that by explaining just what is the explanatory (causal) relation between what is good itself by itself and what is not. It will not be sufficient simply to observe that the value of what is valuable relative to context is valuable in a secondary way. And it will not be enough for that, either, simply to reinstate the importance of practical reason for what is relatively valuable, as an alternative to cultivating indifference. Instead, Zeno needs to settle a metaphysical issue: to show how it is that the real, objective values of things are themselves explained by what is valuable itself by itself. For Zeno supposes that life should be lived according to some rational disposition; and he needs to show that this rational disposition matches some rational order out there in the world.

---

[106] Stobaeus cites the same comparison, 2.84.2.

[107] Long, (n. 14) n. 63 compares this coinage with Stobaeus' account of what it is for something (e.g. health) to be choosable in itself, 2.82.20–83.4. This does not, I believe, account for the strangeness of the expression προηγμένον.

[108] '...and no function or task for wisdom could be found, since there would be no difference at all between the things that concern the living of life, and no choice between them would have to be made' (trans. Long and Sedley (n. 11) 58I).

[109] A point here about chronology: if Zeno first proposed the theory of indifferents, and then Aristo took it over in a heretical manner, then Zeno's account of preference will itself be a response to Aristo. See Schofield (n. 91).

His development of the contrast between προηγμένα indifferents and ἀποπροηγμένα indifferents is, I suggest, designed to fulfil this purpose (that is confirmed by Stobaeus, who defines a preferred indifferent as what we 'select on the basis of a preferential reason',[110] 2.84.18–85.11). Recall that the relation between wisdom and the other goods in the *Euthydemus*, a relation that I have described as a relation of source to derivative, was described as wisdom *leading* the other valuables (this expression was also used in the *Meno*). The same relation is invoked in a rather more complex context: to justify the claim that wisdom turns fewer goods into greater, ignorance turns greater goods into evils.

> ... if ignorance leads them,[111] they are greater evils than their opposites,[112] insofar as they are better able to serve a bad leader; but if intelligence and wisdom lead them, they are greater goods.[113] (*Euthydemus* 281d6–8)

Suppose someone has a collection of putative goods, but is ignorant; then their ignorance will turn those goods bad, and will do their possessor more harm than good. Contrariwise, if someone has wisdom, and yet only a few of the putative goods, those goods will do their possessor more good than we might otherwise expect: for wisdom will make them valuable. So wisdom and ignorance determine the real benefit of possessions and assets. The putative goods are not goods at all without the presence of the source of their value; and the source of their value explains not only how we may compare one extrinsic value with another, but also how we may explain their context-relativity. (Might we find this plausible? We might if we had, not a consequentialist, but an agent-relative bias, in which the source of value is, somehow, the agent, whose happiness is necessarily connected to what he himself brings about.[114] Even so, Socrates' theory is an extreme rationalist or intellectualist one.)

---

[110] Trans. Long and Sedley (n. 11) 58E.

[111] 'them': the antecedent here is the list of *putative* goods, the source of whose value is here under discussion. Plato's discussion up to this point has thoroughly undermined the thought that the original list of putative goods has any objective standing. At this stage in the argument, that is to say, there is no suggestion that these items already have some value, which is increased by wisdom; on the contrary, their value is entirely determined by wisdom.

[112] The 'opposites' are the items that are formally opposite to the original list of putative goods: so they are putative evils (e.g. sickness, poverty). Here the opposition is objective (sickness is objectively opposite to health) but not yet evaluated objectively.

[113] *Cf.* Long (n. 14) n. 59 on this.

[114] An example might be the Kantian notion of the good will. For such a Kantian approach, made more generous about the scope of the good will than the *Groundwork* might be thought to allow, see Korsgaard (n. 87). A different example is to be found in Aristotle's account of the function of man in *Eth. Nic.* 1.

This might press the derivative reading of the *Euthydemus* argument: the items from the list of putative goods that are given objective value derive their value from wisdom. Now Plato explains any possible relation between derivative (extrinsic) goods and the intrinsic good in terms of a metaphor of leader and led, of master and servants, of king and courtiers.[115] So, expressly, the intrinsic evil (ignorance) is conceived as the leader, the extrinsic evils as the led, and conversely, the good itself by itself will be the master, the derivative goods the servants. But to cash this metaphor is to reveal further detail of the theory itself. Recall the distinction between what I called the executive and the regal accounts of leadership. In the regal account, all goods that are not the king himself are extrinsically good. It is the extrinsic goods that serve the intrinsic, and not vice versa; this image, that is to say, fits ill with an instrumental or consequential account of the relation between wisdom and the assets that might constitute the happy life.[116] Second, both the power and the purposes here belong to the leader — the led serve the leader, not the other way about. But the king's purposes (within the metaphor, at least) are not directed at some other, differently defined goods, for there are none such. This gives the leader (wisdom, or virtue) the sort of teleological priority that we should not expect from a consequentialist account. There is, then, an explanatory priority in Plato's image, which Zeno will come to exploit. For the servants serve because they have a master, the led are led because the leader leads them:[117] it is the intrinsic good which explains the extrinsic goods, not the other way about.

Now consider the similarity between Plato's idiom and how Zeno is reported to have explained his use of the expressions προηγμένον and ἀποπροηγμένον. His coinage of προηγμένον may strike us, after all, as initially surprising if his point is merely to emphasise that one asset is preferable (either by nature or by virtue of circumstance) to another (why not say, simply, 'choosable', or selectable: *cf.* Diogenes Laertius 7.105?). But it may after all reflect a conceptual connection between Zeno's προηγμένον ('brought out', 'led out') and Plato's ἡγεῖσθαι ('lead').[118]

---

[115] Hence the interest in kingship in the second Socratic episode, 291b.

[116] This inconcinnity appears even if we concede that extrinsic goods may be final; for even then, we are unlikely to suppose that intrinsic goods are instrumental. Again *cf.* Korsgaard (n. 38).

[117] This is familiar from *Euthyphro* 10a ff.

[118] The idiom of leading is common to both the *Euthydemus* and the *Meno*. In the *Meno*, I suggested, the argument did not imply that wisdom had intrinsic value of its own (but merely an instrumental value, cf. *Meno* 89a1); although it insisted that it is necessary for the achievement of happiness. This is consistent with the (different) idea that wisdom might lead from front, might be the pre-eminent value, rather than its source. However, if the *Euthydemus* alters the terms of this debate, (as I take to

> None of the goods is preferred because they have the greatest value.[119] But what is preferred, having the second place and value, is in some way adjacent to the nature of the goods. For in the court, the king is not one of those who have preferment,[120] but those people have preferment who are ranked after him.[121] (Stobaeus 2.85.11)

> Just as in a royal court — Zeno says — no one says that the king is so to speak promoted to his honour (here 'promoted'[122] translates προηγμένον); but the term is used of those who hold some office which comes close to the primacy of the king, so that they are second; so also in a life it is not those things which are of the first rank, but those which are in second place which are described as προηγμένα, that is to say 'promoted'. (Cicero *Fin.* 3.52)

Zeno's analogy of the king may just be intended to bring out the contrast between the king and even the highest rank of courtiers — the king is always at the top, the courtiers always and necessarily below, the point merely one of hierarchy. But Cicero, I suggest, gives us better elaboration of the point, when he translates προηγμένον into Latin, *productum*. The crucial thing about the first rank of courtiers in a court is not so much that they are, however high-ranking, always behind the king, but that the *explanation* for that fact is that it is the king who promotes them; so, as Cicero observes, no promotion can turn them into the king themselves, any more than the king got to be king by rising up the courtierly ladder. Equally, the disappointed courtier is 'dispreferred', that is demoted and sent away, because he is sent further from the king's presence and the high rank that proximity confers.[123] In a court, the king is the source of value; in Zeno's account, wisdom is the source of value for the indifferents; and in offering that gloss, he fits the theory offered by the *Euthydemus* very well. Zeno, thus, turns away from consequentialism, towards a view of moral value in which the agent is primary, both in importance and in explanation; and he turns, also, away

---

be the case, and as I take to be the point of the positive claim in its conclusion) then the relation of leading to led may be a transitive, not an intransitive one: wisdom does not lead from in front, but by actively bringing on what comes behind.

[119] This claim, that the goods have ἡ μεγίστη ἀξία is, we may note, compared to the derivative ἀξία of the preferred indifferents: once again this suggestion that they differ by degree is incompatible with evaluative dualism. It is, I think, worth noticing also that this notion of the highest value, which is paralleled by Diogenes' account of the goods which are 'at the summit' has strong Platonic echoes (*cf.* e.g. *Rep.* 505 ff.) and may be intended to construe the good αὐτὸ καθ' αὑτό.

[120] This expression is meant to bring out the sense in which προηγμένον is construed, in Zeno's derivation, as a passive. Notice, again, the slight archaism in 'preferred'.

[121] The explicit connection between this analogy and Zeno's coinage is made earlier in Stobaeus' text.

[122] And 'promoted' translates *productum*.

[123] Here the derivation of ἀποπροηγμένον shows up its locative features: and in this respect it fits Zeno's image of the hot heating: the hot heats what is closest to it.

from any idea that there might be two separate types of value in play. When Zeno read Plato he did so with care: evaluative dualism is as out of place in the early Stoa as it is in Plato.

vi

I began by asking about how we should read Plato (section i). I suggested that the significance of this question might appear in consideration of a particular case: two passages in the *Euthydemus* and the *Meno* on the subject of the explanation of value, which appear to be closely related (section ii). This close relation between the two passages, I suggested, could be understood in terms of one 'reading' the other — where one is alluded to in the other, and thereby becomes the subject of critical reflection (section iii). I argued that the *Euthydemus* goes further than the *Meno* in insisting that wisdom is the intrinsic good: the good, that is, which is itself the source of value. Indeed, the careful relations between the two arguments suggests a complex reflection upon, and rejection of, consequentialist accounts of value (section iv).

This case of Plato reading Plato seems to have inspired some central debates in early Stoicism about the nature of the good. Nonetheless, the scope of the *Euthydemus*' contention about the good remains vague; and that is why, when the early Stoics come to read this passage in Plato, they differ in their interpretations. That difference, I claimed (section v), is the source of the disagreement between Zeno and Aristo about the nature of 'ethical indifferents', since different readings of the *Euthydemus*' argument produce different views about whether or not there are any other items of value than the good itself by itself. But in either case, the *Euthydemus* does not encourage what I have called evaluative dualism: the view that there may be two quite different structures of value: for if what is good itself by itself is the source of value for something else — as I argued Zeno to suppose — then the value they have will be of the same kind. Neither Zeno nor Aristo, therefore, were evaluative dualists. Furthermore, if we understand the Stoics as having been engaged upon reading Plato, we may further understand just why they elaborated the theory of indifferents in the language and the terms they did.

So how did the Stoics read Plato? The relation between the *Meno* and the *Euthydemus*, I suggested, is one that encourages critical reflection on the nature and the metaphysics of value. This feature of the Platonic texts was felt by his early Stoic readers. For Zeno and Aristo are not simply influenced by some doctrines they happen to find in the *Euthydemus* and the *Meno*. It is true that Stoic ethical theory would be an ally of the attack on consequentialism in the *Euthydemus*. But the agenda for the debate between Zeno and Aristo is set by the *Euthydemus*, which asks about the source of value. And the conduct of that debate about the source of value is itself informed by the very indeterminacy of the *Euthydemus'* answer. So the Stoic reading of Plato is a rich one; and this is exactly, I submit, what Plato intended to invite.

I should like to thank Malcolm Schofield for his criticisms and encouragement.

16
Galen, Christians, logic

Jonathan Barnes

i

The Emperor Marcus Aurelius described Galen as 'first among physicians and unique among philosophers' — we have Galen's word for it. He was born in Pergamum in AD 129, son of an architect. He enjoyed the best provincial education. Then, guided by a divine dream, his father decided that he should become a physician. He read indefatigably; he served as doctor to a gladiatorial school (it was a pleasure to be able to see the inside of living bodies); he travelled widely — and he visited Rome, where luck, good connections, and his own undeniable talents brought him success. He came to the Emperor's attention, and was appointed doctor-in-waiting to Marcus' son Commodus.

He worked like the devil; and he still found time to write — on pharmacology and anatomy, on diagnostics and therapeutics; commentaries on the works of Hippocrates and essays in the history of medicine; works of philosophy — and of logic. The surviving *œuvre* runs to some ten thousand Greek pages, which are supplemented by several items which have been preserved in Arabic translation. Much is lost. In particular, the 15 books *On Demonstration* (Galen's major work on logic) are known only from a handful of references. But an *Introduction to Logic* survives, in a single Greek manuscript; and although it is elementary in intention, it expounds Galen's own great logical invention — of which more anon.[1]

---

[1] The standard edition of the works of Galen (Greek text and Latin translation) was prepared, for the use of doctors, by C. G. Kühn and published at Leipzig between 1821 and 1833. From a philological point of view, Kühn's edition leaves almost everything to be desired; it contains several late forgeries; and it is incomplete. (The last failing is not to be laid at Kühn's door: several Galenic texts

By the time of Galen's death, in about 210, Christianity had rooted itself in most parts of the Empire. It was still a minority interest, unloved by the authorities. But it was no longer a Jewish splinter group: there were cultivated Greeks and Romans among its adherents; and it was beginning to gather a learned literature.

During Galen's lifetime a number of Christians wrote addresses to their Emperor, and they strove to present the new religion as a philosophy, a system of thought which might be compared — to its own advantage — with Stoicism or Platonism. The *Apology* of Justin and the *Embassy* of Athenagoras demonstrate a certain culture and a certain capacity to write. In the early years of the third century, Clement of Alexandria wrote his *Stromateis* or *Miscellanies*, an endlessly digressive and exuberantly erudite work, in order to show that the Christian religion was the one true philosophy. And thenceforth to the end of antiquity the Church Fathers continued to scribble.[2]

As for logic, the modern term — like its ancient counterparts — is elastic. I use it here in a narrow sense, to denote the theory of argument and proof. In the second century AD, the schools taught logic in two parts: there was 'categorical syllogistic' — essentially a simplified version of the logic found in Aristotle's *Prior Analytics*; and there was 'hypothetical syllogistic', which is associated with the Stoics and in particular with Chrysippus. Galen was dissatisfied with this bipartite discipline; for he found that it could not account for the proofs which scientists — and in particular mathematicians — habitually provide for their theorems. So he invented what he termed 'a third class of syllogism', the class of relational arguments.[3]

---

have been rediscovered since his time.) The series *Corpus Medicorum Graecorum* will eventually replace Kühn (but in its first century of existence it has not reached the half-way point); and there are other modern editions of certain texts. The *Introduction to Logic*, absent from Kühn, is available in a Teubner edition (K. Kalbfleisch (Leipzig 1896)); there is an English translation: J. Kieffer, *Galen's Institutio Logica* (Baltimore 1964). The testimonies to *On Demonstration* are collected and discussed by I. von Müller, 'Ueber Galens Werk vom wissenschaftlichen Beweis', *Abhandlungen der ersten Classe der königlichen Akademie der Wissenschaften* 20 (Munich 1895) 405–78. On Galen's logic see e.g. J. Barnes, 'Galen on logic and therapy', in F. Kudlien and R. Durling (eds.), *Galen's Method of Healing* (Leiden 1991) 50–102; id., 'Galen and the utility of logic', in J. Kollesch and D. Nickel (eds.), *Galen und das hellenistische Erbe* (Stuttgart 1993) 33–52. The compliment paid to Galen by Marcus Aurelius may be found in Galen, *On Prognosis* 14.660 K (i.e., p. 660 of vol. 14 of Kühn's edition of Galen). For this work there is a splendid edition, with English translation and commentary, by Vivian Nutton in the *Corpus Medicorum Graecorum* (Berlin 1979).

[2] Biographical and bibliographical facts about the several Church Fathers mentioned in this chapter may be found in any of the standard handbooks — e.g. J. Quasten, *Patrology* (Utrecht 1960).

[3] See *Inst. log.* 16.1; commentary in J. Barnes, '"A third sort of syllogism": Galen and the logic of relations', in R. W. Sharples (ed.), *Modern Thinkers and Ancient Thinkers* (London 1993) 172–94.

Three examples should make the matter sufficiently clear. First, a categorical syllogism:

> Everyone we invited has come, and we invited some francophones — so some francophones have come.

Secondly, a hypothetical argument:

> He can't both be in Geneva and be at the conference, and he's in Geneva — so he's not at the conference.

Thirdly, from the logic of relations:

> Marie's boots are smaller than mine, and mine are smaller than Ben's — so Marie's are smaller than Ben's.

The examples are valid deductions — that is to say, their conclusion (marked by the word 'so') follows from their premisses. And their validity depends on the force of certain logical elements in them, different types of element in the three different types of case: in the first example, the validity depends on the terms 'everyone' and 'some'; in the second, on the words 'not' and 'and'; in the third, on the expression 'smaller than'. For example, every argument of the same form as the second argument — that is to say, every argument of the form

> Not both A and B, and A — so not B

is valid; and the validity of the second argument is underwritten by the sense or force of the words 'and' and 'not'.

These three subjects — Galen, Christians, logic — have two things in common. First, they are major aspects of the ancient world: Galen was one of the three most influential scientists of antiquity (alongside Aristotle and Ptolemy); the Christians eventually kidnapped the Empire; logic is one of the few ancient sciences which is not entirely out of date.

Secondly, they are of marginal interest to classical scholarship. Galen has his votaries; but there is too much of him, and his case exemplifies one of the iron laws of philology: the more of an author survives, the less he is read. The miserable remains of Heraclitus have spilled more scholarly ink than all the works of Galen. The Christians were yet more voluminous. Who on contemplating the Greek and Latin *Patrologiae* has not groaned: What, will they stretch on to the crack of doom? In any event, that's not our department — there are theologians, church historians, patristic scholars to look after the stuff. As for logic, it has rarely been loved. It is repulsively technical — or else frivolously trifling. In any event, it is dry as dust. In Martianus Capella's *Wedding of Philology and Mercury*, a droll introduction to the seven 'liberal arts' written in the early fifth century AD, Dame Dialectic 'has a pinched body, a sombre dress, rough and uncombed

hair—and she speaks in a way which the common man cannot understand'
(4.329).[4]

ii

Why put the three subjects under one hat? Galen and logic make a pair. But
Galen and Christians? Christians and logic? A Galenic text makes the tie.

In his work on the *Difference of Pulses* Galen thwacks the theories of
Archigenes—whom he had already walloped in a separate work, eight
books long (*Lib. prop.* 19.33 K). Archigenes, he says,

> is wrong from the start: he lists the primary qualities, but he thinks that it is not
> worth proving why there are just so many of them—he is content with a mere
> assertion. (*Diff. puls.* 8.578 K)

No man of science should be so cavalier:

> he ought to have added to his assertion about the eight qualities a proof—or at
> least an argument—in order to avoid the impression that the reader, just as if he
> had entered a school of Moses or of Jesus Christ, was going to hear
> undemonstrated laws. (*Diff. puls.* 8.579 K)

The side-swipe at Jews and Christians is unexpected.

Galen does not distinguish between Jews and Christians, and his
reference is no more than a polemical aside. The claim that Christians have
no time for proofs and arguments, which became one of the platitudes of
anti-Christian propaganda, was made by two of Galen's contemporaries—
Lucian waves at it in his *Peregrinus*, and it is a major theme in the *True
Account* of Celsus, which was the first pagan rebuttal of the new religion.
Perhaps Galen was casually echoing a current commonplace?[5]

But later in *On the Difference of Pulses* Galen returns to the Jews and
Christians:

> You will more readily convert the followers of Moses and of Christ than those
> doctors and philosophers who are stuck to their sects. (8.657 K)

---

[4] English translation by W. H. Stahl, R. Johnson and E. L. Burge in vol. 2 of *Martianus Capella and
the Seven Liberal Arts* (New York 1977).

[5] For Lucian see M. J. Edwards, 'Satire and verisimilitude: Christianity in Lucian's *Peregrinus*',
Historia 38 (1989) 89–98. All that remains of Celsus' *True Account* comes from the long criticism
which Origen wrote some eighty years later: see the annotated translation by H. Chadwick, *Origen:
contra Celsum* (2nd ed., Cambridge 1965).

And elsewhere he refers to 'the doctrine of Moses' about nature and the divine Demiurge: Moses may be no worse than Epicurus, but insofar as 'he deems that everything is possible for God', he is greatly inferior as a theologian to Galen, to Plato, and to all right-thinking Greeks (*Us. part.* 3.904–5 K).

Further references are found in the Arabic tradition. Two texts echo *On the Difference of Pulses*. One is a fragment from Galen's lost treatise *On the Anatomy of Hippocrates*:

> Those who practise medicine without any scientific knowledge they compare to Moses, the Jewish lawgiver; for in his books his method is to write without giving any proofs, saying: God commanded, God spoke.

The second text comes from an anti-Aristotelian essay, *Against the First Unmoved Mover*:

> Were I thinking of those who teach pupils in the manner of the followers of Moses and Christ, ordering them to accept everything on trust, I should not have given you a definition.

Finally, in a passage from his synopsis of Plato's *Republic* (or perhaps of the *Phaedo*) Galen allegedly offered the Christians a bouquet: to be sure, they 'are unable to follow any demonstrative argument'; to be sure, they give credence to stories and parables; yet nevertheless, they face death with an admirable resolution, they are properly self-controlled (even their womenfolk) in sexual matters, they eat and drink modestly, they love justice — in short, in practical life 'they are not at all inferior to genuine philosophers.'[6]

Galen may have been contemptuous of Christian logic, but he admired Christian ethics — and he implicitly defended Christians against the twin charges of cannibalism and incest which were frequently brought against them.[7] It has been inferred that Galen was rather well informed about the followers of Moses and of Christ; that he had some knowledge of the Bible; and that his observations 'probably reflect a discussion which had been going on for

---

[6] The texts are printed, translated and discussed in R. Walzer, *Galen on Jews and Christians*, Oxford Classical and Philosophical Monographs (Oxford 1949); see also e.g. S. Pines, *An Arabic Version of the Testimonium Flavianum and its Implications* (Jerusalem 1971) 73–82; S. Gero, 'Galen on the Christians: a reappraisal of the Arabic evidence', *Orientalia Christiana Periodica* 56 (1990) 371–411.

[7] On cannibalism and incest, Thyestean feasts and Oedipodean intercourse, see e.g. Fronto, in Minucius Felix, *Oct.* 9.6 (*cf.* 8.4, 28.2, 31.2); Justin, *1 Apol.* 26.7; Athenagoras, *Leg.* 3.1; the letter from the church of Vienne and Lyons in Eusebius, *Hist. eccl.* 5.1.14–15; Origen, *C. Cels.* 6.27, 40 (compare Lucian, *Merc. cong.* 41, on choice items of Roman pornography). On the whole matter see A. Henrichs, 'Pagan ritual and the alleged crimes of the early Christians', in P. Granfield and J. A. Jungmann (eds.), *Kyriakon: Festschrift Johannes Quasten* (Münster 1971) 18–35.

some time in the higher strata of Roman society and of which we know merely because Galen inserted these chance remarks into some of his philosophical and medical works'.[8] We might then look again at the Greek corpus. For example, Galen tells a story about the Emperor Hadrian: he once struck a slave in anger and blinded him in one eye; asked to name his compensation, the slave 'boldly asked for nothing else but an eye — for what gift could be worth the loss of an eye?' (*Pecc. an.* 5.17–18 K). Surely a covert allusion to *Deuteronomy*?

All very seductive — but the evidence may be set in its context. From other Arabic texts we learn that St Paul was Galen's nephew; that Galen heard from Mary Magdalene of the miracles of Jesus; that he went to Palestine to interview the surviving disciples; that he foretold the Second Coming; that, a devout Christian himself, his dying wish was that his pupils should follow his own religious example.[9] All this is wild fantasy. Sceptics have supposed, not implausibly, that Galen's alleged praise of Christian morals belongs to the same branch of literature. Nor do the texts give any reason to think that he had read the Bible. In general, according to Tertullian, 'only Christians read our books' (*Test. an.* 1). Tertullian exaggerates, as he always does: Celsus, the declared foe of all things Christian, had read much of the Scriptures, and so had his contemporary, the Platonico-Pythagorean philosopher Numenius — with an approving eye.[10] Yet Tertullian's exaggeration is not far from the truth.

Nonetheless, it is certain that Galen said once, and probable that he said three times, that Christians do not prove their doctrines; and it is possible that the accusation was based on a passing acquaintance with the Christians and their religion.

---

[8] Walzer (n. 6) 2 (a brisk application of scepticism by A. D. Nock, review of Walzer, *Gnomon* 23 (1951) 48–52). The view that Galen had read some of the Christian scriptures seems to derive from E. Norden, *Die antike Kunstprosa* (2nd ed., Leipzig 1909) 518–19 ('it is at least probable — though not certain — that Galen had read in the Gospels'). Norden appeals only to the fragment from *In Rep.* which neither states nor implies anything about reading.

[9] I take these examples from Gero (n. 6) 389, 391 n. 61, 397 n. 76, 398 n. 78. See also [Galen], *Ren. affect.* 19.679 K: 'Because these remedies generally fail, we Christians must go to our greatest and truly mysterious items' — and our Christian cures never fail. The work on the diseases of the kidneys is a late forgery.

[10] For Numenius and the Bible see e.g. M. J. Edwards, 'Atticizing Moses? Numenius, the Fathers and the Jews', *Vigiliae Christianae* 44 (1990) 64–75 (but his scepticism is unconvincing). For pagan citations of the Scriptures see G. Rinaldi, *Biblia Gentium* (Rome 1989), with pp.103–16 for a general survey of the evidence. (The celebrated citation of *Genesis* in 'Longinus' 9.9 is surely an interpolation.)

iii

Whether any Christians had a passing acquaintance with Galen is another question, to which I shall later turn. Before that, some words about the common accusation that Christianity despised and rejected logic.

It must be allowed that innumerable Christian texts appear to give substance to the accusation. Had not St Paul denounced those who are 'doting about questions and strifes of words' (*I Tim.* 6.4)? And was he not there referring to 'the Greek art of logic, which he calls a disease' (Clement, *Strom.* 1.8.40.2)? Many learned Christians thought so.

From the Latin part of the Empire and the late third century you might cite Arnobius, who affirms that Christians have no need of 'syllogisms and enthymemes and definitions and other decorations of that sort' (*Adv. nat.* 1.58); or Lactantius, according to whom

> divine learning has no need of logic, since wisdom is not in the tongue but in the heart, and it is of no account what style you use — it is things, not words, which we seek. (*Div. inst.* 3.13)

And a pair of Greek examples from the fourth century. Gregory of Nazianzus asserts that Christians should express their views 'dogmatically, not antilogically; in a fishermanly fashion, not *à la* Aristotle' (*Orat.* 33.12).[11] And Gregory of Nyssa:

> As for confirming our doctrines by way of the dialectical art, through syllogisms and analytical science, we abjure that form of discourse as rotten and suspect with regard to the demonstration of the truth.

After all, dialectic has 'equal strength in both directions' and is as likely to subvert as to support the truth. A theologian who makes use of logic will only make his doctrines seem dubious (*An. et res.* (PG XLVI 52B)).

In spurning logic, the Christians had pagan predecessors.[12] They adopted the pagan objections. But they also had an objection of their own: logic was the seed-bed of heresy.

Heresy, after all, was grown on Greek philosophy. The *Refutation of all Heresies* compiled by Hippolytus in the early third century is the most sustained essay on the topic (and the one best known to classical scholars);[13] but it

---

[11] Fishermen vs. philosophers: on this favourite trope see H. Hagendahl, 'Piscatorie et non aristotelice: zu einem Schlagwort bei den Kirchenvätern', in *Septentrionalia et Orientalia: studia Bernhardo Kalgren* (Stockholm 1959).

[12] See e.g. J. Barnes, *Logic and the Imperial Stoa* (*Philosophia Antiqua* 75, Leiden 1997) 1–11.

[13] See J. Mansfeld, *Heresiography in Context* (*Philosophia Antiqua* 56, Leiden 1992).

elaborates a commonplace. Tertullian, for example, knew that heretics associate with 'magicians, mountebanks, astrologers and philosophers'.[14] Logic in particular pleases their perverted palates: they love 'wretched Aristotle, who taught them dialectic, the art of proving and refuting' (*De praescr. haeret.* 7.6). Jerome agreed with Tertullian, as he usually did: the heretics 'seek a place and a refuge for themselves amid the thickets of Aristotle and Chrysippus' (*Comm. in Naum* 2.15 (PL XXV 1269C)).

The arch-heretic of the second century, Marcion, called his major work '*Antitheseis*' — a technical term in logic. Apelles, a renegade pupil of Marcion, wrote a work in at least 38 books 'which he entitled *Syllogisms* and in which he hopes to prove that everything which Moses wrote about God is not true but false' ([Tertullian], *Adv. haer.* 6). At about the same time, an adherent of the Valentinian heresy, Alexander, produced a book full of heretical syllogisms.[15]

The fourth-century heretics were worse. Arius was 'a man not unacquainted with logical quibbling' (Socrates, *Hist. eccl.* 1.2). In the nice phrase of Faustinus, Aristotle was the bishop of the Arians (*Trin.* 12 (PL XIII 60B)). Aëtius loved 'the matters set out technically by Aristotle' (Socrates, *Hist. eccl.* 2.35): he learned 'the teachings of Aristotle' in Alexandria, and rapidly became 'a dialectician, good at syllogizing, practised in captious argumentation and wholly devoted to such things' (Sozomen, *Hist. eccl.* 3.15). His *Syntagmation* or *Pamphlet* was copied out by the Catholic bishop of Salamis, Epiphanius, in the course of his exhausting denunciation of every hideous heterodoxy. In the *Panarion* or *Bread-Basket* Epiphanius affirms that Aëtius wrote 'dialectically'; his work was 'a dialectical error' (*Pan.* 76.10.3–4); it was nothing but a 'dialectical ostentation and a syllogistic waste of labour' (25.1).[16]

---

[14] Tertullian, *De praescr. haeret.* 43.1; see also e.g. 7.3; *Adv. Marc.* 1.13. Elsewhere he calls the pagan philosophers the 'patriarchs of the heretics', a phrase which he repeats and which Jerome adopts (*De anima* 3.1; *C. Hermog.* 8.3; Jerome, *Ep.* 133.2). On Tertullian see T. D. Barnes, *Tertullian* (Oxford 1971).

[15] On Marcion see A. von Harnack, *Neue Studien zur Marcion* (*Texte und Untersuchungen zur Geschichte der altchristlichen Literatur* 44, Leipzig 1923); id., *Marcion: das Evangelium vom fremden Gott* (*Texte und Untersuchungen zur Geschichte der altchristlichen Literatur* 45, 2nd ed., Leipzig 1924); on Apelles: von Harnack, *Marcion* 177–96 and 404–20 (testimonia); R. M. Grant, *Heresy and Criticism: the Search for Authenticity in Early Christian Literature* (Louisville, KY 1993) 75–88; on Alexander: Tertullian, *De carne* 17.1, with J.-P. Mahé, *Tertullien: La Chair du Christ* (*Sources chrétiennes* 216, Paris 1975) 58–68.

[16] Aëtius' *Syntagmation*: text, translation, and notes in L. R. Wickham, 'The *Syntagmation* of Aëtius the Anomean', *Journal of Theological Studies* 19 (1968) 532–69. Aëtius was exiled in the 350s for

Eunomius likewise was 'a technician of arguments, given to captiousness, rejoicing in syllogisms' (Sozomen, *Hist. eccl.* 6.26). Gregory of Nazianzus wonders why he 'ties up the weak in spiders' webs, as though that were something grand and clever' (*Orat.* 27.9). According to Jerome, who refers disparagingly to 'those who are trained in the art of dialectic and the arguments of the philosophers',

> Eutychius and Eunomius...attempt with syllogisms and enthymemes — with sophisms and Liars and Sorites — to confirm the errors which others have invented. (*In Amos* 1.1.4)

(It may be noted that Eunomius reversed the charges: the Catholics, he insisted, were 'led astray by the sophisms of the Greeks' — *Apol.* 22; cf. 27.)[17]

iv

A diverting text refers to heretics, to logic — and to Galen. In his *History of the Church* Eusebius transcribes some pages from an attack on the followers of an heretical tanner, Theodotus by name. A part of the transcription is repeated by Theodoretus, who says that it comes from the *Little Labyrinth*, a work which some falsely ascribed to Origen. Other ancient authorities attributed the work to Gaius, of whom we know next to nothing; and some modern scholars have proposed Hippolytus.[18] However that may be, Theodotus is dated to the papacy of Victor, bishop of Rome from 189 to about 200, and his followers had trouble with Victor's successor Zephyrinus.

his heretical opinions — and recalled by the pagan Emperor Julian who remembered their 'old acquaintance and intercourse' (*Ep.* 15 Wright = 46 Bidez (404C)).

[17] On Eunomius and logic see esp. E. Vandenbussche, 'La part de la dialectique dans la théologie d'Eunomius "le technologue"', *Revue d'histoire ecclésiastique* 40 (1944/5) 47–72, with a generous citation of texts. The texts of Eunomius: R. P. Vaggione, *Eunomius: the extant works* (*Oxford Early Christian Texts*, Oxford 1987). On logic and the fourth-century controversies see J. de Ghellinck, *Patristique et moyen âge: études d'histoire littéraire et doctrinale III* (*Museum Lessianum section historique* 7, Brussels 1961) 256–70.

[18] The text: Eusebius, *Hist. eccl.* 5.28.3–19; Theodoretus, *Haer. fab. comp.* 2.5 (note that Theodoretus is independent of Eusebius); Methodius, *Symp.* 8.10. For title and authorship of the *Labyrinth* see e.g. J. Schamp, *Photios historien des lettres* (Liège 1987) 109–15. On Theodotus see D. A. Bertrand, 'L'argument scripturaire de Théodote le Corroyeur (Epiphane, Panarion 54)', in *Lectures anciennes de la Bible* (*Cahiers de Biblia Patristica* 1, Strasbourg 1987) 153–68. On Eusebius see T. D. Barnes, *Constantine and Eusebius* (Cambridge, Mass. 1981).

The Theodotians were charged with several sins. Thus they tampered with the text of the Scriptures, a practice for which heretics (and Jews) were notorious — Celsus was delighted to report that 'some of the believers' altered the text of the Gospels three or four or more times in order to escape refutation (Origen, *C. Cels.* 2.27).[19] A second sin was equally heinous. The Theodotians

> do not inquire what the divine Scripture says. Rather, they diligently practise whatever syllogistic figure can be found to establish their atheism, and if you present them with a text of divine Scripture they investigate whether it can make a conditional or a disjunctive syllogistic figure. Abandoning the holy Scriptures of God, they study geometry — for they are of the earth and speak of the earth and they do not know Him that cometh from above [John 3.31]. Some of them diligently geometrize Euclid; Aristotle and Theophrastus are admired; and Galen no doubt is actually worshipped by some of them. (Eusebius, *Hist. eccl.* 5.28.13–14)

The Theodotians took refuge in logic — and they went to the best pagan authorities.[20]

Among those authorities was Galen, their contemporary, whom they worshipped. The verb is strong — Galen himself refers to intellectual idols

> whom you will not only emulate but worship — Socrates is among them, and Homer, and Hippocrates, and Plato, men whom we revere equally with the gods. (*Protr.* 1.8 K)

It has been inferred that the Theodotians knew Galen in person; that it was from him that they learned the geometry of Euclid and the logic of Aristotle and Theophrastus; and that their penchant for meddling with texts — in other words, for textual criticism — was encouraged by Galen's scholarly work on the text of Hippocrates.[21]

The inferences are fragile. The *Labyrinth* implies no personal contact between the Theodotians and Galen — whose books were readily accessible. It does not suggest that Galen had anything to do with their philological

---

[19] For tampering with the Scriptures see e.g. Justin, *Dial.* 72–3 (the Jews); Eusebius, *Hist. eccl.* 4.29.6 (Tatian); Tertullian, *Adv. Marc.* 4.5.5–6 (the Gnostics); Augustine, *Retract.* 1.8.6; 2.33.1 (Manicheans); Julian, *C. Gal.* 253E. See A. Bludau, *Die Schriftfälschungen der Häretiker* (*Neutestamentliche Abhandlungen* 11.5, Münster 1925).

[20] The passage has amassed a certain literature: see e.g. E. Schwartz, *Zwei Predigten Hippolyts* (*Sitzungsberichte der bayerischen Akademie der Wissenschaften, phil.-hist. Ableitung* 1936.3, Munich 1936); H. Schöne, 'Ein Einbruch der antiken Logik und Textkritik in die altchristliche Theologie', in T. Klauser and A. Rücker (eds.), *Pisciculi: Studien zur Religion und Kultur des Altertums Franz Joseph Dölger dargeboten* (Münster 1939); Walzer (n. 6) 75–86; de Ghellinck (n. 17) 288–96; Grant (n. 15), 59–72.

[21] So Walzer (n. 6) 75–86.

investigations — and there was a horde of pagan commentators from whom they might have sought inspiration. Nor does the text indicate that Galen was the source for all the Theodotians' logical competence: on the contrary, its author, who later insists on the numerous schisms within the heresy, insinuates that one groupuscule ran to Euclid, another to the Peripatetic logicians, and a third to Galen.

The *Labyrinth* is a piece of rude polemic, not a history of logic. Indeed, a solid sceptic might wonder if the reference to Galen was not the author's own invention — does not the phrase 'no doubt' suggest as much? But such an invention is, I think, improbable. Later Fathers of the Church knew Galen; but they knew him as a physician. Efforts to find Galenic influence on earlier Christian authors — on Athenagoras, or on Clement, or on Origen — fail.[22] Nor is Galen often alluded to by pagans. The text of the *Labyrinth* is one of remarkably few early references to Galen. Moreover, it is the only text I know — outside the pages of Galen himself — which celebrates him as a logician.

What of the other pagan logicians to whom the Theodotians applied themselves? Euclid is a surprise; and since geometry is in the text for the sake of the punning allusion to John's Gospel ('geometry' is earthmeasurement, and the Theodotians are of the earth), a sceptic might suspect that Euclid had been imported by the polemicist. At the other extreme, it has been supposed that the Theodotians made use of the *Pseudaria* — a lost work in which Euclid offered a sequence of exercises to guard students against logical fallacies.[23] But neither scepticism nor subtlety is required: geometrical proofs were, after all, the very paradigms of logical demonstration, and the Theodotians will have conned their Euclid in order to hone up their demonstrative prowess.[24]

---

[22] Galen has been found behind Athenagoras (with reference to the Ilkley Moor argument at *Res.* 5–8) by e.g. L. W. Barnard, *Athenagoras: a Study in Second Century Christian Apologetic* (*Théologie historique* 18, Paris 1972) 53–9 — but see *contra*, and incontrovertibly, B. Pouderon, *D'Athènes à Alexandrie: études sur Athénagore et les origines de la philosophie chrétienne* (*Bibliothèque copte de Nag Hammadi*, section Etudes 4, Quebec 1997) 238–44. The best attempt to find Galen in Origen (not in itself an improbable notion) is R. M. Grant, 'Paul, Galen, and Origen', *Journal of Theological Studies* 34 (1983) 533–6 — but his arguments do not stand up. Later Jerome, for example, knows some Galen: A. Lübeck, *Hieronymus quos noverit scriptores et ex quibus hauserit* (Leipzig 1872) 100–4; A. S. Pease, 'Medical allusions in the works of St. Jerome', *Harvard Studies in Classical Philology* 25 (1914) 73–86, at 81–2.

[23] So Schöne (n. 20) 259–60.

[24] See e.g. Gregory of Nazianzus, *Orat.* 28.25, for a Christian reference to Euclid as a celebrated proofmonger.

The name of Aristotle, on the other hand, is expected — who did not know that Aristotle had 'turned philosophy into an expertise and was much given to logic' (Hippolytus, *Ref. haer.* 1.20.1)?[25] Theophrastus might be there as his master's dog; but he was still known at the end of the second century — at any rate, Galen wrote commentaries on his logical writings, and Alexander of Aphrodisias discussed his contribution to hypothetical syllogistic.[26] We may wonder if the old Peripatetics were read in the original — then as now, pagans and Christians got their logic (and most other items) from digests and handbooks. But the use of such conveniences is compatible with study of the original texts; and in truth we have no idea what Theodotus read in his tannery.

There is a startling omission: no Chrysippus — no Stoics at all. At the end of the second century, the Stoic sun still shone bright enough. Hippolytus, for example, remarks casually that the Stoics — not Aristotle — 'made philosophy more syllogistic' (*Ref. haer.* 1.21.1).[27] Moreover, the one logical detail in the text suggests Stoic rather than Peripatetic logic: I mean the reference to conditionals and disjunctions. It is true that conditional propositions ('If . . . , then . . .') and disjunctive propositions ('Either . . . or . . .') had been discussed by Theophrastus; and of course the Theodotians could have learned of them from Galen — or from any textbook — without going back to the Stoic originals. But the *Labyrinth* uses the Stoic terminology rather than the Peripatetic; and it would have been peculiar to go to town on such items without knowing anything about the Stoics. I suspect that the absence of the Stoics from our text is an accident — its author, after all, does not profess to give a comprehensive account of the Theodotians' logical studies.

What he does say about conditionals and disjunctions has puzzled historians of logic:

> . . . if you present them with a text of divine Scripture they investigate whether it can make a conditional or a disjunctive syllogistic figure.

---

[25] On Aristotle among the early Christians, see A. J. Festugière, *L'Idéal religieux des grecs et l'évangile* (2nd ed., Paris 1932) 221–63; D. T. Runia, 'Festugière revisited: Aristotle in the Greek Patres', *Vigiliae Christianae* 43 (1989) 1–34 — Runia finds fewer than 200 references to Aristotle in the Greek Fathers, very few of which suggest a first-hand acquaintance with the texts.

[26] See Galen, *Lib. prop.* 19.47 K; Alexander, *In An. Pr.* 262.28–264.31, 389.31–390.9. The fragments of and testimonies to Theophrastus' logic are in W. W. Fortenbaugh et al., *Theophrastus of Eresus* (*Philosophia Antiqua* 54, Leiden 1992) 115–275.

[27] Early Christian references to Stoic logic are collected by de Ghellinck (n. 17) 282–96. His general thesis is this: 'The way in which they speak of Stoic logic does not point to a first hand acquaintance: it does not go beyond the small change of schoolboy learning characteristic of the culture of the time, or beyond the doxographies or collections of opinions of the philosophers' (p. 284). An exaggeration — Origen, at least, had pretty clearly read the stuff in the original.

There are no such things as conditional or disjunctive 'figures' or forms of syllogism — it is propositions, not argument-forms, which are conditional and disjunctive.

Scholars have therefore canvassed alternative translations.[28] But they are implausible. And they are also superfluous. The *Labyrinth* has no interest in logical niceties, and we should not expect terminological precision from it. What the text means to say is plain enough. The Theodotians asked whether an argument which they found in the Bible should be formalised as a syllogism with a conditional premiss or as a syllogism with a disjunctive premiss. In short, they worried about the logical form of sacred arguments. Did Moses argue by *modus ponens*? Did St Paul syllogize in Barbara?

V

Logic was tainted with heresy, and it was therefore to be rejected by Catholics. But what exactly were they to reject? What exactly were the logical sins of the heretics?

There is no reason to think that the Theodotians theorized about logic or developed any logical techniques of their own. Rather, they applied to the Bible a technique used by commentators on pagan philosophical texts. Neither the *Labyrinth* nor any other of the sparse texts on the Theodotians actually cites one of their syllogisms; but it is easy enough to see what they must have been like. A Platonic commentator, for example, would identify an argument in a patch of Platonic text; he would set out the argument in a clear and explicit fashion; and he would perhaps refer it to one or another syllogistic form or figure.[29] The Theodotians doubtless did the same thing.

Something similar was probably true of Alexander, and certainly true of Apelles.[30] Apelles' *Syllogisms* were a collection of little arguments, each of them self-consciously dressed in the garb of school-logic. But in Apelles' case the arguments were critical rather than exegetical: his syllogisms did not formalise the reasoning of the Prophets — they deduced absurd consequences from the Old Testament. (There was, for example, a detailed criticism of the story of Noah's ark: if we take the Scriptural

[28] See Schöne (n. 20) 257–8 ('... they investigate whether as a conditional or a disjunctive it can make a syllogistic figure').
[29] See, e.g. Galen, *Inst. log.* 15.9–10, 18.2–3; Alcinous, *Didask.* 6 (158–9 H); *cf.* D. J. O'Meara, *Pythagoras Revived* (Oxford 1989) 41–2.
[30] For Alexander and Apelles see above, n. 15.

dimensions seriously, the ark could hardly have accommodated four ele-
phants, let alone animals of every species. The Catholics replied that cubits
were longer in Noah's day.) And at the end of each syllogism, according to
Origen, 'he adds the words: "The story is therefore false; the scripture
therefore does not come from God."'[31] Apelles and the Theodotians had
different aims; but their writings must have had a similar style.

The case of the fourth-century heretics is in some respects rather different. A scrutiny of the surviving fragments of Eunomius will reveal no
remark about logic. What is more, it will scarcely reveal an argument.
Aëtius' pamphlet at first blush makes a similar impression: it consists of a
dozen and a half brief remarks on the unbegotten God. Here is a typical
example:

> If the unbegotten nature is cause of the generated nature, and the unbegotten were
> nothing, how could nothing be cause of the generated? (Epiphanius, *Pan.* 76.12.23)

Now this is not a syllogism, not even in the loosest of senses; it is not even
an argument — it is a question, a conditional question.[32]

Was Epiphanius muddled when he accused Aëtius' pamphlet of being a
nest of logical vipers (*Pan.* 76.10.3–4)? Well, Aëtius alleges that an early
version of the work had been put abroad by his enemies in a corrupted form:
they 'ruined it with interpolations and excisions and altered the run of the
implications' (proem). He therefore prepared a revised version in which, he
says,

> I have distinguished question from question and solution from solution in the form
> of verses so that the arguments may be easy to grasp and clear. (ibid.)

There is indeed a run of implications, or of conditional sentences; and they
are questions. But where are the solutions, and where the arguments?

These are obtuse interrogations. Aëtius' questions are evidently rhetorical questions — they are conditional assertions in interrogative form. And
the conditional assertions are abridged or condensed arguments — the text I
have quoted is to be reconstrued as an argument to the conclusion that the
unbegotten nature is not nothing.

Nonetheless, there are no explicit syllogisms in Aëtius' pamphlet, and to
that extent he is unlike Apelles and unlike the Theodotians. Yet all these
heretics have something in common: a certain address and style. It is a dry
and abstract style, in which propositions are set down with no attention to

---

[31] The passage, from Origen, *In Gen. hom.* 2, is printed in von Harnack, *Marcion* (n. 15) 413*.
[32] For Aëtius and Eunomius see above, n. 16 and n. 17.

literary elegance; it is a spare and abrupt style, in which nothing is decked in rhetorical frippery; it is a pedantic style, in which everything pertinent to the argument and nothing superfluous is laid out as precisely and as plainly as possible. In short, it is a logical style — a style adopted in antiquity by the Stoic masters and affected today by certain logically minded philosophers.[33]

I think that it was this common style, as much as anything of a more strictly logical nature, which roused the ire of the orthodox. Arnobius urges us to do without syllogisms and the like ornaments; Lactantius links a rejection of logic with a recommendation of unadorned speech; Gregory contrasts 'syllogisms and enthymemes' with the plain language of fishermen.[34] Again, Jerome observes of the apostles that

> the grandeur of their saintliness excused their simplicity of speech, while the Dead Man, resurrected, confuted the syllogisms of Aristotle and the twists and spikes of Chrysippus. (*Ep.* 57.12.4)

According to Theodoretus, it would have been easy for the Source of all wisdom to make his heralds 'more sweet-tongued than Plato, more clever than Demosthenes', and to have them 'surpass Thucydides in weight and Aristotle and Chrysippus in the insoluble binding of their syllogisms' (*Cur.* 8.2). Isidore of Pelusium remarks that the clever Greeks 'preen themselves for their style and pride themselves on their logic' (*Ep.* 4.27).

Arnobius and his fellows want to defend plain speaking and to warn against the wiles of clever Greeks. These wiles include cunning ratiocinations as well as mellifluous periods. Conversely, the praise of plain speaking recommends not only humdrum prose but also informal argumentation. It is not the use of argument which the enemies of logic deplored: it is the display of syllogistical technology, it is the logical style of writing. Better imitate the Persians who are an 'extremely syllogistic' people —

> not because they have read the mazes of Chrysippus and of Aristotle, nor because Socrates and Plato have educated them in this area; for they have not been fed on rhetorical and philosophical arguments — their only teacher is nature. (Theodoretus, *Cur.* 5.72)

John Locke would have nodded his accord.

The attitude is intelligible enough. The logical style is meretricious, at once attractive and repugnant: its rapid patter seduces — and yet fails to

---

[33] Grant (n. 15) 80–1, well compares Apelles' argument in Ambrose, *Parad.* 6.30 with Gellius, 2.7 (probably of Stoic origin). On the Stoic style see M. Schofield, 'The syllogisms of Zeno of Citium', *Phronesis* 28 (1983) 31–58; Barnes (n. 12) 12–23.

[34] See the texts cited above, p. 405.

persuade; it leaves the mind stunned and the heart untouched. Many pagans disliked it for such reasons; and the Christians had a further motive: their message was delivered to the masses, for whom such clevernesses are either dangerous or disgusting.

vi

And yet the Christian attitude was humbug. There were no more self-conscious stylists than those Christian writers who most affected to scorn style; there were no more pedantic quibblers than those Christians who objected to heretical logic-chopping. Tertullian, for example, 'attacked dialectic with a tenacious hatred — yet, as we know, he used it himself from the first line of his writings to the last. In the whole history of the early Church there is no more determined dialectician.'[35] Or again, there is a close parallel to Aëtius' *Syntagmation* in the 'Proofs by way of syllogisms', a short pamphlet ascribed to Theodoretus: the text consists of 40 arguments, in the style of Aëtius, which purport to offer formal proofs of the points for which Theodoretus had argued conversationally in his *Eranistes*.[36] Theodoretus sailed close to the wind of heresy; but this pamphlet, for all its technical form and its dialectical structure, is thoroughly Catholic.

Gregory of Nyssa lambasts logic — he also lauds his brother Basil for 'offering profane culture as a gift to the Church of God', and the gift is expressly said to include 'the discipline of logic' (*Vit. Moys.* 2.115). Gregory of Nazianzus scorns logic — he also says admiringly of Basil that he was supreme in rhetoric, in grammar, and

> in that philosophy which is really sublime and ascends on high — the practical and the theoretical and also that which concerns logical proofs and antitheses and tricks, so that it was easier to escape from a maze than to evade the toils of his arguments, should that prove necessary. (*Orat.* 43.23)

To be sure, Basil's writings scarcely suggest such eulogies.

Jerome affected to despise logic. Yet he was sharp enough with an upstart young deacon:

---

[35] A. Labhardt, 'Tertullien et la philosophie, ou la recherche d'une "position pure"', *Museum Helveticum* 7 (1950) 159–80, at 168.

[36] See G. H. Ettlinger, *Theodoret of Cyrus: Eranistes* (Oxford 1975) — the syllogisms are printed at 254–65.

> You say that . . . this dialectician, a pillar of your city and of the family of the
> Plautii, has not even read the *Categories* of Aristotle, nor his *de Interpretatione*,
> nor the *Analytics*, nor indeed Cicero's *Topics*; but in the circles of the ignorant and
> at the tea-parties of little women he weaves his unsyllogistic syllogisms and by
> cunning argumentation unravels my so-called sophisms. . . . In vain did I turn the
> pages of Alexander's commentaries, in vain did my learned teacher introduce me
> to logic by way of Porphyry's *Isagoge*, . . . (*Ep.* 50.1)

Sir Have-it-both-ways was a familiar character in the Church.[37]

But humbug and hypocrisy were not universal. Clement argues that the
study of logic is indispensable to the intelligent Christian.[38] It is childish to
fear pagan logic:

> Most people fear pagan philosophy as children fear the bogeyman — they are
> afraid it will lead them astray. But if their faith is such as to be dissolved by
> plausibilities, then let it be dissolved. (*Strom.* 6.10.80.4)

An intelligent Christian will readily separate rhetoric, which is pernicious,
from dialectic, which is useful (ibid. 1.8.44.2); and he will equally separate
the sophistical and eristical use of logic from its honourable employment
(ibid. 1.10.47.2).

Origen was another such: he mastered logic himself, and in his
school — as one of his parting pupils described it — 'he trained logically that
part of the soul which judges concerning phrases and arguments' (Gregory the
Thaumaturge, *Ad Orig.* 7.106; *cf.* Eusebius, *Hist. eccl.* 6.18.3). Origen
flaunted his logical expertise, and his texts show that this was not mere
vanity.[39]

Or consider Augustine, who was described by his enemy Julianus as the
Carthaginian Aristotle (see Augustine, *C. Iul.* 3.199). He read Aristotle's
Categories when he was 20, and his youthful studies of the liberal arts included logic: he found them easy, his only puzzle (so he later avowed) being
whether they helped him to adore God (*Conf.* 4.16.28–9). However that may
be, he acknowledged that 'I have learned more from dialectic than from any
other part of philosophy' (*C. Acad.* 3.13.29); he once set out to write a book on
the subject, of which 'only the beginning has survived — and even that I have

---

[37] On Jerome see J. N. D. Kelly, *Jerome* (London 1975).

[38] See e.g. *Strom.* 1.28.176.3–177.3; 6.10.80.4–81.1. On Clement and logic see J. Pépin, 'La vraie
dialectique selon Clément', in J. Fontaine and C. Kannengieser (eds.), *Epektasis: Mélanges
patristiques offerts au Cardinal Jean Daniélou* (Paris 1972) 375–83.

[39] See e.g. H. Chadwick, 'Origen, Celsus and the Stoa', *Journal of Theological Studies* 48 (1947)
34–49.

lost, though I think that some people have a copy';[40] and he frequently defends the study of logic.[41]

His enemies exploited this weakness. Petilianus, a heretic of the Donatist variety who detested logic, accused him of being a vile and slippery dialectician (see *C. litt. Petil.* 3.16); and Cresconius seconded the case (see *C. Crescon.* 1.13; 2.18). At the end of Augustine's life, the heretics of the day took an opposite tack, the Pelagians alleging the indispensability of logic for an understanding of the Word of God (e.g. *C. Iul.* 6.20). Augustine must have been tempted to change sides and reject logic as the devil's game — and some scholars have argued that this is just what the old man did.[42] But his reply to the Pelagians follows a different line: he does not argue that logic should be left to the infidels — rather, he urges that Julianus is an incompetent logician (*C. Iul.* 3.7), who shoots himself in the foot (ibid. 6.18).

What did these logical Fathers make of Paul and the Greek disease?[43] Well, a Scriptural score lets you whistle any tune you like. Clement thinks that Paul is rejecting only rhetoric and sophistic, not logic in its entirety; and Eusebius remarks that Paul 'rejects deceptive and sophistical plausibilities and employs plain proofs' (*Praep. evang.* 1.3.5). Origen affirms that Paul used 'sound syllogisms, brought to their conclusions by the art of dialectic' (*Comm. in Rom.* 6.13 (PG XIV 1098A)). After all, the Son of Man was the Word, the Logos; Jesus Christ was Reason Incarnate. How could He not have been a logician? After all — as Augustine pertinently demands — with what if not logic did Jesus confute the Jews?[44]

---

[40] *Retract.* 1.5, recording the events of 387. The opening part of *On Dialectic*, perhaps all that Augustine wrote, has survived — on the question of authenticity see B. D. Jackson, *Augustine: de dialectica* (*Synthèse Historical Library* 16, Dordrecht 1975) 2–5, 26–8, 43–75; J. Pépin, *Saint Augustin et la dialectique* (Villanova, PA 1976) 21–60.

[41] E.g. *Ord.* 2.13.38; *Solil.* 2.11.19–21; *Doct. Christ.* 2.31.48–36.54; *C. Crescon.* 1.14–16; *C. Iul* 6.

[42] See Pépin (n. 40) 243–55. The texts which Pépin adduces are at best guarded. The clearest is this: Julian tries to teach dialectic, *non cogitans quomodo abiciat Christi ecclesia dialecticum quem censet haereticum* (*Op. imperf.* 3.31). Pépin takes this to mean that the Church rejects dialecticians, whom it takes to be heretical; but I think that Augustine rather means that the Church rejects any dialectician whom it takes to be heretical. In written English, a comma makes all the difference; in the Latin, the phrase is ambiguous, but the context prefers the latter interpretation.

[43] See the texts cited above, p. 405.

[44] See *C. Crescon.* 1.17.21–18.22, referring to Matth. 22.21.

vii

Galen, like most pagans who troubled to notice them, was wrong about the Christians. They did not reject proof and argument. Carried away by the sacred duty to refute pagans and heretics, carried along to the rhetorical beat of divine inspiration, carried aloft far above the worldly virtue of self-consistency, they sometimes sneered or snarled at logic. But they could not, and they did not, abjure ratiocination. On the contrary, they literally worshipped Reason.

Christians and logic fit snugly together. And Galen? Did the Christians learn their logic from Galen, the third logician of antiquity after Aristotle and Chrysippus? It would be agreeable to think that they were particularly charmed by his 'third kind of syllogism'. After all, the logic of relations is of apparent pertinence to many of the theological controversies which divided the early Church. The concepts of Father and of Son are relational concepts; the concept of identity, which underlay the long and lacerating dispute over the doctrine of the Trinity, is a relational concept *par excellence*. Now identity, paternity, and sonship are each noticed in Galen's discussion of relational syllogisms (*Inst. log.* 16).

Admittedly, in all the vast patristic library, only one short text associates Christians with Galen the logician. Moreover, the Christians in question are a small and insignificant group of heretics; and the text gives no reason to think that they were especially interested in Galen's logic of relations. But such reticence is wholly unremarkable. Christians took their logic from the pagan authorities — whence else? Origen had read Chrysippus, Jerome says that he had read Aristotle; but in general, the Christians, like their pagan con-temporaries, did not imbibe their logic from those original and distant sour-ces — they drank in derivative streams, their logic came from manuals and handbooks. They do not say so; still less do they name the authors of such little works — whoever would expect them to do so?

One of the few such manuals to survive from antiquity is precisely Galen's *Introduction to Logic*. No ancient author — not even Galen himself — ever refers to the *Introduction*. But it would be a gross error to infer that the work dropped stillborn from the press: for all we know, the thing was sometimes used; for all we know, the thing was sometimes used in Christian schools.

But let me not end on a note of speculative optimism. No surviving text from antiquity, Galen's *Introduction to Logic* apart, ever refers to a logic of relations. Whatever may have been the fortune of the *Introduction* and of his other logical works, his great logical invention was neither admired nor copied.

17
Rhetoric in mid-antiquity

Malcolm Heath

i. From Homer to Byzantium

When the hero Peleus sent his son Achilles to war for the first time he appointed a tutor, prescribing a syllabus of combat skills and rhetoric. In the
words of the tutor, Phoenix, himself (*Iliad* 9.440–3, trans. M. Hammond):

> You were a child, with no knowledge yet of levelling war or of debate, where men
> win distinction. So he sent me out to teach you all these things, to make you a
> speaker of words and a doer of deeds.

It is obvious why combat skills were needed: the *Iliad* is a poem about a war.
But it is also a poem strikingly full of talk, as ancient readers observed.[1] The
heroes confer in large assemblies and in small executive councils; they send
formal embassies and hold informal consultations; and in all of these contexts
they display the capacity to make substantial speeches, well-organised, well-
argued and well-expressed. The poem's plot is set in motion in book 1 by the
miscarriage of Chryses' attempt to persuade Agamemnon, and of the discussion between Agamemnon, Achilles and (as would-be mediator) Nestor. Book
9, from which Peleus' instructions to Phoenix were quoted, is *all* talk: the
Greek army gathers to consider the heavy defeat suffered in the day's fighting;
Nestor shrewdly gets the discussion referred to a closed session of the main
leaders (more likely to reach a constructive result: Agamemnon will be less
sensitive and less defensive, the less public the forum in which his poor leadership is dissected). After talking the situation over this meeting decides
to send three envoys to Achilles. Each of the envoys makes a speech, and
Achilles replies to each; they then report their failure to the leaders' meeting,
and there is further discussion. Later in the poem Patroclus' fateful intervention

---

[1] E.g. Aristotle *Poetics* 24, 1460a5–11.

in the fighting arises from what Nestor says to him (11.655–805) and he to Achilles (16.21–45). So talk is as crucial a determinant of the course of the war as the fighting is: it determines who does and who does not fight, and what they fight for. Later Greeks, looking back to Homer as the fountainhead of rhetoric, were perhaps on the right track.

The *Iliad* is probably the earliest surviving work of European literature.[2] Much later in the Greek tradition, another father offered this advice to his son:

> Nothing could be more beneficial than the knowledge of how to speak well for those who wish to be good rulers, who have sound sense and look towards the common interest, who love what is good and value nothing more than truth. To these men, this is superior straightforwardly to wealth, and far excels the treasures of Croesus so far as security is concerned; it is stronger than Xerxes' multitude of soldiers, and has more force than Gyges' fabled ring and is also honourable; and in sum it is more efficacious than these and of more value.

This is Manuel Palaeologus — Manuel II, the antepenultimate emperor of Byzantium; born in 1350, he reigned from 1391 until his death in 1425.[3] The passage quoted is the beginning of the seven *Ethico-Political Discourses* addressed to his son, the future emperor John.[4] Manuel knew the value of speech to a ruler from personal experience: he had, for example, successfully exhorted the Thessalonians to resist a Turkish attack in 1383 (the city was besieged, and held out until 1387).[5]

Between Homer and Manuel much had changed. Manuel was a Roman emperor: he urged the Thessalonians to 'remember that we are Romans', as

---

[2] The dating of the Homeric poems remains controversial; R. Janko, *Homer, Hesiod and the Hymns* (Cambridge 1982) suggests a date *c.*750–725 BC for the *Iliad*. The minority who date Hesiod earlier than Homer could refer to the section on the eloquence of kings in the proem of *Theogony* (79–93) to reach the same conclusion about the importance of rhetoric.

[3] John W. Barker, *Manuel II Palaeologus: a Study in Late Byzantine Statesmanship* (New Brunswick 1969); L. Petit, 'Manuel II Paléologue', in *Dictionnaire de Théologie Catholique* 9.2 (Paris 1927) 1925–32.

[4] *PG* 156.385a. Barker (n. 3) 344 n. 54 dates this work to about 1406.

[5] Barker (n. 3) 46–60. Manuel's speech is edited by B. Laourdas, 'ὁ συμβουλευτικὸς πρὸς τοὺς Θεσσαλονίκεις τοῦ Μανουὴλ Παλαιολόγου', *Μακεδονικά* 3 (1953–1955) 290–307. Manuel sent a copy to Demetrius Cydones with a covering letter (14: text and translation in G. T. Dennis (ed.), *The Letters of Manuel II Palaeologus* (*Dumbarton Oaks Texts* 4, Washington 1977) 29–31). Cydones' reply is letter 262 in the edition of R.-J. Loenertz (Rome 1956–1960); in another letter (120) Cydones applies *Il.* 9.433 to Manuel (*cf.* Barker 415f.). Manuel also composed declamations rooted in the tradition of older rhetorical schools: we have a fragment of a reply to the embassy speeches of Odysseus and Menelaus (Libanius *Decl.* 3–4, cf. *Il.* 3.203–24), first published by J. F. Boissonade, *Anecdota Graeca* (Paris 1830), vol. 2, 308f. and reprinted in Foerster's edition of Libanius (vol. 5, 226f.), and a complete declamation on an amusing original theme (Boissonade vol. 2, 274–307).

well as that 'your fatherland is that of Philip and Alexander.'[6] Admittedly the Roman empire was by now wholly Greek; it is tempting to think of Rome as a transient aberration which Hellenic culture was in the end able to absorb — discarding in the process not only the Italian city itself, but also such notable eccentricities as the Roman prejudice against calling monarchs 'kings' (the Byzantine emperor's title was *basileus*). If residual unease attached to the term 'Hellenic', it was because of the word's pagan connotations; for Manuel was also a Christian, a fact reflected in the Hebrew derivation of a personal name that Homer would have found outlandish. There had been profound changes, therefore; but these changes coexisted with important continuities, including the crucial role of persuasive speech in Greek culture, and the corresponding importance of rhetoric — that is, of expertise in persuasive speech.

Roughly at the mid-point between Homer and Manuel comes the fourth century AD. Consider, then, how Libanius, the most distinguished fourth-century teacher of rhetoric, echoes Peleus' prescription in celebrating the emperor Julian: 'you have overshadowed men of action by your deeds, and men of speech by your words' (*Or.* 13.51). This is from an oration composed in AD 362; four years earlier Libanius had used the same motif in a letter to Julian, praising his military successes on the Rhine in 357 and his panegyric on the emperor Constantius: 'you have won a double victory, one in arms and the other in speech' (*Ep.* 369.1 = 30 Norman). The Christian theologian Gregory of Nazianzus (who may have been a pupil of Libanius)[7] spoke of Julian in similar terms a few years later: 'great in arms and mighty in forcefulness of speech' (*Or.* 7.12). Gregory, of course, was no admirer of the apostate: the quotation comes from a funeral oration on Gregory's brother Caesarius, whose resistance to the emperor is the more glorious, the more heroic the opposition. The parallel to Peleus' two-part syllabus is not coincidental.

---

[6] Laourdas (n. 5) 297.21 (*cf.* 299.32). On the recovery of the sense of 'Hellenic' identity by the fourteenth century, see S. Runciman, *The Last Byzantine Renaissance* (Cambridge 1970) 14–23, 80 (citing Plethon's address to Manuel at *PG* 160.821–4).

[7] According to the church historians Socrates (4.26) and Sozomen (6.17), Gregory and Basil of Caesarea studied with Libanius in Antioch (Constantinople, in 348/9, is more likely: but if the source knew of a connection with Libanius, Antioch was the natural place to site it by conjecture), as well as with the famous sophists Prohaeresius and Himerius in Athens (perhaps also conjectural: these are the most obvious teachers to supply them with on the basis of a known period of study in Athens). According to Socrates (6.3), Libanius' pupils also included John Chrysostom; Sozomen's report (8.2) of Libanius' death-bed testimonial to John (named as his preferred successor, had he not been 'stolen' by the Christians) might be viewed with scepticism, but it can hardly be denied that the testimonial, if authentic, was merited by John's rhetorical brilliance.

ii. Mid-antiquity

The fourth century is part of what is commonly known as 'late' antiquity — a vague term, sometimes used by scholars whose interests lie elsewhere to disguise their ignorance of what was in truth an important and creative era in the history of Greek culture. I speak here as a repentant sinner. My earliest research was focused on drama in the fifth century BC; the subsequent expansion of my horizons has recapitulated a broader development in the discipline of Classics. Hence in my title I have preferred to speak of 'mid-antiquity', to reflect the period's pivotal significance. It was in the fourth century that the Roman empire of Manuel — Greek, Christian and detached from Rome — began to take root. But the seeds of these developments were already sprouting in the third century.

From the standpoint of most classicists, it is easy to think of the third century as a period of decline and crisis. Looked at from the other end, however, it is a period of crisis and recovery.[8] The empire's successful response to profound challenges is evidence of deep resilience, and the military and political innovations developed to cope with those challenges reflect a robust and creative society. The century began with the extension of Roman citizenship to all free subjects of the empire by Caracalla (AD 212); by the end of the century we have the tetrarchy, the administrative division of empire between East and West, and the shift of its political centre to the East (Constantine's new foundation being foreshadowed by Diocletian's capital at Nicomedia). One other fundamental change remained to be accomplished in the fourth century: the Christian takeover of the empire. Despite the efforts of the heroic Julian,[9] it was to prove irreversible.

Behind this political triumph lay cultural and intellectual advances; for Christians, too, the third century had been a seminal period. Origen, for example, though from a later perspective far from orthodox in many of his views, achieved new levels of sophistication in systematic theology; in the fourth century the heritage of his theology was brought to more orthodox formulation by the Cappadocian fathers — Gregory of Nazianzus (whom we have already met), together with his friend Basil of Caesarea, and Basil's brother Gregory of Nyssa. These developments took place in constant

---

[8] A. Watson, *Aurelian and the Third Century* (London 1999); S. Williams, *Diocletian and the Roman Recovery* (London 1985); S. Corcoran, *The Empire of the Tetrarchs* (Oxford 1996), with further literature.

[9] R. Smith, *Julian's Gods* (London 1995) explores the cultural, religious and philosophical background.

dialogue with their pagan context. Origen replied to the attack on Christianity by the second-century Platonist Celsus. In turn, the third-century philosopher Porphyry wrote a critique of Christianity sufficiently powerful to be banned under Constantine (it survives only in fragments).[10] Despite these mutual polemics the Cappadocian fathers were conscious of their debt to the classical tradition, and sought to bring theology into a (not uncritical) relationship with 'external' philosophy.[11] And the philosophical culture with which they were interacting was itself far from moribund. In the third century Plotinus, Porphyry and Iamblichus gave a new impetus and a new turn to Platonism;[12] in so doing they laid crucial foundations for a flowering of philosophical culture in later antiquity that has attracted increasingly respectful attention in recent years.[13]

Nor were other fields of cultural activity neglected. Consider literary studies. Cassius Longinus, though Plotinus expressed reservations about the depth of his philosophical grasp, was recognised by contemporaries and successors alike as an outstanding literary scholar.[14] The influence of his work can be traced in later Platonists, and also among Christians; Gregory of Nyssa was certainly familiar with his critical writings. If he wrote the treatise *On Sublimity* traditionally attributed to him, the high esteem in which he was held is easy to understand; though the attribution has been disputed since the beginning of the nineteenth century, I believe it may well be correct. Longinus' pupils included Porphyry, a literary scholar as well as a philosopher; his *Homeric Questions* merit more careful study than they have yet

---

[10] M. Frede, 'Celsus' attack on the Christians', in J. Barnes and M. Griffin (eds.), *Philosophia Togata II* (Oxford 1997) 218–40; id., 'Origen's treatise *Against Celsus*', in M. Edwards, M. Goodman and S. Price (eds.), *Apologetics in the Roman Empire* (Oxford 1999) 131–56; A. Meredith, 'Porphyry and Julian against the Christians', *Aufstieg und Niedergang der römischen Welt* 2.23.2 (1980) 1119–49; *cf.* n.16 below. Christian responses: M. Frede, 'Eusebius' apologetic writings', in Edwards, Goodman and Price, 223–50. For the larger background: R. Lane Fox, *Pagans and Christians* (London 1986).

[11] J. Pelikan, *Christianity and Classical Culture* (New Haven 1993).

[12] See the collection of articles in *Aufstieg und Niedergang der römischen Welt* 2.36.2 (1987).

[13] See especially R. Sorabji, *Time, Creation and the Continuum* (London 1983), and *Matter, Space and Motion* (London 1988).

[14] For the account of Longinus in this paragraph, see M. Heath, 'Longinus *On Sublimity*', *Proceedings of the Cambridge Philological Society* 45 (1999) 43–74; 'Echoes of Longinus in Gregory of Nyssa', *Vigiliae Christianae* 53 (1999) 395–400; 'Caecilius, Longinus and Photius', *Greek, Roman, and Byzantine Studies* 39 (1998) 271–92. Testimonia and fragments: L. Brisson and M. Patillon, 'Longinus Platonicus Philosophus et Philologus, I. Longinus Philosophus', *Aufstieg und Niedergang der römischen Welt* 2.36.7 (1994) 5214–99; 'Longinus Platonicus Philosophus et Philologus, II. Longinus Philologus', *Aufstieg und Niedergang der römischen Welt* 2.34.4 (1998) 3023–108.

received.[15] The scholarship and acute critical intellect which Porphyry deployed in his debate with Christianity, notably in his redating of the book of Daniel,[16] no doubt reflects Longinus' philological training: among other areas of expertise, Longinus was an authority on questions of authenticity, and ancient scholarly discussion of the attribution of literary works routinely deployed chronological as well as stylistic evidence.

In rhetoric, too, this was a period of genuine innovation. The second century had seen important developments in the theory of argument and in stylistics; these were summed up, and in the latter case taken to a new level of sophistication, by Hermogenes in the late second and early third centuries. His books *On Issues* and *On Types of Style* became standard works, and the system of rhetorical theory which they established was to remain canonical to the end of the Byzantine era.[17] But canonisation did not entail stagnation: theoretical innovation continued, and new modes of exposition were developed to serve as its medium. Here, too, the astonishingly versatile Porphyry was a key figure. He was, so far as we know, the first to write a commentary on a technical work on rhetoric. Since he adopted as his base-text a treatise by Hermogenes' ultimately unsuccessful rival Minucianus, Porphyry's commentary was superseded and has left only sparse fragments;[18] but he had many successors.

Porphyry's innovative use of commentary as a vehicle for rhetorical theory reflects a general enthusiasm for the commentary format in this period. As we shall see in the next section, it was in the third century that the latest developments in rhetorical theory were applied to the speeches of Demosthenes in the most influential of ancient commentaries on the orator. The philosophers known to modern scholarship as Neoplatonists thought of themselves simply as Platonists. Their thought was rooted in interpretation of Plato (and, especially under Porphyry's influence, of Aristotle), and many of them wrote commentaries; Iamblichus' innovative approach to the hermeneutics of Plato's

---

[15] Book 1 has been edited by A. R. Sodano, *Quaestionum Homericarum liber I* (Naples 1970), and translated by R. R. Schlunk, *Porphyry: the Homeric Questions* (New York 1993); otherwise we still depend on Schrader's deeply flawed edition (Leipzig 1880–1890).

[16] P. M. Casey, 'Porphyry and the origin of the book of Daniel', *Journal of Theological Studies* 27 (1976) 15–33; B. Croke, 'Porphyry's anti-Christian chronology', *Journal of Theological Studies* 34 (1983) 168–85.

[17] M. Heath, *Hermogenes On Issues* (Oxford 1995); C. Wooten, *Hermogenes On Types of Style* (Chapel Hill 1987); *cf.* I. Rutherford, *Canons of Style in the Antonine Age* (Oxford 1998). On the Byzantine reception of Hermogenes: G. L. Kustas, *Studies in Byzantine Rhetoric* (Thessalonica 1973); T. Conley, 'Greek rhetorics after the fall of Constantinople', *Rhetorica* 18 (2000) 265–94.

[18] Not, however, so sparse as one would infer from A. Smith (ed.), *Porphyrius. Fragmenta* (Leipzig 1993); note, for example, the long extract in *RG* 4.397.8–399.26 Walz. See M. Heath, 'Porphyry's rhetoric' (in preparation).

dialogues had immense influence on his successors.[19] For the biblically oriented Christians, too, exegesis was a crucial discipline; Origen was a prolific
and brilliant biblical commentator as well as a systematic theologian. The
Christians' use of techniques shared with pagan exegetes again reflects their
interaction with contemporary culture.[20]

As the prevalence of commentaries shows, the innovations of the third
and fourth centuries did not represent a break with the past; rather, the
resources inherited from a continuing tradition were renewed and developed
further. Philosophers studied Plato and Aristotle; literary scholars studied the
classics; rhetoricians studied the classical orators and taught their pupils to
use them as models;[21] even Christians stood in a close relationship to the
classical, as well as the Biblical, tradition.

This aspiration to continuity with the classical tradition points to one
dimension of the significance of rhetorical education in this period: part at
least of its importance lay in the entry it gave to a specific social and cultural
identity.[22] Through their training in rhetoric students acquired a variety of
proofs of education and Hellenic culture: for example, mastery of a (by now
archaic) form of the language;[23] control of a range of styles approved for use
in educated circles; familiarity with Greek traditions; and participation in
those traditions through imitation of the classical masters.[24] That these things
should depend on a specifically rhetorical training is not, of course, the result

---

[19] B. Dalsgaard Larsen, *Iamblique de Chalcis: Exégéte et Philosophe* (Aarhus 1972); M. Heath,
Unity in Greek Poetics (Oxford 1989) 124–36. For the later commentators on Aristotle: H. J.
Blumenthal, *Aristotle and Neoplatonism in Late Antiquity: Interpretations of the De Anima* (London
1996).

[20] F. Young, 'The rhetorical schools and their influence on patristic exegesis', in R. Williams (ed.),
The Making of Orthodoxy (Cambridge 1989) 182–99, and *Biblical Exegesis and the Formation of
Christian Culture* (Cambridge 1997); B. Neuschäfer, *Origenes als Philologe* (Basel 1987); M. J.
Hollerich, *Eusebius of Caesarea's Commentary on Isaiah* (Oxford 1999). See also B. Metzger, 'The
practice of textual criticism among the Church Fathers', *Studia Patristica* 12 (1975) 1.340–9.

[21] E.g. B. Schouler, *La tradition Hellenique chez Libanius* (Paris 1984); *cf.* n. 24 below.

[22] On the social and cultural importance of rhetoric see variously: G. Anderson, 'The *pepaideumenos*
in action: sophists and their outlook in the early Roman empire', *Aufstieg und Niedergang der
römischen Welt* 2.33.1 (1989) 29–208; P. Brown, *Power and Persuasion in Late Antiquity* (Madison
1992), esp. ch. 2; M. Gleason, *Making Men: Sophists and Self-presentation in Ancient Rome*
(Princeton 1995); T. Schmitz, *Bildung und Macht: zur sozialen und politischen Funktion der zweiten
Sophistik in der griechischen Welt der Kaiserzeit* (*Zetemata* 97, Munich 1997); S. Swain, *Hellenism
and Rome* (Oxford 1996).

[23] On the normative status of the classical Attic form of the language for the educated elite see Swain
(n. 22) 17–64.

[24] D. A. Russell, *'De imitatione'*, in D. A. West and A. J. Woodman (eds.), *Creative Imitation and
Latin Literature* (Cambridge 1979) 1–16; H. Hunger, 'On the imitation (μίμησις) of antiquity
in Byzantine literature', *Dumbarton Oaks Papers* 23.4 (1969/70) 17–38 (= *Byzantinistische*

of any universal necessity. It was a historical contingency — the fact that oratory had been a key social and political skill in the classical period — which made an engagement with rhetoric indispensable for participation in the tradition. Rhetorical training therefore played a crucial role in transmitting a cultural identity rooted in the past. But that raises further questions. Had rhetoric by now become little more than a fossilised reflection of the importance it had enjoyed in the classical period? Or did it retain a continuing practical significance? If the latter, in what social practices was that significance located? In attempting to answer these questions we shall first look into the rhetor's classroom, and then follow his pupils out of the classroom into their careers.

iii. In the rhetor's classroom

In this section I shall examine a lengthy passage from the scholia to Demosthenes' speech *On the False Embassy*. The scholia — notes found in medieval manuscripts — preserve material from a variety of older sources; the passage which concerns me here derives (I shall argue) from a commentary composed in the late third century AD. Apparently originating in lectures to advanced students, this commentary offers us an unexpected glimpse into the rhetorician's classroom. What we find there will not be to everyone's taste: the lecturer deploys, in what may seem obsessive detail, the formidably elaborate apparatus of contemporary rhetorical theory. Readers who find the intricacies of this theory indigestible may prefer to skip to the start of the next section. Though missing an instance of what seems to me elegant and pleasing subtlety, they will at least have acknowledged one of the points I wish to make — that the study of rhetoric in this period was a complex and demanding technical discipline.

In rhetorical theory the term 'conjecture' applies to disputes concerning a question of fact: did the defendant do it or didn't he?[25] The prosecution in such a case will argue that certain acknowledged facts are indicative of the defendant's guilt; for example, the fact that the defendant was seen running away from the scene of the crime shows that he was the criminal. Technically, this head of argument was known as 'sequence of events'. The defence's

---

Grundlageforschungen (London 1973) no. 15) and 'The classical tradition in Byzantine literature: the importance of rhetoric', in M. Mullett and R. Scott (eds.), *Byzantium and the Classical Tradition* (Birmingham 1981) 35–47.

[25] On conjecture in the rhetorical theory of issues see Heath (n. 17) 80–101.

response to the sequence of events must try to show that the allegedly incriminating facts have an innocent explanation; for example, he was running away because he had seen someone he wanted to avoid, not because he had committed the crime. This response is sometimes known as the 'transposition of the cause', sometimes (more perspicuously) as the 'gloss': in it, the defence tries to put an innocent gloss on the suspicious act. So in setting out the sequence of events the prosecution needs to anticipate and undermine the defendant's gloss. There are two ways in which this can be done. The prosecutor may deny that the gloss succeeds in explaining the incriminating act away: in my example, the prosecution, accepting that the defendant had seen the other man, might deny that this was his reason for running away (e.g. 'he has often been in this man's company and never felt it necessary to avoid him before'). Alternatively, the prosecutor may dispute the factual basis of the gloss: so, in the example, he might deny that the defendant had seen the man at all (e.g. 'the man is known to have been elsewhere at the time'). If the prosecutor takes this latter path, then another question of fact arises: did the defendant see the other man? Thus out of the main question (did the defendant commit the crime?) there arises a second, subsidiary conjectural question (did the defendant see the other man?).

This kind of situation is known technically as 'incident conjecture'. We can illustrate it from Demosthenes' *On the False Embassy* — perhaps. In this speech Aeschines is accused of malpractice as ambassador. One fact adduced as evidence of Aeschines' guilt is the misleading assurances about the security of Phocis which he gave the assembly. Aeschines will try to disarm this piece of evidence by claiming that he was himself deceived by Philip, so that he misled the assembly unwittingly. Demosthenes tries to pre-empt that gloss by claiming that Aeschines was bribed. So the main conjectural question is: was Aeschines guilty of deliberate malpractice? From this arises an incident conjecture: was Aeschines bribed?

This interpretation of *On the False Embassy* is attributed to Menander of Laodicea, a rhetorician of the late third century (schol. Dem. 19.1 (1a) = hyp. 2). It was controversial: one commentator on Hermogenes remarks with indignation that 'Menander in his commentary on the orator had the audacity to assert that the *False Embassy* is an incident conjecture' (*RG* 7.374.12–15 Walz). The problem lies in a subtle discrepancy between this way of analysing the speech and the definition of incident conjecture given above. According to the definition the subsidiary question should arise out of the defendant's gloss; but in the *False Embassy* the subsidiary question arises, not out of the gloss itself, but out of the prosecutor's response to the gloss. For the subsidiary question is not whether Aeschines was *deceived* by Philip (as he claims), but whether he was *bribed* by Philip (as Demosthenes alleges). Minute though this discrepancy may appear, it was enough to make Menander's interpretation provocative to his professional peers. It is interesting, therefore, to find a lengthy scholion which maintains the interpretation of the speech as incident conjecture, despite the acknowledged discrepancy with the standard definition (schol. Dem. 19.101 (228)); even more interesting is the finesse with which the problem is handled.

The first part of the scholion (40.10) shows how Demosthenes takes Aeschines' gloss (the claim that he had been deceived by Philip), refutes it, and puts forward an alternative explanation (that he had been bribed by Philip). Then a discussion is introduced, seemingly in passing, of some technical doctrine from Hermogenes: 'It is worth considering what Hermogenes said in his handbook about the sequence of events...' (40.28). What Hermogenes said (*On Issues* 49.7–23) was that the sequence of events might be based on actions, or on utterances, or on displays of emotion. In each case the defence's gloss should take a different form; in particular, when the sequence of events is based on an utterance, the defence should use the tactic of 'letter and intent' — the apparently incriminating literal meaning of the utterance should be explained away by arguing that another, innocent meaning was intended. Our scholion has no problem in proving that this superficial doctrine is 'unsound'. It does so partly by looking at what Demosthenes does in the *False Embassy*: Aeschines' misleading assurances to the assembly were utterances, but the gloss is not based on letter and intent (the defence is technically a plea of mitigation: Aeschines claims that he had been deceived by Philip, so it was not his fault that he misled the assembly). But the scholion also considers some hypothetical cases of the kind that would be set to students as themes for the exercise in oratory known as declamation.[26] Then there is this summing-up (41.16):

> So you should not accept uncritically what is said in the technical handbooks, as if that was laid down as the law. You should apply it to many different cases; and if you find that the precept fits them, then you can use it with confidence; but if it fits a few cases, but not all, then clearly it will be seen to be unsound. For example, the precept doesn't hold water in this fictitious case either: 'A rich man and a poor man were political enemies. At a dinner-party the rich man swore that he would make himself tyrant; in reply the poor man swore that he would kill the tyrant. The poor man is found murdered (but not robbed) on the way back from dinner. The rich man is accused of his murder.' What is the first element in the sequence

---

[26] D. A. Russell, *Greek Declamation* (Cambridge 1983); D. H. Berry and M. Heath, 'Oratory and declamation', in S. Porter (ed.), *A Handbook of Classical Rhetoric* (Leiden 1997) 393–420.

of events? 'The rich man swore that he would make himself tyrant.' Well then: that consists of something said. But the defence here is not based on intent; it is a plea of mitigation — because he claims that he spoke under the influence of alcohol. So how can we say that the author of the handbook laid down the law correctly?

The scholion goes on (41.27) to suggest a more adequate theoretical view of this kind of situation.

Since this critique of Hermogenes coincides with another testimonium to Menander,[27] it seems reasonable to conclude that his commentary on Demosthenes was the source of the scholion with which we are concerned. The exposition clearly has its context in the rhetorical classroom. We can envisage Menander lecturing to fairly advanced students: they have a good grasp of the rules taught in the elementary textbooks, but must now be encouraged to take a more critical view of them. While using theory to interpret Demosthenes' text, therefore, Menander is simultaneously using the text to refine and develop his students' grasp of theory. Moreover, when he illustrates his argument by citing declamation themes he is also linking the discussion to the students' own practical exercises. The purpose of the exposition is thus not primarily philological or theoretical: it is also, and above all, practical.

After this theoretical digression Menander returns to the text, explaining (42.14) how Demosthenes introduces the question of motive. He points out (42.33) that this head of argument has two functions: in the main question (about Aeschines' conduct as ambassador) it helps to refute the gloss, but it also introduces the subsidiary question (about Aeschines taking bribes). It is here, with the subsidiary question arising out of the refutation of the gloss (rather than out of the gloss itself), that the discrepancy with the standard definition of incident conjecture emerges. Menander acknowledges and briefly explains the objection, but is undeterred. Now the true purpose of the preceding critique of textbook dogma becomes clear — Menander was preparing his defence in advance (43.10):

> If the orator's speech does not conform to present-day textbooks, one should not regard the textbooks as more authoritative than Demosthenes' speeches. It is the originals that we should take as our legislators, not those who have borrowed a few ideas from them.

Having made this point, he adds an immediate follow-up:

---

[27] The testimonium, from an unpublished commentary on Hermogenes, can be found in L. Schilling, *Quaestiones rhetoricae selectae* (*Jahrbuch für classische Philologie* Suppl. 28, 1903, 663–778) 745–6.

> After all, in the problem concerning the dissolute son Hermogenes has stated as a general principle that there cannot be a simple conjecture without acts, although Isocrates in his *Against Euthynus* has laid down for us exactly the opposite law.

The technical point in question here need not detain us; it is enough to say that the controversy about incomplete simple conjecture without acts (illustrated by the case of a dissolute son accused of murder when his father mysteriously disappears) was one of the points on which Hermogenes had attacked his rival Minucianus.[28] Menander points out that Hermogenes' objection is overruled by a counter-example in Isocrates; as in the earlier critique of Hermogenes, the handbooks have to be treated critically, in the light of practical experience. So by sandwiching his analysis between two examples of defects in textbook doctrine, Menander has disarmed the objection that his reading of the *False Embassy* goes against the textbook definition of incident conjecture.

There is one further subtlety. To judge from the commentaries on Hermogenes, third-century rhetoricians were almost unanimous in rejecting his views both on the solution to the sequence of events and on incomplete simple conjecture without acts. So Menander has placed his controversial departure from textbook doctrine between two uncontroversial departures. There was an important principle in classical rhetoric that weak arguments should be put between strong ones — a tactic sometimes known as 'Homeric disposition' (alluding to Nestor's advice in *Iliad* 4.297–300 that good troops should be deployed in front of and behind bad ones, to stop the bad ones running away). The scholia often comment on Demosthenes' use of this technique of putting strong arguments first and last; for example, a scholion on the beginning of the *First Olynthiac* singles this out as 'a principle of general application' (schol. Dem. 1.1 (5d)). This and numerous other scholia with similar didactic language reflect the practical orientation of rhetorical commentary: the commentators regularly highlight techniques which can be observed in the orator and which the student should learn from him and imitate.[29] But in this scholion we see a rhetorician going one step further, and exploiting the principle himself. In these lectures Menander was not just talking *about* rhetoric: he was also *using* rhetoric. He was giving his students a live model, and they were surely meant to observe and imitate the technique.

---

[28] Heath (n. 17) 65–6, 92–4.

[29] E.g. schol. Dem. 19.233 (453); 19.237 (455a); 20.1 (5c); 20.56 (138); 20.73 (169); 21.18 (20). Other authors on the students' reading-list were cited too: 21.1 (1) refers to a lost declamation by Aelius Aristides.

iv. From classroom to career

Of all the rhetoricians of this period, Menander of Laodicea is the most familiar to modern scholars; but the account of Menander given in the previous
section will not be recognisable to many. Modern perceptions of Menander's
significance have been dominated by the two treatises on epideictic (the
honorific oratory of ceremonial occasions: welcoming a visiting dignitary,
praising the emperor, celebrating a wedding and so forth) transmitted under his
name.[30] Yet the earliest explicit link between Menander and epideictic is the
superscription to the epideictic treatises in a tenth-century manuscript;[31] the
overwhelming majority of earlier testimonia and fragments relate to his work
as a commentator on Demosthenes. There is also evidence that he wrote
commentaries on technical handbooks by Hermogenes and his rival Minucianus. In other words, his contemporaries and successors saw Menander
primarily as a specialist in the kind of minute analysis of forensic and deliberative oratory that we observed in the previous section; epideictic was a
relatively marginal interest.

   This should come as no surprise. By far the largest part of the vast bulk
of technical literature on rhetoric that survives from late antiquity is concerned with techniques of forensic and deliberative speech. The notion that
rhetoric in this period was primarily concerned with epideictic is therefore a
misconception; that was not the main classroom focus. But this very fact,
when recognised, is sometimes seen as a shortcoming. On the assumption
that late ancient *oratory* was primarily epideictic, it is inferred that the
pattern of rhetorical training reflected in the theorists was ill-adapted to
contemporary reality. For example:[32]

> The educational tradition, in fact, never really caught up with the real situation
> under the empire, when epideictic was the centre of activity for many orators,
> though of course forensic and deliberative speeches were still needed.

---

[30] D. A. Russell and N. G. Wilson, *Menander Rhetor* (Oxford 1981). In fact Menander is not the
author of the first of the two treatises; see L. Pernot, 'Les *topoi* de l'éloge chez Ménandros le
Rhéteur', *Revue des études grecques* 96 (1986) 33–53.

[31] A fifth-century papyrus provides a possible exception: H. Maehler, 'Menander Rhetor and
Alexander Claudius in a papyrus letter', *Greek, Roman, and Byzantine Studies* 15 (1974) 305–11; but
the identification of the works mentioned in this letter is not completely certain. The other explicit
testimonia date to the eleventh century or later.

[32] D. A. Russell, 'The panegyrists and their teachers', in M. Whitby (ed.), *The Propaganda of
Power: the Role of Panegyric in Late Antiquity* (Leiden 1998) 17–49, at 25.

That sentence needs to be read with care. It does not say that epideictic was the centre of activity for *most* orators, or that those who did centre on it did so to the *exclusion* of other kinds of oratory. The observation is perfectly consistent, therefore, with forensic and deliberative speech still being the central activity for most orators, and with few (if any) orators devoting themselves exclusively to epideictic. But if that were the case, it would be difficult to maintain that teaching had become detached from the real situation. The justifiably cautious claims advanced fall short of the conclusion they are meant to sustain.

This is not to deny the importance of epideictic in the functioning of late ancient society.[33] The author of a comprehensive study of the 'rhetoric of praise' has spoken of the 'triumph' of epideictic in this period, and of epideictic as the 'summit' of the art of oratory. Yet he notes the marginal role of epideictic in the curriculum, and recognises that leading sophists (the most distinguished teachers of rhetoric, and especially the virtuoso performers with a flair for public display) were also active in the deliberative and forensic spheres. His conclusion — that the lack of prominence of epideictic in our sources 'paradoxically' confirms its triumph — seems strained.[34] A distinction is needed. Epideictic could be seen as undemanding, since it is easier to embellish a proposition taken as uncontested than it is to argue for or against a proposition that is in dispute. On the other hand, epideictic could be seen as the most difficult kind of oratory, because of its sustained stylistic demands.[35] A sophist, then, could achieve greater glory for the stylistic brilliance of an epideictic speech than for the more pedestrian expression of his forensic or deliberative speeches; but in teaching there was an emphasis on the difficult techniques of argument that were essential to the less prestigious forms. Since most of a rhetorician's pupils would not become sophists, this focus on techniques of argument was realistic. The pattern of training typical of the rhetorician's classroom concentrated on the techniques which most students would need most, while also giving scope for developing skills of display of which most students would have less need, but which a few would need above all.

---

[33] For the social and ideological background to the importance of epideictic: J. E. Lendon, *Empire of Honour: the Art of Government in the Roman World* (Oxford 1997).

[34] L. Pernot, *La rhétorique de l'éloge dans le monde gréco-romain* (Paris 1993) 70–6, 350–2; for the paradox see p. 103.

[35] Undemanding: Anon., *RG* 2.49.14–18 Walz (for the principle *cf.* Theon *Prog.* 65.7–19 Spengel). Difficult: Fronto *Ad M. Caes.* 3.17 (49.9–14 van den Hout[2]).

To illustrate this conclusion, let us return to Libanius. His complaints about the decline of rhetoric under the pressures of social and political change in the late fourth century are well known.[36] But he is a rhetorician, not a social historian, and these complaints need to be interpreted in the light of their rhetorical context; a more complex picture then emerges. In *Oration* 62 Libanius responds to critics of his professional ability thus (62.5):

> Some ... say that I may be good at making speeches, and better than most, but that I am not equally good as a teacher. At once they ask: 'Which of his pupils has distinguished himself in lawsuits? Which in the ranks of politicians? Which from the teacher's chair? Which from the official's chair?' And they pre-empt those they questioned, and make themselves a gift of the answer: 'No one!'

A sophist's pupils would be expected, then, to enter careers in advocacy, in civic life, in teaching rhetoric, or in the imperial administration. This comes as no surprise: his pupils would as a matter of course be drawn largely from the social class that *did* fill such posts.[37] More interesting is the implication that the sophist's training would help to equip his pupils to distinguish themselves in these posts; if this were not the case, it would hardly reflect badly on Libanius as a teacher that his pupils failed to do so. The same implication is found in *Oration* 35, where Libanius rebukes former pupils who, though now members of the political class in Antioch, avoided speaking in court (35.1) and in council (35.6);[38] this default (contrasted with others' readiness to speak) reflects badly on their teacher.

Libanius' initial response in *Oration* 62 is to maintain that the fault lies not with him, but with the context in which he works: changing social and political conditions have brought rhetoric into disfavour with students and their parents, who see shorthand (8–16) or law (21–23) as better routes to social advancement. At first sight this argument may seem to miss the point of a criticism directed, not against rhetorical teaching in general, but against *his* teaching of rhetoric (the critics are, after all, likely to include his professional rivals). Libanius has perhaps expanded the discussion in this way partly to distract attention from the criticism's individual thrust. But the emphasis on the difficulties facing rhetors in general also helps throw into sharper relief the individual success which he goes on to claim when he

---

[36] J. H. W. G. Liebeschuetz, *Antioch: City and Imperial Administration in the Later Roman Empire* (Oxford 1972) 242–55.

[37] See the prosopographical study by P. Petit, *Les Étudiants de Libanius* (Paris 1956). On the social origins of the sophists: G. W. Bowersock, *Greek Sophists in the Roman Empire* (Oxford 1969) 21–8, with E. L. Bowie, 'The importance of the sophists', *Yale Classical Studies* 27 (1982) 29–59.

[38] City councils: Liebeschuetz (n. 36) 101–5, 167–74.

shows that his pupils have in fact distinguished themselves as orators
(27–8) — not, perhaps in great numbers as teachers (30–6), but in civic life
(37–40), the courts (41–9) and imperial government (50–62).[39]

The nature of the problem faced by rhetoricians should also be carefully
noted. When Libanius (*Or.* 62.16) contrasts those trained in rhetoric (who
speak in the courts) and those trained in shorthand (who record the speeches),
there is no implication that rhetorical training has ceased to be a useful preparation for practical advocacy; rather, advocacy has ceased to be the chosen
route to social advancement. So, too, in *Oration* 2.45 the claim that rhetorically
trained advocates who have saved many people's property have now aban-
doned the courts because they can find better opportunities for advancement
elsewhere assumes that rhetoric retains its importance for the advocate. The
point, then, is not that a rhetorical training has no practical relevance in advocacy, but that advocacy no longer offers an attractive career path.

Many of Libanius' pupils did become advocates (e.g. *Ep.* 539, 831, 858).[40]
His letters and speeches show how varied individual cases could be. One pupil
in his second year with Libanius was taken away by his father to begin a career
as an advocate; Libanius regarded this as premature (*Or.* 57.3). Another continued his studies to the point where he did seem ready to speak in court, but
then after going abroad on business returned for more advanced study
(*Or.* 38.3). One practising advocate simultaneously studied with Libanius to
enhance his existing skills (*Ep.* 203.2). So a basic course in rhetoric was sufficient for advocacy, but more advanced study was also available, with potential
relevance to advocacy (as well as, presumably, to a career as a sophist).

But there was another option open for those who wished to undertake
further study. One pupil who had reached the point at which the alternatives of
further rhetorical study or entering advocacy were under consideration ab-
sconded to the law-school at Beirut after a quarrel with his father; the father
had designated him for rhetoric and his older brother for law (*Ep.* 1375). This
incident reflects the fact that a legal training was increasingly seen as desirable; the old separation of roles between rhetorically trained advocates and
legal experts was giving way to a situation in which legal expertise was
essential for advocacy (cf. *Ep.* 1170).[41] But even now it was essential as an

---

[39] Elsewhere (*Or.* 1.151–3) Libanius seems to concede that his pupils were less successful than he
had hoped, and offers by way of excuse that the best died young (though here he does claim to have
trained successful teachers).

[40] On the careers of Libanius' pupils: Petit (n. 37) 154–8, 170–85.

[41] But to render 'advocate' as 'lawyer' (as in Norman's Loeb) is misleading. Even if advocates had
studied law, and even if that study was an advantage in advocacy, it was not by virtue of their legal
expertise that they practised as advocates.

adjunct to rhetoric, not as a substitute. Libanius comments that legal training was previously the preserve of the poor, while the prosperous studied rhetoric; now the latter add legal study to their rhetorical training (*Or.* 62.21–3). He remarks, tendentiously, that this addition makes them forget their rhetorical skill; but elsewhere he acknowledges at least one pupil whose study of law did not eradicate his previous rhetorical training (*Ep.* 339.5–8), and he wrote many letters of recommendation for pupils going on to law school (*Ep.* 117, 533, 1131, 1171, 1203, 1431 = 114 Norman, 1539).

In an entertaining anecdote, Philostratus (*Life of Apollonius* 6.36) describes an encounter between Apollonius of Tyana and an ill-educated young man whose hobby was teaching birds to talk. Apollonius criticises the youth for substituting bad Greek for the beauty of the birds' natural song, but also for putting his property at risk; if harried in the courts, he will have no power to defend himself. The solution is to go to school and learn rhetoric — specifically the rhetoric of the 'market-place' rhetoricians, which he will find easy to learn; he has left it too late to study with philosophers and sophists. The anecdote shows that there were teachers of rhetoric on more than one level of sophistication. But it is important to note that the contrast is not between practical 'market-place' rhetoric and the useless, academic or purely decorative rhetoric of the sophists. On the contrary, Apollonius compares the former to the equipment of light-armed skirmishers, the latter to the more complete and more formidable equipment of the heavy infantry.[42] And although Libanius could complain (*Or.* 62.43–44) that current court practice gives no advantage to properly (that is, sophistically) trained rhetors over the 'market-place' orators, we should again be cautious. He refers especially to the lack of time allocated to advocates, a complaint that goes back at least to the first century (Tacitus *Dial.* 38–9). Indeed, the flourishing rhetorical culture of classical Athens which Libanius so admired was not notably inhibited by the use of water-clocks to time forensic speeches.[43]

---

[42] For these 'market-place' orators see, perhaps, the papyri containing advocates' briefs and trial transcripts from Roman Egypt: references are collected in J. A. Crook, *Legal Advocacy in the Roman World* (London 1995). The techniques of argument used in some of these papyri have points of convergence with those taught in sophistic handbooks, though they are less elaborately developed: see my paper 'Practical advocacy in Roman Egypt', in M. J. Edwards and C. Reid (eds.), *Oratory in Action* (Manchester, forthcoming).

[43] Against the myth of a decline in the importance of advocacy see (for the early empire) E. P. Parks, *The Roman Rhetorical Schools as a Preparation for the Courts under the Early Empire* (*Johns Hopkins University Studies in Historical and Political Science* 43.2, 1945); Crook (n. 42) 180–92. On the courts in later antiquity: J. D. Harries, *Law and Empire in Late Antiquity* (Cambridge 1999).

We know that many sophists were active and successful in forensic and deliberative oratory. Philostratus' *Lives of the Sophists* attests to this for the second and early third centuries;[44] at the end of the third century a similar prospect is disclosed by Menander's treatise on epideictic. One of his illustrative examples envisages a pupil making a farewell speech to a fellow-student (396.2) leaving Athens (396.26) to return home at the end of his studies. The future pictured for the departing student is as follows (397.17–20): 'you will be your city's champion in courts of law, in speakers' contests, on embassies, and in literary rivalry.' Unless the 'speakers' contests' are simply reduplicated by 'literary rivalry', different activities must be in question. Elsewhere (398.6) a 'literary struggle' is a competition-piece of the kind presented at festivals like the Museia;[45] so too in Libanius (*Ep.* 364.4 = 29 Norman) 'literary contests' are rhetorical exercises. Menander's 'speakers' contests', then, should be distinct from these literary competitions, but also (since the list begins with 'courts of law') from forensic oratory; the reference is perhaps to deliberative oratory in the city councils that managed local affairs.[46] Another option open to Menander's pupil is to enter the service of the emperor (399.27).[47] If he is very well educated in rhetoric, he might teach (397.28); but if he does teach, he will not be like Isocrates, Isaeus or Lysias (397.29) — that is, he will not be disengaged from the city's affairs. Menander's addressee, himself a prospective sophist (388.17), will comment on the city's politics in his informal discourses (390.14–17).

This pattern continued into the fourth century: the range of career paths mentioned in Menander is identical to that observed in Libanius' dispute with his critics. Thus Libanius praises his former pupil Priscio for the distinction he has achieved both in legal advocacy and in sophistic display (*Ep.* 1000.1):

> I am grateful to Priscio both for his former and for his latter achievements. The former were contests in the law-courts, the latter contests in the theatres — respectively an advocate's and a sophist's role. Because he was great in both on his own account he also made, and is making, my account greater.

---

[44] References in Heath (n. 17) 12 n. 34. Of course, this was not true of all sophists; like most satirical caricatures, the image of the sophist utterly incompetent in practical affairs (ibid. n. 33) was generalised from a carefully biased sample.

[45] On these competitions: Pernot (n. 34) 63–5.

[46] See n. 38.

[47] Bowersock (n. 37) 43–58; F. Millar, *The Emperor in the Roman World* (London 1977), 83–101, 236–8.

Once more, the teacher gains glory from the pupil's success both as advocate and as declaimer. These were not Priscio's only achievements; elsewhere we learn that he has delivered a panegyric on the emperor (*Ep.* 1053.1 = 185 Norman): 'Priscio who has won many victories in the law-courts, and many in the theatres that receive speeches, and filled the earth with his labours and pleased the emperor by his composition on him . . .'. In this letter Libanius rebukes Priscio for his bad relations with Hilarius, governor of the province in which he is teaching, and himself a former pupil. Despite his critics, Libanius' pupils achieved distinction in public service, too.

v. Conclusion

In Chapter 3 above, Peter Parsons has described how in the last century the study of ancient Greece and Rome has been immeasurably enriched by the discovery of new texts on papyrus. But old texts, too, still offer the classicist scope for discovery. In this chapter I have tried to illustrate the possibility that the scholia on Demosthenes may give access to extensive material from Menander's commentary. The recovery of the rhetor Menander will not, it is true, generate the same level of literary excitement as the recovery of the comic Menander. But it is, in its own way, consequential: it helps us to see in a quite different light an author we thought we had known well; and the adjustment of our perspective on this one individual in turn invites us to reconsider the nature and social significance of a key element in late ancient education and culture — the cultivation of rhetoric.

We did, indeed, already have clues to Menander's importance as a commentator on Demosthenes (it is the dominant message of the testimonia and fragments), and the thought that his commentary might have been a major source of the scholia is not new — that was already conjectured in the nineteenth century.[48] But confirming the conjecture has only recently been made possible by the continuing progress of scholarship. One decisive contribution is a work of traditional philological scholarship: Marvin Dilts's edition of the Demosthenes scholia has made it possible for the first time to get a secure understanding of the structure of the manuscript tradition.[49] But this tradition is not transmitting a *single* work: the scholia conflate material from several

---

[48] W. Nitsche, *Der Rhetor Menandros und die Scholien zu Demosthenes* (*Wissenschaftliche Beilage zum Programm des Leibniz-Gymnasiums zu Berlin* 63, Berlin 1883).

[49] M. R. Dilts (ed.), *Scholia Demosthenica* (Leipzig 1983–1986), superseding Dindorf's pre-critical edition (Oxford 1851).

sources. To separate out these different strands we must also be able to tell apart the sometimes subtly discrepant rhetorical analyses that the scholia have mingled (and sometimes mangled); and that requires an understanding of the technicalities of late ancient rhetorical theory.

Needless to say, my own contribution in this field builds on the achievements of earlier researchers;[50] but it has also — less predictably — been advanced by the opportunity to teach undergraduate courses on ancient rhetoric. As we have seen, rhetorical theory was taught in antiquity above all as a practical tool; an understanding of it should therefore be a practical understanding.[51] There is no more potent mechanism for focusing the mind on the practical dimension than the knowledge that you will have to go before a class and explain *why* the theory is what it is, and show *how* it can be used to generate arguments. Classicists in modern universities address a student body many of whom will know no Greek or Latin, and have accordingly been compelled to develop approaches to the study of the ancient world that are not tied to reading canonical Greek and Latin texts in the original language. In my own experience, this constraint has proved to be a liberating and enlightening opportunity for experiment and discovery.

Technical understanding, even when approached with a view to its practical application, is not enough. We also need to see rhetoric so far as possible in a larger intellectual, cultural and social context. The project on which this chapter is an interim report aims to move outward from the most basic questions about technical writing on rhetoric — who wrote what, when? — to questions of significance: *why*? Proximately, that is a question about the workings of the schools of rhetoric: how do these texts relate (and what do they reveal) about syllabus structures and classroom practices (and about their evolution over time)? When rhetoricians committed their teachings to writing, what purposes were being served and what audiences addressed? Such questions encourage us to look to other contemporary fields of intellectual endeavour: what can we learn from the partially parallel practices of literary scholars, philosophers and theologians? [52] As we have seen, the third and fourth centuries sustained a flourishing and many-sided culture, the different strands of which were closely interlinked; the study of rhetoric soon leads us,

---

[50] Heath (n. 17) inspired especially by Russell (n. 26) and G. A. Kennedy, *Greek Rhetoric under Christian Emperors* (Princeton 1983).

[51] For an attempt to apply this premise see M. Heath, 'Invention', in S. Porter (ed.), *A Handbook of Classical Rhetoric* (Leiden 1997) 89–119.

[52] Or doctors: Galen's essay 'On my own books' (trans. P. N. Singer, *Galen: Selected Works* (Oxford 1997) 3–22) contains much valuable evidence concerning the production, circulation and uses of technical writing.

therefore, into other areas, such as patristics and the history of philosophy. It leads us, too, into social history. For the question of significance also points beyond the rhetorical schools: who was it who studied rhetoric, and to what ends? How far, and in what ways, was that study relevant to the students' subsequent career paths?

The tendency of questions to proliferate and ramify in this way means that classicists typically have to pursue their enquiries within a broad thematic horizon. The opening section of this paper will also (I hope) have helped to suggest how reference to a broad chronological horizon can contribute illuminating new perspectives. Classicists study a tradition spanning more than two millennia, displaying complex patterns of continuity and change. The way in which late antiquity canonised Demosthenes as a paradigm of oratorical brilliance and subjected his speeches to minute analysis as models of persuasive technique is just one illustration of that tradition's constant self-conscious appropriation of its past. One consequence of this process is that every era of antiquity not only presupposes what has gone before, but has also played a part in the preservation of the inheritance, and has left its mark on what was preserved. The study of any one part of the tradition may therefore interact with any other. Add to that a growing corpus of evidence, old evidence read afresh, new techniques of study and new questions ... The future of Classics in the coming century can only be guessed at; but there is little danger that classicists will exhaust their material.

Index of passages

General index

Achilles Tatius, on Egypt   202
Adcock, Fleur   1, 2
Aeschines   25, 267
Aeschylus   3–6, 8–9, 17–19, 52, 265
Aëtius, Aristotelian heretic   406, 412, 414
Aezani, price-edict text at   153, 154–6, 157, 162
agriculture, and slavery   254–5
Agrippa, recipient of ode   312
Agyrrhios, grain law of   242
Alcibiades, friend of Socrates   267, 270
Alexander, heretic   406, 411
Alexander of Aphrodisias, on Theophrastus   410
Alexandria   207, 210, 222
Alexandrian scholarship   23, 25
Alexis, comic poet   46
Ambrose, St   181
Ammianus Marcellinus   207–8
Anchises, status of   356
Antaeus, in Heaney   16
Antimachus, lost author   39
Antinoopolis   195–7
Antinous, death and afterlife of   195
Antonius, M.   142
Anytus, prosecutor of Socrates   267
Apelles, heretical syllogisms of   406, 411–12
Aphrodisias, price-edict text at   156–62
   statues at   65–8, 93, 96
Apollodorus of Athens, book-lover   40, 56
Apollonius of Tyana   182, 435
Appian   143, 287
Apuleius   146
Ara Pacis Augustae   65, 98, 318, 330
Arab conquest   170, 173, 174, 191, 222
Archilochus   30, 43, 49–50
Ariès, Philippe   232
Aristarchus, Alexandrian scholar   23, 30, 56
Aristion of Paros, sculptor   87
Aristo, Stoic philosopher   366, 389–91, 393, 397–8
Aristophanes of Byzantium   23
Aristophanes, late popularity of   48, 198
Aristotle   28–9, 253–4, 261

discovery of his *Ath. Pol.*   41, 43, 49–50
   logic of   400, 405, 406, 408, 410, 413, 415
Arius, heretic   406
Arnobius   405, 413
Arsinoe (Cilicia), foundation of   243–4
Arsinoe (Egypt), Jupiter temple at   204
art history, preconceptions in   64–5, 74–6, 78–82, 93–6
asceticism   181–2
Athenaeus, on Middle Comedy   39
Athenian authors, admiration of   25, 27, 48
Atticus, T. Pomponius   108, 116–17, 118, 125–6
Auden, W. H.   7, 8
Augustine, St   181, 182, 415–16
Augustus, as god   314
   in Horace   312–15, 317–18, 320–2, 324–30, 342
   portraiture of   61–2, 92–3, 98
   as world ruler   326–8, 337
Aurelius Victor, *Caesars* of   146

Bacchylides, discovery of text   41, 46
Bailey, Cyril   356
Bankes, William J., on price-edict   152
barbarian invasions, significance of   169–71
Barchiesi, Alessandro   339, 349, 350, 354
Barns, J. W. B.   220–1
Basil, St   36, 414, 422
Beazley, Sir John   73
Beesly, E. S.   309
Beloch, Karl Julius   226, 229
Bentley, Richard   103–6
Bernal, Martin   194, 221–2
Boeckh, August   230, 231
books, precarious survival of   39–40
Botton, Alain de   34
Boukoloi, brigands   202–3
Bowersock, Glen   171
Bradley, Keith   262
Braudel, Fernand   246
Brown, Peter   166–8, 171, 175, 178, 181, 183, 185
Brunt, P. A.   309